PREFACE

At the twentieth special session of the General Assembly in 1998, States Members agreed to make significant progress towards the control of supply and demand for illicit drugs by the year 2008. They noted that this objective could only be achieved by means of the 'balanced approach' (giving demand as much attention as supply), and on the basis of regular assessments of the drug problem. The aim of the present report is to contribute to such assessments by presenting supply and demand statistics and analysis on the evolution of the global illicit drug problem.

Reliable and systematic data to assess the drug problem, and to monitor progress in achieving the goals set by the General Assembly, however, is not readily available. The present report is based on data obtained primarily from the annual reports questionnaire (ARQ) sent by Governments to the United Nations Office on Drugs and Crime (UNODC) in 2002, supplemented by other sources. Two of the main data limitations are that: (a) these annual questionnaires are not systematic enough, both in terms of the number of countries responding and of content; and (b) most countries lack the monitoring systems required to produce reliable, comprehensive and internationally comparable data. There have been some recent improvements. National illicit coca and opium monitoring systems, supported by UNODC, are now providing annual cultivation estimates for the main producing countries. However, data on other links in the drug chain, particularly on the demand side, are progressively weaker.

This report tries to overcome the data limitations by presenting, annually, estimates and analysis of illicit drug production, trafficking and consumption. The first section deals with Trends in illicit drug production, trafficking and consumption. The second section provides the Statistics on which the globally aggregated estimates and trends are based.

The difficulties of measuring an illicit activity are well known. Although they impose obvious limitations on data, it is possible to make reasonable order-of-magnitude estimates. It is also highly desirable to do so, because such estimates encourage transparency, stimulate discussion and build knowledge. Empirical evidence is the only realistic basis for policy-making. This report, by presenting what we know, and by showing what we do not know, contributes to building the knowledge base for better policy. It also sets the basis for more focussed action to achieve the goals set in 1998 and reiterated at the Ministerial segment of the UN Commission on Narcotic Drugs in April 2003.

Antonio Maria Costa
Executive Director
United Nations *Office on Drugs and Crime*

EXPLANATORY NOTE

This report has been reproduced without formal editing.

The designations employed and the presentation of the material in this publication do not imply the expression of any opinion whatsoever on the part of the Secretariat of the United Nations concerning the legal status of any country, territory, city or area or of its authorities, or concerning the delimitation of its frontiers or boundaries. The names of territories and administrative areas are in italics.

The following abbreviations have been used in this report:

ARQ	annual reports questionnaire
ATS	amphetamine-type stimulants
CICAD	Inter-American Drug Abuse Control Commission
CIS	Commonwealth of Independent States
DEA	United States of America, Drug Enforcement Administration
DMT	N,N - dimethyltryptamine
DOB	brolamfetamine
EMCDDA	European Monitoring Centre for Drugs and Drug Addiction
ESPAD	European School Survey Project on Alcohol and other Drugs
F.O.	UNODC Field Office
ICMP	UNODC Global Illicit Crop Monitoring Programme
IDU	Injecting drug use
INCB	International Narcotics Control Board
INCSR	United States of America, International Narcotics Control Strategy Report
Interpol/ICPO	International Criminal Police Organization
LSD	lysergic acid diethylamide
NAPOL	National Police
ODCCP	United Nations Office for Drug Control and Crime Prevention
PCP	phencyclidine
UNAIDS	Joint and Co-sponsored United Nations Programme on Human Immunodeficiency Virus/Acquired Immunodeficiency Syndrome
UNDCP	United Nations International Drug Control Programme
UNODC	United Nations *Office on Drugs and Crime*
WCO	World Customs Organization
WHO	World Health Organization
Govt.	Government
u.	Unit
lt.	Litre
kg	Kilogram
ha	Hectare
mt	Metric ton

TABLE OF CONTENTS

EXECUTIVE SUMMARY

This summary presents, *first*, an analysis of the main illicit markets for heroin, cocaine, cannabis and amphetamine-type stimulants (ATS); and *secondly* synthesizes the main trends in illicit drug production, trafficking and consumption. The analysis of the main illicit markets focuses on the period between 1998 and 2003 since the international community is presently reviewing progress in achieving the targets set at the twentieth special session of the General Assembly (UNGASS) in 1998. The illicit drug production, trafficking and consumption trends focus on 2001/2002, updating last year's edition of the present publication.

I. Main Trends in Illicit Drug Markets

The evolution of the main illicit drug markets in recent years provides an uneven picture, depending on the drugs and the regions considered. Overall, the evolution of world heroin and cocaine markets shows some positive tendencies. The picture is confused for synthetic drugs and fairly negative for cannabis.

- **Heroin**

Treatment data consistently shows that illicit heroin use has the most severe health consequences for drug abusers. In 2000-2001, UNODC estimated that about 15 million people abused opium and heroin in the world. Although this figure has not changed much since the late 1990s, gaps in the data prevent precise monitoring of changes in global demand for illicit opium and heroin from year to year. The impression of the relative stability of the global heroin market since the end of the 1990s can be supported by an assessment of the supply situation, for which there is more robust data. About 4,400 metric tons (mt) of illicit opium were produced in 1998. Four years later, in 2002, the production (approximately 4,500 mt) is more or less at the same level. Underneath the apparent stability of global production, however, major shifts are at work.

Statistics on agricultural land devoted to illicit opium poppy cultivation in the world show that the market is changing. While global opium production remained basically stable over a four-year period, illicit opium poppy cultivation declined by 25%. The answer to this apparent paradox can be found in a considerable shift of production from South-East to South West Asia. Progress made in Myanmar and the Lao PDR has resulted in a 40% reduction in the area under opium poppy cultivation in that region between 1998 and 2002. This downward trend continued in 2003. If the current rate of reduction in South-East Asia is sustained, the Golden Triangle could well become a minor source of illicit opium it the next few years. This would close a century long chapter in the history of drug control. Meanwhile, a 16% increase was recorded in South West Asia from 1998 to 2002. The higher productivity of the irrigated opium fields in Afghanistan explains why the world's opium output remained stable while the level of cultivation was going down. The result has been an increasing concentration of illicit opium production in a single country, Afghanistan.

Regional shifts have also reshaped the patterns of heroin abuse in the world. There are some improvements in West Europe, but the rapid growth of opium production in Afghanistan has fuelled the development of a large heroin market in the region and, further, in Central Asia, the Russian Federation and East Europe. Largely caused by the increase in intravenous heroin abuse, the HIV/AIDS epidemic has been expanding at an alarming rate.

The new heroin markets in East Europe, Russia and Central Asia are not yet as lucrative as the West European markets. The economic incentive they provide to traffickers is thus lower. They do, however, offer the potential to offset the reduction in profitability per transaction by expanding the consumer base.

There are already more opiate abusers in those regions than in West Europe and the potential for further growth is large.

There is evidence to suggest that the effect of long-term demand reduction efforts can be catalyzed by rapid and shorter-term progress in the reduction of supply. Although stocks delayed and reduced the impact of the short-lived but considerable decline of opium production in Afghanistan in 2001, records show that heroin purity levels in Europe declined that year and that the trend continued in the first two quarters of 2002. One positive consequence was a decline in the number of drug related deaths in a number of West European countries. Similarly, there are indications that in the countries of Central Asia the growth of abuse declined markedly in 2002 as a consequence of reduced supply. Australia provided another illustration. Following the dismantling of a number of trafficking groups supplying the Australian market, the availability of heroin in that country dropped significantly in 2001. As a result, declines in the number of drug related crimes and drug related deaths, as well as increases in the number of heroin addicts seeking treatment, were recorded. In 2003, however, there have been reports of the supply slack in Australia being partly taken up by heroin originating in, or being trafficked *via*, the Democratic People's Republic of Korea (North Korea).

- **Cocaine**

Cocaine is abused by about 14 million people in the world and comes second to heroin in terms of treatment demand. There are some signs of progress in controlling cocaine supply and demand. Of the three countries which supply the world's illicit cocaine, Bolivia has now become an almost marginal source (less than one-tenth of world cocaine production), and Peru has achieved a reduction of about 60 % in coca cultivation since 1995. Although both countries are encountering difficulties in consolidating the decline and eliminating the remaining illicit cultivation on their territory, overall they have not produced more than one-fifth of world illicit cocaine during the past few years.

The main challenge is Colombia, where the production of cocaine from domestic cultivation increased roughly by a factor of five between 1993 and 1999. By then, the country had become the source of almost three-quarters of the world's illicit cocaine. The good news is that, reversing an eight-year trend, and for the second year in a row, Colombia achieved a very significant reduction of coca bush cultivation on its territory in 2002. Cumulatively, this amounts to a 37% decline between 2000 and 2002. Combining the three source countries translates into an overall reduction of 22% of the area under coca between 1999 and 2002. If this trend persists there could be a major change in the dynamics of world cocaine supply.

At the other end of the trafficking chain, some positive evidence is available. In the United States of America (USA), the world's largest cocaine market, student surveys show that the number of cocaine users has tended to stabilize in recent years. Annual prevalence figures for 2002 in that country were reported to be 15% lower than in 1998, and some 60% lower than in 1985.

Nonetheless, there is some cause for concern on the demand side in other regions. Cocaine abuse is increasing in South America and cocaine traffickers have been finding new market outlets in Europe. As in the case of heroin, there are indications of a shifting market. Although the bulk of cocaine trafficking is still in the Americas, there has been an increase in cocaine trafficking towards West Europe. The share of West Europe in global cocaine seizures more than doubled between 1998 and 2001, rising from 8% to 17% during that period. Information on consumption tells the same story. The majority of West European countries reported an increase in cocaine abuse for the year 2001.

- **Cannabis**

Cannabis continues to be the most widely produced, trafficked and consumed illicit drug worldwide.

Given the global spread of cannabis production and the virtual absence of monitoring systems, no reliable production estimates for cannabis are available. (In Morocco, which is one of the largest producers of cannabis resin, UNODC and the Government are launching the first survey of cannabis cultivation this year). Rising levels of cannabis seizures and abuse suggest, however, that production is also increasing.

About two-thirds of the 86 countries which reported cannabis consumption trends to UNODC last year, indicated an increase of cannabis abuse in 2001. Overall seizures of cannabis rose by some 40% between 1998 and 2001.

A distinction should be made between cannabis resin and herb products. Seizure data over the period 1998-2001 suggest a relative stability in the trafficking patterns of cannabis resin, which continues to be primarily seized in West Europe (around three-quarters of all seizures). It was therefore cannabis herb seizures that accounted for the increase noted above. More than 60% of all cannabis herb seizures in 2001 were reported from the Americas. However, the strongest increase was in Africa, probably reflecting a combination of large-scale cultivation of cannabis and increased enforcement efforts in recent years. More than a quarter of all cannabis herb seizures are now reported from countries in Africa, compared to little more than 10% in 1998-99.

Finally, seizures of cannabis plants – an indicator of the efforts made by governments to eradicate cannabis fields– seem to be declining, possibly an indication of lesser priority given to cannabis eradication by some governments.

There are, however, some positive trends. In the USA, for instance, cannabis abuse (annual prevalence) fell in 2002 among high-school students and was almost 10% lower than in 1997 and some 30% lower than in the late 1970s. In Australia, cannabis abuse among the general population declined by 23% over the 1998-2001 period.

- **Amphetamine-type stimulants**

Amphetamine-type-stimulants (ATS) are synthetic drugs that include the chemically related amphetamine, methamphetamine and ecstasy. Unlike the traditional plant-based drugs, the production of ATS starts with readily available chemicals, in easily concealed laboratories. This makes an assessment of the location, extent and evolution of the production of such illicit drugs extremely difficult. In order to obtain a clearer picture of this complex situation, UNODC is presently undertaking a global survey on ATS.

Seizures of laboratories and end-products, as well as reports on consumption, indicate that the expansion of the ATS market is continuing. More laboratories were detected and dismantled worldwide over the last few years than ever before, particularly in the United States. But the market is also changing, partly in response to drug control agencies' efforts to tackle the problem, and partly as a result of the dynamics of abuse patterns.

Trafficking in methamphetamine accounts for the bulk of trafficking in ATS and has been clearly shifting towards East and South-East Asia in recent years. Seizures in 2001 declined, however, possibly a consequence of better controls of ephedrine (one of the main precursors) and first successes in reducing methamphetamine production in the People's Republic of China. The Democratic People's Republic of Korea (North Korea) seems to be emerging as a significant source/transshipment area for methamphetamine going to Japan, which is the region's most lucrative ATS market.

In 2000, close to 90% of all countries reporting to UNODC on trends in the abuse of methamphetamine reported an increase. By 2001 this proportion fell to 52%. Japan reported a stabilization in methamphetamine abuse in 2001, following years of increase. Thailand, in contrast, affected by large-scale methamphetamine imports from neighbouring Myanmar, seized the largest quantity of methamphetamine worldwide in 2001 and reported a further increase in ATS abuse for 2001.

Europe, notably the Netherlands, Poland and Belgium, continues to be the main centre of clandestine amphetamine production. Seizures of amphetamine in West Europe peaked around 1998 and have shown a downward trend since, but production and trafficking continued to increase in East Europe. This could signal an underlying shift of amphetamine production to East Europe, and possibly a less buoyant demand in West Europe. While half of all West European countries reported an increase in amphetamine abuse in 2000, this proportion fell somewhat, to 33%, in 2001.

Trafficking in ecstasy increased strongly throughout the 1990s. In 2001, however, ecstasy seizures declined, mainly in North America and West Europe. Europe (particularly the Netherlands and Belgium) is still the main centre of global ecstasy production. However, its relative importance seems to be declining as ecstasy production is appearing in other parts of the world. In the mid-1990s, West European countries reported around 80% of all ecstasy seizures. This proportion fell to around 50% in 2000 and 2001. Trafficking in ecstasy has increased particularly in the Americas in recent years, though it is now found in other regions as well, notably in South-East Asia, Southern Africa and the Near and Middle East.

Ecstasy abuse, after a period of decline, has again shown signs of increase in West Europe. In the USA it declined, for the first time in years, in 2002. In other regions, particularly the Caribbean and parts of South America, Oceania, South-East Asia, the Near East, and southern Africa, it seems to be accelerating.

II. Main Trends in Production, Trafficking and Consumption, 2001/2002

Production

- After the steep decline recorded in 2001, world illicit opium and heroin production recovered in 2002, despite a reduction of cultivation by 23% in Myanmar and 18% in Laos. This increase was due to the resumption of large-scale opium poppy cultivation in Afghanistan. Global illicit opium poppy cultivation climbed back to about 180,000 hectares in 2002 (against 144,000 ha in 2001 and 222,000 ha in 2000). The resulting opium production was estimated at about 4,500 metric tons (against 1,600 mt in 2001 and 4,700 mt in 2000).

- In 2002, the relative distribution of illicit opium production among the main source countries was: Afghanistan (76%), Myanmar (18%), Laos (2%) and Colombia (1%). The remaining 3% came from other countries (Mexico, Pakistan, Thailand, Vietnam, etc.) where marginal production is reported.

- For the second year in a row, illicit coca cultivation declined in Colombia. The 30% reduction recorded between November 2001 (145,000 ha) and December 2002 (102,000 ha) translated into an 18% decline in world illicit coca cultivation (from 211,000 ha in 2001, to 173,000 ha at the end of 2002).

- Peru's illicit coca cultivation remained relatively stable during the year (52,500 ha in 2002). In Bolivia, where cultivation had recorded a continuous decline between 1996 (48,100 ha) and 2000 (14,600 ha), cultivation increased for the second year in a row (by 23% to 24,400 ha in 2002).

- The relative distribution of potential cocaine production among the three countries in 2002 was estimated as follows: Colombia 72%, Peru 20% and Bolivia 8%.

- The lack of adequate data does not enable UNODC to precisely monitor trends in cannabis and synthetic drug production from year to year. However, indirect indicators suggest that global production of cannabis and amphetamine-type stimulants continued to increase in recent years, although regional variations could be observed.

Trafficking

- Overall trafficking, as reflected in the number of seizure cases reported, continued growing in 2001, though at a slower pace than in the 1990s. (The latest seizure data received from Member States in replies to the Annual Reports Questionnaire (ARQ) refer to the year 2001.)

- The largest quantities seized worldwide were of cannabis herb, followed by cannabis resin. Seized quantities of cannabis remained stable in 2001. The largest cannabis herb seizures in 2001 were reported from Mexico; the largest cannabis resin seizures were made by Spain.

- The third largest quantities of drugs seized worldwide were of cocaine. They remained more or less stable in 2001. The largest cocaine seizures were reported from the USA, followed by Colombia.

- Overall, seizures of opiates declined by 23% in 2001. The decline is attributed to the considerable decline of opium production in Afghanistan that year. Most opiate seizures (opium, morphine and heroin) continued to be made by the Islamic Republic of Iran. The largest seizures of heroin, however, were reported from the People's Republic of China in 2001.

- Following years of massive growth, seizures of amphetamine-type stimulants (excluding ecstasy) fell in 2001 by 36%. This decline was mainly due to lower methamphetamine seizures reported by China, which in recent years accounted for the bulk of such seizures. Nonetheless, global ATS seizures (excluding ecstasy) were still four times as high as in 1995 and eight times as high as in 1990. The largest ATS seizures in 2001 were reported from Thailand.

- Ecstasy seizures fell by around 10% in 2001. Declines were recorded in a number of major markets, including the USA, Canada, Netherlands, France and Italy. The largest ecstasy seizures were reported from the Netherlands, followed by the United States.

Consumption

- UNODC estimates that about 200 million people consume illicit drugs (annual prevalence 2000-2001). This includes about 163 million for cannabis, 34 million for amphetamines, 8 million for Ecstasy, 14 million for cocaine, 15 million for opiates (of which 10 million for heroin). These numbers are not cumulative because of poly-drug use. They should be treated with considerable caution, given the large gaps in the prevalence data reported.

- The main problem drugs in the world, as reflected in demand for treatment, remained the opiates, followed by cocaine. In much of East and South-East Asia, ATS are the main problem drugs. In Africa, treatment demand continues to be concentrated on cannabis.

- Reports indicate that, overall, the global drug problem continues to spread in geographical terms as more countries reported increases rather than decreases in drug abuse. As in previous years, the strongest increase in abuse levels was for cannabis, followed by amphetamine-type stimulants. There are, however, indications that the rate of increase is slowing down, with the exception of ecstasy.

- Heroin abuse declined in East Asia, Oceania and West Europe in 2001, but continued to increase in the countries located on the Afghan heroin trafficking route towards Russia and Europe.

- Cocaine abuse continued to increase in West Europe and in South America, while it was stable in North America and fell among US high-school students in 2001.

- The methamphetamine epidemic appears to be continuing in South East Asia, while abuse has stabilized in Japan.

- Amphetamine abuse stabilized in West Europe, but continued to increase in East and North Europe.

- Most countries reporting on Ecstasy saw increasing levels of abuse.

- Cannabis abuse increased in Africa, South America, Europe and South West Asia. Declines were recorded in Oceania and South East Asia.

1. TRENDS

1.1. PRODUCTION

1.1.1. Overview

After the steep decline recorded in 2001, world's illicit opium and heroin production recovered in 2002 due to the resumption of large-scale opium poppy cultivation in Afghanistan. By the end of 2002, coca bush cultivation had declined by 18%, compared with the end of 2001, thanks to a significant reduction of coca cultivation achieved in Colombia. The lack of adequate data does not enable UNODC to precisely monitor trends in cannabis and synthetic drug production from year to year. However, indirect indicators suggest that global production of cannabis and amphetamine-type stimulants continued to increase in 2002, although regional variations can be observed.

1.1.2. Opium / Heroin

Most of the world's illicit opium and heroin comes from a few countries. Afghanistan ranks first, with about three-quarters of world's production, followed by Myanmar, the Lao People's Democratic Republic (Laos) and Colombia. From 2000 to 2001, the world's illicit opium production declined by 65 %. That considerable decline was primarily the result of a ban on opium poppy cultivation enforced by the Taliban regime that reduced Afghanistan's opium production by 94 %.

The resumption of large-scale opium poppy cultivation in Afghanistan last year brought the world's illicit opium poppy cultivation back to 180,000 hectares (ha) in 2002 (against 222,000 ha in 2000 and 144,000 ha in 2001). The resulting opium production was estimated at about 4,500 metric tons (mt) (against 4,700 mt in 2000 and 1,600 mt in 2001). This one-year setback is however somewhat mitigated by a longer-term decline of 25% in the global area under opium poppy cultivation since 1998, when the total extent was 238,000 ha.

Leaving aside the short-lived exception of 2001, the most significant trend over the last four-year period is the relative shift of illicit opium production from South-East to South West Asia. Afghanistan's irrigated fields typically produce 4 times more opium per hectare than the rain-fed fields of the mountainous Shan States in Myanmar. Between 1999 and 2002, opium poppy cultivation declined by 40 % in South-East Asia. During the same period, the extent of opium

poppy cultivation in Afghanistan increased by 16%. In 2002 alone, cultivation declined by 23 % in Myanmar, from 105,000 ha to about 81,000 ha, and by 18 % in Laos, from about 17,000 ha to about 14,100 ha.

In 2002, the relative distribution of illicit opium production among the main source countries was: Afghanistan (76%), Myanmar (18%), Laos (2%), Colombia (1%). The remaining 3% came from other countries (Mexico, Pakistan, Thailand, Vietnam, etc...) where marginal production is reported.

Potential production of illicit heroin in 2002 would amount to about 450 mt. It should be noted that this figure is only indicative. There are too many uncertainties about a number of important factors to calculate a more reliable estimate. Such factors include the quantity of opium directly consumed in and around the producing countries, and therefore not transformed into heroin, the exact morphine content of the opium produced in the different source countries[a], or the efficiency of the clandestine laboratories which process opium into morphine and then heroin.

Outlook for 2003
At the time of writing of the present report (end of May 2003), the annual opium surveys supported by UNODC in the framework of its global Illicit Crop Monitoring Programme (ICMP) were reaching final stages in Myanmar and Laos, and proceeding in Afghanistan. Preliminary results showed a continuing decline of opium poppy cultivation in Myanmar (about 20%) and Laos (about 15%) in 2003. While it was too early to forecast the results of the ongoing survey in Afghanistan, preliminary indications pointed to some shifts in the relative distribution of opium poppy cultivation in the country. The reports and final results of the annual surveys are expected to be published in June 2003 for Myanmar and Laos and September/October 2003 for Afghanistan.

---

[a] The morphine content of opium is conventionally assumed to be 10 % (10 kg of opium to produce 1 kg of morphine), but there are indications that it could vary significantly from country to country. The ratio for the conversion of morphine into heroin is 1.

OPIUM

GLOBAL ILLICIT CULTIVATION OF OPIUM POPPY AND PRODUCTION OF OPIUM, 1990-2002

	1990	1991	1992	1993	1994	1995	1996	1997	1998	1999	2000	2001	2002
CULTIVATION[(1)] IN HECTARES													
SOUTH-WEST ASIA													
Afghanistan	41,300	50,800	49,300	58,300	71,470	53,759	56,824	58,416	63,674	90,583	82,171	7,606	74,100
Pakistan	7,488	7,962	9,493	7,329	5,759	5,091	873	874	950	284	260	213	622
Subtotal	48,788	58,762	58,793	65,629	77,229	58,850	57,697	59,290	64,624	90,867	82,431	7,819	74,722
SOUTH-EAST ASIA													
Lao PDR	30,580	29,625	19,190	26,040	18,520	19,650	21,601	24,082	26,837	22,543	19,052	17,255	14,000
Myanmar	150,100	160,000	153,700	165,800	146,600	154,070	163,000	155,150	130,300	89,500	108,700	105,000	81,400
Thailand	1,782	3,727	3,016	998	478	168	368	352	716	702	890	820	750
Viet Nam [(2)]	18,000	17,000	12,199	4,268	3,066	1,880	1,743	340	442	442			
Subtotal	200,462	210,352	188,105	197,106	168,664	175,768	186,712	179,924	158,295	113,187	128,642	123,075	96,150
OTHER ASIAN COUNTRIES													
Combined	8,054	7,521	2,900	5,704	5,700	5,025	3,190	2,050	2,050	2,050	2,479	2,500	2,500
Total Asia	257,304	276,635	249,798	268,439	251,593	239,643	247,599	241,264	224,969	206,104	213,552	133,394	173,372
LATIN AMERICA													
Colombia [(3)]		1,160	6,578	5,008	15,091	5,226	4,916	6,584	7,350	6,500	6,500	4,300	4,200
Mexico [(4)]	5,450	3,765	3,310	3,960	5,795	5,050	5,100	4,000	5,500	3,600	1,900	4,400	2,700
Total Latin America	5,450	4,925	9,888	8,968	20,886	10,276	10,016	10,584	12,850	10,100	8,400	8,700	6,900
GRAND TOTAL	262,754	281,560	259,686	277,407	272,479	249,919	257,615	251,848	237,819	216,204	221,952	142,094	180,272
POTENTIAL PRODUCTION IN METRIC TONS													
SOUTH-WEST ASIA													
Afghanistan	1,570	1,980	1,970	2,330	3,416	2,335	2,248	2,804	2,693	4,565	3,276	185	3,400
Pakistan	150	160	181	161	128	112	24	24	26	9	8	5	5
Subtotal	1,720	2,140	2,151	2,491	3,544	2,447	2,272	2,828	2,719	4,574	3,284	190	3,405
SOUTH-EAST ASIA													
Lao PDR	202	196	127	169	120	128	140	147	124	124	167	134	112
Myanmar	1,621	1,728	1,660	1,791	1,583	1,664	1,760	1,676	1,303	895	1,087	1,097	828
Thailand	20	23	14	17	3	2	5	4	8	8	6	6	9
Viet Nam	90	85	61	21	15	9	9	2	2	2			
Subtotal	1,933	2,032	1,862	1,998	1,721	1,803	1,914	1,829	1,437	1,029	1,260	1,237	949
OTHER ASIAN COUNTRIES													
Combined	45	45	-	4	90	78	48	30	30	30	38	40	40
Total Asia	3,698	4,217	4,013	4,493	5,355	4,328	4,234	4,687	4,186	5,633	4,582	1,467	4,394
LATIN AMERICA													
Colombia [(3)]		16	90	68	205	71	67	90	100	88	88	58	50
Mexico	62	41	40	49	60	53	54	46	60	43	21	71	47
Total Latin America	62	57	130	117	265	124	121	136	160	131	109	129	97
GRAND TOTAL	3,760	4,274	4,143	4,610	5,620	4,452	4,355	4,823	4,346	5,764	4,691	1,596	4,491
Potential HEROIN	376	427	414	461	562	445	436	482	435	576	469	160	449

[(1)] Potentially harvestable, after eradication.

[(2)] Due to small production, Viet Nam cultivation and production were included in the category " Other Asian countries" as of 2000.

[(3)] According to the Government of Colombia, cultivation covered 7,350 ha and 6,500 ha and production amounted to 73 mt and 65 mt in 1998 and 1999 respectively.

[(4)] Sources: As its survey system is under development, the Govt of Mexico indicates it can neither provide cultivation estimates nor endorse those published by UNDCP which are derived from US Government surveys.

OPIUM POPPY CULTIVATION (2001-2002)

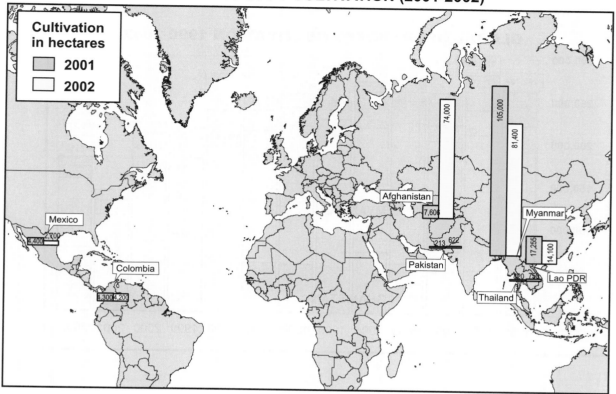

OPIUM PRODUCTION (2001-2002)

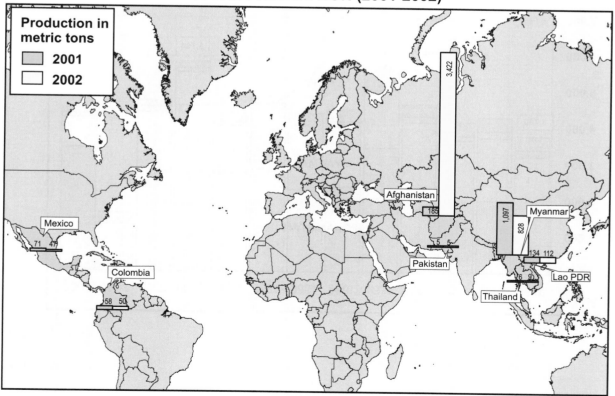

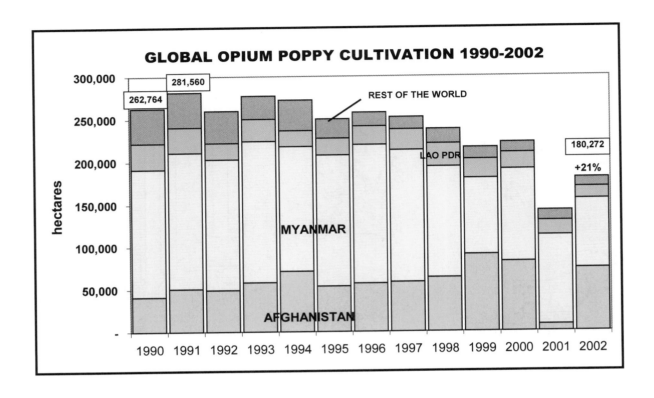

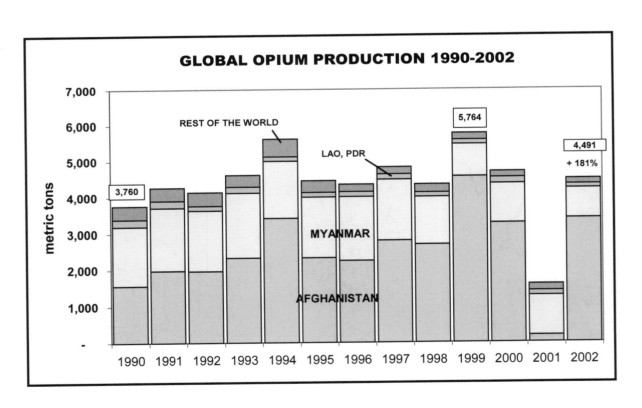

AFGHANISTAN - OPIUM POPPY CULTIVATION, 1991-2002

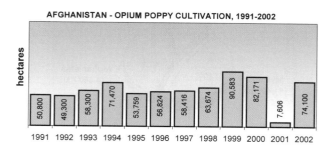

AFGHANISTAN - OPIUM PRODUCTION, 1991-2002

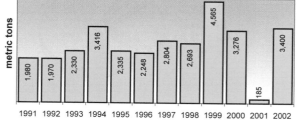

MYANMAR - OPIUM POPPY CULTIVATION, 1991-2002

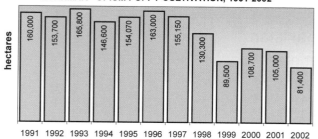

MYANMAR - OPIUM PRODUCTION, 1991-2002

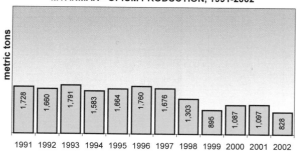

LAO PDR - OPIUM POPPY CULTIVATION, 1991-2002

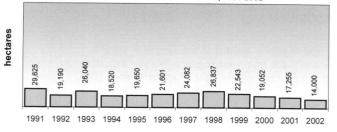

LAO PDR - OPIUM PRODUCTION, 1991-2002

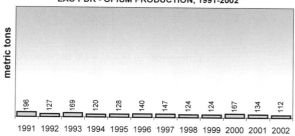

REST OF THE WORLD - OPIUM POPPY CULT. 1991-2002

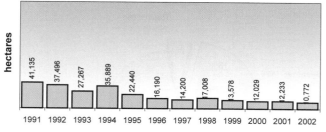

REST OF THE WORLD - OPIUM PRODUCTION, 1991-2002

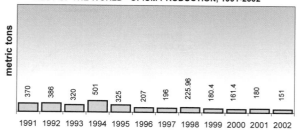

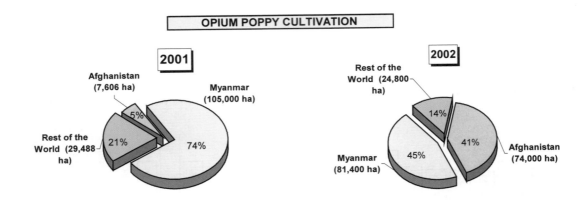

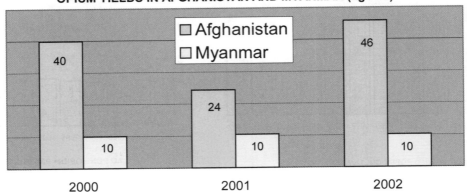

Differences in opium yield between Afghanistan and Myanmar are due to differences in opium poppy varieties and growing conditions. Variations of yields from year to year in the same country are mostly caused by changes in weather conditions and/or, as in the case of Afghanistan in 2001, by a shift in the relative distribution of cultivation from irrigated to rain-fed land.

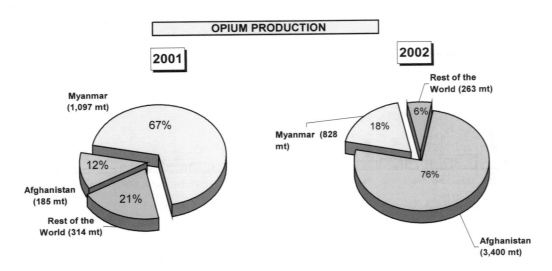

POTENTIAL VALUE OF 2002 FARMGATE PRODUCTION OF OPIUM

(UNODC estimates)

	Farmgate price US$ per kg	Production metric tons	Potential value millions of US$
Myanmar	151	828	125
Afghanistan	350	3,400	1,190
Lao, PDR	122	112	14
Other Asia [1]		54	22
Colombia	194	50	10
Mexico [2]	194	47	9
Total opium		4,491	1,370

[1] Including Pakistan. Thailand. Vietnam and other Asian countries: price is based on estimated average for these countries.
(2) Farmgate price not available: value based on price in Colombia

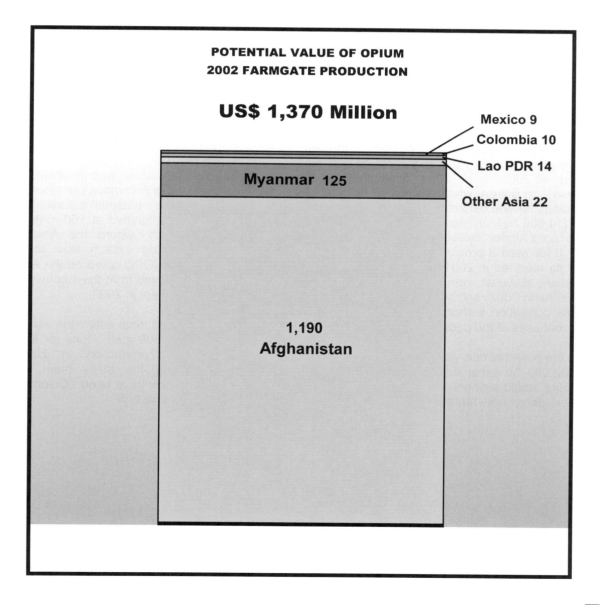

POTENTIAL VALUE OF OPIUM
2002 FARMGATE PRODUCTION

US$ 1,370 Million

Mexico 9
Colombia 10
Lao PDR 14
Other Asia 22
Myanmar 125
1,190 Afghanistan

1.1.3. Coca / cocaine

For the second year in a row, the UNODC supported monitoring system reported a decline in illicit coca cultivation in Colombia. It declined by 30%, to a total of 102,000 ha in December 2002, down from 145,000 ha in November 2001. The two-year decline in Colombia comes after a continuous increase, which took illicit cultivation from less than 40,000 ha in the early 1990's to more than 160,000 ha in 2000. The decline recorded now is attributed primarily to the large-scale eradication campaign implemented by the Colombian government, as well as to field abandonment or voluntary manual eradication by farmers facing declining coca base price or benefiting from alternative development programmes.

As Colombia is by far the largest source of illicit coca in the world, ahead of Peru and Bolivia, this large decline was reflected in globally aggregated coca cultivation, which decreased by 18 % from 211,000 ha in 2001 to 173,000 ha at the end of 2002.

According to the UNODC supported monitoring system, Peru's illicit coca cultivation remained relatively stable during the year, with 46,500 ha, against 46,200 ha in 2001 (less than 1 % increase). In Bolivia, where cultivation recorded a continuous decline between 1996 (48,100 ha) and 2000 (14,600 ha), an increase of 4,500 ha (23%) in the area under cultivation was reported last year. It followed a previous one-year increase of 5,300 ha reported in 2001. The area under coca cultivation, however, remains relatively modest (24,000 ha in 2002) and includes about 12,000 ha of coca cultivation authorized by national law for traditional uses of the coca leaf.

While the potential one-year cocaine production of the 102,000 ha recorded in December 2002 in Colombia would amount to 480 metric tons, this number does not represent actual production

throughout 2002. Estimating the actual production of cocaine in Colombia in 2002 is not easy, because coca fields are harvested more than once in a given year and eradication activities are spread over several months. In order to arrive at a more realistic estimate for Colombia, UNODC calculated an average of the two cultivation figures recorded in November 2001 and in December 2002 by the UNODC supported national monitoring system. This average (123,400 ha) was then multiplied by the estimated yield per hectare and per harvest, and by the average number of harvests per year (4). The result amounted to 580 metric tons of potential cocaine production in Colombia for 2002. While the calculated estimate is not very accurate, it is probably closer to the actual amount produced during the calendar year than a figure derived solely from the extent of cultivation recorded at the end of the year, after an extensive eradication campaign.

It should be noted that, although less than in the past, some of the coca base produced in Peru is still processed into cocaine in Colombian clandestine laboratories.

In Peru, the estimation was relatively simpler, because the level of cultivation remained stable in 2002. The resulting potential cocaine output for that country was estimated at 160 metric tons in 2002. For Bolivia, where the new UNODC supported monitoring system was still in pilot phase last year, UNODC relied on the estimate of 60 metric tons, derived from the survey conducted by the US government in 2002.

Adding the three national estimates would give a tentative figure of 800 metric tons for the world's potential cocaine production in 2002. Its distribution among the three main producing countries would thus have been : Colombia 72 %, Peru 20% and Bolivia 8 %.

COCA

GLOBAL ILLICIT CULTIVATION OF COCA BUSH AND PRODUCTION OF COCA LEAF AND COCAINE, 1990-2002

	1990	1991	1992	1993	1994	1995	1996	1997	1998	1999	2000	2001	2002
CULTIVATION[1] OF COCA BUSH IN HECTARES													
Bolivia [2]	50,300	47,900	45,300	47,200	48,100	48,600	48,100	45,800	38,000	21,800	14,600	19,900	24,400
Colombia [3]	40,100	37,500	37,100	39,700	44,700	50,900	67,200	79,400	101,800	160,100	163,300	144,800	102,000
Peru [4]	121,300	120,800	129,100	108,800	108,600	115,300	94,400	68,800	51,000	38,700	43,400	46,200	46,700
	211,700	**206,200**	**211,500**	**195,700**	**201,400**	**214,800**	**209,700**	**194,000**	**190,800**	**220,600**	**221,300**	**210,900**	**173,100**
POTENTIAL PRODUCTION OF DRY COCA LEAF IN METRIC TONS													
Bolivia	77,000	78,000	80,300	84,400	89,800	85,000	75,100	70,100	52,900	22,800	13,400	20,200	19,800
Colombia	45,300	45,000	44,900	45,300	67,500	80,900	108,900	129,500	165,900	261,000	266,200	236,000	222,100
Peru	196,900	222,700	223,900	155,500	165,300	183,600	174,700	130,600	95,600	69,200	46,200	49,300	52,500
	319,200	**345,700**	**349,100**	**285,200**	**322,600**	**349,500**	**358,700**	**330,200**	**314,400**	**353,000**	**325,800**	**305,500**	**294,400**
POTENTIAL MANUFACTURE OF COCAINE IN METRIC TONS													
Bolivia	189	220	225	240	255	240	215	200	150	70	43	60	60
Colombia	92	88	91	119	201	230	300	350	435	680	695	617	580
Peru	492	525	550	410	435	460	435	325	240	175	141	150	160
	774	**833**	**866**	**769**	**891**	**930**	**950**	**875**	**825**	**925**	**879**	**827**	**800**

[1] Potentially harvestable, after eradication

[2] Source: CICAD and US Department of State, International narcotics Control Strategy Report. Annual estimates include 12,000 hectares authorized by Bolivian law 1008.

[3] Cultivation estimates for 1999 and subsequent years come from the national monitoring system established by the Colombian government with the support of UNODC. Estimates for 2000 refer to the level of cultivation in August 2000, estimates for 2001 refer to the level of cultivation in November 2001 and estimates for 2002 refer to the level of cultivation in December 2002. Due to the change of methodology, figures for 1999 and after cannot be directly compared with data from previous years.

[4] UNODC now relies on the results for 2000, 2001 and 2002 of the illicit crop monitoring system established with the support of UNODC.

COCA BUSH CULTIVATION (2001-2002)

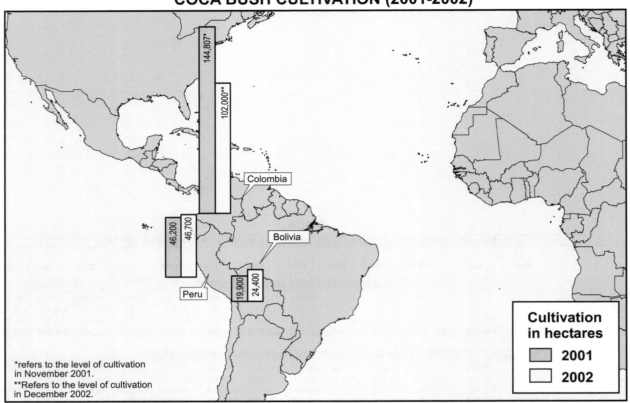

POTENTIAL COCAINE PRODUCTION (2001-2002)

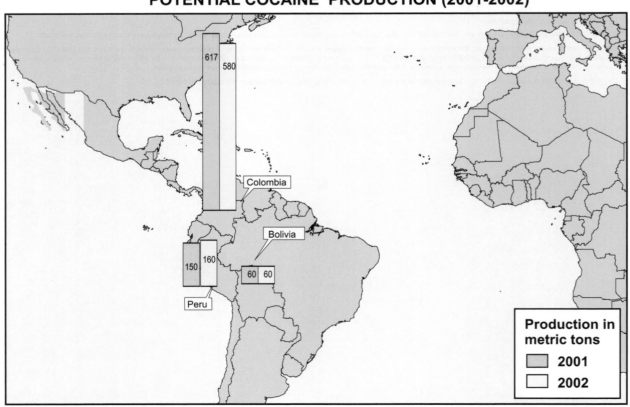

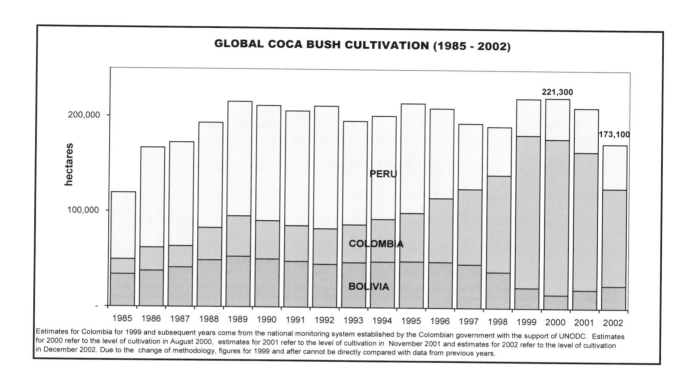

Estimates for Colombia for 1999 and subsequent years come from the national monitoring system established by the Colombian government with the support of UNODC. Estimates for 2000 refer to the level of cultivation in August 2000, estimates for 2001 refer to the level of cultivation in November 2001 and estimates for 2002 refer to the level of cultivation in December 2002. Due to the change of methodology, figures for 1999 and after cannot be directly compared with data from previous years.

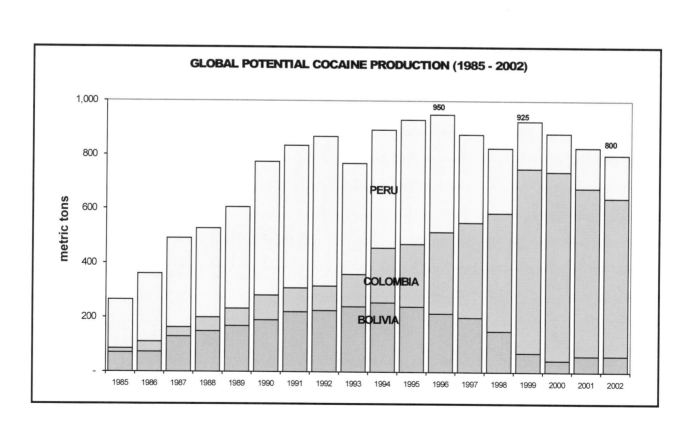

COLOMBIA - COCA BUSH CULTIVATION 1990-2002

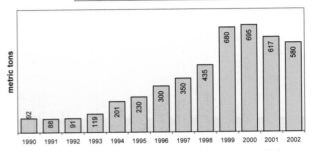

Cultivation estimates for Colombia for 1999 and subsequent years come from the national monitoring system established by the Colombian government with the support of UNDCP. Estimates for 2000 refer to the level of cultivation in August 2000, estimates for 2001 refer to the level of cultivation in November 2001 and estimates for 2002 refer to the level of cultivatin in December 2002, Due to the change of methodology, figures for 1999 and after cannot be directly compared with data from previous years. The production figures are estimates for the entire calendar year.

PERU - COCA BUSH CULTIVATION 1990-2002

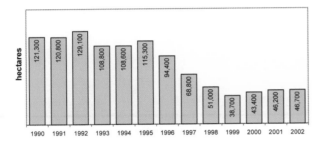

PERU- POTENTIAL COCAINE PRODUCTION 1990-2002

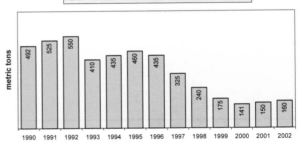

BOLIVIA - COCA BUSH CULTIVATION 1990-2002

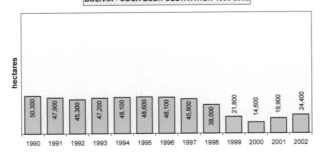

BOLIVIA- POTENTIAL COCAINE PROD. 1990-2002

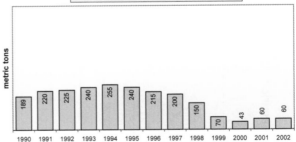

COCA BUSH CULTIVATION

2001

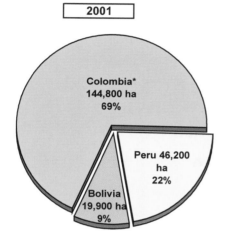

*refers to the level of cultivation in November 2001.

2002

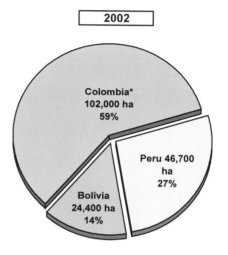

*refers to the level of cultivation in December 2002.

POTENTIAL COCAINE PRODUCTION

2001

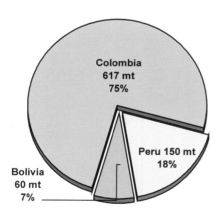

2002

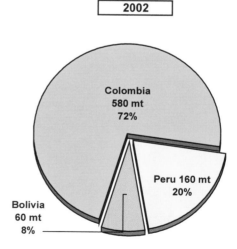

POTENTIAL VALUE OF 2002 FARMGATE PRODUCTION OF COCA BASE

	Farmgate price US$ per kg	Production metric tons	Potential value millions of US$
Colombia	847	580	491
Peru	559	160	89
Bolivia	1,000	60	60
Total opium		800	640

(UNODC estimates)

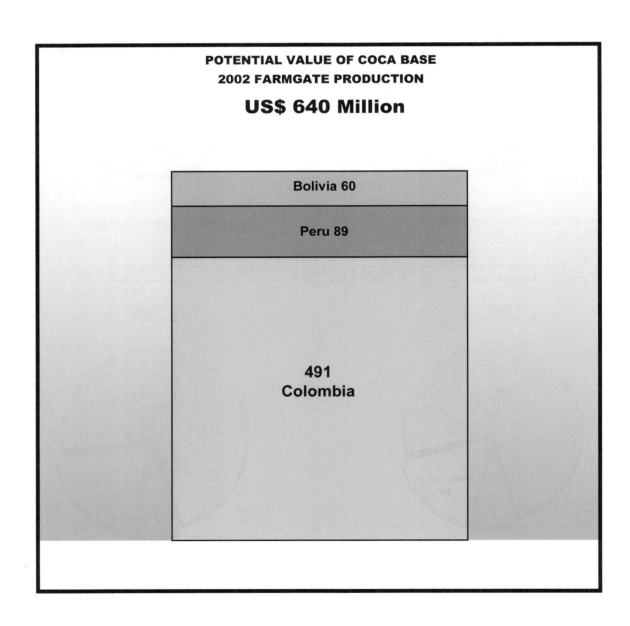

POTENTIAL VALUE OF COCA BASE
2002 FARMGATE PRODUCTION

US$ 640 Million

Bolivia 60

Peru 89

491
Colombia

1.1.4. Cannabis

The wide spread of cannabis cultivation over the world and the virtual absence of cannabis cultivation monitoring systems and surveys make it impossible to have an accurate assessment of the location, extent and evolution of cultivation and production in the world. Indirect indicators related to seizures of illicit cannabis products can help to shed some light on certain aspects of the problem. For instance, the origin of the seized drugs helps to identify the main source countries for cannabis. Overall, the rising level of cannabis seizures seems to indicate a continuing increase in cannabis cultivation worldwide.

Cannabis herb

Ninety-two countries providing information on the main sources of the cannabis herb they seized in 2001, identified 85 different source countries. Considering the same information collected over the 1998-2001 period from 111 countries, 102 different source countries for cannabis were identified. This clearly demonstrates the almost universal problem of cannabis production and trafficking.

The source countries are evenly distributed across Africa, Europe, the Americas and Asia. In contrast to cocaine or heroin trafficking, most of the cannabis herb trafficking is intra-regional. Thus, the main sources of cannabis in the Americas are located in the same region. The same applies to Africa and Asia. Inter-regional trafficking of cannabis herb is largely limited to Europe. About 40% of the source countries mentioned by countries in Europe (44 in total over the 1998-2001 period) were not located in Europe; 6 were located in Africa (incl. South Africa, Morocco, Nigeria and Malawi), 6 in Asia (Central Asia, the Near and Middle East and South-East Asia (Thailand)), 4 in the Americas (incl. Colombia and Jamaica) and 1 in Oceania (Australia).

Overall, the most frequently mentioned source countries at the global level in 2001 included Albania, Colombia, South Africa, the Russian Federation, Jamaica and the Netherlands. For the 1998-2001 period, Thailand, Ghana and Paraguay would have to be added to the list. In addition, in terms of quantities of cannabis herb trafficked, Mexico, Canada and the USA play an important role as source countries. US authorities estimate

that more than 10,000 tons of cannabis herb is produced domestically and that more than 5,000 tons a year are imported from neighbouring Mexico and Canada. Mexico is believed to produce between 7,000 and 8,000 tons of cannabis herb a year according to US estimates (USA, INCSR, March 2003).

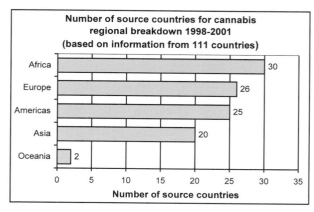

Source: UNODC, Annual Reports Questionnaire Data / DELTA.

Cannabis resin

Over the period 1999–2001, Morocco, as well as Afghanistan and Pakistan, were most often mentioned as source countries for cannabis resin products. In Western Europe, more than 60% of the countries reporting to UNODC (13 out of 21) identified Morocco as a main source of their cannabis resin for that period, and a third identified Afghanistan and Pakistan (7 out of 21) as major sources.

At the global level, other important source countries identified were in Central Asia and the Russian Federation. Lebanon was also mentioned in 2001 by a number of countries, possibly reflecting a revival of cannabis cultivation there. In Europe, Albania still seems to play a role as a source country, as well as Nepal, in South Asia. In addition, a significant number of countries in Europe identified Spain and the Netherlands as the countries where criminal groups obtained their cannabis resin. The only country in the Americas cited as a country of origin of cannabis resin is Jamaica.

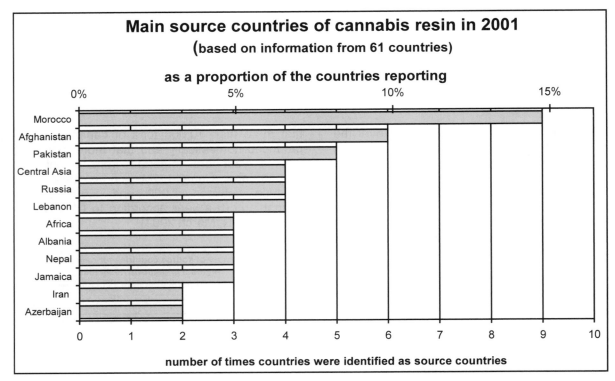

Main source countries of cannabis resin in 2001
(based on information from 61 countries)
as a proportion of the countries reporting

number of times countries were identified as source countries

Source: UNODC, Annual Reports Questionnaire Data / DELTA.

Eradication of cannabis cultivation

In contrast to rising seizures of the cannabis end-products, reported seizures of cannabis plants showed a decline in recent years and is now back at the levels of the early 1990s. This could be an indication that the eradication of cannabis plantations is being given less priority by enforcement agencies. About 18,500 tons of cannabis plant material were reportedly seized in 2001, down from 23,900 tons in 2000. In total 70 countries reported seizure of cannabis plants in 2001 and 95 over the 2000-2001 period.

The largest such seizures of cannabis plants in 2001 were reported by Turkey. In the European Union, Italy reported the largest seizures. In South America, it was Brazil; in the Caribbean, Trinidad & Tobago ; and in Central America, Costa Rica. The largest seizures of cannabis plants in Asia were reported by the Philippines and, in Africa, by the Republic of South Africa. In terms of land under cannabis cultivation eradicated, Mexico reported the highest figures in recent years.

Cannabis plant seizures at the global level 1985-2001

Source: UNODC, Annual Reports Questionnaire Data / DELTA.

1.1.5. Amphetamine-type stimulants (ATS)

Overview

Diversions from licit production of amphetamine-type stimulants are now rare. This is particularly the case with regard to substances controlled under Schedule 1 of the Psychotropic (1971) convention, such as methcathinone, or the ecstasy group (MDMA, MDA, MDME) for which there is hardly any licit production and thus very limited risk of diversion. It is also true for Schedule II substances, such as amfetamine or metamfetamine, even though they are produced in larger quantities (in 2001 : 15.5 tons of amfetamine also used for the production of 6.6 tons of dexamfetamine and 3.5 tons of levamfetamine; 5 tons of metamfetamine; and 0.8 tons of levomethamphetamine)[1].

However, seizure statistics show that the licit production figures mentioned above are dwarfed by illicit production. The overwhelming part of reported seizures of ATS are substances produced in clandestine laboratories. Global seizures of illegal amphetamine and methamphetamine amounted to 41 tons and 26 tons in 2000 and 2001, respectively. Seizures of ecstasy group substances amounted to 5 tons each in 2000 and 2001, respectively.

One indicator for the extent and the trends of illicit manufacture is the number of clandestine laboratories detected and seized. Based on ARQ data about 11,400 clandestine laboratories were

dismantled in 2001, of which 8,600 (75%) produced ATS. For comparison, this proportion was around 18% in the early 1990s. The average annual growth in the number of clandestine ATS laboratories detected and dismantled was 35% p.a. over the 1991-2001 period, while the number of other laboratories (mainly cocaine, morphine and heroin laboratories) grew by just 4½ % p.a. The increase in reported detections of ATS laboratories accelerated during the period 1995-1999.

Most ATS laboratories dismantled produced methamphetamine (almost 95% in 2001). Laboratories producing a combination of ATS (mostly methamphetamine, methcathinone, amphetamine and ecstasy) came next (3%), followed by those producing only amphetamine (1% in 2001) and only 'ecstasy' (close to 1% in 2001). Only 0.1% of the laboratories dismantled produced other synthetic stimulants.

Detections of ATS laboratories increased over the last two decades and showed a relative shift from amphetamine to methamphetamine production. In 1985, 26% of the ATS laboratories seized produced amphetamine, in 1991 14% and in 2001 only 1%. Meanwhile the proportion of methamphetamine laboratories increased from 69% in 1985, to 87% in 1991 and almost 95% in 2001.

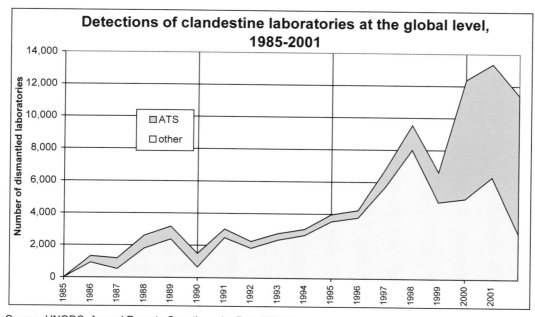

Source: UNODC, Annual Reports Questionnaire Data/DELTA.

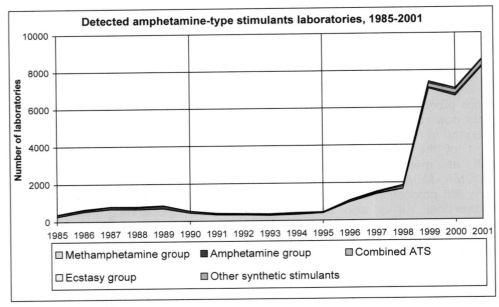

Source: UNODC, Annual Reports Questionnaire Data/DELTA.

Ecstasy production increased as well. The number of dismantled ecstasy laboratories was in 2001 almost six times as high as in 1991. While in the late 1980s and early 1990s laboratories producing MDA, MDME and other ecstasy-type substances still played a role, almost all laboratories seized in the late 1990s and in subsequent years only produced MDMA ('ecstasy').

The number of dismantled amphetamine laboratories, in contrast, was lower in 2001 than in the late 1980s. If, however, laboratories producing amphetamine and "combinations" (i.e. non-specified ATS which are likely to include a significant number of amphetamine laboratories) were analyzed together, the resulting number for 2001 would be more than twice the corresponding one for the late 1980s.

Data on seizures of precursors, the 'raw material' for ATS manufacture, confirm the foregoing analysis.

- Seizures of ATS precursors increased during the 1990s, and, expressed in ATS equivalents, were 12 times larger in 2001 than in 1991.
- A clear majority of the seizures were precursors used to manufacture methamphetamine:
- From 1991 to 2001, 66% of the seizures of precursor chemicals, expressed in ATS equivalents, were ephedrine and pseudoephedrine, used in the manufacture of methamphetamine. The bulk of the ephedrine diverted from licit channels is used for methamphetamine production, though some of it is also used for the manufacture of methcathinone.

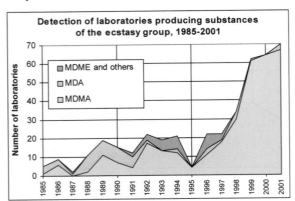

Source: UNODC, Annual Reports Questionnaire Data.

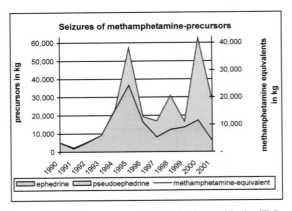

Source: INCB, *Precursors and chemicals used in the illicit manufacture of narcotic drugs and psychotropic substances*, 2002 and previous years.

- P2P, norephedrine and phenylacetic acid, used in the manufacture of amphetamine, accounted for 15% of all ATS precursor seizures expressed in ATS equivalents.
- Precursor chemicals used for ecstasy production – 3.4-MDP-2P, safrole, isosafrole and piperonal – accounted for 19% of all ATS precursor seizures between 1991 and 2001.

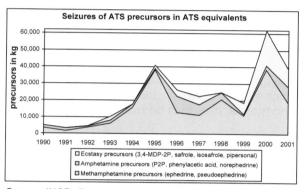

Source: INCB, *Precursors and chemicals used in the illicit manufacture of narcotic drugs and psychotropic substances*, 2002 and previous years.

Since 1990, methamphetamine seizures were characterized by two peaks: one in the mid 1990s and a second one in 2000. (Both peaks were due to exceptionally large seizures made in the USA). Data also suggest that there was a partial replacement of ephedrine by pseudo-ephedrine in recent years, following improved controls of ephedrine. This was notably the case in North America. Methamphetamine production in Asia is still based on ephedrine.

The amounts of precursors seized in 2000 - 17 tons of ephedrine and 45 tons of pseudoephedrine - would have enabled production of about 42 tons of methamphetamine. For comparison, global seizures of the methamphetamine end-product in that year amounted to about 35 tons. In ATS equivalent, precursor seizures were thus larger than end-product seizures and this generally applies to previous years as well. In 2001, however, the ranking was reversed. Both methamphetamine and precursor seizures declined. Methamphetamine seizures amounted to 22 tons; precursor seizures to 19 tons of methamphetamine equivalent. Nonetheless, seizures of precursors and of end-products were still some 12 times larger in 2001 than in 1991.

There was also an increase in amphetamine seizures. Between 1991 and 2001, seizures of amphetamine-precursors, expressed in ATS equivalents, rose six-fold. There was one peak in the mid-1990s and another one in 2001. The main

precursor chemical used in the manufacture of amphetamine is 1-phenyl-2-propanone or P2P (also known as BMK), followed by norephedrine. P2P can be also used for the manufacture of methamphetamine. The regional patterns of P2P seizures suggest, however, that P2P is mainly being used for the manufacture of amphetamine.

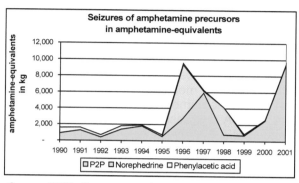

Source: INCB, *Precursors and chemicals used in the illicit manufacture of narcotic drugs and psychotropic substances*, 2002 and previous years.

A stronger increase, although starting from low levels, was reported for seizures of ecstasy precursors. A peak was reached in 2000. Seizures of ecstasy precursors in 2001 - expressed in 'ecstasy equivalents' - were lower than a year earlier. Nonetheless, they were several hundred percent higher in 2001 than in 1991. Average annual growth over this period amounted to 85% p.a. Seizures were mainly 3,4-methylendioxyphenyl-2-propane or 3,4-MDP-2-P (also known as PMK), a direct precursor for the manufacture of MDMA followed by safrole, a 'pre-precursor', used for the manufacture of 3,4-MDP-2-P which then serves as a basis for the manufacture of MDMA, generally known as ecstasy.

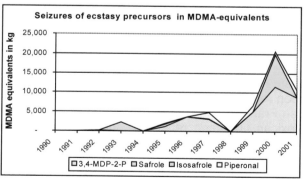

Source: INCB, *Precursors and chemicals used in the illicit manufacture of narcotic drugs and psychotropic substances*, 2002 and previous years.

1.1.5.1. Regional distribution of ATS production

Methamphetamine

North America

Replies to the ARQ show that most methamphetamine laboratories were dismantled in the USA. In 2001, 7,990 methamphetamine laboratories were discovered and dismantled in that country equivalent to 98% of all reported detections of methamphetamine laboratories worldwide. The number of laboratories dismantled in the USA increased strongly over the last decade (24% p.a. over the 1985-2001 period and 38% p.a. over the 1991-2001 period). There was also an increase in the number of laboratories dismantled in Mexico and in Canada over the last decade.

A significant number of the clandestine methamphetamine laboratories in the USA are operated by independent operators. Several of the larger ones are operated by criminal groups from neighbouring Mexico and/or US citizens of Mexican origin, reflecting the ability of these groups to acquire ephedrine from international markets and to smuggle it via Mexico into the USA. Improved controls of ephedrine since the mid-1990s prompted, however, many criminal groups to opt for pseudo-ephedrine as an alternative precursor. Pseudo-ephedrine is most often smuggled into the USA via Canada. In the 1980s, when ephedrine was less strictly controlled, methamphetamine production and distribution were almost exclusively in the hands of US motorcycle gangs.

Clandestine methamphetamine laboratories have been seized in all of the 50 states. There are, nonetheless, concentrations in states along the West coast, notably in California, as well as in a number of other southern states bordering Mexico. The highest levels of methamphetamine related emergency room mentions per capita have been reported for years in California, notably from San Francisco and San Diego located close to the Mexican border, reflecting the close nexus between production and abuse. In addition, production (and consumption) increased in recent years in some of the states bordering Canada, such as Washington, reflecting illegal pseudo-ephedrine imports from Canada. By contrast, states along the East Coast have been less affected by large-scale methamphetamine production and abuse.

In total, the USA dismantled almost 30,000 clandestine methamphetamine laboratories over the 1991-2001 period, equivalent to 97% of all reported detections of methamphetamine laboratories worldwide. There were reports of a few 'super-labs', but the large majority of the laboratories were small-scale production facilities. A simple comparison with some other countries, which have less, but larger clandestine laboratories, may thus be misleading.

Indeed, using alternative indicators based on the importance of methamphetamine production and on the seizures of chemical precursors and end-products shows a different picture. Over the 1991-2001 period, 59% of all ephedrine and pseudo-ephedrine seizures took place in the USA. If seizures of neighbouring countries – Mexico and Canada – are added, the proportion rises to 67%, a number which remains clearly lower than the USA's share in the world's total number of laboratories dismantled. Furthermore, seizures in North America of the methamphetamine end-product accounted for only 16% of global methamphetamine seizures in 2001.

In terms of output, US authorities estimate that the annual methamphetamine production in the USA and Mexico amounts to some 125 tons (range 106 to 144 tons).[2] For comparison, total legal manufacture of methamphetamine worldwide was 5 tons (of which 1.7 tons in the USA) in 2001[3]. A clandestine production of 125 tons in North America suggests that about 3% of the illicit methamphetamine produced is actually seized (3.3 tons in the USA and Mexico in 2001). Including seizures of the methamphetamine raw material, ephedrine and pseudoephedrine, seizures in North America amount to about 15% of methamphetamine production. For comparison, in the case of opiates about 18% of the illicit opium produced globally was seized worldwide (in the form of opium, morphine or heroin) over the 1996-2001 period. In the case of cocaine, which has been the main priority of US enforcement efforts, the proportion is around 40% (1996-2001 period).

South-East Asia

Other important production sites of methamphetamine are located in a number of countries in South-East and East Asia, notably in the People's Republic of China, Thailand and Myanmar. There is ample evidence that methamphetamine production increased strongly throughout the region over the last decade. Compared with the period 1991-1995, the number of clandestine methamphetamine laboratories detected there more than quadrupled over the 1996-2001 period. Methamphetamine precursor seizures increased also, in both absolute and relative terms. While the countries of East and South-East Asia accounted for 21% of all methamphetamine precursor seizures over the 1991-95 period, this proportion rose to 31% for the period 1996-2001.

However, those numbers do not necessarily reveal the whole picture. Several East and South-East Asian countries still have a limited capacity to detect clandestine laboratories and to monitor effectively the movements of precursors. The

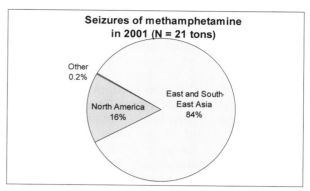

Seizures of methamphetamine in 2001 (N = 21 tons)

Source: UNODC, Annual Reports Questionnaire Data.

importance of East and South-East Asia as, possibly, the world's largest production area of illicit methamphetamine becomes more visible if seizures of the end-products are analyzed. In 2001, 84% of all methamphetamine were seized in that region and similarly high proportions were reported for previous years. The high seizures likely reflect the fairly easy access to precursor chemicals, the existence of large-scale methamphetamine production and consumption in the region, and intensive trafficking across the region.

The largest seizures of methamphetamine in recent years took place in *the People's Republic of China* (50% of all methamphetamine seizures in East and South-East Asia over 1996-2001). In 2001, China reported dismantling 44 clandestine ATS laboratories, up from 26 in 1995, and none before 1990. There is a clear concentration of methamphetamine production in several southeastern provinces, notably Fujian and Guandong (close to Hong Kong), but authorities have also started to report methamphetamine production in other provinces of the country. A number of the Chinese laboratories actually worked for criminal groups located in Hong Kong SAR or Taiwan, province of China.

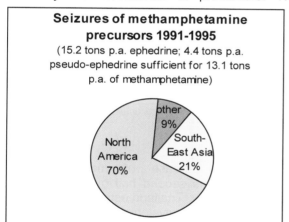

Seizures of methamphetamine precursors 1991-1995

(15.2 tons p.a. ephedrine; 4.4 tons p.a. pseudo-ephedrine sufficient for 13.1 tons p.a. of methamphetamine)

Source: INCB, *1998 Precursors*, New York 1999 and previous years.

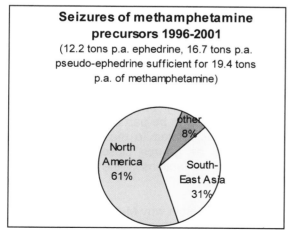

Seizures of methamphetamine precursors 1996-2001

(12.2 tons p.a. ephedrine, 16.7 tons p.a. pseudo-ephedrine sufficient for 19.4 tons p.a. of methamphetamine)

Source: INCB, *2002 Precursors*, New York 2003 and previous years.

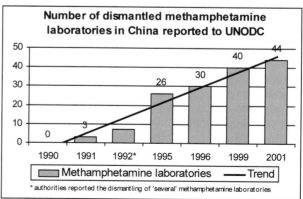

Number of dismantled methamphetamine laboratories in China reported to UNODC

* authorities reported the dismantling of 'several' methamphetamine laboratories

Source: UNODC, Annual Reports Questionnaire Data, CEPAL.

Taiwan, province of China, reported that local criminal groups acquired the know-how to manufacture methamphetamine in the 1970s from Japanese trafficking groups and initially produced methamphetamine for them. Only later (late 1980s), did they also start producing for a rapidly growing local market. When Taiwan improved controls on ephedrine, mainland China increasingly served as the main source for this 'raw material'. In the early 1990s, notably in 1991 and 1992, law enforcement agencies in Taiwan initiated a major crackdown on the local methamphetamine industry.[4] Criminal groups from Taiwan then looked for new production opportunities and – via Hongkong – found them in mainland China. Thus, the initial drive for the development of a methamphetamine industry in China was largely prompted by criminal groups from Taiwan and Hong Kong[5], though in subsequent years, a number of laboratories in the People's Republic of China also started to produce methamphetamine for a growing domestic market. Japan, the Philippines and Taiwan, Province of China, are the main recipients of methamphetamine produced in China.

Some of the laboratories dismantled in China produced very large quantities of methamphetamine. While in the USA, the average amount of methamphetamine seized per dismantled laboratory was just 0.1 kg (in 2000/2001), the comparable figure for China amounted to about 50 kg in the mid 1990s and to significantly larger amounts in recent years. Seizures of methamphetamine in China amounted to 20.9 tons and 4.8 tons in 2000 and 2001, respectively, which is significantly larger than the seizures reported from the USA (less than 2.4 tons in 2000, and 2.9 tons in 2001). Chinese methamphetamine seizures were equivalent to 60% of all methamphetamine seizures in 2000, and 21% in 2001. Moreover, China seized large quantities of ephedrine in recent years: 10.2 tons in 2000, equivalent to 80% of all ephedrine seizures in South-East Asia, or 59% of global ephedrine seizures in that year.

No methamphetamine production estimates are available for China. The seizures and arrest of people involved in methamphetamine manufacture resulted in a massive crack-down of clandestine illicit drug manufacture in recent years, apparently limiting the outflow of methamphetamine from China. Indeed, Japan saw a stabilization of methamphetamine abuse in 2001, following years of increase of illicit methamphetamine imports in the 1990s.

Illegal methamphetamine production is also reported from *Thailand*. Over the 1996-2001

period, Thailand accounted for 29% of all methamphetamine seizures in East and South-East Asia. In 2001, seizures in Thailand reached 8.4 tons, the largest worldwide, and thus surpassing China's (4.8 tons).

Thailand reported dismantling 10 clandestine methamphetamine laboratories in 2001 and more than 120 between 1991 and 2001. The number of clandestine laboratories seized in Thailand between 1996 and 2001 was larger than between 1991 and 1995. Increased enforcement efforts in recent years prompted, however, drug trafficking networks to look for alternative production sites in neighbouring countries, notably in Myanmar. This can explain why, despite a booming local market and increasing exports of methamphetamine from Thailand, local production does not seem to have increased in recent years.

Source: UNODC, Annual reports Questionnaire Data/DELTA.

The largest increase of methamphetamine production in the second half of the 1990s took place in *Myanmar*. Thailand estimated that at least 700 million pills, equivalent to almost 70 tons of methamphetamine, or one third of total methamphetamine production of North America, are smuggled every year into Thailand across the Thai-Myanmar border. Most methamphetamine production in Myanmar takes place in areas where central government control is limited, close to the Thai and Chinese borders. Many of the groups involved in illegal heroin manufacture and trafficking are also involved in the manufacture of methamphetamine. Some reports suggest that among the producers of methamphetamine are groups which used to be part of the Khun Sa drug network, groups related to the United Wa State Army as well as groups close to the Kokang militias and some factions of the former Burmese Communist Party.

This may also explain why Myanmar was only in a position to report a limited number of methamphetamine laboratory seizures to UNODC (5 laboratories in 2001). Thai authorities estimate that some 60 large clandestine laboratories in Myanmar produce the bulk of the illegal methamphetamine shipped to Thailand.

Myanmar, however, reported the seizure of important quantities of ephedrine in recent years: 3.9 tons in 2001, the second largest ephedrine & pseudo-ephedrine seizures reported to INCB, equivalent to 14% of global ephedrine & pseudo-ephedrine seizures in 2001. Over the 1996-2000 period[b] only China reported larger seizures of ephedrine. Most of the countries/territories of East and South-East Asia reported that the seized ephedrine originated in China or India.

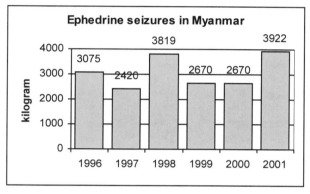

Ephedrine seizures in Myanmar

Source: INCB, *2002 Precursors*, New York 2003 and previous years.

Myanmar also reported the seizure of almost 1 metric ton of methamphetamine in 2001, the fifth largest quantity seized in East and South-East Asia, after Thailand, the People's Republic of China, the Philippines and Taiwan, Province of China, and slightly more than the 0.8-0.9 tons reported in the two previous years.

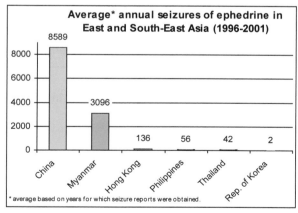

Average* annual seizures of ephedrine in East and South-East Asia (1996-2001)

* average based on years for which seizure reports were obtained.

Source: INCB, *2002 Precursors*, New York 2003 and previous years.

Smaller-scale production of methamphetamine in the region, as confirmed by seizures of clandestine laboratories, also takes place *in Hong Kong*, SAR of China, *the Republic of Korea*, the *Philippines, Indonesia* and *Malaysia*. Particularly in the Philippines and Indonesia, domestic production appears to have increased in recent years.

The Japanese authorities suspect that *North Korea* is a significant supplier of methamphetamine, accounting for up to a third of all methamphetamine smuggled into Japan in recent years (most methamphetamine smuggled into Japan originates in China). So far, however, there has been no evidence to confirm the existence of such production in North Korea.[c]

Cases of manufacturing methamphetamine within *Japan* are rare. In 1994, Japan reported some seizures of ephedrine. Some methamphetamine production in the late 1990s appears to have taken place in connection with the operations of the Aun sect which was subsequently dismantled. In 2001, Japan reported imports of semi-processed methamphetamine. Since it would have required further refining, this suggests that some limited production takes place within Japan itself.

Oceania

A significant and rapidly rising number of clandestine laboratories were dismantled in *Australia* in recent years. The number rose from 10 in 1990, to 201 in 2001. Close to 90% of the recent years' cases concerned laboratories producing ATS.

Most ATS laboratories produced methamphetamine (about 60% of all laboratories or 70% of the ATS laboratories). Laboratories producing amphetamine accounted for about 20% of all clandestine laboratories. There is also some production of MDMA ('ecstasy') and methcathinone in Australia. Although there have been 'imports' of methamphetamine from South-East Asia, most of the methamphetamine found on the local market is produced locally. In contrast, MDMA is still mostly imported from Europe.

---

[b] No seizure reports of ephedrine for the year 2001 were obtained from China.

[c] An INCB mission to North Korea in 2002, for instance, did not find evidence of such production.

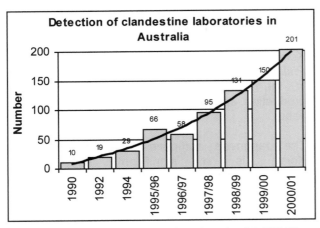

Detection of clandestine laboratories in Australia

Source: UNODC, Annual Reports Questionnaire data/DELTA.

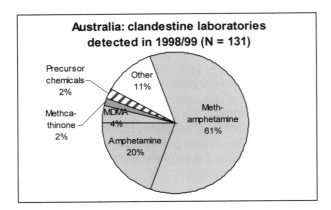

Australia: clandestine laboratories detected in 1998/99 (N = 131)

Source: Australian Bureau of Criminal Intelligence, *Australian Illicit Drug Report 1998/99*, Canberra 2000.

There has apparently been a shift of production, from amphetamine to the more potent methamphetamine, in the 1990s. Throughout the 1980s, Australia only reported the dismantling of amphetamine laboratories. In the early 1990s, production still concerned mainly amphetamine. In 1990, 9 out of 10 laboratories detected produced amphetamine and only one produced methamphetamine. Towards the end of the decade, 7 out of 10 produced methamphetamine and only 2 amphetamine.

Seizures of ATS precursors also seem to provide evidence for such a shift. In 1990, seized ATS precursors were exclusively P2P, usually used in the manufacture of amphetamine. As of 1992, however, pseudo-ephedrine and ephedrine began to be seized. Over the 1996-2001 period, 94% of the ATS precursor seizures (expressed in ATS equivalents) were accounted for by the two methamphetamine precursors, pseudo-ephedrine and ephedrine, and only 4% by the amphetamine precursors, P2P and norephedrine. This would confirm the increasing dominance of methamphetamine production in Australia. Most of

the pseudo-ephedrine used in the production of methamphetmine is reported to be extracted from cough- and cold-suppressant medications such as Sudafed tablets. In addition, Australia reported small seizures of piperonal and safrole, used as pre-precursor for the manufacture of ecstasy (2% of all ATS precursor seizures over the 1996-2001 period).

Methamphetamine production takes place in several parts of Australia. There is, however, a clear concentration in Queensland (north-eastern Australia), notably in the south-eastern corner of this state.[6] In 1998/99, 56 out of 80 methamphetamine laboratories (70%) were dismantled in Queensland. Such high proportions have also been typical for subsequent years. The importance of Queensland as a production site for methamphetamine may also explain why prices there amounted to only Aus$70-90 (US$36-47) per gram in 2001, while higher prices were found in the neighbouring state of New South Wales (Aus$90-120 or US$47-62), in Victoria (south-eastern Australia, Aus$300) or in the Northern Territory (Aus$300 or US$155).

Strong increases in the manufacture of methamphetamine have been also reported in recent years from *New Zealand*. While no clandestine laboratory was detected prior to 1998 (though there were suspicions that motorcycle gangs were producing such drugs) and only 1 in 1998, the number increased to 39 by 2001. That year, 95% of the clandestine laboratories dismantled produced methamphetamine. The rest produced ecstasy. Production of methamphetamine is reported to take place all across New Zealand. Concentrations are in Northland and in the Auckland area. In parallel, New Zealand − like Australia − faced increasing imports of methamphetamine from South-East Asia (notably from Myanmar/Thailand). The expansion of production and imports went hand in

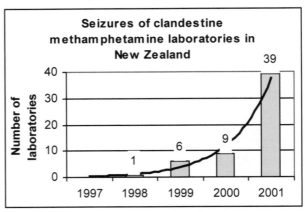

Seizures of clandestine methamphetamine laboratories in New Zealand

Source: UNODC, Annual Reports Questionnaire Data/DELTA.

hand with strong declines of methamphetamine prices. They nearly halved as compared to the mid 1990s.

Europe

Europe is characterized by significant levels of amphetamine production; production of methamphetamine, in contrast, is far more limited. Over the 2000-2001 period, Europe accounted for only only 2% of the clandestine methamphetamine laboratories dismantled globally. Only two European countries report significant levels of methamphetamine production: the Czech Republic and the Russian Federation. Methamphetamine production is also still relatively important in Slovakia. In all three countries production is, however, mainly for local use, not for export. Minor levels of methamphetamine production are reported from the Baltic countries, the Ukraine, Bulgaria, as well as from some West European countries: Belgium, the UK, Germany and France.

The Russian Federation and the Czech Republic were also the only two countries that repeatedly reported seizures of ephedrine. Lower levels of ephedrine/pseudo-ephedrine seizures in recent years have been reported from the Ukraine, Latvia, Lithuania, Estonia, Slovakia, Bulgaria, Hungary, Slovenia as well as from Italy, Spain, France, Germany, the Netherlands and Finland. The overall seizures of ephedrine and pseudo-ephedrine in Europe were, however, rather modest, amounting to 3% of global ephedrine/pseudo-ephedrine seizures over the 2000-2001 period.

Clandestine production of methamphetamine, locally known as *pervitin*, in the *Czech Republic*, and before in Czechoslovakia, was reported since the early 1980s. Local production of ephedrine contributed to the emergence of a clandestine methamphetamine manufacturing industry in the country. By 1993, the number of dismantled laboratories rose to 50, but subsequently fell. Improved controls of ephedrine seem to have contributed to falling levels of production. In recent years, some 30 laboratories were dismantled every year; most were of the so-called kitchen lab-type.

In *Slovakia,* the number of laboratories dismantled used to be less than 10 per year. In 2000, however, the country – in a move to crack down on methamphetamine production - dismantled 95 laboratories. In 2001, the number fell back to 10,

i.e. about one third of the number for the neighbouring Czech Republic.

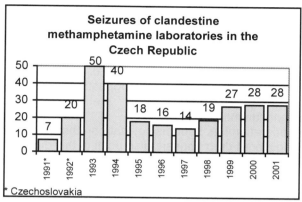

Source: UNODC, Annual Reports Questionnaire Data/DELTA.

In the *Russian Federation,* authorities reported the seizures of laboratories producing various kind of ATS since the 1980s. Most of these ATS laboratories produce either methamphetamine or methcathinone also known as ephedrone. Both substances are produced from ephedrine and most of this production takes place in simple kitchen labs. However, there were also reports in the 1990s that medical doctors, laboratory assistants and technical personnel in scientific research institutes were involved in the illegal production of synthetic drugs, including various ATS. Availability of a well-developed system of research institutes and laboratories that dispose of the required equipment and the existence of a large number of trained specialists in chemistry and pharmacology – some of them unemployed - laid the basis for the development of a thriving cottage industry for the clandestine manufacture of synthetic drugs in the 1990s. St. Petersburg

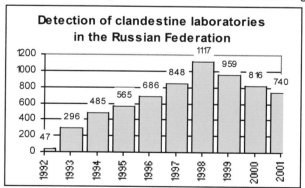

Source: UNODC, Russia Country Profile 2002.

emerged as one of the centres for the illegal production. Several clandestine laboratories were also reported to operate in Moscow and in other towns. The number of dismantled clandestine laboratories producing methamphetamine and methcathinone, totaling 71 in 2001, accounted for about 10% of all clandestine laboratories detected in that year, up from 6% or 17 detected laboratories in 1993, suggesting that the importance of illicit methamphetamine/ methcathinone production in the Russian Federation has been rising. Data on the number of registered drug abusers also point in this direction.

Seizures of ephedrine made by the Russian authorities accounted for 81% of all ephedrine seizures made in Europe over the 1996-2001 period (80% of all ephedrine and pseudo-ephedrine seizures), or for 9% of the world's ephedrine seizures. No seizures of P2P were reported by the Russian authorities over the last decade, suggesting that the production of amphetamine, in contrast, is not widespread in Russia.

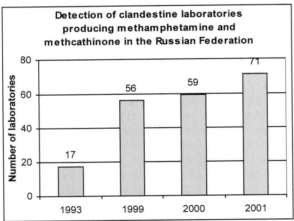

Source: UNODC, Russia Country Profile 2002.

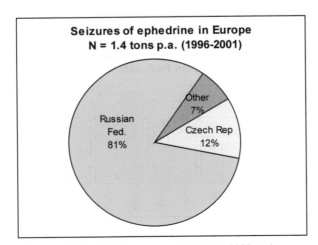

Source: INCB, *2002 Precursors*, New York 2003 and previous years.

Africa

Methamphetamine production in Africa seems to be limited to a few countries, notably Egypt and South Africa, which reported seizures of laboratories in recent years. In addition, Cote d'Ivoire and Zambia reported seizures of ephedrine and Algeria and Uganda seizures of pseudoephedrine in recent years. This is a possible indication that methamphetamine production also takes place in other African countries. Quantities seized were, however, rather small.

In *Egypt,* a pharmaceutical preparation of dexamfetamine, produced in Europe, known under the name of *Maxiton Forte*, became popular and was increasingly abused, prompting the Government to prohibit imports of the substance. Subsequently, domestic clandestine production of ATS began and reached important magnitudes in the late 1980s/early 1990s. Since the mid-1980s, Egypt continuously reported the clandestine manufacture of Maxiton Forte to UNODC. Given the use of ephedrine as the main precursor in the detected clandestine laboratories, it is likely that the ATS produced was methamphetamine. The last detection of a clandestine Maxiton Forte laboratory, in Egypt was in 1999.

A limited number of methamphetamine laboratories were also seized in the Republic of *South Africa*, which also consistently reported seizures of small quantities of ephedrine, since the mid-1990s

Trafficking and abuse of amphetamine-type stimulants is reported to be widespread in Central and West Africa.[7] They are apparently mostly diverted from legal sources and supplied through parallel markets across Africa. This reduces the incentive for clandestine production of ATS in most African countries. South Africa, which has the most advanced monitoring system of the use of psychotropics in Africa and is thus faced with comparatively small levels of diversions of (legal) stimulants, compared to other African countries, showed an overall consumption of (legal) stimulants of 7.2 defined daily doses (DDD) per 1000 inhabitants per day over the 1999-2001 period. This was almost four times the median value (1.9 DDD per 1000 inhabitants) of 45 countries investigated by the INCB. Similarly high or higher levels of ATS consumption could be expected for many other African countries that have far less effective controls in place.

South America

No seizures of methamphetamine precursors and no detections of clandestine methamphetamine laboratories have been reported from countries in South America. This can be explained by the abundant supply of cocaine in the region, another potent stimulant, as well as – until recently - easy access to a number of legal ATS (usually Schedule IV substances), often marketed as anorectics.

- In Brazil, for instance, the consumption of legal stimulants was 7.4 DDD per day per 1000 inhabitants over the 1992-94 period. This figure fell to 5.9 DDD during the 1999-2001 period. But this was still three times the median value of 1.9 of 45 countries investigated by INCB over this period.
- In Argentina, the legal stimulant use per day was as high as 13 DDD per 1000 inhabitants over the 1992-94 period, 11 times the median value of 1.2 at the time (45 countries investigated). Following the introduction of stricter controls, legal stimulant use fell in Argentina to 3.4 DDD per 1000 inhabitants over the 1997-99 period. But this was still three times the median level of consumption at the time (1.2 DDD per 1000 inhabitants of 49 countries investigated). In recent years, however, consumption declined further to just 1.0 DDD per 1000 inhabitants (1999-2001 period).

- Chile reported legal consumption of stimulants of 13.6 DDD per 1000 inhabitants over the 1992-94 period, more than 11 times the median value of 1.2 DDD per 1000 inhabitants. The number fell to 2 DDD per 1000 inhabitants over the 1999-2001 period.

All of this indicates that there has been, for years, an over-supply of ATS from legal sources in several parts of South America, thus making the emergence of a clandestine methamphetamine industry largely redundant. Better controls of legal ATS and curtailed cocaine production could, however, change the situation.

Amphetamine

Clandestine manufacture of amphetamine is mainly concentrated in Europe. The region accounts for close to 60% of all amphetamine laboratories seized over the 1991-2001 period. Production of amphetamine clearly exceeds that of methamphetamine. The proportions are tentative as it is not always clear whether countries, when reporting the dismantling of 'amphetamine' laboratories really meant 'amphetamine' laboratories or the broader category of amphetamine-type laboratories (amphetamine and other ATS).

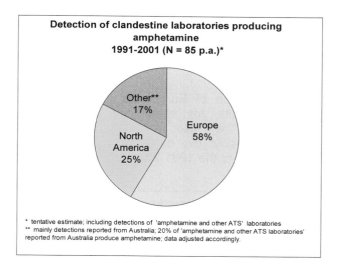

Detection of clandestine laboratories producing amphetamine 1991-2001 (N = 85 p.a.)*

Other** 17%
North America 25%
Europe 58%

* tentative estimate; including detections of 'amphetamine and other ATS' laboratories
** mainly detections reported from Australia; 20% of 'amphetamine and other ATS laboratories' reported from Australia produce amphetamine; data adjusted accordingly.

Source: UNODC, Annual Reports Questionnaire Data/DELTA.

Europe

The overall number of dismantled amphetamine laboratories (including the category of Amphetamine and other ATS laboratories) in Europe increased by about 40% over the 1996-2001 period as compared to the period 1991-95.

Close to 85% of all detections of amphetamine laboratories (excluding 'ATS combinations') over 1991-2001 in Europe were reported from the UK, Germany, Poland and the Netherlands. Other European countries reporting the detection of amphetamine laboratories included Sweden, Spain, Belgium, Lithuania, Bulgaria, Denmark, Finland, Estonia, Latvia, France, Hungary, Italy, Greece, Norway and the Russian Federation. In 2001, the largest numbers of dismantled amphetamine laboratories in Europe were reported from Poland (12), the Netherlands (10) and the UK (5).

The importance of Europe as the world's key production site for clandestine amphetamine manufacture is also reflected in precursor statistics. About two thirds of all amphetamine precursors over the 1991-2001 period were seized in Europe.

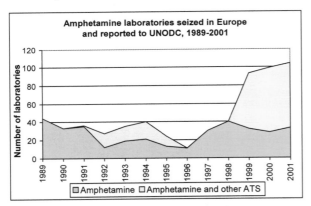

Source: UNODC, Annual Reports Questionnaire Data/DELTA.

North America

About quarter of all clandestine amphetamine laboratories detection occurred in North America. In contrast to Europe, however, amphetamine production only accounts for a small proportion of the overall production of ATS in North America. Production of amphetamine in North America is mainly concentrated in the USA, though some laboratories producing it were also detected in Canada and Mexico. Using the number of dismantled laboratories as an indicator, amphetamine production in the USA appears to have declined over the 1989-1998 period, but rose again thereafter.

P2P is the main precursor for amphetamine production in North America, though norephedrine played an important role in the late 1990s as well.

In three out of the four years of 1997-2000, norephedrine seizures exceeded those of P2P.

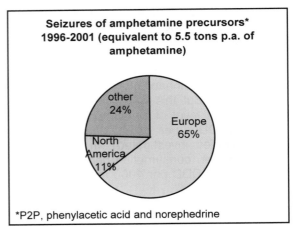

Source: INCB *2002 Precursors* and previous years.

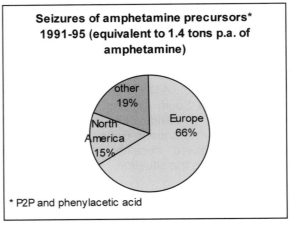

Source: INCB *2002 Precursors* and previous years

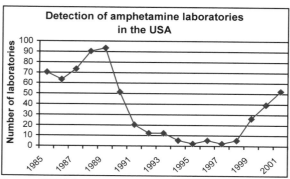

Source: UNODC, Annual Reports Questionnaire Data/DELTA.

Other regions

Significant levels of amphetamine production outside Europe and North America are only found in *Australia*. 26 laboratories, equivalent to 20% of all dismantled clandestine laboratories in Australia in 1998/99, produced amphetamine, up from 9 in 1990 and 4 in 1985. This figure was higher than the corresponding figure for the USA and came close to the figure reported from Europe (excluding 'ATS combinations') in 1998/99. In subsequent years no breakdown of the dismantled laboratories by drug category was provided, but it can be assumed that amphetamine laboratories continued to play a role.

A number of other countries in Asia also reported the detection of a few amphetamine laboratories. However, it is not clear whether these laboratories were, indeed, producing amphetamine or methamphetamine. The seizure of ephedrine in these countries suggests that the laboratories produced methamphetamine rather than amphetamine.

Regular seizures of P2P outside Europe and North America are limited to Australia. In addition, seizures of P2P were in recent years reported from New Zealand (1996) and Hong Kong (1997). Seizures of phenylacetic acid, used for the production of P2P, were reported from Australia (1996 and 2000), New Zealand (1996), Myanmar (1999 and 2001) and South Africa (2001). Seizures of phenylacetic acid and of P2P are indications, though not proof, of amphetamine production as these substances can also be used for the manufacture of methamphetamine.

Ecstasy

Europe

Precursor seizures suggest that ecstasy (MDMA) production is still largely concentrated in Europe, even though it has spread to other regions in recent years. Overall, 87% of all ecstasy precursors – sufficient for the production of 4.7 tons p.a. of MDMA - were seized in Europe over the 1991-2001 period. The main precursor chemical for the production of ecstasy in Europe - expressed in ecstasy equivalents - is 3,4-MDP-2-P, also known as BMK, followed by safrole, a 'pre-precursor' of ecstasy, used for the production of 3,4-MDP-2-P.

The number of detected and dismantled laboratories producing ecstasy showed an upward trend in the late 1990s, peaking in 2000, and declining again in 2001. The strong increase in the late 1990s was largely due to improved reporting as countries – which previously only reported the detection of clandestine laboratories – specified that they seized laboratories producing 'ecstasy'.

A number of indicators suggest that ecstasy production is concentrated in the Netherlands and in Belgium. Over the 1999-2001 period, 75% of all seizures of clandestine laboratories producing ecstasy took place in the Netherlands and 14% in Belgium. The two next prominent production sites of ecstasy are the UK (6%) and Germany (4%). Seizures of ecstasy laboratories and/or ATS laboratories including ecstasy laboratories, were also reported over the 1991-2001 period from Spain, Norway, Lithuania, Latvia, Estonia, Poland, Hungary and the Ukraine. In a couple of cases, Dutch nationals were involved in setting up and/or running such clandestine ecstasy laboratories abroad, which could be a reaction to increased pressure by the Dutch authorities to crack down on domestic production.

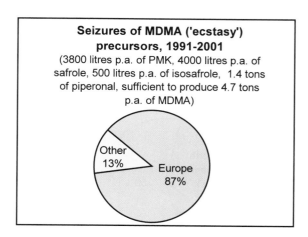

Source: INCB, *2002 Precursors, New York 2003* and previous years

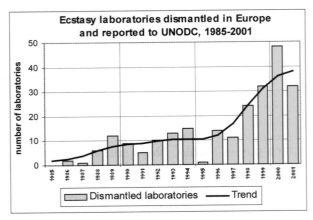

Source: UNODC, Annual Reports Questionnaire Data/DELTA.

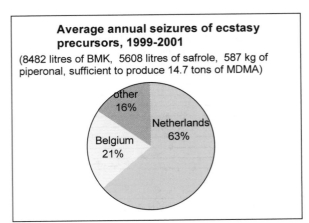

Source: UNODC, Annual Reports Questionnaire Data/DELTA.

Similarly, in terms of seizures of ecstasy precursors, the highest figures have been reported in recent years from the Netherlands (63% of all such seizures over the 1999-2001 period), followed by Belgium (21%). The category of 'other countries' includes Slovakia, which made significant seizures of BMK in 1999, Germany, Spain and Lithuania. No data from the UK are available. Ecstasy precursor seizures were last reported to INCB in 1997, though the UK continued reporting the dismantling of ecstasy laboratories in subsequent years.

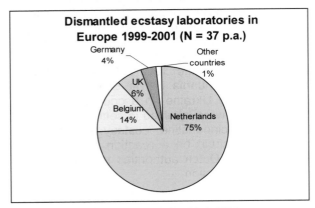

Source: INCB, 2002 Precursors, New York 2003.

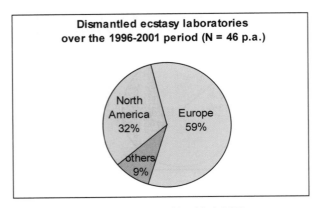

Source: INCB, 2002 Precursors, New York 2003.

North America

The next largest production site of ecstasy after Europe is North America. A third of all clandestine laboratory detection occurred in North America over the 1996-2001 period. The clear increase in the seizure of clandestine laboratories producing ecstasy in the late 1990s is an indication that not only imports of ecstasy from Europe, but also domestic production, increased over this period in North America. In addition to production in the USA, Canada emerged as a production site for ecstasy in the region. One ecstasy laboratory was also seized in Mexico (1995). In contrast to Europe, most of the ecstasy precursor seizures in the USA concerned safrole and only, at far lower levels, BMK and piperonal.

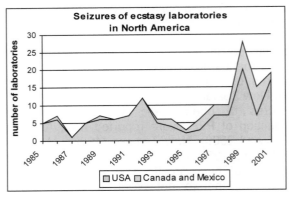

Source: UNODC, Annual Reports Questionnaire Data/DELTA.

Other countries

Seizures of ecstasy laboratories outside Europe and North-America have been reported in recent years from Oceania (specifically from Australia, but also, in 2001, from New Zealand), from East and South-East Asia (Thailand, Indonesia, Hong Kong, SAR of China), from the Near and Middle East (Israel), from South Africa and from Colombia. In 2001, South Africa dismantled 5 ecstasy laboratories. Seizures of ecstasy precursors, however, were only reported - outside Europe and North America - from Australia and Hong Kong in recent years

ENDNOTES

[1] INCB, *Psychotropic Substances*, New York 2003, pp. 105-111.
[2] Office of National Drug Control Policy, National Drug Control Strategy, February 2003, p. 30.
[3] INCB, *Psychotropic Substances*, New York 2003, p. 111.
[4] Taiwan, ROC, National Police Administration, Current Situation and Trends of Drug Abuse in Taiwan, June 1992.
[5] Guilhelm Fabre, *Criminal Prosperity*, New York 2003,.(chapter Drugs and Post-Communism: The Chinese Case), pp. 40.41.
[6] Australian Bureau of Criminal Intelligence, *Australian Illicit Drug Report 1999-2000*, Canberra 2001, p. 48.
[7] INCB, Report 2002, New York 2003, p. 34.

1.2. TRAFFICKING

1.2.1. Overview

Number of seizures

…. continue growing, but at a slower pace

Overall trafficking, as reflected in the number of seizure cases, appears to have continued growing in 2001. Growth rates of reported seizure cases were, however, lower in 2001 than they were in the 1990s. Over the 1990-2000 period, the number of reported seizure cases grew from 0.3 to 1.3 million or 15% p.a. In 2001 the growth rate was 6%. The strong increases in the 1990s were also a reflection of improvements in reporting. In 1990, 55 countries and territories reported seizure cases to UNODC. By the year 2000, reporting improved to 94 countries. The number of countries reporting seizure cases to UNODC fell, however, to 85 for the year 2001. Nonetheless, the total number of reported seizure cases increased further to 1.4 million.

The total at the global level is likely to be even higher. A significant number of countries did not report the number of seizures, though they reported the quantities of drugs seized.

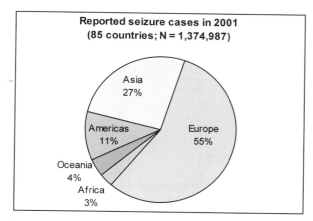

Source: UNODC, Annual Reports Questionnaire Data / DELTA.

In 2001, most seizure cases concerned cannabis (48%), followed by the amphetamine-type stimulants (22% including ecstasy). Opiates accounted for 21% and coca/cocaine-related substances for 7% of the seizures reported. As compared to the mid 1990s, the proportion of ATS doubled (from 11% in 1995 to 22% in 2001) while the proportions of opiates and cannabis declined.

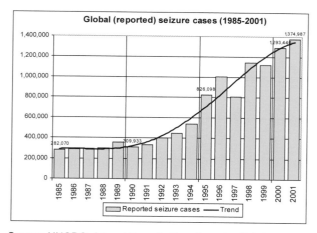

Source: UNODC, Annual Reports Questionnaire Data/ DELTA.

More than half of all seizure cases in 2001 were reported from Europe (close to 39% from Western Europe and close to 17% from Eastern Europe) and more than one quarter from Asia. About 11% of all seizure cases were reported to UNODC from the Americas (of which 80% in North America) and the rest from Oceania (4%) and Africa (3%).

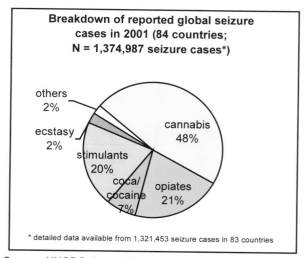

Source: UNODC, Annual Reports Questionnaire Data / DELTA.

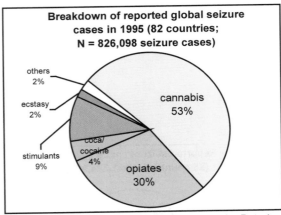

Source: UNODC, Annual Reports Questionnaire Data / DELTA.

Quantities seized

...largest quantities seized worldwide: cannabis, followed by cocaine

Far more countries report the amounts of drugs seized (159 countries and territories in 2001) than the number of seizure cases (85 countries and territories). The data on the quantities seized thus provide a more comprehensive picture of the drug trafficking situation at the global level.

The largest volume of illicit drugs seized concerned cannabis herb and resin, followed by cocaine, the opiates (opium followed by heroin and morphine) and the amphetamine-type stimulants (methamphetamine, followed by amphetamine and ecstasy). This ranking has not changed in recent years.

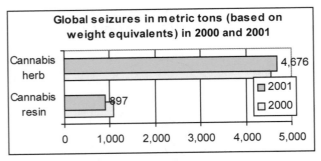

Source: UNODC, Annual Reports Questionnaire Data / DELTA.

... cannabis and cocaine seizures remain stable

The following analysis of quantities seized is based on information provided by 159 countries & territories.[a] Overall cannabis seizures remained almost unchanged in 2001 as compared to a year earlier (close to 5,500 tons). A decline in cannabis resin (hashish) was largely offset by an increase in cannabis herb (marijuana) seizures.

Cocaine seizures amounted to 366 tons in 2001, and were thus slightly higher than in 2000. Seizures of coca leaf, by contrast, showed a strong decline (88%), reflecting declines reported from all three Andean countries.

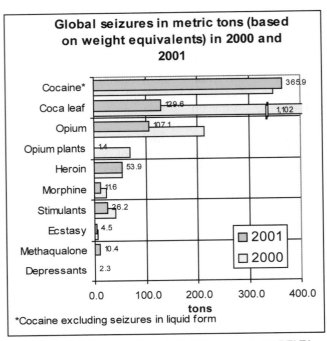

Source: UNODC, Annual Reports Questionnaire Data / DELTA.

---

[a] Data for the year 2000 refer to 164 countries & territories which reported seizures to UNODC.

TRENDS IN WORLD SEIZURES - 1991-2001
(in metric tons)

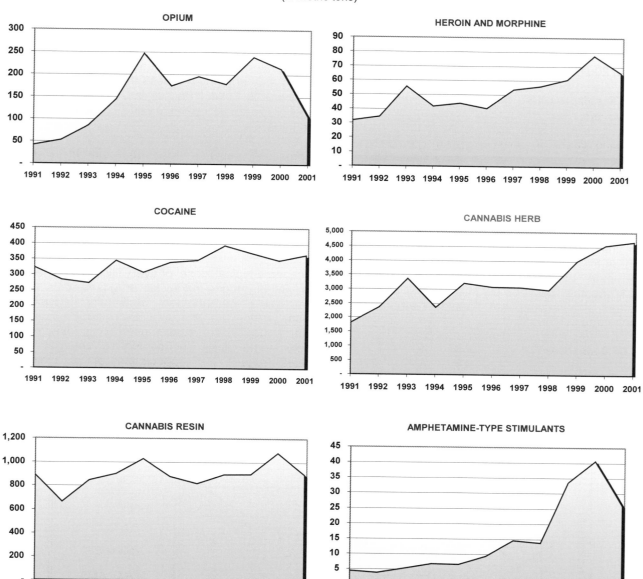

.... seizures of opiates (except heroin) decline in 2001

In contrast to more or less stable cannabis and cocaine seizures, opiate seizures showed a decline in 2001. Expressed in heroin equivalents, opiate seizures fell by 23% in 2001 compared to the year 2000. Both opium and morphine seizures fell by about 50%. The decline was a consequence of the 2000-2001 ban on opium production in Afghanistan. Huge stocks of heroin as well as intensified enforcement efforts by some governments (notably China and Tajikistan), resulted, however, in stable heroin seizures: 54 tons in 2001.[b]

....ATS seizures also fall, though remaining at high levels

Following years of massive growth, seizures of amphetamine-type stimulants (excluding ecstasy) fell in 2001 by 33% from the peak in 2000. This decline was mainly due to lower ATS seizures reported by China, which in recent years accounted for the bulk of such seizures. Nonetheless, global stimulant seizures were still four times as high as in 1995 and eight times as high as in 1990. Ecstasy seizures – according to preliminary estimates - fell by around 10% in 2001.[c] Ecstasy seizures fell in a number of major markets, including the USA, Canada, Netherlands, France and Italy.

... LSD seizures fall strongly

The overall amounts of LSD seized fell by 73% in 2001. Forty countries reported seizures of LSD in 2001, down from 49 countries in 2000. The largest seizures – in kilogram equivalents - took place in the Russian Federation and Canada; the largest numbers of LSD units were seized in the USA, followed by the Netherlands and Spain. Outside North America and Europe, the largest unit seizures took place in South Africa, Hong Kong, SAR of China, and Israel.

... while methaqualone and depressant seizures increase

Seizures of both methaqualone and of depressants rose significantly in 2001. Methaqualone seizures quadrupled in 2001, though they amounted to less than a fifth of what they were in 1994. The rise in 2001 was due to larger seizures of methaqualone in South Africa and India.

Depressant seizures rose four-fold in 2001, reflecting strong rises in West Africa, West Asia and Europe, notably Eastern Europe. Depressant seizures in 2001 were at their highest level since the early 1980s.

Seizures in unit terms

Because a typical 'dose' of every illicit drug differs, the weight of one particular drug seized is not comparable with another. Estimating a typical 'dose' (or consumption unit), even though it may differ a great deal across users and locations, offers some basis for comparing volumes of seized drugs. For the calculations of a 'typical consumption unit' (at street purity) the following conversion ratios were used: cannabis herb: 0.5

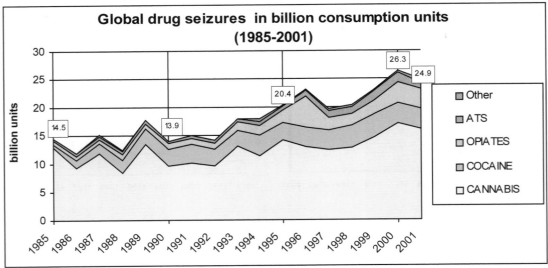

Source: UNODC, Annual Reports Questionnaire Data / DELTA.

[b] Since seizure data for the year 2001 were not received from the UK and Belgium, it was assumed that the seizures of these two countries remained at the same level as 2000.

[c] See footnote above.

grams, cannabis resin: 0.135 grams; cocaine and ecstasy: 0.1 grams, heroin and amphetamines: 0.03 grams, LSD 0.00005 grams (50 micrograms), etc. If global seizures are expressed in such typical consumption units, some 24.9 billion drug units were seized in 2001, down from 26.3 billion in 2000, but up from 13.9 billion in 1990. Thus, overall seizures, expressed in such consumption units, increased by 6.6% p.a. over the 1990-2000 period though falling – according to preliminary data – by 5.4% in 2001. Some of this decline was because less countries and territories reported seizures in 2001 (159) than in 2000 (164).

Comparing data for 1995 and 2001, the overall proportion of cannabis fell from 69% in 1995 to 64% in 2001, reflecting a decline in cannabis resin seizures that was not offset by an increase in cannabis herb seizures. The proportion of opiates increased from 10% to 14%. The increase was due to rising seizures of synthetic opioids. Excluding the synthetic opioids the proportion would have fallen from 10% to 9%. The proportion of cocaine remained unchanged at 15%, though it

fell if compared to the year 1998 (20%). The proportion of ATS in seizures rose between 1995 and 2001 from 3% to 4%, though their proportion fell, if compared to 1999 (8%). The proportion of 'other drugs' remained unchanged between 1995 and 2001 at 3%.

In terms of regional distribution of seizures, the largest volumes are seized in Northern America (27%), followed by Western Europe (26%). Asia accounts for 19% of all seizures; Africa for 12% and South America for 10%. Increases in the proportions of seizures over the 1995-2001 period were observed in Europe, notably Eastern Europe, and in Africa. The proportion of seizures in the Americas remained stable, rising slightly in North America but falling slightly in South America. The proportion of seizures that took place in Asia declined due to lower seizures in the Near & Middle East / South-West Asia subregion, mainly reflecting the lower opiate seizures in 2001 as a consequence of the opium poppy ban in Afghanistan. In all other parts of Asia, seizures increased.

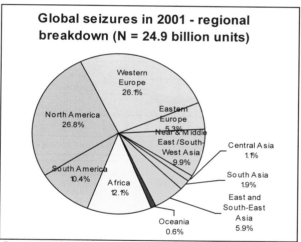

Source: UNODC, Annual Reports Questionnaire Data / DELTA

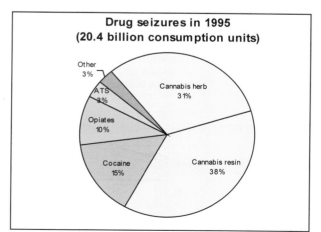

Source: UNODC, Annual Reports Questionnaire Data / DELTA

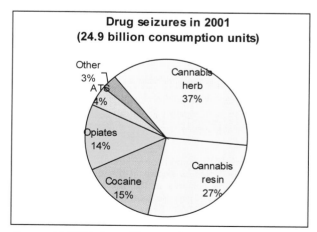

Source: UNODC, Annual Reports Questionnaire Data / DELTA

1.2.2. Trafficking in Opium / Heroin

.... falling in 2001

Global seizures of opiates (heroin, morphine and opium expressed in heroin equivalents) fell by 23% in 2001, the first significant decline in opiate seizures over the last two decades.

This was the result of two different trends. Opium and morphine seizures declined by about 50% in 2001, reflecting the strong reduction in global opium production (-65%) following Afghanistan's opium cultivation ban in the year 2001. Heroin seizures, however, did not decline and remained stable. Given the existence of large heroin stocks, not only in the production countries but also in the transit countries, heroin trafficking continued unabated in 2001. Assuming that seizures of countries which so far have not reported remained at about the same level as a year earlier[a], then overall heroin seizures remained basically stable in 2001.

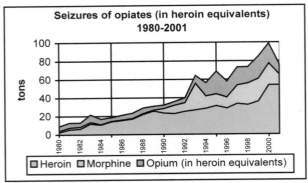

Source: UNODC, Annual Reports Questionnaire Data / DELTA.

.... while remaining concentrated in Asia, notably in South-West Asia

Given the fact that the world's two largest illicit opium production areas are located in Asia, most opiates seizures are also made in Asia (69% of all opiates seizures in 2001). Europe accounts for 25% and the Americas for 6% of global seizures.

Within Asia the largest opiates seizures take place in the Near & Middle East / South-West Asia region which includes Iran and Pakistan, i.e. the two countries which border Afghanistan to its east,

south and west. This subregion accounted for 40% of global opiate seizure in 2001.

If the subregions of South-West Asia (Iran and Pakistan) and Central Asia are combined, to reflect the countries neighbouring Afghanistan, then a decline in opium seizures of more than 50% and of morphine seizures of close to 50% was observed in 2001. Heroin seizures, in contrast, declined by a more moderate rate of 15%, reflecting the existence of important heroin stocks in the region in 2001 that were accumulated over the two previous years of bumper harvests in Afghanistan.

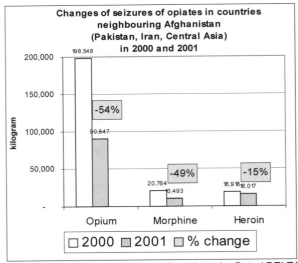

Source: UNODC, Annual Reports Questionnaire Data / DELTA.

The second most important subregion for opiate seizures is the East and South-East Asia sub-region which includes China and Thailand, i.e. countries that share long frontiers with Myanmar, the world's second largest producer of illicit opium (and the largest one in 2001). Other subregions of importance are the consumer markets of West Europe (19%) and North America (3%) and Central Asia (7%). West Europe accounted for 81% of all European opiate seizures. North America's seizures were equivalent to 58% of all opiate seizures in the Americas.

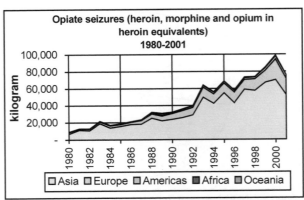

Source: UNODC, Annual Reports Questionnaire Data / DELTA.

[a] The heroin seizures shown in the graph above for 2001 assume that the seizures of the UK and Belgium remained unchanged. The UK and Belgium accounted for 7% of global heroin seizures in 2000. Even if the seizures of these two countries had fallen by 50%, global heroin seizures would have only declined by 3% which could still signal a stabilization of global heroin seizures.

The world's largest opiate seizures – ever since 1988 – have been reported from Iran. Despite an overall decline in opiates seizures in 2001 by 54% (a consequence of Afghanistan's opium ban), Iran alone accounted still for 27% of the world's opiate seizures in 2001, ahead of China (18%), Pakistan (12%), Turkey (7%) and Tajikistan (6%). A year earlier, Iran's share in global opiate seizures was still 45%.

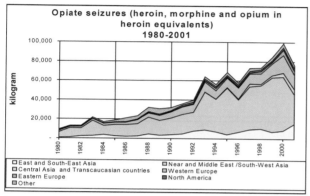

Source: UNODC, Annual Reports Questionnaire Data / DELTA.

.... heroin seizures, in contrast, were highest in South-East Asia in 2001

Overall 59% of the global heroin seizures were made in Asia, 33% in Europe (26% West Europe) and close to 8% in the Americas (4% North America). Africa accounted for 0.4% and the Oceania region for 0.2% in 2001. The highest heroin seizures in Asia were reported from the East-and South-East Asia subregion (27% of global seizures) in 2001, followed by the Near & Middle East / South-West Asia subregion (21%). (97% of all heroin seizures in the latter region took place in the two countries of South-West Asia, Pakistan and Iran). In 2000 and in most previous years over the last two decades, in contrast, heroin seizures made in South-West Asia exceeded those of South-East Asia.

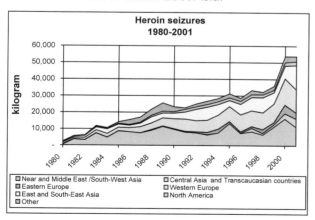

Source: UNODC, Annual Reports Questionnaire Data / DELTA.

The predominance of South-West Asia over the last decade was, however, less pronounced for heroin than for opiate seizures. This reflects the fact that (in contrast to South-East Asia) not all of the opium produced in Afghanistan is actually transformed into heroin within the region of South-West Asia. Some of the heroin is manufactured in Europe. In other words, seizure data suggest that the heroin production capacity of South-West Asia, though growing, has only been slightly higher than that of South-East Asia, even though opium production as such (apart from 2001), and thus opium and morphine seizures, had been significantly higher in South-West Asia than in South-East Asia over the last decade.

It may be also interesting to note that the heroin seizure trends of the two subregions basically show a mirror image. This is a rather surprising result as other indicators do not provide evidence of frequent substitution effects between the heroin markets of South-West Asia and those of South-East Asia. Opium price trends observed in Myanmar and Afghanistan, for instance, have not shown the similarities which one would have to expect if the two opium markets had been linked. In addition, throughout the last two decades the European heroin markets were reported by enforcement agencies to be predominantly sourced from South-West Asia, while the heroin from South-East Asia supplied the growing local markets as well as parts of the markets in North America and the Oceania region. Only a number of criminal West African groups were reported to source heroin from both Pakistan and Thailand for local consumption in Africa and/or final destinations in Western Europe.

The declines of seizures in South-West Asia in 2001 were due to Afghanistan's opium ban, which reduced the supply of trafficked heroin to stocks built up over previous years, while rising seizures in China were largely due to strongly stepped up enforcement efforts. The net result was a stabilization of heroin seizures at the global level. The People's Republic of China reported – for the first time since 1998 (and for the fourth time over the last decade) - the highest heroin seizures worldwide in 2001 (13.2 tons or 25% of global heroin seizures), ahead of Pakistan (6.9 tons or 13%), Turkey (4.4 tons or 8%), Tajikistan (4.2 tons or 8%) and Iran (4 tons or 7%).

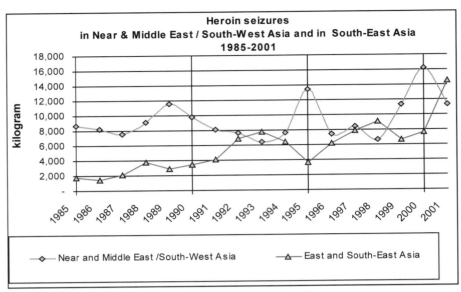

Source: UNODC, Annual Reports Questionnaire Data / DELTA.

.... declines in 2001 mainly in South-West Asia and in countries along the Balkan route

Overall opiate seizures declined in Asia, Europe and Oceania in 2001 and increased in Africa and in the Americas. If only heroin seizures are looked at, data show a decline of seizures in the Near & Middle East / South-West Asia region (-30%), in South Asia (-22%) in Europe (-16%) as well as in the Oceania region (-91%). Heroin seizures increased, in contrast, in South-East Asia (+89%), in Central Asia (+54%), in the Americas (+30%) and in Africa (+10%).

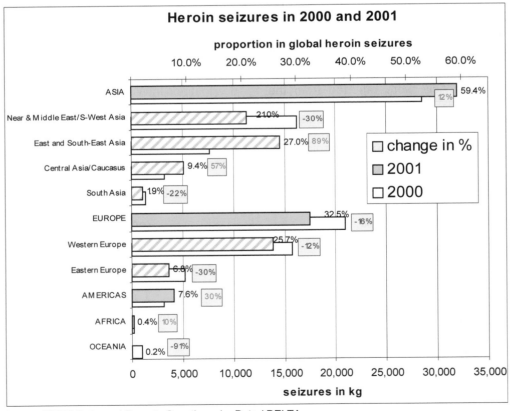

Source: UNODC, Annual Reports Questionnaire Data / DELTA.

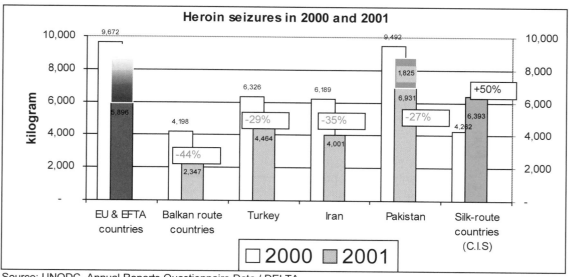

Heroin seizures in 2000 and 2001

Source: UNODC, Annual Reports Questionnaire Data / DELTA.

The declines of heroin seizures in South-West Asia were largely related to the sharply reduced opium production in southern and eastern Afghanistan in 2001. The concentration of opium production in 2001 in northern Afghanistan meant that the northern route gained in importance. Thus heroin seizures in Central Asia rose by more than 55% in 2001.

If heroin seizures of the countries around Afghanistan are aggregated according to the two main trafficking routes to Europe, data clearly show significant declines of heroin seizures along the 'traditional' trafficking route (-32% in 2001), including Pakistan[b], Iran, Turkey and the (East-European) countries along the Balkan route. In contrast, trafficking along the Northern route (or Silk route)[c], clearly increased (+50%), mainly due to significantly higher seizures reported from Tajikistan (+125%) and the Russian Federation (+31%).

The growing importance of the Northern route (silk road) for heroin leaving Afghanistan is a phenomenon that has been reflected in seizure

statistics since the mid 1990s. Between 1998 and 2001 heroin seizures rose five-fold in Central Asia, as trafficking and the response to this increased, in particular by the Tajik authorities. In both 2001 and 2002 about 85% of all heroin seizures reported from Central Asia were made by the authorities in Tajikistan.

Heroin and morphine seizure data for 2002, received for the countries neighbouring Afghanistan, suggest that the overall levels and distribution of the seizures remained largely unchanged, suggesting that trafficking routes – despite important political changes in Afghanistan and the resumption of large-scale opium production – did not change much in 2002. There have been some moderate increases of heroin and morphine seizures in Pakistan and Iran

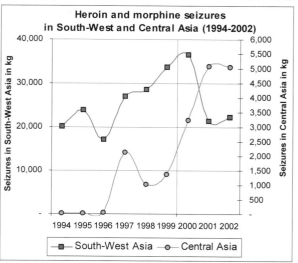

Source: UNODC, Annual Reports Questionnaire Data / DELTA.

---

[b] The Pakistan authorities reported in 2001, for the first time in years, both heroin and morphine seizures to UNODC. The decline of reported heroin seizures between 2000 and 2001 amounted to 27%. However, it cannot be excluded that part of the heroin seizures reported in 2000 (and in previous years) also included morphine seizures. Individual seizure cases, as reported by Interpol, point in this direction. Thus the actual decline of heroin seizures in 2001 may have been less. If heroin and morphine seizures are combined, the decline would have amounted to 8%.

[c] For the purposes of this analysis the Central Asian countries and the other countries forming part of the Commonwealth of Independent States (C.I.S.) were aggregated.

(though remaining significantly below the levels reported in 2000) and some declines compared to 2001 in Tajikistan and Uzbekistan offseting increases reported from Kyrgyzstan and Kazakhstan.

.... while heroin seizures in EU and EFTA countries remain largely stable

Heroin seizures in EU and EFTA countries do not appear to have changed much in 2001[d], possibly reflecting the existence of important heroin depots in several transit countries. Largely stable heroin prices in West European countries in 2001 and 2002 also seem to confirm this. In case of a severe shortage, heroin prices could have been expected to rise in Western Europe.

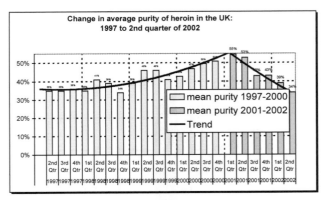

Source: UK Forensic Science Service.

Sources: EUROPOL and UNODC, Annual Reports Questionnaire Data / DELTA.

However, a number of West European countries, including the United Kingdom, reported significant declines in heroin purity levels in 2001 and 2002.

...and seizures decline in the Oceania region

The overall decline of heroin seizures in the Oceania region was mainly linked to the 'Australian heroin drought' of 2001. This had been the result of successful law enforcement interventions in South-East Asia in late 2000 when important trafficking networks, shipping heroin from Myanmar *via* Thailand and Hongkong to Australia, were dismantled. In 2003, however, there have been reports of the supply stack in Australia being partly taken up by heroin originating in, or being trafficked via the Democratic People's Republic of Korea (North Korea).

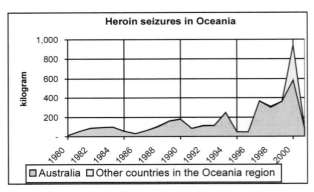

Source: UNODC, Annual Reports Questionnaire Data / DELTA.

... but are rising in South-East Asia, notably in China

In contrast to these declines, strong increases in heroin seizures (close to 90%) were reported from South-East Asia, mainly reflecting the very strong efforts by the Chinese authorities to fight drug trafficking. China accounted for 91% all heroin seizures in the East and South-East Asia region in 2001. Excluding the huge seizures reported from

---

[d]   Data are still preliminary as no seizure data have been obtained so-far from the UK and Belgium; however heroin seizures remained largely stable for the other EU & EFTA countries in 2001. For all of Western Europe, which includes Turkey according to UNODC classification, heroin seizures declined, nonetheless, by about 12%.

China, seizures from other countries of South-East Asia, however, did not show much of change.

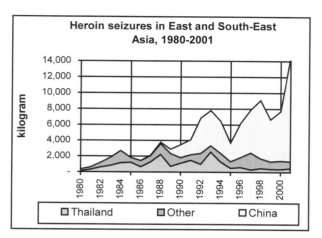

Source: UNODC, Annual Reports Questionnaire Data / DELTA.

... and continue rising in the Americas

Heroin seizures grew, in contrast, in the Americas (30%), and reached the highest level ever. There was an increase in North America (+15%), in South America (+50%). the Caribbean (61%) and in Central America (129%). The US authorities report that the bulk of the heroin found on US markets originates nowadays in the Americas, mainly in Colombia and in Mexico.

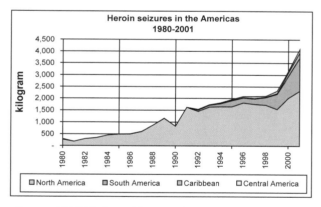

Source: UNODC, Annual Reports Questionnaire Data / DELTA.

... as well as in Africa

There was also an increase of heroin seizures in Africa in 2001 (10% compared to 2000). They rose in all sub-regions of Africa except West Africa. The strongest increase in 2001 was reported from the countries of southern Africa (73%).

Nonetheless, overall heroin seizures remained clearly below the levels reported in the early 1990s. The decline was not necessarily due to lower levels of trafficking but could be because there were fewer resources available in several countries to track drug traffickers.

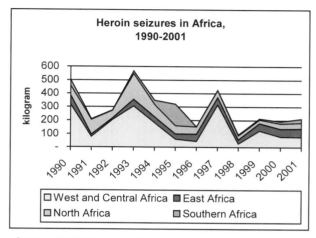

Source: UNODC, Annual Reports Questionnaire Data / DELTA.

...interception rate rises strongly in 2001

The strong reduction of opium production in 2001 by 65% and the more moderate decline of opiate seizures by 23% also had an impact on the calculated interception rate. Comparing global opium production in 2001 to opiate seizures (heroin, morphine and opium re-calculated in heroin equivalents), data suggest that an amount equivalent to 48% of the 2001 opium production was seized in 2001, up from 21% in 2000 and 15% in 1999.

Such a rate of 48%, though impressive, is, however, not a realistic as the trafficking flows – due to the existence of previously built up stocks – clearly exceeded the amounts of opiates produced in that year. It is however not possible to provide any reliable estimates of the size of these stocks. Against this background, the calculation of a meaningful interception rate for 2001, to show the effectiveness of law enforcement, is not possible for the time being. Nonetheless, data for 2001 helps to generate some meaningful orders of magnitude of the average interception rate over the last few years. It amounted to, on average, 17% over the 1995-2001 period, and was thus clearly higher than in previous periods when it fluctuated around 10%.

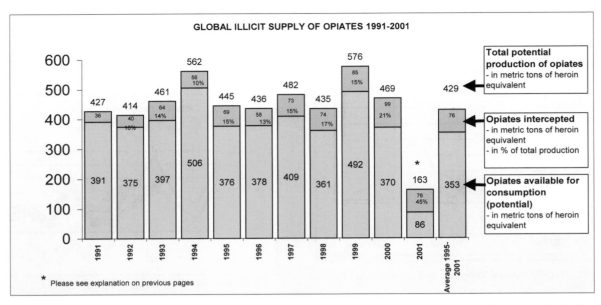

(opiates intercepted = combined seizures of opium, heroin and morphine, in metric tons of heroin equivalent)

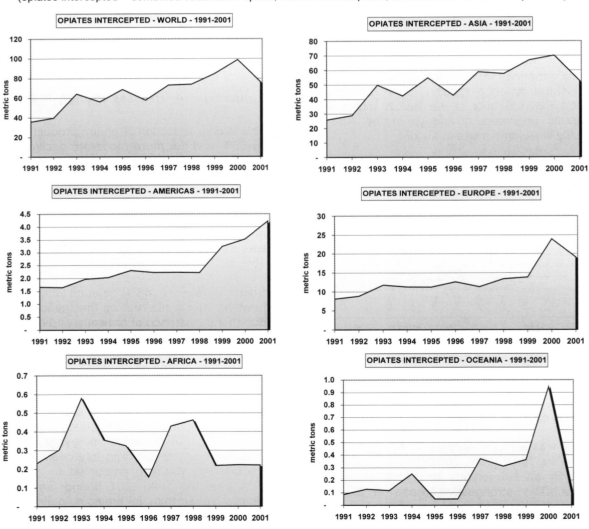

GLOBAL SEIZURES OF OPIUM, 1991-2001

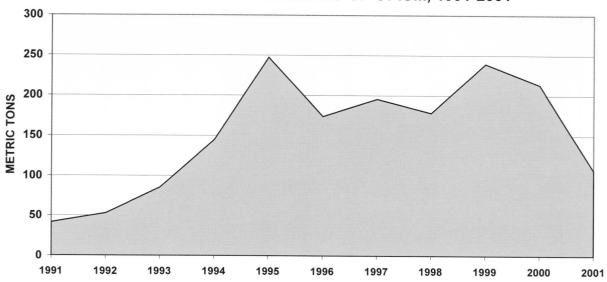

Year	1991	1992	1993	1994	1995	1996	1997	1998	1999	2000	2001
Metric tons	41	53	85	145	247	174	195	178	239	213	107

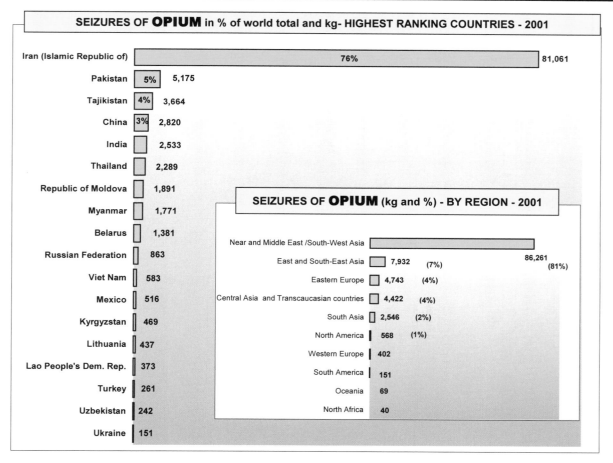

SEIZURES OF OPIUM in % of world total and kg- HIGHEST RANKING COUNTRIES - 2001

Country	%	kg
Iran (Islamic Republic of)	76%	81,061
Pakistan	5%	5,175
Tajikistan	4%	3,664
China	3%	2,820
India		2,533
Thailand		2,289
Republic of Moldova		1,891
Myanmar		1,771
Belarus		1,381
Russian Federation		863
Viet Nam		583
Mexico		516
Kyrgyzstan		469
Lithuania		437
Lao People's Dem. Rep.		373
Turkey		261
Uzbekistan		242
Ukraine		151

SEIZURES OF OPIUM (kg and %) - BY REGION - 2001

Region	kg	%
Near and Middle East /South-West Asia	86,261	(81%)
East and South-East Asia	7,932	(7%)
Eastern Europe	4,743	(4%)
Central Asia and Transcaucasian countries	4,422	(4%)
South Asia	2,546	(2%)
North America	568	(1%)
Western Europe	402	
South America	151	
Oceania	69	
North Africa	40	

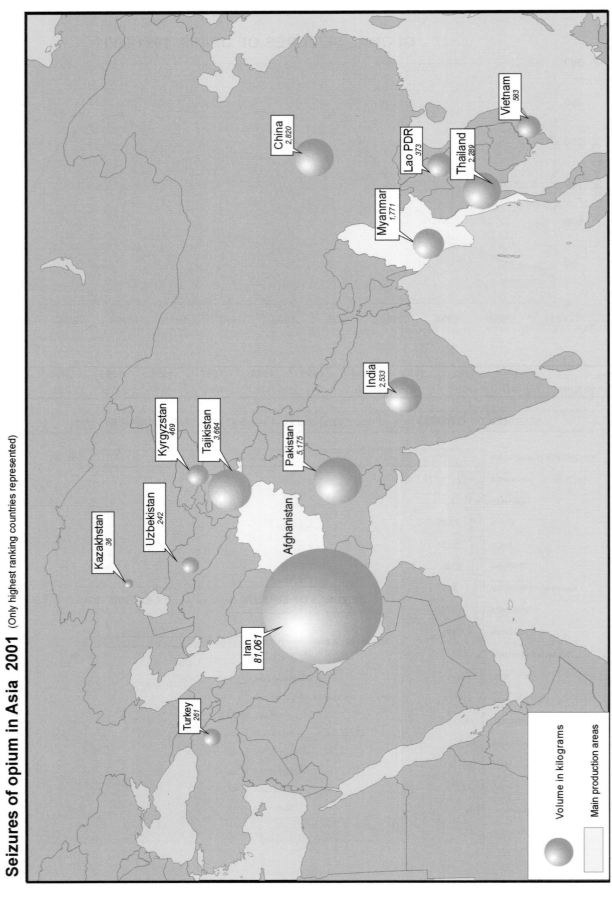

Seizures of opium in Asia 2001 (Only highest ranking countries represented)

Vietnam
583

China
2,820

Lao PDR
373

Thailand
2,289

Myanmar
1,771

India
2,533

Kyrgyzstan
469

Tajikistan
3,664

Pakistan
5,175

Uzbekistan
242

Kazakhstan
36

Afghanistan

Iran
81,061

Turkey
261

Volume in kilograms

Main production areas

Note: The boundaries and names shown and the designations used on this map do not imply official endorsement or acceptance by the United Nations

GLOBAL SEIZURES OF HEROIN AND MORPHINE, 1991-2001

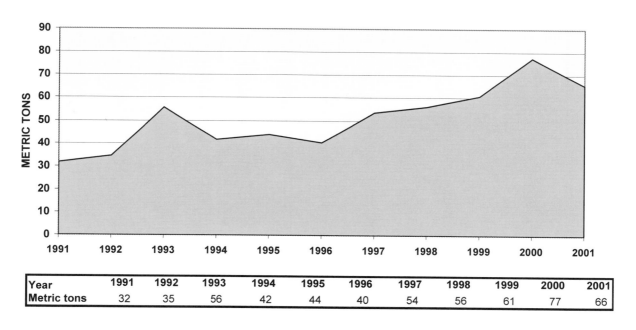

Year	1991	1992	1993	1994	1995	1996	1997	1998	1999	2000	2001
Metric tons	32	35	56	42	44	40	54	56	61	77	66

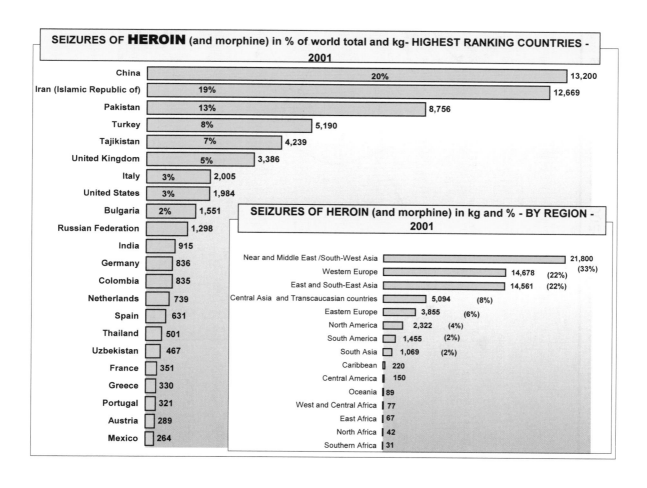

Heroin and morphine trafficking 2000-2001: extent and trends (countries reporting seizures of more than 0.01 tons (10 kg))

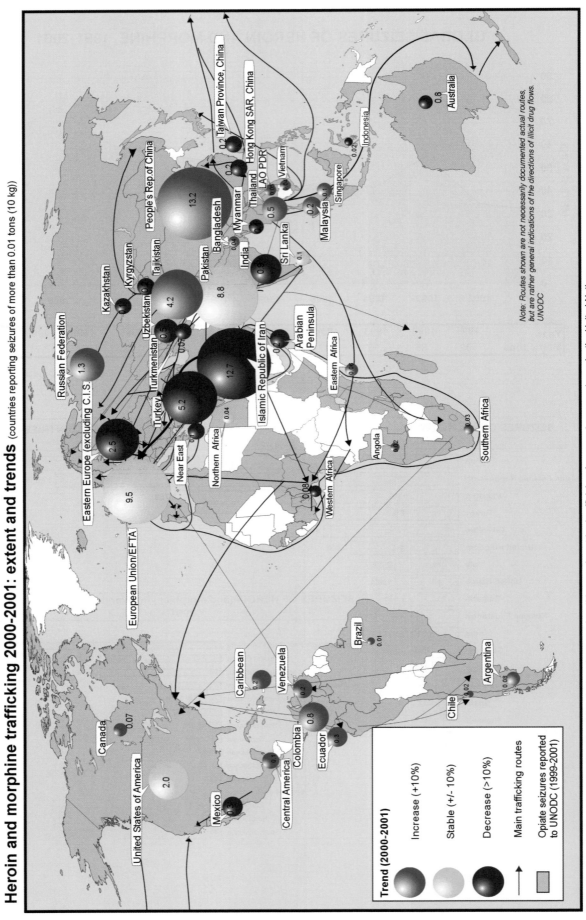

Note: Routes shown are not necessarily documented actual routes, but are rather general indications of the directions of illicit drug flows.
UNODC

Trend (2000-2001)

- Increase (+10%)
- Stable (+/- 10%)
- Decrease (>10%)
- Main trafficking routes
- Opiate seizures reported to UNODC (1999-2001)

1.2.4. Trafficking in coca / cocaine

... stabilizes in recent years

Cocaine seizures increased slightly in 2001 as compared to 2000, but were still some 7% less than in 1998. Given fluctuations from year to year, and some changes in the number of countries reporting, cocaine seizures basically reflected stable to slightly declining cocaine production in recent years after having increased dramatically in the 1980s at the time when cocaine production skyrocketed.

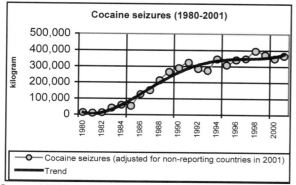

Source: UNODC, Annual Reports Questionnaire Data.

... is concentrated in the Americas and, to a lesser extent, in Western Europe

The bulk of the seizures continue to take place in the Americas, in both north and south. In 2001, 45% of all cocaine seizures took place in South America (including Central America and the Caribbean), 38% in North America and 17% in Europe (of which 99% in Western Europe).

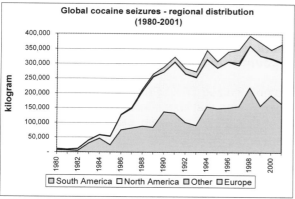

Source: UNODC, Annual Reports Questionnaire Data.

...while cocaine trafficking in North America has been stable/declining, strong increases have been reported from Western Europe

The most striking trend in recent years was, however, the strong increase in European cocaine seizures, reflecting underlying shifts in trafficking. This has been observed for some years and became even more pronounced in 2001. The proportion of cocaine seizures made in Europe rose from 8% of global seizures in 2000 to 17% in 2001. This increase in trafficking was also reflected in rising levels of cocaine abuse in a number of West European countries. Instead of targeting the already saturated and high risk North American market, traffickers have been increasingly turning to the lucrative (and still probably less risky) West European market. Indeed, a comparison of cocaine wholesale and retail prices indicates that from a trafficker's point of view the still growing European market appears to be potentially more attractive than the basically stable to declining US market.

Distribution of cocaine seizures by region in % (1985-2001)					
	1985	1990	1995	2000	2001
Americas	97.8%	94.0%	92.8%	91.1%	82.7%
Europe	2.1%	5.9%	7.0%	8.3%	16.5%
Asia	0.09%	0.04%	0.04%	0.03%	0.32%
Oceania	0.03%	0.04%	0.11%	0.41%	0.32%
Africa	0.00%	0.02%	0.08%	0.12%	0.13%
Total	100%	100%	100%	100%	100%

Source: UNODC, Annual Reports Questionnaire Data.

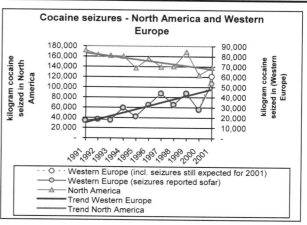

Source: UNODC, Annual Reports Questionnaire Data.

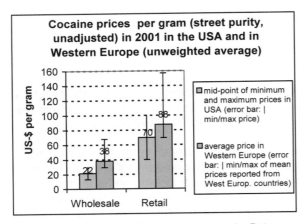

Source: UNODC, Annual Reports Questionnaire Data.

...Cocaine seizures decline in source countries in 2001

With regard to seizures in the Americas, the relative importance of seizures in the source countries (Colombia, Peru and Bolivia) declined in 2001 as compared to 2000. In 2000 cocaine (incl. cocaine base) seizures in the three Andean source countries accounted for 41% of all cocaine seizures in the Americas. In 2001 this proportion fell to 29%. In contrast, seizures in the transit countries (notably Ecuador, Brazil and Mexico) as well as in the main consumer markets of North America (USA and Canada) increased.

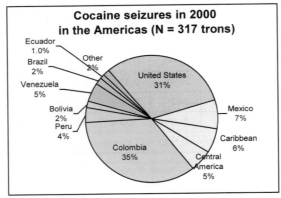

Source: UNODC, Annual Reports Questionnaire Data.

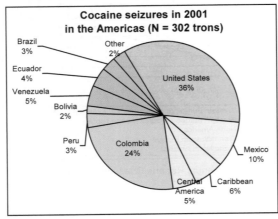

Source: UNODC, Annual Reports Questionnaire Data

... possibly a consequence of improved precursor control

The decline of cocaine seizures in 2001 in the three Andean countries by a third in 2001 as compared to a year earlier may have been a consequence of first results of improved precursor control, notably of potassium permanganate. Poor quality of cocaine and low levels of oxidation of cocaine seized in the Andean region in 2001 point in this direction.

Intensified control efforts at the global level to monitor shipments of potassium permanganate commenced in 2000 as part of 'Operation Purple', a joint endeavor by Interpol, INCB and a number of national law enforcement agencies. Thus a number of major attempted diversions, involving around 1180 tons of potassium permanganate were stopped in 2001 and a similar quantity was stopped again in 2002[a]. These quantities of potassium permanganate would have been sufficient to produce some 5900 tons of cocaine in 2001, equivalent to seven times the total illegal cocaine production in 2001 (827 tons). These huge amounts reflect enforcement efforts, as well as the attitude of many clandestine operators to purchase potassium permanganate far in excess of actual requirements from a number of sellers in different countries, anticipating that most orders will not be fulfilled. Most of the potassium permanganate shipments which were stopped originated in China and were destined for Mexico (apparently for further shipment to Colombia), Colombia itself, and Brazil (possibly intended for ongoing shipments to Bolivia, Colombia and Peru). In addition, seizures of potassium permanganate were reported from most South American countries in recent years, including the three Andean countries; but they showed a declining trend as availability was apparently reduced since the start of Operation Purple.

...Concentration of cocaine seizures in Colombia due to important coca production in the country and strong enforcement efforts

Colombia seized 84%, Peru 11% and Bolivia 5% of the cocaine that was intercepted in the region in 2001. Compared to a year earlier, the proportion fell slightly in Colombia and increased slightly in Peru and Bolivia (86% Colombia, 9% Peru, 4% Bolivia in 2000), possibly a reflection of first successes in 2001 to reduce coca production in Colombia. At the same time, the cocaine seizures in 2001 continued to be disproportionately high in Colombia. Out of the potential cocaine output of

---

[a] Precursors and Chemicals Frequently Used in the Illicit Manufacture of Narcotic Drugs and Psychotropic Substances: Report of the International Narcotics Control Board, 2002.

827 tons in 2001 75% was accounted for by Colombia, 18% by Peru and 7% by Bolivia. This suggests that the cocaine interception rate among all three Andean countries was the highest in Colombia (12% in Colombia, 7% in Bolivia and 6% in Peru in 2001).

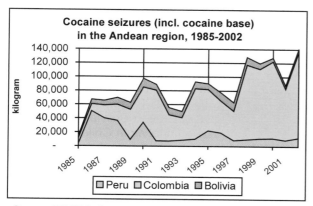

Source: UNODC, Annual Reports Questionnaire Data / DELTA.

...notably in 2002 when cocaine seizures increase despite falling levels of cocaine production

Data for 2002 suggest that parallel to strong eradication efforts in Colombia (some 130,000 hectares in 2002 were sprayed, up from 96,000 ha in 2001 and 62,000 ha in 2000), clandestine laboratories were also targeted by the authorities. A total of 1574 clandestine laboratories were dismantled in 2001 (of which 1085 were involved in the production of cocaine HCL and 470 in the production of cocaine base), up from 647 in 2000 and 316 in 1999. According to preliminary figures, a further 587 cocaine laboratories were dismantled in 2002. Interception of cocaine was also stepped up and cocaine seizures rose. Thus, despite falling coca production in Colombia, seizures of cocaine (including cocaine base) rose by almost 70% in 2002 to a new record high of 124 tons, probably exceeding those of the USA in that year. Colombia accounted for 88% of all cocaine seizures in the Andean region in 2002; Peru for 9% and Bolivia for 4%. The cocaine interception rate in Colombia rose from 12% in 2001 to 21% in 2002.

This triple strategy, focussing on eradication, the seizures of laboratories and on the dismantling of trafficking networks, contributed to a net decline in the area under coca cultivation by 30% in Colombia in 2002. The intensified dismantling of clandestine laboratories in 2000 and 2001 reduced demand for coca produced by farmers and thus prevented a rise in coca base prices

which otherwise could have been expected as a result of intensified eradication efforts. Thus, the paradoxical trend observed in previous periods in Colombia (and in some other countries), of a net expansion of cultivation parallel to intensified eradication efforts, was successfully prevented.

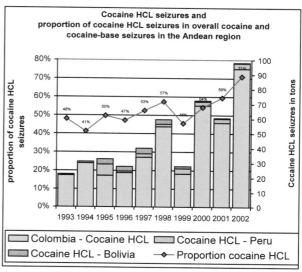

Source: US Dept. of State, International Narcotics Control Strategy Report 2002, March 2003.

If only the seizures of cocaine HCL (the 'end product' of cocaine) are considered, the dominance of Colombia is even more pronounced. Colombia accounted for 95% of all cocaine HCL seizures in the Andean region in 2001 and this proportion rose to 96% in 2002.

Overall 71% of all 'cocaine' (cocaine HCL and cocaine base) in the Andean region was seized in the form of cocaine HCL in 2002, up from 59% in 2001 and 48% in 1993. This could be an indication that within the region a higher proportion of the coca leaf is now being transformed into the end-product, cocaine HCL. However, the trends among the three Andean countries were not uniform. Colombia has for years reported the highest proportions of cocaine HCL in 'cocaine' seizures, indicating that most of the cocaine manufacture in the Andean region - even prior to the strong increase of coca cultivation in the country in the late 1990s – took place in Colombia. The proportion of cocaine HCL seizures in Peru was always significantly lower, indicating that not much of the final production happened in Peru. However, there was a strong increase in 2002, giving rise to fears that increasing amounts of cocaine HCL may be now produced in Peru. The proportion of cocaine HCL seizures in Bolivia increased in the early 1990s but showed a downward trend over the last few years. This trend also continued in 2001 and 2002. Less domestic coca production together with a shortage in the supply of precursor chemicals were probably responsible.

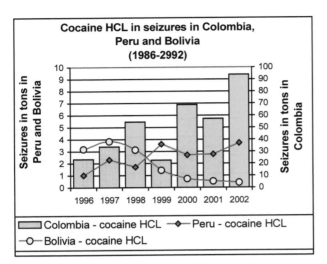

Cocaine HCL in seizures in Colombia, Peru and Bolivia (1986-1992)

Source: US Dept. of State, *International Narcotics Control Strategy Report* , March 2003.

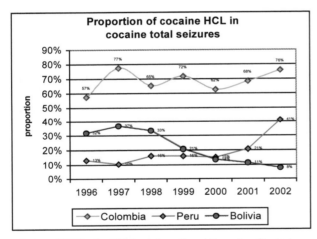

Proportion of cocaine HCL in cocaine total seizures

Source: US Dept. of State, *International Narcotics Control Strategy Report* , March 2003.

...Colombia's cocaine production also reflected in reports from transit countries of Central America and the Caribbean

Despite Colombian successes in eradicating coca cultivation and intercepting cocaine, most countries of Central America, the Caribbean and North America cited Colombia as the predominant source of the cocaine found on their markets in 2001 (close to 100%). The US authorities estimate that about 90% of the cocaine which enters the

USA originates or passes through Colombia[b]. The Colombian authorities also report that the main cocaine trafficking routes continue to go from Colombia *via* Mexico (either *via* the Pacific Ocean or Central America) to the USA and/or *via* the Caribbean (often using go-fast boats). The final destination, in general, is the USA, though some of the cocaine is also destined for Europe. If the cocaine is transported by air, Venezuela and Brazil are common transshipment points.

The situation is different south of Colombia. In Peru and Bolivia most of the cocaine is of domestic origin (100% in Peru, 76% in Bolivia; 24% of the seized cocaine in Bolivia originated in Peru in 2001). The authorities in Chile reckon that about 50% of the cocaine they seize comes from Peru. In Argentina, 80% of the cocaine is believed to originate in Bolivia, 10% in Peru and 10% in Colombia in 2001. In Brazil the authorities reckon that about 70% originates in Colombia, 20% in Bolivia and 10% in Peru (2000).

...Spain and the Netherlands continue to be Europe's main entry points for South American cocaine

Throughout the 1990s Spain and the Netherlands reported the highest cocaine seizures in Europe and were mentioned by most other European countries as important transshipment points. Data for 2000 and 2001 confirm this pattern. The analysis of seizure data for 2001 is complicated by the fact that two countries, the UK and Belgium, which accounted for about a quarter of all European cocaine seizures in 2000, have not so far provided seizure data for 2001. However, even if these two countries had not made any cocaine seizures in the year, overall European cocaine seizures would have doubled in 2001. Assuming that the seizures of the UK and Belgium remained at similar levels in 2001 as in 2000, overall cocaine seizures in Europe would have risen by some 120% in 2001. The increase was mainly due to a quadrupling of cocaine seizures in Spain. Thus the proportion of Spain in overall European cocaine seizures rose from 21% in 2000 to more than 50% in 2001. Seizures in the Netherlands, traditionally the second largest entry point for South American cocaine, increased by 30%. Spain and the Netherlands thus accounted for about 70% of all cocaine seizures in 2001. Strong increases in cocaine seizures were also reported by Portugal (81%), France (58%) and Germany (41%). Among the larger countries only Italy reported a decline (-23%)

---

[b] USA/ONDCP, National Drug Control Strategy, February 2003.

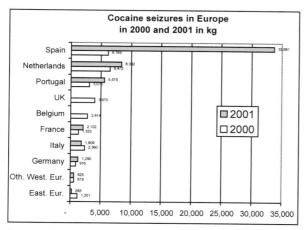

Cocaine seizures in Europe in 2000 and 2001 in kg

Source: UNODC, Annual Reports Questionnaire Data.

...Multiple sources and trafficking routes of cocaine to Europe

Almost half of all European countries which reported on the origin of the cocaine, identified Colombia as the main source (11 out of 24 reporting countries in 2001); 7 European countries cited Bolivia as a source and five cited Peru. Six countries were not able to differentiate and simply reported South America as the origin. The ranking provided by Spain, Europe's main entry point of cocaine, cites Colombia first, followed by Peru and only then Bolivia. The UK reported 80% of the cocaine to originate in Colombia, 12% in Peru and only 8% in Bolivia. The authorities in Sweden reported that 80% of the cocaine came from Colombia. The authorities in Belgium cite almost 100% originating in Colombia. The Czech authorities reported 90% originating in Colombia and about 10% in Bolivia.

Typical transshipment countries from which cocaine came to the European market in 2001 were reported to be Venezuela (four countries), Ecuador (three), Brazil (three), Suriname (1) as well as countries/territories in the Caribbean (such as the Netherland Antilles or Martinique) and countries in Central America (such as Panama or Nicaragua). In 2000, in addition, Costa Rica and Aruba were reported as transshipment points where criminal groups purchased the cocaine.

Most countries in the Americas saw the USA, neighbouring countries as well as their own country as important final destinations of the cocaine trafficked *via* their territory. However, a number of countries, in addition, identified countries in Europe as important destinations. They included in 2000/2001 Colombia, Peru, Bolivia, Brazil, Chile, Argentina and Uruguay in

South America, the Dominican Republic, Costa Rica, Guatemala in Central America, and a number of countries/territories in the Caribbean (Trinidad and Tobago, Jamaica, the Bahamas, the British Virgin Islands, Grenada and Saint Lucia). Spain was identified by most countries as the main European destination.

...including via Africa

In addition, a number of African countries, including Nigeria, Togo, Ghana, Gambia, Rep. of South Africa, Zimbabwe, Swaziland, Tanzania, Kenya, and Uganda reported South American cocaine being transshipped *via* their territory to Europe (1999-2001).

The rather large number of countries reporting seizures of cocaine in Africa indicates that trafficking is widespread. Over the 1991-2001 period 41 African countries reported seizures of cocaine, up from 24 countries over the 1980-1990 period. The largest cocaine seizures in Africa were reported from Nigeria and South Africa in 2001. In addition, cocaine seizures in 2001 were reported by Benin and Togo, Gambia and the Côte d'Ivoire in Western Africa, Angola, Namibia, Swaziland, Malawi and Mozambique in Southern Africa, Kenya and Tanzania in Eastern Africa, and Morocco and Algeria in Northern Africa.

...Limited trafficking of cocaine in Asia

In contrast, only one country in Asia, the Philippines, reported regularly transshipments of cocaine to Europe and to North America. Overall trafficking in cocaine in Asia region is still small though increasing. Cocaine seizures in Asia amounted to 0.3% of global cocaine seizures in 2001, up from 0.1% in 2000. Seizures in 2001 were mainly reported from the countries of the Near and Middle East, notably Syria, Israel, Lebanon, and – at lower levels - Jordan. Cocaine seizures in South Asia have been reported from India and Sri Lanka and cocaine seizures in South-East Asia are concentrated in Indonesia, Hong Kong (SAR of China) and Thailand.

Authorities of Indonesia reported transshipments of cocaine to Australia. More cocaine arriving in Australia, however, appears to be shipped *via* the Caribbean and the Panama Canal. Other transshipment points identified were the USA, Argentina, South Africa and the Netherlands (2000).

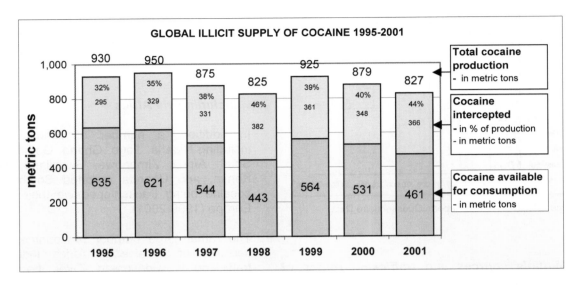

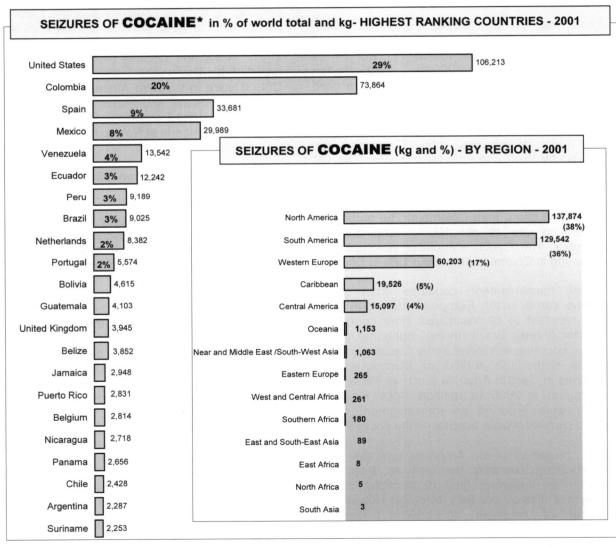

* excluding seizures in liquid form.

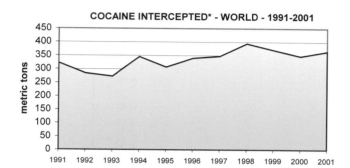

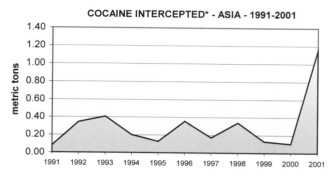

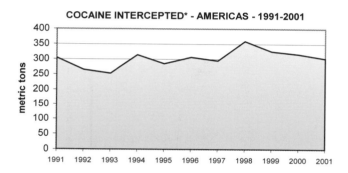

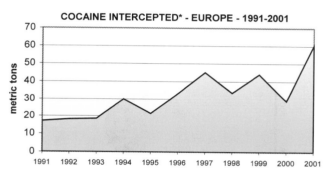

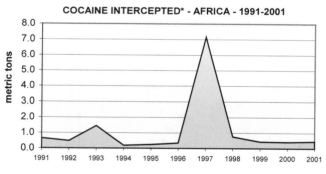

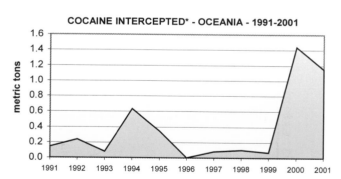

*excluding seizures in liquid form.

Cocaine* trafficking 2000-2001: extent and trends (countries reporting seizures of more than 0.01 tons (10 kg))

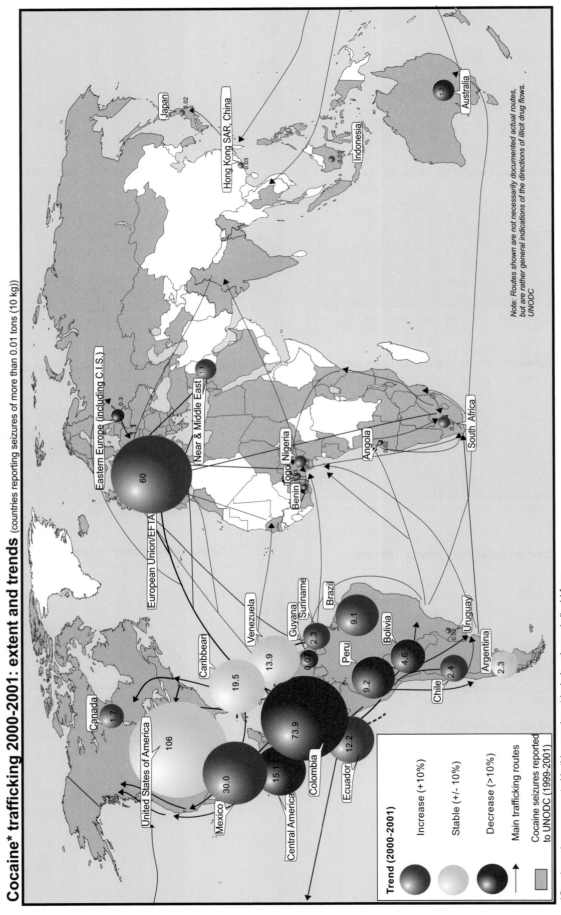

Note: Routes shown are not necessarily documented actual routes, but are rather general indications of the directions of illicit drug flows. UNODC

Trend (2000-2001)

- Increase (+10%)
- Stable (+/- 10%)
- Decrease (>10%)
- Main trafficking routes
- Cocaine seizures reported to UNODC (1999-2001)

*Cocaine seizures presented in this map do not include seizures in liquid form.
Note: The boundaries and names shown and the designations used on this map do not imply official endorsement or acceptance by the United Nations.

1.2.4. Trafficking in cannabis

... the most extensively trafficked drug worldwide

The two cannabis products, cannabis herb (marijuana) and cannabis resin (hashish) continue to be the main drugs trafficked worldwide. Almost all countries are affected by cannabis trafficking and in almost all countries seizures of cannabis exceed those of other drugs. In total almost 5600 tons of cannabis products were seized in 2001, i.e.15 times the amount cocaine and more than 100 times the amount of heroin. Seizures of cannabis herb amounted to almost 4700 tons and seizures of cannabis resin amounted to about 900 tons in 2001. In addition, about 3 tons of cannabis oil were seized in 2001.

... rising seizures of cannabis herb and stable / declining trend for cannabis resin

The rise of cannabis seizures in recent years was concentrated on herb while the resin seizures remained basically stable. In 2001 seizures of marijuana continued rising while hashish seizures declined. Overall cannabis seizures remained stable.

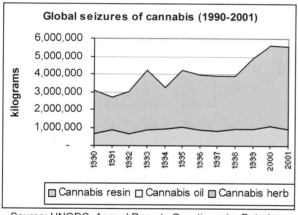

Source: UNODC, Annual Reports Questionnaire Data / DELTA.

... concentrated in the Americas and in Africa where seizures rose strongly in recent years

In 2001, 53% of all seizures were reported from countries in the Americas, 23% from Africa, 15% from Europe, 8% from Asia and less than 1% from the countries in Oceania. The most striking feature in recent years was the increase of seizures reported from countries in Africa. Between 1998 and 2001 the proportion of Africa in seizures almost doubled, from 12% to 23%. In contrast, the proportion of Europe declined over the same

period from 24% to 15%. Given reports of ongoing increases in consumption, a possible explanation for this could be changes in the priorities of enforcement agencies in several European countries.

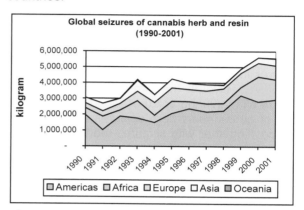

Source: UNODC, Annual Reports Questionnaire Data / DELTA.

Trafficking in cannabis herb

... strong rise in cannabis herb seizures in recent years

Cannabis herb (marijuana) is the by far most widely trafficked drug worldwide. Over the 1991-2001 period 194 countries and territories reported seizures of cannabis herb to UNODC, more than for cocaine (174 countries), heroin (172 countries), cannabis resin (143 countries), or stimulants (120 countries). Cannabis herb seizures rose by about 50% between 1998-2000 and by a further 3% in 2001.

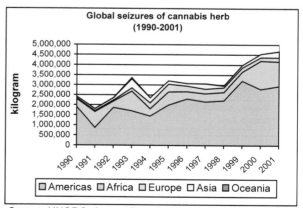

Source: UNODC, Annual Reports Questionnaire Data / DELTA.

Compared to the year 2000, seizures increased strongly in the Oceania region (+90%), and in Asia (+72%), more moderately in Europe (+22%) and slightly in the Americas (+6%). Seizures in Africa fell in 2001 as compared to 2000 (-13%), but were still three times as high as in 1998. No other region reported similarly high increases over the 1998-2001 period.

... concentration in the Americas, notably in North America

There is a concentration of cannabis herb seizures in the Americas, notably in Mexico and in the USA. Overall the Americas accounted for 63% of all marijuana seizures worldwide. In 2001, 39% of all cannabis herb seizures were made in Mexico. Together with seizures made in the USA, accounting for 15% of global marijuana seizures, North America was thus responsible for 54% of global marijuana seizures. Seizures in North America have shown an upward trend in the 1990s while those of South America have been stable to declining since the mid 1990s and significantly lower than in the mid 1980s. Thus overall cannabis herb seizures in the Americas are still less than they were in the early to mid 1980s. The shift in seizures seems to reflect underlying shifts in cannabis production which shifted from countries in South America and the Caribbean closer to the lucrative market of the United States, including Mexico, Canada and the United States itself. US authorities estimate that some 10,000 tons of cannabis herb is produced domestically and more than 5000 tons are imported annually into the country from neighbouring Mexico and Canada.

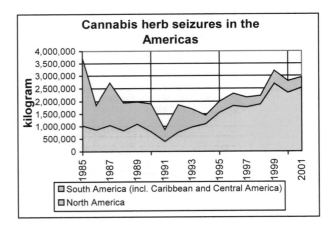

Source: UNODC, Annual Reports Questionnaire Data / DELTA.

... and a concentration in Africa, notably in southern Africa

The next largest region for cannabis production, trafficking and consumption is Africa, accounting for 26% of global cannabis herb seizures in 2001. Compared to other drugs, the proportion is particularly high for Africa. The largest seizures in 2001 were reported from Kenya, Nigeria, and the Republic of South Africa. Cannabis is produced and trafficked throughout Africa. Thirty African countries reported cannabis herb seizures over the 2000-2001 period to UNODC, more than for any other drug. The bulk of cannabis was seized throughout the 1990s by the countries of southern Africa, notably the Republic of South Africa, followed by Malawi. Since the mid 1990s significant seizures were also reported from countries in West Africa, notably Nigeria, followed by Ghana. In 2001, East Africa emerged, for the first time, as the subregion in Africa which had the largest cannabis herb seizures. In particular Kenya and Tanzania reported huge cannabis herb seizures in 2001. Cannabis herb seizures in North Africa were particularly strong over the last decade in Morocco and Egypt.

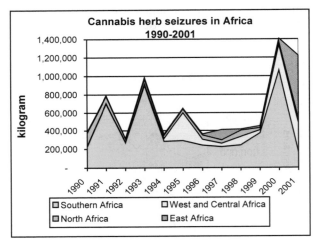

Source: UNODC, Annual Reports Questionnaire Data / DELTA.

... cannabis herb seizures in Asia are concentrated in South Asia and show a rising trend over the last few years

Asia accounted for 6% of global cannabis herb seizures in 2001. The largest seizures in Asia were reported from Sri Lanka and India. Overall seizures of cannabis herb were largest (in most years) over the last two decades in South Asia. Though falling between 1993 and 1999, they rose again in 2000 and 2001. Seizures in South-East Asia have been basically stable in recent years. Increases, by contrast, were reported from countries in Central Asia.

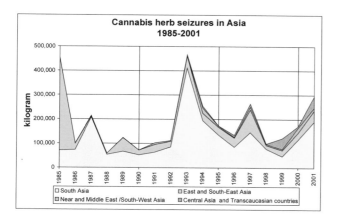

Source: UNODC, Annual Reports Questionnaire Data / DELTA.

Based on US government production estimates in Mexico and the USA, the interception rate of cannabis herb would have been around 25% of annual domestic production in Mexico in 2001 and around 5% in the USA (domestic production and imports), and thus significantly lower than for cocaine.

... falling cannabis herb seizures in West Europe and rising seizures in East Europe

Europe accounted for 4% of global cannabis herb seizures. Only the Oceania region reported less seizures (less than 1%). Cannabis herb seizures in Europe have shown an upward trend until 1995. Since then, however, the trend was clearly towards a decline even though seizures in 2001 exceeded those reported in 2000. The decline of seizures since the mid-1990s appears to be linked to changes in enforcement policies in a number of West European countries rather than a decline in trafficking. Seizures in East Europe, in contrast, have shown a rising trend. The largest seizures in Europe were reported from the Russian Federation for the year 2001. In West Europe the largest cannabis herb seizures were reported by the Italian authorities in 2001.

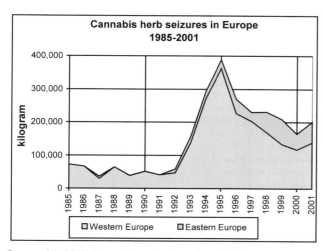

Source: UNODC, Annual Reports Questionnaire Data / DELTA.

GLOBAL SEIZURES OF CANNABIS HERB, 1991-2001

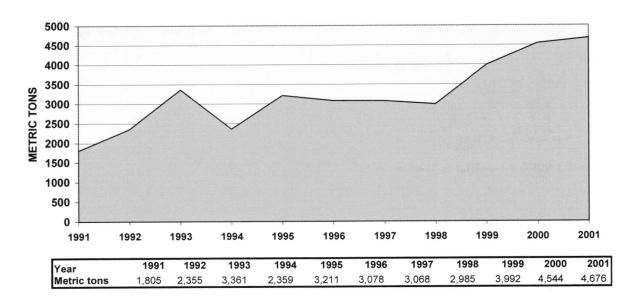

Year	1991	1992	1993	1994	1995	1996	1997	1998	1999	2000	2001
Metric tons	1,805	2,355	3,361	2,359	3,211	3,078	3,068	2,985	3,992	4,544	4,676

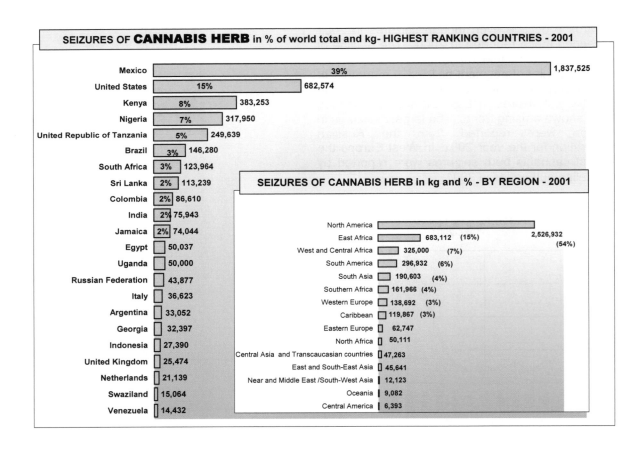

SEIZURES OF CANNABIS HERB in % of world total and kg- HIGHEST RANKING COUNTRIES - 2001

Country	%	kg
Mexico	39%	1,837,525
United States	15%	682,574
Kenya	8%	383,253
Nigeria	7%	317,950
United Republic of Tanzania	5%	249,639
Brazil	3%	146,280
South Africa	3%	123,964
Sri Lanka	2%	113,239
Colombia	2%	86,610
India	2%	75,943
Jamaica	2%	74,044
Egypt		50,037
Uganda		50,000
Russian Federation		43,877
Italy		36,623
Argentina		33,052
Georgia		32,397
Indonesia		27,390
United Kingdom		25,474
Netherlands		21,139
Swaziland		15,064
Venezuela		14,432

SEIZURES OF CANNABIS HERB in kg and % - BY REGION - 2001

Region	kg	%
North America	2,526,932	(54%)
East Africa	683,112	(15%)
West and Central Africa	325,000	(7%)
South America	296,932	(6%)
South Asia	190,603	(4%)
Southern Africa	161,966	(4%)
Western Europe	138,692	(3%)
Caribbean	119,867	(3%)
Eastern Europe	62,747	
North Africa	50,111	
Central Asia and Transcaucasian countries	47,263	
East and South-East Asia	45,641	
Near and Middle East /South-West Asia	12,123	
Oceania	9,082	
Central America	6,393	

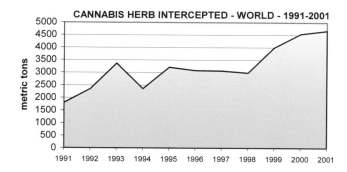

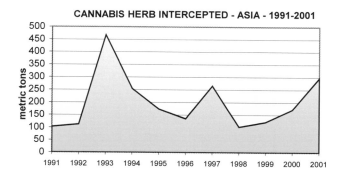

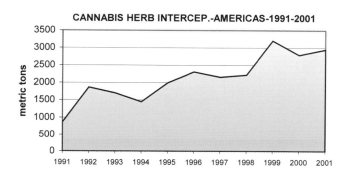

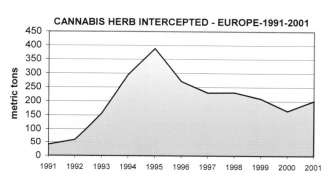

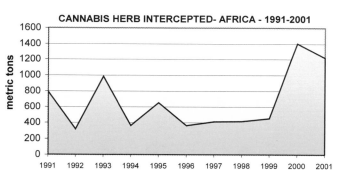

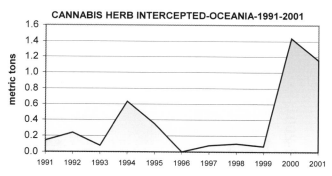

Cannabis herb trafficking 2000-2001: extent and trends (countries reporting seizures of more than 0.1 tons (100 kg))

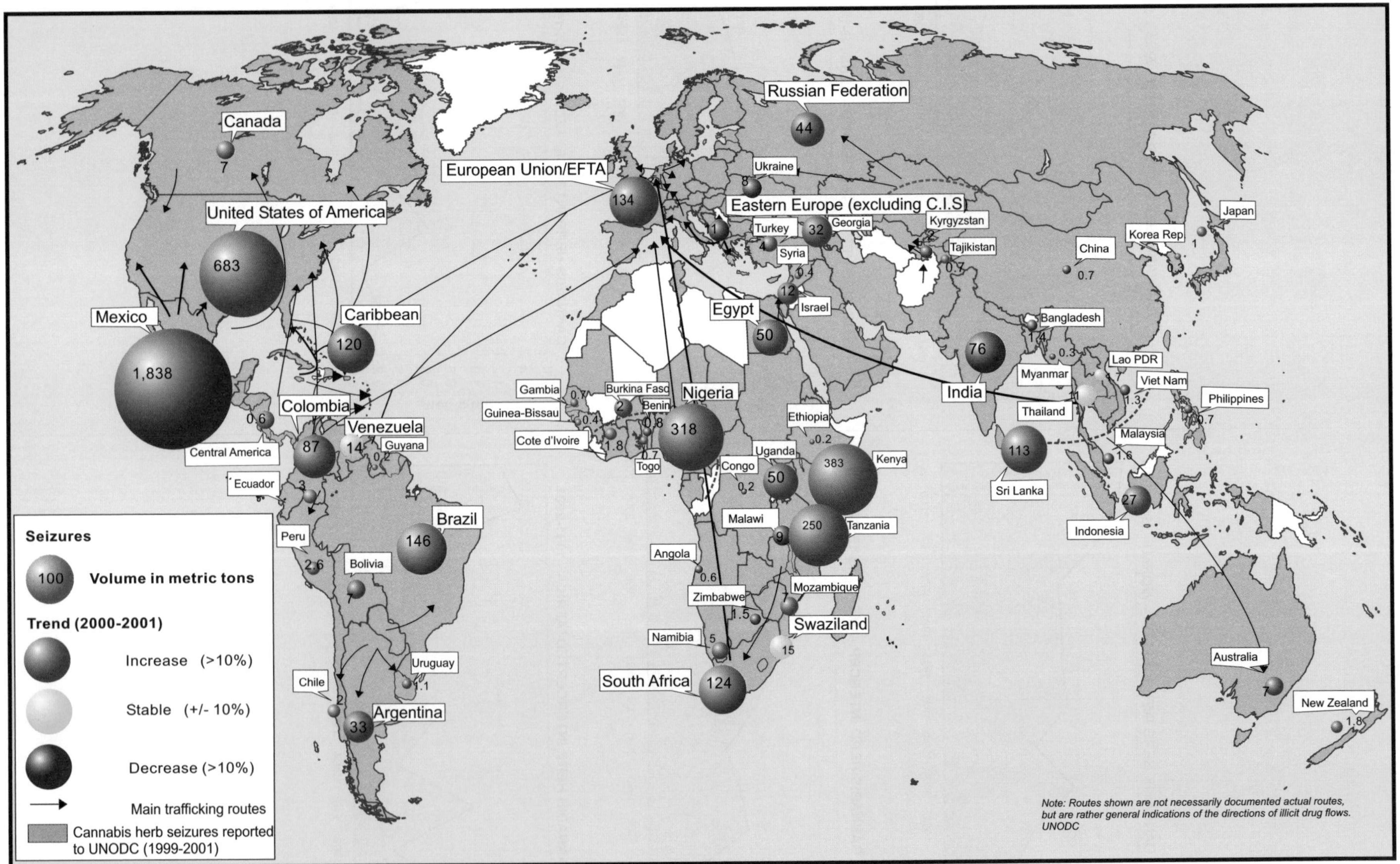

Note: Routes shown are not necessarily documented actual routes, but are rather general indications of the directions of illicit drug flows. UNODC

Seizures

100 — Volume in metric tons

Trend (2000-2001)

Increase (>10%)

Stable (+/- 10%)

Decrease (>10%)

Main trafficking routes

Cannabis herb seizures reported to UNODC (1999-2001)

Selected country values: New Zealand 1.8, Australia 27, Japan 1, Korea Rep., China 0.7, Bangladesh 1.4, Philippines 0.7, Viet Nam 1.3, Malaysia 1.6, Indonesia, Myanmar 0.3, Thailand, Sri Lanka 113, India 76, Russian Federation 44, Tajikistan, Kyrgyzstan, Georgia, Ukraine 8, Turkey 4, Syria, Israel 12, Egypt 50, Eastern Europe (excluding C.I.S) 32, European Union/EFTA 134, Nigeria 318, Kenya 383, Tanzania 250, Mozambique 7, Swaziland 15, Malawi 9, Zimbabwe 1.5, Namibia 5, South Africa 124, Angola 0.6, Congo 0.2, Uganda, Ethiopia 0.2, Benin 0.8, Togo 0.7, Burkina Faso 2, Cote d'Ivoire 1.8, Guinea-Bissau 0.4, Gambia 0.7, Canada 7, United States of America 683, Mexico 1,838, Central America 0.6, Ecuador, Colombia 87, Venezuela 14, Guyana, Peru 2.6, Bolivia, Brazil 146, Chile 2, Uruguay 0.1, Argentina 33, Caribbean 120

Note: The boundaries and names shown and the designations used on this map do not imply official endorsement or acceptance by the United Nations.

Trafficking in cannabis resin

...Cannabis resin seizures show signs of stabilization

At the global level about 900 tons of cannabis resin ('hashish') were seized in 2001. Seizures in 2001 were at about the same level as in 1999, though 17% less than in 2000. Overall seizures of cannabis resin showed signs of stabilization since the mid 1990s after having increased strongly between 1980 and 1995. In contrast to cannabis herb, production, trafficking and consumption of cannabis resin is far more concentrated. There are basically two main areas of production: Morocco in North Africa and Pakistan/Afghanistan in South-West Asia. Europe is the main consumer region outside the production countries. The largest seizures at the global level have been repeatedly reported from Spain, followed by Pakistan and Morocco.

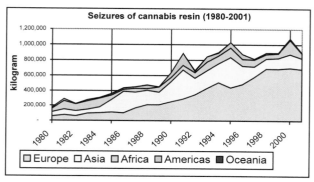

Source: UNODC, Annual Reports Questionnaire Data / DELTA.

...Concentration in Europe, notably in Spain

Throughout the 1990s as well as in 2000 and 2001, the bulk of cannabis resin was seized in Europe: 76% of all cannabis resin seizures took place there, 16% in Asia and 7% in Africa in 2001. In contrast, trafficking of cannabis resin in the Americas and Oceania is almost negligible. In Europe, cannabis resin seizures were more than three times larger than cannabis herb seizures in 2001. Ninety eight percent of all European cannabis resin seizures take place in West Europe. The largest hashish seizures have been reported for years from Spain, reflecting its position as a transit country of Moroccan hashish to other countries of West Europe. Cannabis resin seizures made by the authorities in Spain accounted for 57% of world seizures and 75% of

seizures in Europe in 2001. While hashish seizures in other European countries have shown a falling trend since the mid 1990s, they continued to rise in Spain. This resulted in an overall flat trend for Europe as a whole in the last few years.

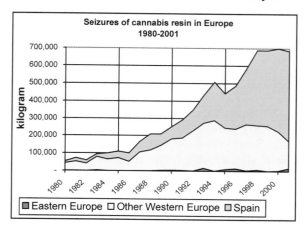

Source: UNODC, Annual Reports Questionnaire Data / DELTA

... and in North Africa, notably in Morocco

Seizures of cannabis resin in Africa have been concentrated in Morocco over the last decade, reflecting the concentration of hashish production in the country. In 2000 Morocco accounted for 13% of global cannabis resin seizures. In 2001, however, they fell back to the levels reported in 1998 and 1999. Compared to the record seizures in 2000, this was equivalent to a decline by 57%. Nonetheless, 94% of all cannabis resin seizures reported from African countries were made by the Moroccan authorities in that year. (Over the 1991-2001 period Morocco accounted for 86% of all African cannabis resin seizures). The only other

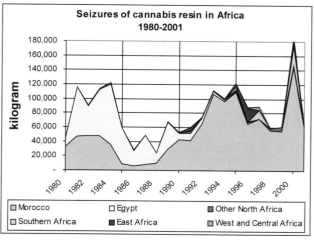

Source: UNODC, Annual Reports Questionnaire Data / DELTA.

African country which used to report similarly high hashish seizures in the 1980s was Egypt. However, following the end of large-scale cannabis resin production in the Bekaa Valley of Lebanon in the early 1990s, Egypt's traditional hashish problem, and related trafficking, appears to have largely disappeared.

.... and in the Near & Middle East / South-West Asia region, notably in Pakistan

The largest cannabis resin seizures in this region have been continuously reported from countries in South-West Asia, and to a lesser extent from countries in Central Asia and South Asia. Over the 1991-2001 period seizures of the Near & Middle East / South-West Asia subregion accounted for 94% of all cannabis resin seizures made in Asia. Pakistan alone was responsible for 74% of all such seizures and Iran for a further 7%, reflecting large scale cannabis resin production in both Afghanistan and Pakistan. Lebanon and its neighbours in the Near East used to report considerable cannabis resin seizures, but declined following the end of large-scale production in the Bekaa Valley in the early 1990s. The overall decline of cannabis resin seizures in South-West Asia in the second half of the 1990s was possibly linked to the Taliban policy to prohibit cannabis production while tolerating / promoting opium production during the first few years of the regime.

In 2001, Pakistan's cannabis resin seizures were equivalent to 53% of all Asian seizures. Iran's proportion in Asian cannabis resin seizures rose to 33% in 2001 as the country was targeted by Afghan traffickers who shifted their 'traditional' cannabis resin exports to the more lucrative Iranian market instead, for domestic production and/or further shipments to markets in Western Europe. Pakistan and Iran together accounted for 86% of all Asian cannabis resin seizures in 2001.

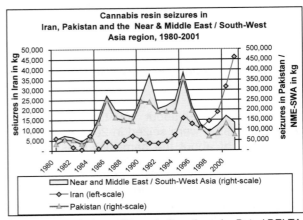

Source: UNODC, Annual Reports Questionnaire Data / DELTA.

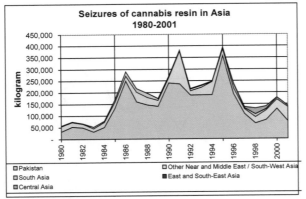

Source: UNODC, Annual Reports Questionnaire Data / DELTA

GLOBAL SEIZURES OF CANNABIS RESIN, 1990-2001

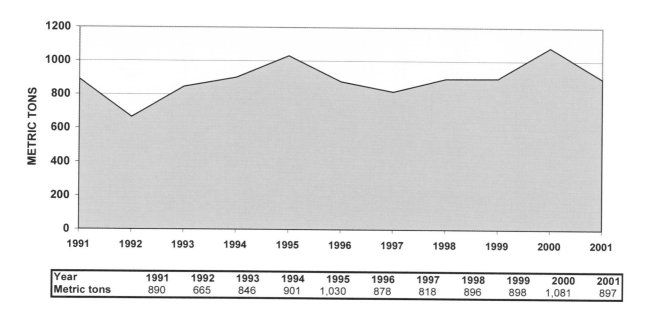

Year	1991	1992	1993	1994	1995	1996	1997	1998	1999	2000	2001
Metric tons	890	665	846	901	1,030	878	818	896	898	1,081	897

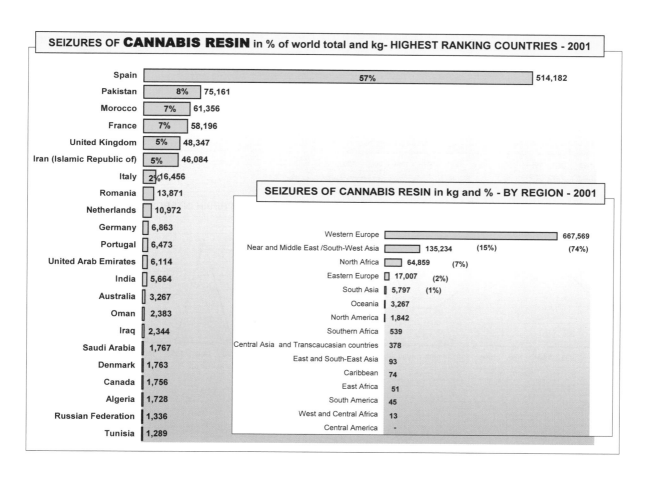

SEIZURES OF **CANNABIS RESIN** in % of world total and kg- HIGHEST RANKING COUNTRIES - 2001

Spain	57%	514,182
Pakistan	8%	75,161
Morocco	7%	61,356
France	7%	58,196
United Kingdom	5%	48,347
Iran (Islamic Republic of)	5%	46,084
Italy	2%	16,456
Romania		13,871
Netherlands		10,972
Germany		6,863
Portugal		6,473
United Arab Emirates		6,114
India		5,664
Australia		3,267
Oman		2,383
Iraq		2,344
Saudi Arabia		1,767
Denmark		1,763
Canada		1,756
Algeria		1,728
Russian Federation		1,336
Tunisia		1,289

SEIZURES OF CANNABIS RESIN in kg and % - BY REGION - 2001

Western Europe	667,569	(74%)
Near and Middle East /South-West Asia	135,234	(15%)
North Africa	64,859	(7%)
Eastern Europe	17,007	(2%)
South Asia	5,797	(1%)
Oceania	3,267	
North America	1,842	
Southern Africa	539	
Central Asia and Transcaucasian countries	378	
East and South-East Asia	93	
Caribbean	74	
East Africa	51	
South America	45	
West and Central Africa	13	
Central America	-	

CANNABIS RESIN INTERCEPTED- WORLD - 1991-2001

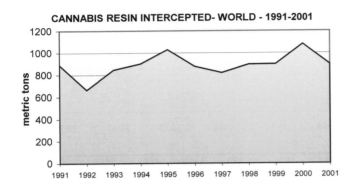

CANNABIS RESIN INTERCEPTED - ASIA - 1991-2001

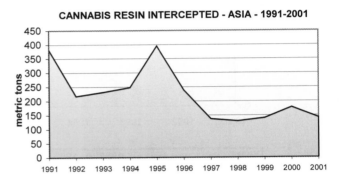

CANNABIS RESIN INTERCEP. AMERICAS-1991-2001

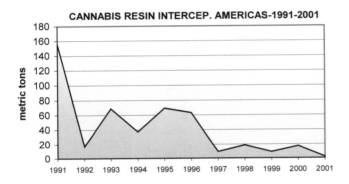

CANNABIS RESIN INTERCEPT. - EUROPE-1991-2001

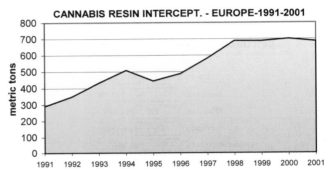

CANNABIS RESIN INTERCEPTED- AFRICA - 1991-2001

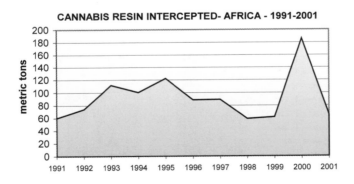

CANNABIS RESIN INTERCEPTED-OCEANIA-1991-2001

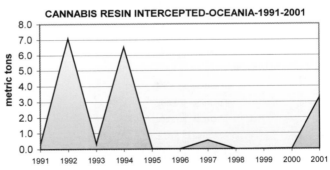

Cannabis resin trafficking 2000-2001: extent and trends (countries reporting seizures of more than 0.01 tons (10 kg))

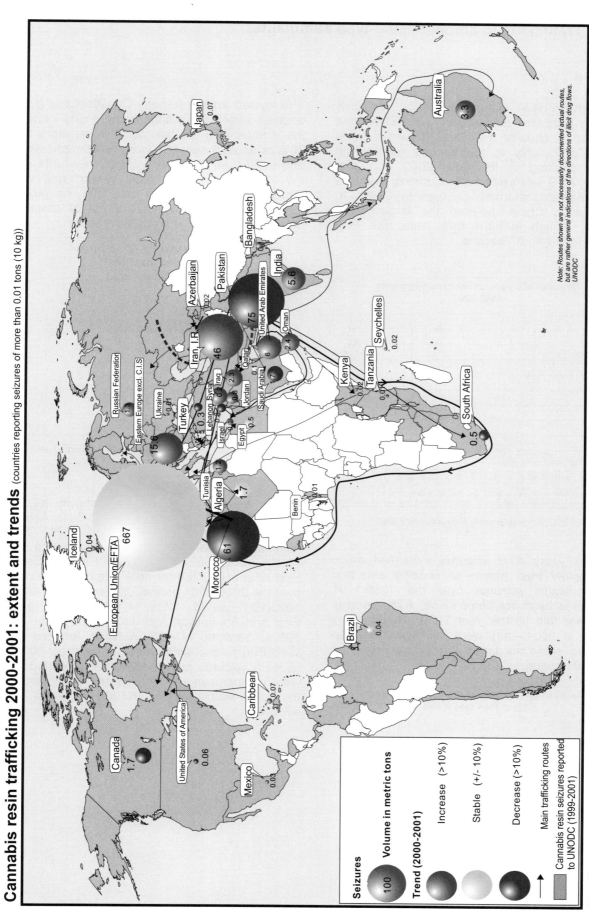

Note: Routes shown are not necessarily documented actual routes, but are rather general indications of the directions of illicit drug flows.
UNODC

Seizures		
Volume in metric tons		
100		
Trend (2000-2001)		
	Increase (>10%)	
	Stable (+/- 10%)	
	Decrease (>10%)	
	Main trafficking routes	
	Cannabis resin seizures reported to UNODC (1999-2001)	

Japan 0.07
Australia 3.3
Bangladesh
India 5.6
Azerbaijan 0.02
Pakistan
United Arab Emirates 75
Oman 2.4
Iran, I.R 46
Qatar 6
Seychelles 0.02
Tanzania 0.07
Kenya 0.02
Russian Federation
Eastern Europe excl. C.I.S
Ukraine 0.01
Turkey 15.6
Iraq 2.3
Syria 0.7
Jordan 0.03
Saudi Arabia 0.7
Egypt 0.5
Israel 0.1
Lebanon 0.3
South Africa 0.5
Iceland 0.04
European Union/EFTA 667
Tunisia 1.2
Algeria 1.7
Benin 0.01
Morocco 61
Brazil 0.04
Canada 1.7
United States of America 0.06
Mexico 0.03
Caribbean 0.07

Note: The boundaries and names shown and the designations used on this map do not imply official endorsement or acceptance by the United Nations

1.2.5. Trafficking in amphetamine-type stimulants

Overview

Amphetamine-type stimulants (ATS) seizures reflecting increases in production, trafficking and consumption, showed a marked upward trend in the 1990s, notably in the second half of the decade, peaking in the year 2000. In 2001, however, ATS seizures declined, mainly due to a fall of methamphetamine seizures in China. In recent years China reported the largest ATS seizures, though in 2001 they were less than those reported from Thailand.

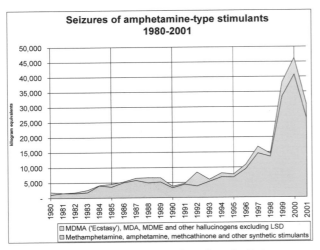

Source: UNODC, Annual Reports Questionnaire Data.

In recent years ATS seizures increased much more rapidly than heroin or cocaine seizures. Using average seizures over the 1989-1991 period as a basis for comparison, ATS seizures rose nine fold till the year 2000. Though they declined in 2001, they were still higher than in 1998 and some six times larger than over the 1989-1991 period.

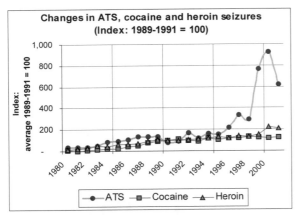

Source: UNODC, Annual Reports Questionnaire Data.

The revised Annual Reports Questionnaire (ARQ) enables better distinctions to be made between the various ATS. At the global level, more than 70% of all ATS seizures were methamphetamine and more than 10% were ecstasy seizures over the 2000/2001 period. Most of the rest were amphetamine (between 9 and 16%; no precise proportion can be given since not all countries detail the type of ATS which they seized).

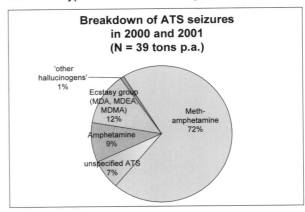

Source: UNODC, Annual Reports Questionnaire Data.

Overall seizures of ATS have shown a clear concentration in East and South-East Asia in recent years, including 2000 and 2001. Other regions of importance are North America and West Europe. Seizures of ATS in East and South-East Asia accounted for 66% of all such seizures over the 2000-2001 period, up from 32% over the 1990-1991 period. Most of the increase in the East and South-East Asia took place in the late 1990s. Seizures of ATS in North America and West Europe accounted together for about 30% of all such seizures over the 2000-2001 period and were of approximately equal size. Other parts of the world accounted for just 4% of global ATS seizures.

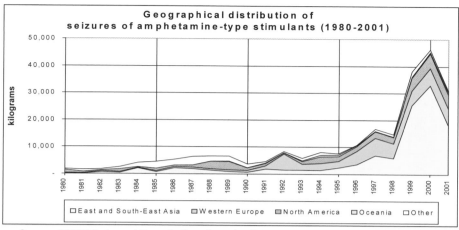

Source: UNODC, Annual Reports Questionnaire Data

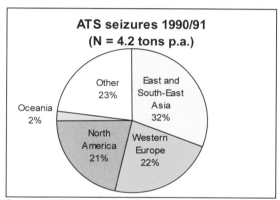

Source: UNDODC, Annual Reports Questionnaire Data.

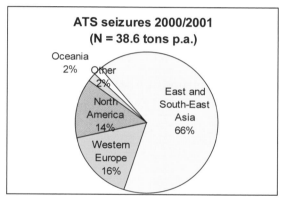

Source: UNODC, Annual Reports Questionnaire Data and US Drug Enforcement Administration, Federal-wide Drug Seizure System.

Methamphetamine

Methamphetamine seizures are mainly concentrated in East and South-East Asia, as well as in North America. Over the 2000-2001 period, about 86% of all seizures took place in the East and South-East Asia region and 14% in North America (these proportions take the 'federal-wide drug seizures' of methamphetamine, for both 2000 and 2001, into account)[a].

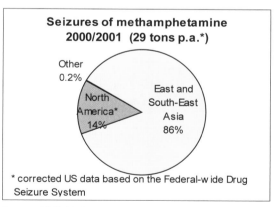

Source: UNDODC, Annual Reports Questionnaire Data.

---

[a] In the official reply to the UNODC ARQ, in contrast, the US authorities reported all ATS seizures for the year 2000 as a lump-sum.

If these data are broken down by country, then clearly the largest methamphetamine seizures over the 2000-2001 period took place in the People's Republic of China, followed by Thailand and the USA. The three countries together accounted for 84% of all methamphetamine seizures worldwide.

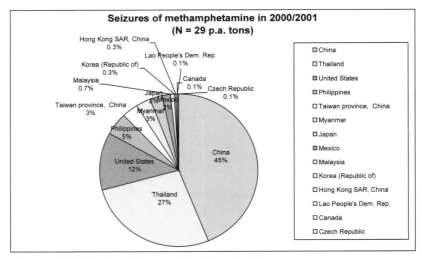

Source: UNODC, Annual Reports Questionnaire Data.

Trafficking of South-East Asian methamphetamine within and without the region			
Country reporting	**Year**	**Origin of methamphetamine**	**Source**
a) within East and South-East Asia			
Japan	2000	China	UNODC ARQ
	2000	Republic of Korea	UNODC ARQ
	2000	Democratic People's Republic of Korea	UNODC/Interpol/WCO Individual Seizures
Rep. of Korea	2001	Philippines	UNODC ARQ
	2001	China	UNODC ARQ
Hong Kong SAR of China	2001	China	UNODC ARQ
People's Rep. of China	2001	Myanmar	UNODC ARQ
Thailand	2000	Myanmar	UNODC/Interpol/WCO Individual Seizures
Indonesia	2001	Thailand	UNODC ARQ
Malaysia	2001	Thailand	UNODC ARQ
	2001	China	UNODC ARQ
Brunei Darussalam	2001	Philippines	UNODC ARQ
Singapore	1999	Philippines	UNODC ARQ
b) outside East and South-East Asia			
India	2001	Myanmar	UNODC ARQ
Australia	2001	Philippines	UNODC/Interpol/WCO Individual Seizures
	2001	Indonesia	UNODC/Interpol/WCO Individual Seizures
New Zealand	2001	Malaysia	UNODC/Interpol/WCO Individual Seizures
Canada	2001	China	UNODC ARQ
UK	1999	Philippines	UNODC ARQ
Switzerland	2000	Thailand	UNODC/Interpol/WCO Individual Seizures
Germany	2001	Thailand	UNODC/Interpol/WCO Individual Seizures
Austria	2000	Philippines	UNODC/Interpol/WCO Individual Seizures
USA	2001	Thailand	UNODC/Interpol/WCO Individual Seizures
Guam	2000	Philippines	UNODC/Interpol/WCO Individual Seizures
France	2001	China	UNODC/Interpol/WCO Individual Seizures

The countries most frequently mentioned as source countries for methamphetamine from South-East Asia are China, the Philippines, Myanmar and Thailand, both by countries within the East and South-East Asia region as well as by countries from other parts of the world.

A number of indicators suggest that China was the main source for illegal methamphetamine in South-East Asia until 2000. In 2001, however, seizures declined. There are no indications that the decline was a result of lower priority given by law enforcement to the ATS issue in the China. The decline may well have been the result of an actual reduction in trafficking activities, intensified efforts to dismantle both clandestine laboratories and as well as criminal groups in trafficking methamphetamine.

Authorities in Hong Kong SAR confirmed this view and reported a stabilization of methamphetamine trafficking *via* their territory in 2001. Similarly, methamphetamine seizures reported from Japan indicate a marked decline in 2001, indirectly confirming the thesis that trafficking of methamhetamine out of China declined in 2001. The authorities in Japan, who for years reported China to be the main source of methamphetamine, are now increasingly concerned about illegal methamphetamine imports which are believed to originate in the Democratic People's Republic of Korea.

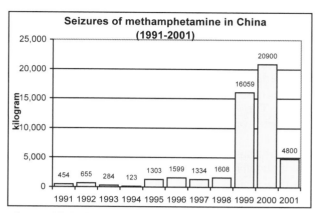

Source: UNODC, Annual Reports Questionnaire Data.

Methamphetamine seizures, in contrast, continued growing in Thailand. As a consequence, the ranking of the first two countries reporting the highest methamphetamine seizures, was reversed in 2001. The Thai authorities made the largest methamphetamine seizures worldwide in 2001, reflecting large-scale methamphetamine imports from neighbouring Myanmar. Methamphetamine found in Thailand is for domestic consumption as well as for transhipment to other countries of South-East Asia. Smaller quantities are also trafficked to other regions, notably to North America and Western Europe.

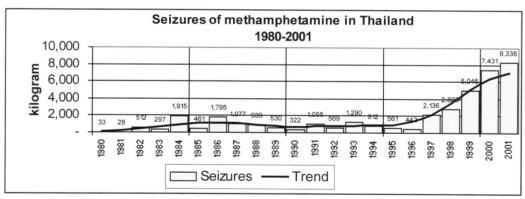

Source: UNODC, Annual Reports Questionnaire Data.

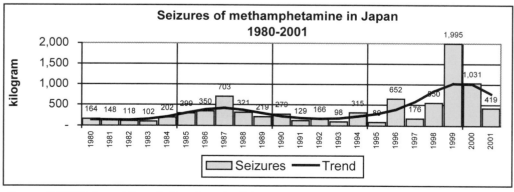

Source: UNODC, Annual Reports Questionnaire Data.

The third largest seizures of methamphetamine worldwide have been reported in recent years from the USA, the only non-Asian country among the group of countries reporting large-scale methamphetamine trafficking and abuse. Methamphetamine seizures continued growing in 2001. The increase in seizures reflected both improved enforcement efforts and increases in domestic production and trafficking. Methamphetamine is largely manufactured domestically though some of it also originates in Mexico.

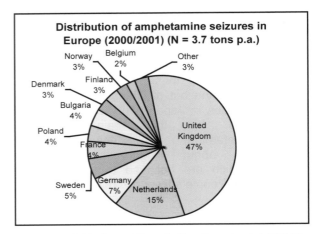

Regional distribution of amphetamine seizures 2000/2001 (N = 4.6* tons p.a.)

* tentative estimate based on adjusted results

Source: UNODC, Annual Reports Questionnaire Data.

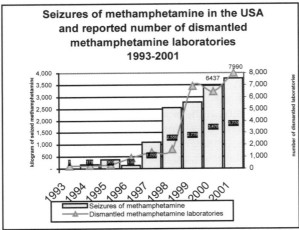

Source: UNODC, Annual Reports Questionnaire Data and US Drug Enforcement Administration, *Federal-wide Drug Seizure System*.

Distribution of amphetamine seizures in Europe (2000/2001) (N = 3.7 tons p.a.)

Sources: UNODC, Annual Reports Questionnaire data/DELTA.

Amphetamine

About three quarters of all amphetamine seizures take place in Europe. West Europe accounts for more than two thirds of all amphetamine seizures (2000/2001 average).

Almost half of all amphetamine seizures within Europe over the 2000-2001 period were accounted for by the UK, reflecting large-scale consumption and trafficking of amphetamine in the country. The next largest seizures were reported by the Netherlands (15%), followed by Germany (7%) and Sweden (5%). The largest amphetamine seizures in East Europe were reported by Poland (4%), accounting for more than 40% of all amphetamine seizures reported from countries in East Europe. Seizures made in East Europe were responsible for 9½ % of all amphetamine seizures made in Europe over the 2000-2001 period.

Seizures of amphetamine in West Europe showed a marked upward trend over the 1990-1997 period, rising more than eight fold over this period. Given the fact that a number of epidemiological surveys also found a significant upward trend during this period, the increase appears to have been a reflection of more trafficking, though greater enforcement efforts also played a role. Following a peak in 1997, amphetamine seizures declined, however, in subsequent years and appear to have levelled off over the 1999-2001 period. (Seizure data for the year 2001 are not as yet complete. The estimate shown in graph assumes that for all countries which have not as yet reported their 2001 seizures (UK, Belgium), the magnitude remained the same as in the previous year).

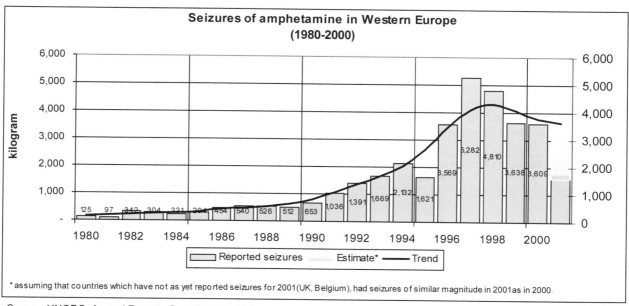

Source: UNODC, Annual Reports Questionnaire Data.

The patterns found in data for West Europe are largely a reflection of seizure patterns reported by the UK. A breakdown of UK seizure data by enforcement agency shows that both police and customs reported significant increases in amphetamine seizures in the early 1990s. Police seizures peaked in 1996 and 1997, which was, *inter alia,* linked to some large-scale amphetamine production by clandestine laboratories in the UK. These labortories were subsequently dismantled, prompting an increased demand for illicit amphetamine imports from continental Europe (mainly from the Netherlands). This resulted in customs seizures peaking in 1998. Since then amphetamine seizures reported by H.M. Customs & Excise have shown a downward trend, which continued in 2001 as well as in 2002.

Other indicators for the availability of drugs are prices and purity. Drug prices in consumer markets tend to remain rather stable in the short-term and are thus only an interesting indicator for the analysis of long-term trends. In contrast, short-term adjustments to changes in supply (or demand) usually take place through changes in purity.

In line with seizure and prevalence data, the development of the mean purity of amphetamine seized by the police suggests that this drug became increasingly available on the UK market in the 1990s. The upward trend lasted until 1998. Subsequently, in line with falling seizures reported by customs, purity - and thus availability - declined in 1999 and remained at the far lower level in 2000 as well. This seems to confirm that the reported decline of amphetamine seizures by customs in 1999 and 2000 was, indeed, a consequence of lower levels of clandestine imports into the UK. Increased enforcement efforts by other European countries, including the Netherlands, Europe's largest illegal amphetamine producer, seem to have been largely responsible for this.

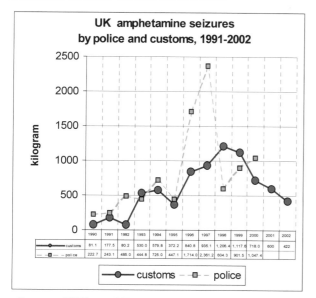

Source: UK Home Office, *Drug Seizure and Offender Statistics*, 2002 and H.M. Customs & Excise data.

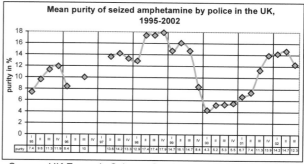

Source: UK Forensic Science Service.

However, the increases of purity levels in 2001 and 2002 signal, once again, improved availability of amphetamine on the UK market. The mean purity of both police seizures and customs seizures improved in 2001 and in 2002. This, *prima facie,* does not seem to fit with reports of still declining customs seizures. It indicates either that criminal groups have become more successful in smuggling amphetamine into Europe's largest amphetamine market, frustrating

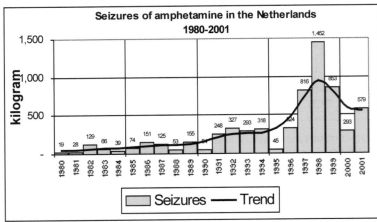

Seizures of amphetamine in the Netherlands 1980-2001

Source: UNODC, Annual Reports Questionnaire Data.

the efforts of the enforcement authorities, or that the recent improvements of availability were actually the result of significantly lower levels of demand for this substance as drug users shifted to other drugs. Indeed, annual prevalence data from the British Crime Survey show that

amphetamine use fell from 2.6% of the population (15-69) in 1998 to 1.9% in 2000 and 1.6% in 2001/2002, i.e. a decline by almost 40% over the 1998-2002 period. But the data also show that the decline of amphetamine use was stronger during the period when availability was scarce (1998-2000) than during the time when availability was no longer a limiting factor (2001-2002).

The analysis of amphetamine seizures reported by the Dutch authorities shows a basically similar pattern as that found by the UK customs. In both the Netherlands and the UK (customs) seizures of amphetamine increased in the early 1990s and peaked in 1998 before falling back to lower levels. Similar patterns are also found in a number of other West European countries.

Though the importance of the Netherlands as a source country of amphetamine has declined in recent years due to increases of amphetamine production in a number of East European countries, the Netherlands is still the main source country for the export of illicit amphetamine in Europe: 70% of all European countries, reporting to UNODC, cited the Netherlands as the main source of their illegally imported amphetamine in 2001. Other countries frequently mentioned in this context are Poland, Belgium and Germany.

Reported origin of 'imported' amphetamine in Europe in 2001			
Year	**Reporting country**	**Origin of 'imported' amphetamine**	**Source**
2001	UK	Netherlands, Belgium	UNODC, ARQ
2001	Ireland	Netherlands	UNODC, ARQ
1999/2000	Iceland	Netherlands, Poland	UNODC, ARQ
		Germany	
2001	Belgium	Netherlands	UNODC, ARQ
2001	Germany	Netherlands, Poland	UNODC, ARQ
1999	France	Netherlands, Belgium	UNODC, ARQ
2001	Italy	Netherlands	EMCDDA
2001	Spain	Netherlands, Germany, Belgium	UNODC, ARQ
2000	Denmark	Netherlands, Poland, Czech Rep., Belgium	UNODC, ARQ
2001	Sweden	Netherlands, Poland	UNODC, ARQ
2001	Norway	Netherlands	UNODC, ARQ
2001	Finland	Estonia	UNODC, ARQ
2001	Estonia	Poland	UNODC, ARQ
2001	Latvia	Lithuania, Poland	UNODC, ARQ
2001	Lithuania	Netherlands, Poland	UNODC, ARQ
2001	Poland	Netherlands, United Kingdom	UNODC, ARQ
2001	Austria	Poland, Hungary	UNODC, ARQ
2001	Hungary	Netherlands	UNODC, ARQ
2001	Croatia	Netherlands, Germany, Czech Rep., Belgium, Slovakia	UNODC, ARQ
2001	Bulgaria	Hungary, Romania	UNODC, ARQ
2001	Turkey	Bulgaria, Romania	UNODC, ARQ
2001	Ukraine	Poland	UNODC, ARQ
2001	Russian Federation	Netherlands, Lithuania, Poland	UNODC, ARQ

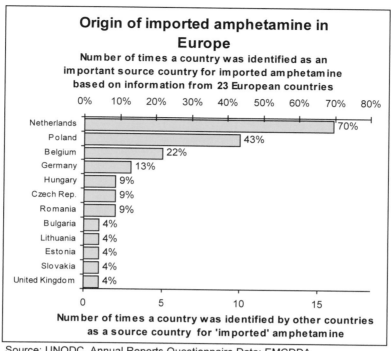

Source: UNODC, Annual Reports Questionnaire Data; EMCDDA.

In contrast to either stable or falling amphetamine seizures in recent years in West Europe, most countries of East Europe reported an upward trend. This reflects improved enforcement capabilities as well as an increase in clandestine amphetamine manufacture and trafficking in the sub-region.

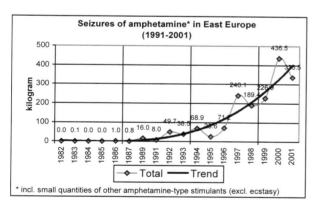

Source: UNODC, Annual Reports Questionnaire Data.

In Poland, which was identified by European countries as the second most frequent source country for imported amphetamine, seizures showed a marked increase, including in 2001. The Polish authorities estimate that around 35% of the amphetamine produced is for domestic purposes and 65% for export. About half of the amphetamine produced is thought to be destined for Germany, i.e. for the German market as such as well as for further distribution to other West European countries, notably Denmark and

Sweden. Most of the rest is destined for the three Baltic countries (often with final destination again in the Nordic countries), the Ukraine, the Russian Federation and Austria. About 10% of domestic production is believed by the Polish authorities to be destined for the United States.

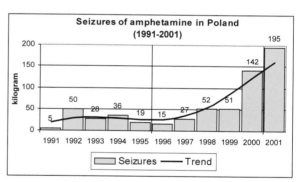

Source: UNODC, Annual Reports Questionnaire Data.

In addition to significant levels of intra-regional trafficking in amphetamine, Europe is also a source zone for amphetamine exports to some overseas countries. In addition to some for the US market (most amphetamine found on the US market appears to be of domestic origin), amphetamine imports from Europe have been reported by Mexico, Costa Rica, Malaysia, the Philippines, South Africa, Nigeria as well as some countries in the Near and Middle East region. In general, the quantities of amphetamine trafficked out of Europe are, however, relative small compared to the large volumes trafficked within Europe.

GLOBAL SEIZURES OF AMPHETAMINE-TYPE STIMULANTS*, 1991-2001

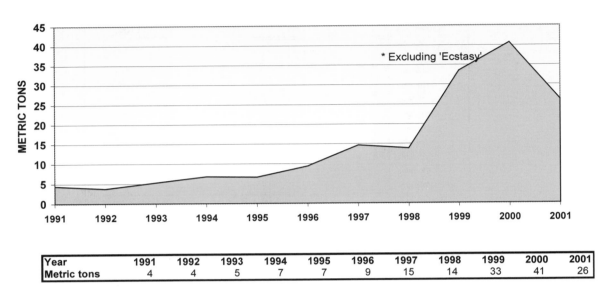

* Excluding 'Ecstasy'

Year	1991	1992	1993	1994	1995	1996	1997	1998	1999	2000	2001
Metric tons	4	4	5	7	7	9	15	14	33	41	26

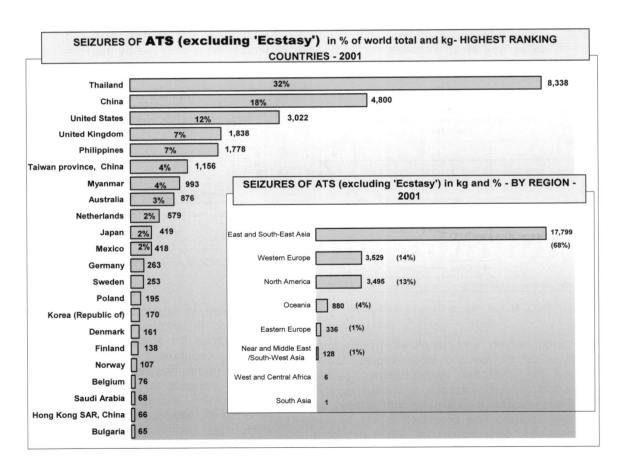

SEIZURES OF **ATS (excluding 'Ecstasy')** in % of world total and kg- HIGHEST RANKING COUNTRIES - 2001

Country	%	kg
Thailand	32%	8,338
China	18%	4,800
United States	12%	3,022
United Kingdom	7%	1,838
Philippines	7%	1,778
Taiwan province, China	4%	1,156
Myanmar	4%	993
Australia	3%	876
Netherlands	2%	579
Japan	2%	419
Mexico	2%	418
Germany		263
Sweden		253
Poland		195
Korea (Republic of)		170
Denmark		161
Finland		138
Norway		107
Belgium		76
Saudi Arabia		68
Hong Kong SAR, China		66
Bulgaria		65

SEIZURES OF ATS (excluding 'Ecstasy') in kg and % - BY REGION - 2001

Region	kg	%
East and South-East Asia	17,799	(68%)
Western Europe	3,529	(14%)
North America	3,495	(13%)
Oceania	880	(4%)
Eastern Europe	336	(1%)
Near and Middle East /South-West Asia	128	(1%)
West and Central Africa	6	
South Asia	1	

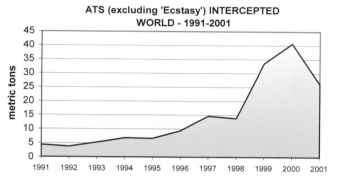

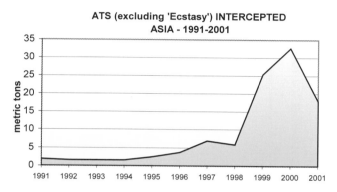

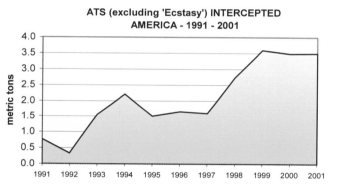

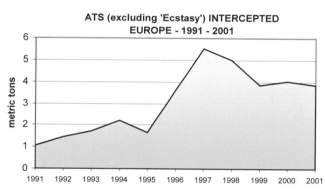

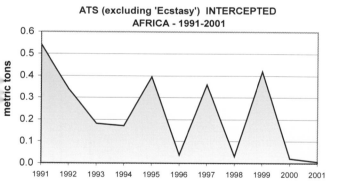

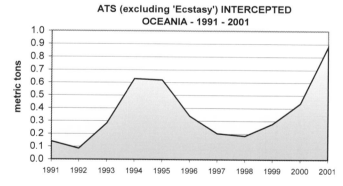

Trafficking of amphetamine-type stimulants (excluding ecstasy) 2000-2001: extent and trends
(countries reporting seizures of more than 0.001 tons (1kg))

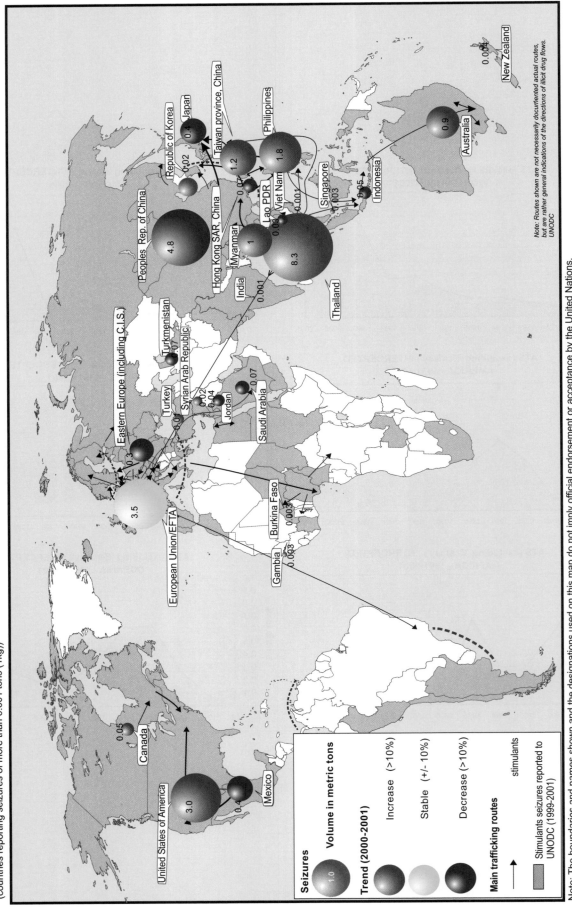

Note: Routes shown are not necessarily documented actual routes, but are rather general indications of the directions of illicit drug flows. UNODC

Seizures

Volume in metric tons

1.0

Trend (2000-2001)

Increase (>10%)

Stable (+/- 10%)

Decrease (>10%)

Main trafficking routes

stimulants

Stimulants seizures reported to UNODC (1999-2001)

Note: The boundaries and names shown and the designations used on this map do not imply official endorsement or acceptance by the United Nations.

Ecstasy

Prior to the introduction of the revised Annual Reports Questionnaire and the creation of a separate reporting category for the substances of the 'ecstasy group' (MDMA, MDA, MDME) as part of the broader category of ATS, ecstasy seizures were reported to UNODC under the category of 'hallucinogens other than LSD'. Analysis of the seizure data for 2000 and 2001 shows that the bulk of the category of 'other hallucinogens' is actually accounted for by ecstasy seizures (93%), so that this category seems to be a reasonably good proxy for the development of 'ecstasy seizures' over the last couple of years.

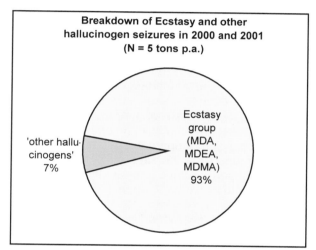

Breakdown of Ecstasy and other hallucinogen seizures in 2000 and 2001 (N = 5 tons p.a.)

Source: UNODC, Annual Reports Questionnaire Data.

Using this data-set, seizures of ecstasy showed a clear upward trend in the 1990s, reaching a peak in 2000. This increase went parallel with increases in reported seizures of clandestine laboratories producing ecstasy and a number of reports of

rising levels of abuse. In 2001, however, seizures fell slightly as compared to a year earlier. Practically all regions showed either stable or declining seizures in 2001 as compared to a year earlier.

While in the early 1990s ecstasy trafficking was almost exclusively concentrated in Europe, recent years have shown a spread across the world. Thus, expressed a percentage of total seizures, the proportion of West Europe in ecstasy seizures fell from three-quarters of all such seizures in 1993-1994 to about half in 2000-2001. (98% of the ecstasy seized in Europe was in West Europe). Over the same period, the proportion of North America rose from about a fifth of all ecstasy seizures to close to 40%. Around 8% of all ecstasy seizures were reported from countries in Asia.

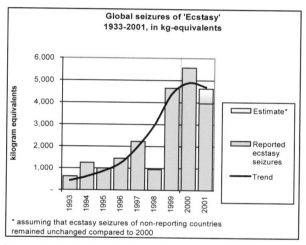

Source: UNODC, Annual Reports Questionnaire Data/DELTA.

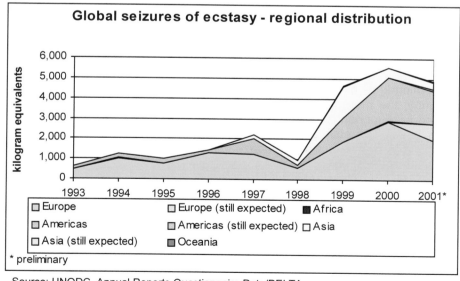

Source: UNODC, Annual Reports Questionnaire Data/DELTA.

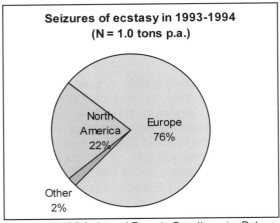

Source: UNODC, Annual Reports Questionnaire Data.

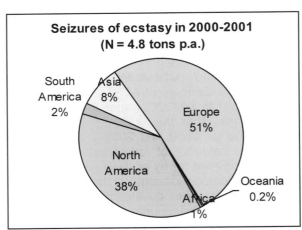

Source: UNODC, Annual Reports Questionnaire Data.

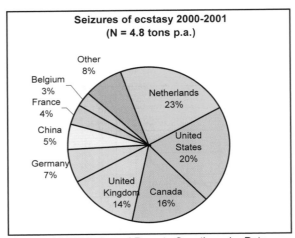

Source: UNODC, Annual Reports Questionnaire Data.

only the responses of the countries within Europe are considered, the proportion of the Netherlands as a source country rises to 86%, and is thus higher for ecstasy than for amphetamine (70%). The next most frequently mentioned country of origin was Belgium, apparently reflecting a shift of criminal groups from the Netherlands as controls were tightened. Other frequently mentioned source countries were Germany, the UK, Spain and the USA. The most frequently mentioned source countries located in East Europe were the Baltic countries, Poland and Belarus. The People's Republic of China, Indonesia and Thailand were the most frequently reported source countries located in Asia. The Republic of South Africa in Africa and Colombia in South America were identified as source countries for ecstasy.

Another key indicator in this context is the 'origin' of the ecstasy seized by the authorities. Available data from the ARQ complemented by information from the UNODC/Interpol/WCO individual seizures database, allowed analysis of 'country of origin' information of seized ecstasy for 52 countries (largely for the year 2001). The more often a country is mentioned by other countries as a major source country, the more likely it is that this country is indeed an important producer and exporter of ecstasy. In total 21 source countries located in Europe, the Americas, Asia and Africa could be identified as producing and exporting 'Ecstasy'. However, there is a clear concentration: 92% of all countries providing information on the origin of their ecstasy, reported a European country to be the main source. In Europe all countries reported that ecstasy imports originated from within Europe.

Three quarters of the countries reported that their imported ecstasy originated in the Netherlands. If

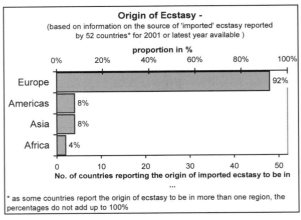

Sources: UNODC, Annual Reports Questionnaire Data, UNODC/INTERPOL/WCO, Individual Seizures Database.

Origin of 'imported' Ecstasy				
Reporting countries		**Year**	**Main origin of imported ecstasy**	**Source**
Region	**Country**			
Western Europe	UK	2001	Netherlands, Germany, Belgium	UNODC ARQ
	Ireland	2001	Netherlands	UNODC ARQ
	Belgium	2001	Netherlands	UNODC ARQ
	Luxembourg	1999	Netherlands, Belarus	UNODC ARQ
	France	2001	Netherlands, Belgium	UNODC ARQ
	Germany	1999	Netherlands, Switzerland, Belgium	UNODC ARQ
	Austria	2001	Netherlands	UNODC ARQ
	Switzerland	1999	UK, Belgium, Netherlands	UNODC/INTERPOL/WCO
	Italy	2001	Netherlands, Belgium	UNODC ARQ
	Malta	2001	Netherlands	UNODC ARQ
	Spain	1999	Netherlands	UNODC/INTERPOL/WCO
	Portugal	2001	Netherlands, Spain	UNODC ARQ
	Greece	2000	Belgium, UK	UNODC ARQ
	Cyprus	2000	Netherlands	UNODC/INTERPOL/WCO
	Turkey	2001	Netherlands, Germany, Belgium	UNODC ARQ
	Denmark	2000	Netherlands, Germany, Belgium, Spain	UNODC ARQ
	Sweden	2001	Netherlands, Belgium, Germany, Spain	UNODC ARQ
	Norway	2001	Netherlands, UK	UNODC ARQ
	Iceland	2000	Netherlands, UK, Germany	UNODC ARQ
	Finland	2001	Estonia	UNODC ARQ
Eastern Europe	Estonia	2001	Netherlands,Belgium	UNODC ARQ
	Lithuania	2000	Netherlands, Latvia	UNODC ARQ
	Russian Federation	2001	Netherlands, Lithuania, Poland, Germany	UNODC ARQ
	Ukraine	2001	Lithuania, Poland, Latvia	UNODC ARQ
	Czech Republic	2000	Netherlands	UNODC ARQ
	Hungary	2001	Netherlands	UNODC ARQ
	Croatia	2001	Netherlands, Germany, Czech Republic, Belgium, Slovakia	UNODC ARQ
	Serbia & Montenegro	2001	Europe	UNODC ARQ
	Romania	2001	Netherlands	UNODC ARQ
North America	USA	2001	Netherlands, Belgium	UNODC ARQ
	Canada	2001	Netherlands, Belgium	UNODC ARQ
	Mexico	2001	Netherlands, Germany	UNODC ARQ
South America (incl. Central America and the Caribbean)				
	Peru	2001	Netherlands, Spain	UNODC ARQ
	Venezuela	2001	Mexico	UNODC ARQ
	Panama	2001	Colombia, USA	UNODC ARQ
	Costa Rica	2001	Netherlands	UNODC ARQ
	Dominican Rep.	2001	Netherlands	UNODC ARQ
	Cayman Islands	1999	Europe, USA	UNODC ARQ
	Jamaica	2001	Europe	UNODC ARQ
Africa	South Africa	2001	Netherlands, UK	UNODC ARQ
	Namibia	2001	South Africa, Germany	UNODC ARQ
	Zimbabwe	2001	Netherlands, South Africa, UK	UNODC ARQ

Origin of 'imported' Ecstasy				
	Reporting countries	**Year**	**Main origin of imported ecstasy**	**Source**
Region		**Country**		
Near and Middle East	Israel	2000	Netherlands, Belgium	UNODC ARQ
East and South-East Asia	Philippines	2001	Europe	UNODC ARQ
	Singapore	2000	Europe	UNODC ARQ
	Hong Kong, SAR of China	1999	Netherlands, Belarus	UNODC ARQ
		2001	Europe, China	UNODC ARQ
	Indonesia	2001	Netherlands, Thailand, China	UNODC ARQ
	Korea (Rep.)	2001	Thailand, USA	UNODC ARQ
	China (Peoples Rep.)	2001	Europe, Indonesia	UNODC ARQ
	Malaysia	1999	Netherlands	UNODC/INTERPOL/WCO
Oceania	Australia	2000	UK, Malaysia, Netherlands, Indonesia, USA, Germany, Belgium	National Report
	New Zealand	2001	Netherlands, Belgium	UNODC ARQ
Sources: UNODC, Annual Reports Questionnaire Data, UNODC/INTERPOL/WCO Individual Seizures Database.				

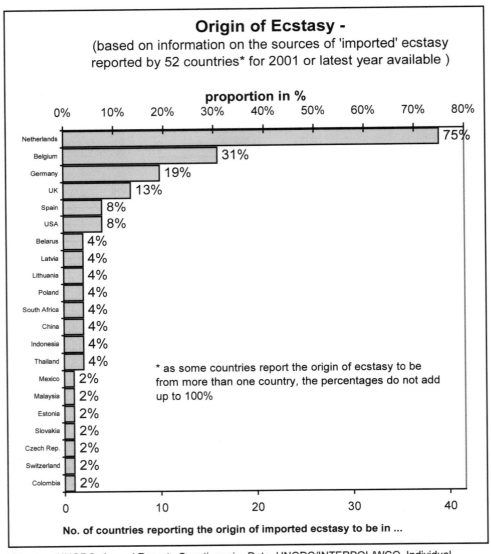

Sources: UNODC, Annual Reports Questionnaire Data, UNODC/INTERPOL/WCO, Individual Seizures Database.

Though there has been a spread of ecstasy production across the globe, data also show that there is still a strong concentration in Europe which has implications for the supply of overseas markets. It is thus interesting to see that the overall ecstasy seizures made by the authorities in West Europe and in North America followed a largely similar pattern over the last few years. Following an increase until 1997, a temporary drop in 1998 and a very strong upward trend over the 1998-2000 period, ecstasy seizures declined both in West Europe and in North America in 2001. US prevalence data seem to confirm this pattern. Following an increase in 1997, the 'Monitoring the Future Study' found a relatively strong reduction in the annual ecstasy prevalence rates of high school students by about 15% in 1998, a subsequent increase over the 1998-2001 period by more than 100% and in 2002 a reduction by about 20% (i.e. one year after seizures had again indicated a decline in availability). In parallel, students actually confirmed a decline in the availability of ecstasy in the USA in 2002.

In other words, the decline of seizures in 2001 seems to reflect an actual reduction in global ecstasy production in that year. Ecstasy seizures did not only decline in 2001 in West Europe (including in the Netherlands) and in North America but also in the rest of the world taken together. This can be linked to intensified efforts by the Dutch authorities in recent years to improve precursor control, identify criminal groups operating in this business and dismantle clandestine laboratories. Over the 2000-2001 period, 75% of all clandestine laboratories in West

Europe producing ecstasy were dismantled by the Dutch authorities. While in the early 1990s about seven clandestine laboratories producing ecstasy were seized by the Dutch authorities per year, intensified efforts led to the dismantling of 24 ecstasy producing laboratories in 1999, 34 in 2000 and 25 in 2001.

The seizure trends, however, are less uniform among countries, even when they are located in the same region. Thus ecstasy seizures fell in 2001 within West Europe in the Netherlands, France, Spain, Switzeland, Italy, Austria, Sweden, Finland, Ireland as well as within North America in the USA and Canada, while increases were reported from Germany, Denmark, Norway, Greece, Turkey as well as, in North America, from Mexico. A mixed picture was also shown in South America. Overall, however, more countries reported declines of ecstasy seizures in 2001 than increases. In East Europe, by contrast, more countries reported increases than declines. Increases were reported by the Czech Republic, Poland, Bulgaria, Romania, Hungary, Estonia, Latvia and the Russian Federation and only some of the smaller countries reported declines, possibly reflecting increasing levels of local ecstasy production. In Asia increases were reported from China, Japan and the Rep. of Korea while Thailand, Malaysia and the Philippines reported declines. In Africa and the Near & Middle East, significant increases were reported from Egypt and Israel, while seizures in the Republic of South Africa declined, though they rose in Namibia and Zimbabwe.

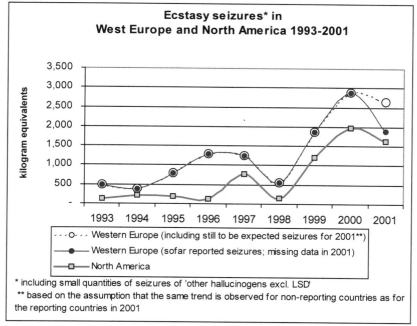

Sources: UNODC, Annual Reports Questionnaire Data, UNODC/INTERPOL/WCO, Individual Seizures Database.

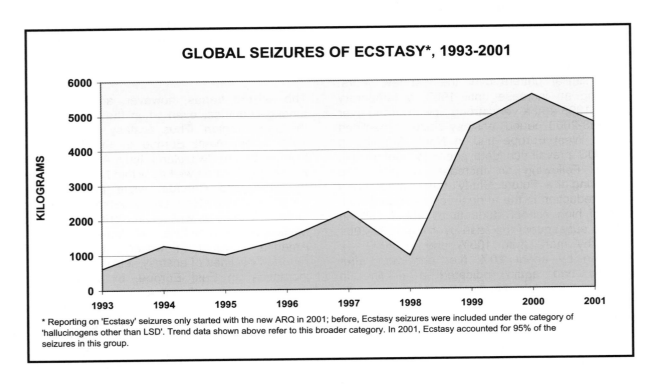

GLOBAL SEIZURES OF ECSTASY*, 1993-2001

* Reporting on 'Ecstasy' seizures only started with the new ARQ in 2001; before, Ecstasy seizures were included under the category of 'hallucinogens other than LSD'. Trend data shown above refer to this broader category. In 2001, Ecstasy accounted for 95% of the seizures in this group.

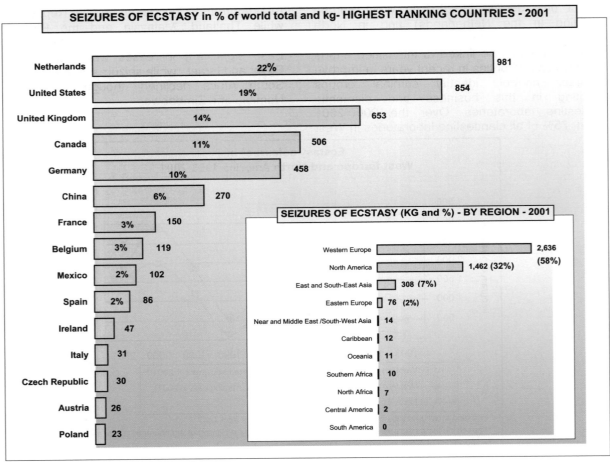

SEIZURES OF ECSTASY in % of world total and kg- HIGHEST RANKING COUNTRIES - 2001

Country	%	kg
Netherlands	22%	981
United States	19%	854
United Kingdom	14%	653
Canada	11%	506
Germany	10%	458
China	6%	270
France	3%	150
Belgium	3%	119
Mexico	2%	102
Spain	2%	86
Ireland		47
Italy		31
Czech Republic		30
Austria		26
Poland		23

SEIZURES OF ECSTASY (KG and %) - BY REGION - 2001

Region	KG (%)
Western Europe	2,636 (58%)
North America	1,462 (32%)
East and South-East Asia	308 (7%)
Eastern Europe	76 (2%)
Near and Middle East /South-West Asia	14
Caribbean	12
Oceania	11
Southern Africa	10
North Africa	7
Central America	2
South America	0

Trafficking of Ecstasy (MDA, MDEA, MDMA) 2000-2001: extent and trends (countries reporting seizures of more than 1kg)

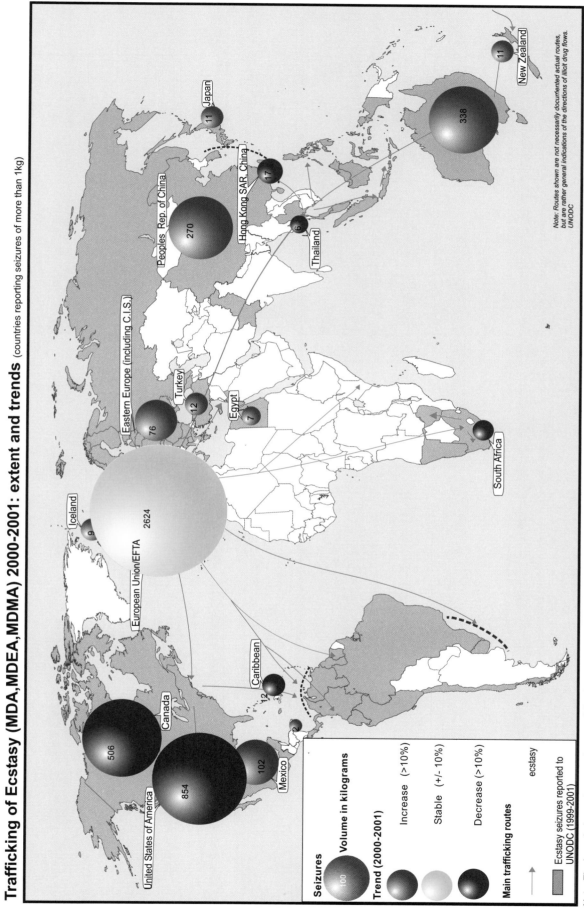

Note: Routes shown are not necessarily documented actual routes, but are rather general indications of the directions of illicit drug flows.
UNODC

Seizures

Volume in kilograms

Trend (2000-2001)

Increase (>10%)

Stable (+/- 10%)

Decrease (>10%)

Main trafficking routes

ecstasy

Ecstasy seizures reported to UNODC (1999-2001)

Note: The boundaries and names shown and the designations used on this map do not imply official endorsement or acceptance by the United Nations.

1.3. CONSUMPTION

1.3.1. OVERVIEW

Extent

UNODC has thus far done three rounds of estimating the global extent of drug abuse, and published them in the 1997 and 2000 *World Drug Reports,* as well as in last year's version of the present publication, *Global Illicit Drug Trends 2002.* The first round of estimates was based on information received by early 1997, covering the period from the early to mid 1990s; the second round was based on information received by mid 2000, covering the period from the mid 1990s to 1997/1998; and the third round covered the period from 1998 to 2000. The fourth round has now been initiated and the preliminary estimates are presented here. They are based on the latest available information, primarily covering the period 2000-2001.

The new estimates show, once again, that the most widely abused substances worldwide are cannabis (around 160 million people), followed by the amphetamine-type stimulants (34 million people abusing amphetamines, notably methamphetamine and amphetamine, and 8 million abusing ecstasy). The number of opiate and cocaine abusers are approximately the same (cocaine: more than 14 million people and opiates less than 15 million people, of whom close to 10 million are taking heroin).

The total number of drug abusers is estimated at some 200 million people, equivalent to 3.4% of the global population or 4.7% of the population age 15 and above. As drug abusers frequently take more than one substance, it should be noted that the total is not identical to the sum of the individual drug categories. A more detailed geographical breakdown of these estimates is provided in the substance-specific sub-chapters below.

The new estimates are slightly higher than those of last year. Annual prevalence of drug abuse is now estimated to be 4.7% of the world population age 15 and above, compared to 4.3% last year. This is primarily the result of more people abusing cannabis, though estimates for other drugs, in absolute numbers, are slightly higher as well. Expressed as a percentage of the population age 15 and above, the estimates for other drugs, however, remained largely stable.

Changes in the two sets of estimates should not be over-interpreted because they do not necessarily reflect increases in the number of drug abusers. They could also reflect changes in the methodology used by Member States reporting to UNODC. For instance, an overall improvement of reporting could either increase or decrease the number of abusers estimated for a particular country. In fact, many countries have, over the last few years, changed or improved the way their national estimates are derived. Further changes can be still expected as countries switch from simple "guesstimates" to more robust estimates based on rigorous scientific criteria. The global estimates presented here must therefore be treated with a high degree of caution.

Extent of drug abuse (annual prevalence) - estimates 2000-2001							
	Illicit drugs of which:	Cannabis	Amphetamine-type stimulants		Cocaine	Opiates	of which heroin
			Amphetamines	Ecstasy			
GLOBAL (million people)	200.0	162.8	34.3	7.7	14.1	14.9	9.5
in % of global population	3.4%	2.7%	0.6%	0.1%	0.2%	0.3%	0.16%
in % of global population age 15 and above	4.7%	3.9%	0.8%	0.2%	0.3%	0.4%	0.22%
Sources: UNDCP, Annual Reports Questionnaire data, various Govt. reports, reports of regional bodies, UNDCP estimates.							

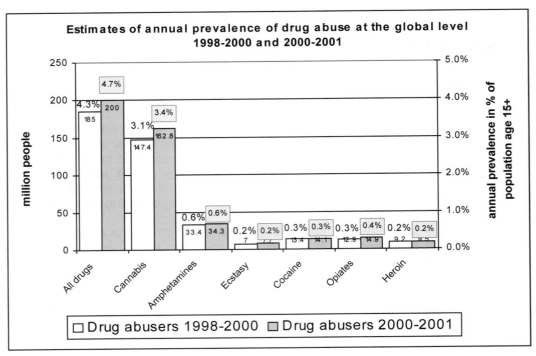

Sources: UNODC, Annual Reports Questionnaire data, National Reports, UNODC estimates.

Main 'problem drugs' as reflected in treatment demand

One way of assessing the impact of illicit drugs is to use the category of 'problem drugs' as an indicator. There are different definitions of 'problem drugs'[a]. They rely primarily on the criteria of treatment for addiction, drug related mortality as well as drug related crime, notably drug related violence. The definition of 'problem drug' used here is the extent to which abuse of a certain drug leads to treatment demand. 'Problem drug' use does not necessarily relate to the size of the population consuming it. Cannabis, for example, is the most widely consumed illicit drug worldwide; it is not, however, the main 'problem drug' for which people seek treatment.

The opiates are the most serious problem drug in the world, and are responsible for most treatment demand. On average 70% of all treatment demand in Asia, 64% in Europe and 62% in Australia is related to opiate abuse. In much of South East Asia, however, methamphetamine emerged over the last decade as the main

problem drug. In the Americas, cocaine is still the main problem drug accounting for 58% of treatment demand in South America and around 40% in North America. [b] In the USA, however, the number of people admitted to treatment institutions for heroin abuse has started to exceed the number of people admitted for cocaine abuse (1999 and 2000). In Africa, cannabis is the main problem drug, accounting for 61% of treatment demand.

Most of the data presented here covers the 1998-2000 period, though some countries also reported their treatment data for 2001. Compared to previous calculations, covering the 1995-97 period, and presented in *Global Illicit Drug Trends 2002*, there has been a general decline of the importance opiates in Europe and (to a lesser extent) in Asia. In the Americas, the relative importance of cocaine has declined. In general, poly-drug abuse seems to be on the rise.

---

[a] For instance, the EMCDDA defines problem drug use as 'injecting drug use or long duration/regular use of opiates, cocaine and/or amphetamines', and excludes ecstasy and cannabis users; *2001 Annual report on the state of the drugs problem in the European Union*, p.11.

[b] The regional averages were calculated as a simple unweighted average of the proportions reported from individual countries.

Main problem drugs (as reflected in treatment demand) in the late 1990s (updated in 2003)

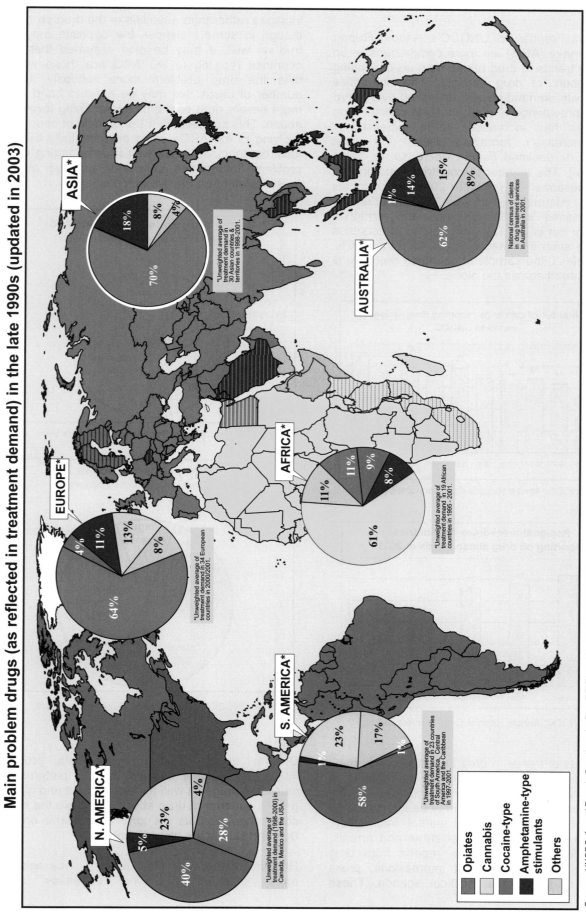

ASIA*

18% / 8% / 4% / 70%

*Unweighted average of treatment demand in 30 Asian countries & territories in 1998-2001.

AUSTRALIA*

1% / 14% / 15% / 8% / 62%

National census of clients in drug treatment services in Australia in 2001.

AFRICA*

11% / 11% / 9% / 8% / 61%

*Unweighted average of treatment demand in 19 African countries in 1995 - 2001.

EUROPE*

4% / 11% / 13% / 8% / 64%

*Unweighted average of treatment demand in 34 European countries in 2000/2001.

S. AMERICA*

1% / 23% / 17% / 1% / 58%

*Unweighted average of treatment demand in 23 countries of South America, Central America and the Caribbean in 1997-2001.

N. AMERICA*

5% / 23% / 4% / 28% / 40%

*Unweighted average of treatment demand (1998-2000) in Canada, Mexico and the USA.

Legend:
- Opiates
- Cannabis
- Cocaine-type
- Amphetamine-type stimulants
- Others

Sources: UNODC., Annual Reports Questionnaire Data/DELTA and National Government Reports.

Trends

In general, replies to UNODC's Annual Report Questionnaire (ARQ) are more comprehensive on reporting trends in drug abuse than on estimating the numbers of drug abusers. The authorities dealing with demand issues are asked every year whether prevalence of drug abuse in various drug categories has increased ('large increase' or 'some increase'), remained stable ('no great change') or declined ('some decrease' or 'large decrease'). The number of countries reporting on these questions has grown in 2001: 92 countries provided information, up from 52 in 1992. As questionnaires to 191 countries and territories were sent out in 2001, the proportion of countries providing such information is still less than 50%. Nevertheless, the sample of countries reporting is evenly spread across the globe.

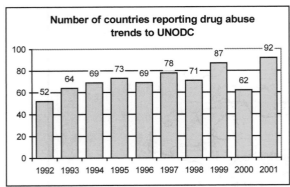

Source: UNODC, Annual Reports Questionnaire Data.

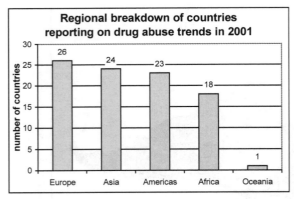

Source: UNODC, Annual Reports Questionnaire Data.

factors may induce a bias towards reporting an increase rather than a decline of the drug problem though in some instances the opposite may be true as well. It may be also assumed that the countries replying to the ARQ are those which take the drug problem more seriously. In a number of cases this may go hand in hand with more severe drug problems and/or rising levels of abuse. This suggests that the sample of countries replying to the ARQs could be potentially biased towards countries faced with a deteriorating drug problem. Information on trends of drug abuse must therefore be treated with caution.

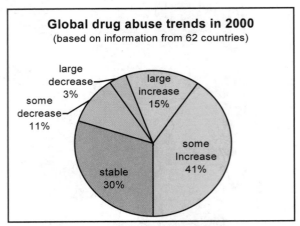

Source: UNODC, Annual Reports Questionnaire Data.

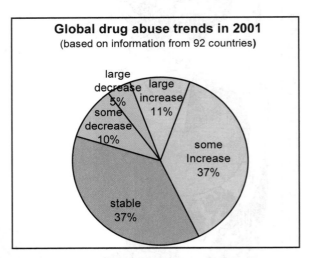

Source: UNODC, Annual Reports Questionnaire Data.

Indications of trends in drug abuse are - for many countries - primarily a reflection of 'perceptions' of the development of the drug problem by the authorities. The perceptions may be influenced by a number of factors and partial information, including police reports on seizures and arrests, reports from social workers, reports from drug treatment centres, personal impressions, press reports, or a particular political agenda. These

Despite these caveats, trend data provide interesting insights into the growth patterns of individual drugs as well as into regional and global growth patterns of drug abuse. They are the most comprehensive data set currently available on the demand side at the global level.

Results for the year 2001 show - once again - more countries reporting increases than

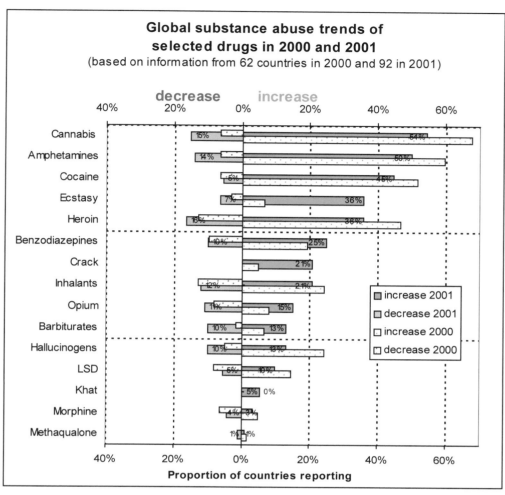

**Global substance abuse trends of
selected drugs in 2000 and 2001**
(based on information from 62 countries in 2000 and 92 in 2001)

Source: UNODC, Annual Reports Questionnaire Data.

decreases in drug abuse. This indicates that the drug problem, at the global level, continues to spread in geographical terms. It does not necessarily mean that the number of drug abusers at the global level is rising as increases in smaller countries could be offset by declines in a few larger countries.

A comparison of trend data received for the years 2000 and 2001, suggests that the spread of drug abuse may have lost momentum. While in 2000, 56% of all drug abuse trends reported by member states indicated an increase, the proportion fell to 48% in 2001. In parallel, countries indicating stable or declining levels of drug abuse were on the rise: those showing a stable trend increased from 30% to 37% and those indicating a decline grew from 14% to 15% of all reporting countries.

The spread of drug use in 2001, like in previous years, concerned mainly cannabis and the group of amphetamine-type stimulants. More than half of

all countries (54%) which provided UNODC with their perception of drug trends, reported an increase in cannabis use. Half of all countries reported an increase in the use of amphetamines (methamphetamine and amphetamine). This is followed by cocaine, ecstasy and heroin. 45% of the countries saw an increase in cocaine use and 36% in both ecstasy use and in the abuse of heroin. Less than a third of the countries reported increases in other substance (25% benzodiazepines, 21% inhalants, 15% opium, 13% hallucinogens, and barbiturates etc.).

Overall, countries continued to report increases more often than declines. The number of countries reporting declines in heroin (16%), amphetamines (16%), cannabis (15%) ecstasy (7%) or cocaine (5%) did not offset the number of countries reporting increases in these substances. For opium, morphine, hallucinogens and barbiturates, the number of countries reporting increases and declines was more evenly distributed.

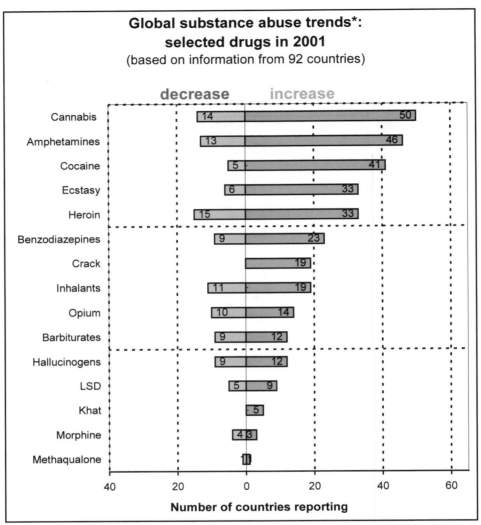

Global substance abuse trends*:
selected drugs in 2001
(based on information from 92 countries)

Source: UNODC, Annual Reports Questionnaire Data.

If the proportions for the year 2001 are compared to those of 2000, data show a net decline in the growth of cannabis, heroin, amphetamines, cocaine and the abuse of hallucinogens. There was, however, an increase in the growth of ecstasy, crack-cocaine and the abuse of benzodiazepines reported for the year 2001. The strong increases reported for ecstasy and crack-cocaine abuse, however, are partly reporting issues as both substances were not mentioned in the old ARQ but are explicitly mentioned in the revised ARQ.

1.3.2. OPIUM / HEROIN

EXTENT

The opiates, notably heroin, continue to be the main problem drugs in the world. In Asia, Europe and Oceania, which together have about three quarters of the world's total population, about two thirds of treatment demand is related to the abuse of opiates. Even in the USA, where cocaine was traditionally the main problem drug, more people were admitted for heroin abuse treatment (28% of all treatment demand excluding alcohol) than for cocaine abuse (25%) in 1999 and 2000.

Opiate abuse (including heroin) over the 2000-2001 period is estimated to affect almost 15 million people or 0.4% of the population age 15 and above. About 10 million people are estimated to be abusing heroin, slightly more than 0.2% of the population age 15 and above.

Most opiate abusers (about 7½ million or half of the world's total opiate abusing population) are found in Asia, primarily in the countries around Afghanistan and Myanmar. The highest prevalence rates have been reported from Iran, the Lao PDR and from Kyrgyzstan. The overall largest number of opiate users, however, is found in India, though prevalence rates in India are lower than in neighbouring Pakistan or Myanmar. A recently conducted national household survey in India found that 0.7% of the male population age 10 and above consumed opiates, which is equivalent to about 0.4% of the total population age 15 and above. The total number of opiate abusers in Europe is estimated to amount some 4½ million people, accounting for some 30% of the global total. Two thirds of Europe's opiate users are found in East Europe, reflecting very high levels of opiate abuse reported from the Russian Federation. IDU related HIV data and independently conducted school surveys under the ESPAD project in 1999 also seem to confirm this[a]. Nonetheless, some of the difference in the overall prevalence rates of the general population between West and East Europe is also due to

differences in methods for calculating national estimates and the differences are far less significant if only heroin consumption is considered. The West European estimates are largely based on the concept of "problem" drug users, applying various estimation techniques: different multiplier methods, capture-recapture methods, multivariate indicators, etc. The estimate for the Russian Federation is derived from the number of registered drug abusers and the reported proportion of opiate abusers. The majority of opiate abusers in the Russian Federation (and in some other C.I.S. countries) consume a brew of poppy straw (known as 'kompot') which is injected. Heroin abuse, however, is on the rise, accounting for more than 20% of all registered drug opiate abusers and for more than 40% of all opiate abusers undergoing treatment in the Russian Federation.

Opiate abuse levels in Oceania (not taking the heroin drought of 2001 into account) and of North America are above the global average, and so is Europe if taken as a whole. Abuse levels in South America and Africa are below the global average.

The rather high rates traditionally reported from the Oceania region, compared to West Europe, possibly reflect methodological differences more than underlying differences in the level of drug abuse. In 2001, the reported household data for Australia showed a large decline in the levels of heroin abuse, to levels below the West European average. It remains to be seen, however, whether abuse will stay at these lower levels. As the circumstances of the heroin drought and the consequent decline were exceptional, the lower figures have not yet been used in the calculation of UNODC global estimates.

Methodological issues also appear to play a role in the different prevalence rates of West Europe and North America. Estimates for the United States, the largest heroin market in North America, combine occasional and chronic use. If only heroin 'problem use' (West Europe) and heroin 'chronic use' (USA) are considered, then the rates in North America and West Europe are very similar.

---

[a] The weighted average (by the size of the youth population) of life-time prevalence of heroin use among 15-16 years old in West Europe (ESPAD survey data and other surveys for Germany, Spain, and the Benelux countries) was 1.7%, less than half the average rate found in Eastern Europe (3.8%). (UNODC, *Global Illicit Drug Trends 2002*).

Annual prevalence estimates of opiate abuse: 2000-2001				
	Opiates		of which heroin	
	Number of people (in million)	in % of population age 15 and above	Number of people (in million)	in % of population age 15 and above
EUROPE	4.56	0.70	3.23	0.50
- West Europe	1.57	0.42	1.30	0.35
- East Europe	2.99	1.08	1.66	0.60
OCEANIA	0.14	0.63	0.14	0.63
ASIA	7.46	0.29	3.59	0.14
AMERICAS	1.86	0.30	1.86	0.30
- North America	1.50	0.48	1.50	0.48
- South America	0.36	0.12	0.36	0.12
AFRICA	0.92	0.20	0.95	0.20
GLOBAL	14.94	0.35	9.47	0.22

▨ Opiate abuse above global average
☐ Opiate abuse close to global average
▨ Opiate abuse below global average

Sources: UNODC, Annual Reports Questionnaire data, various Govt. reports, reports of regional bodies, UNODC estimates.

Abuse of opiates (including heroin)

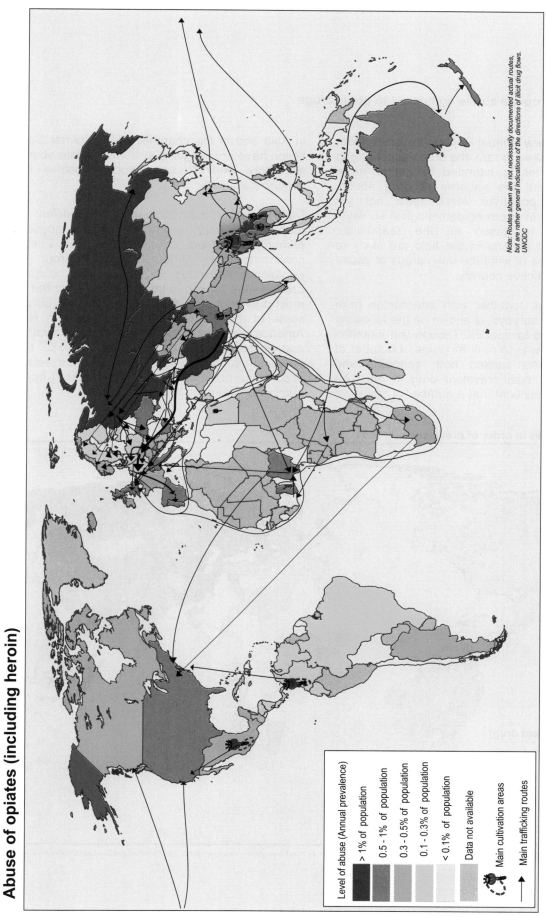

Note: Routes shown are not necessarily documented actual routes, but are rather general indications of the directions of illicit drug flows.
UNODC

Level of abuse (Annual prevalence)
> 1% of population
0.5 - 1% of population
0.3 - 0.5% of population
0.1 - 0.3% of population
< 0.1% of population
Data not available

Main cultivation areas

Main trafficking routes

Note: The boundaries and names shown and the designations used on this map do not imply official endorsement or acceptance by the United Nations.

Importance of opiate abuse compared to other drugs

As part of the new Annual Reports Questionnaire, countries are asked to rank the drugs according to prevalence. This is intended to gather more information about the patterns of drug abuse, particularly in countries which have not yet undertaken any in-depth epidemiological surveys. The question is based on the reasonable assumption that experts in the field are likely to have a good idea of what the main drugs of abuse are in their respective country.

This information, together with information from epidemiological surveys, is shown on the following map with regard to opiates. Though the intention of the question was to rank all drugs, a number of countries in Asia ranked both cannabis and opiates as the most prevalent drug. It must be also taken into account that a number of countries

in Asia and in the countries of the former Soviet Union have drug-registry systems. Opiate abusers are more likely to enter such registries than cannabis abusers.

Despite some methodological deficiencies, the map shows very clearly that opiate abuse is primarily a problem in Asia and in East Europe, confirming the patterns derived from the prevalence estimates. In most of the countries, opiates were ranked to be either the 1st or the 2nd. most prevalent drug. By contrast, in West Europe, some of the EU candidate countries, in North America, Oceania and parts of eastern, southern and western Africa, heroin is the 4th to 6th most prevalent substance of abuse. A lower relative importance of heroin abuse was reported from a number of countries in South America.

Ranking of opiates in order of prevalence in 2001

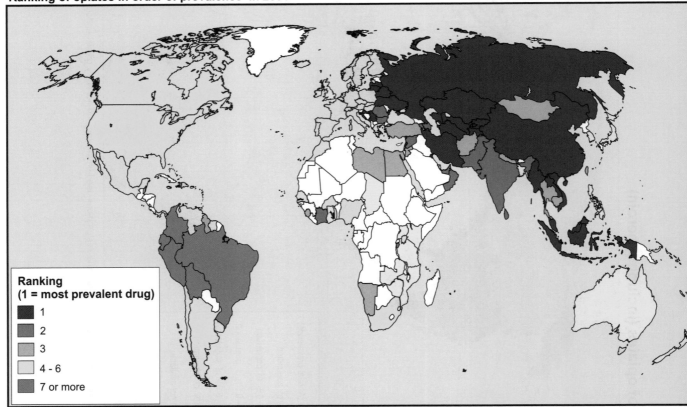

Ranking
(1 = most prevalent drug)
- 1
- 2
- 3
- 4 - 6
- 7 or more

Sources: UNODC Annual Reports Questionnaires data, SAMSHA US National Household Survey on Drug Abuse, Iranian Ministry of Health, Rapid Assessement Study and UNODC ARQ,Council of Europe,

TRENDS

At the global level, there are still more countries reporting increases than there are countries reporting declines in the abuse of opiates (heroin, morphine and opium). This is particularly the case for heroin. Nonetheless, some progress appears to have been made in recent years. If the difference of the number of countries reporting increases in heroin abuse and those reporting stable or declining trends, is calculated, the resulting balance used to be clearly in favor of those reporting increases, but shifted over the 1998-2001 period towards an equilibrium. The results in 2001 were thus the best ones since 1993.

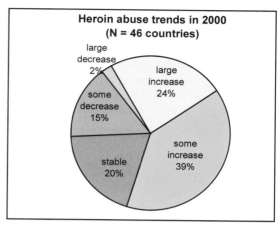

Source: UNODC, Annual Reports Questionnaire Data.

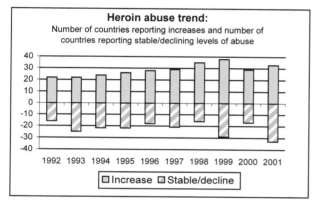

Source: UNODC, Annual Reports Questionnaire Data.

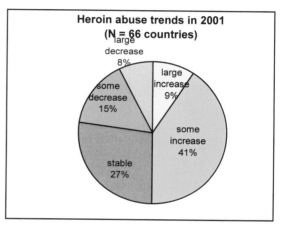

Source: UNODC, Annual Reports Questionnaire Data.

A comparison between the trend reports for the year 2000 and the year 2001 shows that the number of countries reporting 'large increases' declined markedly, while those reporting 'large decreases' were clearly on the rise. While in 2000, 24% of all countries reported a 'large increase' of heroin abuse, this proportion fell to 9% in 2001 which suggests that the heroin epidemic lost momentum in 2001, the year in which global opium production fell by 65%.

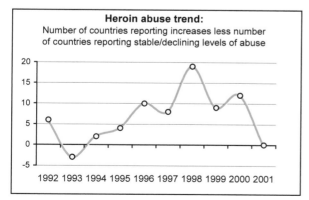

Source: UNODC, Annual Reports Questionnaire Data.

Europe

Heroin abuse reported to UNDOC from countries of West Europe showed generally stable to declining trends. These trends are indirectly confirmed by a number of statistical data, including household surveys, proportion of people in treatment for heroin abuse, age of people in treatment, development of HIV/AIDS among drug addicts, first time offenders against the drug laws and drug related deaths. Most of these indicators showed a deterioration in the 1980s. However, in the 1990s they indicated a stabilization or a decline of abuse levels, and these trends also continued in 2000 and 2001.

The trend towards a decline in heroin abuse has been most pronounced in Spain over the last decade, including in 2000 and 2001. Spain used to have one of the highest, if not the highest prevalence rates of heroin abuse in Europe in the 1980s. However, annual prevalence of heroin abuse, as measured by household surveys, fell from a level of around 0.9% in the late 1980s/early 1990s (estimate based on pooled results of regional surveys conducted in Spain over the 1987-1993 period) to 0.5% in 1995 and to 0.1% in 2001. Though household surveys are not very suitable instruments to identify the total number of heroin users (which is usually higher), they still provide – if done repeatedly - important

information on trends, that are confirmed by a number of other indicators as well. The number of new admissions for treatment of heroin abuse declined by 60% between 1992 and 2000. The incidence of injecting drug use related AIDS declined by 54% over the 1992-2000 period and by a further 16% in 2001. The number of heroin related deaths fell by 55% between 1992 and 2000 and continued to fall in 2001.

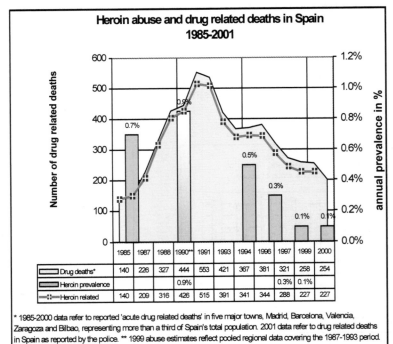

Heroin abuse and drug related deaths in Spain 1985-2001

	1985	1987	1988	1990**	1991	1993	1994	1996	1997	1999	2000
Drug deaths*	140	226	327	444	553	421	367	381	321	258	254
Heroin prevalence				0.9%					0.3%	0.1%	
Heroin related	140	209	316	426	515	391	341	344	288	227	227

* 1985-2000 data refer to reported 'acute drug related deaths' in five major towns, Madrid, Barcelona, Valencia, Zaragoza and Bilbao, representing more than a third of Spain's total population. 2001 data refer to drug related deaths in Spain as reported by the police. ** 1999 abuse estimates reflect pooled regional data covering the 1987-1993 period.

Sources: UNODC, Annual Reports Questionnaire Data, Observatorio Español Sobre Drogas, *Informe No. 5*, July 2002, Plan Nacional Sobre Drogas, *Encuesta Domiciliaria sobre Consumo de Drogas en Espana, 2001*, December 2002, Plan Nacional Sobre Drogas, 'Resultados obtenidos en la lucha contra la oferta de drogas durante 1997-2001', EMCDDA, 2002 *Annual Report on the state of the drugs problem in the European Union and Norway.*

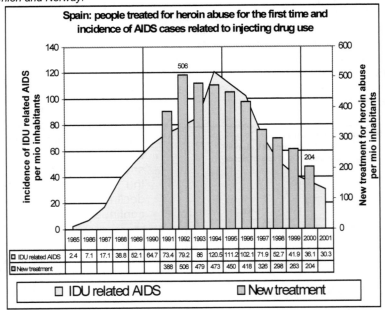

Spain: people treated for heroin abuse for the first time and incidence of AIDS cases related to injecting drug use

	1985	1986	1987	1988	1989	1990	1991	1992	1993	1994	1995	1996	1997	1998	1999	2000	2001
IDU related AIDS	2.4	7.1	17.1	38.8	52.1	64.7	73.4	79.2	86	120.5	111.2	102.1	71.9	52.7	41.9	36.1	30.3
New treatment							388	506	479	473	450	418	326	298	263	204	

☐ IDU related AIDS   ☐ New treatment

Source: Observatorio Español Sobre Drogas, *Informe No. 5*, July 2002, EMCDDA, Extended annual Report on the State of the Drugs Problem 1999 and EuroHIV, *HIV/AIDS Surveillance in Europe*, Mid-Year Report 2002, No. 67.

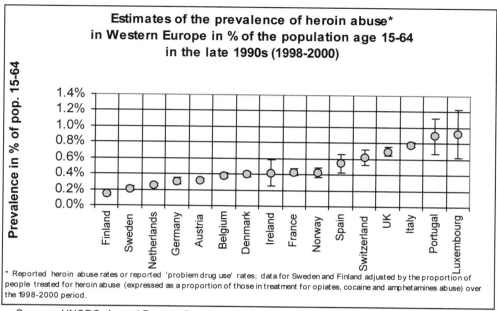

Estimates of the prevalence of heroin abuse*
in Western Europe in % of the population age 15-64
in the late 1990s (1998-2000)

* Reported heroin abuse rates or reported 'problem drug use' rates; data for Sweden and Finland adjusted by the proportion of people treated for heroin abuse (expressed as a proportion of those in treatment for opiates, cocaine and amphetamines abuse) over the 1998-2000 period.

Sources: UNODC, Annual Reports Questionnaire Data, EMCDDA, 2002 Annual report on the state of the drugs problem in the European Union and Norway.

Following Spain (high levels of heroin abuse in the 1980s, and a strong reduction in the 1990s), Italy seems to have been confronted with the most severe heroin abuse problem among the larger EU countries in the 1990s and subsequent years. Thus Italy had, in absolute numbers, the largest heroin abusing population of all West European countries over the 1998-2000 period.

Italy, like all other West European countries, was confronted with strong increases of heroin abuse in the 1980s. A number of indicators suggest that progress has been made in recent years in stabilizing the levels of heroin abuse. The underlying trend pattern is, however, more complex than in many other West European countries and requires a more detailed discussion.

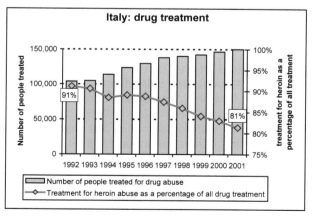

Italy: drug treatment

Source: Ministero del Lavoro e delle Politiche Sociali, *Relazione Annuale al Parlamento Sullo Stato delle Tossicodipendenze in Italia , 2001 and previous years.*

Overall treatment demand for heroin abuse increased between 1992 and 2001 in Italy, but less than overall treatment demand for drug abuse. In 1992 heroin accounted for 91% of all treatment demand in the country. By the year 2001, the proportion fell to 81%. Over the last few years the overall number of people treated for heroin abuse remained roughly stable. The number of IDU related AIDS cases declined by 80% over the 1994-2001 period.

The number of drug related deaths, which are mainly related to heroin abuse, fell by almost 50% between 1996 and 2001. (However, the number of drug related deaths recorded in 1996 was exceptionally high). In 1999/2000 the downward trend of drug related deaths came to a temporary halt, possibly a consequence of the bumper harvests of Afghan opium in 1999 and 2000 which resulted in increased supply of higher purity heroin on the Italian market. In 2001, the year of Afghanistan's opium poppy ban, the number of drug related deaths fell by nearly 20% in Italy. This decline went hand in hand with some indications of decreases in heroin availability, reflected, inter alia, in a fall in average heroin purity from 36% in 2000 to 31% in 2001.[b] Successes by the Italian authorities in seizing considerable quantities of heroin in that year (2 tons in 2001, up from 1 ton in 2000 and 0.5 tons in 1997) also contributed to reducing the over-supply.

---

[b] Ministero del Laboro e delle Politiche Sociale, Report to the EMCDDA, Italy, Drug situation 2001.

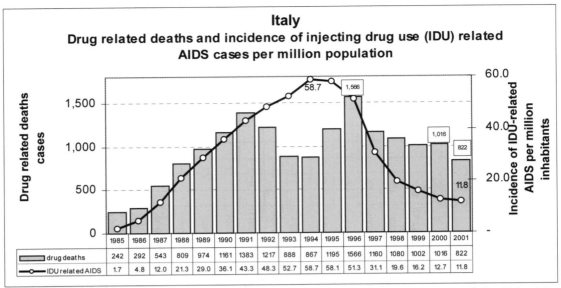

Sources: Ministero del Lavoro e delle Politiche Sociali, *Relazione Annuale al Parlamento Sullo Stato delle Tossicodipendenze in Italia , 2001*, EMCDDA, *2002 Annual Report on the State of the Drugs Problem in the European Union and Norway*, EuroHIV, *HIV-AIDS, Surveillance in Europe, Mid-Year Report 2002, No. 67*.

Estimates of the number of heroin abusers in Italy, based on a number of different indirect methods (capture-recapture method, multivariate indicator method, back calculation HIV/AIDS multiplier method, treatment multiplier and extrapolations from Ministry of the Interior data), did not find a decline in heroin abuse over the 1996-2000 period. There seems to have been a slight increase over the 1996-99 period, followed by a stronger increase in 2000. In 2001, however, the year of Afghanistan's opium poppy ban, data show a decline of the number of heroin users in the general population by about 15%.

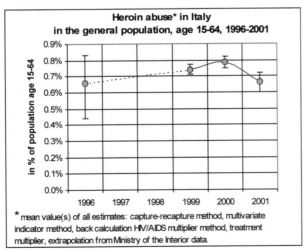

Source: Ministero del Lavoro e delle Politiche Sociali, Report to the EMCDDA, Italy Drug Situation 2001 and United Nations Population Division, World Population Prospects, the 2000 Revision. Feb. 2001.

Another source of information on heroin trends is the development of drug use in the military. This data is collected by the ministry of defence, arising from disciplinary proceedings and from requests for treatment. It shows that the proportion of heroin among all registered drug abuse cases in the army increased quite strongly over the 1995-1998 period (from 3.2% to 6.9%) but fell again thereafter (4.3% in 2001). The total number of army personnel identified to have been using heroin fell by 55% in 2001[c].

Finally, national school surveys (ESPAD) were conducted over the 1999-2001 period. They found a strong increase in heroin abuse in 2000, apparently related to large-scale availability and a perception that smoking heroin was not particularly dangerous. This upward trend, however, did not continue in 2001. The results of the ESPAD study indicate that herion abuse among students (15-19) fell by about 50% in 2001 (from 4.2% to 2%), possibly also a result of the temporary end of the heroin glut on the Italian market. A negative side-effect of decreased availability, however, was an increase in injecting drugs, which rose from 0.2% in 1999 to 0.4% in 2001. Another warning signal is that the approval rates for using heroin continued to grow (from 6% in 1999, 7% in 2000 to 9% in 2001). Thus more than four times as many students as have experience with heroin (2% in 2001) approve of using it. This is a cause for concern, because heroin abuse among youth may grow again if large-scale supply is re-established.

---

[c] Ministero del Lavoro e delle Politiche Sociali, Report to the EMCDDA, Italy Drug Situation 2001.

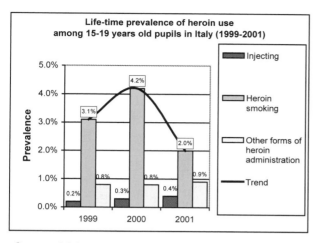

Life-time prevalence of heroin use among 15-19 years old pupils in Italy (1999-2001)

Source: Ministero del Lavoro e delle Politiche Sociali, *Relazione Annuale al Parlamento Sullo Stato delle Tossicodipendenze in Italia , 2001.*

some 60%, down from levels around 90% in the early 1990s. Treatment demand for abuse of heroin declined in relative terms from 76% of all drug related treatment demand to slightly less than 70% between 1997 and 1999. (OFDT, *Drogues et Dependances, Indicateurs et Tendances 2002*).

Over the last few years heroin abuse appears to have stabilised at lower levels. Within this overall positive macro-trend, studies in France found, however, a disturbing new trend of new groups of occasional users of ecstasy and amphetamine, usually linked to the clubbing scene, starting to experiment with sniffing or smoking heroin as well. In this context, heroin is often used as a substance to 'come down' from ATS or (crack-cocaine), and is initially used as a quasi-therapeutic substance to deal with the problems arising from the abuse of other drugs.[d]

France, like other West European countries, reported increases of heroin abuse in the 1980s and a decline in the second half of the 1990s. The number of drug related deaths, mostly linked to heroin, fell by more than 75% between 1995 and 2000, and within these smaller numbers of drug related deaths, the proportion of opiates fell to

Overall positive trends were also reported from Switzerland. Research in country's largest heroin market, Zürich[e], based on methadone registry data and in-depth analyses of the latency period of different groups of drug abusers between start of heroin abuse ('incidence') and prescription of methadone (average 6 years), found a strong

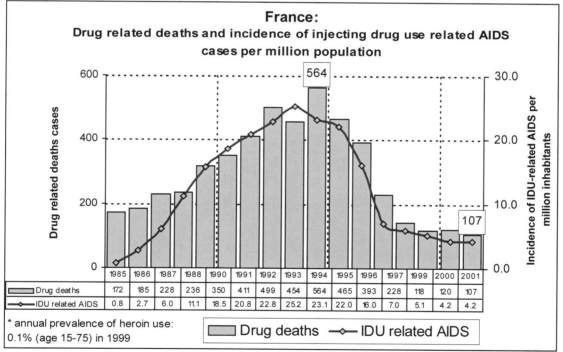

France:
Drug related deaths and incidence of injecting drug use related AIDS cases per million population

	1985	1986	1987	1988	1990	1991	1992	1993	1994	1995	1996	1997	1999	2000	2001
Drug deaths	172	185	228	236	350	411	499	454	564	465	393	228	118	120	107
IDU related AIDS	0.8	2.7	6.0	11.1	18.5	20.8	22.8	25.2	23.1	22.0	16.0	7.0	5.1	4.2	4.2

* annual prevalence of heroin use: 0.1% (age 15-75) in 1999

☐ Drug deaths   —◇— IDU related AIDS

Sources: Ministero del Lavoro e delle Politiche Sociali, *Relazione Annuale al Parlamento Sullo Stato delle Tossicodipendenze in Italia , 2001*, EMCDDA, *2002 Annual Report on the State of the Drugs Problem in the European Union and Norway*, EuroHIV, *HIV-AIDS, Surveillance in Europe, Mid-Year Report 2002, No. 67.*

[d] OFDT, Phénomènes émergents liés aux drogues en 2001, Rapport TREND, Juin 2002, pp. 184-187.

(almost three-fold) increase in the incidence of heroin abuse in the second half of the 1980s, leading – with regard to injecting drug users - to a peak in 1990 and a strong decline thereafter. The incidence rates for non-injecting heroin use, also rose strongly in the second half of the 1980s. But the peak was slightly later (1991-93). A significant decline took place after 1996.

The massive increase in the heroin incidence rates in the 1980s and the decline in the 1990s, had also repercussions for the development of drug related deaths in the country. Following a tripling in the number of drug related deaths over the 1985-1992 period, which went parallel to the development of an open drug scene (notably in Zürich) and thus a strong overall expansion of the heroin market, the number of drug related deaths fell by about 50% between 1992 and 2001. In parallel, the number of injecting drug use related AIDS cases fell by 80% between 1995 and 2001. The closure of the open drug scene in the mid 1990s and improved access to treatment as well as changes in the perception of heroin played a role in this outcome. Some Swiss researchers argue that government policies may have played a role in the changing image of heroin, replacing its aura of rebellion against society, enforced by the persecution of heroin addicts, by the image of heroin addicts being disenfranchised invalids, thus reducing the attractiveness of heroin for potentially new consumers.[f]

The positive downward trend in the number of drug related deaths came to a halt in 2000. Large-scale supply from Afghanistan's record harvests seems to have caused this. However, following Afghanistan's opium ban in 2001 and additional supply problems related to the dismantling of some criminal Albanian groups which had control of important parts of the Swiss market, heroin availability fell. Drug related deaths declined by 20% in 2002.

In neighbouring Austria, heroin abuse is still at one of the lowest levels in West Europe, and the heroin epidemic took place a few years later than in most of the sub-region. Heroin trafficking in Austria grew after the fall of the iron curtain in 1989/1990, which enabled the establishment of a number of new trafficking routes, notably from Slovakia and Hungary, providing additional links between the Balkan route countries and the markets of West Europe. Increasing spill-overs were the consequence. Thus the number of registered heroin related violations against the narcotics law and the number of drug related deaths (which are to 98% related to opiate abuse, alone or in combination with alcohol and other drugs) moved more or less in parallel over the last decade. They peaked in 1994, the year of the first opium bumper harvest in Afghanistan, and fell in subsequent years as treatment and counselling services improved. However, drug related deaths

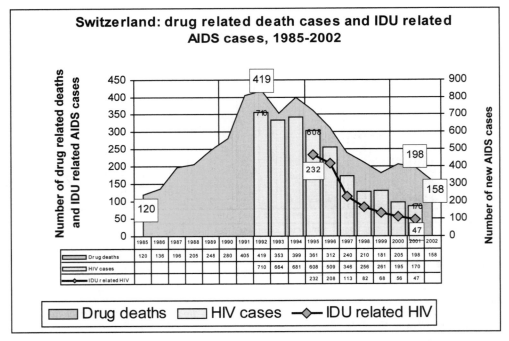

Sources: UNODC, Annual Reports Questionnaire Data, Bundesamt für Polizei (Switzerland),
EuroHIV, *HIV-AIDS, Surveillance in Europe, Mid-Year Report 2002, No. 67 and previous years*

[e] Michael Stauffacher *et al*, "Trend in heroin use in Zurich (Switzerland), using methadone maintenance treatment admission data to estimate onset incidence" (2003, Draft).
[f] ibid.

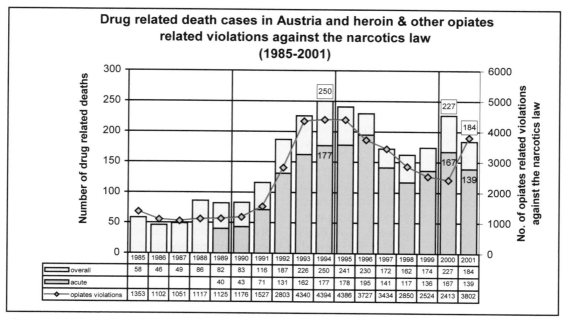

Drug related death cases in Austria and heroin & other opiates related violations against the narcotics law (1985-2001)

	1985	1986	1987	1988	1989	1990	1991	1992	1993	1994	1995	1996	1997	1998	1999	2000	2001
overall	58	46	49	86	82	83	116	187	226	250	241	230	172	162	174	227	184
acute					40	43	71	131	162	177	178	195	141	117	136	167	139
opiates violations	1353	1102	1051	1117	1125	1176	1527	2803	4340	4394	4386	3727	3434	2850	2524	2413	3802

Sources: UNODC, Annual Reports Questionnaire Data, Bundesministerium für Inneres, Österreichisches Bundesinstitut für Gesundheitswesen, Bericht zur Drogensituation 2002.

peaked again in 2000, following Afghanistan's bumper harvests of 1999 and 2000. In 2001, the year of the Taliban opium ban, drug related deaths declined by about 20%. Increased enforcement efforts preventing the consolidation of an open drug scene, seem to have been additional contributory factors in reducing availability of heroin in 2001. Estimates, based on a capture-recapture method, found in both 1994/95 and in 1999, 15,000-20,000 problematic heroin users, equivalent to 0.3% of the population age 15-64 and thus less than half the corresponding rates reported from Switzerland or Italy.

Available trend data for Germany show a partly mixed picture. General population household surveys indicate a fall in heroin abuse over the 1995-1997 and the 1997-2000 periods. (Given the small numbers - and thus the large error margins of such data – it is only safe to state that there was no (significant) increase in the second half of

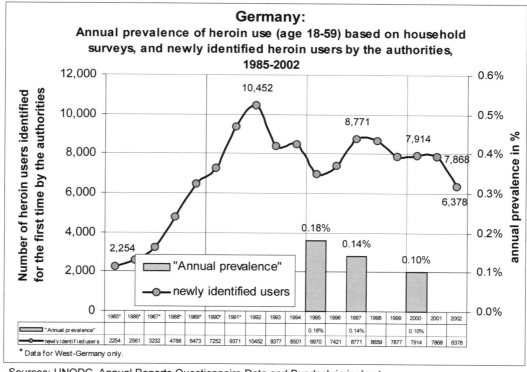

Germany: Annual prevalence of heroin use (age 18-59) based on household surveys, and newly identified heroin users by the authorities, 1985-2002

	1985*	1986*	1987*	1988*	1989*	1990*	1991*	1992	1993	1994	1995	1996	1997	1998	1999	2000	2001	2002
"Annual prevalence"											0.18%		0.14%			0.10%		
newly identified users	2254	2561	3232	4788	6473	7252	9371	10452	8377	8501	6970	7421	8771	8659	7877	7914	7868	6378

* Data for West-Germany only.

Sources: UNODC, Annual Reports Questionnaire Data and Bundeskriminalamt.

the 1990s). In any case, data indicate that increased availability of heroin in the late 1990s did not affect the spread of heroin in the general population. The number of new heroin abusers identified by the authorities remained practically stable in recent years until 2001, and was lower than in the early 1990s. In 2002 (the year following Afghanistan's opium poppy ban) the number of newly identified heroin abusers, declined, however, by 19% and was 39% less than in the peak year of 1991.

There are, however, no indications for a similar decline of problematic heroin abuse in Germany. Though still low by West European standards, problematic heroin abuse appears to have increased slightly over the 1996-2000 period. (Existing margins of errors for these estimates, however, limit any firm conclusion). In parallel, the number of drug related deaths rose over the same period.

Drug related deaths, after having increased strongly over the 1985-1991 period (rising more than six-fold), declined over the 1991-1997 period by 30%, mainly reflecting improved treatment services, including substitution treatment. However, faced with increased heroin supply in the late 1990s as a consequence of Afghanistan's expansion of opium production and an ongoing increase in the number of drug related deaths in the new provinces, this positive trend was not maintained. The number of drug related deaths rose by 35% over the 1997-2000 period. In parallel, average heroin purity in Germany increased (from 12.8% in 1997 to 18.5% in 2000) while prices continued to show a slightly falling trend, indicating an overall rise in heroin availability on the German market. However, in 2001 (and even more so in 2002) heroin supply for the German market, like in other West European countries, seems to have fallen. The number of drug related deaths fell by 10% in 2001 and by almost 18% in 2002.

In other words, available data suggest that rising levels of heroin availability over the 1997-2000 period did not affect the general population (as the image of heroin in the general population continued to be negative), but led to higher levels of heroin consumption among established heroin abusers. This led to a larger number of drug related deaths. Similarly, first signs of ending the heroin oversupply for the German market in 2001 (purity stopped increasing in 2001) did not affect the heroin incidence rate, but reduced consumption levels of those already taking heroin, and thus contributed to lower levels of drug related deaths in 2001. For 2002, however, all indicators, both on the demand and the supply side, showed a decline.

In contrast to a basically stable heroin market in most other West European countries, the UK was confronted with rapidly rising heroin abuse in the 1990s and emerged, together with Italy, as one of the largest heroin markets of the sub-region. British Crime Survey data suggest that heroin abuse almost tripled over the 1998-2000 period. Heroin seizures rose 6-fold over the 1990-2000 period; the number of persons arrested for heroin related violations (possession and trafficking) increased 8-fold over the same period; demand for treatment for heroin abuse increased substantially; and the number of heroin related deaths rose 5-fold between 1993 and 2000. For comparison, the overall number of drug related deaths rose by just 32% over the same period.

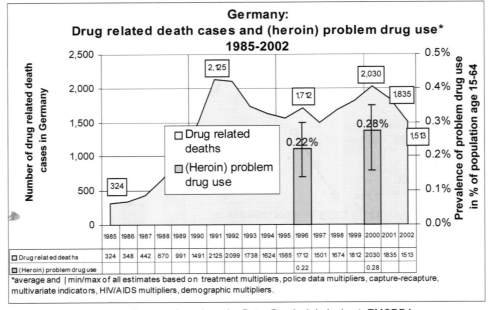

Germany:
Drug related death cases and (heroin) problem drug use*
1985-2002

	1985	1986	1987	1988	1989	1990	1991	1992	1993	1994	1995	1996	1997	1998	1999	2000	2001	2002
Drug related deaths	324	348	442	670	991	1491	2125	2099	1738	1624	1565	1712	1501	1674	1812	2030	1835	1513
(Heroin) problem drug use												0.22				0.28		

*average and | min/max of all estimates based on treatment multipliers, police data multipliers, capture-recapture, multivariate indicators, HIV/AIDS multipliers, demographic multipliers.

Sources: UNODC, Annual Reports Questionnaire Data, Bundeskriminalamt, EMCDDA.

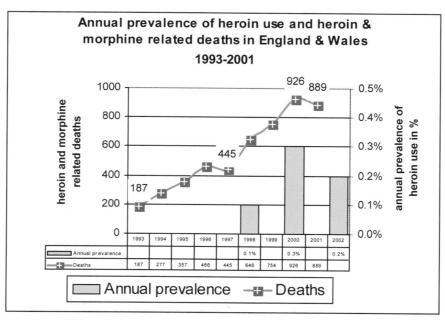

Sources: UK Home Office, *Prevalence of Drug Use: Key Findings from the 2001/2002 British Crime Survey*; UK Home Office, *British Crime Survey data suggest that heroin use tripled over the 1998-2000 period and* National Statistics, *Health Statistics Quarterly, Spring 2003 and Spring 2002.*

Afghanistan's opium poppy ban in 2001, however, seems to have stopped this trend from continuing. Following an average annual growth in the number of heroin related deaths of 26% p.a. over the 1993 to 2000 period in England & Wales, heroin related deaths fell by 4% in 2001. The 2001/2002 data of the latest British Crime survey also found a statistically significant decrease as compared to the data of the previous survey, conducted in 2000. This also applied to the group of 16-24 year olds: a comparison of the 2000 and the 2002 data shows a decline in the number of heroin abusers in this age group by about 60%. Though 40% of those 16-24 year olds found it very easy to get access to cannabis and 19% reported that it was very easy to get access to ecstasy, only 8% said the same for heroin and 36% considered it to be difficult if not impossible to get access to heroin in 2001/2002.[9]

Reported increases of heroin abuse in the rest of West Europe were limited to a few Nordic countries, which traditionally had very low levels of it, as well as to a few countries in southern Europe (Portugal, Greece and Andorra), which were affected by trafficking activities.

Drug abuse trends in Central and Eastern Europe were less clear-cut than in previous years. Over the last few years, heroin abuse trends were reported to be stable or declining in most of West

Europe and strongly rising in almost all countries of East Europe. For 2001, abuse trends were far more mixed. A number of countries along the Balkan route, including Turkey, Croatia and Slovakia reported either stable or declining levels of abuse, while others, including Greece, Bulgaria, Romania, Hungary and the Czech Republic reported an ongoing increase. Strong increases in 2001 were reported from Poland and from Belarus, possibly an indication of a growing importance of heroin shipments via Russia, leading to local spill-overs. Increases in heroin abuse were also reported from Tajikistan and Kyrgyzstan which are transit countries between Afghanistan and the Russian market. The Ukraine, in contrast, reported a large decrease in heroin abuse in 2001.

The total number of opiate abusers is estimated by the authorities to be several times more than the amount reported in the registries. One set of estimates provided by the ministry of internal affairs, suggests that the total number of drug addicts was around 2.4 million people in 2001, up from 1.3 million in 1996. Expressed as a percentage of the total population, the number of (problem) drug users in the Russian Federation would thus amount to 1.6%. Expressed as a proportion of the population age 15-64, the typical age range used in West European countries, the rate amounted to 2.3% in 2001. This rate is almost three times larger than similar rates of problem drug users reported from West European countries such as Italy or the UK. Registry data

---

[9] Home Office, *Findings 182 – Prevalence of drug use: key findings from the 2001/2002 British Crime Survey*, London 2002.

show that around 89% of the registered drug addicts have been abusing opiates in recent years. This suggests that abuse of opiates affected 2.1% of the population age 15-64 in 2001. However, registry data also show that in 1999 close to 80% of the opiate abusers were still using opium in its various forms and only slightly more than 20% were addicted to heroin. Thus in

terms of heroin abuse, several West European countries appear to have higher levels than the Russian Federation, even though opiate abuse is significantly more widespread in Russia than in West Europe. The number of heroin abusers among the opiate abusers is, however, rising rapidly in Russia.

Trends in abuse of heroin in Europe, incl. C.I.S. countries, in 2001 (or latest year available) (countries sorted according to size of population)			
Stable or declining abuse levels		**Rising abuse levels**	
Germany, 2000, stable	WE*	Russian Fed., 2000, strong increase	CEE*
Turkey, 2000, stable	WE*	Poland, 2001, large increase	CEE*
UK, 2000, stable	WE*	Romania, 2000, large increase	CEE*
France, 2001, stable	WE*	Greece, 2001, some increase	WE*
Italy, 2001, some decrease	WE*	Czech Rep., 2001, some increase	CEE*
Ukraine, 2001, large decrease	CEE*	Portugal, 2001, some increase	WE*
Spain, 2000, some decrease	WE*	Belarus, 2001, large increase	CEE*
Netherlands, 2001, stable	WE*	Hungary, 2001, some increase	WE*
Belgium, 2000, stable	WE*	Sweden, 2001, some increase	WE*
Austria, 2001, stable	WE*	Bulgaria, 2001, some increase	CEE*
Azerbaijan, 2001, large decrease	CEE*	Tajikistan, 2001, some increase	CEE
Switzerland, 2001, some decrease	WE*	Georgia, 1999, some increase	CEE*
Slovakia, some decrease	CEE	Kyrgyzstan, large increase	CEE
Denmark, 2001, stable	WE*	Norway, 1999, some increase	WE*
Finland, 2001, stable	WE*	Moldova, 2000, large increase	CEE*
Croatia, 2001, some decrease	CEE	Latvia, 2000, large increase	CEE*
Armenia, 2001, some decrease	WE	Macedonia FYR, 1999, large increase	CEE*
Ireland, 1999, stable	WE*	Estonia, 2000, some increase	CEE*
Cyprus, 2000, stable	WE*	Andorra, some increase	WE
Luxembourg, 2001, stable	WE*		
Malta, 2001, stable	WE*		
Iceland, 2000, stable	WE*		
Liechtenstein, 2001, stable	WE*		
* WE = West Europe; CEE = Central and East Europe Sources: UNDCP, Annual Reports Questionnaire Data; official reports.			

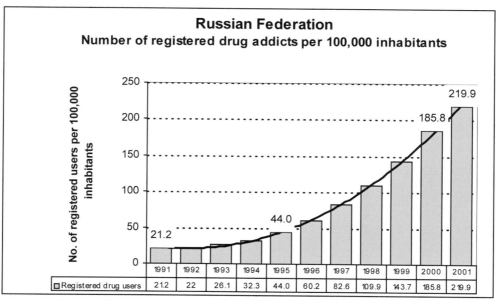

Sources: Ministry of Health, Drug addicts registered with state treatment facilities and MIA, Russia 2001.

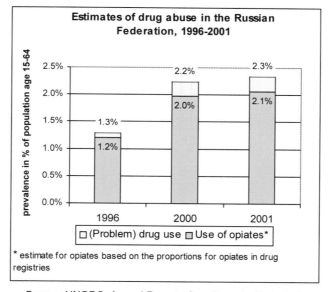

Source: UNODC, Annual Reports Questionnaire Data and MIA, Russia 2001.

Increase in number of drug abusers in the Russian Federation

		1996	1997	1998	1999	2000	2001
Estimate number of drug abusers (in thousands)		1,272	1,537	2,243	2,222	2,269	2,365
Number of drug abusers registered by medical institutions		243,670	219,173	287,689	359,067	451,603	506,850
Including	Diagnosed as drug addicts	90,409	113,349	156,231	198,345	297,598	364,010
	Aged from 18 to 30	148,194	130,896	160,535	220,487	254,123	
	Children and teenagers	38,843	39,230	47,170	52,598	50,079	

Source: MIA, Russia, 2000.

Over the 1995-2000 period, demand for new treatment was particularly high - and grew strongest in Orenburg, located close to the border with Kazakhstan along one of the main trafficking routes of opiates from Central Asia to Moscow. In general, towns close to the border with Kazakhstan as well as in the very south of the country, the city of Krasnodar, close the Caucasus countries and the Ukraine, have been confronted in recent years with the most serious problems of opiate abuse, followed by Moscow and, at lower levels, St. Petersburg

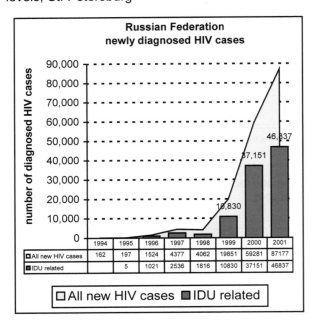

The Russian Federation also has one of the highest injecting drug use (IDU) related HIV rates in the world, which shows signs of rapid increase. In 2000 the numbers more than tripled and a further rise – though not as rapid - was also reported in 2001. In total, 319 persons per million inhabitants, up from 7 in 1996, were registered for HIV infection as a consequence of IDU. This compares with levels of less than 10 cases per million inhabitants in the UK, Germany or the Nordic countries. Injecting drug use accounted in the year 2000 for 63% of all HIV infections in the Russian Federation. A deceleration in the growth rated of IDU related HIV cases in the following year meant that the IDU related proportion of HIV cases declined to 54% in 2001, suggesting that a HIV epidemic, once spreading to the population at large, becomes extremely difficult to contain, even if the underlying cause – infections through drug injections - were to be removed. At the same time, the proportion of IDU related HIV cases in all HIV cases continued to be substantially higher in Russia than in West Europe. In 14 West European

countries[h] the proportion was, on average, 14% in 2001, and even smaller in some countries (3% in the UK, 7% in Germany, 12% in Switzerland and 14% in Sweden).

High numbers of IDU related HIV cases in per capita terms, are also reported from the Baltic region (Latvia and Estonia) as well as from the Ukraine and from Kazakhstan. The number of AIDS cases in Russia and the other countries of the former Soviet Union is still low, but there is a danger that the current IDU related HIV epidemic could grow into a major AIDS epidemic.

---

[h] Belgium, Denmark, Finland, Germany, Greece, Iceland , Ireland, Luxembourg, Malta, Norway, Portugal, Sweden, Switzerland and the UK.

Newly diagnosed injecting drug use related HIV infections per million inhabitants in 2001 (data for 1996 in brackets)

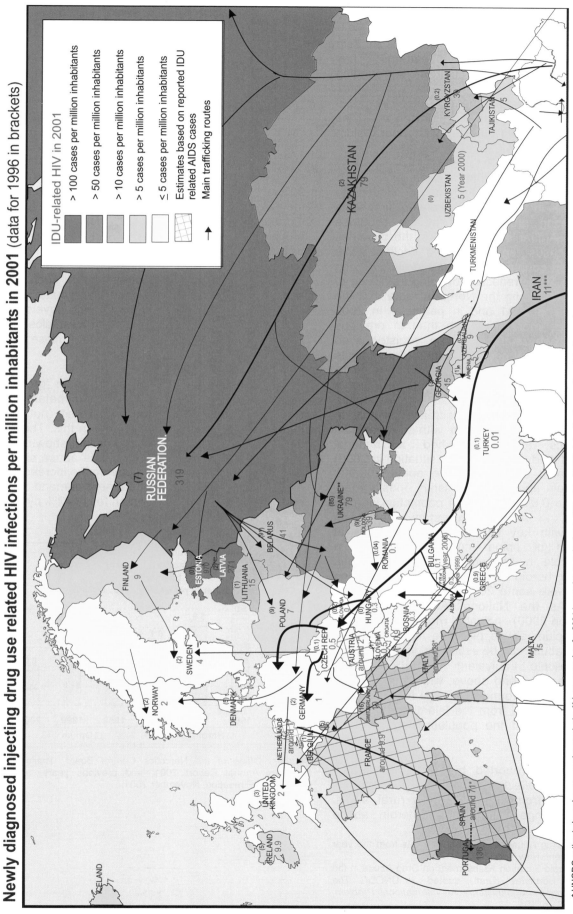

* UNODC estimate based on regression analysis ** Lower number for 2001 is not due to a decline in IDU related HIV but due to changes in registration system.

Sources: EuroHIV, HIV/AIDS Surveillance in Europe End-year report 2001, June 2002 and previous years.

Asia and the Pacific (Oceania)

In 1999 and 2000, opiate abuse trends in Asia showed two distinct sub-regional patterns. They rose strongly in the countries surrounding Afghanistan, notably in the countries of Central Asia, in line with Afghanistan's bumper harvests of 1999 and 2000. They declined in the countries surrounding Myanmar, in line with poor opium harvests in the region.

These regional abuse patterns changed in 2001. Countries surrounding Myanmar continued to show declines in abuse. But there were first signs of decelerating growth rates in the countries surrounding Afghanistan. Several of the countries in the Caucasus region reported declines. The Central Asian countries continued to show strong increases in 2001, reflecting ongoing trafficking of Afghan opiates along the Northern route. But the growth rates in 2001 and in particular in 2002 tended to be more moderate than in previous years. In Kyrgyzstan the drug registry even showed a decline of newly registered drug addicts in 2002, the first such decline in more than a decade. Authorities in Pakistan reported heroin abuse to have stabilized in 2001 while opium abuse was reported to have decreased slightly. In 2002, UNODC in partnership with the Pakistan Anti-Narcotics Force published a national assessment study (based on the situation in 2000) which revealed that there were about 500,000 chronic heroin abusers in Pakistan[i], mostly men, equivalent to 0.6% of the total population age 15 and above. In addition, the study, based on interviews with key informants, suggested that consumption of opium continued to play a significant role in the country, though less than cannabis or heroin. Previous studies suggested that there were some 200,000 opium abusers in Pakistan. As the National Assessment study (conducted in 2000) indicated more or less stable trends in opium abuse over the last five years, total opiate abuse can be estimated to affect some 700,000 people equivalent to 0.9% of the population age 15 and above, which is similar to opiate abuse rates found in Central Asia[j], but less than those reported from the Islamic Republic of Iran (1.7%-2.8% of the population age 15 and above).

Increases were reported by the authorities in India, mainly reflecting an ongoing spread of heroin abuse from metropolitan to rural areas. However, stronger increases in heroin abuse

appear to have taken place earlier, over the 1997-2000 period, as documented in a Rapid Assessment Study, conducted on behalf of UNODC, which is due to be released soon. A national household survey conducted in India in 2002, found that overall 0.7% of the male population, age 12-60, were 'current users' (at least once in the last month) of opiates, including 0.2% of the male population abusing heroin, 0.4% taking opium and 0.1% using other opiates. Life-time prevalence of opiate abuse among males stood at 1%. (Other studies showed that around 90% of all drugs in India are consumed by males). India has thus – in absolute terms- the largest number of opiate abusers worldwide, though prevalence rates are smaller than in Pakistan, Iran or Myanmar. Abuse of opiates was less common than cannabis (3% current users), but more common that abuse of other drugs such as sedatives/hypnotics, hallucinogens, stimulants or volatile substances. States with high levels of opiate abuse are mainly in the north west, close to Afghanistan, and the north east, close to Myanmar.

In East and South East Asia the main 'growth sector' was not opiates but methamphetamine. Poor opium harvests in South East Asia, notably Myanmar, apparently played a role in this. This is clearly reflected in data from Thailand, showing a continuing downward trend in opiate abuse since the mid 1990s while methamphetamine increased. While in 1995, 95% of all treatment demand was related to opiates, the proportion fell to 42% by the year 2000.

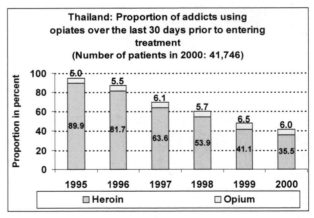

Sources: Office of the Narcotics Control Board, Thailand Narcotics Annual Report 2001, and previous years, and UNODC GAP meeting, November 2001.

---

[i] UNODCCP, Drug Abuse in Pakistan - Results from the year 2000 Assessment, New York 2002
[j] UNODC, "Rapid Situation Assessment on Drug Abuse in the Central Asian Countries" (Draft), quoted in UNODC, *The Opium Economy in Afghanistan - An International Problem*, New York 2003, p. 191

UNODC, as part of its regular opium poppy surveys in the Lao PDR, also conducts general population surveys in the northern provinces of the country. These surveys showed that after a strong increase over the 1992-98 period, prevalence of opium abuse fell again, parallel to falling opium production. Opium production in the Lao PDR declined by 20% in 2001; the number of opiates users fell by 8% in 2001 as compared to a year earlier. The link between opium production and consumption was also found in a more in-depth analysis of the prevalence rates in northern Laos. Villages with opium production had, on average, a prevalence rate that was 27% higher than was found in non-producing villages in the same region (based on 2000 data). It should be noted that the prevalence rates in these surveys are given as percentage of the total population. For the year 2000, a population breakdown for the northern provinces is available, showing that 44% of the population are children below the age of 15. Based on these data, internationally more comparable rates of the number of people taking opiates as a percentage of the population age 15 and above was 4.8% in 2000. Results for the year 2001 translate, accordingly, into a prevalence rate of 4.4%. This is still very high compared to other countries, though not uncommon for poppy

Declines in opiate abuse, notably opium but also heroin, were also reported by the authorities in Myanmar. In 2000, Indonesia, Malaysia, Singapore, Brunei Darussalam and Hong-Kong SAR also reported declining levels of opiate abuse. Japan reported a stabilization of heroin abuse in 2000. In 2001 declines in abuse of heroin were reported from Myanmar, Vietnam, Indonesia, Macao as well as Japan.

In contrast, authorities in the People's Republic of China continued to report an upward trend in the abuse of opiates, even though the main 'growth sector', like in other countries of South-East Asia, is ATS. The increasing levels of opiate abuse reflect the long-term trend of increasing trafficking of opiates out of Myanmar via China which was noticeable in most of the 1990s. Thus, the number of registered drug addicts in China - mostly heroin - rose more than ten-fold in the 1990s, reaching 860,000 in the year 2000 and more than 900,000 in 2001. In proportional terms, these levels (0.1% of the population age 15 and above) are still small compared to other countries, even if one takes into account the possibility that the total number of opiate abusers may exceed those officially registered.

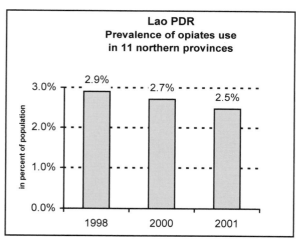

Lao PDR
Prevalence of opiates use
in 11 northern provinces

Source: UNODC, Lao Annual Opium Poppy Survey 2001 and previous years (2000, 1998).

growing areas in Asia. On the assumption of no opium abuse in the rest of the country (which, of course, would not be completely true), Laos has a prevalence rate of opiates abuse of at least 2%, age 15 and above, in 2001. Thus Laos, despite the decline over the last few years, has still a prevalence rate that is significantly above the Asian and the global average and - according to present estimates - the world's second highest rate after the Islamic Republic of Iran.

Opiate use is also still low compared to the levels reported in the 19th century and the first half of the 20th century in China. Then the estimates of opiates users - at a time when the population of China was substantially smaller – ranged between 12 million and 20 million. However, China - like many other countries - is confronted with an additional drug-related problem: by the end of 2000, some 22,500 HIV positives were recorded of whom 71% - a far higher percentage than in Europe - had contracted the virus through intravenous injection.(NNCC, *Annual Report on Drug Control in China, 2000*).

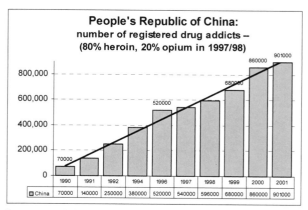

People's Republic of China:
number of registered drug addicts –
(80% heroin, 20% opium in 1997/98)

	1990	1991	1992	1994	1996	1997	1998	1999	2000	2001
China	70000	140000	250000	380000	520000	540000	596000	680000	860000	901000

Sources: UNODC, Annual Reports Questionnaire, China National Narcotics Control Commission, *Annual Report on Drug Control in China 2000*, U.S. Dept. of State, *International Narcotics Control Strategy Report(s)*, Washington 2001 and previous years.

In contrast to still rising levels of heroin abuse in China, Australia reported in 2001 a strong decline which lasted well into 2002, and has not returned to levels experienced before the heroin shortage. All available data clearly showed a downward trend. The shortage of heroin in Australia's domestic market was largely the result of successful law enforcement operations in late 2000 which, in co-operation with the authorities of other countries/territories, notably Hong Kong SAR of China, Myanmar and Thailand, dismantled major heroin trafficking rings which for years had supplied the Australian market (Sydney) with heroin from South-East Asia. This supply shortage was reflected in Australia's new Drug Use Monitoring (DUMA) system which tests offenders by means of urine analysis within 48 hours after arrest at a police station, as well as in a number of other indicators. Overall heroin-related overdoses, for instance, fell by around 66% in 2001, to the lowest level since the early 1990s. The total number of drug related deaths fell by a third. Data from the national household survey showed a decline of annual prevalence from 0.8% of the population (age 14 and above) in 1998 to 0.2% in 2001. Initial fears that such a heroin shortage could entail more crime and health risks by drug addicts, did not materialize. Drug addicts made use of treatment, notably of substitution treatment. Overall crime rates moved downwards rather than upwards. (NSW Bureau of Crime statistics and Research, "The Australian Heroin Drought and its Implications for Drug Policy", *Crime and Justice Bulletin*, October 2001).

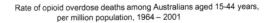
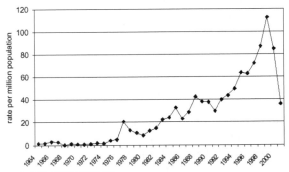

Rate of opioid overdose deaths among Australians aged 15-44 years, per million population, 1964 – 2001

Source: Australian Bureau of Statistics

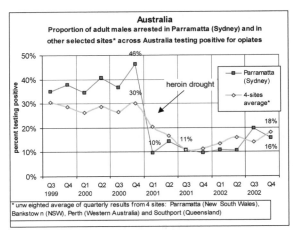

Source: Drug Use Monitoring in Australia (DUMA)

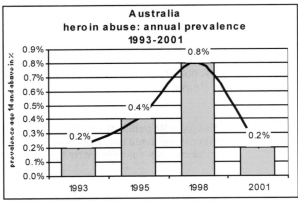

Source: AIHW, *Statistics on Drug Use in Australia* 2002.

Africa

Levels of opiate abuse in Africa still seem to be low compared to most other regions, mostly due to rather high prices by local purchasing power standards. The overall abuse trend, however, appears to go upwards.

Relatively few countries reported on heroin abuse trends in 2001. Data available from previous years, however, suggest that abuse was rising in the 1990s. In 2001, 2 African countries reported a strong increase (Namibia and Zimbabwe), 5 'some increase' (in East Africa: Uganda and Mauritius and in West Africa: Togo, Ghana and Gambia), 2 countries saw a stable trend (Benin and Burundi). South Africa, however, which has a well established system of monitoring drug abuse trends, reported a strong decline in heroin abuse, following years of increase.

Americas

Reported opiate abuse remained basically stable in North America though a number of countries in South America, including Colombia, Venezuela, Panama, Chile and Argentina reported increases in 2001. However, overall levels of heroin abuse in South America continue to be low. Indicators for the USA showed a mixed picture in 2001. General population surveys found an increase while high-school surveys found a strong decline. The overall trend thus seems to be rather stable. In 2002, the national high-school surveys (Monitoring the Future) remained at the levels found in the second half of the 1990s and were significantly lower than in 2000, though marginally higher than in 2001. However, as highlighted in reports of the Community Epidemiology Work-Group (CEWG), there is an ongoing increase in problem drug use, including heroin, in rural and suburban areas while the situation is improving in the urban areas which so-far had suffered more from the social consequences of large-scale substance abuse.

Occasional heroin abuse in 2001, as reflected in the household survey, affected 0.2% of the population age 12 and above. Overall heroin abuse estimates, including chronic heroin abuse, are around 0.5% of the population age 12 and above.

The increases of heroin prevalence in the early 1990s are still observed in treatment demand which has gradually increased over the last couple of years. Though drug related emergency visits to hospitals are still almost twice as common for cocaine as for heroin, treatment admissions for curing heroin dependence exceeded the number of cocaine related admissions in both 1999 and 2000. In 2000, 31% of all treatment demand (excluding alcohol) in the USA was related to abuse of opiates. Heroin alone was responsible for 28% of all treatment demand, and thus again more important than treatment demand for cocaine (25%).

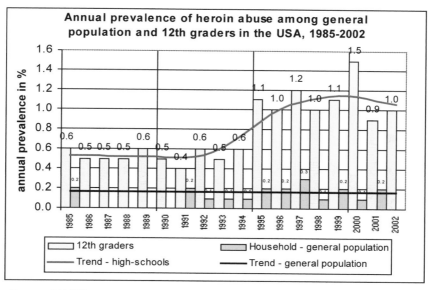

Source: SAMHSA, *National Household Survey on Drug Abuse*, 2001 an previous years , NIDA, Monitoring the Future 2002 and previous years.

Changes in abuse of heroin and other opiates, 2001 (or latest year available)

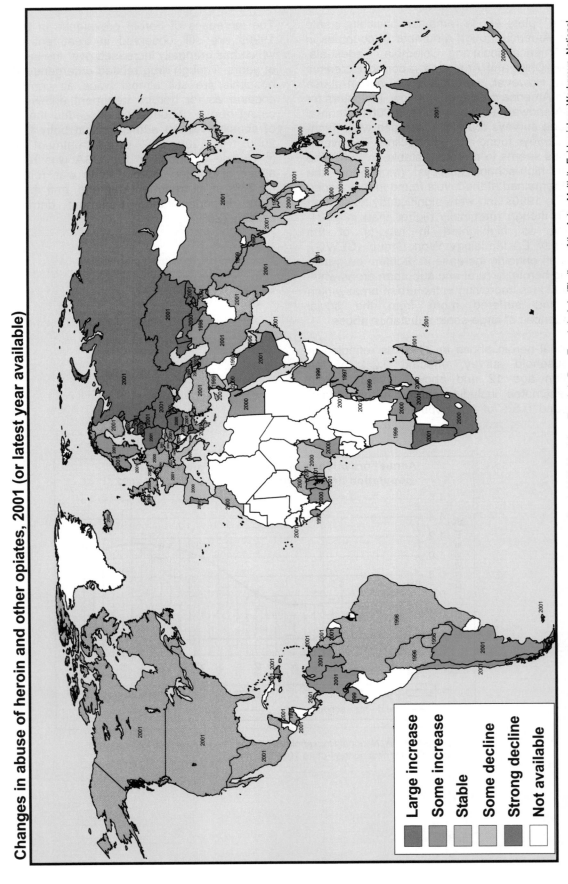

Legend:
- Large increase
- Some increase
- Stable
- Some decline
- Strong decline
- Not available

Sources: UNODC Annual Reports Questionnaires data, UNODC (Regional Centre Bangkok) Epidemiology Trends in Drug Trends in Asia (Findings of the Asian Multicity Epidemiology Workgroup, National Household Surveys submitted to UNODC, United States Department of State (Bureau for International Narcotics and Law Enforcement Affairs) International Narcotics Control Strategy Report, Bundeskriminalamt (BKA) and other Law Enforcement Reports, SACENDU (South African Community Epidemiology Network, UNODC, Meetings of Heads of Law Enforcement Agencies (HONLEA), UNODC, Global Workshop on Drug Information Systems.

1.3.3. COCA / COCAINE

EXTENT

Cocaine is world-wide the second most common problem drug in the world. It is the main problem drug in the Americas (56%[a] of all treatment demand in the Americas). In several countries of West Europe, cocaine is the second or third most common problem drug, and its importance has grown in recent years.

Cocaine consumption is estimated to affect some 14 million people or 0.3% of the population age 15 and above (estimate for 2000-2001). Most of the increase from the UNODC estimates of 13.4 million (for the 1998-2000 period) took place in West Europe. Most cocaine, nonetheless, continues to be consumed in the Americas (65%), notably in North America (45%). The 3.7 million cocaine abusers of Europe account for about a quarter of the global total of cocaine abuse. More than 90% of Europe's cocaine abusers are in West Europe. In terms of annual prevalence, the overall rate for North America is estimated at around 2% (age 15 and above), compared with about 1% in West Europe, South America and the Oceania region. However, in some of the West European countries (Spain, UK), annual household surveys showed figures which exceed those reported in annual household surveys in the USA. But chronic cocaine use is still significantly larger in the USA than in other countries. In all other regions, cocaine abuse is below the global average of 0.3%. The lowest spread of cocaine abuse is in Asia. Cocaine abuse in Africa is largely linked to spill-overs of cocaine being shipped from South America via Africa to Europe.

Annual prevalence estimates of cocaine abuse: 2000-2001		
	Number of people (in million)	in % of population age 15 and above
AMERICAS	9.08	1.50
- North America	6.35	2.03
- South America	2.74	0.94
OCEANIA	0.23	1.03
EUROPE	3.71	0.57
- West Europe	3.43	1.06
- East Europe	0.29	0.09
AFRICA	0.91	0.20
ASIA	0.15	0.01
GLOBAL	14.08	0.33

Abuse above global average
Abuse close to global average
Abuse below global average

Sources: UNODC, Annual Reports Questionnaire data, various Govt. reports, reports of regional bodies, UNODC estimates.

---

[a] Unweighted average of the proportions of treatment demand reported from 26 countries.

Abuse of cocaine

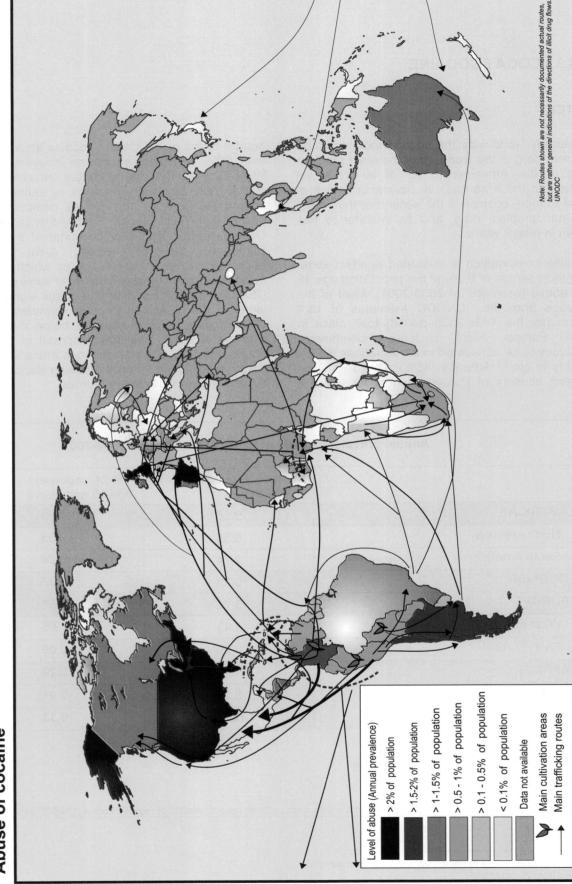

Level of abuse (Annual prevalence)

> 2% of population
> 1.5-2% of population
> 1-1.5% of population
> 0.5 - 1% of population
> 0.1 - 0.5% of population
< 0.1% of population
Data not available

Main cultivation areas
Main trafficking routes

Note: Routes shown are not necessarily documented actual routes, but are rather general indications of the directions of illicit drug flows. UNODC

Note: The boundaries and names shown and the designations used on this map do not imply official endorsement or acceptance by the United Nations.

Importance of cocaine abuse compared to other drugs

In terms of the spread of cocaine abuse as compared to other drugs, most countries in the Americas see cocaine as the second or third most widely abused substance in their own territories. In most countries of West Europe, cocaine is the third most widely consumed drug after cannabis and the ATS. In Spain, it is the second most widespread drug after cannabis. Cocaine is of less importance only in the Nordic countries. It ranks 4 to 6 in most of East Europe, except the Russian Federation where it is even less important. The same applies to a number of Asian countries. In a number of western and southern African countries, its relative importance, compared to other drugs, is significantly higher.

Ranking of cocaine-type substances in order of prevalence in 2001 (or latest year available)

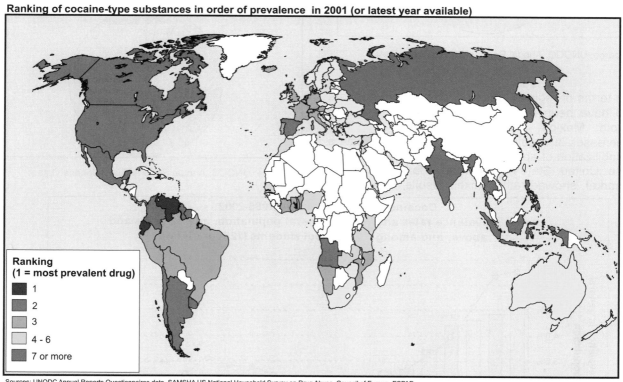

Sources: UNODC Annual Reports Questionnaires data, SAMSHA US National Household Survey on Drug Abuse, Council of Europe, ESPAD.

TRENDS

In 2001 56% of all countries reporting on cocaine trends (N = 61) saw an increase and only 7% reported a decline. As compared to 2000, this seems to reflect some progress because 62% of countries had reported an increase at that time.

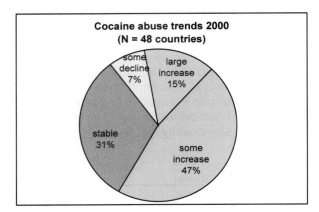

Source: UNODC, Annual Reports Questionnaire Data.

In terms of regional patterns, drug abuse appears to have been basically stable in North America. Both Mexico and Canada, which reported increases in cocaine consumption in 2000, saw a stabilization of abuse levels in 2001. Trends within the United States, the world's largest cocaine market, showed rather mixed results. The annual household survey on drug abuse in the USA, conducted in 2001, found 1.9% of the population age 12 and above to have used cocaine in year prior to the survey[b]. This was an increase as compared to a year earlier but some 25% less than a decade earlier and more than 60% less than in the mid 1980s (5.1% in 1985). According to high-school surveys cocaine abuse was creeping upward over the 1992-1999, but did not continue in subsequent years. High-school surveys found an annual prevalence rate of 5% in 2002, down from 6.2% in 1999 and some 60% less than in the mid 1980s (13.1% in 1985). The overall cocaine abuse trends in the USA can be thus considered to be more or less stable while abuse is at significantly lower levels than in the 1980s.

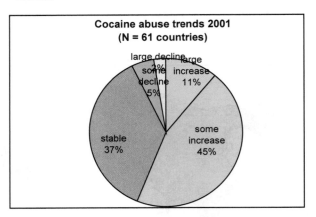

Source: UNODC, Annual Reports Questionnaire Data.

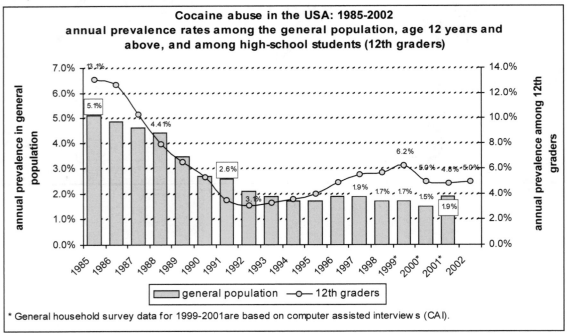

Source: SAMHSA, *National Household Survey on Drug Abuse 2001* and previous years, NIDA, *Monitoring the Future, 2002* and previous years.

---

[b] It should be noted that the overall estimate of cocaine abuse in the USA is still higher, as chronic cocaine users are not usually found in households.

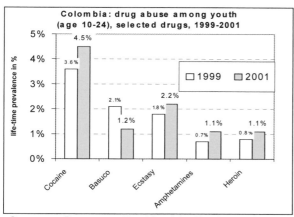

Sources: Programa Presidencial Rumbos, Sondeo Nacional del Consumo de Drogas en Jovenes, 1999-2000 and Programa Presidencial Rumbos, Encuesta Nacional sobre consumo de sustancias psicoactivas en jóvenes de 10 a 24 años, 2001.

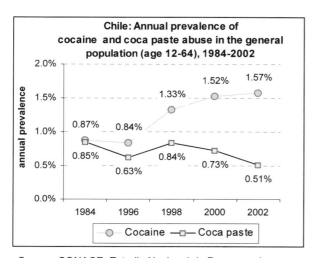

Source: CONACE, Estudio Nacional de Drogas en la Población Nacional de Chile, 2002.

Cocaine abuse trends from countries in South America show a mixed, but not necessarily positive picture. Overall stabilization of cocaine production does not appear – as yet – to have limited the spread of cocaine abuse in the region. There have been stable cocaine abuse trends reported from Chile and Bolivia for 2001, apparently reflecting lower levels of cocaine production in the latter country, as well as from Guyana, Belize and the Bahamas. Increases were reported from Colombia, Venezuela, Surinam, Costa Rica, El Salvador, several countries in the Caribbean, as well from Argentina. Crack-cocaine abuse appears to be spreading more rapidly, notably in the Caribbean and Central America, than the abuse of cocaine. Bazuco, a cocaine-type side-product in the manufacture of cocaine, in contrast, appears to be loosing in popularity, including in Colombia and in Chile.

In Europe, two thirds of all countries reported an increase of cocaine consumption in 2001 while only 8% of the countries reported a decline. The

proportions were largely the same in Western and in Eastern Europe. A number of recently published household surveys in Spain, the UK and the Netherlands confirm this upward trend quite clearly.

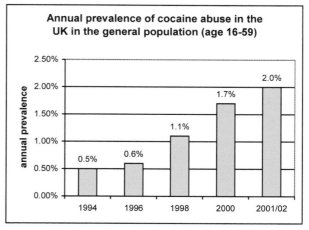

Source: UK Home Office, Results from the British Crime Survey 2001/02 and previous years.

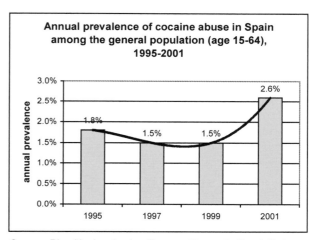

Source: Plan Nacional sobre Drogas, *Encuesta Domiciliaria sobre Consumo de Drogas en Espana, 2001*

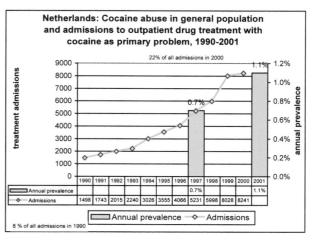

Source: Trimbos Instituut, National Drug Monitor – National Report 2002.

Upward trends in consumption were also reported from France and Luxembourg, from the Nordic countries (Denmark, Norway, Sweden), a number of southern countries (Portugal, Greece and Malta) as well as a number of East European countries (Bulgaria, Serbia & Montenegro, Croatia as well as Slovakia, Poland and Belarus).

Stable or declining levels of cocaine abuse were reported from Germany, Austria, Switzerland and Liechtenstein as well as from the Czech Republic and Hungary. This almost uniform reporting trend of several neighbouring countries in the centre of Europe suggests that supply to this area may not have been as abundant as in previous years. Stable or declining trends were also reported from Turkey, the Ukraine and Latvia.

In Africa, only the Republic of South Africa reported a stable trend for 2001. All other reporting countries (Benin, Gambia, Ghana and Togo from western Africa and Namibia and Zimbabwe from southern Africa) saw a rise. No East African or North-African country reported on trends of cocaine abuse, possibly reflecting the fact that cocaine abuse in Africa is only a problem in the west and south.

For the whole of Asia only 7 countries reported on cocaine abuse trends, reflecting the low prevalence of cocaine abuse in that region. They saw mostly stable or declining levels of abuse. Only India and Saudi Arabia reported an increase. Relatively large cocaine seizures reported by the Syrian authorities in 2001 suggest that a local market could develop in the Near and Middle East.

Changes in abuse of cocaine, 2001 (or latest year available)

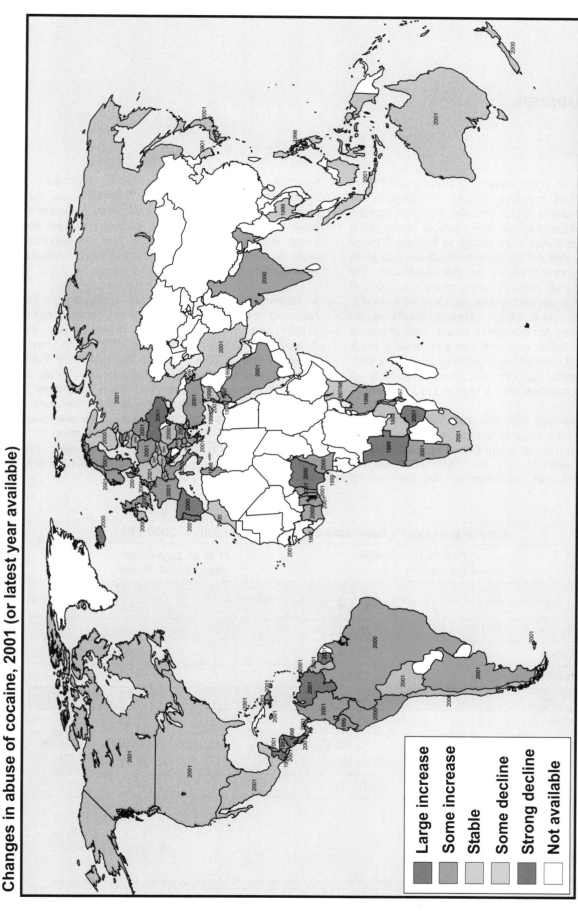

Large increase

Some increase

Stable

Some decline

Strong decline

Not available

Sources: UNODC Annual Reports Questionnaires data, UNODC (Regional Centre Bangkok) Epidemiology Trends in Drug Trends in Asia (Findings of the Asian Multicity Epidemiology Workgroup, December 1999, National Household Surveys submitted to UNODC, United States Department of State (Bureau for International Narcotics and Law Enforcement Affairs) International Narcotics Control Strategy Report, 1999;Bundeskriminalamt (BKA) and other Law Enforcement Reports, SACENDU (South African Community Epidemiology Network July - December 1998,UNODC and Ministerio de Educacion,Estudio Epidemiologico 1999, CEDRO, Epidemiologia de Drogas en la poblacion urbana Peruana - 1995, INCB, Annual Report for 1999.

1.3.4. CANNABIS

EXTENT

Cannabis is the most widely consumed illicit drug worldwide. The number of patients treated for cannabis abuse is much smaller than for opiates or cocaine. Nonetheless, the number is far from negligible and it has been rising. In Europe 13% of patients are treated for cannabis abuse (up from 10% in the mid 1990s); in the Americas the proportion is 23%, and in Africa more than 60% of all treatment is cannabis related. Only in Asia it is comparatively low (8%). The proportions of patients treated for cannabis abuse has shown a clear upward trend in recent years in several parts of the world, reflecting growing consumption, almost unlimited supply and the availability of more potent varieties with a higher THC content.

UNODC estimates that about 163 million people or 3.9% of those 15 and above, abused cannabis in 2000/2001. This is a significant increase on the 147 million estimate for the 1998-2000 period. There was a net increase in the number of cannabis abusers in recent years, as reflected in a number of surveys, but that is definitely less than indicated by the data above. As more countries have started to report on substance abuse, the initial estimates (probably on the conservative side) are being replaced by actual study results, thus leading to overall higher numbers.

In terms of average annual prevalence, the reported rates are highest in the Oceania region (17%) and in Africa (8.6%), followed by the Americas (6.1%) and Europe (5.2%). In North America and in West Europe the rates are 7.5% and 7.2% respectively. Relatively low levels of cannabis abuse are reported from countries in Asia (2.2%). Nonetheless, the largest numbers – in absolute terms – of cannabis abusers are found in Asia (some 55 million people), accounting for a third of all cannabis abusers worldwide. The Americas account for 22% of all cannabis abusers and Africa for about 20%.

Annual prevalence estimates of abuse of cannabis: 2000-2001		
	Number of people (in million)	in % of population age 15 and above
OCEANIA	3.93	16.89
AFRICA	33.21	8.60
AMERICAS	36.70	6.10
- North America	23.54	7.53
- South America	13.16	4.56
EUROPE	34.09	5.20
- West Europe	23.21	7.16
- East Europe	10.88	3.29
ASIA	54.88	2.17
GLOBAL	162.81	3.88

Abuse above global average

Abuse close to global average

Abuse below global average

Sources: UNODC, Annual Reports Questionnaire data, various Govt. reports, reports of regional bodies, UNODC estimates.

Abuse of Cannabis

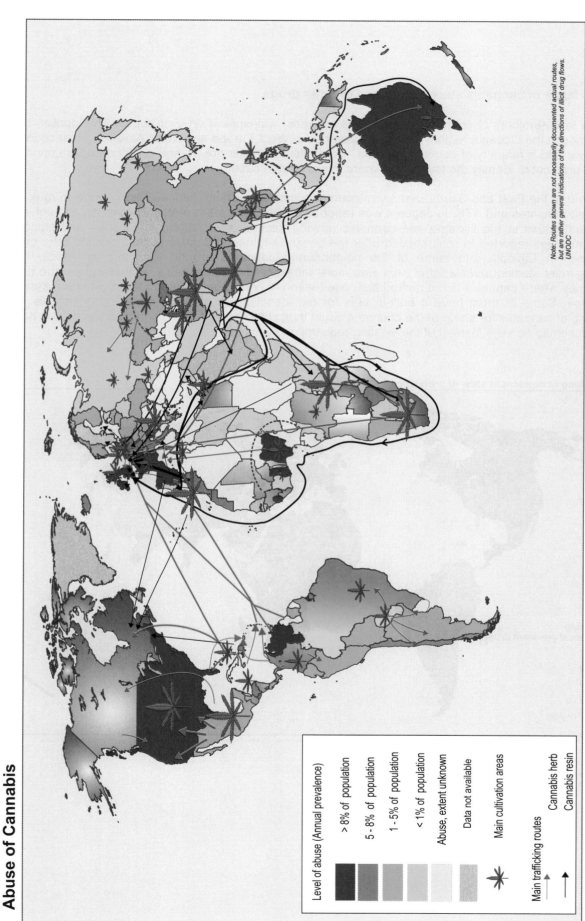

Note: Routes shown are not necessarily documented actual routes, but are rather general indications of the directions of illicit drug flows.
UNODC

Level of abuse (Annual prevalence)

- > 8% of population
- 5 - 8% of population
- 1 - 5% of population
- < 1% of population
- Abuse, extent unknown
- Data not available
- Main cultivation areas

Main trafficking routes

Cannabis herb
Cannabis resin

Note: The boundaries and names shown and the designations used on this map do not imply official endorsement or acceptance by the United Nations.

Importance of cannabis abuse compared to other drugs

In the large majority of countries, cannabis is the most widespread drug of abuse. This applies to all countries in the Oceania region, almost all countries in West Europe and North America, most countries in Africa and a majority of countries in Asia. The difficulty is thus not to find countries where cannabis ranks first, but to identify the few cases where this is not the case.

In some of the East and South East Asian countries, including China, cannabis is reported to rank only third after opiates and ATS. In Japan it was reported to rank third after methamphetamine and solvents. The authorities in the Ukraine see cannabis ranking second after opium. In Sweden and Hungary, cannabis was reported to rank second after the benzodizepines and in Venezuela second after crack-cocaine. In Ethiopia and some of the neighbouring countries around the Horn of Africa, rapid assessment studies revealed that Khat was more widespread than cannabis. However, in some of the countries where cannabis is not ranked first, one reason may also be related to the registration systems in place. Some of them have a built-in bias for the identification of drugs other than cannabis. The ranking of cannabis for some of the countries could thus still change if the information were to be based on household surveys instead of the existing registration systems.

Ranking of cannabis in order of prevalence in 2001

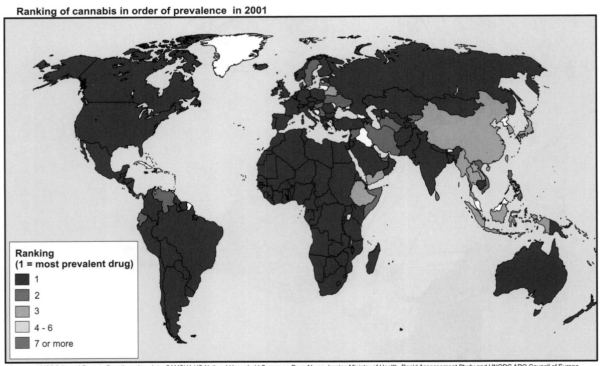

Ranking
(1 = most prevalent drug)
1
2
3
4 - 6
7 or more

Sources: UNODC Annual Reports Questionnaires data, SAMSHA US National Household Survey on Drug Abuse, Iranian Ministry of Health, Rapid Assessement Study and UNODC ARQ,Council of Europe,

TRENDS

In total 53% of all countries reporting on cannabis abuse trends in 2001 (N = 92 countries), saw an increase while 14% reported a decline. In 2000, 77% of the countries providing such information reported an increase and only 8% a decline, suggesting that in relative terms, at least, the spread of cannabis abuse may have weakened in 2001.

In all regions, the countries that reported increasing cannabis abuse exceeded those reporting. The largest proportion of countries reporting increases is found in Africa (64%), followed by the Americas (59%). Europe (51%) is close to the global average while the number of countries reporting increases in Asia (36%) is

clearly below the global average. Asia also has the largest number of countries reporting declines in cannabis abuse (21%).

Reported increases in cannabis use were particularly widespread in Africa, Latin America, West and East Europe, as well as in Turkey, Iran, Pakistan and India. The Iranian authorities reported that part of the increase was due to increased efforts by Afghan opium traders to substitute opium with cannabis in 2001.

In contrast, cannabis use in North America remained stable at high levels and was reported to have declined significantly in Australia between 1998 and 2001.

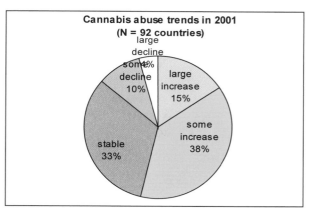

Source: UNODC, Annual Reports Questionnaire Data.   Source: UNODC, Annual Reports Questionnaire Data.

Changes in abuse of cannabis, 2001 (or latest year available)

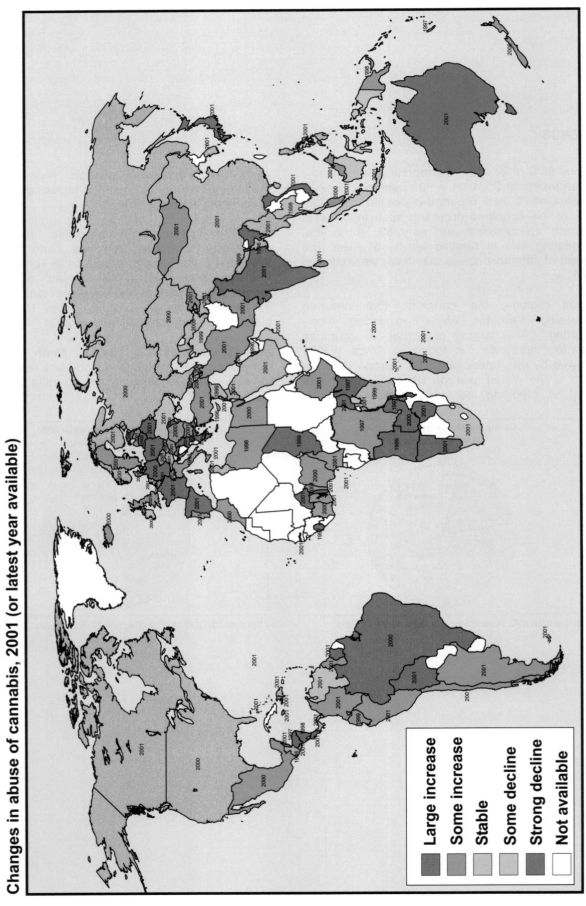

Legend:
- Large increase
- Some increase
- Stable
- Some decline
- Strong decline
- Not available

Note: The boundaries and names shown and the designations used on this map do not imply official endorsement or acceptance by the United Nations.

1.3.5. AMPHETAMINE-TYPE STIMULANTS

Amphetamine-type stimulants (ATS), i.e. mainly "amphetamines" (amphetamine/methamphetamine) and "ecstasy" (MDMA; related products such as MDA and MDME, grouped together with MDMA under the heading of "ecstasy-group substances") are chemically and partly also pharmacologically related, and consumed by similar user populations in several countries.

The typical 'profiles' of different amphetamine-type stimulants are, however, different. In addition to the recreational use of both amphetamine and MDMA, a number of countries suffer from a serious methamphetamine problem, and related issues of violence, serious health degradation and treatment demand. Methamhetamine is in general more potent than amphetamine and thus causes more serious health problems and problems of drug related violence.

Extent

Amphetamines

Amphetamines (ATS excluding ecstasy) account, on average, for some 10% of treatment demand at the global level. The highest proportion of treatment demand for ATS abuse is found in Asia (18%), ahead of Australia (14%), Europe (11%), Africa (8%) and the Americas (5%), including 9½ % in the USA. In a number of countries in East and South-East Asia, particularly Thailand, the Philippines, Japan, the Republic of Korea (and to a lesser extent in Taiwan Province of China), amphetamines, notably methamphetamine, are already the main problem drugs and play a similar role as opiates in Europe or cocaine in the Americas. In parallel, a strong spread of recreational use of amphetamines took place in a large number of countries in the 1990s.

Abuse of amphetamines is estimated to affect some 34 million people or 0.8% of the global population age 15 and above over the 2000-2001 period. In addition, some 8 million people are estimated to take ecstasy. Abuse of amphetamine-type stimulants is thus at a higher level than abuse of opiates (15 million people, or 0.3%) or cocaine (14 million people, or 0.3%), though less than consumption of cannabis (163 million people or 3.9%) over the 2000-2001 period.

Though rates differ significantly from country to country, the regional averages are rather close to the global average. About two thirds of the abusers of amphetamines are found in Asia, in East and South-East Asia. The Americas and Europe together account for a quarter of global abuse of amphetamines.

Relatively high levels of ATS consumption also continue being reported from countries in South America and in Africa. While supply of amphetamines in North America, Europe and Asia is largely from clandestine manufacture, supply in South America and Africa is still mainly from licit channels where the dividing line between licit and illicit consumption is not always clear. There are indications that in a number of countries in South America abuse of licit ATS has been curtailed significantly in recent years. However, there is cause for concern that this curtailed supply could be replaced by illicitly manufactured ATS.

Substances differ as well. While in Europe amphetamine is the ATS of choice, in South-East Asia and North America it is methamphetamine, which is generally more potent and carries more health risks than amphetamine.

Abuse of Amphetamine-type stimulants

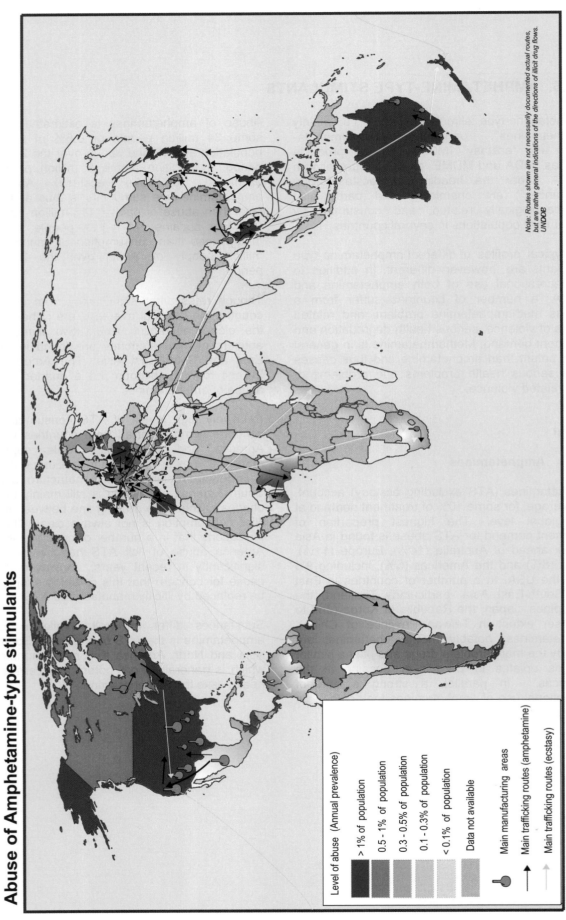

Note: Routes shown are not necessarily documented actual routes,
but are rather general indications of the directions of illicit drug flows.
UNDCP

Level of abuse (Annual prevalence)

- > 1% of population
- 0.5 - 1% of population
- 0.3 - 0.5% of population
- 0.1 - 0.3% of population
- < 0.1% of population
- Data not available

- Main manufacturing areas
- → Main trafficking routes (amphetamine)
- → Main trafficking routes (ecstasy)

The boundaries and names shown and the designations used on this map do not imply official endorsement or acceptance by the United Nations.

<u>Note</u>: The boundaries and names shown and the designations used on this map do not imply official endorsement or acceptance by the United Nations.

Annual prevalence estimates of abuse of amphetamines: 2000-2001		
	Number of people (in million)	in % of population age 15 and above
OCEANIA	0.62	2.78
EUROPE	3.31	0.51
- West Europe	2.25	0.50
- East Europe	2.4	0.50
AMERICAS	5.6	0.93
- North America	2.56	0.82
- South America	3.04	1.04
AFRICA	2.25	0.50
ASIA	22.5	0.89
GLOBAL	34.28	0.81

▨ Abuse above global average

☐ Abuse close to global average

▨ Abuse below global average

Sources: UNODC, Annual Reports Questionnaire data, various Govt. reports, reports of regional bodies, UNODC estimates.

Ecstasy

About 0.2% of the global population (age 15 and above) consume ecstasy. Rates significantly above the global average have been reported from countries in Oceania, West Europe and North America. Some 40% of global consumption is concentrated in Europe and, following strong growth rates in recent years, almost 50% in North America. West Europe and North America together account for around 90% of global abuse. Ecstasy abuse, however, is spreading to East Europe as well as to developing countries, notably in the Americas, southern Africa, the Near and Middle East as well as South-East Asia. A number of school surveys in countries outside West Europe, North America and Oceania confirm the increasing importance of ecstasy as a drug of choice among youth.

Annual prevalence estimates of abuse of ecstasy: 2000-2001		
	Number of people (in million)	in % of population age 15 and above
OCEANIA	0.56	2.15
EUROPE	3.25	0.50
- West Europe	2.91	0.78
- East Europe	0.35	0.13
AMERICAS	3.73	0.64
- North America	3.46	1.11
- South America	0.31	0.12
AFRICA	0.01	0.002
ASIA	0.14	0.01
GLOBAL	7.74	0.18

▨ Abuse above global average

☐ Abuse close to global average

▨ Abuse below global average

Sources: UNODC, Annual Reports Questionnaire data, various Govt. reports, reports of regional bodies, UNODC estimates.

Importance of ATS abuse compared to other drugs

The relative importance of ATS abuse (including ecstasy) is strongest in the East and South-East Asia and in Australia, being ranked there as either first or second drugs of choice.

Amphetamine and ecstasy are ranked as the second most widespread drug in several countries of West Europe, including the UK, Ireland, Germany, Switzerland, Austria, Belgium and Iceland; in the Nordic countries, they are ranked third.

In East Europe, the United States and some countries of South America and Africa, ATS are ranked as the third most widespread drugs of abuse.

Ranking of amphetamine-type stimulants in order of prevalence in 2001 (or latest year available)

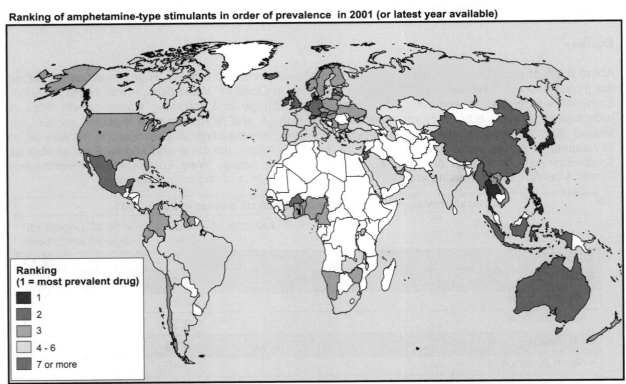

Sources: UNODC Annual Reports Questionnaires data, National Household Surveys on Drug Abuse, UNODC Rapid Assessement Studies, Council of Europe, ESPAD.

TRENDS

The number of countries reporting on trends in ATS abuse tripled between 1992 and 2001, reflecting the rising importance of ATS across countries. A majority of the countries reporting on ATS trends saw an increase in abuse levels over the 1992-2001 period. If the number of countries reporting increases less those reporting decreases in ATS are plotted, the trend line goes clearly upwards.

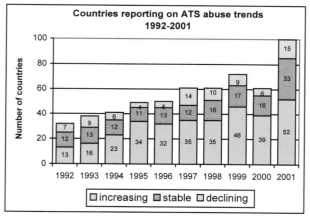

Source: UNODC, Annual Reports Questionnaire Data.

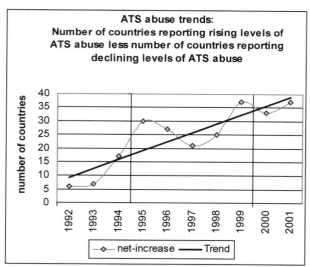

Source: UNODC, Annual Reports Questionnaire Data.

The upward trend is also reflected in UNODC estimates on the number of ATS abusers. The total number of abusers of amphetamines increased by about 40%; the total number of ecstasy abusers rose by about 70% if UNODC estimates for the 1995-1997 period are compared with those for the 2000-2001 period. The rise in ATS consumption was thus the strongest such increase among all major drug categories. For comparison, the estimated number of cannabis abusers increased by 13%, the number of opiate

abusers by 10% and the number of cocaine abusers remained basically stable.

However, there are also indications that the strongest growth rates actually happend in the mid-1990s and that growth in ATS abuse has lost momentum more recently. In 1995, 27% of all countries reporting on ATS trends saw a strong increase; by 2001 this proportion declined to 18%. Overall 73% of the countries reporting on ATS trends saw an increase in 1995; by 2001 this proportion fell to 57%. In parallel the number of countries reporting declines in ATS abuse rose from 7% in 1995 to 14% in 2001.

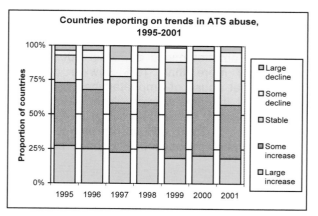

Source: UNODC, Annual Reports Questionnaire Data.

The new Annual Reports Questionnaire allows for a clearer distinction between amphetamine, methamphetamine and the substances of the ecstasy group. If abuse trends among the individual substances are analyzed, data show that the strongest increase was reported for ecstasy: of the countries reporting on ecstasy trends, 63% reported an increase in 2001. In the case of methamphetamine the proportion of countries reporting an increase was 55% and in the case of amphetamine it was 52%.

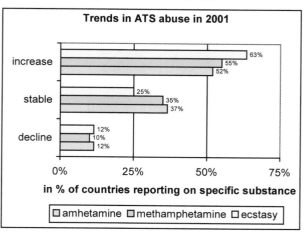

Source: UNODC, Annual Reports Questionnaire Data.

If the proportions are calculated on the basis of all countries reporting on drug abuse trends (reporting on any drug), then half the countries showed increasing levels of 'amphetamines' (amphetamine and methamphetamine) abuse in 2001; 36% of all countries showed increasing levels of ecstasy abuse.

'Amphetamines' abuse trends

For the purposes of this section, amphetamine and methamphetamine are combined, and dealt with under the heading of 'amphetamines' (ATS excluding ecstasy). The subsequent section will then deal with ecstasy abuse.

More than half of all countries (55%) reported an increase in amphetamines abuse in 2001 while only slightly more than 10% saw a decline, indicating that abuse of amphetamines continues to spread at the global level. Nonetheless, the situation appears to be improving, at least in relative terms. In 2000, 68% of replying countries reported amphetamines abuse to have been on the rise.

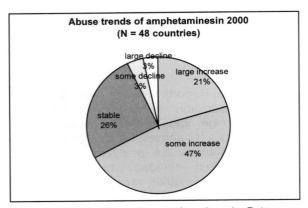

Source: UNODC, Annual Reports Questionnaire Data.

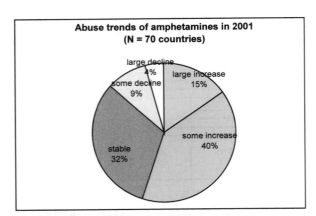

Source: UNODC, Annual Reports Questionnaire Data.

Most countries reporting on amphetamines trends in 2001 were located in Europe, in the Americas and in Asia. In almost all continents, more countries reported increases than decreases in the abuse of amphetamines, except for the Oceania.

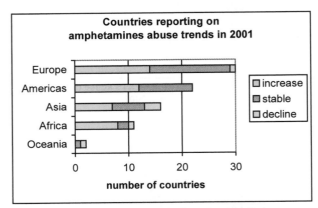

Source: UNODC, Annual Reports Questionnaire Data.

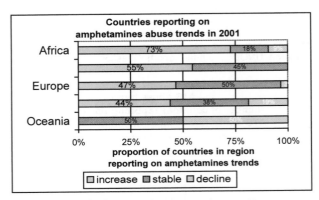

Source: UNODC, Annual Reports Questionnaire Data.

The proportions of countries reporting increases for 2001 were above the global average in Africa (73% of the counties reporting on amphetamines' trends). Strong increases for 2001 among African countries were reported by Burkina Faso, by Namibia and Zimbabwe. Only Madagaskar reported a decline. The proportions of countries reporting increases in the Americas were at about the global average (55%); in Europe (47%) and Asia (44%) they were slightly below average in 2001.

Asia and the Pacific

In 2001, more than 70% of the countries in Asia reporting on amphetamines abuse trends were located in the East and South-East Asia subregion, known to have the highest levels of amphetamines abuse in the world. Large increases in the consumption of methamphetamine were reported from China, and some increases were reported from Myanmar, the Philippines, the Republic of Korea and Vietnam. Authorities in Indonesia saw a decline.

Some of the strongest increases in recent years were reported from *Thailand*. Estimates provided by the authorities suggest that the number of methamphetamine abusers rose 10-fold between 1993 and 2001. Thailand also reported the highest methamphetamine prevalence rate worldwide (2½ million people[a] or 5.6% of the population age 15-64, though some estimates reported in the press go up to 3 million people[b]) as well as the world's highest methamphetamine seizures in 2001. The proportion of people admitted to treatment for abusing methamphetamine rose from 2.1% in 1995 to 50.5% in 2001 (Out of 39,931 admissions for treatment of substance abuse, 20,157 patients consumed methamphetamine in 2001).

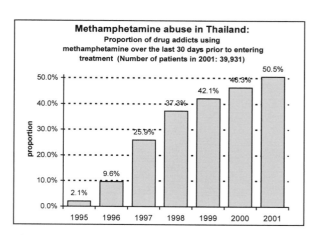

Methamphetamine abuse in Thailand:
Proportion of drug addicts using methamphetamine over the last 30 days prior to entering treatment (Number of patients in 2001: 39,931)

Source: ONCB, *Thailand Narcotics Annual Report 2002* and previous years

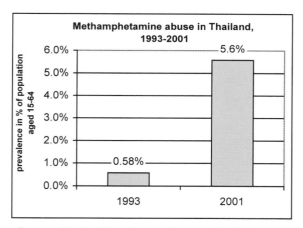

Methamphetamine abuse in Thailand, 1993-2001

Sources: Thailand Development Research Institute, 1995 and ONCB, Thailand Narcotics Annual Report 2002.

---

[a] The number of all drug abusers was estimated at 2.65 million people, 90% among them were methamphetamine abusers (derived from the number of drug addicts who applied for treatment in 2001. (Office of the Narcotics Control Board, Thailand Narcotics Annual Report 2002, p. 9.)

[b] On the other hand, the Thai authorities also published preliminary results of a household survey, conducted in 2001, which showed significantly lower levels of methamphetamine abuse. According to this survey, 1,092,500 people used Ya-ba (methamphetamine tablets) within the last year, equivalent to 2.4% of the population age 12-65. (ONCB in collaboration of Assumption University, Chiang Mai University, Chulalongkorn University, Khon Kaen University, Rajapat Institute Pibulsongkram, Rajapat Instittue Uttaradit and Songkhla University, "Preliminary Report of Estimation of Population

Another major market for methamphetamine in South-East Asia is the *Philippines*. Various estimates suggest that drug abuse, in general, and abuse of methamphetamine, in particular, increased over the last decades, from negligible levels in the 1970s and still relatively low levels in the 1980s, to high levels in the 1990s. Estimates on the number methamphetamine users in the Phillippines, cited in various reports, range from 500,000 people (1.1% of the population age 15-64, a conservative estimate provided by the National Drug Law Enforcement and Prevention Center for the late 1990s) to 1.8 milllion people (4% of the population age 15-64), cited in various press reports. According to the US *International Narcotics Control Strategy Report 2002*, the figure of 1.8 million people reflects estimates provided by the Government of the Philippines referring to the overall level of drug abuse in the Philippines in 2001/2002. Based on the number of people in treatment and other indicators (seizures, arrests), it can be estimated that 70% to 90% of drug abuse in the Philippines is related to abuse of methamphetamine. (The proportion of treatment admissions for abuse of methamphetamine is significantly higher in Thailand). Youth surveys, conducted in the mid 1990s and again in 1997/98, found an increase in life-time prevalence from 7% (1.4 million) to 10% (2.1 million) of those aged 15-30. Based on all this information, UNODC estimates that about 1.3 million people or 2.8% of the population age 15-64 may be using methamphetamine in the Philippines.

Japan is another important East Asian market for methamphetamine. Japan was the first country in East Asia affected by methamphetamine abuse epidemics, first in the early 1950s, then in the

---

Related with Substance Abuse", quoted in ONCP, *Thailand Country Report*, February 2003.)

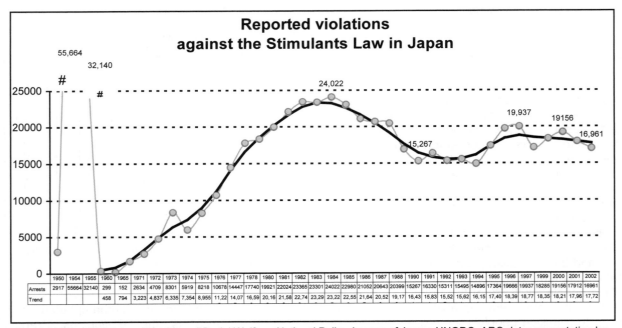

Reported violations against the Stimulants Law in Japan

	1950	1954	1955	1960	1965	1971	1972	1973	1974	1975	1976	1977	1978	1980	1981	1982	1983	1984	1985	1986	1987	1988	1990	1991	1992	1993	1994	1995	1996	1997	1999	2000	2001	2002
Arrests	2917	55664	32140	299	152	2634	4709	8301	5919	8218	10678	14447	17740	19921	22024	23365	23301	24022	22980	21052	20643	20399	15267	16330	15311	15495	14896	17364	19666	19937	18285	19156	17912	16961
Trend				458	794	3,223	4,837	6,335	7,354	8,955	11,22	14,07	16,59	20,16	21,58	22,74	23,29	23,22	22,55	21,64	20,52	19,17	16,43	15,83	15,52	15,62	16,15	17,40	18,39	18,77	18,35	18,21	17,96	17,72

Sources: Japan, Ministry of Health and Social Welfare; National Policy Agency of Japan; UNODC, ARQ data; presentation by the Japanese delegation to the Commission on Narcotic Drugs, April 2003.

1970s and early 1980s, and again in the second half of the 1990s. However, over the last few years methamphetamine abuse appears to have been stabilizing or even declining in Japan. Both prevalence surveys undertaken by the Japanese Ministry of Health, and arrest and seizure statistics collected by the police, point in this direction.

Overall prevalence estimates, however, differ substantially depending on the source, ranging from 260,000 persons or 0.3% of the population age 15-64 (Japanese Ministry of Health) to 2.8 million or 3.2% of the population age 15-64, based on other official estimates cited in the US *International Narcotics Control Strategy Report* for the year 2002. According the latter estimates, the number of methamphetamine addicts is around 600,000; the number of casual users amounts about 2.18 million. UNODC's estimate, the average of these and other estimates received from Japanese Government sources over the 2000-2002 period, amounts to about 1½ million people or 1.7% of those age 15-64.

Australia is also an important market for ATS, notably methamphetamine. According to national household survey data, 3.4% of the population age 14 and above or 4% of the population age 15-64 abused amphetamines (methamphetamine and/or amphetamine) in 2001, the second highest rate worldwide after Thailand (or the largest rate if only estimates from household surveys are used). However, the national household survey data also show that the strong upward trend, reported over the 1995-1998 period, did not continue in

subsequent years, but gave way to a period of stabilization. The DUMA surveys ('Drug Use Monitoring in Australia' testing police detainees for drug consumption based on urine analysis) showed that in the course of 2001 amphetamines abuse increased for a short period of time - reflecting substitution effects resulting from the heroin shortage in 2001[c], before declining again in 2002.

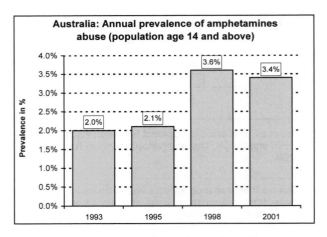

Sources: UNODC, Annual Reports Questionnaire Data, Australian Institute for Health and Welfare, 1998 National Drug Strategy Household Survey, August 1999 and previous years.

---

[c] The decline in heroin abuse in 2001 was, however, far more pronounced than the temporary increase in the use of amphetamines.

Americas

In South America, Argentina and Bolivia reported rising amphetamine abuse levels. In most other countries, including Colombia and Venezuela and Panama, abuse levels were stable. In North America, an increase in amphetamines consumption was found in the USA and Mexico while Canada saw basically stable abuse levels.

Overall abuse of stimulants showed a slight upward trend in the USA in the 1990s (from an annual prevalence rate of 0.7% of the general population (age 12 and above) in 1992 to 1.1% in 2001. This followed a period of strong decline over the 1985-1992 period (from 2.9% to 0.7%).

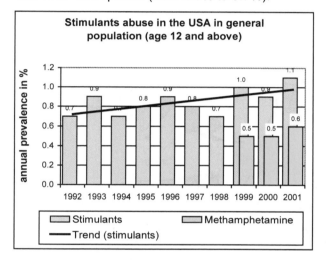

Source: SAMHSA, US Household Survey on Drug Abuse, 2001 and previous years.

Embedded in the overall increase of stimulants use has been a trend of rising levels of

methamphetamine abuse. Life-time prevalence of methamphetamine abuse more than doubled, from 1.8% in 1994 to 4.3% in 2001. About half of all stimulants consumption in the USA is now already related to methamphetamine abuse (measured by annual prevalence).

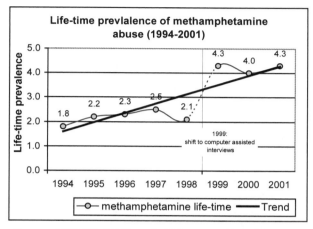

Source: SAMHSA, US Household Survey on Drug Abuse, 2001 and previous years.

Rising levels of methamphetamine abuse were also reflected in treatment demand. The overall treatment admission rate for primary amphetamine/methamphetamine abuse rose from 10 admissions per 100,000 population aged 12 and above in 1992 to 36 per 100,000 in 2000. Excluding alcohol, methamphetamine accounted for 2.3% of all admissions for drug abuse treatment in 1992 and 7.5% in 2000; including amphetamine the proportion rose from 3.5% in 1992 to 9.5% in 2000. About 80% of all ATS related treatment demand is due to abuse of methamphetamine.

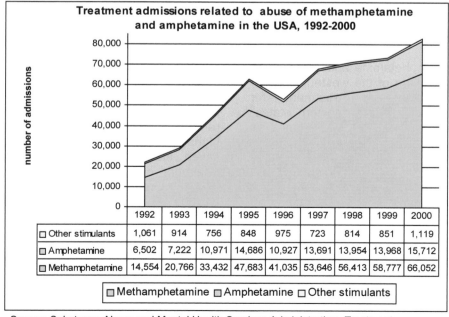

Source: Substance Abuse and Mental Health Services Administration, *Treatment Episode Data Set (TEDS) 1992-2000* , December 2002.

Another trend over the last decade has been the spread of methamphetamine abuse from the Pacific States into the rest of the United States.

USA: primary methamphetamine/amphetamine admissions rates for treatment by state per 100,000 population age 12 and above, 1992-2000

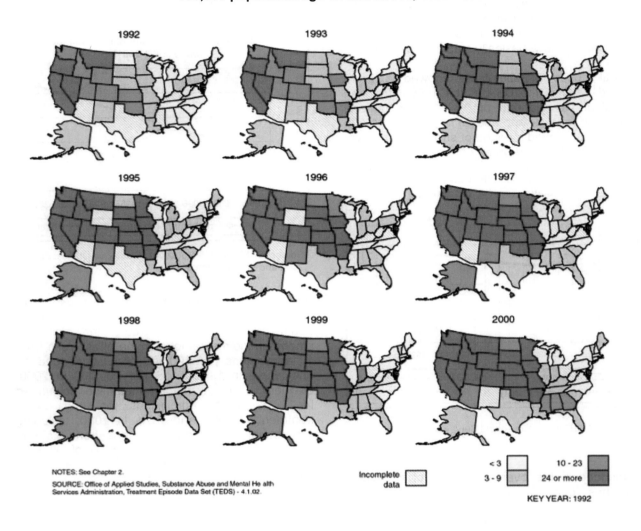

NOTES: See Chapter 2.
SOURCE: Office of Applied Studies, Substance Abuse and Mental He alth Services Administration, Treatment Episode Data Set (TEDS) - 4.1.02.

Incomplete data

< 3   10 - 23
3 - 9   24 or more

KEY YEAR: 1992

Nonetheless, methamphetamine abuse continues to be primarily a problem of the western parts of the USA. Admissions to treatment for methamphetamine abuse in the western states[d] was in 2000, on average, about three times as high as the national average. By far the largest abuser population requiring treatment was reported from California, accounting for 40% of all methamphetamine treatment demand in the USA in 2000. Most of the production of methamphetamine in the USA, as reflected in the dismantling of clandestine laboratories, was also reported to take place in California. California's treatment admissions of 125 per 100,000 population age 12 and above, were 3½ times the national average (36). The treatment admission rates on a per 100,000 population basis are even higher in a number of other western states. Of the seven states reporting the highest levels of treatment demand in 2000, six were western states - Oregon (267), Utah (197), Hawaii (178), Nevada (153), Washington (141) and California (125) - and one was a mid-western state (Iowa). Overall treatment demand in the mid-western[e]

[d] Western States: a) Mountain states (Idaho, Nevada, Arizona, New Mexico, Utah, Colorado, Wyoming, Montana) and the b) Pacific states (California, Oregon, Washington, Hawaii, Alaska) as defined in the US National Household Survey on Drug Abuse.

[e] Mid-Western States: East-North Central Division (Wisconsin, Illinois, Michigan, Indiana, Ohio) and the West North Central Division (North Dakota, South Dakota, Nebraska, Kansas, Minnesota, Iowa, Missouri).

states was at about the national average. In the southern states[f], treatment demand, though rising, continues to be below the national average. The lowest spread of methamphetamine abuse and treatment demand is in the eastern states[g]. They continue to have the highest heroin and cocaine abuse levels and thus the highest treatment demand for those drugs.

If high-school data are analyzed, the overall trends – at first sight - appear to be less problematic. Though average high-school consumption of amphetamines increased in the early 1990s, it stabilized, or even fell since 1996/97, including in 2002. Nonetheless, amphetamines use levels among high-school students in the USA are still more than five times as widespread as in Europe, measured by life-time prevalence among 10th graders (15-16 year olds). Even the European countries with the highest levels of amphetamines abuse (UK in Western Europe and Poland and Estonia in Eastern Europe) still show significantly lower levels of amphetamines use among high-school students than the USA (about half the US figures).

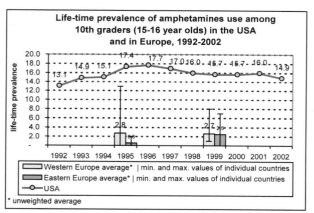

Sources: NIDA, Monitoring the Future 2002 and previous years, Council of Europe, *The 1995 ESPAD Report – the European School Survey Project on Alcohol and Other Drugs*, Stockholm 1997 and on Council of Europe *The 1999 ESPAD Report. – the European School Survey Project on Alcohol and Other Drugs – Alcohol and other Drug Use Among Students in 30 European countries*, Stockholm December 2000 and national youth surveys conducted in Spain, Germany and the Netherlands.

Comparable school surveys are also available from some provinces of neighbouring *Canada*. Probably the most representative surveys for

Canada as a whole are those conducted in the province of Ontario which accounts for a third of Canada's total population. The basic patterns observed among high-school students in Ontario have been similar to those in the USA. Between 1999 and 2001 data for Ontario indicate a significant decline for amphetamines consumption in general, including methamphetamine abuse. Overall abuse of amphetamines in the general population was considered by the Canadian authorities to have remained stable in 2001.

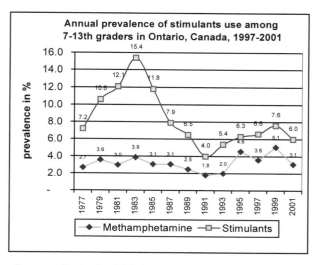

Sources: Centre for Addiction and Mental Health, *Drug Use among Ontario Students 1977-2001*, Toronto, 2001.

Europe

Countries of Eastern Europe reported ongoing increases in amphetamine abuse for 2001. In Western Europe, by contrast, the predominant trend reported by member states to UNODC in 2001 was towards stabilization, or even decline.

In the *United Kingdom*, which used to be Europe's largest market for amphetamine, prevalence rates increased strongly until 1996, but showed a downward trend thereafter. Prevalence rates fell over the 1996-98 period, declined strongly over the 1998-2000 period, and – though more moderately – continued falling over the 2000-2002 period. Over the 1996-2002 period, amphetamine use fell by 45% in the UK. However, the decline in the use of amphetamine went hand in hand with an increase in ecstasy abuse and an increase in cocaine abuse. In 2001/2002 abuse of amphetamine was – for the first time ever – lower than ecstasy or cocaine abuse in the UK.

---

[f] Southern States: South-Atlantic Division (West Virginia, Virginia, Maryland, Delaware, District of Columbia, North Carolina, South Carolina, Georgia, Florida) and East-South Central Division (Mississippi, Tennessee, Kentucky, Alabama).
[g] Eastern States: New England Division (Maine, New Hampshire, Vermont, Massuchusetts, Rhode Island, Connecticut) and Middle Atlantic Division (New York, New Jersey, Pennsylvania).

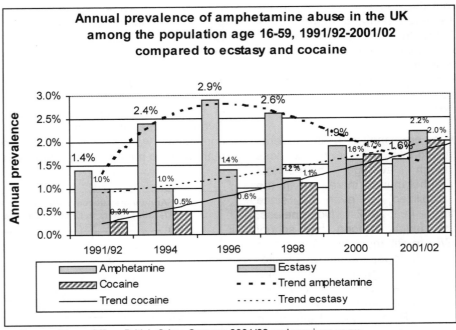

Annual prevalence of amphetamine abuse in the UK among the population age 16-59, 1991/92-2001/02 compared to ecstasy and cocaine

Source: Home Office, British Crime Surveys 2001/02 and previous years.

In *Germany*, annual prevalence of amphetamine abuse increased strongly in the early 1990s and less strongly, over the 1997-2000 period. The number of first time registered amphetamine users, reached a peak in 1998, and remained basically stable over the next few years.

The highest per capita arrests for the possession/consumption of amphetamine were reported from the province of Rheinland-Pfalz bordering Belgium, followed by neighbouring Saarland and, more towards the east, by Bavaria and Sachsen (as well as Thüringen), the

provinces bordering (or close to) the Czech Republic. Thus annual prevalence of amphetamine abuse in the 'new provinces' (former East Germany) was almost as high (0.5% of those age 18-59) as in the 'old provinces' (0.6%) in 2001 while overall drug abuse is still higher in the old provinces than in the new provinces.

In *Sweden*, one of the first countries in Europe affected by an amphetamine epidemic, surveys undertaken among military recruits found declining levels of amphetamine abuse in the 1970s and in

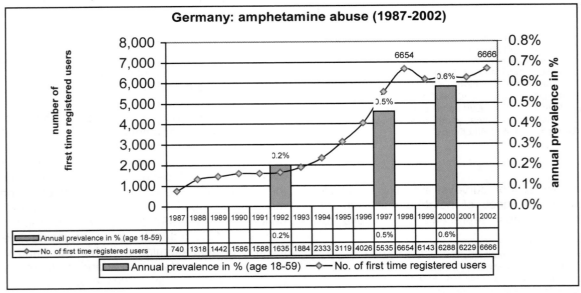

Germany: amphetamine abuse (1987-2002)

Sources: UNODC, Annual Reports Questionnaire Data, *Bundesministerium für Gesundheit, Repräsentativeerhebung 1997,* L. Kraus and R. Augustin, Repräsentativerhebung zum Gebrauch psychoaktiver Substanzen bei Erwachsenen in Deutschland 2000, Sucht, Sonderheft 1, Sept. 2001, and Bundeskriminalamt, Rauschgiftjahresbericht 2001 Bundesrepublik Deutschland, June 2002 and BKA,.*Daten zur Rauschgiftkriminalität in der Bundesrepublik Deutschland 2002.*

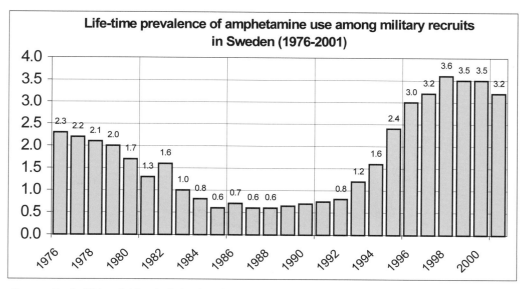

Life-time prevalence of amphetamine use among military recruits in Sweden (1976-2001)

Source: Centralförbundet för alcohol och narkotikaupplysning, Drogutvecklingen I Sverige – Rapport 2002, Trends in Alcohol and other Drugs in Sweden, Report 2002.

the 1980s, followed by strong increases in the early 1990s. However, a peak was reached in 1998. Since then the trend has been towards stabilization / decline.

In *Italy*, life-time prevalence of amphetamine abuse among those aged 15-19 also showed increases in the early 1990s, but declined over the 1999-2001 period. Similarly, data on drug users identified in military service, showed an increase in amphetamine abuse until 1998 and a decline/stabilization thereafter.

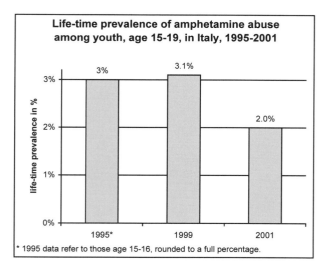

Life-time prevalence of amphetamine abuse among youth, age 15-19, in Italy, 1995-2001

* 1995 data refer to those age 15-16, rounded to a full percentage.

Sources: Council of Europe, The 1995 ESPAD report and 1999 and 2001 ESPAD Italy surveys, quoted in Ministerio del Lavoro e della Politiche Sociali, Relazione Nazionale al OEDT sullo Stato delle Tossicodipendenze in Italia in 2001.

Changes in abuse of amphetamine-type stimulants (excluding ecstasy), 2001 (or latest year available)

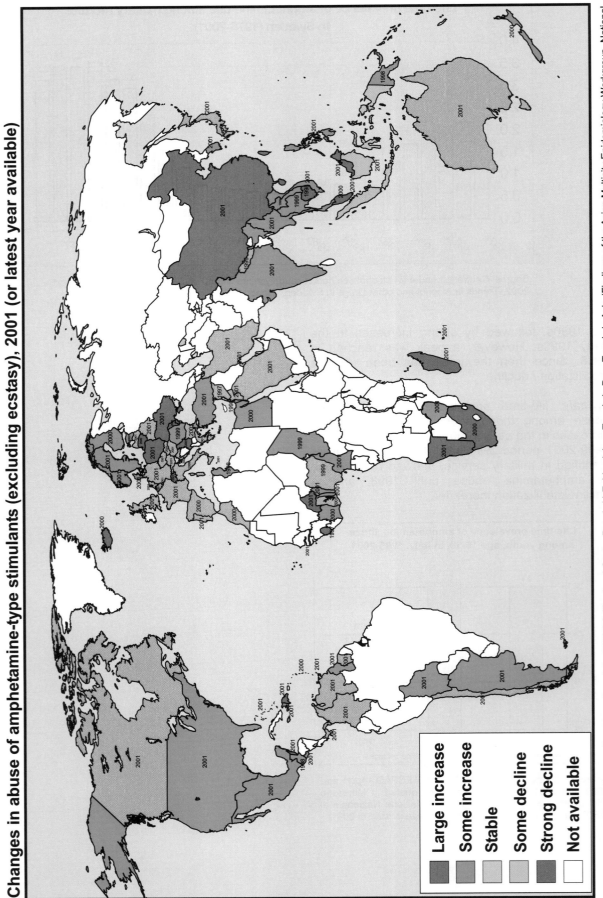

Legend:
- Large increase
- Some increase
- Stable
- Some decline
- Strong decline
- Not available

Sources: UNODC Annual Reports Questionnaires data, UNODC (Regional Centre Bangkok) Epidemiology Trends in Drug Trends in Asia (Findings of the Asian Multicity Epidemiology Workgroup, National Household Surveys submitted to UNODC, United States Department of State (Bureau for International Narcotics and Law Enforcement Affairs) International Narcotics Control Strategy Report;Bundeskriminalamt (BKA) and other Law Enforcement Reports.

Ecstasy abuse trends

Ecstasy was, for the first time, explicitly mentioned in the new Annual Reports Questionnaire. It is therefore not really possible to make comparisons with previous years when reporting on ecstasy trends was sporadic. In 2001, 63% of all countries reporting on ecstasy abuse trends saw an increase. This included 29% reporting a large increase, the highest such proportion for all drugs. Only 12% reported a decline, including 6% reporting a strong decline.

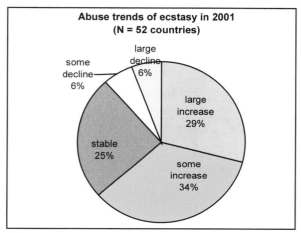

Source: UNODC, Annual Reports Questionnaire Data.

In practically all regions, abuse of ecstasy was reported to have increased in 2001, including in Western and Eastern Europe, in North America, and in the Oceania region. Outside Europe, North America and Australia, ecstasy appears to be becoming more popular in the countries of South America and in South-East Asia. In addition, there are markets for ecstasy in the Near East and in southern Africa. In contrast, in most of the rest of

Sub-Saharan Africa and in several parts of Asia (except South-East Asia and some countries in the Near and Middle East), abuse of ecstasy still seems to be uncommon. Except Europe, North America and Australia, which have been faced with widespread ecstasy abuse for more than a decade, as many as 28 countries reported on ecstasy trends, indirectly confirming the ongoing spread of this substance across the globe. Among these countries, only Indonesia in South-East Asia, Venezuela in South America and Madagascar in Africa reported a decline of ecstasy abuse in 2001.

Changes in abuse of Ecstasy (MDA,MDEA,MDMA), 2001 (or latest year available)

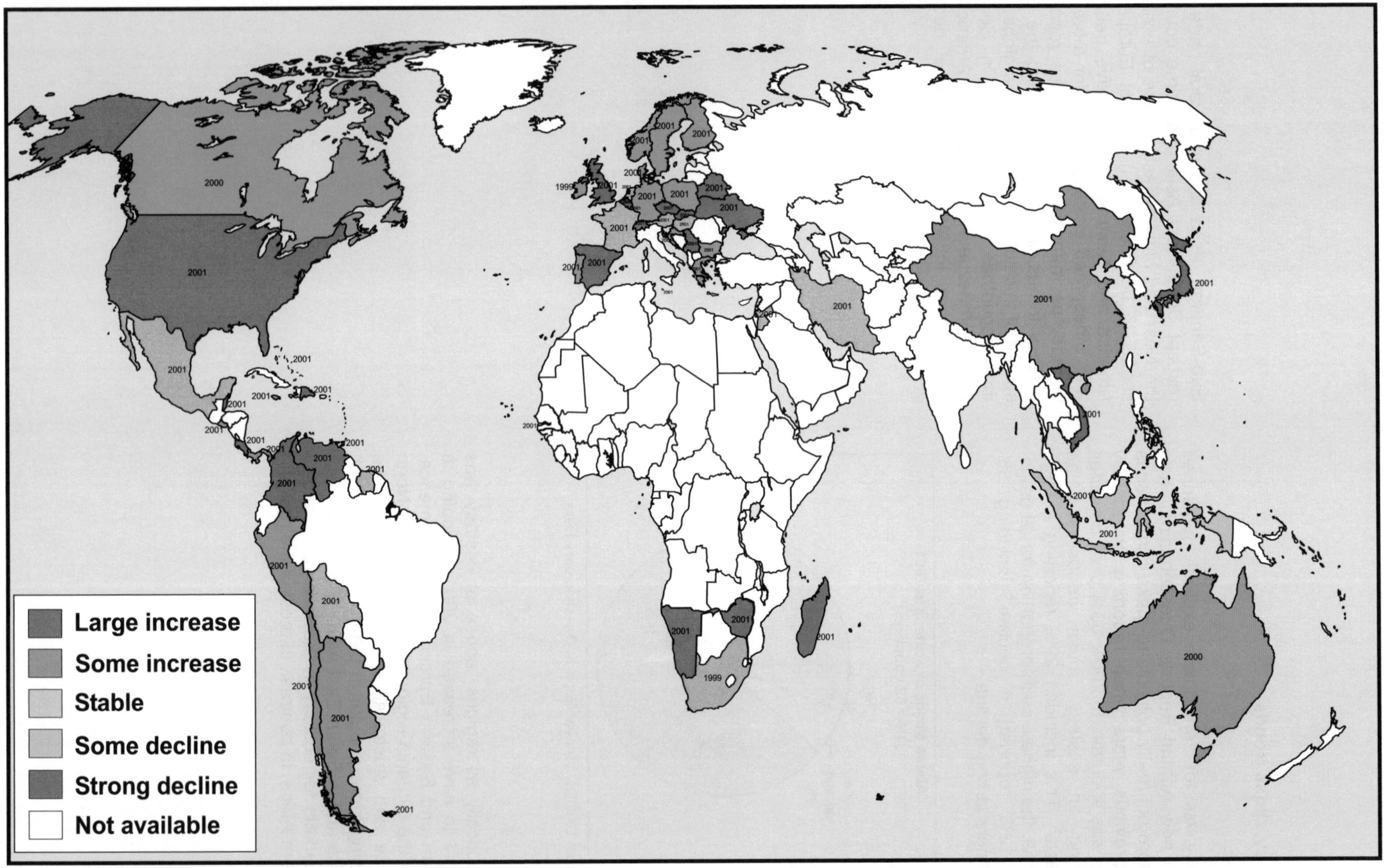

Large increase
Some increase
Stable
Some decline
Strong decline
Not available

Sources: UNODC Annual Reports Questionnaires data,
UNODC (Regional Centre Bangkok) Epidemiology Trends in Drug Trends in Asia (Findings of the Asian Multicity Epidemiology Workgroup, National Household Surveys submitted to UNODC, United States
Department of State (Bureau for International Narcotics and Law Enforcement Affairs) International Narcotics Control Strategy Report;Bundeskriminalamt (BKA) and other Law Enforcement Reports.

Europe

Western Europe was first affected by rapidly rising levels of ecstasy consumption in the early 1990s, starting in Spain and the UK (late 1980s) and then spreading to the rest of the continent. In the second half of the 1990s, overall ecstasy abuse continued to increase in Europe, as was clearly reflected in the ESPAD (European School Survey Project on Alcohol and Other Drugs) studies, conducted among 15 to 16 year olds in some 30 countries on behalf of the Council of Europe. The overall increase in ecstasy abuse in the second half of the 1990s was due to rapidly growing levels in practically all countries of Eastern Europe, notably Latvia, Lithuania, the Czech Republic, Slovenia, Estonia and Hungary.

In contrast, a number of West European countries, including the UK, Ireland, the Netherlands, Italy, Iceland and Cyprus reported falling levels of ecstasy abuse over the 1995-1999 period. Stable to falling levels of ecstasy abuse between 1996 and 1998 were also reported from Spain and over the 1997-2001 period from Germany.

However, the trend towards stabilization does not appear to have continued in subsequent years. General population surveys in the UK showed a temporary decline of ecstasy abuse between 1996 and 1998, followed by an upward trend over the 1998-2002 period. Annual prevalence of ecstasy abuse was found to affect 2.2% of the population age 16-59 in the UK in 2002, more than twice the level reported in 1994.

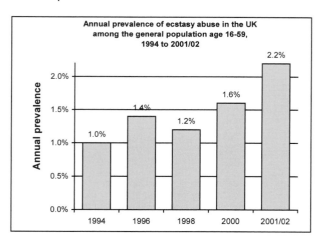

Source: Home Office, *British Crime Surveys 2001/02* and previous years.

In *Spain*, ecstasy abuse increased strongly from the late 1980s to the mid 1990s. In subsequent years, both household surveys and school surveys showed, however, a decline. Between

1995 and 1999 annual prevalence of ecstasy abuse fell by a third. However, the downward trend ended after 1999. Between 1999 and 2001 annual prevalence of ecstasy abuse more than doubled, from 0.8% to 1.8% in 2001 of the population age 15-64, close to the levels reported from the UK.

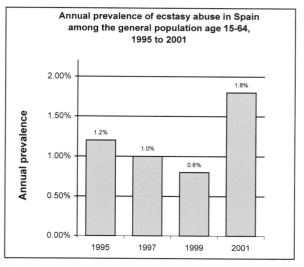

Source: Delegación del Gobierno para el Plan Nacional sobre Drogas, Encuesta Domiciliaria sobre Consumo de Drogas en España, 2001, Deciembre 2002.

A similar pattern is also found in *the Netherlands*. The national survey on illicit drug abuse found an increase in ecstasy abuse between 1997 and 2001 of more than 50% (from 0.3% to 0.5% in terms of monthly prevalence, from 0.7% to 1.1% in terms of annual prevalence and from 1.9% to 2.9% in terms of life-time prevalence of the population age 12 and above). Annual prevalence of ecstasy abuse in Amsterdam more than doubled between 1994 and 2001 and rose about 5-fold over the 1990-2001 period.

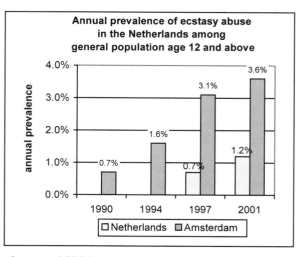

Source: CEDRO, *Licit and illicit drugabuse in the Netherlands 2001*, Amsterdam 2002 and CEDRO, *Licit and illicit drugabuse in Amsterdam III. Developments in drugabuse 1987 – 1997*, Amsterdam 1998.

Data for *Sweden*, based on life-time prevalence of drug abuse among military recruits, also show a clear upward trend for ecstasy abuse. There was a strong increase in the early 1990s until 1997 and following a temporary stabilization between 1997 and 1999, ecstasy abuse again rose strongly in 2000. Between 1997 and 2001 life-time ecstasy abuse among military recruits rose by more than 70%.

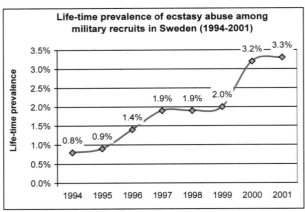

Source: Centralförbundet för alcohol och narkotikaupply-sning, Drogutvecklingen I Sverige – Rapport 2002, Trends in Alcohol and other Drugs in Sweden, Report 2002.

Data for *Germany* show a trend in the opposite direction. After having increased strongly in the first half of the 1990s, general population surveys as well as independently conducted youth surveys actually found a decline in ecstasy abuse between 1997 and 2000/2001. The readiness to experiment with ecstasy among youth also apparently fell between 1997 and 2001. Nonetheless, there are still three times as many youths who consider experimenting with ecstasy at some stage in the future compared to youths who have already experimented with this drug, indicating a strong growth potential. Ecstasy remains the second most widely abused drug after cannabis among 12-25 year olds in Germany, ahead of amphetamine and cocaine. Among the general population, ecstasy was the second most widely consumed illicit drug in the new provinces and the third most widely consumed drug in the old provinces after cannabis and cocaine in 2000.

Annual prevalence of ecstasy abuse in the general population (age 18-59) fell from 0.8% in 1997 to 0.6% in 2000. This was the outcome of two opposing trends. While ecstasy abuse declined in the 'old provinces' (former West-Germany), it increased in the 'new provinces' (former East Germany). By the year 2000, prevalence of ecstasy abuse in the new provinces

already exceeded ecstasy abuse in the old provinces. Police arrest data, however, are not fully in line with the survey results. More people – in both absolute and relative terms – are still arrested for ecstasy possession in the old provinces than in the new provinces. The number of persons registered for the first-time for ecstasy abuse, rose by 60% between 1997 and 2001. In 2002, however, this number fell by 22% as compared to a year earlier.

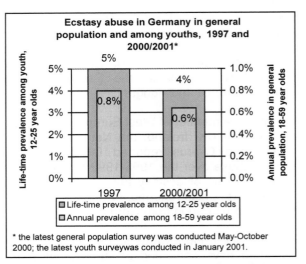

* the latest general population survey was conducted May-October 2000; the latest youth survey was conducted in January 2001.

Sources: Bundesministerium für Gesundheit, *Repräsentativ-erhebung 1995, 1997* und *2000*; Bundeszentrale für gesundheitliche Aufklärung, *Die Drogenaffinität Jugendlicher in der Bundesrepublik Deutschland 2001*.

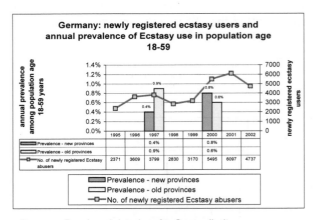

Sources: Bundesministerium für Gesundheit, *Repräsentativerhebung 1997* und 2000; Bundeskriminalamt, *Rauschgiftjahresbericht 2001, June 2002*.

Similar trends were also reported from *Italy*. Ecstasy abuse showed strong increases in the early 1990s, like in the rest of Europe, but it appears to have leveled off, or declined in subsequent years, as reflected in the data of the Italian ESPAD school-surveys. The proportion of ecstasy abuse among all drug abusers identified by the military service, showed, however, a less clear-cut picture: there has been a proportional decline in 1999, an increase in 2000 and again a decline in 2001.

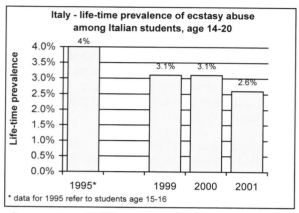

Italy - life-time prevalence of ecstasy abuse among Italian students, age 14-20

* data for 1995 refer to students age 15-16

Sources: Council of Europe, *The 1995 ESPAD Report*, Stockholm 1997 and 1999-2001 Italian ESPAD reports quoted in Ministerio del Lavoro e delle politiche sociali, *Italy Drug Situation 2001*, Rome 2002.

Americas

Ecstasy abuse in the Americas was first reported in the early 1980s, in the USA, leading to the control of MDMA in that country in 1985. Following the control of ecstasy, its spread was halted for several years. The next wave of ecstasy abuse – this time among youth - was only noticed as of the mid 1990s, and in particular over the 1998-2001 period. Life-time prevalence of ecstasy abuse among the general population more than doubled between 1998 and 2001.

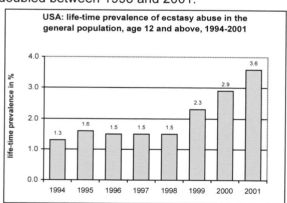

USA: life-time prevalence of ecstasy abuse in the general population, age 12 and above, 1994-2001

Source: SAMHSA, *National Household Survey on Drug Abuse* 2001 and previous years

The Monitoring the Future survey results on young adults (age 19-32) revealed that ecstasy abuse is still more widespread in the north-eastern[h] parts of

the United States, possibly reflecting closer links to Europe where most of the ecstasy originates. Prevalence of ecstasy abuse in the north-eastern parts of the USA was about a third higher than the national average. Ecstasy abuse in the western[i] parts of the USA was slightly above average, whereas it was below average in the southern[j] and north-central parts[k] of the USA.

In 2001, the US National Household Survey on Drug Abuse also had a question on annual prevalence of ecstasy abuse. It found that 1.4% of the population age 12 and above abused ecstasy in the 12 months prior to the survey. This was higher than the European average (0.8%), though still lower than data reported from the UK or Spain. Abuse of ecstasy in the USA was only slightly less frequent than abuse of cocaine (1.9%) and more widespread than abuse of stimulants (1.1%). or heroin (0.2%) in the general population. If the number of the abusers of ecstasy over the last twelve months are compared to life-time prevalence rates, the proportion is 40%. For comparison, the corresponding proportions are: 25% for cannabis, 16% for stimulants, 15% for both cocaine and heroin, and 8% for LSD. All of this indicates that ecstasy abuse is a far more recent phenomenon than the abuse of most other drugs.

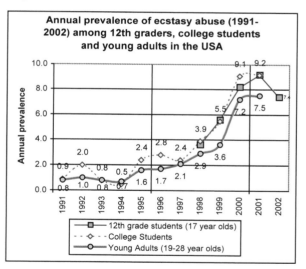

Annual prevalence of ecstasy abuse (1991-2002) among 12th graders, college students and young adults in the USA

- ■ 12th grade students (17 year olds)
- ◇ College Students
- ○ Young Adults (19-28 year olds)

Source: NIDA, Monitoring the Future, Volume II: College Students & Young Adults , 2001 and NIDA, The Monitoring the Future National Survey Results on Adolescent Drug abuse: Overview of Key Findings, 2002.

---

[h] North-East: Maine, New Hampshire, Vermont, Massachusetts, Rhode Island, Connecticut, New York, New Jersey and Pennsylvania.

[i] West: Montana, Idaho, Wyoming, Colorado, New Mexico, Arizona, Utah, Nevada, Washington, Oregon and California.
[j] South: Delaware, Maryland, District of Columbia, Virginia, West Virginia, North Carolina, South Carolina, Georgia, Florida, Kentucky, Tennessee, Alabama, Mississippi, Arkansas, Louisiana, Oklahoma and Texas.
[k] North Central: Ohio, Indiana, Illinois, Michigan, Wisconsin, Minnesota, Iowa, Missouri, North Dakota, South Dakota, Nebraska and Kansas.

Indeed, annual prevalence of ecstasy abuse rose 10-fold between 1991 and 2002, for both US college students and young adults (age 19-28). Most of the increase took place between 1998 and 2001.

Annual prevalence of ecstasy abuse among 8th and 10th graders almost doubled between 1998 and 2001 in the USA. Among 12th graders ecstasy abuse more than doubled, the highest such increase for any drug in recent years. In 2002, however, ecstasy abuse declined by about 20%, the first decline among high-school students since 1998. Nonetheless, it remains significantly higher than cocaine, methamphetamine or heroin abuse among high school students (7.4% for ecstasy versus 5% for cocaine, 3.6% for methamphetamine and 1% for heroin among 12th graders in 2002).

showed a massive increase over the 1998-2001 period, followed by a decline in 2002. Availability of ecstasy on the US market and the perceived risks apparently played a role. In 1998 38% of 12th grade students perceived ecstasy to have been easily available. By 2001, this ratio rose to 62% in 2001, but in 2002 it declined to 59%. In parallel, the perceived medical risks from consuming ecstasy, which had started to increase in 2001, rose strongly in 2002. The combination of perceived increases in health risks and lower availability appear to have prompted the decline of ecstasy abuse in 2002.

Nonetheless, ecstasy prevalence rates among high-school students in the USA are higher than those in Europe. While average life-time prevalence of ecstasy abuse in 32 European countries among 15-16 year olds was 2.5% in 1999 (range 0% – 6%), the corresponding average rate in the USA was 6% in 1999, rising to 8% by 2001 before falling back to 6.6% in 2001. Only Ireland (9%) and the UK (8%) reported in the mid 1990s still higher life-time levels of ecstasy abuse among 15-16 year old students than the USA has had in recent years.

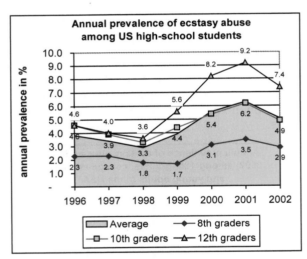

Sources: NIDA, *Monitoring the Future* 2002.

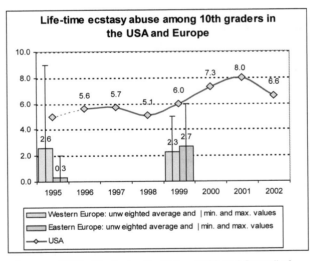

Sources: NIDA, *Monitoring the Future* 2002 and Council of Europe, *The 1995 ESPAD Report* and Council of Europe, *The 1999 ESPAD Report.*

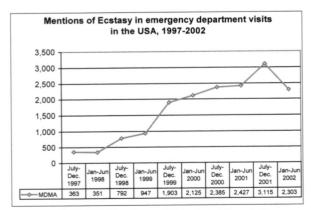

Source: SAMHSA, Emergency Department Trends From the Drug Abuse Warning Network, Preliminary Estimates January–June 2002

These growth pattern are also reflected in US emergency department statistics. They also

In contrast, high school surveys in the most populous province of Canada, Ontario, found prevalence rates that are very close to those reported from the USA, also suggesting that ecstasy abuse in Canada is already higher than in Europe. The annual prevalence data from the Ontario high school surveys show that ecstasy abuse among the sample of 7,9,11 and13 graders amounted to 6% in 2001 (as compared to 6.3% among 8, 10 and 12th graders in the USA), reflecting a ten-fold increase between 1993 and 2001. Like in the USA, abuse of ecstasy among high-school students (6%) is more widespread than cocaine (3.8%), methamphetamine (3.1%) or heroin (1.2%).

High and rising levels of ecstasy abuse were also reported from *New Zealand*. In 2001 3.4% of those age 14-45 abused ecstasy in the previous twelve months, up from 1.5% in 1998. This would be equivalent to an increase in the population age 15-65 from 1% in 1998 to 2.3% in 2001.

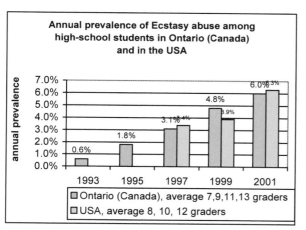

Sources: Ontario School Survey, NIDA, *Monitoring the Future* 2002

Oceania

The highest levels of ecstasy abuse in 2001, however, were reported from *Australia*. The 2001 national household survey revealed an annual prevalence rate of 2.9% among the general population, age 14 and above (or 3.4% among those age 15-64), higher than the corresponding rates of the UK (2.3%) or Spain (1.8%) and about twice the rate of ecstasy abuse reported from the USA (1.4%). Over the 1995-2001 period ecstasy abuse tripled in Australia, from 0.9% to 2.9%. Most of the increase took place over the 1995-1998 period.

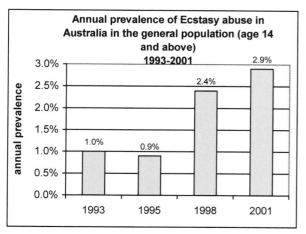

Source: Australian Institute of Health and Welfare (AIHW), *National Drug Strategy Household Survey 2001* and previous years.

2. STATISTICS

2.1. PRODUCTION

2.1.1. OPIUM / HEROIN

OPIUM

GLOBAL ILLICIT CULTIVATION OF OPIUM POPPY AND PRODUCTION OF OPIUM, 1990-2002													
	1990	1991	1992	1993	1994	1995	1996	1997	1998	1999	2000	2001	2002
CULTIVATION[(1)] IN HECTARES													
SOUTH-WEST ASIA													
Afghanistan	41,300	50,800	49,300	58,300	71,470	53,759	56,824	58,416	63,674	90,583	82,171	7,606	74,100
Pakistan	7,488	7,962	9,493	7,329	5,759	5,091	873	874	950	284	260	213	622
Subtotal	48,788	58,762	58,793	65,629	77,229	58,850	57,697	59,290	64,624	90,867	82,431	7,819	74,722
SOUTH-EAST ASIA													
Lao PDR	30,580	29,625	19,190	26,040	18,520	19,650	21,601	24,082	26,837	22,543	19,052	17,255	14,000
Myanmar	150,100	160,000	153,700	165,800	146,600	154,070	163,000	155,150	130,300	89,500	108,700	105,000	81,400
Thailand	1,782	3,727	3,016	998	478	168	368	352	716	702	890	820	750
Viet Nam [(2)]	18,000	17,000	12,199	4,268	3,066	1,880	1,743	340	442	442			
Subtotal	200,462	210,352	188,105	197,106	168,664	175,768	186,712	179,924	158,295	113,187	128,642	123,075	96,150
OTHER ASIAN COUNTRIES													
Combined	8,054	7,521	2,900	5,704	5,700	5,025	3,190	2,050	2,050	2,050	2,479	2,500	2,500
Total Asia	257,304	276,635	249,798	268,439	251,593	239,643	247,599	241,264	224,969	206,104	213,552	133,394	173,372
LATIN AMERICA													
Colombia [(3)]		1,160	6,578	5,008	15,091	5,226	4,916	6,584	7,350	6,500	6,500	4,300	4,200
Mexico [(4)]	5,450	3,765	3,310	3,960	5,795	5,050	5,100	4,000	5,500	3,600	1,900	4,400	2,700
Total Latin America	5,450	4,925	9,888	8,968	20,886	10,276	10,016	10,584	12,850	10,100	8,400	8,700	6,900
GRAND TOTAL	262,754	281,560	259,686	277,407	272,479	249,919	257,615	251,848	237,819	216,204	221,952	142,094	180,272
POTENTIAL PRODUCTION IN METRIC TONS													
SOUTH-WEST ASIA													
Afghanistan	1,570	1,980	1,970	2,330	3,416	2,335	2,248	2,804	2,693	4,565	3,276	185	3,400
Pakistan	150	160	181	161	128	112	24	24	26	9	8	5	5
Subtotal	1,720	2,140	2,151	2,491	3,544	2,447	2,272	2,828	2,719	4,574	3,284	190	3,405
SOUTH-EAST ASIA													
Lao PDR	202	196	127	169	120	128	140	147	124	124	167	134	112
Myanmar	1,621	1,728	1,660	1,791	1,583	1,664	1,760	1,676	1,303	895	1,087	1,097	828
Thailand	20	23	14	17	3	2	5	4	8	8	6	6	9
Viet Nam	90	85	61	21	15	9	9	2	2	2			
Subtotal	1,933	2,032	1,862	1,998	1,721	1,803	1,914	1,829	1,437	1,029	1,260	1,237	949
OTHER ASIAN COUNTRIES													
Combined	45	45	-	4	90	78	48	30	30	30	38	40	40
Total Asia	3,698	4,217	4,013	4,493	5,355	4,328	4,234	4,687	4,186	5,633	4,582	1,467	4,394
LATIN AMERICA													
Colombia [(3)]		16	90	68	205	71	67	90	100	88	88	58	50
Mexico	62	41	40	49	60	53	54	46	60	43	21	71	47
Total Latin America	62	57	130	117	265	124	121	136	160	131	109	129	97
GRAND TOTAL	3,760	4,274	4,143	4,610	5,620	4,452	4,355	4,823	4,346	5,764	4,691	1,596	4,491
Potential HEROIN	376	427	414	461	562	445	436	482	435	576	469	160	449

[(1)] Potentially harvestable, after eradication.

[(2)] Due to small production, Viet Nam cultivation and production were included in the category " Other Asian countries" as of 2000.

[(3)] According to the Government of Colombia, cultivation covered 7,350 ha and 6,500 ha and production amounted to 73 mt and 65 mt in 1998 and 1999 respectively.

[(4)] Sources: As its survey system is under development, the Govt of Mexico indicates it can neither provide cultivation estimates nor endorse those published by UNDCP which are derived from US Government surveys.

2.1.1.1. AFGHANISTAN

The information presented below is based on abstracts from the UNODC report Afghanistan, Opium Survey 2002, October 2002. The full report can be accessed on UNODC's website (http://www.unodc.org/odccp/crop_monitoring.html).

Background

Annual opium survey in Afghanistan

The United Nations Office on Drugs and Crime (UNODC) has conducted an annual opium poppy survey in Afghanistan since 1994. The survey collects and analyses information on the location and extent of opium poppy cultivation, on the potential production of opium, as well as on opium prices in that country. The results provide a detailed picture of the current year's opium season and enable the identification of trends. This information is essential for planning, implementing and monitoring the impact of the measures required for tackling a problem which, in a country that has become by far the largest source of illicit opium and heroin trafficked in the world, has clearly assumed international dimensions.

UNODC's opium survey in Afghanistan is implemented in the technical framework of its global Illicit Crop Monitoring Programme (ICMP). The objective of ICMP is to assist the international community in monitoring the extent and evolution of illicit crops in the context of the elimination objective adopted at the General Assembly Special Session on Drugs in June 1998.

The high level of opium poppy cultivation in Afghanistan

During the 1990s, Afghanistan firmly established itself as the largest source of illicit opium and its derivative, heroin, in the world. By the end of the 1990s, Afghanistan provided about 70% of global illicit opium production, well ahead of Myanmar (about 22%) and Lao PDR (about 3%). Primarily supplying countries in South West Asia, Central Asia, East and West Europe, as well as in South Asia, the Arabian peninsula and Africa, illicit opiates of Afghan origin were consumed by an estimated 9 million abusers, which is two-thirds of all opiate abusers in the world. It can be estimated that, all along the trafficking chain, about half a million people have been involved in the trade of illicit Afghan opiates in recent years. Although these numbers are only approximate, UNODC also estimates that the overall turnover of illicit international trade in Afghan opiates can be roughly estimated at US$ 25 billion annually.

An abrupt decline of illicit opium poppy cultivation was recorded in Afghanistan in 2001, following the ban imposed by the Taliban regime in its last year in power. Despite the existence of significant stocks of opiates accumulated during previous years of bumper harvests, the beginning of a heroin shortage became apparent on some European markets by the end of 2001. Furthermore, the absence of the usual harvest in Afghanistan in spring 2001 and the subsequent depletion of stocks pushed opium prices upwards to unprecedented levels in the country (prices increased by a factor of 10), creating a powerful incentive for farmers to plant the 2002 crop.

The power vacuum in Kabul caused by the aftermath of 11 September 2001 enabled farmers to replant opium poppy (starting in October/November 2001). By the time the Afghan Interim Administration was established and issued a strong ban on opium poppy cultivation, processing, trafficking and consumption (17 January 2002), most opium poppy fields had already started to sprout.

In February 2002, a two-week rapid assessment survey launched by UNODC in the traditional opium growing areas of southern and eastern Afghanistan provided the basic evidence to confirm the resumption of opium poppy cultivation on a large scale. This survey did not cover all the growing areas. Due to a later and more staggered planting than usual, some opium fields could not even be seen during the February 2002 field visits by the UNODC surveyors. A full survey was therefore required for a comprehensive and reliable assessment of the problem. It was launched by UNODC in March 2002 and completed in September 2002. The present text summarizes the findings.

Methodology

Due to the events of 11 September 2001 and the subsequent armed conflict, UNODC's annual survey faced a difficult and dangerous security environment on the ground.

In April 2002, at the onset of the opium harvest in eastern and southern Afghanistan, the Afghan Interim Administration (AIA) launched an eradication campaign (with compensations). Some farmers' reactions to this measure resulted in a temporary deterioration of the security situation for UNODC's surveyors who were withdrawn from the opium poppy growing areas. As the field work stopped, UNODC quickly adapted the methodology to ensure a continuation of the survey. Instead of running a census ground survey complemented with limited satellite imagery, the 2002 survey was based on high-resolution satellite images complemented by extensive ground truthing and targeted ground surveys. In total, UNODC field surveyors visited 923 villages in 84 districts of 16 provinces.

High-resolution satellite images ensured a sample-based coverage of all the main opium growing areas, regardless of the security situation. To improve the interpretation of the images as well as to account for staggered planting, images of the same areas were acquired twice, with a one-month interval. As soon as the security situation permitted, UNODC surveyors went back to the opium growing areas where they collected GPS coordinates of opium poppy fields in about 600 different locations. This information was crucial to ensure an accurate interpretation of the satellite images (ground truthing). Independent of the satellite-based survey, a sample ground survey was carried out in the North of Afghanistan. It provided similar results as the satellite-based survey, confirming the validity of the methodology used. Some ground survey activities were also carried out in the East in Nangarhar and in central Afghanistan in the province of Ghor.

Data on yield and productivity were collected for both irrigated and rain-fed poppy cultivation through farmer interviews by UNODC surveyors in three provinces: Helmand, Nangarhar and Badakhshan. The yield survey was conducted on a random sample basis during or after the main opium harvest period. Data on opium prices were collected at various locations.

Findings

Opium poppy cultivation

The total opium poppy cultivation in Afghanistan in 2002 was estimated to range from 69,000 hectares (ha) to 79,000 ha, with a mean estimate of 74,000 ha.

This level of opium poppy cultivation compares with levels reached during the mid to late 1990s. Although it remains lower than the record levels of 1999 (about 90,500 ha) and 2000 (about 82,000 ha), it confirms that opium poppy cultivation has resumed to high levels, after the considerable decline recorded in 2001.

Afghanistan opium poppy cultivation from 1994 to 2002 (in ha)									
	1994	**1995**	**1996**	**1997**	**1998**	**1999**	**2000**	**2001**	**2002**
Rounded total	71,000	54,000	57,000	58,000	64,000	91,000	82,000	8,000	74,000

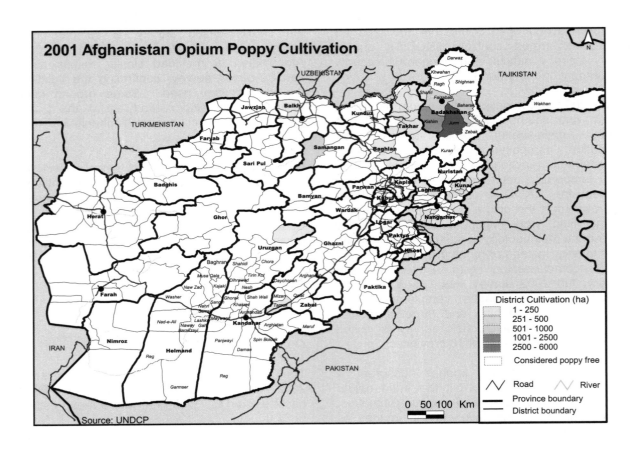

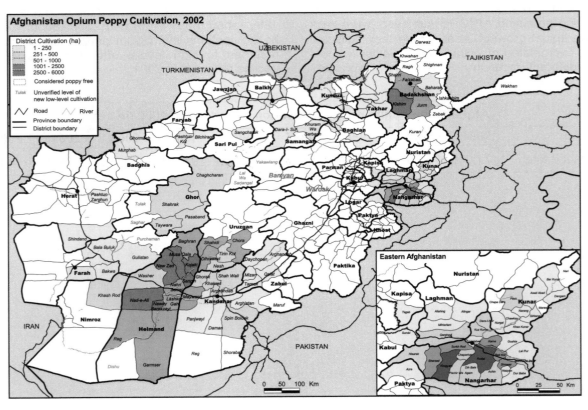

Afghanistan opium poppy cultivation estimates (ha), 2002

Province	District	Former district reference	Previous UNDCP survey estimates								2002		
			1994	1995	1996	1997	1998	1999	2000	2001	Low	Avg	High
Badakhshan	Baharak	Baharak	111	64	116	9	202	23	86	345	170	180	190
	Fayzabad	Faizabad	77	2,344	1,592	1,634	1,282	906	1,073	868	2,070	2,370	2,660
	Ishkashim	Eshkashem	0	0	3	0	0	0	0	0	-	-	-
	Jurm	Jurm	433	555	1,326	1,051	1,198	1,249	773	2,897	2,300	2,690	3,070
	Khwahan	Khvahan								0	-	-	-
	Kishim	Keshem	1,093	3	177	62	62	385	507	2,191	2,570	2,840	3,120
	Ragh	Ragh	0	0	8	31	2	8	0	0	-	-	-
	Shahri Buzurg	Shahr-e-Bozorg	0	0	0	0	71	113	19	41	160	170	180
	Zebak	Zebak	0	4	8	115	0	0	0		-	-	-
Badakhshan Total			**1,714**	**2,970**	**3,230**	**2,902**	**2,817**	**2,684**	**2,458**	**6,342**	**7,270**	**8,250**	**9,220**
Badghis	Ghormach	Ghowrmach							20	0	3	4	5
	Murghab	Morghab							21	0	21	22	23
Badghis Total			**0**	**0**	**0**	**0**	**0**	**0**	**41**	**0**	**25**	**26**	**28**
Baghlan	Andarab	Anderab								81	30	31	31
	Baghlan	Baghlan							152	0	115	120	124
	Dahana-I- Ghori	Dahaneh-e-Ghowri				328	929	967	27	0	0	0	0
	Nahrin	Nahrin								1	-	-	-
	Puli Khumri	Pul-e-Khumri						38	20	0	1	1	2
Baghlan Total			**0**	**0**	**0**	**328**	**929**	**1,005**	**199**	**82**	**147**	**152**	**157**
Balkh	Balkh	Balkh				13	29	29	82	1	21	22	23
	Chahar Bolak	Char Bulaq				165	530	2,600	53	0	0	0	0
	Chimtal	Chemtal			1,065	532	485	1,428	2,451	0	152	153	154
	Dawlat Abad	Dowlatabad								3	-	-	-
	Dihdadi	Dehdadi							22	0	7	8	8
	Nahri Shahi	Naher Shahi							33	0	14	14	15
	Sholgara	Shulgarah							28	0	19	19	20
Balkh Total			**0**	**0**	**1,065**	**710**	**1,044**	**4,057**	**2,669**	**4**	**214**	**217**	**219**
Farah	Anar Dara	Anar Darreh								0	-	-	-
	Bakwa	Bakwah		1	13	129	31	129	259	0	-	-	-
	Bala Buluk	Bala Balok		8	19	169	36	186	183	0	-	-	-
	Farah	Farah			18	18	10	44	73	0	-	-	-
	Gulistan	Gulestan			581	252	94	428	849	0	-	-	-
	Khaki Safed	Khak-e Safid							0	0	-	-	-
	Lash Wa Juwayn	Lash-e Joveyn								0	-	-	-
	Pur Chaman	Purchaman								0	-	-	-
	Qalay-I-Kah	Qalae Koh								0	-	-	-
Farah Total			**0**	**9**	**631**	**568**	**171**	**787**	**1,364**	**0**	**300**	**500**	**700**
Faryab	Bilchiragh	Belcheragh							6	0	19	26	33
	Maymana	Meymaneh							1	0	0	0	0
	Pashtun Kot	Pashtun Kowt							11	0	1	1	2
	Qaysar	Qeysar							16	0	-	-	-
	Shirin Tagab	Shirin Tagab							3	0	-	-	-
Faryab Total			**0**	**0**	**0**	**0**	**0**	**0**	**36**	**0**	**20**	**28**	**35**
Ghazni	Ajristan	Ajristan	313	0	0	0	0	0	0	0	-	-	-
Ghazni Total			**313**	**0**	**0**	**0**	**0**	**0**	**0**	**0**	**0**	**0**	**0**
Ghor	Chaghcharan										630	700	770
	Pasaband										630	700	770
	Shahrak										270	300	330
	Taywara										450	500	550
Ghor Total											**1,980**	**2,200**	**2,420**
Helmand	Baghran	Baghran		2,519	1,267	2,754	2,910	2,794	2,653	0	1,660	1,800	1,930
	Dishu	Deh Shu								0	-	-	-
	Garmser	Garmser	786	725	942	1,993	1,205	2,643	2,765	0	1,900	2,020	2,140
	Kajaki	Kajaki	979	4,087	2,814	3,904	3,959	5,746	4,625	0	2,500	2,640	2,780
	Lashkar Gah	Bust	2,256	885	1,054	1,325	1,869	2,528	3,145	0	1,070	1,140	1,220
	Musa Qala	Musa Qala	1,154	5,137	3,924	4,360	5,574	7,013	5,686	0	3,500	3,690	3,890
	Nad-e-Ali	Nad-e-Ali	12,529	5,983	4,035	5,102	5,156	8,667	8,323	0	5,690	5,880	6,080
	Nahri Sarraj	Nahr-e-Saraj	590	4,716	4,309	4,807	2,426	4,041	4,378	0	1,720	1,850	1,980
	Naw Zad	Naw Zad	2,345	2,799	3,596	1,585	3,605	4,424	5,085	0	2,550	2,650	2,780
	Naway Barakzayi	Nawa Barakzai	6,074	1,254	505	722	1,150	2,581	3,246	0	2,540	2,730	2,910
	Reg	Khan Neshin							222		1,810	1,940	2,070
	Sangin	Sarban Qala	2,866	973	1,909	1,971	1,734	2,646	1,711	0	2,650	2,810	2,960
	Washer	Washir		676	555	877	1,084	1,469	1,014	0	780	800	820
Helmand Total			**29,579**	**29,754**	**24,910**	**29,400**	**30,672**	**44,552**	**42,853**	**0**	**28,370**	**29,950**	**31,560**

Province	District	Former district reference	Previous UNDCP survey estimates								2002		
			1994	1995	1996	1997	1998	1999	2000	2001	Low	Avg	High
Herat	Obe	Obey								0	-	-	-
	Pashtun Zarghun	Pashtun Zarghun	0	0	0	38	0	0	38	0	-	-	-
	Shindand	Shindand							146	0	-	-	-
	Zinda Jan	Zendeh Jan								0	-	-	-
Herat Total			0	0	0	38	0	0	184	0	30	50	70
Jawzjan	Aqcha	Aqchah						532	208	0	46	47	47
	Faysabad	Faizabad						43	105	0	23	24	25
	Khamyab	Khamyab							6		29	30	31
	Mardyan	Mardian						43	111	0	4	4	4
	Mingajik	Manga Jek						1,789	141	0	7	7	7
	Qarqin	Qarqin						186	10	0	24	24	24
	Shibirghan	Sheberghan							19	0	1	1	1
Jawzjan Total			0	0	0	0	0	2,593	600	0	134	137	139
Kabul	Surobi	Sarobi						132	340	29	57	58	59
Kabul Total			0	0	0	0	0	132	340	29	57	58	59
Kandahar	Arghandab	Arghandab	211	87	331	561	399	750	459	0	320	330	340
	Arghistan	Arghistan						38	13	0	70	80	90
	Daman	Daman						110	50	0	170	190	210
	Ghorak	Ghorak	347	803	692	1,503	1,126	1,109	574	0	270	380	320
	Kandahar	Qandahar+Dand	320	53	234	21	73	227	156	0	480	640	810
	Khakrez	Khakrez	362	274	627	286	518	632	320	0	520	560	610
	Maruf	Maruf	30	16	1	0	3	5	17	0	-	-	-
	Maywand	Maiwand	256	333	618	1,278	2,497	2,022	995	0	950	1,090	1,240
	Panjwayi	Panjwai	250	357	266	255	134	132	184	0	140	150	170
	Shah Wali Kot	Shah Wali Kot	678	97	94	127	162	236	238	0	240	260	290
	Spin Boldak	Spin Boldak	1,170	107	194	91	317	261	26	0	260	290	320
Kandahar Total			3,624	2,127	3,057	4,122	5,229	5,522	3,034	0	3,420	3,970	4,400
Kapisa	Tagab	Tagab						5	104	0	206	207	208
Kapisa Total			0	0	0	0	0	5	104	0	206	207	208
Khost	Spera	Speyrah								0	-	-	-
	Tani	Tani								6	-	-	-
Khost Total			0	0	0	0	0	0	0	6	0	0	0
Kunar	Asad Abad	Asadabad						73	239	1	120	140	150
	Bar Kunar	Bar Kunar						47	72	31	40	40	50
	Chawkay	Chawki	13	11	0	0	8	9	50	8	120	140	160
	Dangam	Dangam								4	46	49	52
	Khas Kunar	Khas Kunar	75	82	10	0	12	50	173	0	60	70	80
	Narang	Narang		15	1	0	13	27	84	10	90	100	120
	Nari	Naray								1	-		
	Nurgal	Mazar (Nur Gul)	27	19	5	0	8	28	98	9	60	70	80
	Pech	Peche								11	260	263	266
	Sirkanay	Sarkani		25	2	0	34	54	71	8	90	100	110
Kunar Total			115	152	18	0	75	288	786	82	886	972	1,068
Kunduz	Ali Abad	Aliabad						5	51	0	2	3	3
	Chahar Dara	Chahar Darreh						8	30	0	6	6	7
	Imam Sahib	Emam Saheb						3	0			-	
	Khan Abad	Khanabad						2	36	0		-	
	Kunduz	Kunduz						9	51	0	3	3	3
	Qalay-I- Zal	Qala-e Zal						11	321	0	4	5	5
Kunduz Total			0	0	0	0	0	38	489	0	16	16	17
Laghman	Alingar	Alingar	0	0	0	0	2	71	131	3	142	146	150
	Alishing	Alishang	0	0	0	0	3	26	88	0	101	104	107
	Dawlat Shah	Dowlat Shah								12		-	
	Mihtarlam	Metarlam	0	0	0	0	14	72	190	0	190	240	290
	Qarghayi	Qarghai	0	0	0	0	58	128	298	0	300	460	610
Laghman Total			0	0	0	0	77	297	707	15	733	950	1,157
Nangarhar	Achin	Achin	5,354	2,187	2,315	1,640	1,693	2,209	1,317	1	920	940	960
	Bati Kot	Bati Kot	3,797	529	392	1,013	2,034	603	535	0	2,210	2,390	2,570
	Chaparhar	Chaparhar	1,089	1,377	1,750	1,234	1,365	977	832	2	970	990	1,010
	Dara-I-Nur	Darae Noor	1,302	392	199	73	199	734	421	0	370	380	400
	Dih Bala	Deh Bala	307	646	354	569	511	468	439	11	640	650	660
	Dur Baba	Durbaba	29	78	38	39	56	50	33	0	40	40	40
	Goshta	Goshta	1,249	467	116	77	122	240	238	99	150	150	160
	Hisarak	Hesarak	202	453	253	370	436	741	541	2	600	620	650

Province	District	Former district reference	Previous UNDCP survey estimates								2002		
			1994	1995	1996	1997	1998	1999	2000	2001	Low	Avg	High
	Jalalabad	Behsud+Jalalabad	458	31	51	123	397	979	1,021	0	89	90	90
	Kama	Kama	0	18	0	0	198	389	589	0	1,080	1,120	1,170
	Khogyani	Khogiani	4,347	2,577	2,628	3,385	3,808	5,338	4,913	3	2,630	2,640	2,650
	Kuz Kunar	Kuz Kunar	293	233	115	15	105	236	399	0	490	500	520
	Lal Pur	La'lpur	302	267	79	66	137	270	248	95	240	250	260
	Muhmand Dara	Mohmand Dara	1,630	0	156	83	125	290	255	0	690	720	750
	Nazyan	Nazian	343	138	251	111	252	184	177	0	150	150	150
	Pachir Wa Agam	Pachier wa Agam	768	571	681	400	488	731	630	3	400	420	430
	Rodat	Rodat	1,026	2,038	1,959	1,583	2,147	3,649	2,302	0	2,760	2,760	2,760
	Sherzad	Sherzad	1,954	2,351	1,646	1,689	1,302	1,741	1,719	2	1,470	1,470	1,470
	Shinwar	Shinwar	3,884	1,265	2,075	1,478	1,374	1,559	1,300	0	2,060	2,060	2,060
	Surkh Rod	Sorkh Rod	747	106	587	619	1,072	1,602	1,840	0	1,340	1,440	1,540
Nangarhar Total			**29,081**	**15,724**	**15,645**	**14,567**	**17,821**	**22,990**	**19,747**	**218**	**19,299**	**19,780**	**20,300**
Nimroz	Chahar Burjak	Char Borjak								0	-	-	-
	Kang	Kang	10	2	1	107	5	2	0	0	-	-	-
	Khash Rod	Khash Rud	672	117	135	535	6	201	219	0	-	-	-
Nimroz Total			**682**	**119**	**136**	**642**	**11**	**203**	**219**	**0**	**180**	**300**	**420**
Paktya	Azra	Azro					4	29	46	1	37	38	39
	Chamkani	Chamkani								0		-	
	Jaji	Jaji								0		-	
	Lija Mangal	Hasan Kheyl								0		-	
	Sayid Karam	Seyed Karam								0		-	
Paktya Total			**0**	**0**	**0**	**0**	**4**	**29**	**46**	**1**	**37**	**38**	**39**
Samangan	Dara-I- Suf	Darae Souf								614	-	-	-
	Khuram Wa Sarbagh	Khuram+Samangan							54	0	-	-	-
Samangan Total			**0**	**0**	**0**	**0**	**0**	**0**	**54**	**614**	**60**	**100**	**140**
Sari Pul	Sangcharak	Sar-e Pol							146	0	57	57	57
Sari Pul Total			**0**	**0**	**0**	**0**	**0**	**0**	**146**	**0**	**57**	**57**	**57**
Takhar	Bangi	Bangi							8	0		-	
	Chah Ab	Chah Ab						17	45	19		-	
	Chal	Chal						8	17	20		-	
	Farkhar	Farkhar						6	6	26		-	
	Ishkamish	Eshkamesh							10	19		-	
	Kalafgan	Kalafgan						101	93	27		-	
	Khwaja Ghar	Khvajeh Ghar						9	57	32		-	
	Rustaq	Rostaq						10	151	24		-	
	Taluqan	Taloqan						16	97	16		-	
	Warsaj	Warsaj						12	9	10		-	
	Yangi Qala	Yangi Qala						22	154	20		-	
Takhar Total			**0**	**0**	**0**	**0**	**0**	**201**	**647**	**211**	**782**	**788**	**794**
Uruzgan	Chora	Chora	694	424	1,574	233	652	932	1,179	0	1,220	1,330	1,330
	Day Kundi	Dai Kundi								0		-	
	Dihrawud	Dehrawud	909	938	2,923	1,870	1,033	1,243	726	0	1,250	1,340	1,420
	Gizab	Gezab	1,476	16	8	0	0	0	0	0		-	
	Khas Uruzgan	Khas Oruzgan	0	4	0	0	0	0	130	0		-	
	Kijran	Kajran								0		-	
	Nesh	Nesh	410	334	104	399	373	510	394	0	460	490	520
	Shahidi Hassas	Char Chashma	1,337	12	0	0	1,158	1,110	802	0	1,130	1,190	1,240
	Shahristan	Shahrestan								1			
	Tirin Kot	Tirin Kot	1,428	1,180	3,271	2,484	1,445	1,194	1,494	0	680	750	830
Uruzgan Total			**6,254**	**2,908**	**7,880**	**4,986**	**4,661**	**4,989**	**4,725**	**1**	**4,740**	**5,100**	**5,340**
Zabul	Arghandab	Arghandab	0	0	0	0	0	74	139	0	-	-	-
	Daychopan	Dai Chopan	0	0	0	0	0	41	114	0	-	-	-
	Mizan	Mizan	54	0	255	154	160	373	383	0	-	-	-
	Qalat	Qalat	0	0	0	0	1	46	40	0	-	-	-
	Shahjoy	Shah Juy								0	-	-	-
	Tarnak Wa Jaldak	Jaldak	0	0	0	0	0	77	48	1	-	-	-
Zabul Total			**54**	**0**	**255**	**154**	**161**	**611**	**725**	**1**	**120**	**200**	**280**
TOTAL			**71,416**	**53,763**	**56,827**	**58,417**	**63,672**	**90,983**	**82,172**	**7,606**	**69,082**	**74,045**	**78,827**

| **ROUNDED TOTAL** | | | **71,000** | **54,000** | **57,000** | **58,000** | **64,000** | **91,000** | **82,000** | **8,000** | **69,000** | **74,000** | **79,000** |

Potential opium production

The average opium yield was estimated at 46 kg per hectare, a significant increase compared to last year's overall yield of 24 kg/ha. The reasons for this increase are twofold : (a) opium poppy cultivation has resumed on irrigated land in southern and eastern Afghanistan, which are significantly more productive; and (b) climatic conditions were more favourable than before, after the end of the drought which affected Afghanistan over the last few years.

As a result, the total potential opium production in Afghanistan in 2002 is estimated to amount to 3,400 metric tons (range: from 3,200 mt to 3,600 mt), a considerable increase compared to 2001, but a 25% decline from the record production of 1999 (4,600 mt).

Afghanistan opium production from 1994 to 2002 (in tons)									
	1994	**1995**	**1996**	**1997**	**1998**	**1999**	**2000**	**2001**	**2002**
Rounded total	3,400	2,300	2,200	2,800	2,700	4,600	3,300	185	3,400

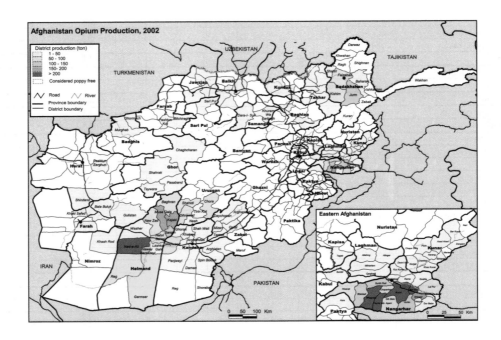

Geographical distribution

Opium poppy cultivation was found in 24 out of a total of 32 provinces in Afghanistan. However, in line with the usual pattern (with the exception of 2001), almost 95% of the cultivation was concentrated in just five provinces. Helmand in the South came first, with nearly 30,000 ha, followed by Nangarhar in the East (about 20,000 ha), Badakshan in the North (about 8,000 ha), Uruzgan in the South/Center (about 5,000 ha) and Kandahar in the South (about 4,000 ha).

Provincial ranking of opium poppy cultivation and production in 2002				
Province	**Cultivation (in ha)**	**% of country total**	**Production (in tons)**	**% of country total**
Helmand	29,950	40%	1,300	38%
Nangarhar	19,780	27%	1,030	30%
Badakhshan	8,250	11%	300	9%
Uruzgan	5,100	7%	230	7%
Kandahar	3,970	5%	180	5%
Country	74,000		3,400	

Opium prices

Opium prices in Afghanistan changed considerably during the last two years. After a long period of relative stability (1994-2000) and prices as low as US$ 30 per kg, opium prices skyrocketed in 2001 following the enforcement of a ban on opium poppy cultivation. Between mid-2000 and the harvest time of 2001, opium prices increased ten-fold from US$ 30 per kg to about US$ 300 per kg, and then doubled again to reach a record-high of about US$ 700 per kg in early September 2001. Immediately after 11 September, opium prices declined quickly to about US$100 per kg, reflecting the closing of Afghanistan's borders and the off-loading of stocks by traders.

In early 2002, as measured by the survey, the average price for Afghan fresh opium increased again to US$ 350 per kg. As the opium harvest is not brought at once to the markets and as opium prices movements are difficult to anticipate, the final average price for the 2002 opium production could differ from this estimate.

At current price levels, and as a result of the combination of high level cultivation (74,000 ha) and good opium yield (46 kg/ha), the total income for the Afghan opium poppy farmers could reach several hundreds million US dollars this year. The value of the 2002 production will then reach a record high, far above earlier years (from 1994 to 2000, the estimated total annual income varied between a minimum of about US$ 50 million and a maximum of about US$ 200 million at the time of the bumper harvest in 1999).

At surveyed prices, and on the basis of an estimated average of 0.3 ha of opium poppy cultivation per opium poppy farmer, the 2002 average income per opium poppy farmer could amount to a few thousand dollars in 2002. In previous years the typical income was estimated at several hundred dollars, from US$ 400 to 600. It is essential to bear in mind that these estimates do not refer to the country at large (where the average per family income remains one of the lowest in the world). Rather, the relatively high level of farming revenues refers to the few regions where the opium poppy cultivation is concentrated.

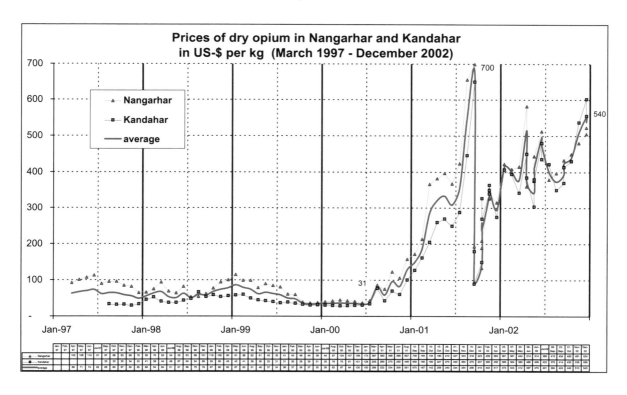

Prices of dry opium in Nangarhar and Kandahar in US-$ per kg (March 1997 - December 2002)

Afghanistan opium prices (US$/kg), 2002

Province	District	Former district reference	2001 Dry	2001 Fresh		2002 Dry	2002 Fresh	2002 Dry	2002 Fresh
						May		July-August	
Badakhshan	Baharak	Baharak	397	238		274		250	200
	Fayzabad	Faizabad	353	281		230		260	210
	Ishkashim	Eshkashem						220	190
	Jurm	Jurm	398	327		207	80	297	228
	Kishim	Keshem	392	326		275			
	Shahri Buzurg	Shahr-e-Bozorg	286	339		270			
Badakhshan average			**365**	**302**		**238**	**80**	**257**	**207**
Badghis	Ghormach	Ghowrmach	174			514			
	Murghab	Morghab	174			649	431		
Badghis average			**174**			**595**	**431**		
Baghlan	Andarab	Anderab	242	201		327			
	Baghlan	Baghlan	206				202		
	Dahana-I- Ghori	Dahaneh-e-Ghowri	197						
	Puli Khumri	Pul-e-Khumri	205			274	215		
Baghlan average			**212**	**201**		**312**	**208**		
Balkh	Balkh	Balkh	237	201		137	103		
	Chahar Bolak	Char Bulaq	235			172			
	Chimtal	Chemtal	239			158	98		
	Dihdadi	Dehdadi				236	176		
	Nahri Shahi	Naher Shahi	250			210	145		
	Sholgara	Shulgarah	213			200	151		
Balkh average			**235**	**201**		**179**	**123**		
Faryab	Bilchiragh	Belcheragh	180			346			
	Maymana	Meymaneh	175						
	Pashtun Kot	Pashtun Kowt	186						
	Qaysar	Qeysar	161						
	Shirin Tagab	Shirin Tagab	164						
Faryab average			**173**						
Ghazni	Ajristan	Ajristan	360						
Ghazni average			**360**						
Ghor	Chaghcharan							349	331
	Pasaband							352	331
	Shahrak							353	332
	Taywara							346	321
Ghor average								**349**	**328**
Helmand	Baghran	Baghran	237					394	370
	Dishu	Deh Shu							
	Garmser	Garmser	259					437	396
	Kajaki	Kajaki	257					407	370
	Lashkar Gah	Bust	234					426	389
	Musa Qala	Musa Qala	236					437	400
	Nad-e-Ali	Nad-e-Ali	268					426	389
	Nahri Sarraj	Nahr-e-Saraj	242					426	389
	Naw Zad	Naw Zad	265					433	385
	Naway Barakzayi	Nawa Barakzai	277					437	396
	Reg	Khan Neshin						437	396
	Sangin	Sarban Qala	247					407	370
	Washer	Washir						407	370
Helmand average			**252**					**423**	**385**
Herat	Obe	Obey	335						
	Pashtun Zarghun	Pashtun Zarghun	331						
	Shindand	Shindand	342						
	Zinda Jan	Zendeh Jan	314						
Herat average			**327**						
Jawzjan	Aqcha	Aqchah	169			88	68		
	Faysabad	Faizabad	230			152	108		
	Khamyab	Khamyab	194			56	44		
	Mardyan	Mardian	217			42	43		
	Mingajik	Manga Jek	198			92	66		
	Qarqin	Qarqin	195			76	46		

Province	District	Former district reference	2001 Dry	2001 Fresh		2002 Dry	2002 Fresh	2002 Dry	2002 Fresh
						May		July-August	
	Shibirghan	Sheberghan	176			41	41		
Jawzjan average			**194**			**100**	**61**		
Kabul	Surobi	Sarobi	362						
Kabul average			**362**						
Kandahar	Arghandab	Arghandab	316						
	Ghorak	Ghorak	234						
	Kandahar	Qandahar+Dand	245						
	Khakrez	Khakrez	262						
	Maywand	Maiwand	288						
	Panjwayi	Panjwai	257						
Kandahar average			**270**						
Kapisa	Tagab	Tagab	403						
Kapisa average			**403**						
Khost	Tani	Tani	325	291					
Khost average				**291**					
Kunar	Bar Kunar	Bar Kunar	302	155					
	Chawkay	Chawki	370	200					
	Narang	Narang	301	187					
	Nurgal	Mazar (Nur Gul)	354	188					
	Pech	Peche	373	268					
Kunar average			**339**	**200**					
Kunduz	Ali Abad	Aliabad	210			243	118		
	Chahar Dara	Chahar Darreh	234			250	107		
	Kunduz	Kunduz	219			263	149		
	Qalay-I- Zal	Qala-e Zal	236			225	112		
Kunduz average			**229**			**247**	**125**		
Laghman	Alingar	Alingar	404						
	Alishing	Alishang	318						
	Dawlat Shah	Dowlat Shah	365						
	Mihtarlam	Metarlam	336						
	Qarghayi	Qarghai	350						
Laghman average			**354**						
Nangarhar	Achin	Achin	330					388	341
	Bati Kot	Bati Kot	331					410	336
	Chaparhar	Chaparhar	317					385	344
	Dara-I-Nur	Darae Noor	282					378	334
	Dih Bala	Deh Bala	335					378	332
	Dur Baba	Durbaba	329					388	340
	Goshta	Goshta	350					391	343
	Hisarak	Hesarak	297					340	240
	Jalalabad	Behsud+Jalalabad	355					385	344
	Kama	Kama	348					385	338
	Khogyani	Khogiani	301					490	350
	Kuz Kunar	Kuz Kunar	303					378	334
	Lal Pur	La'lpur	346	188					
	Muhmand Dara	Mohmand Dara	379					422	337
	Nazyan	Nazian	396					378	341
	Pachir Wa Agam	Pachier wa Agam	315					398	344
	Rodat	Rodat	347					385	337
	Sherzad	Sherzad	304						
	Shinwar	Shinwar	321					478	351
	Surkh Rod	Sorkh Rod	312					390	310
Nangarhar average			**330**	**188**				**397**	**333**
Nimroz	Chahar Burjak	Char Borjak							
	Kang	Kang							
	Khash Rod	Khash Rud	378						
Nimroz average			**378**						
Paktya	Azra	Azro	389	292					
Paktya average			**389**	**292**					
Samangan	Dara-I- Suf	Darae Souf	240	207		386			

Province	District	Former district reference	2001 Dry	2001 Fresh		2002 Dry	2002 Fresh	2002 Dry	2002 Fresh
						May		July-August	
	Khuram Wa Sarbagh	Khuram+Samanga	339			299			
Samangan average			**290**	**207**		**328**			
Sari Pul	Sangcharak	Sar-e Pol	175			169	125		
Sari Pul average			**175**			**169**	**125**		
Takhar	Bangi	Bangi	235						
	Chah Ab	Chah Ab	246	100					
	Chal	Chal	223	151					
	Farkhar	Farkhar	251	113					
	Ishkamish	Eshkamesh	222	73					
	Kalafgan	Kalafgan	232	141		223	171		
	Khwaja Ghar	Khvajeh Ghar	233	110		202	185		
	Rustaq	Rostaq	253	141					
	Taluqan	Taloqan	235	90					
	Warsaj	Warsaj	238	100					
	Yangi Qala	Yangi Qala	251	111					
Takhar average			**238**	**113**		**216**	**176**		
Uruzgan	Chora	Chora	307						
	Day Kundi	Dai Kundi							
	Dihrawud	Dehrawud	259						
	Gizab	Gezab	292						
	Khas Uruzgan	Khas Oruzgan	254						
	Kijran	Kajran	269						
	Nesh	Nesh	291						
	Shahidi Hassas	Char Chashma	262						
	Shahristan	Shahrestan	271						
	Tirin Kot	Tirin Kot	248						
Uruzgan average			**280**						
Zabul	Arghandab	Arghandab	276						
	Daychopan	Dai Chopan	274						
	Mizan	Mizan	253						
	Qalat	Qalat	258						
	Shahjoy	Shah Juy	264						
	Tarnak Wa Jaldak	Jaldak	255						
Zabul average			**264**						

Agricultural land in opium growing areas

Another interesting finding of the survey is the evolution of the total agricultural land in Afghanistan during the last decade. Based on an update of the FAO 1993 land cover figures made by UNODC for the opium growing areas, it is estimated that the decline in arable land amounted to 37 % between the early and the late 1990s. This places the increased levels of opium poppy cultivation in a clearer perspective as it further illustrates the shift of some regions in Afghanistan to an illicit opium economy during the last decade.

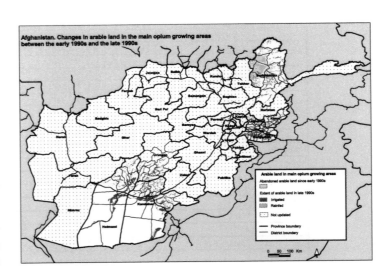

2.1.1.2. PAKISTAN

UNODC interim report on the status of opium poppy cultivation in Pakistan as of 16 May 2003.

According to Government reports the total estimated area under poppy cultivation in Pakistan during 2003 was approx. 5,691 hectares. Forty one percent (2,358 hectares) is reported to have been eradicated by 16 May 2003.

The NWFP Government confirmed that 3,870 hectares had been planted with opium poppy in the areas of the North-West Frontier Province of Pakistan, thirty seven percent (1,450 hectares) of which had been eradicated by 16 May 2003. Of the 1,821 hectares estimated to have been cultivated in Baluchistan Province, ANF/Narcotics Control Division reported the eradication of about 50 percent of the opium poppy crop by end of April 2003. The bulk of poppy cultivation in Baluchistan Province was concentrated in the Gulistan area of Pishin District close to the border with Afghanistan. It is noteworthy that this is the first time that significant cultivation has been reported from Baluchistan Province. The poppy eradication effort in Baluchistan could not be monitored by UNODC due to security constraints.

The Government of the North-West Frontier Province (NWFP) of Pakistan organized opium poppy monitoring missions in March and April 2003. The United Nations Office on Drugs and Crime (UNODC) participated in the missions in an observer's capacity. The missions assessed 41 sites. UNODC was represented in the assessment missions to Upper and Lower Dir, Khyber Agency and South Waziristan Agency (see map for location of the 41 sites).

Field-by-field visual assessments were conducted by experts from the agencies concerned, including agriculture extension specialists. In some areas, due to security or time limitations, the number of opium poppy fields was counted from a vantage point and the estimated size of each field was noted. Aerial assessments were subsequently carried out to monitor the extent of cultivation and eradication. Details of poppy eradication status as of 16 May 2003 are presented in the table attached.

It is also important to note that the eradication campaign is in the final phase at the time of reporting. The situation presented in this interim report can therefore not be considered as complete and final.

NWFP: POPPY ERADICATION STATUS
as of May 16, 2003

Number	Location	in Hectares		
		Eradicated	Standing crop	Total
	Upper & Lower Dir District			
1	Nehag Valley	76.89	4.05	80.94
2	The Rest of Upper Dir District	22.26	2.02	24.28
3	Lower Dir	18.62	0.00	18.62
	Total	117.77	6.07	123.84
	Bajaur Agency			
4	Salarzai Area	16.19	0.00	16.19
5	Asil Targhao, Ghar Shamozai	7.28	0.00	7.28
6	Chamarkand	0.81	0.00	0.81
	Total	24.28	0.00	24.28
	Mohmand Agency			
7	Ambar	20.23	0.00	20.23
8	Prang Ghar	16.19	0.00	16.19
9	Dawazai	14.16	0.00	14.16
10	Halimzai	26.31	0.00	26.31
11	Safi Area	8.09	0.00	8.09
12	Danish Kool	4.05	0.00	4.05
	Total	89.03	0.00	89.03
	Khyber Agency			
13	Choora Valley	6.07	6.07	12.14
14	Bazar Zakakhel Area	0.00	28.33	28.33
15	Bara River Valley	0.00	1214.08	1214.08
	Total	6.07	1248.48	1254.55
	Orakzai Agency			
16	Toi Mushti	36.42	0.00	36.42
17	Bulend Khel	202.35	0.00	202.35
18	Sultan Zai,Daulat Zai Area	8.09	0.00	8.09
	Total	246.86	0.00	246.86
	Karram Agency			
19	Masozai Area	113.31	696.07	809.39
20	Para Chamkani	4.05	149.74	153.78
21	Ali Sherzai	80.94	0.00	80.94
22	Zia Musht	60.70	0.00	60.70
	Total	259.00	845.81	1104.82
	North Waziristan Agency			
23	Shewa, Pipli, Miami	16.19	0.00	16.19
24	Kaitu Valley	40.47	0.00	40.47
25	Boya	0.81	0.00	0.81
26	Ghulam Khan (Bangi Dar)	0.40	0.00	0.40
	Total	57.87	0.00	57.87
	South Waziristan Agency			
27	Makin, Bazai	1.62	0.00	1.62
28	Tiarza	2.43	0.00	2.43
29	Wana Plain	242.82	0.00	242.82
30	Zarmalan Plain	28.33	0.00	28.33
31	Kazha Panga	8.09	16.19	24.28
	Total	283.29	16.19	299.47
	Frontier Regions Kohat			
32	Bazi Khel	4.05	6.07	10.12
33	Akhor Wal	8.09	8.09	16.19
	Total	12.14	14.16	26.31
	Frontier Regions Peshawar			
34	Jana Kor & Hasan Khel	0.00	2.83	2.83
35	Rest of FR (Bazi Khel)	0.81	3.24	4.05
	Total	0.81	6.07	6.88
	Kala Dhaka			
36	Kala Dhaka	161.88	0.00	161.88
	Total	161.88	0.00	161.88
	Kohistan District			
37	Kohistan	121.41	283.29	404.69
	Total	121.41	283.29	404.69
	Buner District			
38	Nawagai & Totalai area	29.14	0.00	29.14
	Total	29.14	0.00	29.14
	Swabi District			
39	Gadoon Area	18.21	0.00	18.21
40	Nuranzi	21.45	0.00	21.45
41	Matten Bala, Pabani, Marghuz	0.81	0.00	0.81
	Total	40.47	0.00	40.47
	Total NWFP	1450.02	2420.07	3870.09

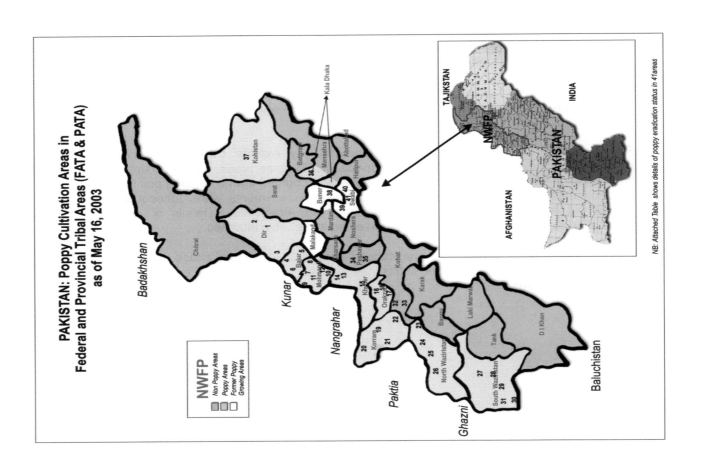

PAKISTAN: Poppy Cultivation Areas in Federal and Provincial Tribal Areas (FATA & PATA) as of May 16, 2003

NB: Attached Table shows details of poppy eradication status in 41areas

2.1.1.3. MYANMAR

The information presented below is based on abstracts from the UNODC report Myanmar, Opium Survey 2002, August 2002. The full report can be accessed on UNODC's website *(http://www.unodc.org/odccp/crop_monitoring.html)*.

The 2002 opium poppy survey was the first comprehensive survey implemented throughout the Shan State of Myanmar by the Central Committee for Drug Abuse Control (CCDAC) of the Government of Myanmar in co-operation with UNODC, in the framework of UNODC's Illicit Crop Monitoring Programme (ICMP). The Shan State represents more than 90% of the total opium poppy cultivation in Myanmar.

The survey relied on a combination of extensive fieldwork and satellite imagery. The fieldwork took place from January to March 2002 in a sample of villages, including the Wa Special Region. During this period, 169 surveyors visited 1,861 villages, measured 5,687 opium poppy fields, collected data for opium yield assessment from 1,269 fields and measured 37,061 opium poppy capsules. The surveyors also collected data on opium farm-gate prices and opium addiction by gender and age.

After analysis of the survey data, the total opium poppy cultivation in Myanmar was estimated to range from 65,600 ha to 97,700 ha in 2002, with a mean estimate of 81,400 ha.

The opium yield for the Shan State was found to range from 6.9 kg/ha to 13.1 kg/ha with a mean of 10.0 kg/ha. The total opium production in Myanmar was estimated to range from 670 to 992 tons, with an mean estimate of 828 tons in 2002.

The February 2002 average opium farm gate price of 109,500 Kyat/kg[a] (or 151 US$/kg) was used as the best estimate for the farm gate opium price for the 2002 opium season. As a result, the total farm gate value of opium in Myanmar in 2002 would range from US$100 to 150 million, with an overall mean value of US$ 125 million.

Population statistics for the Shan State are very limited, but assuming a total population of 5,000,000 inhabitants and an estimated 241,700 households growing opium poppy, the average annual household income from opium would range from US$400 to US$600, with an overall mean value of US$500 per household.

The analysis revealed that about 80,000 persons, representing 1.6% of the total population or 2.4% of the population age 15 and above, were smoking opium on a daily basis.

At the country level, eradication has been reported to reach a total of 7,469 ha. As the estimates for cultivation were made after eradication, the total area under poppy cultivation in Myanmar would amount to 88,900 ha. This would correspond to an eradication level of about 8%.

Detailed findings of the survey which covered 328 villages of the UNODC Wa Alternative Development Programme were included for the establishment of national estimates presented here but are detailed and analysed in a separate survey report.

---

[a] At the February 2002 exchange rate of 725 Kyat/US$

Myanmar opium poppy cultivation and opium production estimate 2002

Township	District	Region	Cultivation (ha)	YIELD (kg/ha)	Production (kg)
Kalaw**	Taunggyi	Southern	-		-
Kunhin	Loilem	Southern	60	11.6	696
Kunlong	Kunlon	Northern	991	10.0	9,910
Kutkai	Muse	Northern	7,955	12.5	99,438
Konkyan	Lawkai	Northern	5,402	15.9	85,892
Kengtung	Kengtung	Eastern	1,385	16.0	22,160
Kyakme	Kyakme	Northern	607	10.0	6,070
Kehsi	Loilem	Southern	67	10.0	670
Hsihseng	Taunggyi	Southern	203	12.6	2,558
Yawnghwe	Taunggyi	Southern	305	10.0	3,050
Tachilek	Tachilek	Eastern	337	5.9	1,988
Tangyan	Lashio	Northern	5,395	7.3	39,384
Taunggyi**	Taunggyi	Southern	-		-
Narphant	Lashio	Northern	4,772	7.3	34,836
Namkham	Muse	Northern	122	12.5	1,525
Namsang (south)	Loilem	Southern	387	10.0	3,870
Namhsan (North)	Namsang	Northern	1,416	10.0	14,160
Namtu	Kyakme	Northern	904	10.0	9,040
Nawnghkio**	Kyakme	Northern	-		-
Pinlaung	Tauungyi	Southern	920	5.6	5,152
Pindaya**	Taunggyi	Southern	-		-
Pangyan	Lashio	Northern	1,641	11.9	19,528
Pangwaing	Lashio	Northern	6,796	10.6	72,038
Pekhon	Taunggyi	Southern	2,465	4.9	12,079
Mabein**	Namsang	Northern	-		-
Manphant	Lashio	Northern	933	8.4	7,837
Mongnai	Loilem	Southern	1,181	10.0	11,810
Mongmit	Namsang	Northern	80	10.0	800
Muse	Muse	Northern	3,925	10.0	39,250
Mongkung	Loilem	Northern	452	6.8	3,074
Mongkhak	Kengtung	Eastern	42	10.0	420
Monghsat	Monghsat	Eastern	661	10.0	6,610
Mongtung	Monghsat	Eastern	132	4.8	634
Mongpan	Loilem	Southern	2,052	10.0	20,520
Mongping	Monghsat	Eastern	899	11.3	10,159
Mongphak	Mongphak	Eastern	1,105	15.5	17,128
Mongmao	Lashio	Northern	1,255	8.7	10,919
Mongyawng	Mongphak	Eastern	1,641	10.0	16,410
Mongyang	Kengtung	Eastern	1,076	9.6	10,330
Monghsu	Loilem	Southern	378	18.5	6,993
Mongyai	Lashio	Northern	142	10.0	1,420
Mawkmai	Loilem	Southern	895	10.0	8,950
Lawksawk	Taunggyi	Southern	437	10.0	4,370
Ywangan**	Taunggyi	Southern	-		-
Lashio	Lashio	Northern	2,127	5.5	11,699
Laikha	Loilem	Southern	749	10.0	7,490
Langkho	Loilem	Southern	177	10.0	1,770
Loilem	Loilem	Southern	381	10.0	3,810
Hsipaw	Kyakme	Northern	101	10.0	1,010
Hsenwi	Lashio	Northern	1,200	5.6	6,720
Hopong	Taunggyi	Southern	973	9.3	9,049
Hopang	Kunlon	Northern	1,110	10.0	11,100
Lawkai	Lawkai	Northern	6,279	9.9	62,162
Manton	Namsang	Northern	402	9.8	3,940
Mantman	Monghsat	Eastern	1,641	11.8	19,364
Shan State Total			**74,556**		**759,786**
Estimates Outside Shan State			6,837	10.0	68,360
National Estimates (ha)			**81,393**		**828,146**

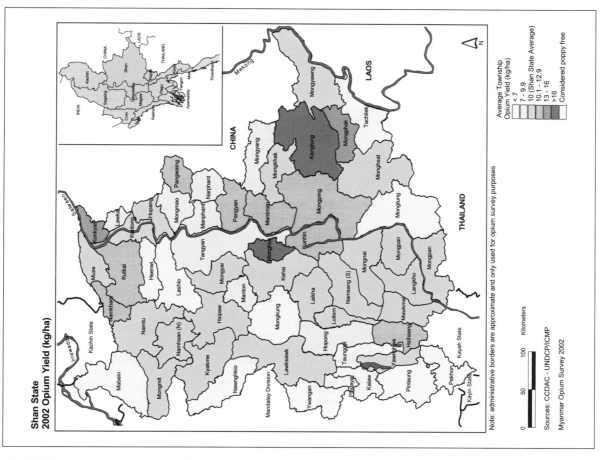

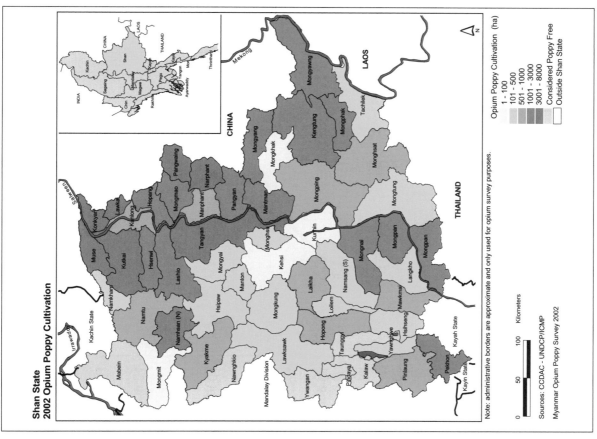

Myanmar 2002 Opium prices

RegionName	ID	Township	March 01	April 01	May 01	June 01	July 01	Aug 01	Sept 01	Oct 01	Nov 01	Dec 01	Jan 02	Feb 02
Northern Shan State	3	Kunlong	132,665											129,458
	4	Kutkai	118,007	132,519	136,018	135,931	131,464	135,931	127,125	125,199	123,821	123,378	121,625	122,859
	12	Tangyan	79,933	80,381	83,126	85,178	88,784	91,526	94,060	96,553	99,565	105,273	87,380	90,437
	15	Namkham	84,052	86,835	88,227	90,036	104,091	111,049	114,528	116,059	123,434	124,269	107,333	100,669
	29	Muse	120,659	95,672	98,989	104,091	106,132	101,487	144,604	112,695				137,304
	30	Mongkung	64,292	66,843	69,394	72,456	73,986	76,538	79,089	78,579	80,109	80,109	59,189	61,740
	37	Mongmao	75,925	75,925	75,925	75,925	75,925	75,925	75,925	75,925	75,925	75,925	82,048	81,640
	41	Mongyai	118,888	113,276	139,298	138,788		110,214	110,214	132,155	128,583	110,214	101,370	99,193
	45	Lashio	97,968	91,845	90,314									91,845
	50	Hsenwi	112,255	112,255	112,255	112,255	112,595	114,976	117,698	117,698	120,079	118,378	124,161	125,181
	52	Hopang	117,212	122,460	116,337								101,030	111,132
	53	Lawkai	252,101	252,101									144,958	144,958
Northern Shan State average			109,379	105,224	94,844	95,019	97,600	100,347	104,747	105,586	105,413	107,195	102,274	104,903
Southern Shan State	2	Kunhin	85,722	85,883	86,528	88,300	92,328	94,423	96,840	100,868	111,986	117,304	85,722	68,884
	8	Kehsi	54,636	56,520	59,817	61,701	64,998	70,650	72,534	77,951	80,070	81,954	84,780	83,171
	9	Hsihseng						91,845		91,845		91,845	91,845	91,845
	10	Yawnghwe										82,661		
	16	Namsang (south)	91,845									77,558	74,497	75,007
	20	Pinlaung	69,977	71,602	72,979	74,433	75,836	77,850	76,163	72,902	71,976	72,711	81,130	84,641
	24	Pekhon	68,260	68,260	68,260	69,848	74,837	78,465	79,599	82,320	85,042	82,027	78,374	82,661
	27	Mongnai										85,722	72,796	74,497
	34	Mongpan										122,460		
	40	Monghsu	71,896	71,896	71,896	75,451	80,192	92,043	96,783	102,708	117,522	122,460	122,460	122,460
	46	Laikha	85,722										112,255	113,276
	47	Langkho									122,460	84,191	61,230	
	48	Loilem	76,538	82,661	76,538	81,130	88,018	80,364	89,549	103,326	90,314	88,784	84,191	86,487
	51	Hopong									73,476	92,525	100,349	82,661
Southern Shan State average			71,715	72,164	72,662	74,839	78,425	82,661	84,222	86,898	90,961	92,181	93,915	87,427
Wa Region	39	Mongyang	144,851	124,856	133,105	125,219	159,020	162,105	186,653	152,690	148,466	136,738	111,273	110,829
Wa Region average			144,851	124,856	133,105	125,219	159,020	162,105	186,653	152,690	148,466	136,738	111,273	110,829
Eastern Shan State	6	Kengtung	104,091										95,598	104,648
	11	Tachilek	306,096	306,645	306,645	306,645	323,872	334,701	334,701	334,701	329,779	317,473	307,834	307,834
	31	Mongkhak	85,722			97,968	97,968					110,214		
	32	Monghsat	117,856	114,759	114,759	114,759	114,759	114,759	114,759	114,759	114,759	111,501	116,694	116,694
	33	Mongtung	112,735	114,536	119,579	126,422	130,744	136,147	146,232	151,994	157,757	161,359	104,451	108,413
	35	Mongping	78,671	79,785	83,681	90,268	94,257	102,792	107,802	109,472	99,638	90,361	79,228	74,960
	36	Mongphak	102,083	105,560	109,038	131,435	116,140	119,702	123,412	127,058	130,662	155,389	137,849	130,444
	38	Mongyang	88,784											61,230
	39	Mongyawng	122,460	153,075	153,075		153,075	153,075	142,870	153,075	153,075	183,690	112,255	114,806
	56	Mant Man	67,727	67,727	67,727	68,237	114,976	115,827	117,017	117,358	121,950	117,698	97,288	77,558
Eastern Shan State average			123,069	122,892	124,814	129,999	141,611	146,756	149,582	151,379	150,966	149,660	127,802	124,791
AVERAGE FOR THE SHAN STATE			115,084	101,447	99,974	102,909	111,664	116,542	122,565	118,379	119,022	118,127	110,356	109,649
Exchange Rate Kyat/USD			530	653	685	650	640	683	705	732	739	740	710	725
AVERAGE FOR THE SHAN STATE IN USD			217	155	146	158	174	171	174	162	161	160	155	151

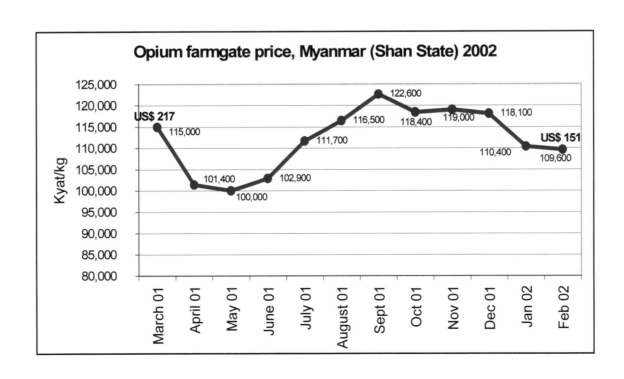

Opium farmgate price, Myanmar (Shan State) 2002

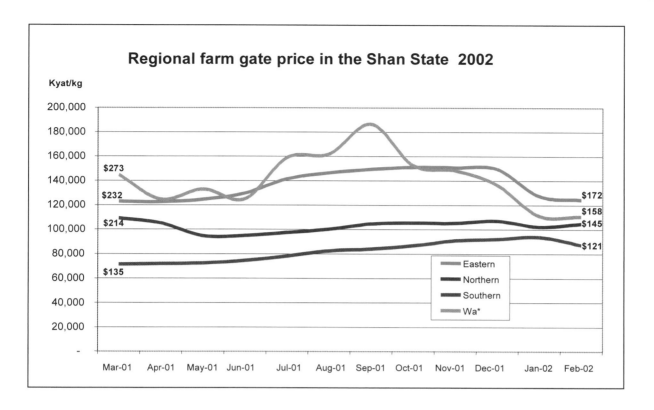

FARMGATE PRICES, 1991-2002
(in constant 2002 US$, per kilogramme)

1991	1992	1993	1994	1995	1996	1997	1998	1999	2000	2001	2002
153	181	198	195	208	146	106	112	167	267	211	128

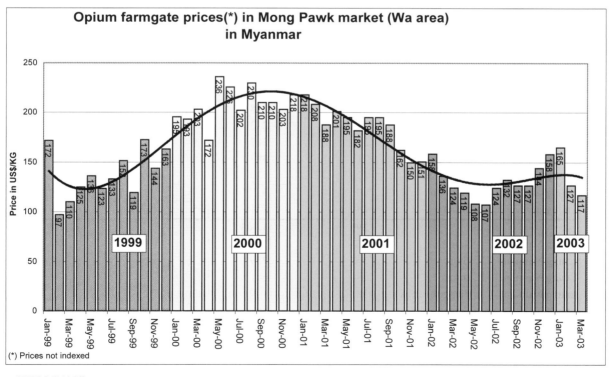

Source: UNODC Field Office.

2.1.1.4. LAO, PDR

The information presented below is based on abstracts from the UNODC report Laos PDR, Opium Survey 2002, August 2002.   The full report can be accessed on UNODC's website (http://www.unodc.org/odccp/crop_monitoring.html).

The 2002 opium poppy survey was the third consecutive annual survey since 2000. It was implemented by the Lao National Commission for Drug Control and Supervision, with technical support from the UNODC Illicit Crop Monitoring Programme.

Like in previous surveys, the 2002 opium survey used a sampling methodology. A total of 421 villages (out of 6008) were surveyed in the 11 provinces of northern Laos, through interviews of village headmen and opium poppy farmers, as well as physical measuring of opium poppy fields and capsules.

Nationally, the survey estimated that there were 14,052 hectares of opium poppy under cultivation for the 2002 season. This represented a reduction in total opium poppy area of 18.6% compared with the 2001 estimate of 17,255 hectares. This confirmed the downward trend of opium poppy cultivation in Laos since 1998 when the cultivation of opium poppy was estimated at 26,800 hectares.

The survey confirmed that opium poppy cultivation mainly took place in the 6 provinces targeted by the Opium Elimination Programme launched in 1998. The cultivation in these 6 provinces accounted for 88 % of the total area under cultivation.

The total potential opium production was estimated at about 112 tons, representing a 16% decrease compared to last year. The national average yield was estimated at 8 kg/ha. This figure should be understood as a potential yield.

The estimate for opium addiction indicated similar patterns as previous surveys. The total number of opium addicts was estimated at 52,613 persons, against 58,175 persons in 2001, representing an encouraging 9.6% decrease.

At the country level, the farm gate price of opium was estimated at 1,160,000 KIP/kg (or 122 USD/kg) for February 2002. The estimated farm gate price for the previous year was 1,400,00 KIP/kg (or 165 USD/kg) for March 2001.

Estimates of Opium cultivation and productionat province and district levels

Province	District	No. of villages Growing Opium	Estimated Area	Yield	(*)	Production
			ha	kg/ha		kg
Phongsaly	Phongsaly	45	318	7.9	*	2,521
Phongsaly	May	39	213	7.9	*	1,682
Phongsaly	Khua	38	207	7.9	*	1,639
Phongsaly	Samphanh	71	387	7.9	*	3,062
Phongsaly	Boon Neua	22	120	7.9	*	949
Phongsaly	Nhot Ou	60	327	7.9	*	2,588
Phongsaly	Boontai	24	131	7.9	*	1,035
		299	**1,703**			**13,475**
Luang Namtha	Namtha	25	207	6.7	**	1,390
Luang Namtha	Sing	35	289	6.7	**	1,946
Luang Namtha	Long	58	661	7.3		4,829
Luang Namtha	Viengphoukha	18	149	6.7	**	1,001
Luang Namtha	Nalae	6	50	6.7	**	334
		142	**1,355**			**9,498**
UdomXay	Xay	41	369	5.6	**	2,054
UdomXay	La	31	279	5.6	**	1,553

Province	District	No. of villages Growing Opium	Estimated Area	Yield	(*)	Production
			ha	kg/ha		kg
UdomXay	Namor	41	369	5.6	**	2,054
UdomXay	Nga	21	189	5.6	**	1,052
UdomXay	Beng	17	153	5.6	**	852
UdomXay	Hoon	34	306	4.4		1,348
UdomXay	Pakbeng	26	234	5.6	**	1,303
		211	**1,901**			**10,216**
Bokeo	Huoixai	4	38	7.9	*	300
Bokeo	Tonpheung	4	38	7.9	*	300
Bokeo	Meung	4	38	7.9	*	300
Bokeo	Pha Oudom	6	57	7.9	*	450
Bokeo	Paktha	15	142	7.9	*	1,126
Bokeo	Special Region	2	19	7.9	*	150
		35	**332**			**2,626**
Luang Prabang	Luang Prabang	8	173	10.4	**	1,803
Luang Prabang	Xieng Ngeun	16	275	10.4	**	2,866
Luang Prabang	Nan	7	100	10.4	**	1,042
Luang Prabang	Park Ou	16	268	10.4	**	2,793
Luang Prabang	Nambak	18	329	10.4	**	3,429
Luang Prabang	Ngoi	28	520	10.4	**	5,420
Luang Prabang	Pak Xeng	13	179	10.4	**	1,866
Luang Prabang	Phonxay	20	403	10.4	**	4,200
Luang Prabang	Chomphet	16	299	10.4	**	3,116
Luang Prabang	Viengkham	37	457	10.4	**	4,763
Luang Prabang	Phoukhoune	16	397	10.4	**	4,138
		195	**3,400**			**35,437**
Huapanh	Xamneua	101	816	7.9	*	6,462
Huapanh	Xiengkhor	20	162	7.9	*	1,280
Huapanh	Viengthong	36	291	7.9	*	2,303
Huapanh	Viengxay	38	307	7.9	*	2,431
Huapanh	Huameuang	51	412	7.9	*	3,263
Huapanh	Xamtay	77	622	7.9	*	4,926
Huapanh	Sopbao	20	162	7.9	*	1,280
Huapanh	Add	20	162	7.9	*	1,280
		363	**2,934**			**23,225**
Xayabouri	Xayabury	30	257	6.1	**	1,560
Xayabouri	Khop	12	103	6.1	**	624
Xayabouri	Hongsa	23	197	6.1	**	1,196
Xayabouri	Ngeun	12	103	6.1	**	624
Xayabouri	Xienghone	14	120	6.1	**	728
Xayabouri	Phiang	9	77	6.1	**	468
Xayabouri	Parklai	-	-	6.1	**	-
Xayabouri	Kenethao	-	-	6.1	**	-
Xayabouri	Botene	-	-	6.1	**	-
Xayabouri	Thongmyxay	-	-	6.1	**	-
		100	**857**			**5,199**
Xieng Khuang	Pek	25	164	7.9	*	1,301
Xieng Khuang	Kham	34	223	7.9	*	1,769

Province	District	No. of villages Growing Opium	Estimated Area	Yield	(*)	Production
			ha	kg/ha		kg
Xieng Khuang	Nonghed	61	138	7.9	*	1,092
Xieng Khuang	Khoune	39	256	7.9	*	2,029
Xieng Khuang	Morkmay	23	151	7.9	*	1,197
Xieng Khuang	Phookood	12	79	7.9	*	624
Xieng Khuang	Phaxay	10	66	7.9	*	520
		204	**1,078**			**8,532**
Vientiane	Phonhong	-	-	7.9	*	-
Vientiane	Thoulakhom	-	-	7.9	*	-
Vientiane	Keo Oudom	-	-	7.9	*	-
Vientiane	Kasy	-	-	7.9	*	-
Vientiane	Vangvieng	-	-	7.9	*	-
Vientiane	Feuang	-	-	7.9	*	-
Vientiane	Xanakharm	-	-	7.9	*	-
Vientiane	Mad	-	-	7.9	*	-
Vientiane	Viengkam	-	-	7.9	*	-
Vientiane	Hinhurp	-	-	7.9	*	-
Vientiane	Hom	10	100	7.9	*	790
Vientiane	Longxan	11	110	7.9	*	875
		21	**210**			**1,664**
Bolikhamsay	Pakxanh	-	-	7.9	*	-
Bolikhamsay	Thaphabath	-	-	7.9	*	-
Bolikhamsay	Pakkading	-	-	7.9	*	-
Bolikhamsay	Bolikhanh	-	-	7.9	*	-
Bolikhamsay	Khamkheuth	-	-	7.9	*	-
Bolikhamsay	Viengthong	11	42	7.9	*	331
		11	**42**			**331**
Xaisombun	Saysomboun	20	40	7.9	*	317
Xaisombun	Thathom	-	-	7.9	*	-
Xaisombun	Phoon	4	200	7.9	*	1,583
		24	**240**			**1,900**
	TOTAL	**1,605**	**14,052**	**8.0**	***	**112,104**

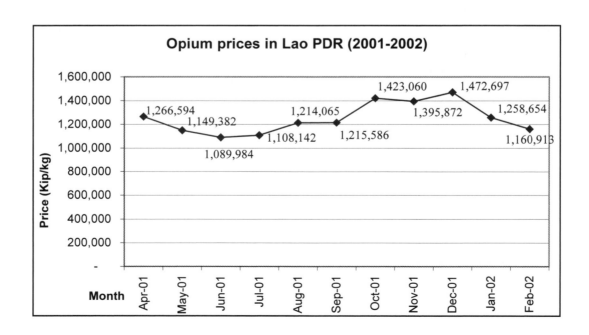

Opium prices in Lao PDR (2001-2002)

2.1.1.5. REPORTED ERADICATION OF OPIUM POPPY

ERADICATION REPORTED, 1992-2002										
(in hectares)										
	1993	1994	1995	1996	1997	1998	1999	2000	2001	2002
Opium poppy										
Afghanistan							400	121		17,300
Colombia	9,400	5,314	5,074	7,412	7,333	3,077	8,434	9,279	2,583	3,371
Mexico	13,015	10,959	15,389	14,671	17,732	17,449	15,461	15,717	15,350	
Myanmar	160	1,041	3,310	1,938	3,093	3,172	9,824	1,643	9,317	7,469
Pakistan	856	463		867	654	2,194	1,197	1,704	1,484	n/a
Thailand	1,706	1,313	580	886	1,053	716	808	757	832	507
Vietnam		672	477	1,142	340	439		426		

2.1.1.6. MANUFACTURE
SEIZURES OF ILLICIT LABORATORIES
REPORTED FOR 2000 - 2001

Remark: For convenience, an attempt was made to group the reported estimates by drug categories. however, due to inconsistencies and gaps in the reporting, no overall analysis of the data set was performed. Numbers are presented as reported to UNDCP and should be interpreted with caution.

Source: Annual Report Questionnaire if not otherwise indicated

Country or Territory	Year	Name of drug seized	Number of laboratories (and quantity of drug) seized	Source
			OPIATE GROUP	
Americas				
North America				
Mexico	2001	Heroin	1 Lab.	
Subtotal North America			1 Lab.	
South America				
Colombia	2000	Heroin	10 Lab.	
	2001	Heroin	6 Lab.(1.400 kg)	
Subtotal South America			16 Lab.(1.400 kg)	
Total Americas			17 Lab.(1.400 kg)	
Asia				
East and South-East Asia				
Hong Kong SAR, China	2000	Heroin	16 Lab.(46.690 kg)	
	2001	Heroin	12 Lab.	
Korea (Republic of)	2000	Opium	789 Lab.	ICPO
Malaysia	2000	Heroin	(3.640 kg)	
Myanmar	2000	Opium	(69.400 kg)	
	2000	Heroin	3 Lab.(0.042 kg)	
	2001	Heroin	16 Lab.	
Subtotal East and South-East Asia			836 Lab.(119.772 kg)	
South Asia				
India	2000	Heroin	2 Lab.	ICPO
	2001	Heroin	6 Lab.	
	2001	Morphine	1 Lab.	
Subtotal South Asia			9 Lab.	
Total Asia			845 Lab.(119.772 kg)	
Europe				
Eastern Europe				
Lithuania	2000	Opium liquid	7 Lab.(0.581 lt.)	
Poland	2000	Polish heroin	168 Lab.(388.000 lt.)	
	2001	Polish heroin	408 Lab.(280.000 lt.)	

Country or Territory	Year	Name of drug seized	Number of laboratories (and quantity of drug) seized	Source
Republic of Moldova	2001	Opium	11 Lab.	
Russian Federation	2000	Opium	243 Lab.	Govt
	2000	Heroin	8 Lab.	Govt
	2001	Opium	232 Lab.(24.114 kg)	
Subtotal Eastern Europe			1077 Lab.(24.114 kg)(668.581 lt.)	
Western Europe				
Italy	2000	Heroin	2 Lab.(0.150 kg)(3 u.)	
Turkey	2000	Heroin	9 Lab.(284.572 kg)	
Subtotal Western Europe			11 Lab.(284.722 kg)(3 u.)	
Total Europe			1088 Lab.(308.836 kg)(668.581 lt.)(3 u.)	
Opiate group			1950 Lab.(430.008 kg)(668.581 lt.)(3 u.)	

2.1.2. COCA / COCAINE

COCA

GLOBAL ILLICIT CULTIVATION OF COCA BUSH AND PRODUCTION OF COCA LEAF AND COCAINE, 1990-2002												
	1990	1991	1992	1993	1994	1995	1996	1997	1998	1999	2000	2001	2002

CULTIVATION[1] OF COCA BUSH IN HECTARES													
Bolivia [2]	50,300	47,900	45,300	47,200	48,100	48,600	48,100	45,800	38,000	21,800	14,600	19,900	24,400
Colombia [3]	40,100	37,500	37,100	39,700	44,700	50,900	67,200	79,400	101,800	160,100	163,300	144,800	102,000
Peru [4]	121,300	120,800	129,100	108,800	108,600	115,300	94,400	68,800	51,000	38,700	43,400	46,200	46,700
	211,700	**206,200**	**211,500**	**195,700**	**201,400**	**214,800**	**209,700**	**194,000**	**190,800**	**220,600**	**221,300**	**210,900**	**173,100**

POTENTIAL PRODUCTION OF DRY COCA LEAF IN METRIC TONS													
Bolivia	77,000	78,000	80,300	84,400	89,800	85,000	75,100	70,100	52,900	22,800	13,400	20,200	19,800
Colombia	45,300	45,000	44,900	45,300	67,500	80,900	108,900	129,500	165,900	261,000	266,200	236,000	222,100
Peru	196,900	222,700	223,900	155,500	165,300	183,600	174,700	130,600	95,600	69,200	46,200	49,300	52,500
	319,200	**345,700**	**349,100**	**285,200**	**322,600**	**349,500**	**358,700**	**330,200**	**314,400**	**353,000**	**325,800**	**305,500**	**294,400**

POTENTIAL MANUFACTURE OF COCAINE IN METRIC TONS													
Bolivia	189	220	225	240	255	240	215	200	150	70	43	60	60
Colombia	92	88	91	119	201	230	300	350	435	680	695	617	580
Peru	492	525	550	410	435	460	435	325	240	175	141	150	160
	774	**833**	**866**	**769**	**891**	**930**	**950**	**875**	**825**	**925**	**879**	**827**	**800**

[1] Potentially harvestable, after eradication

[2] Source: CICAD and US Department of State, International narcotics Control Strategy Report. Annual estimates include 12,000 hectares authorized by Bolivian law 1008.

[3] Cultivation estimates for 1999 and subsequent years come from the national monitoring system established by the Colombian government with the support of UNODC. Estimates for 2000 refer to the level of cultivation in August 2000, estimates for 2001 refer to the level of cultivation in November 2001 and estimates for 2002 refer to the level of cultivation in December 2002. Due to the change of methodology, figures for 1999 and after cannot be directly compared with data from previous years.

[4] UNODC now relies on the results for 2000, 2001 and 2002 of the illicit crop monitoring system established with the support of UNODC.

2.1.2.1. COLOMBIA

The information presented below is based on abstracts from the UNODC report *Colombia, Coca Survey for 2002, April 2003.*   The full report can be accessed on UNODC's website (http://www.unodc.org/odccp/crop_monitoring.html).

The Illicit Crop Monitoring Programme (ICMP) of the United Nations *Office on Drugs and Crime* (UNODC) presently covers the six countries where most illicit cultivation of the coca bush and opium poppy takes place (Colombia, Bolivia and Peru for coca; Afghanistan, Laos and Myanmar for opium).With illicit coca cultivation expanding steadily during the 1980's and 1990's, Colombia has become the country with the largest illicit coca growing area and cocaine production in the world.

UNODC implements an Illicit Crop Monitoring System (SIMCI) in Colombia since 1999, with the logistical support of the Colombian Anti-Narcotics Police (DIRAN), and in coordination with the National Narcotics Office in Colombia (DNE).

The 2002 census of illicit coca cultivation implemented by SIMCI covered the whole territory of Colombia. The methodology was based on the analysis of satellite images taken during the period August 2002 – January 2003, complemented with verification flights over coca growing areas. The reliability of the results is estimated at 90% (accuracy checks are still proceeding at the time of preparation of the present preliminary report, but the final figure should not vary significantly).

The results of the census show that, at the end of December 2002, about 102,000 hectares of coca were cultivated in 21 out of the 32 Colombian departments. This represents approximately 0.09% of the national territory's 1.14 million square km.

Although Colombia remains the country with the largest area under coca bush cultivation, ahead of Peru and Bolivia, the new figure reflects a decrease of about 43,000 ha (30%) since November 2001, when about 145,000 ha of illicit coca bush cultivation were reported by SIMCI. The decline recorded last year (about 18,000 ha, or 11 %) thus continued and accelerated in 2002. The national trend masks however important variations at department level, as well as within departments.

Very significant reductions in coca cultivation were recorded in the departments of Putumayo (- 33,000 ha), Meta (- 2,000 ha), and Caquetá (- 6,000 ha), where eradication activities implemented by the government took place in 2002. Other departments also show reductions attributed to abandonment of fields or voluntary manual eradication, such as Bolívar (-2,000 ha), Cauca (-1,000 ha) and Vichada (-4,000 ha).

Guaviare has now become the most important coca-growing department of the country, with a total of about 27,000 ha of coca bush and a one-year increase of about 2,000 ha. The second ranking department, Nariño, recorded an even larger increase of about 8,000 ha.

With an average of four harvests per year, the potential cocaine output of the 102,000 ha recorded in December 2002 is estimated at 480 metric tons (against 617 mt in November 2001). This figure does not represent the entire production for 2002, but the production potential of the hectares of coca bush under cultivation in December 2002. The actual production for the year 2002 is likely to have been higher, in the range between today's estimate (480 mt, Dec. 2002) and last year's (617 mt, Nov. 2001).

Illicit opium poppy cultivation is concentrated in the central and southern mountainous areas of the country, in Cauca, Nariño, Huila and Tolima. SIMCI has not yet established a reliable remote-sensing methodology for the detection of opium poppy. Based on visual reconnaissance, the DIRAN estimates that approximately 4,200 ha were under opium poppy cultivation in November 2002, which would translate in a reduction of about 1,900 ha compared with 2001. Based on an estimated average yield of 15kg/ha and two harvests per year, the <u>potential opium production</u> would have reached about <u>128 metric tons</u>, equivalent <u>to about 5 metric tons of heroin</u>.

In 2002, the DIRAN carried out a large-scale eradication campaign. The DIRAN reported the spraying of 130,364 hectares of coca bush and 3,371 hectares of opium poppy in 2002. Compared with 2001, this represents increases of 45% and 67%, respectively.

Cultivation of coca bush in hectares, Colombia, 1994 - 2002

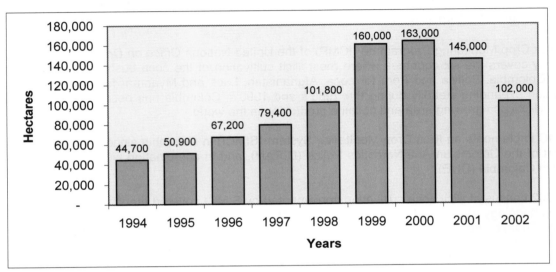

Remark: Estimates for 1999 and subsequent years come from the national monitoring system established by the Colombian government with the support of UNODC. Due to the change of methodology, figures for 1999 and after cannot be directly compared with data from previous years (based on US government surveys).

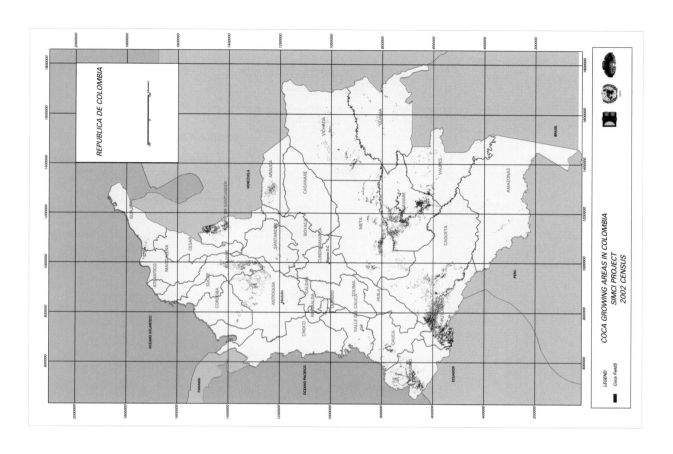

COCA GROWING AREAS IN COLOMBIA
SIMCI PROJECT
2002 CENSUS

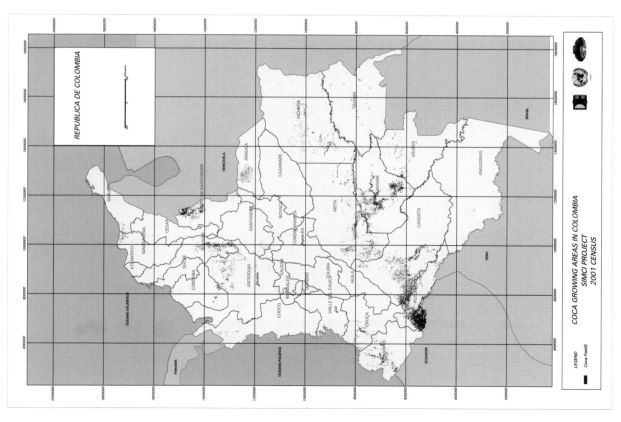

COCA GROWING AREAS IN COLOMBIA
SIMCI PROJECT
2001 CENSUS

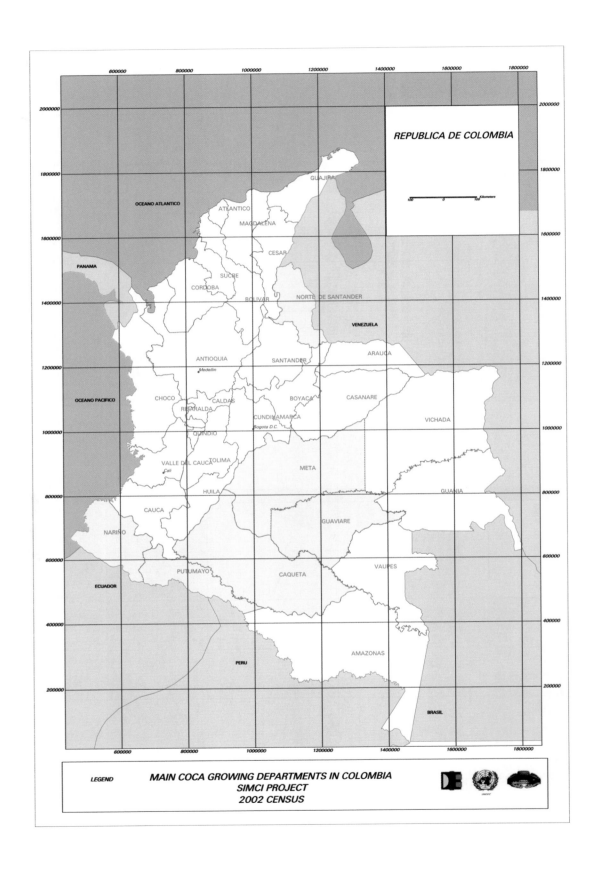

MAIN COCA GROWING DEPARTMENTS IN COLOMBIA
SIMCI PROJECT
2002 CENSUS

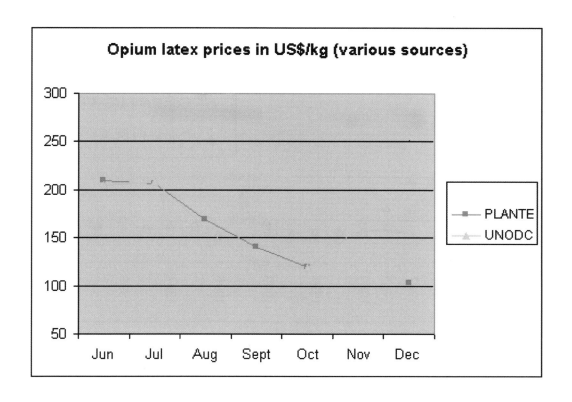

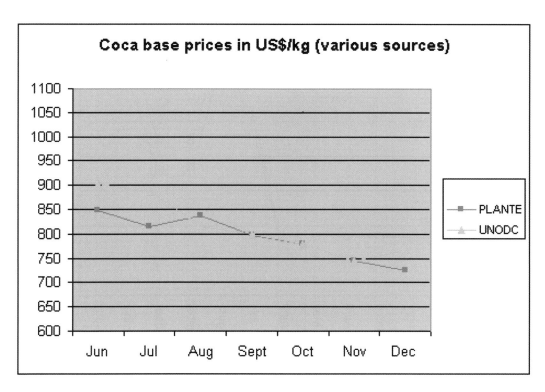

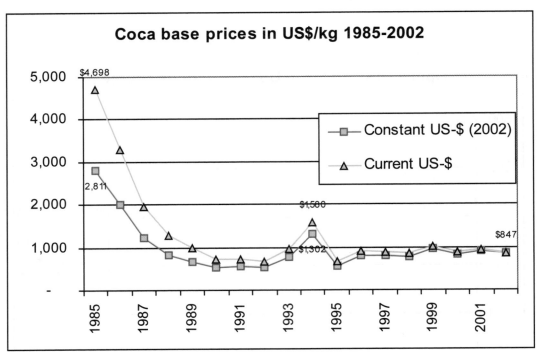

Coca base prices in US$/kg 1985-2002

Source: UNODC, DELTA and UNODC Field Office

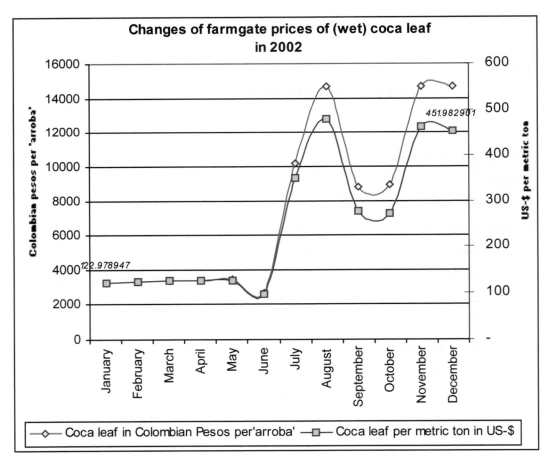

Changes of farmgate prices of (wet) coca leaf in 2002

Source: UNODC, Field Office.

2.1.2.2. PERU

The information presented below is based on abstracts from the UNODC report *Peru, Coca Survey for 2002, April 2003.*   The full report can be accessed on UNODC's website (http://www.unodc.org/odccp/crop_monitoring.html).

Under its global Illicit Crop Monitoring Programme, UNODC has been assisting the Peruvian Government in the development of a national coca monitoring system since 1998. Annual surveys have been implemented since 2000. The report presents the findings of the coca survey for 2002.

In Peru, coca cultivation is concentrated in six main areas (Apurimac, the upper Huallaga, La Convention-Lares, Sandia, Aguaytia and Central Selva). The estimation of coca cultivation is based on the interpretation of satellite images covering the entire coca growing areas, complemented by field verifications and the use of a previously established detailed cartography of the coca cultivation areas.

The total area under coca cultivation in Peru was estimated at about 46,700 ha in 2002. This represented an increase of 1% compared to the 2001 estimates of 46,200 ha. Despite the small increase, the level of coca cultivation remained well below the cultivation levels recorded in the mid-1990s.

Coca cultivation in Peru, 1992-2002 (ha)

1992	1993	1994	1995	1996	1997	1998	1999	2000	2001	2002
129,100	108,800	108,600	115,300	94,400	68,800	51,000	38,700	43,400	46,200	46,700

The overall stability masked variations at regional level. Decreases in coca cultivation were observed in the areas of La Convention-Lares (-13%) and in Sandia (-4%), while increases were recorded in other areas, such as Apurimac (+12%), the upper Huallaga (+6%) and Aguaytia (+1%). Coca cultivation remained stable in other areas such as Central Selva.

The total production of dry coca leaf for 2002 was estimated at 52,500 metric tons, with a country average yield of about 1,100 kg of dry leaf harvested per hectare. There are however regional variations: annual yields varied from 400 kg/ha (La Convention-Lares) to 2,200 kg/ha (Apurimac).

After the steep decline in coca prices in 1995-96, a progressive recovery has now brought prices back to the relatively high level of 1994. The average price for dry coca leaf on the illicit market reached 2.5 US$/kg in 2002, with a maximum of 2.9 US$/kg in August and a minimum of 2.1 US$/kg in April. In some areas, increasing coca prices have created an incentive for farmers to reactive abandoned coca fields.

In 2002, the government reported the eradication of 7,200 ha of coca fields. This represents the third largest report of eradication since 1983. In Peru, eradication is conducted manually as chemical eradication is prohibited.

Although, probably still at relatively low levels, there are indications that opium poppy cultivation has spread in recent years in Peru. Given this trend, the monitoring system will develop a methodology to detect opium poppy fields in future years.

Annual coca cultivation since 1992 (in ha)

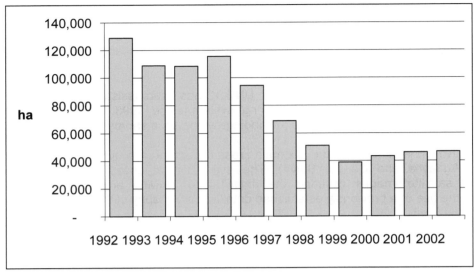

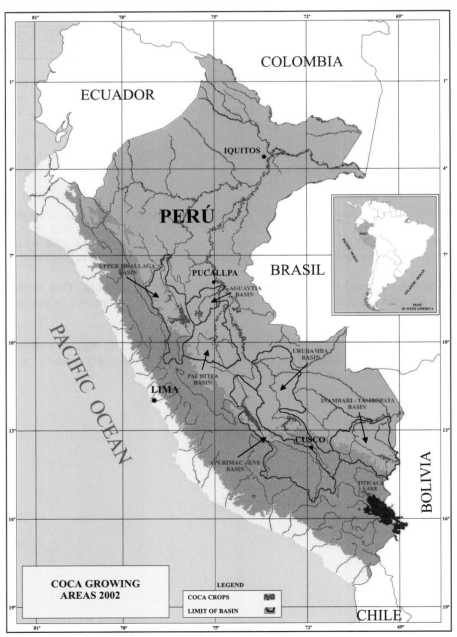

COCA GROWING
AREAS 2002

LEGEND

COCA CROPS

LIMIT OF BASIN

PERU: FARMGATE PRICES OF COCA LEAF, 1991-2002

(in constant 2002 US$, per kilogramme)

1991	1992	1993	1994	1995	1996	1997	1998	1999	2000	2001	2002
1.93	3.19	2.43	3.00	1.41	0.75	0.88	1.60	2.29	2.16	2.41	2.48

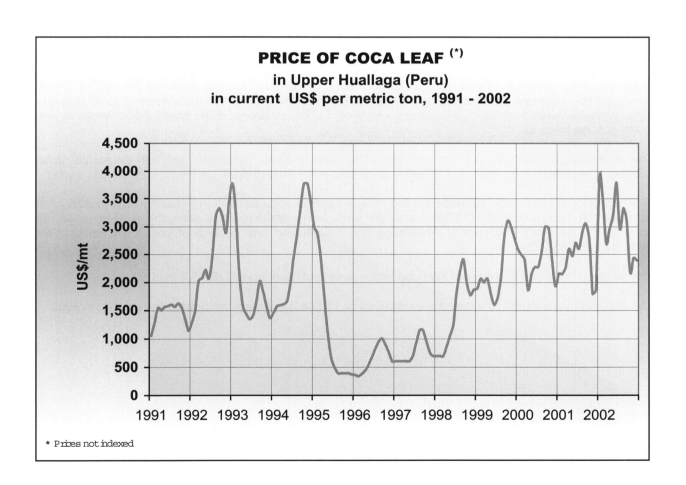

PRICE OF COCA LEAF (*)

in Upper Huallaga (Peru)
in current US$ per metric ton, 1991 - 2002

* Prices not indexed

2.1.2.3. BOLIVIA

The information presented below is based on abstracts from the UNODC report *Bolivia, Coca Survey in the Yungas of Lapaz in 2002, March 2003.* The full report can be accessed on UNODC's website (http://www.unodc.org/odccp/crop_monitoring.html).

The report presents the findings of the UNODC project "Land use management and monitoring system in the Yungas of La Paz" for the year 2002. This project is part of UNODC's Illicit Crop Monitoring Programme and was launched at the end of 2001, as a pilot phase, over one of the two main coca growing areas in Bolivia. A project extension is being prepared to develop a system that will produce annual national estimates of coca cultivation in Bolivia, as of 2003.

The first survey identified 13,800 hectares of coca bush cultivated in the Yungas of La Paz in 2002. In the traditional coca growing area, as defined under the Bolivian law 1008 which authorises up to 12,000 ha of coca cultivation within its limits, the survey identified 11,300 hectares, while about 2,500 hectares were found outside the area.

The methodology relied on the interpretation of satellite images, complemented with extensive ground truthing. It enabled the identification of every coca field in the survey area.

In the traditional area, coca cultivation is the main crop, and coca cultivation generally covers 30% of the land, with an average density of 30 hectares per km². In the non-traditional area, the density varied from 10 to 30 ha per km². The cost of developing and maintaining one hectare of coca bush in 2002 was estimated at US$ 2,000.

The average price of a kilogram of dry coca leaf was estimated at about US$ 5.7 in 2002.

The Bolivian Government reported the eradication of 11,848 ha of coca throughout the country in 2002.

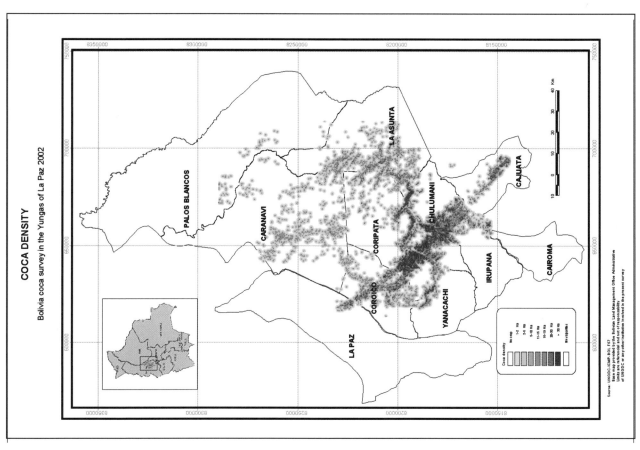

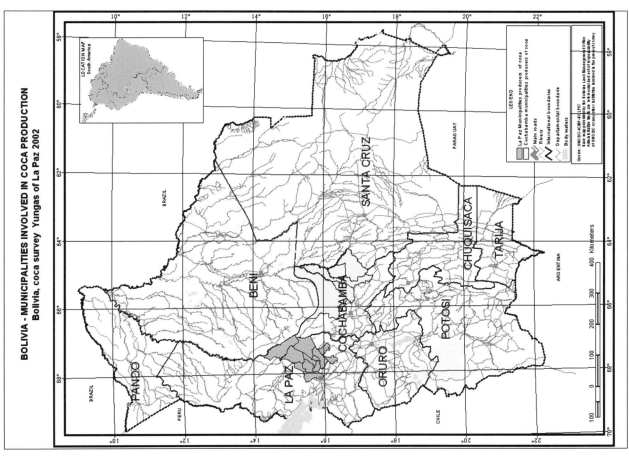

BOLIVIA: FARMGATE PRICES OF COCA LEAF, 1991-2002

(in constant 2002 US$, per kilogramme)

1991	1992	1993	1994	1995	1996	1997	1998	1999	2000	2001	2002
1.32	1.14	1.59	1.36	1.65	1.28	1.72	1.67	3.31	5.86	5.66	5.60

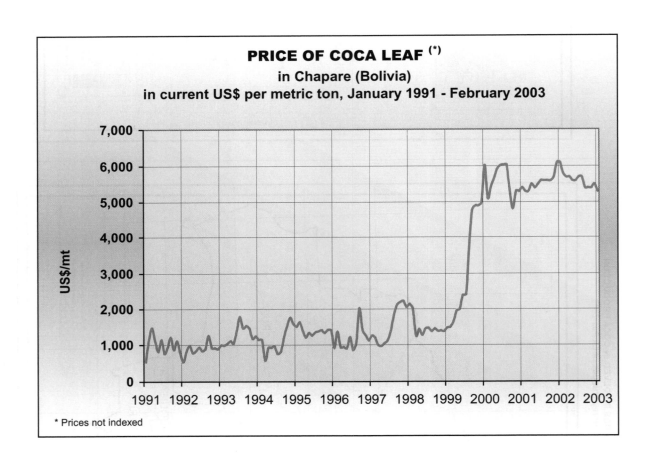

PRICE OF COCA LEAF [*]

in Chapare (Bolivia)

in current US$ per metric ton, January 1991 - February 2003

* Prices not indexed

2.1.2.4. ERADICATION REPORTED

ERADICATION OF COCA BUSH REPORTED, 1992-2002

(in hectares)

	1993	1994	1995	1996	1997	1998	1999	2000	2001	2002
Bolivia	2,400	1,100	5,493	7,512	7,000	11,620	15,353	7,653	9,435	11,853
Colombia	946	4,904	25,402	23,025	44,123	69,155	44,157	61,574	95,898	130,364
Peru		240	7,512	7,512	3,462	17,800	13,800	6,200	3,900	7,200

2.1.2.5 MANUFACTURE
SEIZURES OF ILLICIT LABORATORIES
REPORTED FOR 2000 - 2001

Remark: For convenience, an attempt was made to group the reported estimates by drug categories. however, due to inconsistencies and gaps in the reporting, no overall analysis of the data set was performed. Numbers are presented as reported to UNDCP and should be interpreted with caution.

Source: Annual Report Questionnaire if not otherwise indicated

Country or Territory	Year	Name of drug seized	Number of laboratories (and quantity of drug) seized	Source
			COCA GROUP	
Americas				
Central America				
Guatemala	2000	Cocaine (crack)	3 Lab.(12000.000 kg)	
Subtotal Central America			3 Lab.(12000.000 kg)	
North America				
United States	2001	Cocaine	3 Lab.(0.456 kg)	
Subtotal North America			3 Lab.(0.456 kg)	
South America				
Argentina	2000	Coca paste	2 Lab.	
	2000	Cocaine	8 Lab.	
	2001	Cocaine	6 Lab.	
Bolivia	2000	Cocaine base	628 Lab.(5043.200 kg)	F.O
	2000	Cocaine	6 Lab.(555.300 kg)	F.O
	2001	Cocaine	5 Lab.(334.100 kg)	F.O
	2001	Cocaine base	1006 Lab.(4280.400 kg)	F.O
Chile	2000	Cocaine	2 Lab.(33.000 kg)(35.000 lt.)	
Colombia	2000	Cocaine	631 Lab.(949.971 kg)(974.842 lt.)	
	2001	Cocaine	1085 Lab.(5335.000 kg)	
Venezuela	2001	Cocaine	2 Lab.	
Subtotal South America			3381 Lab.(16530.971 kg)(1009.842 lt.)	
Total Americas			3387 Lab.(28531.427 kg)(1009.842 lt.)	
Asia				
East and South-East Asia				
Thailand	2001	Cocaine	1 Lab.	Govt.
Subtotal East and South-East Asia			1 Lab.	
Total Asia			1 Lab.	
Europe				
Western Europe				
Germany	2000	Cocaine (crack)	6 Lab.(0.191 kg)	
	2001	Cocaine	1 Lab.	
Italy	2000	Cocaine	6 Lab.(2.447 kg)	
Portugal	2000	Cocaine	1 Lab.	ICPO

Country or Territory	Year	Name of drug seized	Number of laboratories (and quantity of drug) seized	Source
Spain	2000	Cocaine	7 Lab.(1744.797 kg)	
	2001	Cocaine	4 Lab.	
Subtotal Western Europe			25 Lab.(1747.435 kg)	
Total Europe			25 Lab.(1747.435 kg)	
Coca group			3413 Lab.(30278.862 kg)(1009.842 lt.)	

2.1.3. CANNABIS

2.1.3.1. ERADICATION REPORTED

ERADICATION REPORTED, 1992-2002										
(in hectares)										
Cannabis plant										
	1993	1994	1995	1996	1997	1998	1999	2000	2001	2002
Mexico	16,645	14,207	21,573	22,769	23,576	23,928	33,569	31,046	33,000	n/a

2.1.3.2. MANUFACTURE
SEIZURES OF ILLICIT LABORATORIES
REPORTED FOR 2000 - 2001

Remark: For convenience, an attempt was made to group the reported estimates by drug categories. however, due to inconsistencies and gaps in the reporting, no overall analysis of the data set was performed. Numbers are presented as reported to UNDCP and should be interpreted with caution.

Source: Annual Report Questionnaire if not otherwise indicated

Country or Territory	Year	Name of drug seized	Number of laboratories (and quantity of drug) seized	Source
CANNABIS GROUP				
Europe				
Eastern Europe				
Russian Federation	2000	Cannabis resin	123 Lab.	Govt
	2000	Cannabis herb	145 Lab.	Govt
	2001	Cannabis herb	137 Lab.(920.549 kg)	
Subtotal Eastern Europe			405 Lab.(920.549 kg)	
Total Europe			405 Lab.(920.549 kg)	
Cannabis group			405 Lab.(920.549 kg)	

2.1.4. AMPHETAMINE-TYPE STIMULANTS

MANUFACTURE
SEIZURES OF ILLICIT LABORATORIES
REPORTED FOR 2000 - 2001

Remark: For convenience, an attempt was made to group the reported estimates by drug categories. however, due to inconsistencies and gaps in the reporting, no overall analysis of the data set was performed. Numbers are presented as reported to UNDCP and should be interpreted with caution.

Source: Annual Report Questionnaire if not otherwise indicated

Country or Territory	Year	Name of drug seized	Number of laboratories (and quantity of drug) seized	Source
COMBINED AMPHETAMINE, METHAMPHETAMINE GROUP				
Europe				
Western Europe				
Germany	2000	Amphetamine, methamphetamine	7 Lab.(0.043 kg)	
Subtotal Western Europe			7 Lab.(0.043 kg)	
Total Europe			7 Lab.(0.043 kg)	
Oceania				
Australia	2001	Amphetamine, Methamphetamine	201 Lab.	
Total Oceania			201 Lab.	
Combined amphetamine, methamphetamine group			208 Lab.(0.043 kg)	
AMPHETAMINE GROUP				
Americas				
North America				
Canada	2000	Amphetamine	22 Lab.	ICPO
Mexico	2000	Amphetamine	26 Lab.	ICPO
United States	2000	Amphetamine	39 Lab.	
	2001	Amphetamine	52 Lab.(5.300 kg)	
Subtotal North America			139 Lab.(5.300 kg)	
Total Americas			139 Lab.(5.300 kg)	
Europe				
Eastern Europe				
Bulgaria	2000	Amphetamine	1 Lab.	ICPO
Lithuania	2000	Amphetamine	3 Lab.(18.200 kg)	
Poland	2000	Amphetamine	14 Lab.(0.003 kg)	
	2001	Amphetamine	12 Lab.(86.000 kg)	
Subtotal Eastern Europe			30 Lab.(104.203 kg)	
Western Europe				
Belgium	2000	Amphetamine	1 Lab.(0.420 kg)(25.000 lt.)	
	2001	Amphetamine	1 Lab.	
Denmark	2001	Amphetamine	1 Lab.	
Germany	2001	Amphetamine	1 Lab.	
Greece	2000	Amphetamine	1 Lab.(1.994 kg)	
Netherlands	2001	Amphetamine	10 Lab.	
Sweden	2001	Amphetamine	3 Lab.	
United Kingdom	2000	Amphetamine	5 Lab.(1000.000 kg)	

Country or Territory	Year	Name of drug seized	Number of laboratories (and quantity of drug) seized	Source
United Kingdom	2001	Amphetamine	5 Lab.	
Subtotal Western Europe			28 Lab.(1002.414 kg)(25.000 lt.)	
Total Europe			58 Lab.(1106.617 kg)(25.000 lt.)	
Amphetamine group			197 Lab.(1111.917 kg)(25.000 lt.)	

COMBINED AMPHETAMINE, METHAMPHETAMINE AND ECSTASY GROUP

Europe

Eastern Europe

Estonia	2000	Amphetamine, methamphetamine	5 Lab.(17.000 kg)	
Subtotal Eastern Europe			5 Lab.(17.000 kg)	
Total Europe			5 Lab.(17.000 kg)	
Combined amphetamine, methamphetamine and ecstasy group			5 Lab.(17.000 kg)	

METHAMPHETAMINE GROUP

Americas

North America

Canada	2000	Methamphetamine	(16.902 kg)	
	2001	Methamphetamine	13 Lab.	
Mexico	2000	Methamphetamine	23 Lab.	
	2001	Methamphetamine	19 Lab.	
United States	2000	Methamphetamine	6437 Lab.	
	2001	Methamphetamine	7990 Lab.(865.400 kg)	
Subtotal North America			14482 Lab.(882.302 kg)	
Total Americas			14482 Lab.(882.302 kg)	

Asia

East and South-East Asia

China	2001	Methamphetamine	44 Lab.	
Hong Kong SAR, China	2000	Methamphetamine	1 Lab.	ICPO
Korea (Republic of)	2001	Methamphetamine	1 Lab.(10.000 kg)	
Malaysia	2000	Methamphetamine	(37.190 kg)	
	2000	Methamphetamine	1 Lab.	ICPO
Myanmar	2001	Methamphetamine	5 Lab.	
Philippines	2001	Methamphetamine	3 Lab.	
Thailand	2000	Methamphetamine	10 Lab.	ICPO
	2001	Methamphetamine	10 Lab.	Govt.
Subtotal East and South-East Asia			75 Lab.(47.190 kg)	
Total Asia			75 Lab.(47.190 kg)	

Europe

Eastern Europe

Bulgaria	2001	Methamphetamine	1 Lab.	INCB
Czech Republic	2000	Methamphetamine	28 Lab.(12512.000 kg)	
	2001	Methamphetamine	28 Lab.	
Lithuania	2000	Methamphetamine	1 Lab.(6.500 kg)	

Country or Territory	Year	Name of drug seized	Number of laboratories (and quantity of drug) seized	Source
Slovakia	2000	Methamphetamine	95 Lab.	
	2001	Methamphetamine	10 Lab.	
Subtotal Eastern Europe			163 Lab.(12518.500 kg)	
Western Europe				
Germany	2001	Methamphetamine	3 Lab.	
United Kingdom	2000	Methamphetamine	3 Lab.	
Subtotal Western Europe			6 Lab.	
Total Europe			169 Lab.(12518.500 kg)	
Oceania				
Oceania				
New Zealand	2000	Methamphetamine	9 Lab.	
	2001	Methamphetamine	39 Lab.	
Subtotal Oceania			48 Lab.	
Total Oceania			48 Lab.	
Methamphetamine group			14774 Lab.(13447.992 kg)	

ECSTASY GROUP

Country or Territory	Year	Name of drug seized	Number of laboratories (and quantity of drug) seized	Source
Africa				
Southern Africa				
South Africa	2000	MDMA (Ecstasy)	1 Lab.	
	2001	MDMA	5 Lab.(857.000 kg)	
Subtotal Southern Africa			6 Lab.(857.000 kg)	
Total Africa			6 Lab.(857.000 kg)	
Americas				
North America				
Canada	2000	MDMA (Ecstasy)	8 Lab.(2200000 u.)	
	2001	MDA	2 Lab.	
United States	2000	MDMA (Ecstasy)	7 Lab.	
	2001	MDMA	17 Lab.(4.400 kg)	
Subtotal North America			34 Lab.(4.400 kg)(2200000 u.)	
Total Americas			34 Lab.(4.400 kg)(2200000 u.)	
Asia				
East and South-East Asia				
Hong Kong SAR, China	2001	MDMA	3 Lab.	
Malaysia	2000	MDMA (Ecstasy)	(10538 u.)	
Subtotal East and South-East Asia			3 Lab.(10538 u.)	
Total Asia			3 Lab.(10538 u.)	
Europe				
Eastern Europe				
Lithuania	2000	MDMA (Ecstasy)	1 Lab.(0.100 kg)	
Subtotal Eastern Europe			1 Lab.(0.100 kg)	
Western Europe				
Belgium	2000	MDMA (Ecstasy)	8 Lab.(22.500 kg)(9300.000 lt.)(500000 u.)	

Country or Territory	Year	Name of drug seized	Number of laboratories (and quantity of drug) seized	Source
Germany	2001	MDMA	2 Lab.	
Netherlands	2000	MDMA (Ecstasy)	34 Lab.	
	2001	MDMA	25 Lab.	
United Kingdom	2000	MDMA (Ecstasy)	5 Lab.	
Subtotal Western Europe			74 Lab.(22.500 kg)(9300.000 lt.)(500000 u.)	
Total Europe			75 Lab.(22.600 kg)(9300.000 lt.)(500000 u.)	
Ecstasy group			118 Lab.(884.000 kg)(9300.000 lt.)(2710538 u.)	

2.1.5. OTHER DRUGS

MANUFACTURE

SEIZURES OF ILLICIT LABORATORIES

REPORTED FOR 2000 - 2001

Remark: For convenience, an attempt was made to group the reported estimates by drug categories. however, due to inconsistencies and gaps in the reporting, no overall analysis of the data set was performed. Numbers are presented as reported to UNDCP and should be interpreted with caution.

Source: Annual Report Questionnaire if not otherwise indicated

Country or Territory	Year	Name of drug seized	Number of laboratories (and quantity of drug) seized	Source
OTHER SYNTHETIC STIMULANTS				
Americas				
North America				
United States	2000	Methcathinone	19 Lab.	
Subtotal North America			19 Lab.	
Total Americas			19 Lab.	
Other synthetic stimulants			19 Lab.	
DEPRESSANT GROUP				
Africa				
Southern Africa				
South Africa	2000	Methaqualone	4 Lab.(8000.000 kg)	
Subtotal Southern Africa			4 Lab.(8000.000 kg)	
Total Africa			4 Lab.(8000.000 kg)	
Europe				
Western Europe				
Belgium	2000	GHB	1 Lab.	
Subtotal Western Europe			1 Lab.	
Total Europe			1 Lab.	
Depressant group			5 Lab.(8000.000 kg)	
HALLUCINOGEN GROUP				
Americas				
North America				
Canada	2000	LSD	(2124 u.)	
United States	2000	Phencyclidine (PCP)	1 Lab.	
	2000	LSD	1 Lab.	
Subtotal North America			2 Lab.(2124 u.)	
Total Americas			2 Lab.(2124 u.)	
Europe				
Western Europe				
Denmark	2001	LSD	1 Lab.	
Subtotal Western Europe			1 Lab.	

Country or Territory	Year	Name of drug seized	Number of laboratories (and quantity of drug) seized	Source
Total Europe			1 Lab.	
Hallucinogen group			3 Lab.(2124 u.)	
			OTHER	
Africa				
Southern Africa				
South Africa	2001	Methaqualone	5 Lab.(198419 u.)	
Subtotal Southern Africa			5 Lab.(198419 u.)	
Total Africa			5 Lab.(198419 u.)	
Other			5 Lab.(198419 u.)	
			PRECURSORS	
Asia				
East and South-East Asia				
Indonesia	2000	Unspecified	2 Lab.	
Subtotal East and South-East Asia			2 Lab.	
Total Asia			2 Lab.	
Europe				
Eastern Europe				
Slovakia	2000	Ephedrine	3 Lab.	
Subtotal Eastern Europe			3 Lab.	
Total Europe			3 Lab.	
Precursors			5 Lab.	
			UNSPECIFIED	
Americas				
North America				
Canada	2000	Unspecified	14 Lab.	CICAD
Subtotal North America			14 Lab.	
South America				
Bolivia	2000	Unspecified	1424 Lab.	CICAD
Colombia	2000	Unspecified	647 Lab.	CICAD
Peru	2000	Unspecified	1177 Lab.	CICAD
Subtotal South America			3248 Lab.	
Total Americas			3262 Lab.	
Unspecified			3262 Lab.	

2.2. TRAFFICKING

2.2.1. Opiates: Seizures 1996-2001

Region/country or territory	SEIZURES 1996 - 2001 Opium (raw and prepared)					
	1996	1997	1998	1999	2000	2001
AFRICA						
East Africa						
Mauritius	0.000 kg	No Report	No Report	No Report	No Report	0.001 kg
Sub-Total						0.001 kg
North Africa						
Egypt	16.272 kg	31.156 kg	25.894 kg	24.702 kg	75.283 kg	40.000 kg
Tunisia	No Report	No Report	No Report	No Report	0.017 kg [ICPO]	No Report
Sub-Total	16.272 kg	31.156 kg	25.894 kg	24.702 kg	75.300 kg	40.000 kg
Southern Africa						
Zambia	2.344 kg [Govt]	0.102 kg [Govt]	6.770 kg [Govt]	8.622 kg	0.000 kg [Govt]	0.000 kg [Govt]
Sub-Total	2.344 kg	0.102 kg	6.770 kg	8.622 kg		
West and Central Africa						
Benin	No Report	No Report	No Report	No Report	No Report	0.414 kg [ICPO]
Gabon	0.001 kg [ICPO]	No Report	No Report	No Report	No Report	No Report
Niger	No Report	No Report	No Report	0.013 kg [ICPO]	No Report	No Report
Sub-Total	0.001 kg			0.013 kg		0.414 kg
Total region	18.617 kg	31.258 kg	32.664 kg	33.337 kg	75.300 kg	40.415 kg
AMERICAS						
North America						
Canada	1.150 kg	11.925 kg	61.310 kg	57.000 kg 10061 u.	18.788 kg 140 u.	27.307 kg
Mexico	196.421 kg	342.081 kg	149.640 kg	801.180 kg	469.445 kg	516.369 kg
United States	61.925 kg	39.010 kg	No Report	68.970 kg	No Report	24.500 kg
Sub-Total	259.496 kg	393.016 kg	210.950 kg	927.150 kg 10061 u.	488.233 kg 140 u.	568.176 kg
South America						
Colombia	102.772 kg	121.550 kg	99.950 kg	29.203 kg	16.063 kg	3.700 kg
Peru	No Report	No Report	11.528 kg	No Report	No Report	146.950 kg
Sub-Total	102.772 kg	121.550 kg	111.478 kg	29.203 kg	16.063 kg	150.650 kg
Total region	362.268 kg	514.566 kg	322.428 kg	956.353 kg 10061 u.	504.296 kg 140 u.	718.826 kg
ASIA						
Central Asia and Transcaucasian countries						
Armenia	1.906 kg	2.054 kg	No Report	2.032 kg [Govt.]	2.188 kg	0.090 kg
Azerbaijan	39.039 kg [ICPO]	83.328 kg [ICPO]	48.541 kg	52.218 kg	87.617 kg [ICPO]	10.500 kg
Georgia	17.593 kg [ICPO]	No Report	No Report	14.700 kg [ICPO]	33.500 kg [ICPO]	No Report

Source: Annual Report Questionnaire if not otherwise indicated

SEIZURES 1996 - 2001
Opium (raw and prepared)

Region/country or territory	1996	1997	1998	1999	2000	2001
ASIA						
Central Asia and Transcaucasian countries						
Kazakhstan	500.000 kg [Govt.]	1000.000 kg [Govt.]	296.574 kg	170.236 kg	136.000 kg [F.O]	36.000 kg [F.O]
Kyrgyzstan	1489.684 kg	1639.476 kg	171.872 kg	151.174 kg	1405.232 kg	469.225 kg
Tajikistan	3405.000 kg	3455.510 kg [F.O]	1190.400 kg	1269.278 kg [F.O]	4778.448 kg [F.O]	3664.277 kg
Turkmenistan	No Report	1410.000 kg [Govt.]	1412.000 kg [Govt.]	4600.000 kg [F.O]	2300.000 kg [F.O]	No Report
Uzbekistan	1865.000 kg [Govt.]	2364.167 kg	1935.315 kg	3292.342 kg	2008.200 kg	241.680 kg [F.O]
Sub-Total	7318.222 kg	9954.535 kg	5054.702 kg	9551.979 kg	10751.190 kg	4421.772 kg
East and South-East Asia						
Cambodia	No Report	15.006 kg [ICPO]	No Report	No Report	No Report	No Report
China	1745.000 kg	1880.000 kg	1215.000 kg	1193.000 kg [ICPO]	2428.000 kg [Govt.]	2820.000 kg [Govt.]
Hong Kong SAR, China	12.800 kg	3.400 kg	No Report	0.100 kg	0.090 kg	2.500 kg
Indonesia	0.030 kg	No Report	0.030 kg [HNLP]	3.097 kg [HNLP]	0.034 kg [ICPO]	0.009 kg
Japan	31.106 kg	39.061 kg	19.811 kg	7.688 kg	8.979 kg	11.020 kg
Korea (Republic of)	0.567 kg	6.805 kg	1.035 kg	3.064 kg	14996 u. [ICPO]	0.218 kg
Lao People's Dem. Rep.	199.001 kg [Govt.]	200.100 kg [Govt.]	442.000 kg [INCSR]	225.800 kg [HNLP]	78.000 kg [INCSR]	372.600 kg [Govt]
Malaysia	2.640 kg [Govt.]	150.311 kg	32.747 kg	21.066 kg	0.710 kg	69.270 kg [ICPO]
Myanmar	1300.002 kg	7883.975 kg	5705.881 kg	1759.538 kg	1773.652 kg	1770.773 kg
Singapore	28.464 kg	1.545 kg	22.781 kg	98.144 kg	4.504 kg	13.375 kg
Thailand	381.322 kg [ICPO]	1150.582 kg	1631.124 kg	421.939 kg	1591.991 kg [ICPO]	2289.000 kg [HNLP]
Viet Nam	839.850 kg [ICPO]	No Report	No Report	495.350 kg [F.O]	460.000 kg [ICPO]	583.005 kg
Sub-Total	4540.782 kg	11330.790 kg	9070.408 kg	4228.786 kg	6345.960 kg 14996 u.	7931.770 kg
Near and Middle East /South-West Asia						
Bahrain	No Report	0.007 kg	0.014 kg [ICPO]	0.323 kg [ICPO]	0.001 kg [ICPO]	No Report
Iran (Islamic Republic of)	149577.000 kg	162413.953 kg	154453.569 kg	204485.000 kg	179053.000 kg [NAPOL]	81061.000 kg
Iraq	1.000 kg	4.815 kg	No Report	No Report	10.511 kg	0.993 kg
Israel	0.003 kg	5.100 kg	0.556 kg	0.005 kg [ICPO]	0.194 kg	4.405 kg
Jordan	43.350 kg	22.671 kg	No Report	61.700 kg	No Report	0.327 kg
Kuwait	40.804 kg [ICPO]	11.710 kg [ICPO]	4.720 kg	14.000 kg [INCB]	32.500 kg [ICPO]	No Report
Lebanon	3.000 kg	7.625 kg	No Report	44.226 kg	0.052 kg	7.028 kg
Oman	12.000 kg [INCB]	0.060 kg [INCB]	No Report	No Report	1.647 kg [ICPO]	0.308 kg
Pakistan	7422.772 kg [ICPO]	7300.000 kg [Govt.]	5021.712 kg	16319.918 kg	8867.407 kg	5175.000 kg [F.O]
Qatar	0.340 kg	0.962 kg [ICPO]	0.030 kg [ICPO]	0.100 kg [ICPO]	2.700 kg [ICPO]	No Report
Saudi Arabia	23.038 kg [ICPO]	16.127 kg [ICPO]	16.721 kg [(1]	No Report	13.472 kg	0.954 kg
Syrian Arab Republic	1.802 kg [Govt]	6.003 kg [Govt]	1.200 kg [Govt]	5.876 kg [Govt]	35.400 kg [Govt]	1.862 kg [Govt]

Source: Annual Report Questionnaire if not otherwise indicated

SEIZURES 1996 - 2001
Opium (raw and prepared)

Region/country or territory	1996	1997	1998	1999	2000	2001
ASIA						
Near and Middle East /South-West Asia						
United Arab Emirates	16.269 kg	3.822 kg	9.717 kg	8.389 kg	27.236 kg	8.899 kg
Sub-Total	157141.300 kg	169792.800 kg	159508.300 kg	220939.500 kg	188044.100 kg	86260.770 kg
South Asia						
Bangladesh	0.073 kg	No Report	No Report	0.072 kg [F.O]	No Report	11.535 kg [ICPO]
India	2867.000 kg [F.O]	3316.000 kg	2031.000 kg	1588.000 kg	2684.000 kg	2533.000 kg
Nepal	0.441 kg	No Report	0.950 kg	1.440 kg	No Report	No Report
Sri Lanka	0.145 kg	1571 u.	0.020 kg	0.008 kg	36.452 kg	1.658 kg
Sub-Total	2867.659 kg	3316.000 kg 1571 u.	2031.970 kg	1589.520 kg	2720.452 kg	2546.193 kg
Total region	171868.000 kg	194394.200 kg 1571 u.	175665.300 kg	236309.800 kg	207861.700 kg 14996 u.	101160.500 kg
EUROPE						
Eastern Europe						
Albania	No Report	No Report	No Report	0.026 kg [ICPO]	No Report	No Report
Belarus	No Report	1.124 kg [INCB]	0.001 kg	0.033 kg	0.090 kg	1381.000 kg [ICPO]
Bulgaria	0.080 kg	8.240 kg	1.970 kg	4.466 kg	No Report	1.980 kg
Croatia	[(2]	0.001 kg	[(2]	0.103 kg	0.011 kg	No Report
Czech Republic	1.000 kg	No Report	No Report	No Report	No Report	No Report
Estonia	0.001 kg [ICPO]	No Report	No Report	No Report	19.426 kg 20 u.	No Report
FYR of Macedonia	2.000 kg [NAPOL]	44.783 kg [NAPOL]	19.985 kg	12.239 kg [NAPOL]	27.395 kg [NAPOL]	3.494 kg [Govt]
Hungary	No Report	No Report	No Report	2.149 kg	17.905 kg	0.003 kg
Latvia	0.001 kg	0.230 kg	0.755 kg	0.005 kg	0.005 kg	No Report
Lithuania	0.278 kg	0.236 kg	0.101 kg	0.190 kg	0.129 kg	436.505 kg
Poland	No Report	No Report	No Report	No Report	55.000 kg	No Report
Republic of Moldova	No Report	20.000 kg	No Report	28.000 kg [ICPO]	1485.000 kg [ICPO] 98.550 lt.	1891.000 kg
Romania	1.442 kg	2.488 kg [ICPO]	0.728 kg	2.470 kg	0.060 kg	15.530 kg
Russian Federation	1400.500 kg	222.706 kg	1803.700 kg [F.O]	1506.966 kg	2186.000 kg [F.O]	862.645 kg
Ukraine	194.528 kg	No Report	No Report	No Report	166.056 kg [ICPO]	151.009 kg
Sub-Total	1599.830 kg	299.808 kg	1827.240 kg	1556.647 kg	3957.077 kg 98.550 lt. 20 u.	4743.166 kg
Western Europe						
Austria	17.667 kg	9.041 kg	10.447 kg	33.646 kg	69.873 kg	4.488 kg

Source: Annual Report Questionnaire if not otherwise indicated

215

SEIZURES 1996 - 2001
Opium (raw and prepared)

Region/country or territory	1996	1997	1998	1999	2000	2001
EUROPE						
Western Europe						
Belgium	No Report	No Report	0.011 kg	0.200 kg	No Report	No Report
Cyprus	0.654 kg	1.913 kg	0.021 kg	0.062 kg	0.575 kg	0.367 kg
Denmark	0.052 kg	0.105 kg	5.428 kg	0.330 kg	1.405 kg	5.000 kg
Finland	0.254 kg	No Report	0.007 kg	No Report	No Report	No Report
France	4.326 kg	2.696 kg	3.194 kg	0.503 kg	18.701 kg	2.720 kg
Germany	45.387 kg	41.656 kg	286.074 kg	79.500 kg	30.900 kg	4.115 kg
Greece	0.235 kg	2.559 kg	No Report	46.208 kg [ICPO]	1.742 kg	0.955 kg
Italy	0.617 kg	9.821 kg 54 u.	2.895 kg	0.401 kg [ICPO]	28.672 kg	0.189 kg 6 u.
Norway	1.288 kg	0.023 kg	2.498 kg	1.661 kg	9.800 kg	3.214 kg
Portugal	No Report	0.012 kg	0.001 kg	No Report	2.850 kg [ICPO]	0.015 kg 77 u.
Spain	2.857 kg	26.287 kg	0.002 kg	1.080 kg	5.264 kg	84.900 kg
Sweden	30.679 kg	7.709 kg 139 u.	15.641 kg	9.867 kg	24.030 kg	16.153 kg
Switzerland	0.168 kg	0.042 kg	0.015 kg	0.775 kg	0.009 kg [ICPO]	No Report
Turkey	233.000 kg	93.356 kg	141.665 kg	318.624 kg	362.950 kg [Govt.]	261.176 kg
United Kingdom	11.400 kg	17.800 kg	54.263 kg	37.700 kg [NCIS]	18.481 kg	18.481 kg [UNODC (3]
Sub-Total	348.584 kg	213.020 kg 193 u.	522.162 kg	530.557 kg	575.252 kg	401.773 kg 83 u.
Total region	1948.414 kg	512.828 kg 193 u.	2349.402 kg	2087.204 kg	4532.329 kg 98.550 lt. 20 u.	5144.938 kg 83 u.
OCEANIA						
Oceania						
Australia	8.072 kg	2.095 kg	No Report	3.000 kg [INCB]	2.279 kg	68.410 kg 397 u.
New Zealand	No Report	0.016 kg [INCB]	0.006 kg	No Report	No Report	0.008 kg
Sub-Total	8.072 kg	2.111 kg	0.006 kg	3.000 kg	2.279 kg	68.418 kg 397 u.
Total region	8.072 kg	2.111 kg	0.006 kg	3.000 kg	2.279 kg	68.418 kg 397 u.
TOTAL	174205.400 kg	195454.900 kg 1764 u.	178369.800 kg	239389.700 kg 10061 u.	212975.900 kg 98.550 lt. 15156 u.	107133.100 kg 480 u.

1) Including other opiates. 2) Small quantity. 3) Due to unavailability of 2001 data, year 2000 data were used for analysis purposes.

Source: Annual Report Questionnaire if not otherwise indicated

SEIZURES 1996 - 2001

Opium (liquid)

Region/country or territory	1996	1997	1998	1999	2000	2001
AFRICA						
North Africa						
Egypt	0.017 lt.	0.009 lt.	0.030 lt.	0.001 lt.	0.005 lt.	No Report
Sub-Total	0.017 lt.	0.009 lt.	0.030 lt.	0.001 lt.	0.005 lt.	
Total region	0.017 lt.	0.009 lt.	0.030 lt.	0.001 lt.	0.005 lt.	
AMERICAS						
Caribbean						
Cayman Islands	No Report	No Report	No Report	No Report	0.628 kg 1 u.	No Report
Sub-Total					0.628 kg 1 u.	
South America						
Peru	36.921 kg	No Report	No Report	66.088 kg	508.358 kg	No Report
Sub-Total	36.921 kg			66.088 kg	508.358 kg	
Total region	36.921 kg			66.088 kg	508.986 kg 1 u.	
ASIA						
Central Asia and Transcaucasian countries						
Armenia	No Report	No Report	2.000 kg	No Report	0.002 kg	No Report
Kazakhstan	No Report	No Report	1.265 kg	No Report	No Report	No Report
Kyrgyzstan	No Report	15000 u.	No Report	No Report	No Report	No Report
Sub-Total		15000 u.	3.265 kg		0.002 kg	
East and South-East Asia						
Hong Kong SAR, China	No Report	No Report	No Report	No Report	2 u.	No Report
Indonesia	No Report	No Report	0.030 kg	3.097 kg	0.034 kg	No Report
Japan	5.912 lt.	No Report	0.130 lt.	No Report	No Report	No Report
Myanmar	No Report	1027.685 kg	383.251 kg	332.495 kg	16.086 kg	18.684 kg
Sub-Total	5.912 lt.	1027.685 kg	383.281 kg 0.130 lt.	335.592 kg	16.120 kg 2 u.	18.684 kg
Near and Middle East /South-West Asia						
Jordan	No Report	No Report	No Report	No Report	41.150 kg	No Report
Lebanon	No Report	No Report	35.840 kg	No Report	0.000 kg [1]	No Report
Sub-Total			35.840 kg		41.150 kg	
Total region	5.912 lt.	1027.685 kg 15000 u.	422.386 kg 0.130 lt.	335.592 kg	57.272 kg 2 u.	18.684 kg

Source: Annual Report Questionnaire if not otherwise indicated

SEIZURES 1996 - 2001
Opium (liquid)

Region/country or territory	1996	1997	1998	1999	2000	2001
EUROPE						
Eastern Europe						
Belarus	82.196 kg	No Report	330.882 kg	244.034 kg [2]	220.520 kg	No Report
Croatia	No Report	2.000 lt.	8.600 lt.	No Report	1.500 kg	No Report
Estonia	20.701 lt. [ICPO]	No Report	19.200 kg / 293 u.	0.276 kg / 61 u.	0.027 kg / 19 u.	No Report
Latvia	89.000 lt.	0.133 lt.	64.800 kg	17.300 kg	7.170 kg	No Report
Lithuania	96.085 lt.	86.000 lt.	49.490 lt.	190.000 lt.	77.000 lt.	No Report
Republic of Moldova	27.104 kg	No Report	13.480 kg	No Report	No Report	No Report
Ukraine	No Report	171.200 kg	127.000 kg	No Report	No Report	No Report
Sub-Total	109.300 kg / 205.786 lt.	171.200 kg / 88.133 lt.	555.362 kg / 58.090 lt. / 293 u.	261.610 kg / 190.000 lt. / 61 u.	229.217 kg / 77.000 lt. / 19 u.	
Western Europe						
Austria	No Report	No Report	No Report	No Report	0.075 kg	No Report
Denmark	0.005 kg	0.030 kg	0.004 kg	2.640 kg	No Report	No Report
Italy	No Report	No Report	No Report	No Report	35 u.	No Report
Sweden	No Report	No Report	0.326 lt.	16.000 lt.	0.018 kg	No Report
Sub-Total	0.005 kg	0.030 kg	0.004 kg / 0.326 lt.	2.640 kg / 16.000 lt.	0.093 kg / 35 u.	
Total region	109.305 kg / 205.786 lt.	171.230 kg / 88.133 lt.	555.366 kg / 58.416 lt. / 293 u.	264.250 kg / 206.000 lt. / 61 u.	229.310 kg / 77.000 lt. / 54 u.	
OCEANIA						
Oceania						
Australia	0.080 kg	1.630 kg	No Report	No Report	No Report	No Report
Sub-Total	0.080 kg	1.630 kg				
Total region	0.080 kg	1.630 kg				
TOTAL	146.306 kg / 211.715 lt.	1200.545 kg / 88.142 lt. / 15000 u.	977.752 kg / 58.576 lt. / 293 u.	665.930 kg / 206.001 lt. / 61 u.	795.568 kg / 77.005 lt. / 57 u.	18.684 kg

1) Small quantity. 2) Includes liquid heroin (1.160kg)

Source: Annual Report Questionnaire if not otherwise indicated

SEIZURES 1996 - 2001
Opium (plant,capsule)

Region/country or territory	1996	1997	1998	1999	2000	2001
AFRICA						
North Africa						
Egypt	3639320832 u.	No Report	0.352 kg 30214000 u.	14.552 kg	No Report	No Report
Sub-Total	3639321000 u.		0.352 kg 30214000 u.	14.552 kg		
West and Central Africa						
Niger	No Report	No Report	0.040 kg [ICPO]	No Report	No Report	No Report
Sao Tome and Principe	No Report	0.300 kg	No Report	0.300 kg	No Report	No Report
Sub-Total		0.300 kg	0.040 kg	0.300 kg		
Total region	3639321000 u.	0.300 kg	0.392 kg 30214000 u.	14.852 kg		
AMERICAS						
Central America						
Guatemala	No Report	2.600 kg [Govt.] 69119 u.	114238 u.	23100 u.	20619 u.	No Report
Sub-Total		2.600 kg 69119 u.	114238 u.	23100 u.	20619 u.	
North America						
Canada	4.757 kg	18 u.	2.016 kg	15000 u.	No Report	No Report
United States	No Report	50.685 kg 0.109 lt.	No Report	No Report	No Report	No Report
Sub-Total	4.757 kg	50.685 kg 0.109 lt. 18 u.	2.016 kg	15000 u.		
South America						
Argentina	301 u. [Govt.]	2.470 kg	408 u.	No Report	No Report	No Report
Colombia	75000 u.	104818496 u.	No Report	No Report	No Report	No Report
Ecuador	No Report	No Report	100873 u.	No Report	No Report	No Report
Peru	534.253 kg	1754 u.	964 u.	63703.614 kg	20837.016 kg	No Report
Sub-Total	534.253 kg 75301 u.	2.470 kg 104820200 u.	102245 u.	63703.610 kg	20837.020 kg	
Total region	539.010 kg 75301 u.	55.755 kg 0.109 lt. 104889400 u.	2.016 kg 216483 u.	63703.610 kg 38100 u.	20837.020 kg 20619 u.	

Source: Annual Report Questionnaire if not otherwise indicated

SEIZURES 1996 - 2001
Opium (plant,capsule)

Region/country or territory	1996	1997	1998	1999	2000	2001
ASIA						
Central Asia and Transcaucasian countries						
Armenia	76.826 kg	4.460 kg	18.725 kg	No Report	No Report	No Report
Azerbaijan	No Report	38750.000 kg ICPO	6.200 kg	No Report	No Report	No Report
Georgia	19.168 kg ICPO	No Report	7.500 kg ICPO	No Report	No Report	No Report
Kazakhstan	335.719 kg ICPO	No Report	113.895 kg	No Report	No Report	No Report
Uzbekistan	863.767 kg ICPO	118.285 kg	54.496 kg	No Report	14.700 kg	No Report
Sub-Total	1295.480 kg	38872.750 kg	200.816 kg		14.700 kg	
East and South-East Asia						
Hong Kong SAR, China	No Report	No Report	No Report	32 u.	3.001 kg	No Report
Indonesia	No Report	1620 u.	0.030 kg	No Report	No Report	No Report
Japan	No Report	6803 u.	0.063 kg 6807 u.	No Report	0.022 kg 11571 u.	No Report
Korea (Republic of)	72645 u.	24301 u.	21944 u.	No Report	No Report	No Report
Malaysia	No Report	321 u.	No Report	No Report	No Report	No Report
Thailand	No Report	205.234 kg	No Report	312.837 kg	No Report	No Report
Viet Nam	No Report	919.000 kg ICPO	1.100 kg ICPO	No Report	No Report	No Report
Sub-Total	72645 u.	1124.234 kg 33045 u.	1.193 kg 28751 u.	312.837 kg 32 u.	3.023 kg 11571 u.	
Near and Middle East /South-West Asia						
Saudi Arabia	0.038 kg ICPO	No Report	No Report	No Report	No Report	No Report
United Arab Emirates	No Report	129 u.	No Report	No Report	No Report	No Report
Yemen	No Report	No Report	ICPO	No Report	No Report	No Report
Sub-Total	0.038 kg	129 u.				
South Asia						
Nepal	No Report	0.693 kg ICPO	No Report	No Report	No Report	No Report
Sub-Total		0.693 kg				
Total region	1295.518 kg 72645 u.	39997.670 kg 33174 u.	202.009 kg 28751 u.	312.837 kg 32 u.	17.723 kg 11571 u.	
EUROPE						
Eastern Europe						
Belarus	1792.000 kg	327.744 kg INCB	1621.000 kg	1056.000 kg	1084.000 kg	No Report
Bulgaria	48.500 kg	No Report	No Report	No Report	No Report	1415.000 kg
Croatia	No Report	769 u.	3504 u.	6206 u.	1.607 kg 519 u.	No Report
Estonia	135.428 kg ICPO	165.800 kg	36.011 kg 111 u.	No Report	37.883 kg 69 u.	No Report

Source: Annual Report Questionnaire if not otherwise indicated

SEIZURES 1996 - 2001					
Opium (plant,capsule)					
Region/country or territory	1996	1997	1998	1999	2000	2001
EUROPE						
Eastern Europe						
Latvia	0.180 kg	218.000 kg	192.000 kg	30.200 kg	145.950 kg	No Report
Lithuania	1652.000 kg	1291.000 kg	1525.000 kg	744.000 kg	623.000 kg	No Report
Poland	1000.000 kg	8500.000 kg	4000.000 kg	3553.000 kg	No Report	No Report
Republic of Moldova	No Report	597.000 kg	406.550 kg	No Report	No Report	No Report
Russian Federation	19469.801 kg	853.019 kg	16511.359 kg	18366.055 kg	No Report	No Report
Ukraine	No Report	34003.262 kg	26632.801 kg	No Report	No Report	No Report
Sub-Total	24097.910 kg	45955.820 kg 769 u.	50924.720 kg 3615 u.	23749.260 kg 6206 u.	1892.440 kg 588 u.	1415.000 kg
Western Europe						
Austria	1103.859 kg	1.193 kg	9.367 kg	9.349 kg	No Report	No Report
Finland	No Report	No Report	1.000 kg	No Report	No Report	No Report
Greece	130 u.	640 u.	No Report	No Report	No Report	No Report
Italy	No Report	1448 u.	5991 u.	No Report	4449 u. [1]	No Report
Norway	No Report	0.115 kg	0.070 kg	No Report	0.001 kg	No Report
Portugal	150 u.	No Report	28848 u.	351 u.	2.850 kg 1348 u.	No Report
Spain	11185.998 kg	862.112 kg [2]	4.800 kg	1003.004 kg	22755.700 kg	No Report
Sweden	No Report		No Report	3615 u.	No Report	No Report
Turkey	No Report	No Report	No Report	No Report	1820.000 kg 3550 u.	No Report
Sub-Total	12289.860 kg 280 u.	863.420 kg 2088 u.	15.237 kg 34839 u.	1012.353 kg 3966 u.	24578.550 kg 9347 u.	
Total region	36387.770 kg 280 u.	46819.250 kg 2857 u.	50939.960 kg 38454 u.	24761.610 kg 10172 u.	26470.990 kg 9935 u.	1415.000 kg
OCEANIA						
Oceania						
Australia	0.001 kg	0.095 kg	No Report	No Report	0.407 kg 2083 u.	No Report
New Zealand	No Report	No Report	20249 u.	338 u.	No Report	No Report
Sub-Total	0.001 kg	0.095 kg	20249 u.	338 u.	0.407 kg 2083 u.	
Total region	0.001 kg	0.095 kg	20249 u.	338 u.	0.407 kg 2083 u.	

Source: Annual Report Questionnaire if not otherwise indicated

221

SEIZURES 1996 - 2001					
Opium (plant,capsule)					
Region/country or territory	**1996**	**1997**	**1998**	**1999**	**2000**	**2001**
TOTAL	38222.290 kg 3639469000 u.	86873.060 kg 0.109 lt. 104925400 u.	51144.380 kg 30517940 u.	88792.910 kg 48642 u.	47326.130 kg 44208 u.	1415.000 kg

1) 221buds(1), 4,228 plants(6) 2) Including depressants.

Source: Annual Report Questionnaire if not otherwise indicated

SEIZURES 1996 - 2001
Opium (poppy seed)

Region/country or territory	1996	1997	1998	1999	2000	2001
AFRICA						
North Africa						
Egypt		No Report	No Report	180.022 kg	185.088 kg	No Report
Sub-Total				180.022 kg	185.088 kg	
Total region				180.022 kg	185.088 kg	
AMERICAS						
Central America						
Guatemala	No Report	0.014 kg [Govt.]	2.003 kg	54.886 kg 121 u.	1.400 kg	No Report
Sub-Total		0.014 kg	2.003 kg	54.886 kg 121 u.	1.400 kg	
North America						
Canada	0.045 kg	0.014 kg	No Report	0.000 kg	0.018 kg	No Report
Mexico	1155.152 kg	587.282 kg	702.551 kg	749.985 kg	1036.274 kg	No Report
Sub-Total	1155.197 kg	587.296 kg	702.551 kg	749.985 kg	1036.292 kg	
South America						
Argentina	No Report	No Report	30.000 kg	No Report	0.010 kg	No Report
Colombia	No Report	411.200 kg	12.600 kg	49.945 kg	17.000 kg	No Report
Peru	No Report	No Report	1.047 kg	193.739 kg	4.890 kg	No Report
Venezuela	No Report	No Report	No Report	No Report	50.000 kg	No Report
Sub-Total		411.200 kg	43.647 kg	243.684 kg	71.900 kg	
Total region	1155.197 kg	998.510 kg	748.201 kg	1048.555 kg 121 u.	1109.592 kg	
ASIA						
Central Asia and Transcaucasian countries						
Armenia	No Report	2.330 kg	No Report	0.117 kg	2.614 kg	4.370 kg
Azerbaijan	No Report	No Report	No Report	2577.008 kg	No Report	No Report
Georgia	No Report	No Report	No Report	83.500 kg [ICPO]	No Report	No Report
Kazakhstan	No Report	No Report	No Report	141.159 kg	No Report	No Report
Kyrgyzstan	32392 u.	No Report	No Report	No Report	No Report	No Report
Turkmenistan	No Report	No Report	No Report	17996.000 kg [F.O]	No Report	No Report
Uzbekistan	No Report	No Report	No Report	61.400 kg [ICPO]	No Report	No Report
Sub-Total	32392 u.	2.330 kg		20859.180 kg	2.614 kg	4.370 kg
East and South-East Asia						
China	29754.000 kg	No Report	No Report	No Report	No Report	No Report

Source: Annual Report Questionnaire if not otherwise indicated

SEIZURES 1996 - 2001
Opium (poppy seed)

Region/country or territory	1996	1997	1998	1999	2000	2001
ASIA						
East and South-East Asia						
Japan	12425 u.	No Report	No Report	28256 u.	No Report	0.246 kg 4608 u.
Korea (Republic of)	No Report	0.036 kg	No Report	28268 u.	No Report	12566 u.
Thailand	No Report	No Report	60.393 kg	No Report	No Report	No Report
Sub-Total	29754.000 kg 12425 u.	0.036 kg	60.393 kg	56524 u.		0.246 kg 17174 u.
Near and Middle East /South-West Asia						
Bahrain	0.020 kg	No Report	No Report	1.200 kg ICPO	No Report	No Report
Kuwait	No Report	No Report	No Report	13.695 kg ICPO	No Report	No Report
Lebanon	No Report	No Report	10.000 kg	59.000 kg	No Report	No Report
Saudi Arabia	No Report	No Report	No Report	5.697 kg ICPO	No Report	No Report
United Arab Emirates	No Report	No Report	No Report	0.122 kg	No Report	No Report
Sub-Total	0.020 kg		10.000 kg	79.714 kg		
South Asia						
Sri Lanka	58.250 kg	No Report	No Report	No Report	No Report	No Report
Sub-Total	58.250 kg					
Total region	29812.270 kg 44817 u.	2.366 kg	70.393 kg	20938.900 kg 56524 u.	2.614 kg	4.616 kg 17174 u.
EUROPE						
Eastern Europe						
Croatia	14.000 kg	No Report	No Report	0.002 kg	No Report	No Report
Czech Republic	No Report	No Report	No Report	91.400 kg	No Report	No Report
Estonia	No Report	No Report	No Report	128.934 kg 249 u.	No Report	50.595 kg
FYR of Macedonia	No Report	No Report	No Report	No Report	No Report	128 u. Govt
Latvia	No Report	No Report	No Report	No Report	No Report	182.900 kg
Republic of Moldova	2264.000 kg	No Report	No Report	706.000 kg ICPO	No Report	No Report
Russian Federation	No Report	No Report	No Report	No Report	18564.000 kg F.O	No Report
Ukraine	No Report	No Report	No Report	133.000 kg ICPO	No Report	No Report
Sub-Total	2278.000 kg			1059.336 kg 249 u.	18564.000 kg	233.495 kg 128 u.
Western Europe						
Austria	No Report	No Report	No Report	No Report	1.140 kg	No Report
Finland	No Report	6.518 kg	0.220 kg	No Report	No Report	No Report
Italy	15919 u.	No Report	No Report	ICPO	No Report	No Report

Source: Annual Report Questionnaire if not otherwise indicated

SEIZURES 1996 - 2001
Opium (poppy seed)

Region/country or territory	1996	1997	1998	1999	2000	2001
EUROPE						
Western Europe						
Norway	41.100 kg	No Report	No Report	0.008 kg 49 u.	No Report	No Report
Portugal	0.035 kg	No Report	No Report	No Report	No Report	No Report
Sub-Total	41.135 kg 15919 u.	6.518 kg	0.220 kg	0.008 kg 49 u.	1.140 kg	
Total region	2319.135 kg 15919 u.	6.518 kg	0.220 kg	1059.344 kg 298 u.	18565.140 kg	233.495 kg 128 u.
OCEANIA						
Oceania						
Australia	No Report	1.410 kg	No Report	No Report	No Report	No Report
Sub-Total		1.410 kg				
Total region		1.410 kg				
TOTAL	33286.600 kg 60736 u.	1008.804 kg	818.814 kg	23226.820 kg 56943 u.	19862.440 kg	238.111 kg 17302 u.

Source: Annual Report Questionnaire if not otherwise indicated

SEIZURES 1996 - 2001
Heroin

Region/country or territory	1996	1997	1998	1999	2000	2001
AFRICA						
East Africa						
Burundi	0.800 kg [Govt.]	No Report	No Report	0.006 kg [ICPO] 260 u.	No Report	No Report
Ethiopia	27.472 kg [ICPO]	36.112 kg	8.987 kg	12.582 kg	18.042 kg	5.650 kg
Kenya	15.492 kg	7.787 kg	9.954 kg	17.459 kg	28.657 kg	19.438 kg [Govt]
Madagascar	No Report	No Report	No Report	0.005 kg [ICPO]	No Report	No Report
Mauritius	5.235 kg	6.920 kg	6.060 kg	3.067 kg	4.062 kg	24.532 kg
Rwanda	2.520 kg [Govt.]	No Report	No Report	No Report	No Report	No Report
Uganda	2.722 kg	No Report	1.302 kg	14.170 kg	3.400 kg	5.772 kg
United Republic of Tanzania	No Report	4.852 kg	2.745 kg	7.583 kg	5.322 kg [ICPO]	7.997 kg [Govt]
Sub-Total	54.241 kg	55.671 kg	29.048 kg	54.872 kg 260 u.	59.483 kg	63.389 kg
North Africa						
Algeria	0.222 kg [ICPO]	No Report	0.256 kg [ICPO]	0.002 kg	No Report	0.006 kg [ICPO]
Egypt	48.256 kg	51.222 kg 0.225 lt.	24.416 kg 0.266 lt.	23.627 kg	37.114 kg	38.000 kg 385 u.
Libyan Arab Jam.	No Report	No Report	4.809 kg	No Report	No Report	No Report
Morocco	0.362 kg 6 u.	0.318 kg [Govt.]	1.282 kg	0.437 kg	0.152 kg	3.971 kg 110 u.
Tunisia	4.575 kg [ICPO]	0.308 kg [ICPO]	0.474 kg	1.391 kg	1.020 kg [ICPO]	No Report
Sub-Total	53.415 kg 6 u.	51.848 kg 0.225 lt.	31.237 kg 0.266 lt.	25.457 kg	38.286 kg	41.977 kg 495 u.
Southern Africa						
Angola	No Report	0.010 kg [ICPO]	No Report	(1	0.005 kg [ICPO]	21.500 kg [ICPO]
Botswana	No Report	0.228 kg [ICPO]	No Report	No Report	No Report	No Report
Lesotho	No Report	No Report	No Report	0.500 kg [ICPO]	No Report	No Report
Malawi	No Report	No Report	0.200 kg	0.500 kg	No Report	No Report
Mozambique	No Report	No Report	No Report	No Report	232 u. [ICPO]	0.005 kg [ICPO]
Namibia	No Report	No Report	No Report	0.003 kg [ICPO]	0.100 kg	0.003 kg
South Africa	0.811 kg	1.548 kg	5.383 kg	7.435 kg [ICPO]	15.386 kg	8.465 kg
Swaziland	0.002 kg [ICPO]	1.041 kg [ICPO]	0.010 kg	0.097 kg	1.919 kg	0.093 kg
Zambia	0.939 kg [Govt]	0.000 kg [Govt]	0.001 kg [Govt]	0.369 kg	0.005 kg	0.002 kg [Govt]
Zimbabwe	0.032 kg [ICPO]	No Report	0.740 kg	No Report	No Report	No Report
Sub-Total	1.784 kg	2.827 kg	6.334 kg	8.904 kg	17.415 kg 232 u.	30.068 kg
West and Central Africa						
Benin	2.271 kg [Govt]	0.143 kg [Govt]	0.888 kg	18.670 kg [Govt]	7.572 kg [F.O]	0.079 kg [ICPO]
Burkina Faso	1.144 kg [Govt]	222.000 kg [Govt]	No Report	No Report	No Report	0.038 kg

Source: Annual Report Questionnaire if not otherwise indicated

SEIZURES 1996 - 2001
Heroin

Region/country or territory	1996	1997	1998	1999	2000	2001
AFRICA						
West and Central Africa						
Cameroon	No Report	No Report	2.150 kg	0.400 kg	No Report	No Report
Chad	0.500 kg [Govt.]	No Report	No Report	1.800 kg [ICPO]	No Report	No Report
Congo	No Report	0.070 kg	No Report	No Report	No Report	0.010 kg
Côte d'Ivoire	4.531 kg	0.538 kg	0.060 kg 16 u.	1.889 kg 19 u.	3.035 kg [ICPO]	10.394 kg
Democratic Republic of the Congo	2.654 kg [Govt.]	No Report	No Report	No Report	No Report	No Report
Gabon	0.005 kg [ICPO]	No Report	No Report	0.106 kg [ICPO]	No Report	No Report
Gambia	0.084 kg [ICPO]	0.088 kg [ICPO]	0.590 kg [ICPO]	0.039 kg	No Report	4.000 kg
Ghana	3.850 kg [F.O.]	0.005 kg	18.023 kg	21.020 kg	No Report	No Report
Guinea	No Report	No Report	No Report	No Report	2.215 kg [ICPO]	0.592 kg [ICPO]
Mali	2.710 kg [Govt.]	No Report	No Report	No Report	No Report	No Report
Mauritania	0.173 kg [Govt.]	0.005 kg [Govt]	0.005 kg [Govt]	No Report	No Report	No Report
Niger	0.100 kg [ICPO]	0.100 kg [ICPO]	0.412 kg [ICPO]	No Report	No Report	No Report
Nigeria	19.379 kg [ICPO]	10.490 kg	362.000 kg [Govt]	81.035 kg	55.100 kg	46.639 kg
Senegal	7.830 kg [F.O.]	No Report	0.234 kg [ICPO]	0.071 kg [ICPO] 382 u.	198 u. [ICPO]	No Report
Sierra Leone	0.002 kg	No Report	No Report	No Report	No Report	No Report
Togo	0.027 kg	81.601 kg [Govt.]	No Report	No Report	10.808 kg	15.253 kg
Sub-Total	45.260 kg	315.040 kg	384.362 kg 16 u.	125.030 kg 401 u.	78.730 kg 198 u.	77.005 kg
Total region	154.700 kg 6 u.	425.386 kg 0.225 lt.	450.981 kg 0.266 lt. 16 u.	214.263 kg 661 u.	193.914 kg 430 u.	212.439 kg 495 u.
AMERICAS						
Caribbean						
Aruba	No Report	3.298 kg [INCB]	No Report	6.000 kg [F.O]	78.000 kg [F.O]	65.000 kg [F.O]
Barbados	No Report	No Report	No Report	3.230 kg [HONLC]	No Report	No Report
Bermuda	0.100 kg	0.398 kg	No Report	0.836 kg	0.292 kg	2.000 kg [F.O]
British Virgin Islands	No Report	No Report	No Report	No Report	No Report	1.200 kg 1 u.
Cayman Islands	No Report	No Report	No Report	No Report	1.000 kg [F.O]	0.213 kg
Cuba	1.630 kg	0.700 kg [ICPO]	No Report	3.000 kg [F.O]	No Report	No Report
Dominican Republic	12.158 kg	11.328 kg	6.891 kg	11.909 kg	24.000 kg [F.O]	33.003 kg
Guadeloupe	No Report	No Report	No Report	No Report	No Report	4.000 kg [F.O]
Jamaica	0.600 kg [ICPO]	No Report	No Report	No Report	No Report	0.450 kg

Source: Annual Report Questionnaire if not otherwise indicated

SEIZURES 1996 - 2001
Heroin

Region/country or territory	1996	1997	1998	1999	2000	2001
AMERICAS						
Caribbean						
Netherlands Antilles	No Report	No Report	No Report	2.000 kg [INCB]	2.032 kg [ICPO]	72.000 kg [F.O]
Puerto Rico	No Report	No Report	No Report	No Report	24.000 kg [F.O]	42.000 kg [F.O]
Saint Lucia	No Report	No Report	No Report	No Report	2.000 kg	No Report
Trinidad Tobago	0.719 kg [ICPO]	No Report	No Report	No Report	5.000 kg [INCSR]	No Report
Sub-Total	15.207 kg	15.724 kg	6.891 kg	26.975 kg	136.324 kg	219.866 kg 1 u.
Central America						
Belize	No Report	No Report	No Report	No Report	No Report	3.399 kg
Costa Rica	18.000 kg [CICAD]	26.000 kg [CICAD]	13.500 kg	2.400 kg	7.787 kg	20.280 kg
El Salvador	No Report	2.151 kg [ICPO]	0.697 kg [ICPO]	0.099 kg	6.900 kg [ICPO]	9.368 kg
Guatemala	13.479 kg	17.420 kg [Govt.]	3.650 kg	53.000 kg	9.740 kg	21.170 kg
Nicaragua	1.000 kg	2.000 kg	No Report	2.000 kg [CICAD]	2.000 kg [CICAD]	8.422 kg [ICPO]
Panama	10.697 kg	33.307 kg	22.825 kg	46.456 kg	39.045 kg	87.000 kg
Sub-Total	43.176 kg	80.878 kg	40.672 kg	103.954 kg	65.472 kg	149.639 kg
North America						
Canada	83.000 kg	95.000 kg	22.295 kg 0.176 lt. 994 u.	88.000 kg 91 u.	6.970 kg 0.117 lt. 2 u.	73.979 kg
Mexico	363.457 kg	114.903 kg	120.896 kg	260.191 kg	299.102 kg	263.152 kg
United States	1366.300 kg	1542.000 kg	1580.700 kg [Govt.]	1200.000 kg 437 u.	1705.188 kg 1.850 lt. 593 u.	1983.700 kg
Sub-Total	1812.757 kg	1751.903 kg	1723.891 kg 0.176 lt. 994 u.	1548.191 kg 528 u.	2011.260 kg 1.967 lt. 595 u.	2320.831 kg
South America						
Argentina	No Report	38.580 kg	31.040 kg	7.962 kg	47.664 kg	84.683 kg
Bolivia	No Report	No Report	0.760 kg	No Report	No Report	No Report
Brazil	No Report	No Report	0.950 kg	No Report	No Report [ICPO]	12.500 kg [Govt]
Chile	No Report	No Report	No Report	No Report	21.088 kg	33.234 kg
Colombia	80.772 kg	129.735 kg	239.154 kg	514.592 kg	563.054 kg	787.600 kg
Ecuador	80.980 kg	53.096 kg	58.248 kg	80.559 kg	108.715 kg [ICPO]	254.639 kg
Peru	No Report	No Report	No Report	No Report	2.186 kg	0.004 kg
Suriname	No Report	No Report	0.030 kg	No Report	No Report	No Report
Uruguay	No Report	No Report	No Report	No Report	No Report	5.872 kg [ICPO]
Venezuela	56.002 kg	16.086 kg [CICAD]	No Report	41.514 kg	195.580 kg	228.430 kg
Sub-Total	217.754 kg	237.497 kg	330.182 kg	644.627 kg	938.287 kg	1406.962 kg

Source: Annual Report Questionnaire if not otherwise indicated

SEIZURES 1996 - 2001

Heroin

Region/country or territory	1996	1997	1998	1999	2000	2001
AMERICAS						
Total region	2088.894 kg	2086.002 kg	2101.636 kg 0.176 lt. 994 u.	2323.748 kg 528 u.	3151.343 kg 1.967 lt. 595 u.	4097.298 kg 1 u.
ASIA						
Central Asia and Transcaucasian countries						
Armenia	0.171 kg	0.429 kg	0.065 kg	0.191 kg	0.109 kg	0.016 kg
Azerbaijan	0.098 kg [ICPO]	0.170 kg [ICPO]	4.332 kg	4.018 kg	9.917 kg [ICPO]	4.000 kg
Georgia	0.310 kg [ICPO]	No Report	0.083 kg [ICPO]	2.300 kg [ICPO]	3.993 kg [ICPO]	5.518 kg [ICPO]
Kazakhstan	No Report	43.000 kg [Govt.]	24.196 kg	54.264 kg	262.400 kg [F.O]	136.700 kg [F.O]
Kyrgyzstan	1.500 kg [F.O]	4.404 kg	24.732 kg	26.870 kg	216.780 kg	170.898 kg
Tajikistan	6.350 kg	60.000 kg	271.471 kg	708.820 kg	1882.929 kg [F.O]	4239.005 kg
Turkmenistan	No Report	1948.000 kg [Govt.]	495.000 kg [Govt.]	240.000 kg [F.O]	200.000 kg [F.O]	71.000 kg [NAPOL]
Uzbekistan	18.000 kg [Govt.]	70.269 kg	194.679 kg	324.843 kg	675.000 kg	466.601 kg [F.O]
Sub-Total	26.429 kg	2126.272 kg	1014.558 kg	1361.306 kg	3251.128 kg	5093.738 kg
East and South-East Asia						
Brunei Darussalam	0.032 kg	0.001 kg	0.003 kg	No Report	0.001 kg	No Report
Cambodia	No Report	16.000 kg [ICPO]	No Report	No Report	No Report	No Report
China	4347.000 kg	5477.000 kg	7358.000 kg	5364.000 kg [ICPO]	6281.000 kg [Govt.]	13200.000 kg
Hong Kong SAR, China	309.100 kg	202.200 kg	209.000 kg [Govt.]	284.001 kg 0.003 lt.	339.003 kg	156.400 kg
Indonesia	1.709 kg 20 u.	20.433 kg	27.761 kg	14.049 kg	22.655 kg	16.641 kg
Japan	3.974 kg	5.990 kg	3.947 kg	2.150 kg	7.006 kg	4.944 kg
Korea (Republic of)	1.791 kg	0.599 kg	2.126 kg	0.342 kg	No Report	0.567 kg
Lao People's Dem. Rep.	16.200 kg [Govt.]	72.300 kg [Govt.]	80.000 kg [INCSR]	14.750 kg [HNLP]	20.000 kg [INCSR]	49.700 kg [Govt]
Macau SAR, China	0.348 kg [ICPO]	0.231 kg [ICPO]	2.217 kg [ICPO]	1.000 kg [INCB]	0.147 kg	0.069 kg
Malaysia	240.734 kg [Govt.]	276.154 kg	289.664 kg	200.937 kg	109.170 kg	227.058 kg [ICPO]
Myanmar	504.603 kg	1401.079 kg	403.805 kg	273.193 kg	158.921 kg	96.744 kg
Philippines	1.534 kg	3.014 kg [ICPO]	1.741 kg [ICPO]	0.022 kg	No Report	0.010 kg
Singapore	121.291 kg	82.613 kg	141.852 kg	56.730 kg	52.083 kg	106.678 kg
Taiwan province, China	No Report	No Report	No Report	No Report	273.000 kg [PRESS]	153.000 kg [PRESS]
Thailand	597.650 kg [ICPO]	323.287 kg	507.769 kg	405.034 kg	385.962 kg [ICPO]	501.000 kg [F.O]
Viet Nam	54.750 kg [ICPO]	24.300 kg [ICPO]	60.000 kg [ICPO]	66.663 kg [F.O]	49.320 kg [ICPO] 70000 u.	40.300 kg
Sub-Total	6200.717 kg 20 u.	7905.201 kg	9087.884 kg	6682.871 kg 0.003 lt.	7698.267 kg 70000 u.	14553.110 kg

Source: Annual Report Questionnaire if not otherwise indicated

SEIZURES 1996 - 2001
Heroin

Region/country or territory	1996	1997	1998	1999	2000	2001
ASIA						
Near and Middle East /South-West Asia						
Bahrain	12.703 kg	4.165 kg	3.982 kg [ICPO]	2.856 kg [ICPO]	1.643 kg [ICPO]	0.001 kg [ICPO]
Iran (Islamic Republic of)	804.500 kg	1986.042 kg	2894.462 kg	6030.000 kg	6189.000 kg [NAPOL]	4001.000 kg
Iraq	No Report	No Report	8.300 kg	No Report	1.020 kg	No Report
Israel	80.404 kg	75.100 kg	137.800 kg	111.830 kg [ICPO]	80.000 kg	67.625 kg
Jordan	67.387 kg	82.449 kg	52.397 kg	41.397 kg	127.712 kg	35.545 kg
Kuwait	47.525 kg [ICPO]	23.590 kg [ICPO]	21.601 kg	35.000 kg [INCB]	No Report	No Report
Lebanon	50.771 kg	2.361 kg	3.093 kg	8.149 kg	2.363 kg	13.002 kg
Oman	8.000 kg [INCB]	0.756 kg [INCB]	No Report	54.109 kg	14.008 kg [ICPO]	8.485 kg
Pakistan	5872.105 kg [ICPO]	6156.000 kg [ICPO]	3363.723 kg	4973.711 kg	9492.029 kg	6931.470 kg
Qatar	0.338 kg	No Report	1.480 kg [ICPO]	0.108 kg [ICPO]	0.534 kg [ICPO]	0.404 kg [ICPO]
Saudi Arabia	483.416 kg [ICPO]	115.667 kg [ICPO]	63.107 kg	No Report	200.922 kg	178.825 kg
Syrian Arab Republic	9.783 kg [Govt]	12.263 kg [Govt]	36.204 kg [Govt]	57.659 kg [Govt]	50.441 kg [Govt]	30.342 kg [Govt]
United Arab Emirates	21.635 kg	35.767 kg	34.450 kg	65.909 kg	82.176 kg	40.100 kg
Yemen	No Report	No Report	0.027 kg [ICPO]	No Report	No Report	No Report
Sub-Total	7458.567 kg	8494.159 kg	6620.626 kg	11380.730 kg	16241.850 kg	11306.800 kg
South Asia						
Bangladesh	16.800 kg	No Report	No Report	28.840 kg [F.O]	8.031 kg	42.290 kg [ICPO]
India	1257.000 kg [Govt.]	1332.000 kg	655.000 kg	839.000 kg	1240.000 kg	889.000 kg
Maldives	No Report	No Report	1.142 kg	0.357 kg	No Report	0.167 kg
Nepal	9.989 kg	11.117 kg [Govt]	9.400 kg [Govt]	1.515 kg [Govt]	1.705 kg [Govt]	9.360 kg [ICPO]
Sri Lanka	39.815 kg	55.015 kg	56.942 kg	68.500 kg	94.150 kg	102.216 kg
Sub-Total	1323.604 kg	1398.132 kg	722.484 kg	938.212 kg	1343.886 kg	1043.033 kg
Total region	15009.320 kg 20 u.	19923.770 kg	17445.550 kg	20363.120 kg 0.003 lt.	28535.130 kg 70000 u.	31996.680 kg
EUROPE						
Eastern Europe						
Albania	No Report	No Report	No Report	7.122 kg [ICPO]	47.000 kg [Govt]	4.500 kg [Govt]
Belarus	No Report	0.635 kg [INCB]	0.907 kg	1.977 kg	3.442 kg	3.257 kg [ICPO]
Bosnia Herzegovina	0.643 kg [NAPOL]	0.017 kg [NAPOL]	0.686 kg [NAPOL]	1.125 kg [ICPO]	0.375 kg [NAPOL]	1.900 kg [ICPO] 5 u.
Bulgaria	248.265 kg	322.691 kg	219.632 kg	265.249 kg	2067.201 kg	1550.629 kg
Croatia	2.273 kg	3.040 kg	50.095 kg	13.232 kg	7.041 kg	19.569 kg
Czech Republic	20.125 kg	21.442 kg	240.000 kg	108.380 kg	114.520 kg	88.590 kg 478 u.

Source: Annual Report Questionnaire if not otherwise indicated

SEIZURES 1996 - 2001
Heroin

Region/country or territory	1996	1997	1998	1999	2000	2001
EUROPE						
Eastern Europe						
Estonia	No Report	No Report	0.091 kg 129 u.	0.518 kg 1269 u.	0.438 kg 2129 u.	1.163 kg
FYR of Macedonia	29.155 kg [NAPOL]	15.425 kg [NAPOL]	91.672 kg	14.375 kg [NAPOL]	90.789 kg [NAPOL]	110.882 kg [Govt]
Hungary	319.205 kg	206.160 kg [Govt.]	634.613 kg	172.703 kg	819.000 kg	154.410 kg
Latvia	No Report	0.011 kg	0.098 kg	0.768 kg	0.775 kg	0.465 kg
Lithuania	No Report	0.089 kg	0.423 kg	0.923 kg	0.943 kg	2.740 kg
Poland	43.189 kg	142.812 kg	67.405 kg	44.947 kg	120.063 kg [(2] 388.000 lt.	208.106 kg
Republic of Moldova	No Report	10.000 kg	No Report	No Report	1.313 kg [ICPO]	0.041 kg
Romania	103.347 kg	117.922 kg [ICPO]	412.327 kg	63.630 kg	52.940 kg	41.770 kg
Russian Federation	18.100 kg	24.027 kg	442.900 kg	695.085 kg	984.000 kg [F.O]	1287.226 kg
Serbia and Montenegro	No Report	15.425 kg [ICPO]	No Report	No Report	No Report	62.518 kg
Slovakia	11.000 kg [INCB]	90.450 kg	13.671 kg	5.808 kg	98.507 kg	15.680 kg
Slovenia	24.571 kg	29.828 kg	46.106 kg	32.270 kg	392.065 kg	88.930 kg
Ukraine	4.025 kg	3.728 kg	8.940 kg	21.530 kg [ICPO.]	21.743 kg [ICPO]	8.669 kg
Sub-Total	823.898 kg	1003.702 kg	2229.566 kg 129 u.	1449.642 kg 1269 u.	4822.155 kg 388.000 lt. 2129 u.	3651.045 kg 483 u.
Western Europe						
Andorra	No Report	0.005 kg [ICPO]	0.003 kg [ICPO]	0.013 kg	0.009 kg [ICPO]	0.009 kg
Austria	81.326 kg	102.138 kg	118.213 kg	78.914 kg	230.747 kg	288.312 kg
Belgium	133.000 kg	55.000 kg	75.790 kg	73.537 kg	187.739 kg	187.739 kg [UNODC (3]
Cyprus	0.004 kg	No Report	0.035 kg	2.193 kg	4.949 kg	1.638 kg
Denmark	61.400 kg	37.900 kg	55.136 kg	96.040 kg	32.080 kg	25.125 kg
Finland	6.450 kg	2.532 kg	1.965 kg	2.884 kg	6.026 kg	7.500 kg
France	617.241 kg	415.453 kg	343.783 kg	203.313 kg	443.935 kg	351.055 kg
Germany	898.191 kg	722.211 kg	685.920 kg	796.400 kg	796.000 kg	835.836 kg
Gibraltar	0.001 kg	No Report	0.011 kg 1 u.	0.021 kg 2 u.	[(1]	1.200 kg
Greece	193.656 kg 38 u.	146.311 kg 38 u.	232.110 kg 6 u.	98.401 kg 10 u.	1179.526 kg 14 u.	329.725 kg
Iceland	No Report	No Report	No Report	0.001 kg	No Report	No Report
Ireland	10.800 kg	8.184 kg	36.963 kg	15.921 kg	23.942 kg	29.527 kg
Italy	1251.432 kg	470.335 kg 5360 u.	703.335 kg 3069 u.	1313.708 kg [ICPO]	980.379 kg 1678 u.	2004.588 kg 1423 u.
Liechtenstein	9.303 kg	18.680 kg	No Report	14.388 kg	0.005 kg	0.003 kg
Luxembourg	2.934 kg	2.525 kg	3.592 kg	1.914 kg	11.358 kg [ICPO]	No Report

Source: Annual Report Questionnaire if not otherwise indicated

SEIZURES 1996 - 2001
Heroin

Region/country or territory	1996	1997	1998	1999	2000	2001
EUROPE						
Western Europe						
Malta	2.658 kg	4.535 kg	0.498 kg	1.724 kg	5.912 kg	2.599 kg
Monaco	0.003 kg	0.011 kg	[4]	No Report	No Report	No Report
Netherlands	516.000 kg [Govt]	999.000 kg [Govt]	784.000 kg [Govt]	770.000 kg [Govt]	896.000 kg [Govt]	739.000 kg
Norway	74.080 kg	55.509 kg	37.347 kg	45.810 kg	51.500 kg	67.905 kg
Portugal	46.697 kg	57.389 kg	96.666 kg	76.417 kg	567.577 kg [5]	316.039 kg 5.000 lt.
Spain	537.219 kg	479.450 kg	444.243 kg	1159.297 kg	484.854 kg	630.600 kg
Sweden	39.621 kg	11.509 kg	70.927 kg 0.011 lt.	63.009 kg 0.509 lt.	27.649 kg	32.627 kg
Switzerland	405.732 kg	209.261 kg	403.680 kg	397.527 kg	372.061 kg	227.515 kg
Turkey	4422.000 kg	3509.851 kg	4651.486 kg	3605.123 kg	6052.582 kg [Govt.]	4392.103 kg
United Kingdom	1070.100 kg	2234.900 kg	1345.804 kg	2341.700 kg [NCIS]	3382.392 kg	3382.392 kg [UNODC] [3]
Sub-Total	10379.850 kg 38 u.	9542.689 kg 5398 u.	10091.510 kg 0.011 lt. 3076 u.	11158.260 kg 0.509 lt. 12 u.	15737.220 kg 1692 u.	13853.040 kg 5.000 lt. 1423 u.
Total region	11203.750 kg 38 u.	10546.390 kg 5398 u.	12321.070 kg 0.011 lt. 3205 u.	12607.900 kg 0.509 lt. 1281 u.	20559.380 kg 388.000 lt. 3821 u.	17504.080 kg 5.000 lt. 1906 u.
OCEANIA						
Oceania						
Australia	46.604 kg 278 u.	365.370 kg	298.690 kg [Govt. (6]	360.145 kg	583.456 kg	82.729 kg
Fiji	No Report	No Report	No Report	No Report	357.700 kg [ICPO]	No Report
New Zealand	1.000 kg [INCB]	0.171 kg [INCB]	10.859 kg	0.544 kg	0.066 kg	5.536 kg
Sub-Total	47.604 kg 278 u.	365.541 kg	309.549 kg	360.689 kg	941.222 kg	88.265 kg
Total region	47.604 kg 278 u.	365.541 kg	309.549 kg	360.689 kg	941.222 kg	88.265 kg
TOTAL	28504.260 kg 342 u.	33347.090 kg 0.225 lt. 5398 u.	32628.790 kg 0.453 lt. 4215 u.	35869.710 kg 0.512 lt. 2470 u.	53380.980 kg 389.967 lt. 74846 u.	53898.770 kg 5.000 lt. 2402 u.

1) Small quantity. 2) 388 lt. Polish heroin 3) Due to unavailability of 2001 data, year 2000 data were used for analysis purposes. 4) Including depressants. 5) heroin with 44gm of cocaine 6) Provisional figures.

Source: Annual Report Questionnaire if not otherwise indicated

SEIZURES 1996 - 2001
Morphine

Region/country or territory	1996	1997	1998	1999	2000	2001
AFRICA						
East Africa						
Ethiopia	No Report	No Report	0.001 kg 6 u.	No Report	No Report	No Report
United Republic of Tanzania	No Report	0.283 kg	No Report	0.020 kg	No Report	3.338 kg [Govt]
Sub-Total		0.283 kg	0.001 kg 6 u.	0.020 kg		3.338 kg
North Africa						
Egypt	0.024 lt.	0.001 kg	0.012 lt.	0.007 kg	No Report	4 u.
Morocco	0.110 kg	0.318 kg	0.997 kg	No Report	No Report	247 u.
Sub-Total	0.110 kg 0.024 lt.	0.319 kg	0.997 kg 0.012 lt.	0.007 kg		251 u.
Southern Africa						
Mozambique	No Report	No Report	No Report	0.085 kg [ICPO]	No Report	No Report
Zambia	0.000 kg [Govt]	0.000 kg [Govt]	3.200 kg [Govt]	0.028 kg	0.061 kg	0.860 kg [Govt]
Sub-Total			3.200 kg	0.113 kg	0.061 kg	0.860 kg
West and Central Africa						
Benin	No Report	No Report	3.190 kg	No Report	No Report	No Report
Chad	No Report	No Report	No Report	No Report	0.090 kg	No Report
Nigeria	0.019 kg [ICPO]	0.130 kg	No Report	No Report	21.120 kg	No Report
Sub-Total	0.019 kg	0.130 kg	3.190 kg		21.210 kg	
Total region	0.129 kg 0.024 lt.	0.732 kg	7.388 kg 0.012 lt. 6 u.	0.140 kg	21.271 kg	4.198 kg 251 u.
AMERICAS						
Caribbean						
Cuba	23 u.	No Report	No Report	No Report	No Report	No Report
Dominican Republic	No Report	No Report	No Report	No Report	19.000 kg [CICAD]	No Report
Sub-Total	23 u.				19.000 kg	
Central America						
Guatemala	No Report	0.720 kg [Govt.]	No Report	No Report	No Report	No Report
Sub-Total		0.720 kg				
North America						
Canada	0.100 kg 0.172 lt. 329 u.	1.076 kg 2468 u.	1.662 kg 0.433 lt. 1166 u.	1.000 kg 1.016 lt. 1826 u.	0.751 kg 1.285 lt. 1842 u.	0.267 kg 3807 u.
Mexico	No Report	2.068 kg	No Report	1.130 kg	4.480 kg	0.539 kg

Source: Annual Report Questionnaire if not otherwise indicated

SEIZURES 1996 - 2001
Morphine

Region/country or territory	1996	1997	1998	1999	2000	2001
AMERICAS						
North America						
United States	0.081 kg 482 u.	0.006 lt. 560 u.	No Report	3.134 kg 998 u.	180.108 kg 15.723 lt. 134 u.	812 u.
Sub-Total	0.181 kg 0.172 lt. 811 u.	3.144 kg 0.006 lt. 3028 u.	1.662 kg 0.433 lt. 1166 u.	5.264 kg 1.016 lt. 2824 u.	185.339 kg 17.008 lt. 1976 u.	0.806 kg 4619 u.
South America						
Argentina	No Report	No Report	No Report	650.000 kg	No Report	No Report
Brazil	No Report	No Report	No Report	0.150 kg	No Report	No Report
Chile	No Report	No Report	29 u.	1 u. [ICPO]	No Report	No Report
Colombia	94.120 kg	87.122 kg	79.111 kg	154.023 kg	91.017 kg	47.300 kg
Peru	0.001 kg	No Report	No Report	No Report	11.979 kg	0.492 kg
Sub-Total	94.121 kg	87.122 kg	79.111 kg 29 u.	804.173 kg 1 u.	102.996 kg	47.792 kg
Total region	94.302 kg 0.172 lt. 834 u.	90.986 kg 0.006 lt. 3028 u.	80.773 kg 0.433 lt. 1195 u.	809.437 kg 1.016 lt. 2825 u.	307.335 kg 17.008 lt. 1976 u.	48.598 kg 4619 u.
ASIA						
Central Asia and Transcaucasian countries						
Armenia	12 u.	3 u.	[1]	No Report	0.000 kg [1]	0.351 kg
Azerbaijan	No Report	No Report	No Report	0.085 kg	No Report	No Report
Georgia	0.022 kg [ICPO] 0.057 lt. 1659 u.	No Report	No Report	0.003 kg [ICPO]	0.262 kg [ICPO]	0.107 kg [ICPO]
Kazakhstan	No Report	No Report	4.172 kg	1.493 kg	No Report	No Report
Kyrgyzstan	21 u.	No Report	No Report	No Report	No Report	No Report
Uzbekistan	No Report	8 u.	0.030 kg	3.400 kg [ICPO]	No Report	No Report
Sub-Total	0.022 kg 0.057 lt. 1692 u.	11 u.	4.202 kg	4.981 kg	0.262 kg	0.458 kg
East and South-East Asia						
China	178.000 kg	358.000 kg	146.000 kg	No Report	No Report	No Report
Hong Kong SAR, China	17.300 kg	No Report	No Report	[1]	No Report	1462 u.
Indonesia	0.002 kg	0.320 kg	No Report	3.174 kg 202 u.	0.223 kg	0.001 kg
Japan	0.835 kg	0.011 kg 1.107 lt. 229 u.	0.363 kg 0.002 lt. 146 u.	0.002 kg	200 u.	1.275 kg 117 u.

Source: Annual Report Questionnaire if not otherwise indicated

SEIZURES 1996 - 2001
Morphine

Region/country or territory	1996	1997	1998	1999	2000	2001
ASIA						
East and South-East Asia						
Mongolia	No Report	No Report	No Report	No Report	0.270 kg [ICPO]	No Report
Myanmar	No Report	45.728 kg 200 u.	95.087 kg	24.001 kg	22.696 kg	6.052 kg 107 u.
Singapore	No Report	No Report	No Report	No Report	No Report	0.076 kg 24 u.
Thailand	No Report	0.005 kg	No Report	0.200 kg [ICPO]	0.005 kg [ICPO]	No Report
Viet Nam	12937 u. [ICPO]	No Report	No Report	No Report	No Report	No Report
Sub-Total	196.137 kg 12937 u.	404.064 kg 1.107 lt. 429 u.	241.450 kg 0.002 lt. 146 u.	27.377 kg 202 u.	23.194 kg 200 u.	7.404 kg 1710 u.
Near and Middle East /South-West Asia						
Iran (Islamic Republic of)	10430.000 kg	18949.754 kg	22291.102 kg	22764.000 kg	20764.000 kg [NAPOL]	8668.000 kg
Israel	0.005 kg 25 u.	No Report	No Report	0.028 kg [ICPO]	18 u.	0.041 kg
Kuwait	0.007 kg [ICPO]	No Report	No Report	34.813 kg [ICPO]	10.611 kg [ICPO]	No Report
Oman	No Report	No Report	No Report	1.006 kg	No Report	No Report
Pakistan	No Report	No Report	No Report	No Report	No Report	1824.000 kg 7850 u.
Qatar	No Report	0.133 kg [ICPO]	No Report	No Report	No Report	No Report
Saudi Arabia	No Report	No Report	No Report	149.491 kg [ICPO]	No Report	No Report
United Arab Emirates	No Report	No Report	0.018 kg	0.030 kg	No Report	No Report
Sub-Total	10430.010 kg 25 u.	18949.890 kg	22291.120 kg	22949.370 kg	20774.610 kg 18 u.	10492.040 kg 7850 u.
South Asia						
Bangladesh	No Report	No Report	No Report	No Report	No Report	108 u. [ICPO]
India	4.000 kg [Govt.]	128.000 kg	19.000 kg	30.000 kg	39.000 kg	26.000 kg
Nepal	No Report	11.126 kg [ICPO]	No Report	No Report	No Report	No Report
Sub-Total	4.000 kg	139.126 kg	19.000 kg	30.000 kg	39.000 kg	26.000 kg 108 u.
Total region	10630.170 kg 0.057 lt. 14654 u.	19493.080 kg 1.107 lt. 440 u.	22555.770 kg 0.002 lt. 146 u.	23011.720 kg 202 u.	20837.070 kg 218 u.	10525.900 kg 9668 u.
EUROPE						
Eastern Europe						
Albania	No Report	No Report	No Report	No Report	10 u. [ICPO]	No Report
Belarus	No Report	0.001 kg [INCB]	0.154 kg	0.005 kg	0.078 kg	192.000 kg [ICPO]

Source: Annual Report Questionnaire if not otherwise indicated

SEIZURES 1996 - 2001
Morphine

Region/country or territory	1996	1997	1998	1999	2000	2001
EUROPE						
Eastern Europe						
Bulgaria	No Report	4.000 kg	No Report	16 u.	No Report	No Report
Croatia	17 u.	No Report	79 u.	652 u.	27 u.	No Report
Czech Republic	No Report	No Report	No Report	No Report	No Report	0.049 kg
Estonia	0.508 lt. [ICPO]	(2	0.003 kg 5 u.	No Report	0.011 kg 40 u.	1.066 kg
Hungary	0.209 kg	0.686 kg [Govt.]	No Report	0.200 kg	No Report	10 u.
Lithuania	0.365 lt.	No Report	No Report	No Report	No Report	No Report
Poland	No Report	No Report	No Report	No Report	0.588 kg [ICPO] 174 u.	No Report
Republic of Moldova	No Report	31 u.	No Report	No Report	No Report	No Report
Romania	74 u.	71 u. [ICPO]	86 u.	132 u.	0.112 kg	248 u.
Russian Federation	45.141 kg	6.037 kg 8 u.	15.000 kg [F.O]	2.427 kg	2.000 kg [F.O]	11.024 kg
Slovakia	No Report	No Report	3 u.		0.288 kg	
Sub-Total	45.350 kg 0.873 lt. 91 u.	10.724 kg 110 u.	15.157 kg 173 u.	2.632 kg 800 u.	3.077 kg 251 u.	204.139 kg 258 u.
Western Europe						
Austria	0.815 kg	0.327 kg	1.522 kg	0.328 kg	0.220 kg	0.200 kg
Belgium	No Report	10.000 kg	0.098 kg		17.400 kg [ICPO]	17.400 kg [UNODC] (3
Cyprus	No Report	No Report	No Report	No Report	No Report	15 u.
Denmark	0.981 kg	1.560 lt.	3.000 kg	No Report	1.405 kg [ICPO]	No Report
Finland	0.066 kg 2422 u.	0.005 kg	No Report	0.910 kg 60 u.	0.054 kg 60 u.	No Report
France	0.080 kg	0.020 kg	0.088 kg	1.566 kg	0.222 kg	0.218 kg
Greece	0.004 kg	No Report	No Report	No Report	No Report	No Report
Ireland	1261 u.	0.003 kg 528 u.	0.004 kg	90 u. [ICPO]	No Report	No Report
Italy	0.042 kg	0.095 kg 9 u.	2.270 kg 12 u.	1.314 kg [ICPO]	0.752 kg 5 u.	0.015 kg 452 u.
Norway	No Report	0.011 kg	0.008 kg 33 u.	0.001 kg 1219 u.	2005 u.	1963 u.
Portugal	11 u.	No Report	0.005 kg	85 u.	241 u.	0.043 kg 97 u.
Spain	74 u.	8 u.	3 u.	13 u.	33 u.	16 u.
Sweden	0.170 kg	0.003 kg 104 u.	0.154 lt.	0.011 kg 0.202 lt. 120 u.	0.074 kg 320 u.	0.070 kg
Switzerland	0.040 kg	No Report	0.054 kg	0.537 kg	0.135 kg	0.492 kg

Source: Annual Report Questionnaire if not otherwise indicated

SEIZURES 1996 - 2001
Morphine

Region/country or territory	1996	1997	1998	1999	2000	2001
EUROPE						
Western Europe						
Turkey	1157.000 kg	662.816 kg	754.494 kg	1010.328 kg	2484.934 kg [Govt.]	797.493 kg
United Kingdom	1.600 kg	0.400 kg	41.251 kg	1.300 kg [NCIS]	3.278 kg	3.278 kg [UNODC] (3
Sub-Total	1160.798 kg	673.680 kg	802.794 kg	1016.295 kg	2508.474 kg	819.209 kg
	3768 u.	1.560 lt.	0.154 lt.	0.202 lt.	2664 u.	2543 u.
		649 u.	48 u.	1587 u.		
Total region	1206.148 kg	684.404 kg	817.951 kg	1018.927 kg	2511.552 kg	1023.348 kg
	0.873 lt.	1.560 lt.	0.154 lt.	0.202 lt.	2915 u.	2801 u.
	3859 u.	759 u.	221 u.	2387 u.		
OCEANIA						
Oceania						
Australia	1.086 kg	2.049 kg	No Report	No Report	3.205 kg	0.036 kg
	56 u.				104 u.	73 u.
New Zealand	No Report	1.422 kg [INCB]	1.166 kg	0.312 kg	0.713 lt.	0.954 kg
					396 u.	1285 u.
Sub-Total	1.086 kg	3.471 kg	1.166 kg	0.312 kg	3.205 kg	0.990 kg
	56 u.				0.713 lt.	1358 u.
					500 u.	
Total region	1.086 kg	3.471 kg	1.166 kg	0.312 kg	3.205 kg	0.990 kg
	56 u.				0.713 lt.	1358 u.
					500 u.	
TOTAL	11931.840 kg	20272.670 kg	23463.050 kg	24840.540 kg	23680.430 kg	11603.040 kg
	1.126 lt.	2.673 lt.	0.601 lt.	1.218 lt.	17.721 lt.	18697 u.
	19403 u.	4227 u.	1568 u.	5414 u.	5609 u.	

1) Small quantity. 2) Including depressants. 3) Due to unavailability of 2001 data, year 2000 data were used for analysis purposes.

Source: Annual Report Questionnaire if not otherwise indicated

SEIZURES 1996 - 2001
Other opiates

Region/country or territory	1996	1997	1998	1999	2000	2001
AFRICA						
East Africa						
Mauritius	No Report	26 u. [ICPO]	No Report	No Report	No Report	No Report
Sub-Total		26 u.				
North Africa						
Egypt	0.030 lt. [1]	0.060 lt. [1]	No Report	0.030 lt. [1]	1.140 lt. [ICPO]	No Report
Sub-Total	0.030 lt.	0.060 lt.		0.030 lt.	1.140 lt.	
West and Central Africa						
Benin	No Report	No Report	No Report	No Report	1.650 kg [ICPO]	No Report
Sub-Total					1.650 kg	
Total region	0.030 lt.	0.060 lt.		0.030 lt.	1.650 kg	
		26 u.			1.140 lt.	
AMERICAS						
Caribbean						
Cayman Islands	No Report	No Report	No Report	0.003 kg [ICPO]	2 u.	No Report
Dominican Republic	No Report	No Report	No Report	8.000 kg [ICPO]	No Report	No Report
Sub-Total				8.003 kg	2 u.	
North America						
Canada	1.355 kg	0.912 kg	1.446 kg	0.594 kg	0.682 kg	1.124 kg
	2524 u.	0.301 lt.	0.093 lt.	8805 u.	1.050 lt.	22045 u.
		4826 u.	8880 u.		4784 u.	
United States	6.112 kg	No Report	No Report	9338 u. [ICPO (1]	No Report	10778580 u.
	72075 u.					
Sub-Total	7.467 kg	0.912 kg	1.446 kg	0.594 kg	0.682 kg	1.124 kg
	74599 u.	0.301 lt.	0.093 lt.	18143 u.	1.050 lt.	10800630 u.
		4826 u.	8880 u.		4784 u.	
South America						
Argentina	No Report	No Report	No Report	No Report	No Report	0.200 kg
Chile	No Report	No Report	25 u.	No Report	No Report	No Report
Colombia	No Report	No Report	No Report	3.500 kg [1]	No Report	1.000 kg [1]
Peru	No Report	No Report	No Report	38.693 kg [ICPO]	No Report	No Report
Sub-Total			25 u.	42.193 kg		1.200 kg
Total region	7.467 kg	0.912 kg	1.446 kg	50.790 kg	0.682 kg	2.324 kg
	74599 u.	0.301 lt.	0.093 lt.	18143 u.	1.050 lt.	10800630 u.
		4826 u.	8905 u.		4786 u.	

Source: Annual Report Questionnaire if not otherwise indicated

SEIZURES 1996 - 2001
Other opiates

Region/country or territory	1996	1997	1998	1999	2000	2001
ASIA						
Central Asia and Transcaucasian countries						
Armenia	50 u.	No Report	No Report	0.017 kg [ICPO]	1.679 kg	No Report
Azerbaijan	No Report	No Report	No Report	No Report	72.590 kg [ICPO]	No Report
Georgia	30.150 kg [ICPO] 3980 u.	No Report	No Report	25.003 kg [ICPO (2]	12.871 kg [ICPO]	No Report
Kazakhstan	No Report	No Report	3.219 kg	7.944 kg	No Report	No Report
Kyrgyzstan	7.484 kg	No Report	No Report	No Report	No Report	No Report
Tajikistan	66.000 kg	No Report	No Report	No Report	No Report	No Report
Uzbekistan	0.169 kg [ICPO]	0.019 kg	No Report	No Report	288.000 kg [ICPO]	No Report
Sub-Total	103.803 kg 4030 u.	0.019 kg	3.219 kg	32.964 kg	375.140 kg	
East and South-East Asia						
Brunei Darussalam	309.272 lt. 3714 u.	85.173 kg 554 u.	0.057 kg 474 u.	12.970 lt. 2377 u.	23.000 lt.	1413 u.
Hong Kong SAR, China	No Report	No Report	No Report	187 u. [(2]	7.600 lt. [ICPO] 1873 u.	5.200 lt. 3306 u.
Indonesia	No Report	No Report	7179 u.	564 u. [ICPO (1]	No Report	No Report
Japan	0.004 kg 88 u.	0.141 kg 1809 u.	0.006 kg 0.030 lt. 5557 u.	0.005 kg	No Report	No Report
Macau SAR, China	159 u. [ICPO]	64 u. [ICPO]	8.000 lt. [ICPO] 45 u.	No Report	2.000 lt. [ICPO] 1 u.	No Report
Malaysia	No Report	No Report	No Report	18453 u.	17982.480 lt. [(1]	No Report
Myanmar	No Report	194.377 kg	No Report	555.000 kg 121.000 lt.	222.089 lt. [(3]	No Report
Singapore	525 u.	136 u.	301 u.	0.438 kg [(2]	1127 u. [(4]	6382.000 kg
Thailand	No Report	No Report	No Report	381.600 lt. [ICPO (1]	569.505 kg [ICPO]	No Report
Viet Nam	1.400 kg [ICPO]	No Report	No Report	No Report	No Report	No Report
Sub-Total	1.404 kg 309.272 lt. 4486 u.	279.691 kg 2563 u.	0.063 kg 8.030 lt. 13556 u.	555.443 kg 515.570 lt. 21581 u.	569.505 kg 18237.170 lt. 3001 u.	6382.000 kg 5.200 lt. 4719 u.
Near and Middle East /South-West Asia						
Iran (Islamic Republic of)	No Report	255.065 kg	No Report	1088.000 kg	1459.000 kg [ICPO]	No Report
Iraq	No Report	No Report	No Report	No Report	No Report	1.000 kg [(1]
Israel	No Report	No Report	No Report	2.121 lt. [ICPO (1] 7 u.	3.843 kg [ICPO] 15 u.	No Report
Jordan	1349.464 kg	894.738 kg	No Report	No Report	No Report	No Report
Lebanon	No Report	No Report	No Report	No Report	0.300 kg [ICPO]	No Report

Source: Annual Report Questionnaire if not otherwise indicated

SEIZURES 1996 - 2001
Other opiates

Region/country or territory	1996	1997	1998	1999	2000	2001
ASIA						
Near and Middle East /South-West Asia						
Qatar	0.016 kg 42 u.	No Report	No Report	No Report	No Report	No Report
Sub-Total	1349.480 kg 42 u.	1149.803 kg		1088.000 kg 2.121 lt. 7 u.	1463.143 kg 15 u.	1.000 kg
South Asia						
Bangladesh	85903 u.	No Report	No Report	No Report	No Report	No Report
Nepal	No Report	4971 u. [ICPO]	3676 u.	No Report	No Report	No Report
Sub-Total	85903 u.	4971 u.	3676 u.			
Total region	1454.687 kg 309.272 lt. 94461 u.	1429.513 kg 7534 u.	3.282 kg 8.030 lt. 17232 u.	1676.407 kg 517.691 lt. 21588 u.	2407.788 kg 18237.170 lt. 3016 u.	6383.000 kg 5.200 lt. 4719 u.
EUROPE						
Eastern Europe						
Albania	No Report	No Report	No Report	No Report	0.480 lt. [ICPO] 7 u.	No Report
Bosnia Herzegovina	No Report	No Report	1 u. [ICPO]	No Report	No Report	No Report
Bulgaria	No Report	No Report	No Report	No Report	3650 u. [ICPO]	No Report
Croatia	No Report	No Report	No Report	No Report	29 u.	No Report
Estonia	73.529 lt. [ICPO]	23.332 lt.	No Report	2 u.	0.003 kg 20 u.	No Report
FYR of Macedonia	No Report	No Report	No Report	3.988 kg [ICPO] 2.250 lt. 135 u.	No Report	No Report
Hungary	No Report	No Report	438 u.	120 u. [ICPO (2]	No Report	262 u.
Latvia	No Report	0.134 kg	No Report	No Report	No Report	No Report
Lithuania	0.001 kg	No Report	13 u.	0.210 kg 92 u.	0.888 lt. [(2]	No Report
Poland	2801.000 kg	1004.000 lt.	395.000 lt.	389.000 lt. [(5]	3.500 lt. [ICPO] 174 u.	No Report
Republic of Moldova	No Report	1000 u.	2100 u.	682 u. [ICPO]	0.858 kg [ICPO]	No Report
Romania	No Report	No Report	19494 u.	26 u. [(2]	0.840 lt. [(2] 387 u.	No Report
Russian Federation	106.400 kg	4.925 kg 11 u.	167.700 kg [F.O]	54.575 kg	18.000 kg [F.O]	21469.675 kg
Slovakia	No Report	No Report	922 u.	278 u.	38 u. [ICPO]	No Report
Slovenia	No Report	No Report	No Report	0.552 lt.	1.545 lt. [ICPO] 245 u.	No Report

Source: Annual Report Questionnaire if not otherwise indicated

SEIZURES 1996 - 2001
Other opiates

Region/country or territory	1996	1997	1998	1999	2000	2001
EUROPE						
Eastern Europe						
Ukraine	486.500 kg	No Report	No Report	11600 u. [ICPO (1]	No Report	No Report
Sub-Total	3393.901 kg	5.059 kg	167.700 kg	58.773 kg	18.861 kg	21469.680 kg
	73.529 lt.	1027.332 lt.	395.000 lt.	391.802 lt.	7.253 lt.	262 u.
		1011 u.	22968 u.	12935 u.	4550 u.	
Western Europe						
Austria	0.477 kg	0.083 kg	No Report	No Report	No Report	No Report
Belgium	No Report	No Report	0.109 kg	9.100 kg [ICPO]	15.070 kg [ICPO]	15.070 kg [UNODC (6]
				0.200 lt.		
				307500 u.		
Cyprus	No Report	No Report	No Report	55 u. [ICPO]	No Report	No Report
Denmark	No Report	No Report	6.000 kg	No Report	No Report	No Report
Finland	No Report	No Report	No Report	46 u. [ICPO]	13808 u.	31967 u.
France	No Report	No Report	No Report	521 u. [ICPO (2]	4134 u. [ICPO]	No Report
Gibraltar	No Report	No Report	No Report	8 u. [ICPO (2]	558 u. [(1]	No Report
Greece	0.280 kg	2.308 kg	1.529 kg	0.132 kg	0.472 kg	0.070 kg
	5089 u.	15322 u.	6774 u.	7795 u.	5162 u.	1466 u.
Ireland	No Report	No Report	No Report	0.320 kg [ICPO (2]	No Report	No Report
				579 u.		
Italy	0.170 kg	0.002 kg	0.554 kg	2.426 kg [ICPO (2]	2.967 kg [(7]	No Report
		7 u.	7538 u.		7220 u.	
Luxembourg	No Report	No Report	No Report	0.180 lt. [ICPO (2]	0.098 lt. [ICPO]	No Report
Malta	No Report	No Report	77 u.	No Report	98 u.	No Report
Netherlands	491 u. [Govt (2]	2.000 kg [Govt (2]	4093 u. [Govt (2]	50.000 kg [Govt (2]	16.000 kg [Govt (2]	No Report
		16748 u.		186437 u.	5543 u.	
Norway	No Report	No Report	No Report	0.017 kg	0.001 kg	0.255 kg
				9657 u.	8007 u.	18879 u.
Portugal	No Report	21 u.	35 u.	21 u.	15 u. [(8]	20.910 kg
						22 u.
Spain	373 u.	1159 u.	No Report	966 u. [ICPO]	No Report	7708 u.
Sweden	No Report	No Report	0.003 kg	0.053 kg	0.052 kg	No Report
			1.312 lt.	783 u.	631 u.	
Switzerland	4305 u.	0.010 kg	No Report	5006 u.	5472 u. [(2]	No Report
Turkey	No Report	No Report	No Report	34090 u. [ICPO (2]	0.234 kg [Govt. (2]	No Report
United Kingdom		1.000 kg	0.064 kg	60.600 kg [NCIS (2]	0.548 kg	0.548 kg [UNODC (6]
		1.000 lt.				
		1 u.				
Sub-Total	0.927 kg	5.403 kg	8.259 kg	122.648 kg	35.344 kg	36.853 kg
	10258 u.	1.000 lt.	1.312 lt.	0.380 lt.	0.098 lt.	60042 u.
		33258 u.	18517 u.	553464 u.	50648 u.	

Source: Annual Report Questionnaire if not otherwise indicated

SEIZURES 1996 - 2001

Other opiates

Region/country or territory	1996	1997	1998	1999	2000	2001
EUROPE						
Total region	3394.828 kg 73.529 lt. 10258 u.	10.462 kg 1028.332 lt. 34269 u.	175.959 kg 396.312 lt. 41485 u.	181.421 kg 392.182 lt. 566399 u.	54.205 kg 7.351 lt. 55198 u.	21506.530 kg 60304 u.
OCEANIA						
Oceania						
Australia	0.115 kg	[9	22.243 kg $_{(10}^{Govt.}$	6.792 kg $_{(10}^{Govt.}$	0.384 kg	6.786 kg $_{(11}^{Govt.}$
New Zealand	No Report	No Report	No Report	0.100 kg	No Report	No Report
Sub-Total	0.115 kg		22.243 kg	6.892 kg	0.384 kg	6.786 kg
Total region	0.115 kg		22.243 kg	6.892 kg	0.384 kg	6.786 kg
TOTAL	4857.097 kg 382.831 lt. 179318 u.	1440.887 kg 1028.693 lt. 46655 u.	202.930 kg 404.435 lt. 67622 u.	1915.510 kg 909.903 lt. 606130 u.	2464.709 kg 18246.710 lt. 63000 u.	27898.640 kg 5.200 lt. 10865650 u.

1) Codeine 2) Methadone 3) Phensedyl 4) Methadone and dihydrocodeine 5) Polish heroin (also called "compot") 6) Due to unavailability of 2001 data, year 2000 data were used for analysis purposes. 7) 2.933 kg,7208 u. methadone 8) 15 u. liquid heroin, 92 u. methadone 9) Small quantity. 10) Provisional figures. 11) Fiscal year

Source: Annual Report Questionnaire if not otherwise indicated

2.2.2. Opiates: Wholesale and street prices

WHOLESALE AND STREET PRICES OF
OPIUM

Retail and wholesale prices and purity levels:
breakdown by drug, region and country or territory
(prices expressed in US$ or converted equivalent, and purity levels in percentage)

Region / country or territory	RETAIL PRICE (per gram)				WHOLESALE PRICE (per kilogram)			
	Range	Average	Purity	Year	Range	Average	Purity	Year
Africa								
North Africa								
Egypt		1.6	-	2001		760.0	-	2001
East Africa								
Uganda	17.0 - 30.0	23.5	-	1996				
Southern Africa								
Zambia		10.7	-	1999				
Americas								
Central America								
Guatemala						1,888.7	-	1996
North America								
Canada	19.6 - 97.9	58.8	-	2001	14,400.0 - 22,900.0	18,600.0	-	2001
United States	30.0 - 80.0	55.0	-	2001	20,000.0 - 30,000.0	25,000.0	-	2001
South America								
Colombia		0.3	-	2001	260.0 - 304.0	282.0	-	2001
Peru					3,000.0 - 4,000.0	3,500.0	80.0	2001
Asia								
Central Asia and Transcaucasia								
Armenia		10.0	-	2000		1,000.0	-	1999
Azerbaijan	5.0 - 7.0	6.0	-	2001	3,000.0 - 5,000.0	4,000.0	-	2001
Kyrgyzstan	0.6 - 0.8	0.7	14.0 - 22.0	2001	450.0 - 600.0	525.0	14.0 - 22.0	2001
Tajikistan	0.2 - 1.0	0.6	-	2001	120.0 - 500.0	310.0	-	2001
Turkmenistan	0.7 - 2.7	1.7	-	2001	700.0 - 2,700.0	1,700.0	-	2001
Uzbekistan	1.0 - 2.5	1.8	-	2001	600.0 - 1,500.0	1,050.0	-	1999
East and South-East Asia								
Malaysia						513.3	-	1998
Myanmar	0.3 - 0.6	0.5	-	2001		241.3	-	1999
Republic of Korea		90.8	-	2001		78,980.0	-	2001
Singapore						4,490.0	-	2001
Viet Nam					400.0 - 1,506.7	953.3	-	2001
Near and Middle East /South-West Asia								
Afghanistan					27.0 - 72.0	49.5	-	1999
Bahrain		2.3	-	1996				
Iran (Islamic Republic of)	2.4 - 2.9	2.7	-	2000		1,090.0	-	2001
Jordan	84.7 - 113.0	98.9	-	2001	9,900.0 - 12,700.0	11,300.0	-	2001
Lebanon					15,000.0 - 20,000.0	17,500.0	-	2001
Pakistan	0.1 - 0.2	0.1	80.0 - 100.0	1999	470.0 - 750.0	610.0	-	2001
Saudi Arabia					114,700.0 - 152,000.0	133,300.0	5.0 - 50.0	2001
South Asia								
India	0.3 - 0.4	0.3	-	1999	110.0 - 540.0	320.0	-	2001

WHOLESALE AND STREET PRICES OF
OPIUM

Retail and wholesale prices and purity levels:
breakdown by drug, region and country or territory
(prices expressed in US$ or converted equivalent, and purity levels in percentage)

Region / country or territory	RETAIL PRICE (per gram)				WHOLESALE PRICE (per kilogram)			
	Range	Average	Purity	Year	Range	Average	Purity	Year
Europe								
Eastern Europe								
Estonia		45.6	-	2001				
Republic of Moldova		0.8	80.0	2001		800.0	90.0	2001
Romania	2.0 - 4.0	3.0	-	2001	2,000.0 - 4,000.0	3,000.0	-	2001
Russian Federation		40.0	-	1999	2,700.0 - 4,000.0	3,350.0	-	2001
Ukraine	5.0 - 7.0	6.0	-	2001	2,000.0 - 3,000.0	2,500.0	-	2001
Western Europe								
Cyprus		43.0	-	1996		12,903.0	-	1996
France		13.5	-	2001				
Greece		7.3	70.0 - 80.0	1997		5,474.0	80.0 - 90.0	1997
Norway		26.9	-	2001	8,100.0 - 11,700.0	9,900.0	-	2001
Sweden	24.8 - 49.6	37.2	-	2001	5,000.0 - 5,900.0	5,500.0	-	2001
Turkey	17.5 - 19.7	18.6		1999	400.0 - 600.0	500.0	-	2001
United Kingdom	11.5 - 14.4	13.0	-	2001				

HEROIN WHOLESALE AND RETAIL PRICES PER GRAM IN WESTERN EUROPE (*), 1987 - 2001

	1987	1988	1989	1990	1991	1992	1993	1994	1995	1996	1997	1998	1999	2000	2001
Wholesale	135	136	121	128	92	101	70	74	67	60	44	40	40	31	30
Retail	311.0	280.2	228.9	238.6	196.9	187.9	132.8	143.4	140.4	134.7	104.5	104.0	93.6	66.5	60.7

(*) Weighted average (by population) of: Austria, Belgium, Denmark, Finland, France, Germany, Greece, Iceland, Ireland, Italy, Luxembourg, Netherland, Norway, Portugal, Spain, Sweden, Switzerland, United Kingdom.

Source: UNODC, Annual Reports Questionnaire data.

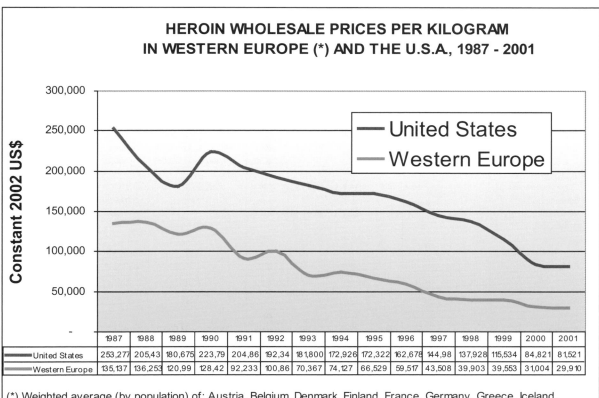

HEROIN WHOLESALE PRICES PER KILOGRAM IN WESTERN EUROPE (*) AND THE U.S.A., 1987 - 2001

	1987	1988	1989	1990	1991	1992	1993	1994	1995	1996	1997	1998	1999	2000	2001
United States	253,277	205,43	180,675	223,79	204,86	192,34	181,800	172,926	172,322	162,678	144,98	137,928	115,534	84,821	81,521
Western Europe	135,137	136,253	120,99	128,42	92,233	100,86	70,367	74,127	66,529	59,517	43,508	39,903	39,553	31,004	29,910

(*) Weighted average (by population) of: Austria, Belgium, Denmark, Finland, France, Germany, Greece, Iceland, Ireland, Italy, Luxembourg, Netherland, Norway, Portugal, Spain, Sweden, Switzerland, United Kingdom.

Source: UNODC, Annual Reports Questionnaire data.

WHOLESALE AND STREET PRICES OF
HEROIN

Retail and wholesale prices and purity levels:
breakdown by drug, region and country or territory
(prices expressed in US$ or converted equivalent, and purity levels in percentage)

Region / country or territory	RETAIL PRICE (per gram)				WHOLESALE PRICE (per kilogram)			
	Range	Average	Purity	Year	Range	Average	Purity	Year
Africa								
East Africa								
Kenya	10.0 - 13.0	11.5	-	1999		13,000.0	-	1999
Mauritius	358.7 - 717.4	538.05	-	2001	161,414.3 - 197,284.1	179,349.2	40.0 - 60.0	2001
Uganda (Heroin no.3)	8.0 - 10.0	9.0	15.0 - 25.0	2001	10,000.0 - 20,000.0	15,000.0	25.0 - 40.0	2001
(Heroin no.4)	10.0 - 20.0	15.0	40.0 - 60.0	2001	20,000.0 - 40,000.0	30,000.0	60.0 - 95.0	2001
United Republic of Tanzania		25.0	-	1999		18,800.0	-	1999
North Africa								
Algeria						189,193.9	-	1999
Egypt	31.3 - 47.0	39.2	-	2001	26,119.4 - 39,179.1	32,649.2	-	2001
Southern Africa								
Namibia (Heroin no.4)	44.4 - 50.8	47.6	-	2001	4,441.6 - 5,076.1	4,758.9	-	2001
South Africa		30.5	-	2001		20,300.0		2001
Swaziland		75.0	-	1998		50,000.0	-	1998
Zimbabwe	272.7 - 363.6	318.2	-	2001	270.0 - 360.0	320.0	-	2001
West and Central Africa								
Benin		20.2	-	1998		18,500.0	-	1998
Côte d'Ivoire (Heroin no.3)					136.0 - 13,603.4	6,869.7	-	2001
(Heroin no.4)	4.8 - 476.1	240.4	10.0	2001	136.0 - 13,603.4	6,869.7	10.0	2001
Ghana	23.5 - 31.4	27.4	60.0 - 90.0	1999		36,000.0	90	1997
Nigeria (Heroin no.3)		0.9	20.0 - 30.0	2001		100.0	70.0 - 100.0	2001
(Heroin no.4)		1.8	20.0 - 30.0	2001		100.0	70.0 - 100.0	2001
Americas								
Central America								
Costa Rica					65,137.9 - 111,665.0	88,401.5	60.0	2001
El Salvador	69.9 - 80.0	75.0	60.0 - 100.0	2001		70,000.0	60.0 - 100.0	2001
Guatemala	51.6 - 77.4	64.5	70.0 - 90.0	2001	25,797.9 - 38,696.8	32,247.4	80.0 - 100.0	2001
Panama (Heroin no.3)	10.0 - 15.0	12.5	80.0 - 90.0	2001	10,000.0 - 15,000.0	12,500.0	80.0 - 90.0	2001
(Heroin no.4)	10.0 - 15.0	12.5	80.0 - 90.0	2001	10,000.0 - 15,000.0	12,500.0	80.0 - 90.0	2001
North America								
Canada	104.5 - 391.8	248.1	40.0 - 90.0	2001	52,238.8 - 91,417.9	71,828.4	50.0 - 90.0	2001
Mexico						32,850.0	-	2001
United States	35.0 - 100.0	67.5	11.0 - 25.0	2001	18,000.0 - 40,000.0	29,000.0	36.0	2001
(Heroin no.4)	60.0 - 200.0	130.0	24.0 - 71.0	2001	60,000.0 - 120,000.0	90,000.0	72.0 - 79.0	2001
(black tar heroin)	80.0 - 600.0	211.5		2000	24,000.0 - 175,000.0	70,500.0		2000
South America								
Colombia (Heroin no.4)	10.4 - 18.3	14.3	80.0 - 93.0	2001	8,262.0 - 9,566.0	8,914.0	-	2001
Ecuador						5,000.0	96.0	1999
Venezuela		21.2	20.0 - 40.0	2001		19,989.6	-	1999
Caribbean								
Bermuda		220.0	-	1997				
Dominican Republic		30.0	-	2001		30,000.0	-	2001
Saint Lucia		30.0	-	2000		25,000.0	-	2000
Asia								
Central Asia and Transcaucasia								
Armenia	120.0 - 150.0	135.0	-	2000				
Azerbaijan	50.0 - 100.0	75.0	-	1999	35,000.0 - 37,000.0	36,000.0	-	2001

WHOLESALE AND STREET PRICES OF

HEROIN

Retail and wholesale prices and purity levels:
breakdown by drug, region and country or territory
(prices expressed in US$ or converted equivalent, and purity levels in percentage)

Region / country or territory	RETAIL PRICE (per gram)				WHOLESALE PRICE (per kilogram)			
	Range	Average	Purity	Year	Range	Average	Purity	Year
Kazakhstan					12,000.0 - 15,000.0	13,500.0	-	2001
Kyrgyzstan	4.0 - 6.0	5.0	4.0 - 6.0	2001	3,200.0 - 4,500.0	3,850.0	4.0 - 6.0	2001
Tajikistan	5.0 - 9.0	7.0	-	2001	1,000.0 - 5,000.0	3,000.0	-	2001
Turkmenistan	9.0 - 17.6	13.3	-	2001	9,000.0 - 18,000.0	13,500.0	-	2001
Uzbekistan	10.0 - 20.0	15.0	-	1999	2,000.0 - 10,000.0	5,666.7	-	2000
East and South-East Asia								
Brunei Darussalam (Heroin no.4)		112.0	-	2001		239,521.0	-	1998
China		121.0	-	2001	9,678.2 - 30,244.4	19,961.3	-	2001
Hong Kong SAR, China (Heroin no.4)	39.3 - 54.8	47.1	-	2001	20,568.6 - 25,229.3	22,898.9	33.8 - 58.0	2001
Indonesia	45.5	45.5	-	1999		42,223.7	-	1999
Japan	388.9 - 583.3	486.1	-	2001				
Macau SAR, China (Heroin no.3)	37.0 - 62.0	49.5	-	2001				
(Heroin no.4)	37.0 - 62.0	49.5	-	2001				
Malaysia	81.3 - 609.8	355.7	32.5	1997		1,340.0	-	1998
Myanmar (Heroin no.4)	7.8 - 12.5	10.1	-	2001		3,619.9	-	1999
Philippines	90.1 - 128.7	109.4	90	1999				
Republic of Korea	94.8 - 189.6	142.2	-	2001		27,640.0	-	2001
Singapore (Heroin no.3)	56.2 - 70.2	63.2	1.0 - 4.4	2001	2,528.1 - 3,370.8	2,949.4	-	2001
Thailand	14.7 - 79.4	47.0	-	2001	7,292.2 - 9,722.9	8,507.5	70.0 - 90.0	1998
Vietnam	24.3 - 25.7	25.0	-	2001	16,800.0 - 24,000.0	20,400.0	-	2001
Near and Middle East/ South- West Asia								
Afghanistan		2.8	-	1996		2,727.0	-	1996
Iran (Islamic Republic of)	0.8 - 1.5	1.1	4.0 - 20.0	2001	2,875.0 - 3,750.0	3,312.5	5.0 - 70.0	2001
Israel	24.3 - 72.8	48.6	-	2001	14,568.2 - 29,136.3	21,852.2	-	2001
Jordan	42.4 - 56.5	49.4	-	2001	18,361.6 - 21,186.4	19,774.0	-	2001
Kuwait						98,684.2	-	1998
Lebanon (Heroin no.3)	30.0 - 40.0	35.0	40.0 - 60.0	2001	15,000.0 - 25,000.0	20,000.0	30.0 - 50.0	2001
(Heroin no.4)	35.0 - 45.0	40.0	-	2001	35,000.0 - 45,000.0	40,000.0	70.0 - 80.0	2001
Oman	52.1 - 78.1	65.1	-	2001	117,187.5 - 130,208.3	123,697.9	-	2001
Pakistan					108.4 - 2,251.8	1,180.1	-	2001
(Heroin no.3)	1.0 - 1.3	1.2	-	2001	934.1 - 1,084.2	1,009.2	-	2001
(Heroin no.4)	1.5 - 2.0	1.1	-	2001	3,919.8 - 4,670.4	4,295.1	-	2001
Qatar	137.0 - 164.1	150.6	-	1996	54,945.0 - 82,420.0	68,682.5	-	1996
Saudi Arabia	213.3 - 266.7	240.0	-	2001		266,666.0	25	1998
Syrian Arab Republic		43.5	-	1999		32,608.7	-	1999
South Asia								
India	2.7 - 7.3	5.0	-	2000	2,155.8 - 8,623.1	5,389.5	-	2001
Maldives						85,324.2	-	1999
Nepal	14.3 - 26.9	20.6	-	1996	15,000.0 - 25,000.0	20,000.0	-	1998
Sri Lanka	12.2 - 29.1	20.7	-	2001	11,452.1 - 14,315.2	12,883.6	-	1999
Europe								
Eastern Europe								
Belarus	30.0 - 40.0	35.0	30.0 - 60.0	2000	20,000.0 - 25,000.0	22,500.0		2000
Bulgaria		9.2	12.0 - 18.0	2001	5,521.6 - 6,902.0	6,211.8	55.0 - 72.0	2001
Croatia	41.5 - 53.3	47.4	10.0 - 15.0	2001	15,992.6 - 17,769.5	16,881.0	50.0 - 80.0	2001
Czech Republic (Heroin no.4)	20.7 - 25.9	23.3	10.0 - 40.0	2001	15,510.8 - 20,681.0	18,095.9	45.0 - 75.0	2001
Estonia (Heroin no.4)	45.6 - 85.5	65.6	-	2001	4,562.4 - 8,554.5	6,558.5	3.0 - 100.0	2001
Hungary	20.4 - 30.7	25.6	4.0 - 60.0	2001	8,520.0 - 11,928.0	10,223.9	7.0 - 75.0	2001
Latvia (Heroin no.4)	32.1 - 80.3	56.2	-	2001	3,214.0 - 8,034.9	5,624.4	-	2001
Lithuania	35.0 - 45.0	40.0	-	2001	20,000.0 - 35,000.0	27,500.0	40.0 - 89.0	2001

WHOLESALE AND STREET PRICES OF
HEROIN
Retail and wholesale prices and purity levels:
breakdown by drug, region and country or territory
(prices expressed in US$ or converted equivalent, and purity levels in percentage)

Region / country or territory	RETAIL PRICE (per gram)				WHOLESALE PRICE (per kilogram)			
	Range	Average	Purity	Year	Range	Average	Purity	Year
Poland (Heroin no.3)	50.4 - 75.6	63.0	-	2001	25,207.1 - 30,248.5	27,727.8	-	2001
(Heroin no.4)					25,207.1 - 30,248.5	27,727.8	-	2001
Republic of Moldova		30.0	-	2001				
(Heroin no.3)						30,000.0	80.0	2001
Romania		14.0	-	2001		8,000.0	15.0 - 50.0	2001
Russian Federation	25.0 - 30.0	27.5	6.0 - 12.0	2001	20,000.0 - 25,000.0	22,500.0	-	2001
Serbia and Montenegro	17.9 - 44.8	24.7	5.0 - 15.0	2001	16,143.5 - 30,493.3	23,318.4	5.0 - 15.0	2001
Slovakia	17.4 - 26.1	21.8	12.0 - 50.0	2000	8,320.1 - 12,480.1	10,400.1	1.0 - 10.0	2001
Slovenia		39.5	-	2001		12,560.0	-	2001
The form.Yug.Rep of Macedonia	28.3 - 39.6	33.9	-	1998	10,175.2 - 12,436.2	11,305.8	-	1998
Ukraine	60.0 - 100.0	80.0	3.0 - 75.0	2001	32,000.0 - 152,000.0	92,000.0	3.0 - 75.0	2001
Western Europe								
Andorra		128.5	-	1999				
Austria (Heroin no.3)	38.6 - 52.0	45.3	1.0 - 55.0	2001	13,035.0 - 26,070.9	19,552.9	20.0 - 51.0	2001
(Heroin no.4)					33,640.0 - 47,095.0	40,370.0	40.0	2000
Belgium (Heroin no.3)	19.0 - 35.7	27.3	-	2001	16,726.5 - 23,856.5	20,291.5	-	2001
Cyprus	92.9 - 154.9	123.9	-	2001	30,973.4 - 38,716.8	34,845.1	-	2001
Denmark (Heroin no.3)	35.9 - 119.6	77.7	-	2001	17,939.5 - 47,838.7	32,889.1	-	2001
(Heroin no.4)	95.7 - 191.4	143.5	-	2001	59,798.4 - 95,677.4	77,737.9	-	2001
Finland (Heroin no.4)	89.7 - 152.5	121.1	20.0	2001		44,840.0	-	2001
France (Heroin no.3)	26.9 - 40.4	33.6	-	2001	13,452.9 - 40,358.7	26,905.8	-	2001
Germany	21.4 - 54.7	38.1	-	2001	11,865.8 - 23,766.3	17,816.1	-	2001
Gibraltar		72.0	-	2001		117,000.0	20.0	1997
Greece (Heroin no.3)	39.5 - 67.3	53.4	8.0 - 35.0	2001	10,762.3 - 18,834.1	14,798.2	-	2001
(Heroin no.4)	39.5 - 67.3	53.4	8.0 - 35.0	2001	13,452.9 - 23,318.4	18,385.7	65.0 - 81.0	2001
Iceland		372.0	-	1998				
Ireland (Heroin no.3)	161.4 - 179.4	170.4	25.0 - 35.0	2001		43,478.3	60.0 - 70.0	1999
Italy (Heroin no. 3)	54.7 - 68.3	61.5	-	2001	25,243.9 - 29,644.2	27,444.0	35.0	2001
(Heroin no. 4)	70.4 - 80.1	75.3	-	2001	36,360.4 - 40,668.1	38,514.3	-	2001
Liechtenstein	34.7 - 62.4	48.5	-	1997		27,760.0	-	1997
Luxembourg	108.0 - 170.5	138.5	-	1998	47,717.5 - 53,019.5	50,368.5	-	1999
Malta (Heroin no.3)		70.0	20.0	2001		45,200.0	60.0	2001
Monaco		86.5	65.0	1997		87,100.0	65.0	1997
Netherlands	24.3 - 60.7	42.5	-	1999	12,376.2 - 17,708.3	15,757.4	-	1998
Norway	89.7 - 224.2	157.0	10.0 - 80.0	2001	26,905.8 - 44,843.1	35,874.4	10.0 - 80.0	2001
Portugal (Heroin no.3)		45.1	10.3 - 63.7	2001		31,310.0	-	2001
Spain		56.7	34.0	2001		32,000.0	71.0	2001
Sweden (Heroin no.3)	99.1 - 148.7	123.9	-	2001	19,824.4 - 29,736.6	24,780.5	-	2001
(Heroin no.4)	99.1 - 198.2	148.7	-	2001	59,473.2 - 79,297.7	69,385.4	-	2001
Switzerland	17.5 - 128.7	73.1	3.0 - 52.0	2001	11,695.9 - 20,467.8	16,081.9	11.0 - 65.0	2001
Turkey	15.0 - 20.0	17.5	-	2001	4,500.0 - 7,000.0	5,750.0	-	2001
United Kingdom	57.6 - 115.2	86.4	43.0 - 51.8	2001	23,045.3 - 28,806.6	25,925.9	38.2 - 53.8	2001
Oceania								
Australia	63.9 - 319.7	191.8	-	1999	84,030.0 - 127,880.0	105,955.0	-	1999
New Zealand	296.0 - 422.8	359.4	-	2001				

2.2.3. Cocaine: Seizures 1996-2001

	SEIZURES 1996 - 2001					
	Cocaine (base and salts)					
Region/country or territory	1996	1997	1998	1999	2000	2001
AFRICA						
East Africa						
Burundi	3.819 kg [Govt.]	No Report	No Report	No Report	No Report	No Report
Kenya	3.440 kg	0.410 kg	1.240 kg	0.110 kg	4.017 kg	0.207 kg [Govt]
Uganda	4.000 kg	No Report	No Report	0.412 kg	1.910 kg	No Report
United Republic of Tanzania	No Report	0.200 kg	No Report	1.161 kg	2.103 kg [ICPO]	7.389 kg [Govt]
Sub-Total	11.259 kg	0.610 kg	1.240 kg	1.683 kg	8.030 kg	7.596 kg
North Africa						
Algeria	No Report	No Report	No Report	No Report	No Report	0.288 kg [ICPO]
Egypt	0.934 kg	0.914 kg	1.860 kg	0.792 kg	14.288 kg	No Report
Libyan Arab Jam.	No Report	No Report	0.136 kg	No Report	No Report	No Report
Morocco	91.195 kg	6055.550 kg	30.111 kg	1.742 kg	0.898 kg	4.298 kg 103 u.
Sudan	No Report	No Report	No Report	No Report	0.001 kg 2 u.	No Report
Tunisia	0.001 kg [ICPO]	0.047 kg [ICPO]	0.127 kg	0.017 kg [ICPO]	No Report	No Report
Sub-Total	92.130 kg	6056.511 kg	32.234 kg	2.551 kg	15.187 kg 2 u.	4.586 kg 103 u.
Southern Africa						
Angola	64.360 kg [Govt.]	536.000 kg [ICPO]	38.007 kg [ICPO]	15.901 kg	173.724 kg [ICPO]	20.745 kg [ICPO]
Botswana	3.000 kg [ICPO]	0.982 kg [ICPO]	0.700 kg [ICPO]	1.696 kg [ICPO]	No Report	No Report
Lesotho	No Report	2.346 kg [ICPO]	No Report	0.632 kg [ICPO]	No Report	No Report
Malawi	No Report	No Report	1.500 kg	1.200 kg	No Report	0.250 kg
Mozambique	No Report	No Report	2.134 kg [ICPO]	0.385 kg [ICPO]	0.100 kg [ICPO]	0.012 kg [ICPO]
Namibia	5.953 kg	23.932 kg [INCB]	2.110 kg	No Report	0.093 kg	3.036 kg 100 u.
South Africa	106.629 kg	151.519 kg	635.908 kg 3825 u.	345.549 kg [ICPO] 12940 u.	91.202 kg	155.305 kg 3470 u.
Swaziland	6.745 kg [ICPO]	9.650 kg [ICPO]	No Report	3.609 kg	6.832 kg	1.006 kg
Zambia	4.443 kg [Govt]	6.498 kg [Govt]	0.000 kg [Govt]	1.116 kg	0.005 kg 27 u.	Govt (1
Zimbabwe	0.597 kg [ICPO]	No Report	0.501 kg	0.166 kg	0.593 kg	No Report
Sub-Total	191.727 kg	730.927 kg	680.860 kg 3825 u.	370.254 kg 12940 u.	272.549 kg 27 u.	180.354 kg 3570 u.
West and Central Africa						
Benin	3.189 kg [Govt]	0.015 kg [Govt]	0.628 kg	No Report	21.494 kg [F.O]	31.741 kg [ICPO]
Burkina Faso	0.260 kg [F.O.]	278.000 kg [Govt.]	No Report	No Report	No Report	No Report
Cameroon	No Report	No Report	3.780 kg	No Report	No Report	No Report
Chad	No Report	No Report	No Report	0.015 kg [ICPO]	0.028 kg	No Report
Congo	No Report	No Report	No Report	No Report	40.010 kg	0.020 kg

Source: Annual Report Questionnaire if not otherwise indicated

SEIZURES 1996 - 2001
Cocaine (base and salts)

Region/country or territory	1996	1997	1998	1999	2000	2001
AFRICA						
West and Central Africa						
Côte d'Ivoire	33.147 kg	22.028 kg	19.015 kg	9.287 kg 16 u.	3.442 kg [ICPO]	1.048 kg
Democratic Republic of the Congo	1.101 kg [Govt.]	No Report	No Report	No Report	No Report	No Report
Gabon	0.022 kg [ICPO]	No Report	No Report	0.216 kg [ICPO]	No Report	No Report
Gambia	0.880 kg [ICPO]	0.057 kg [ICPO]	0.074 kg [ICPO]	0.060 kg	No Report	7.000 kg
Ghana	0.785 kg	6.350 kg [F.O.]	5.035 kg	7.062 kg	No Report	No Report
Mali	4.300 kg [Govt.]	No Report	No Report	No Report	No Report	No Report
Mauritania	0.334 kg [Govt.]	No Report	No Report	No Report	No Report	No Report
Niger	0.020 kg [ICPO]	28.866 kg [ICPO]	0.233 kg [ICPO]	No Report	No Report	No Report
Nigeria	6.160 kg [ICPO]	31.900 kg [CICAD]	9.260 kg [Govt.]	15.064 kg	53.950 kg	195.823 kg
Sao Tome and Principe	No Report	0.100 kg	No Report	0.100 kg	No Report	No Report
Senegal	8.110 kg [F.O.]	No Report	5.321 kg [ICPO]	31.564 kg [ICPO] 110 u.	0.207 kg [ICPO]	No Report
Sierra Leone	0.002 kg	No Report	No Report	No Report	No Report	No Report
Togo	1.081 kg	13.873 kg [Govt.]	No Report	No Report	6.213 kg	29.927 kg
Sub-Total	59.391 kg	381.189 kg	43.346 kg	63.368 kg 126 u.	125.344 kg	265.559 kg
Total region	354.507 kg	7169.237 kg	757.680 kg 3825 u.	437.856 kg 13066 u.	421.110 kg 29 u.	458.095 kg 3673 u.
AMERICAS						
Caribbean						
Anguilla	289.000 kg [F.O]	0.003 kg 8 u.	0.108 kg	0.020 kg [F.O]	No Report	926.000 kg [F.O]
Antigua and Barbuda	6.000 kg [F.O]	126.000 kg [F.O]	1.000 kg [F.O]	26.000 kg [F.O]	24.000 kg [F.O]	767.000 kg [F.O]
Aruba	203.000 kg [NAPOL]	408.307 kg [INCB]	794.000 kg [NAPOL]	465.000 kg [F.O]	346.000 kg [F.O]	266.000 kg [F.O]
Bahamas	115.000 kg [NAPOL]	2579.040 kg [ICPO]	3343.054 kg	1857.000 kg [F.O]	2759.510 kg	1469.000 kg 3238 u.
Barbados	37.000 kg [INCB]	88.050 kg [INCB]	35.000 kg [NAPOL]	132.760 kg [HONLC]	81.000 kg [F.O]	83.000 kg [F.O]
Bermuda	24.662 kg	4.516 kg	4.330 kg	8.076 kg	11.574 kg	667.000 kg [F.O]
British Virgin Islands	1765.000 kg [NAPOL]	838.000 kg [NAPOL]	20.000 kg [NAPOL]	432.000 kg [F.O]	534.000 kg [F.O]	2159.040 kg 34 u.
Cayman Islands	2219.090 kg	1054.000 kg 319 u.	1195.142 kg 1824 u.	1926.129 kg	1813.000 kg [F.O]	1006.817 kg 40874 u.
Cuba	7923.373 kg	1444.000 kg [F.O]	669.000 kg [NAPOL]	2444.000 kg [F.O]	3145.000 kg [F.O]	1278.000 kg [F.O]

Source: Annual Report Questionnaire if not otherwise indicated

SEIZURES 1996 - 2001
Cocaine (base and salts)

Region/country or territory	1996	1997	1998	1999	2000	2001
AMERICAS						
Caribbean						
Dominica	2.947 kg	101.000 kg [F.O]	29.000 kg [F.O]	82.769 kg [ICPO]	10.000 kg [F.O]	6.000 kg [F.O]
Dominican Republic	1341.300 kg	1234.206 kg	2341.916 kg	1075.953 kg	1310.000 kg [CICAD]	1913.944 kg
French Guiana	9.000 kg [F.O]	213.000 kg [F.O]	3.000 kg [F.O]	446.000 kg [F.O]	25.000 kg [F.O]	No Report
Grenada	9.000 kg [F.O]	6.995 kg [INCB]	26.500 kg	43.000 kg [F.O]	103.000 kg [F.O]	53.389 kg
Guadeloupe	91.000 kg [F.O]	66.000 kg [F.O]	3222.000 kg [F.O]	593.000 kg [F.O]	292.000 kg [F.O]	593.000 kg [F.O]
Haiti	956.000 kg [NAPOL]	2100.000 kg [NAPOL]	1272.000 kg [NAPOL]	436.000 kg	594.000 kg [F.O]	414.000 kg
Jamaica	253.530 kg [ICPO] 2321 u.	414.680 kg [ICPO] 6296 u.	1143.000 kg [F.O]	2455.000 kg [ICPO] 3543 u.	1656.000 kg [F.O]	2950.910 kg 3099 u.
Martinique	17.000 kg [F.O]	37.000 kg [F.O]	46.000 kg [F.O]	36.000 kg [F.O]	15.000 kg [F.O]	No Report
Montserrat	No Report	0.130 kg 1 u.	No Report	No Report	No Report	No Report
Netherlands Antilles	710.000 kg [NAPOL]	1302.000 kg [F.O]	639.000 kg [NAPOL]	18.000 kg [F.O]	965.353 kg [ICPO]	1043.000 kg [F.O]
Puerto Rico	11072.000 kg [F.O]	15153.000 kg [F.O]	10344.000 kg [F.O]	9977.000 kg [F.O]	5516.000 kg [F.O]	2831.000 kg [F.O]
Saint Kitts and Nevis	0.000 kg [F.O]	150.000 kg [F.O]	1.000 kg [F.O]	10.000 kg [F.O]	53.000 kg [INCSR]	20.000 kg [F.O]
Saint Lucia	19.800 kg	7.782 kg	78.137 kg	133.000 kg [CICAD]	110.473 kg	63.000 kg [F.O]
Saint Vincent and the Grenadines	2.000 kg [F.O]	1.000 kg [F.O]	13.000 kg [F.O]	15.000 kg [F.O]	51.000 kg [INCSR]	207.000 kg [F.O]
Trinidad Tobago	179.380 kg [ICPO]	71.000 kg [CICAD]	77.680 kg	137.000 kg [CICAD]	203.000 kg [INCSR]	821.880 kg
Turks and Caicos Islands	400.000 kg	1.500 kg	2075.000 kg	3.000 kg	0.136 kg [ICPO]	4.000 kg [F.O]
US Virgin Islands	No Report	No Report	No Report	432.028 kg [ICPO]	No Report	No Report
Sub-Total	27645.080 kg 2321 u.	27401.210 kg 6624 u.	27372.870 kg 1824 u.	23183.730 kg 3543 u.	19618.050 kg	19542.980 kg 47245 u.
Central America						
Belize	720.000 kg [CICAD]	2691.000 kg [CICAD]	1221.000 kg [NAPOL]	39.515 kg [ICPO]	13.000 kg [F.O]	3854.857 kg
Costa Rica	1872.719 kg 45327 u.	7857.000 kg [ICPO] 52170 u.	7387.140 kg 102844 u.	1998.720 kg 56514 u.	5780.730 kg 64998 u.	1747.960 kg 45283 u.
El Salvador	99.000 kg [CICAD]	234.431 kg [ICPO]	45.256 kg [ICPO]	38.649 kg	434.700 kg [ICPO]	31.544 kg
Guatemala	3950.870 kg	5098.466 kg [Govt.] 17 u.	9217.070 kg	9964.788 kg	1537.360 kg	4107.913 kg
Honduras	3275.000 kg [CICAD]	2187.673 kg 209 u.	1804.000 kg [CICAD] 603 u.	709.000 kg [CICAD] 662 u.	1215.000 kg [CICAD] 1031 u.	No Report
Nicaragua	398.444 kg 3531 u.	2790.200 kg 7109 u.	4750.265 kg 21235 u.	833.000 kg [CICAD]	963.000 kg [CICAD]	2717.971 kg [ICPO]
Panama	8658.732 kg	11324.740 kg	11828.085 kg	3139.889 kg	7413.455 kg	2660.000 kg
Sub-Total	18974.770 kg 48858 u.	32183.510 kg 59505 u.	36252.820 kg 124682 u.	16723.560 kg 57176 u.	17357.240 kg 66029 u.	15120.250 kg 45283 u.

Source: Annual Report Questionnaire if not otherwise indicated

SEIZURES 1996 - 2001
Cocaine (base and salts)

Region/country or territory	1996	1997	1998	1999	2000	2001
AMERICAS						
North America						
Canada	3123.467 kg	2090.000 kg 312 u.	562.983 kg 0.007 lt.	1650.518 kg 0.407 lt. 19 u.	280.866 kg 5.156 lt. 26 u.	1678.488 kg 167 u.
Mexico	23833.204 kg	34952.714 kg	22597.072 kg	34622.602 kg	23195.942 kg [2]	29988.684 kg
United States	128725.102 [Govt.] kg	102000.000 [Govt.] kg	117000.000 [Govt.] kg	132318.000 kg	99700.000 kg 1514.386 lt. 5326 u.	106212.500 kg
Sub-Total	155681.800 kg	139042.700 kg 312 u.	140160.100 kg 0.007 lt.	168591.100 kg 0.407 lt. 19 u.	123176.800 kg 1519.542 lt. 5352 u.	137879.700 kg 167 u.
South America						
Argentina	2451.250 kg [Govt.]	5192.570 kg	1766.900 kg	1660.776 kg	2351.359 kg	2286.858 kg
Bolivia	11938.000 kg [F.O]	12325.000 kg [F.O]	11346.000 kg [F.O]	7712.000 kg [F.O]	5599.000 kg [F.O]	4615.000 kg [F.O]
Brazil	4070.504 kg	4309.378 kg	6560.414 kg	7646.103 kg	5555.925 kg	9137.265 kg [Govt]
Chile	2962.098 kg	2660.720 kg	2952.471 kg	2930.000 kg [CICAD]	2076.100 kg	2428.090 kg
Colombia	45779.000 kg [Govt.]	42044.000 kg	107480.000 kg	63945.000 kg [3] 36411.949 lt.	110428.000 kg	73863.500 kg
Ecuador	9533.970 kg	3697.160 kg	3854.229 kg	10161.831 kg	3308.420 kg [ICPO]	12242.329 kg
Guyana	91.503 kg	167.000 kg [F.O]	3222.000 kg [NAPOL]	40.163 kg [ICPO]	167.000 kg [CICAD]	73.000 kg [ICPO]
Paraguay	47.490 kg	77.083 kg	222.352 kg	95.058 kg	96.000 kg [CICAD]	No Report
Peru	19694.666 kg	8795.617 kg	9936.968 kg	11307.116 kg	11847.611 kg	9189.362 kg
Suriname	1412.690 kg	116.099 kg	283.444 kg	185.000 kg [CICAD]	207.000 kg [INCSR]	2253.000 kg
Uruguay	84.793 kg	27.968 kg [Govt.]	23.604 kg	18.698 kg	20.642 kg	24.758 kg [ICPO]
Venezuela	5906.451 kg	16741.000 kg [CICAD]	8159.000 kg [CICAD]	12418.839 kg	15063.194 kg	13950.940 kg
Sub-Total	103972.400 kg	96153.600 kg	155807.400 kg	118120.600 kg 36411.950 lt.	156720.300 kg	130064.100 kg
Total region	306274.000 kg 51179 u.	294781.000 kg 66441 u.	359593.100 kg 0.007 lt. 126506 u.	326619.000 kg 36412.360 lt. 60738 u.	316872.300 kg 1519.542 lt. 71381 u.	302607.000 kg 92695 u.
ASIA						
Central Asia and Transcaucasian countries						
Armenia	0.004 kg	No Report	No Report	No Report	No Report	No Report
Azerbaijan	No Report	No Report	No Report	0.005 kg	No Report	No Report
Georgia	0.002 kg [ICPO]	No Report	No Report	0.002 kg [ICPO]	No Report	No Report
Kazakhstan	No Report	No Report	20.000 kg	0.035 kg	No Report	0.054 kg [F.O]
Turkmenistan	No Report	No Report	1.000 kg [Govt.]	No Report	No Report	No Report

Source: Annual Report Questionnaire if not otherwise indicated

SEIZURES 1996 - 2001

Cocaine (base and salts)

Region/country or territory	1996	1997	1998	1999	2000	2001
ASIA						
Central Asia and Transcaucasian countries						
Sub-Total	0.006 kg		21.000 kg	0.042 kg		0.054 kg
East and South-East Asia						
Hong Kong SAR, China	13.900 kg	31.300 kg	167.700 kg [Govt.]	11.990 kg	9.004 kg	29.700 kg
Indonesia	0.388 kg	3.301 kg	4.748 kg	0.500 kg	17.415 kg	30.793 kg
Japan	37.110 kg	25.455 kg	20.846 kg	10.349 kg	15.580 kg	23.716 kg
Korea (Republic of)	0.766 kg	11.218 kg	2.080 kg	2.251 kg	No Report	0.111 kg
Macau SAR, China	No Report	No Report	No Report	No Report	0.008 kg	No Report
Malaysia	No Report	No Report	No Report	No Report	No Report	0.017 kg [ICPO]
Mongolia	No Report	No Report	No Report	2.800 kg [ICPO]	No Report	0.400 kg
Philippines	1.593 kg	1.000 kg [ICPO]	1.080 kg [ICPO]	0.227 kg	0.588 kg	No Report
Singapore	No Report	No Report	1.050 kg	No Report	No Report	No Report
Thailand	2.264 kg [HNLP]	2.426 kg	3.555 kg	0.619 kg [ICPO]	4.003 kg [ICPO]	4.625 kg [HNLP]
Sub-Total	56.021 kg	74.700 kg	201.059 kg	28.736 kg	46.598 kg	89.362 kg
Near and Middle East /South-West Asia						
Bahrain	No Report	No Report	No Report	No Report	0.010 kg [ICPO]	No Report
Iran (Islamic Republic of)	No Report	1.700 kg	No Report	No Report	No Report	No Report
Israel	73.339 kg	43.700 kg	99.800 kg	28.229 kg [ICPO]	11.659 kg	23.617 kg
Jordan	1.100 kg	No Report	0.940 kg	1.912 kg	0.803 kg	0.505 kg
Kuwait	0.016 kg [ICPO]	0.010 kg [ICPO]	0.003 kg	No Report	36.000 kg [ICPO]	No Report
Lebanon	166.690 kg	4.804 kg	11.898 kg	32.013 kg	0.466 kg	7.207 kg
Pakistan	No Report	No Report	0.100 kg	1.100 kg	No Report	No Report
Saudi Arabia	11.809 kg [ICPO]	0.347 kg [ICPO]	2.202 kg	4.908 kg [ICPO]	0.708 kg 3 u.	0.046 kg
Syrian Arab Republic	1.673 kg [Govt]	0.240 kg [Govt]	0.235 kg [Govt]	32.102 kg [Govt]	7.177 kg [Govt]	1031.880 kg [Govt]
United Arab Emirates	0.040 kg	No Report	0.146 kg	0.840 kg	0.537 kg	0.007 kg
Sub-Total	294.635 kg	50.801 kg	115.324 kg	101.104 kg	57.360 kg 3 u.	1063.262 kg
South Asia						
Bangladesh	No Report	No Report	No Report	No Report	0.550 kg	No Report
India	3.000 kg [Govt.]	24.000 kg	1.000 kg	1.000 kg [ICPO]	0.350 kg [F.O]	2.000 kg
Nepal	No Report	24.000 kg [ICPO]	No Report	No Report	No Report	No Report
Sri Lanka	0.050 kg	No Report	No Report	No Report	No Report	0.640 kg
Sub-Total	3.050 kg	48.000 kg	1.000 kg	1.000 kg	0.900 kg	2.640 kg

Source: Annual Report Questionnaire if not otherwise indicated

SEIZURES 1996 - 2001
Cocaine (base and salts)

Region/country or territory	1996	1997	1998	1999	2000	2001
ASIA						
Total region	353.712 kg	173.501 kg	338.383 kg	130.882 kg	104.858 kg 3 u.	1155.318 kg
EUROPE						
Eastern Europe						
Albania	No Report	No Report	No Report	2.159 kg ICPO	4.000 kg Govt	0.266 kg Govt
Belarus	No Report	2.074 kg INCB	No Report	No Report	No Report	142.000 kg ICPO
Bosnia Herzegovina	No Report	No Report	0.014 kg ICPO	No Report	164.392 kg NAPOL	No Report
Bulgaria	21.515 kg	2.011 kg	685.585 kg	17.010 kg	4.333 kg	12.752 kg
Croatia	1.525 kg	563.009 kg	6.426 kg	1.807 kg	913.127 kg	1.487 kg
Czech Republic	23.358 kg	66.828 kg	42.000 kg	140.800 kg	14.712 kg	5.170 kg 9 u.
Estonia	No Report	0.006 kg	2.565 kg 71 u.	0.128 kg 139 u.	0.108 kg 37 u.	0.137 kg
FYR of Macedonia	13.744 kg ICPO	0.011 kg NAPOL	0.040 kg	2.955 kg NAPOL	4.689 kg NAPOL	5.860 kg Govt
Hungary	4.985 kg	6.995 kg Govt.	26.385 kg	121.147 kg	9.200 kg	6.015 kg
Latvia	0.012 kg	0.024 kg 0.895 lt.	0.063 kg	1.915 kg	0.027 kg	1.024 kg
Lithuania	1.056 kg	2.049 kg	10.133 kg	0.275 kg	1.841 kg	0.129 kg
Poland	31.378 kg	15.501 kg	21.157 kg	20.082 kg	5.664 kg	No Report
Republic of Moldova	No Report	No Report	No Report	No Report	No Report	0.001 kg
Romania	712.611 kg	69.556 kg ICPO	1.203 kg	9.670 kg	13.140 kg	2.524 kg
Russian Federation	73.800 kg	70.825 kg	100.340 kg	12.749 kg	65.000 kg F.O	82.502 kg
Serbia and Montenegro	No Report	No Report	No Report	No Report	No Report	3.623 kg
Slovakia	No Report	9.580 kg ICPO	1.642 kg	2.508 kg	0.166 kg	No Report
Slovenia	0.830 kg	3.573 kg	3.522 kg	1.580 kg	0.098 kg	1.080 kg
Ukraine	No Report	625.010 kg	250.586 kg	26.263 kg ICPO	0.520 kg ICPO	0.018 kg
Sub-Total	884.814 kg	1437.052 kg 0.895 lt.	1151.661 kg 71 u.	361.048 kg 139 u.	1201.017 kg 37 u.	264.589 kg 9 u.
Western Europe						
Andorra	No Report	0.108 kg ICPO	0.064 kg ICPO	0.060 kg	0.023 kg ICPO	0.086 kg
Austria	72.794 kg	86.902 kg	99.140 kg	63.377 kg	20.375 kg	108.278 kg
Belgium	838.000 kg	3329.000 kg	2088.312 kg	1761.709 kg	2813.991 kg	2813.991 kg UNODC (4
Cyprus	0.004 kg	0.020 kg	0.018 kg	5.361 kg	57.599 kg	0.123 kg
Denmark	32.000 kg	58.000 kg	44.133 kg	24.200 kg	35.910 kg	25.624 kg
Finland	0.072 kg	0.121 kg	1.987 kg	1.703 kg	38.575 kg	6.500 kg
France	1752.702 kg	860.599 kg	1076.000 kg	3697.372 kg	1333.119 kg	2102.257 kg

Source: Annual Report Questionnaire if not otherwise indicated

SEIZURES 1996 - 2001
Cocaine (base and salts)

Region/country or territory	1996	1997	1998	1999	2000	2001
EUROPE						
Western Europe						
Germany	1378.435 kg	1721.189 kg	1133.243 kg	1979.100 kg	915.600 kg	1290.087 kg
Gibraltar	0.035 kg	0.098 kg	0.007 kg 7 u.	0.026 kg	0.028 kg	0.016 kg
Greece	155.254 kg	16.734 kg	283.971 kg	45.485 kg 8 u.	156.245 kg 2 u.	227.287 kg
Iceland	No Report	No Report	No Report	0.955 kg	0.942 kg	0.257 kg
Ireland	642.000 kg	11.044 kg	334.230 kg	85.553 kg	18.041 kg	5.325 kg
Italy	2147.347 kg	1639.542 kg 887 u.	2143.804 kg 1341 u.	2997.611 kg [ICPO] 14 u.	2359.715 kg 2329 u.	1808.910 kg 612 u.
Liechtenstein	0.010 kg	1.065 kg	0.151 kg	0.003 kg	0.010 kg	0.750 kg
Luxembourg	12.891 kg	8.983 kg	5.995 kg	0.327 kg	10.757 kg [ICPO]	No Report
Malta	0.171 kg	0.301 kg	0.058 kg	1.366 kg	0.028 kg	2.542 kg
Monaco	0.003 kg	0.001 kg	0.012 kg	0.056 kg [ICPO]	0.001 kg [ICPO]	No Report
Netherlands	9222.000 kg [Govt]	11495.000 kg [Govt]	8998.000 kg [Govt]	10361.000 kg [Govt]	6472.000 kg [Govt]	8382.000 kg
Norway	24.140 kg	4.633 kg	93.020 kg	60.477 kg	12.215 kg	20.753 kg
Portugal	811.568 kg	3162.641 kg	624.949 kg	822.560 kg	3075.374 kg	5574.658 kg
Spain	13742.901 kg	18418.760 kg	11687.623 kg	18110.883 kg	6164.770 kg	33681.091 kg
Sweden	28.702 kg	33.920 kg	18.505 kg	413.945 kg 1.944 lt. 430 u.	52.257 kg	47.388 kg
Switzerland	255.677 kg	349.435 kg	251.616 kg	288.013 kg	207.476 kg	168.637 kg
Turkey	13.000 kg	9.637 kg	604.880 kg	13.153 kg	8.444 kg [Govt.]	1.010 kg
United Kingdom	1219.300 kg	2350.200 kg	2985.323 kg [(5]	2972.700 kg [NCIS]	3970.220 kg	3970.220 kg [UNODC (4]
Sub-Total	32349.000 kg	43557.930 kg 887 u.	32475.040 kg 1348 u.	43707.000 kg 1.944 lt. 452 u.	27723.720 kg 2331 u.	60237.790 kg 612 u.
Total region	33233.820 kg	44994.980 kg 0.895 lt. 887 u.	33626.700 kg 1419 u.	44068.040 kg 1.944 lt. 591 u.	28924.730 kg 2368 u.	60502.380 kg 621 u.
OCEANIA						
Oceania						
Australia	1.764 kg 24 u.	81.944 kg	103.162 kg [Govt. (6]	70.725 kg	1437.869 kg	1151.255 kg
Fiji	No Report	No Report	No Report	No Report	0.347 kg [ICPO]	2.000 kg [ICPO]
New Zealand	No Report	0.037 kg [INCB]	0.015 kg	0.454 kg	0.249 kg	0.008 kg
Tonga	No Report	0.001 kg [INCB]	No Report	No Report	No Report	No Report

Source: Annual Report Questionnaire if not otherwise indicated

SEIZURES 1996 - 2001
Cocaine (base and salts)

Region/country or territory	1996	1997	1998	1999	2000	2001
OCEANIA						
Oceania						
Sub-Total	1.764 kg 24 u.	81.982 kg	103.177 kg	71.179 kg	1438.465 kg	1153.263 kg
Total region	1.764 kg 24 u.	81.982 kg	103.177 kg	71.179 kg	1438.465 kg	1153.263 kg
TOTAL	340217.800 kg 51203 u.	347200.700 kg 0.895 lt. 67328 u.	394419.100 kg 0.007 lt. 131750 u.	371326.900 kg 36414.300 lt. 74395 u.	347761.500 kg 1519.542 lt. 73781 u.	365876.000 kg 96989 u.

1) Small quantity. 2) Includes crack. 3) The 36411.949 litres correspond to 4,737 gallons coca base liquid and 4,882 gallons cocaine liquid 4) Due to unavailability of 2001 data, year 2000 data were used for analysis purposes. 5) Included in cannabis seeds. 6) Provisional figures.

Source: Annual Report Questionnaire if not otherwise indicated

SEIZURES 1996 - 2001
Coca leaf

Region/country or territory	1996	1997	1998	1999	2000	2001
AMERICAS						
Central America						
Guatemala	28903 u.	No Report	No Report	No Report	No Report	No Report
Sub-Total	28903 u.					
North America						
Canada	No Report	0.192 kg	No Report	0.316 kg	0.056 kg	0.050 kg
United States	No Report	No Report	No Report	58.436 kg	45.608 kg [1] 2.181 lt.	0.600 kg
Sub-Total		0.192 kg		58.752 kg	45.664 kg 2.181 lt.	0.650 kg
South America						
Argentina	56853.820 kg [Govt.]	49754.102 kg	47847.961 kg	68492.192 kg	95901.272 kg	91352.081 kg
Bolivia	45940.000 kg [F.O]	80090.000 kg [F.O]	110202.000 kg [F.O]	63911.000 kg [F.O]	59704.000 kg [F.O]	8072.056 kg
Brazil	No Report	0.035 kg	No Report	No Report	0.018 kg [ICPO]	No Report
Chile	4.867 kg	No Report	No Report	No Report	No Report	No Report
Colombia	686018.000 kg	117817.000 kg	340564.000 kg	307783.000 kg [2]	897911.000 kg	583.165 kg
Ecuador	No Report	No Report	0.050 kg	5000 u.	No Report	No Report
Peru	99104.242 kg	146824.953 kg	132209.875 kg	34792.500 kg	48609.597 kg	29324.293 kg
Venezuela	No Report	No Report	No Report	No Report	No Report	180.000 kg
Sub-Total	887920.900 kg	394486.100 kg	630823.900 kg	474978.700 kg 5000 u.	1102126.000 kg	129511.600 kg
Total region	887920.900 kg 28903 u.	394486.300 kg	630823.900 kg	475037.400 kg 5000 u.	1102172.000 kg 2.181 lt.	129512.200 kg
ASIA						
Central Asia and Transcaucasian countries						
Armenia	No Report	No Report	0.163 kg	No Report	No Report	No Report
Sub-Total			0.163 kg			
Near and Middle East /South-West Asia						
Bahrain	0.012 kg	No Report	No Report	No Report	No Report	No Report
Sub-Total	0.012 kg					
Total region	0.012 kg		0.163 kg			
EUROPE						
Eastern Europe						
Hungary	No Report	No Report	No Report	No Report	No Report	1.049 kg

Source: Annual Report Questionnaire if not otherwise indicated

SEIZURES 1996 - 2001
Coca leaf

Region/country or territory	1996	1997	1998	1999	2000	2001
EUROPE						
Eastern Europe						
Poland	No Report	No Report	No Report	No Report	No Report	45.298 kg
Sub-Total						46.347 kg
Western Europe						
Denmark	No Report	No Report	No Report	No Report	0.043 kg	0.000 kg
France	0.005 kg	No Report	No Report	11.133 kg	No Report	No Report
Italy	1.660 kg	No Report	0.049 kg	0.109 kg [ICPO]	0.445 kg	0.055 kg
Norway	No Report	No Report	0.001 kg	3.420 kg	No Report	No Report
Portugal	No Report	0.043 kg	0.020 kg	No Report	No Report	No Report
Sweden	1.054 kg	No Report	No Report	No Report	0.268 kg	No Report
Sub-Total	2.719 kg	0.043 kg	0.070 kg	14.662 kg	0.756 kg	0.055 kg
Total region	2.719 kg	0.043 kg	0.070 kg	14.662 kg	0.756 kg	46.402 kg
OCEANIA						
Oceania						
Australia	0.019 kg	0.590 kg	No Report	No Report	No Report	0.019 kg
New Zealand	No Report	No Report	0.019 kg	0.011 kg	No Report	4.253 kg
Sub-Total	0.019 kg	0.590 kg	0.019 kg	0.011 kg		4.272 kg
Total region	0.019 kg	0.590 kg	0.019 kg	0.011 kg		4.272 kg
TOTAL	887923.700 kg 28903 u.	394486.900 kg	630824.100 kg	475052.100 kg 5000 u.	1102172.000 kg 2.181 lt.	129562.900 kg

1) Includes cocaine other 2) Do not include 9702 gallons (36726 litres) of coca leaf in process

Source: Annual Report Questionnaire if not otherwise indicated

2.2.4. Cocaine: Wholesale and street prices

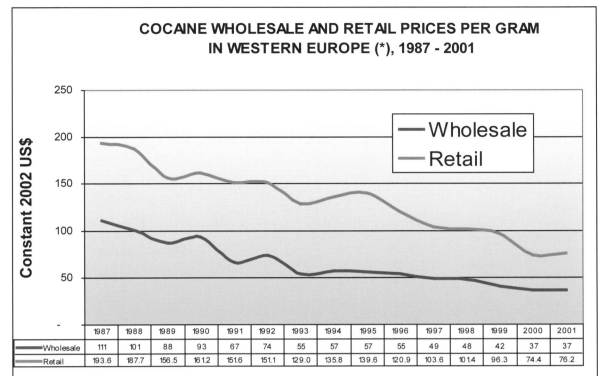

COCAINE WHOLESALE AND RETAIL PRICES PER GRAM IN WESTERN EUROPE (*), 1987 - 2001

Constant 2002 US$

	1987	1988	1989	1990	1991	1992	1993	1994	1995	1996	1997	1998	1999	2000	2001
Wholesale	111	101	88	93	67	74	55	57	57	55	49	48	42	37	37
Retail	193.6	187.7	156.5	161.2	151.6	151.1	129.0	135.8	139.6	120.9	103.6	101.4	96.3	74.4	76.2

(*) Weighted average (by population) of: Austria, Belgium, Denmark, Finland, France, Germany, Greece, Iceland, Ireland, Italy, Luxembourg, Netherland, Norway, Portugal, Spain, Sweden, Switzerland, United Kingdom.

Source: UNODC, Annual Reports Questionnaire data.

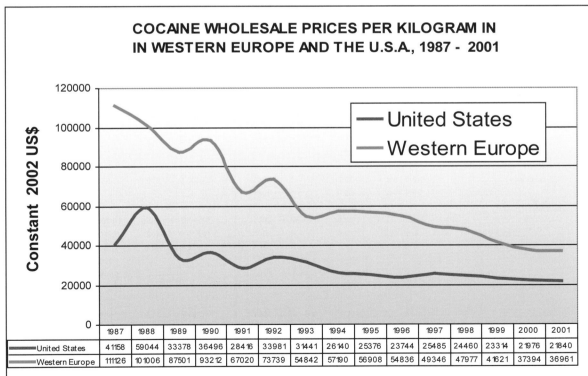

COCAINE WHOLESALE PRICES PER KILOGRAM IN IN WESTERN EUROPE AND THE U.S.A., 1987 - 2001

Constant 2002 US$

	1987	1988	1989	1990	1991	1992	1993	1994	1995	1996	1997	1998	1999	2000	2001
United States	41158	59044	33378	36496	28416	33981	31441	26140	25376	23744	25485	24460	23314	21976	21840
Western Europe	111126	101006	87501	93212	67020	73739	54842	57190	56908	54836	49346	47977	41621	37394	36961

(*) Weighted average (by population) of: Austria, Belgium, Denmark, Finland, France, Germany, Greece, Iceland, Ireland, Italy, Luxembourg, Netherland, Norway, Portugal, Spain, Sweden, Switzerland, United Kingdom.

Source: UNODC, Annual Reports Questionnaire data.

WHOLESALE AND STREET PRICES OF
COCAINE

Retail and wholesale prices and purity levels:
breakdown by drug, region and country or territory
(prices expressed in US$ or converted equivalent, and purity levels in percentage)

Region / country or territory	RETAIL PRICE (per gram)				WHOLESALE PRICE (per kilogram)			
	Range	Average	Purity	Year	Range	Average	Purity	Year
Africa								
East Africa								
Kenya		60.0	-	2000		50,000.0	-	2000
Uganda		100.0	-	2000		200,000.0	90.0	2000
North Africa								
Egypt	156.7 - 261.2	209.0	-	2001	130,597.0 - 182,835.8	156,716.4	-	2001
Southern Africa								
Namibia	44.4 - 50.8	47.6	-	2001	4,441.6 - 5,076.1	4,758.8	-	2001
(Crack)	44.4 - 50.7	47.6	-	2001				
South Africa		28.4	-	2001		19,040.0	-	2001
(Crack)						5,080.0	-	2001
Swaziland (Coca Base)	190.4 - 380.7	285.5	-	2001		7,600.0	-	1999
(Crack)	0.3 - 0.4	0.3	-	2001				
Zambia		26.8	90.0	1999				
Zimbabwe	36.4 - 81.8	59.1	-	2001	18,181.8 - 81,818.2	50,000.0	-	2001
West and Central Africa								
Côte d'Ivoire	6.8 - 68.0	34.0	10.0	2001	204.1 - 20,405.1	10,304.6	10.0	2001
Ghana					31,368.5 - 47,052.8	39,210.7	80.0	1999
Nigeria		4.4	30.0 - 40.0	2001	16,588.0 - 18,334.0	17,461.0	70.0 - 100.0	2001
Americas								
Central America								
Costa Rica		24.8	-	2001	3,412.0 - 5,273.1	4,342.5	70.0 - 90.0	2001
(Crack)	10.3 - 20.7	15.5	-	2001	1,550.0 - 3,100.0	2,330.0	-	2001
El Salvador (Coca Base)	24.6 - 26.3	25.4	60.0 - 90.0	2001	24,571.4 - 26,285.7	25,428.6	70.0 - 90.0	2001
(Crack)	24.6 - 26.3	25.4	60.0 - 90.0	2001	24,571.4 - 26,285.7	25,428.6	70.0 - 90.0	2001
Guatemala	10.3 - 12.9	11.6	60.0 - 80.0	2001	3,869.7 - 6,449.5	5,159.6	85.0 - 100.0	2001
(Crack)	6.5 - 13.0	9.7	50.0 - 70.0	2001	5,160.0 - 6,450.0	5,800.0	-	2001
Honduras						4,690.0	-	1997
Panama	1.0 - 2.0	1.5	40.0 - 80.0	2001	1,200.0 - 2,000.0	1,600.0	-	2001
(Coca Base)	1.0 - 2.0	1.5	40.0 - 80.0	2001	1,200.0 - 2,000.0	1,600.0	-	2001
(Crack)	1.0 - 2.0	1.5	40.0 - 80.0	2001	1,200.0 - 2,000.0	1,600.0	-	2001
North America								
Canada	32.6 - 130.6	81.6	-	2001	20,895.5 - 39,179.1	30,037.3	85.0 - 95.0	2001
(Crack)	65.3 - 130.6	98.0	-	2001				
Mexico						7,880.0	-	2001
United States	40.0 - 100.0	70.0		2001	13,000.0 - 30,000.0	21,500.0	68.0	2001
(Crack)	30.0 - 100.0	65.0	-	2001				
South America								
Argentina	18.0 - 22.0	20.0	4.0 - 20.0	2001	9,500.0 - 10,500.0	10,000.0	40.0 - 90.0	2001
(Coca Base)	8.0 - 12.0	10.0	-	2001	4,510.0 - 5,510.0	5,010.0	-	2001
(Crack)	13.0 - 17.0	15.0	-	2001	5,010.0 - 6,510.0	5,760.0	-	2001
Bolivia		8.0	80.0	2001		1,300.0	90.0	2001
(Coca Base)		5.0	70.0	2001		1,100.0	70.0	2001
Brazil		4.9	-	1997		2,500.0	-	1996
Chile		2.4	-	1997		6,000.0	95.0	1998
Colombia	1.5 - 2.3	1.9	78.0 - 80.0	2001	1,391.0 - 1,739.0	1,565.0	-	2001
(Coca Base)	0.9 - 1.3	1.1	-	2001	830.0 - 1,040.0	940.0	-	2001
Ecuador		1.0	70.0	1999		2,000.0	96.0	1999

WHOLESALE AND STREET PRICES OF
COCAINE

Retail and wholesale prices and purity levels:
breakdown by drug, region and country or territory
(prices expressed in US$ or converted equivalent, and purity levels in percentage)

Region / country or territory	RETAIL PRICE (per gram)				WHOLESALE PRICE (per kilogram)			
	Range	Average	Purity	Year	Range	Average	Purity	Year
Guyana	6.0 - 10.0	8.0	-	1996	4,500.0 - 6,210.0	5,360.0	-	1996
Paraguay		6.5	-	1999		3,500.0	-	1999
Peru	**4.0 - 6.0**	**5.0**	80.0	2001	**900.0 - 1,000.0**	**950.0**	95.0	2001
(Coca Base)	**1.5 - 2.5**	**2.0**	75.0	2001	**300.0 - 400.0**	**350.0**	70.0	2001
Suriname (Coca Base)	**3.0 - 4.5**	**3.8**	-	2001	**3,000.0 - 5,000.0**	**4,000.0**	-	2001
(crack)	**0.5 - 1.0**	**0.8**	-	2001				
Uruguay		12.0	-	2000		5,200.0	85.0 - 90.0	2000
Venezuela		5.0	-	2001	3,435.0 - 5,175.0	5,200.0	-	2000
(crack)		**2.8**	-	2001				
Caribbean								
Bahamas (Coca Base)					**13,000.0 - 20,000.0**	**16,500.0**	-	2001
(crack)	**50.0 - 70.0**	**60.0**	-	2001				
Bermuda		105.8	-	1999	70,550.0 - 141,100.0	105,830.0	70.0 - 90.0	1997
Cayman Islands	**15.0 - 25.0**	**20.0**	85.0 - 95.0	2001	**8,000.0 - 12,000.0**	**10,000.0**	85.0 - 95.0	2001
Cuba		100.0	-	1996	5,000.0 - 10,000.0	7,500.0	70.0 - 90.0	1996
Dominican Republic		10.0	-	2001		10,000.0	-	2001
Grenada (Coca Base)	**16.7 - 22.2**	**19.4**	-	2001	**6,666.7 - 7,407.4**	**7,037.0**	-	2001
Haiti (Coca Base)	**6.0 - 7.0**	**6.5**	-	2001	**5,000.0 - 6,000.0**	**5,500.0**	-	2001
Jamaica	**6.0 - 8.0**	**7.0**	90.0	2001	**5,000.0 - 6,000.0**	**5,500.0**	90.0	2001
(crack)	**1.2 - 1.5**	**1.4**	-	2001	**210.0 - 220.0**	**215.0**	-	2001
Saint Lucia		10.0	-	2000		8,000.0	-	2000
Trinidad Tobago		**50.0**	5.1	2001		**27,000.0**	75.0	2001
Turks and Caicos Islands		100.0	-	1997		150,000.0	-	1999

Asia
Central Asia and Transcaucasia

Region / country or territory	Range	Average	Purity	Year	Range	Average	Purity	Year
Azerbaijan		125.0	-	1999				

East and South-East Asia

Region / country or territory	Range	Average	Purity	Year	Range	Average	Purity	Year
Hong Kong SAR, China	**102.7 - 166.9**	**134.8**	-	2001	**26,320.6 - 41,727.8**	**34,024.2**	-	2001
Republic of Korea	593.0 - 847.1	720.1	85.0	1999	**55,290.0 - 62,390.0**	**58,840.0**	-	2001
Indonesia		70.0	-	1998				
Japan	**58.3 - 83.3**	**70.8**	-	2001				
(Coca Base)	**125.0 - 2,500.0**	**1,312.5**	-	2001				
Mongolia (Coca Base)						27,390.0	-	2001
Philippines	90.1 - 128.7	109.4	-	1999				

Near and Middle East /South-West Asia

Region / country or territory	Range	Average	Purity	Year	Range	Average	Purity	Year
Israel (Coca Base)	**48.6 - 109.3**	**78.9**	-	2001	**24,280.3 - 58,272.6**	**41,276.5**	-	2001
Jordan (Coca Base)		141.2	-	1998	**63,559.3 - 77,683.6**	**70,621.5**	-	2001
Lebanon	**50.0 - 90.0**	**70.0**	50.0 - 90.0	2001	**50,000.0 - 80,000.0**	**65,000.0**	80.0 - 90.0	2001
(Coca Base)	**40.0 - 60.0**	**50.0**	60.0 - 90.0	2001	**30,000.0 - 70,000.0**	**50,000.0**	70.0 - 90.0	2001
Saudi Arabia						9,070.0	0.2	1998

South Asia

Region / country or territory	Range	Average	Purity	Year	Range	Average	Purity	Year
India (Coca Base)					**25,869.2 - 75,451.9**	**50,660.6**	-	2001

Europe
Eastern Europe

Region / country or territory	Range	Average	Purity	Year	Range	Average	Purity	Year
Bulgaria		36.8	75.0	2001	**27,608.0 - 36,810.6**	**32,209.3**	90.0 - 92.0	2001
Croatia	**59.2 - 82.9**	**71.1**	20.0 - 50.0	2001	**26,061.9 - 35,539.0**	**30,800.5**	70.0 - 80.0	2001

WHOLESALE AND STREET PRICES OF
COCAINE

Retail and wholesale prices and purity levels:
breakdown by drug, region and country or territory
(prices expressed in US$ or converted equivalent, and purity levels in percentage)

Region / country or territory	RETAIL PRICE (per gram)				WHOLESALE PRICE (per kilogram)			
	Range	Average	Purity	Year	Range	Average	Purity	Year
Czech Republic	55.5 - 69.4	62.5	-	2000	46,290.0 - 55,550.0	50,920.0		2000
Estonia		97.0	8.5 - 83.0	2001				
Hungary	51.1 - 61.3	56.2	-	2001	27,263.9 - 30,671.9	28,967.9	-	2001
Latvia	56.2 - 80.3	68.3	-	2001				
Lithuania					30,000.0 - 45,000.0	37,500.0	60.0 - 80.0	2001
(Coca Base)	50.0 - 75.0	62.5	30.0 - 50.0	2001				
Poland (Coca Base)	40.3 - 75.6	58.0	-	2001	25,207.1 - 30,248.5	27,727.8	-	2001
Republic of Moldova (Coca Base)		60.0	90.0	2001		30,000.0	90.0	2001
Romania		40.0	-	2001		50,000.0	70.0	2001
Russian Federation	100.0 - 120.0	110.0	-	2001	60,000.0 - 100,000.0	80,000.0	70.0 - 90.0	2001
Serbia and Montenegro	26.9 - 44.8	35.9	-	2001	31,400.0 - 44,800.0	38,100.0	-	2001
(Coca Base)	67.3 - 112.1	89.7	5.0 - 10.0	2001	35,870.0 - 67,260.0	51,570.0	35.0 - 50.0	2001
Slovakia (Crack)	41.6 - 72.8	57.2	10.0 - 30.0	2001	41,600.3 - 166,401.2	104,000.8	60.0 - 95.0	2001
Slovenia		59.2	-	2001		29,600.0	-	2001
Ukraine (Coca Base)	1.5 - 200.0	100.8	3.0 - 32.0	2001	100,000.0 - 170,000.0	135,000.0	3.0 - 32.0	2001
Western Europe								
Andorra	53.6 - 64.4	59.0	-	2001				
Austria	58.3 - 97.8	78.0	3.0 - 94.0	2001	35,847.5 - 52,141.7	43,994.6	1.0 - 92.0	2001
Belgium	44.2 - 58.0	51.1	-	2001	22,309.4 - 31,233.2	26,771.3	-	2001
Cyprus (Coca Base)	108.4 - 170.4	139.4	-	2001	30,973.5 - 38,716.8	34,845.1	-	2001
Denmark	59.8 - 179.4	119.6	-	2001	23,919.4 - 71,758.1	47,838.7	-	2001
Finland	89.7 - 152.5	121.1	-	2001				
France	62.8 - 112.1	87.4	-	2001	26,905.8 - 43,049.3	34,977.6	-	2001
(Crack)	4.5 - 9.0	6.7	-	2001				
Germany	33.8 - 81.2	57.5	-	2001	23,914.6 - 42,554.6	33,234.6	-	2001
Gibraltar	43.2 - 72.0	57.6	-	2001		117,000.0	90.0	1997
Greece	53.8 - 89.7	71.7	-	2001	31,390.1 - 49,327.3	40,358.7	-	2001
Iceland	87.0 - 130.0	108.5	-	2001				
Ireland	80.7 - 98.7	89.7	60.0 - 70.0	2001		29,891.3	60.0 - 70.0	1999
Italy	80.6 - 97.2	88.9	-	2001	35,665.6 - 45,392.6	40,529.1	60.0	2001
Liechtenstein	67.6 - 101.4	84.5	40.0 - 50.0	1998	33,780.0 - 47,300.0	40,540.0	70.0 - 80.0	1998
Luxembourg	79.5 - 159.1	119.3	15.0 - 35.0	1999	42,415.6 - 53,019.5	47,717.5	85.0 - 90.0	1999
Malta		79.1	40.0	2001		67,810.0	60.0	2001
Monaco		203.0	-	1997				
Netherlands	48.5 - 72.8	60.7	-	1999	25,000.0 - 30,000.0	27,500.0	-	1999
Norway	89.7 - 224.2	157.0	10.0 - 70.0	2001	35,874.4 - 67,264.6	51,569.1	20.0 - 90.0	2001
Portugal		48.0	15.6 - 98.8	2001		29,080.0	-	2001
Spain		51.6	50.0	2001		38,898.1	75.0	1999
Sweden	69.4 - 89.2	79.3	-	2001	29,736.6 - 39,648.8	34,692.7	-	2001
Switzerland	20.5 - 117.0	68.7	10.0 - 85.0	2001	17,543.9 - 29,239.8	23,391.8	35.0 - 85.0	2001
Turkey (Coca Base)	70.0 - 90.0	80.0	-	2001	75,000.0 - 85,000.0	80,000.0	-	1999
United Kingdom	72.0 - 115.2	93.6	51.4 - 57.7	2001	28,806.6 - 43,209.9	36,008.2	68.1 - 73.1	2001
(Crack)	21.6 - 36.0	28.8	70.3 - 75.5	2001	28,800.0 - 49,000.0	38,900.0	71.5 - 82.1	2001
OCEANIA								
Australia	159.9 - 511.5	335.7	-	1999	70,330.0 - 83,120.0	76,725.0	-	1999
New Zealand	126.8 - 169.1	148.0	-	2001				

2.2.5. Cannabis: Seizures 1996-2001

	SEIZURES 1996 - 2001					
	Cannabis herb					
Region/country or territory	**1996**	**1997**	**1998**	**1999**	**2000**	**2001**
AFRICA						
East Africa						
Burundi	No Report	No Report	No Report	45.847 kg ^{ICPO}	No Report	No Report
Ethiopia	2.117 kg ^{ICPO}	135.346 kg	331.561 kg	807.364 kg	181.821 kg	152.064 kg
Kenya	8238.000 kg	11250.000 kg	2375.240 kg	8762.033 kg	5649.000 kg	383253.486 ^{Govt (1} kg
Madagascar	3320.000 kg ^{INCB}	510.460 kg ^{INCB}	No Report	1265.332 kg ^{ICPO}	No Report	No Report
Mauritius	8.792 kg	18435.000 kg	3.090 kg	5.592 kg	21.931 kg	66.985 kg
Seychelles	0.162 kg ^{ICPO}	No Report	2.056 kg ^{ICPO}	1.005 kg	22.014 kg	0.067 kg ^{ICPO}
Uganda	258.810 kg	No Report	5530.000 kg	5530.000 kg ^{ICPO}	6100.000 kg	50000.000 kg
United Republic of Tanzania	No Report	82539.539 kg	4617.862 kg	6021.273 kg	24293.304 kg ^{ICPO}	249639.026 ^{Govt} kg
Sub-Total	11827.880 kg	112870.300 kg	12859.810 kg	22438.450 kg	36268.070 kg	683111.600 kg
North Africa						
Algeria	0.036 kg ^{ICPO}	No Report	58.300 kg ^{ICPO}	No Report	No Report	No Report
Egypt	6624.000 kg	10185.538 kg	31078.387 kg	22588.505 kg	30397.591 kg	50037.000 kg
Morocco	38521.145 kg	27955.979 kg	37160.879 kg	No Report	No Report	73.810 kg ^{ICPO}
Sudan	1202.812 kg ^{ICPO}	No Report	No Report	No Report	1887.805 kg	No Report
Tunisia	0.066 kg ^{ICPO}	18.163 kg ^{ICPO}	2.000 kg	1893.381 kg ^{ICPO}	No Report	No Report
Sub-Total	46348.060 kg	38159.680 kg	68299.560 kg	24481.890 kg	32285.400 kg	50110.810 kg
Southern Africa						
Angola	63.850 kg ^{Govt.}	518.006 kg ^{ICPO}	1.975 kg ^{ICPO}	2829.167 kg	4733.667 kg ^{ICPO}	621.278 kg ^{ICPO}
Botswana	1588.198 kg ^{ICPO}	1446.153 kg ^{ICPO}	1186.000 kg ^{ICPO}	1229.000 kg ^{ICPO}	No Report	No Report
Lesotho	15390.089 kg ^{Govt.}	l0472.073 kg ^{ICPO}	21583.824 kg ^{ICPO}	7243.697 kg ^{ICPO}	No Report	No Report
Malawi	8453.497 kg	10320.105 kg	5201.971 kg	27141.583 kg	312471.845 kg	8663.694 kg
Mozambique	No Report	184.024 kg ^{ICPO}	462.000 kg ^{ICPO}	894.406 kg ^{ICPO}	1700.562 kg ^{ICPO}	6721.550 kg ^{ICPO}
Namibia	No Report	298.830 kg ^{INCB}	361.395 kg	282.363 kg	302.981 kg	5386.189 kg
South Africa	203353.953 kg	171929.328 kg	197116.297 kg	289943.561 ^{ICPO} kg	717701.918 kg	123964.058 kg
Swaziland	440.485 kg ^{ICPO}	l1302.505 kg ^{ICPO}	5943.293 kg	33283.707 kg	14946.718 kg	15064.342 kg
Zambia	7794.402 kg ^{Govt}	l1176.308 kg ^{Govt}	3256.366 kg ^{Govt}	7000.653 kg	7318.199 kg	14.600 kg ^{Govt}
Zimbabwe	2428.647 kg ^{ICPO}	4667.320 kg ^{ICPO}	6117.086 kg	1816.001 kg	3045.908 kg	1530.254 kg
Sub-Total	239513.100 kg	222314.600 kg	241230.200 kg	371664.200 kg	1062222.000 kg	161966.000 kg
West and Central Africa						
Benin	44.404 kg ^{Govt}	26.862 kg ^{Govt}	611.077 kg ^{Govt}	25.138 kg ^{Govt}	971.781 kg ^{F.O}	809.408 kg ^{ICPO}
Burkina Faso	2967.410 kg ^{F.O.}	2402.734 kg ^{Govt.}	No Report	No Report	No Report	2404.713 kg
Cameroon	581.870 kg ^{ICPO}	No Report	112.875 kg	1154.560 kg	No Report	No Report
Central African Republic	No Report	No Report	57.551 kg ^{ICPO}	No Report	No Report	No Report
Chad	435.200 kg ^{Govt.}	No Report	No Report	686.000 kg ^{ICPO}	378.000 kg	No Report

Source: Annual Report Questionnaire if not otherwise indicated

SEIZURES 1996 - 2001
Cannabis herb

Region/country or territory	1996	1997	1998	1999	2000	2001
AFRICA						
West and Central Africa						
Congo	No Report	No Report	No Report	1.000 kg	259.000 kg	222.000 kg
Côte d'Ivoire	1482.549 kg	853.871 kg	898.960 kg	1650.189 kg	1236.644 kg [ICPO]	1876.658 kg
Democratic Republic of the Congo	1.066 kg [Govt.]	No Report	No Report	No Report	No Report	No Report
Equatorial Guinea	No Report	3.500 kg [INCB]	24.000 kg 6 u.	26.000 kg 46 u.	No Report	No Report
Gabon	160.189 kg [ICPO]	24.255 kg [ICPO]	114.336 kg [ICPO]	45.648 kg [ICPO]	No Report	No Report
Gambia	11.164 kg [ICPO]	566.971 kg [ICPO]	376.145 kg [ICPO]	No Report	No Report	700.000 kg
Ghana	8294.190 kg [F.O.]	1409.470 kg [F.O.]	4375.098 kg	4080.049 kg	No Report	No Report
Guinea	No Report	No Report	No Report	No Report	640.345 kg [ICPO]	No Report
Guinea-Bissau	No Report	No Report	No Report	No Report	No Report	367.000 kg
Mali	80.000 kg [Govt.]	404.270 kg [ICPO]	No Report	No Report	No Report	No Report
Mauritania	6765.170 kg [F.O.]	92.006 kg [Govt]	17.200 kg [Govt]	No Report	No Report	No Report
Niger	777.384 kg [ICPO]	499.887 kg [ICPO]	682.173 kg [ICPO]	1356.162 kg [ICPO]	No Report	No Report
Nigeria	18604.000 kg [ICPO]	15904.721 kg	16170.500 kg [Govt.]	17691.014 kg	272260.020 kg	317950.204 kg
Saint Helena	No Report	3.009 kg	0.183 kg	No Report	0.075 kg	
Sao Tome and Principe	No Report	0.200 kg	No Report	No Report	No Report	15.000 kg
Senegal	24803.230 kg [F.O.]	13627.390 kg [F.O.]	69652.000 kg [F.O.]	7165.830 kg [ICPO]	No Report	No Report
Togo	156.848 kg	1066.189 kg [Govt.]	No Report	No Report	429.056 kg	655.247 kg
Sub-Total	65164.670 kg	36885.330 kg	93092.090 kg 6 u.	33881.590 kg 46 u.	276174.900 kg	325000.200 kg
Total region	362853.800 kg	410230.000 kg	415481.700 kg 6 u.	452466.100 kg 46 u.	1406950.000 kg	1220189.000 kg
AMERICAS						
Caribbean						
Anguilla	1.000 kg [F.O]	0.644 kg	5.037 kg	8.000 kg [F.O]	No Report	1.000 kg [F.O]
Antigua and Barbuda	1485.000 kg [F.O]	628.000 kg [F.O]	105.000 kg [F.O]	94.000 kg [F.O]	67.000 kg [F.O]	662.000 kg [F.O]
Aruba	77.000 kg [F.O]	13.000 kg [F.O]	No Report	142.000 kg [F.O]	12.000 kg [F.O]	1159.000 kg [F.O]
Bahamas	2606.000 kg [F.O]	3763.000 kg [F.O]	2591.065 kg	3610.000 kg [F.O]	4093.000 kg	4174.000 kg 9203 u.
Barbados	3118.000 kg [INCB] 118 u.	1132.027 kg [INCB]	1650.000 kg [CICAD]	333.580 kg [HONLC]	2948.000 kg [F.O]	5748.925 kg [ICPO]
Bermuda	107.050 kg	91.800 kg	91.800 kg	87.067 kg	136.579 kg	32.000 kg [F.O]

Source: Annual Report Questionnaire if not otherwise indicated

SEIZURES 1996 - 2001
Cannabis herb

Region/country or territory	1996	1997	1998	1999	2000	2001
AMERICAS						
Caribbean						
British Virgin Islands	119.000 kg [F.O]	85.000 kg [F.O]	84.000 kg [F.O]	354.000 kg [F.O]	26.000 kg [F.O]	151.950 kg
						80 u.
Cayman Islands	3188.018 kg	3422.073 kg 427 u.	4063.009 kg 650 u.	5100.371 kg	6621.000 kg	11818.000 kg
Cuba	3931.682 kg	6023.000 kg [F.O]	4610.000 kg [F.O]	5559.000 kg [F.O]	8802.000 kg [F.O]	6121.000 kg [F.O]
Dominica	136.249 kg	404.000 kg [F.O]	361.000 kg [F.O]	192.000 kg [F.O]	468.000 kg [CICAD]	521.000 kg [F.O]
Dominican Republic	245.900 kg	800.660 kg	110.298 kg	184.333 kg	1526.000 kg [CICAD]	3815.900 kg
French Guiana	191.000 kg [F.O]	123.000 kg [F.O]	127.000 kg [F.O]	134.000 kg [F.O]	58.000 kg [F.O]	No Report
Grenada	191.000 kg [F.O]	123.199 kg [INCB]	84.000 kg	219.000 kg [F.O]	103.000 kg [INCSR]	133.690 kg
Guadeloupe	52377.000 kg [F.O]	20179.000 kg [F.O]	8860.000 kg [F.O]	515.000 kg [F.O]	1017.000 kg [F.O]	516.000 kg [F.O]
Haiti	No Report	9000.000 kg [F.O]	9255.000 kg [F.O]	71.030 kg	401.000 kg [F.O]	1705.000 kg [F.O]
Jamaica	31587.000 kg [F.O]	24729.000 kg [F.O]	35911.000 kg [F.O]	56226.940 kg [ICPO]	55870.000 kg [F.O]	74044.000 kg
Martinique	166.000 kg [F.O]	355.000 kg [F.O]	136.000 kg [F.O]	199.000 kg [F.O]	749.000 kg [F.O]	No Report
Montserrat	1.000 kg [F.O]	3.285 kg 14090 u.	No Report	2677.000 kg [F.O]	0.497 kg	No Report
Netherlands Antilles	650.000 kg [F.O]	1553.310 kg [INCB]	No Report	541.000 kg [F.O]	39.782 kg [ICPO]	3772.000 kg [F.O]
Puerto Rico	8635.000 kg [F.O]	1337.000 kg [F.O]	1285.000 kg [F.O]	12605.000 kg [F.O]	1982.000 kg [F.O]	24.000 kg [F.O]
Saint Kitts and Nevis	5.000 kg [F.O]	67.000 kg [F.O]	31.000 kg [F.O]	14124.000 kg [F.O]	119.000 kg [INCSR]	330.000 kg [F.O]
Saint Lucia	326.048 kg	621.684 kg	363.663 kg	267.000 kg [CICAD]	1803.610 kg	753.000 kg [F.O]
Saint Vincent and the Grenadines	1227.000 kg [F.O]	527.000 kg [F.O]	1321.000 kg [F.O]	7180.000 kg [F.O]	1709.000 kg [INCSR]	1962.000 kg [F.O]
Trinidad Tobago	11408.000 kg [F.O]	1430.000 kg [CICAD]	3483.545 kg	8287.000 kg [CICAD]	1546.000 kg [F.O]	2393.950 kg
Turks and Caicos Islands	25.000 kg	22.000 kg	8.000 kg	68.500 kg	27.000 kg [F.O]	24.000 kg [F.O]
US Virgin Islands	No Report	No Report	No Report	48.123 kg [ICPO]	No Report	No Report
Sub-Total	121803.900 kg 118 u.	76433.690 kg 14517 u.	74536.420 kg 650 u.	118826.900 kg	90124.470 kg	119862.400 kg 9283 u.
Central America						
Belize	184.000 kg [CICAD]	263.000 kg [CICAD]	1557.000 kg [F.O]	392.000 kg [F.O]	249.000 kg [F.O]	269.909 kg
Costa Rica	387.053 kg	107.000 kg [CICAD]	469.340 kg	1693.550 kg	1140.650 kg	2848.620 kg
El Salvador	650.000 kg [CICAD]	971.247 kg [ICPO]	291.202 kg [ICPO]	604.581 kg	455.700 kg [ICPO]	463.917 kg
Guatemala	16388.295 kg	256.222 kg [Govt.]	193.970 kg	814.212 kg	158.450 kg	584.550 kg
Honduras	472.000 kg [CICAD]	2.147 kg	1293.000 kg [CICAD]	1583.000 kg [CICAD]	1112.000 kg [CICAD]	No Report
Nicaragua	853.961 kg	285.198 kg	613.027 kg	754.000 kg [CICAD]	737.000 kg [CICAD]	586.560 kg [ICPO]
Panama	18126.550 kg	14102.067 kg	16536.006 kg	3477.268 kg	3657.498 kg	1639.000 kg
Sub-Total	37061.860 kg	15986.880 kg	20953.550 kg	9318.610 kg	7510.298 kg	6392.556 kg

Source: Annual Report Questionnaire if not otherwise indicated

SEIZURES 1996 - 2001
Cannabis herb

Region/country or territory	1996	1997	1998	1999	2000	2001
AMERICAS						
North America						
Canada	176673.000 kg	50624.000 kg	27299.990 kg	44541.000 kg	70221.600 kg	6833.524 kg
			8 u.	52 u.	738 u.	18 u.
Mexico	1015755.538 kg	1038470.414 kg	1062143.980 kg	1471959.958 kg	2050402.078 kg	1837524.728 kg
United States	638661.313 kg	684745.375 kg	799000.875 kg [Govt.]	1175373.000 kg	218256.453 kg	682574.100 kg
Sub-Total	1831090.000 kg	1773840.000 kg	1888445.000 kg	2691874.000 kg	2338880.000 kg	2526932.000 kg
			8 u.	52 u.	738 u.	18 u.
South America						
Argentina	8893.190 kg [Govt.]	13709.620 kg	10920.230 kg	18301.339 kg	25538.966 kg	33052.239 kg
Bolivia	175.000 kg [F.O]	3617.000 kg [F.O]	320.000 kg [F.O]	2160.000 kg [F.O]	3745.000 kg [F.O]	7054.500 kg [F.O]
Brazil	22430.588 kg	31828.432 kg	28982.492 kg	69171.506 kg	159073.232 kg	146279.636 kg [Govt]
Chile	912.634 kg	784.430 kg	2238.325 kg	2105.000 kg [CICAD]	3277.341 kg [(2]	2418.496 kg
Colombia	238943.000 kg	178132.000 kg [Govt.]	70025.000 kg	70124.000 kg	75465.000 kg	86610.000 kg
Ecuador	175.240 kg	224.206 kg	17734.697 kg	2976.910 kg	18263.357 kg [ICPO]	3079.376 kg
Guyana	196.225 kg	40.000 kg [F.O]	51.000 kg [F.O]	3528.000 kg [F.O]	4387.000 kg [F.O]	243.000 kg [ICPO]
Paraguay	43325.414 kg	17218.105 kg	80077.914 kg	199282.319 kg	51081.000 kg [CICAD]	No Report
Peru	No Report	20910.326 kg	19880.324 kg	4055.732 kg	1635.419 kg	2601.446 kg
Suriname	42.916 kg	65.000 kg [F.O]	104.754 kg	177.000 kg [CICAD]	107.000 kg [INCSR]	46.000 kg
Uruguay	269.675 kg [Govt.]	25601.006 kg [Govt.]	424.778 kg	493.783 kg	805.843 kg	1115.222 kg [ICPO]
Venezuela	2983.943 kg	No Report	4500.000 kg [CICAD]	13055.778 kg	14999.634 kg	14431.800 kg
Sub-Total	318347.800 kg	292130.100 kg	235259.500 kg	385431.300 kg	358378.800 kg	296931.700 kg
Total region	2308303.000 kg	2158391.000 kg	2219195.000 kg	3205451.000 kg	2794894.000 kg	2950119.000 kg
	118 u.	14517 u.	658 u.	52 u.	738 u.	9301 u.
ASIA						
Central Asia and Transcaucasian countries						
Armenia	90.245 kg	No Report	0.888 kg	46.675 kg [Govt.]	53.798 kg	14.081 kg
Azerbaijan	10.950 kg [ICPO]	37.475 kg [ICPO]	40.287 kg	55.395 kg	2773.104 kg [ICPO]	61.500 kg
Georgia	642.088 kg [ICPO]	No Report	No Report	31972.800 kg [ICPO]	No Report	32397.000 kg [ICPO]
Kazakhstan	6800.000 kg [Govt.]	11800.000 kg [Govt.]	716.236 kg	10481.505 kg	No Report	11789.000 kg [F.O]
Kyrgyzstan	560.065 kg	694.100 kg [F.O]	1569.243 kg [F.O]	1716.475 kg [(3]	3748.220 kg [(4]	2250.663 kg [(4]
Tajikistan	22.000 kg [F.O]	336.311 kg [F.O]	323.331 kg [F.O]	No Report	No Report	750.486 kg
Uzbekistan	512.910 kg [ICPO]	374.496 kg	358.558 kg	288.689 kg	No Report	No Report
Sub-Total	8638.258 kg	13242.380 kg	3008.543 kg	44561.540 kg	6575.122 kg	47262.730 kg

Source: Annual Report Questionnaire if not otherwise indicated

SEIZURES 1996 - 2001

Cannabis herb

Region/country or territory	1996	1997	1998	1999	2000	2001
ASIA						
East and South-East Asia						
Brunei Darussalam	1.132 kg	0.139 kg	3.288 kg	0.364 kg	0.054 kg	0.007 kg
Cambodia	No Report	53751.000 kg [ICPO]	No Report	No Report	No Report	No Report
China	4876.000 kg	2408.000 kg	5079.000 kg	No Report	4493.000 kg [Govt.]	751.000 kg [Govt.]
Hong Kong SAR, China	8822.700 kg	1002.100 kg	585.000 kg [Govt.]	24.727 kg	226.007 kg	No Report
Indonesia	443.856 kg	715.735 kg	1071.862 kg	3741.068 kg	6332.908 kg	27390.075 kg
Japan	172.659 kg	155.246 kg	120.884 kg	565.904 kg	310.246 kg	1070.248 kg
Korea (Republic of)	44.434 kg	59.548 kg	32.751 kg	39.442 kg	39.371 kg [ICPO]	283.869 kg
Lao People's Dem. Rep.	1896.300 kg [Govt.]	7026.000 kg [Govt.]	410.000 kg [INCSR]	2187.000 kg [HNLP]	1860.000 kg [INCSR]	1702.000 kg [Govt]
Macau SAR, China	21.690 kg [ICPO]	5.519 kg [ICPO]	1.661 kg [ICPO]	3.000 kg [INCB]	16.381 kg	0.519 kg
Malaysia	1425.728 kg [Govt.]	3889.132 kg	1781.010 kg	2064.498 kg	1885.450 kg	1570.526 kg [ICPO]
Mongolia	No Report	No Report	No Report	5.000 kg [ICPO]	5.800 kg [ICPO]	No Report
Myanmar	263.786 kg	288.034 kg	380.970 kg	274.282 kg	601.508 kg	284.387 kg
Philippines	2044.572 kg	2172.452 kg [Govt (5]	2057.974 kg [Govt (5]	1187.870 kg	1429.474 kg [Govt (5]	706.418 kg [Govt (5]
Singapore	70.868 kg	4363.452 kg	21.831 kg [(3]	7.432 kg [(3]	23.903 kg	8.843 kg
Thailand	16720.000 kg [Govt.]	9141.927 kg	5581.840 kg	14706.198 kg	9803.128 kg [ICPO]	10584.000 kg [F.O]
Viet Nam	581.100 kg [ICPO]	7986.000 kg [ICPO]	379.000 kg [ICPO]	400.100 kg [F.O]	2139.000 kg [ICPO]	1289.005 kg
Sub-Total	37384.830 kg	92964.290 kg	17507.070 kg	25206.890 kg	29166.230 kg	45640.900 kg
Near and Middle East /South-West Asia						
Bahrain	6.529 kg	7.382 kg	0.041 kg [ICPO]	0.042 kg [ICPO]	7.417 kg [ICPO]	No Report
Iran (Islamic Republic of)	No Report	No Report	No Report	No Report	1495.000 kg [ICPO]	No Report
Iraq	No Report	No Report	No Report	270.000 kg [INCB]	569.970 kg [ICPO]	No Report
Israel	1075.181 kg	10635.000 kg	3581.000 kg	3400.000 kg [ICPO]	9855.000 kg	11685.000 kg
Jordan	1.040 kg	0.106 kg	No Report	No Report	No Report	55.034 kg
Kuwait	124.623 kg [ICPO]	28.580 kg [ICPO]	0.246 kg	[ICPO]	3.099 kg [ICPO]	No Report
Lebanon	No Report	No Report	No Report	1.379 kg	0.017 kg	0.011 kg
Oman	No Report	No Report	No Report	0.269 kg	6823.000 kg [ICPO]	0.001 kg
Pakistan	No Report	No Report	No Report	No Report	1223.205 kg [ICPO]	No Report
Qatar	0.027 kg	No Report	146.250 kg [ICPO]	3.297 kg [ICPO]	0.300 kg [ICPO]	No Report
Syrian Arab Republic	1569.293 kg [Govt]	1714.634 kg [Govt]	231.759 kg [Govt]	819.058 kg [Govt]	222.016 kg [Govt]	379.957 kg [Govt]
United Arab Emirates	No Report	No Report	0.095 kg	0.341 kg	No Report	2.566 kg
Yemen	No Report	0.569 kg [ICPO]	11.350 kg [ICPO]	No Report	24.990 kg [ICPO]	No Report
Sub-Total	2776.693 kg	12386.270 kg	3970.741 kg	4494.386 kg	20224.010 kg	12122.570 kg
South Asia						
Bangladesh	121.939 kg	No Report	No Report	724.070 kg [F.O]	2657.899 kg	1421.200 kg [ICPO]

Source: Annual Report Questionnaire if not otherwise indicated

SEIZURES 1996 - 2001
Cannabis herb

Region/country or territory	1996	1997	1998	1999	2000	2001
ASIA						
South Asia						
India	62992.000 kg [Govt.]	30866.000 kg	68221.000 kg	38610.000 kg	100056.000 kg	75943.000 kg [Govt (6]
Maldives	No Report	No Report	0.001 kg	0.022 kg	No Report	0.004 kg
Nepal	2271.923 kg	2040.894 kg [ICPO]	6409.669 kg	4064.650 kg	8025.308 kg [ICPO]	No Report
Sri Lanka	20332.385 kg	63338.734 kg	3450.686 kg	4062.421 kg	5026.336 kg	113238.733 kg
Sub-Total	85718.240 kg	146245.600 kg	78081.360 kg	47461.160 kg	115765.500 kg	190602.900 kg
Total region	134518.000 kg	264838.600 kg	102567.700 kg	121724.000 kg	171730.900 kg	295629.100 kg
EUROPE						
Eastern Europe						
Albania	No Report	No Report	No Report	4395.156 kg [ICPO]	6604.000 kg [Govt]	6915.000 kg [Govt]
Belarus	56.000 kg	90.802 kg [INCB]	No Report	425.000 kg	124.000 kg	103.000 kg [ICPO]
Bosnia Herzegovina	15.919 kg [NAPOL]	1.002 kg [NAPOL]	53.815 kg [NAPOL]	59.144 kg [ICPO]	127.982 kg [NAPOL]	467.585 kg [ICPO]
Bulgaria	5475.649 kg	227.440 kg	1527.562 kg	29365.000 kg	295.947 kg	183.061 kg
Croatia	40.651 kg	135.868 kg	20342.877 kg	200.898 kg	797.501 kg	737.911 kg
Czech Republic	11900.000 kg [Govt.]	5.403 kg	5.500 kg	111.200 kg	16.648 kg	190.450 kg
Estonia	1.236 kg [ICPO]	3.439 kg	4.789 kg / 358 u.	1.468 kg / 491 u.	4.190 kg / 673 u.	0.903 kg
FYR of Macedonia	131.400 kg [NAPOL]	57.989 kg [NAPOL]	1136.752 kg	698.098 kg [NAPOL]	1333.399 kg [NAPOL]	99.115 kg [Govt]
Hungary	3.084 kg	2140.000 kg [Govt.]	42.930 kg	65.725 kg	51.000 kg	131.030 kg
Latvia	793.000 kg	22.000 kg	2.480 kg	231.200 kg	6.780 kg	193.580 kg
Lithuania	0.826 kg	8.063 kg	30.357 kg	25.667 kg	14.428 kg	15.540 kg
Poland	2631.156 kg	62.476 kg	62.146 kg	847.901 kg	139.000 kg	74.306 kg
Republic of Moldova	906.510 kg	435.500 kg	No Report	416.000 kg [ICPO]	No Report	No Report
Romania	1737.213 kg	40.186 kg [ICPO]	7.478 kg	4.530 kg [ICPO]	321.000 kg [ICPO]	155.000 kg
Russian Federation	18967.801 kg	22976.000 kg	23510.650 kg	33801.919 kg	23313.000 kg [F.O]	43877.267 kg
Serbia and Montenegro	No Report	No Report	No Report	No Report	No Report	1230.224 kg
Slovakia	24.000 kg [INCB]	865.615 kg	12539.934 kg	156.000 kg	168.196 kg	No Report
Slovenia	34.596 kg	47.555 kg	2772.604 kg	249.156 kg	3413.025 kg	177.880 kg
Ukraine	1279.200 kg	No Report	No Report	4045.000 kg [ICPO. (6]	11609.932 kg [ICPO]	8195.320 kg
Sub-Total	43998.240 kg	27119.340 kg	62039.880 kg / 358 u.	75099.070 kg / 491 u.	48340.030 kg / 673 u.	62747.170 kg
Western Europe						
Andorra	2.000 kg [INCB]	1.892 kg [ICPO]	0.116 kg [ICPO]	0.046 kg	0.237 kg [ICPO]	0.200 kg
Austria	270.659 kg	668.071 kg	1211.031 kg	341.402 kg	1562.828 kg	282.255 kg

Source: Annual Report Questionnaire if not otherwise indicated

SEIZURES 1996 - 2001
Cannabis herb

Region/country or territory	1996	1997	1998	1999	2000	2001
EUROPE						
Western Europe						
Belgium	56791.000 kg	39072.000 kg	2463.270 kg	2914.749 kg	8206.746 kg	8206.746 kg [7] UNODC
Cyprus	5.915 kg	17.582 kg	128.905 kg	30.108 kg	28.875 kg	37.537 kg
Denmark	No Report	No Report	No Report	52.830 kg	739.819 kg 14032 u.	762.262 kg
Finland	3.152 kg	12.153 kg	8.014 kg	18.167 kg	13.825 kg	16.100 kg
France	31279.678 kg	3452.210 kg	3521.790 kg	3382.205 kg	4865.558 kg	3922.370 kg
Germany	6108.577 kg	4167.282 kg	14897.189 kg	15021.800 kg	5870.900 kg	2078.703 kg
Gibraltar	0.026 kg	[8]	0.084 kg	0.028 kg	0.038 kg	0.005 kg
Greece	2565.959 kg 542 u.	12409.776 kg 482 u.	17510.434 kg	12038.938 kg 10 u.	14908.448 kg	11653.193 kg
Iceland	49.000 kg [INCB]	No Report	No Report	0.503 kg	5.092 kg	0.030 kg
Ireland	2.400 kg	34.824 kg	38.909 kg	68.290 kg	207.954 kg	11590.057 kg
Italy	5722.201 kg	45011.035 kg 2675 u.	38785.988 kg 1192 u.	21248.982 kg [ICPO]	26071.488 kg 2068 u.	36622.637 kg 967 u.
Liechtenstein	25.919 kg	1.530 kg	No Report	No Report	0.972 kg [3]	422.470 kg
Luxembourg	16.460 kg	34.387 kg	4.956 kg	3.932 kg	8.383 kg [ICPO]	No Report
Malta	7217.046 kg	0.163 kg	0.069 kg	0.161 kg	No Report	0.022 kg
Monaco	0.011 kg	0.028 kg	0.032 kg	0.013 kg [ICPO]	0.024 kg [ICPO]	No Report
Netherlands	64903.000 kg [Govt]	35315.000 kg [Govt]	55463.000 kg [Govt]	49115.000 kg [Govt]	10330.000 kg [Govt]	21139.000 kg
Norway	70.000 kg	44.095 kg	88.172 kg	16.471 kg	20.905 kg	35.384 kg
Portugal	35.971 kg	72.240 kg	7.115 kg	65.766 kg	223.212 kg	234.533 kg
Spain	13267.759 kg	24890.311 kg	412.866 kg	761.342 kg	353.292 kg	532.420 kg
Sweden	148.423 kg	30.705 kg	98.431 kg	28.228 kg 4 u.	45.597 kg	13.981 kg
Switzerland	3559.769 kg	6634.843 kg	13163.982 kg	7800.229 kg	18313.602 kg	11106.537 kg
Turkey	No Report	No Report	No Report	5458.350 kg [ICPO]	1.000 kg	4561.533 kg
United Kingdom	34189.102 kg	31120.199 kg	21660.666 kg	15410.048 kg [ICPO] 20 u.	25473.979 kg	25473.979 kg [7] UNODC
Sub-Total	226234.000 kg 542 u.	202990.300 kg 3157 u.	169465.000 kg 1192 u.	133777.600 kg 34 u.	117252.800 kg 16100 u.	138692.000 kg 967 u.
Total region	270232.300 kg 542 u.	230109.700 kg 3157 u.	231504.900 kg 1550 u.	208876.700 kg 525 u.	165592.800 kg 16773 u.	201439.100 kg 967 u.
OCEANIA						
Oceania						
Australia	1747.722 kg 1922 u.	4398.986 kg [9]	15996.628 kg [Govt. (6)]	3340.917 kg [Govt. (6)]	4365.089 kg [Govt.]	6918.357 kg
Fiji	6.989 kg	No Report	No Report	45.618 kg [ICPO]	106.200 kg [ICPO]	316.750 kg [ICPO]

Source: Annual Report Questionnaire if not otherwise indicated

SEIZURES 1996 - 2001
Cannabis herb

Region/country or territory	1996	1997	1998	1999	2000	2001
OCEANIA						
Oceania						
New Caledonia	138.000 kg [INCB]	133.610 kg [INCB]	No Report	132.000 kg [INCB]	No Report	No Report
New Zealand	455.000 kg [INCB]	285.012 kg	389.182 kg [(9]	323.649 kg	332.396 kg	1847.000 kg
Tonga	150.000 kg [Govt.]	0.297 kg [INCB]	No Report	No Report	No Report	No Report
Sub-Total	2497.711 kg 1922 u.	4817.905 kg	16385.810 kg	3842.184 kg	4803.685 kg	9082.107 kg
Total region	2497.711 kg 1922 u.	4817.905 kg	16385.810 kg	3842.184 kg	4803.685 kg	9082.107 kg
TOTAL	3078405.000 kg 2582 u.	3068387.000 kg 17674 u.	2985135.000 kg 2214 u.	3992360.000 kg 623 u.	4543972.000 kg 17511 u.	4676458.000 kg 10268 u.

1) Includes plants,resin & seeds 2) No. of seizures include seizures of cannabis plant 3) Including cannabis resin. 4) Including cannabis resin and plants 5) Including cannabis resin 6) Provisional figures. 7) Due to unavailability of 2001 data, year 2000 data were used for analysis purposes. 8) Including depressants. 9) Including cannabis resin, liquid cannabis. 10) Fiscal year

Source: Annual Report Questionnaire if not otherwise indicated

SEIZURES 1996 - 2001
Cannabis resin

Region/country or territory	1996	1997	1998	1999	2000	2001
AFRICA						
East Africa						
Kenya	19633.000 kg	7.007 kg	No Report	3.200 kg [ICPO]	6356.000 kg	21.000 kg [ICPO]
Mauritius	No Report	No Report	0.130 kg	[(1]	0.007 kg	0.040 kg
Seychelles	6.600 kg [ICPO]	No Report	1.073 kg [Govt.]	72.883 kg	32.962 kg	17.934 kg [ICPO]
Uganda	No Report	No Report	25.000 kg	8.797 kg	No Report	No Report
United Republic of Tanzania	No Report	No Report	42.162 kg	No Report	15.000 kg [ICPO]	12.500 kg [Govt]
Sub-Total	19639.600 kg	7.007 kg	68.365 kg	84.880 kg	6403.969 kg	51.474 kg
North Africa						
Algeria	712.160 kg [ICPO]	No Report	1217.179 kg [ICPO]	4080.662 kg	1694.127 kg [ICPO]	1728.258 kg [ICPO]
Egypt	2055.000 kg [F.O]	441.588 kg	628.434 kg	626.000 kg	525.000 kg	486.000 kg
Libyan Arab Jam.	No Report	No Report	471.955 kg	No Report	No Report	No Report
Morocco	64769.098 kg	71887.469 kg	55519.734 kg	54755.235 kg	143946.033 kg	61355.736 kg
Tunisia	555.162 kg [ICPO]	201.074 kg [ICPO]	806.324 kg	1893.381 kg	536.684 kg [ICPO]	1288.877 kg
Sub-Total	68091.420 kg	72530.130 kg	58643.630 kg	61355.280 kg	146701.800 kg	64858.870 kg
Southern Africa						
Lesotho	No Report	3.942 kg [ICPO]	No Report	No Report	No Report	No Report
Malawi	No Report	No Report	3.000 kg	3.000 kg	No Report	No Report
Mozambique	No Report	12000.000 kg [ICPO]	14.160 kg [ICPO]	11.000 kg [ICPO]	i5542.000 kg [ICPO]	0.200 kg [ICPO]
South Africa	1.068 kg	2.150 kg	20.568 kg	22.612 kg [ICPO]	i1500.000 kg	534.146 kg
Swaziland	No Report	No Report	No Report	No Report	No Report	5.056 kg
Zambia	15.724 kg [Govt]	40.269 kg [Govt]	3.111 kg [Govt]	4.201 kg	14.604 kg	0.016 kg [Govt]
Zimbabwe	No Report	No Report	3.191 kg	No Report	No Report	0.081 kg
Sub-Total	16.792 kg	12046.360 kg	44.030 kg	40.813 kg	27056.600 kg	539.499 kg
West and Central Africa						
Benin	No Report	No Report	No Report	No Report	350.000 kg [ICPO]	13.000 kg [ICPO]
Burkina Faso	No Report	4647.000 kg [Govt.]	No Report	No Report	No Report	No Report
Gambia	No Report	0.048 kg [ICPO]	0.420 kg [ICPO]	0.007 kg	No Report	No Report
Sao Tome and Principe	No Report	4.000 kg	No Report	No Report	No Report	No Report
Senegal	No Report	No Report	No Report	No Report	5390.000 kg [ICPO]	No Report
Sierra Leone	987.000 kg	No Report	No Report	No Report	No Report	No Report
Sub-Total	987.000 kg	4651.048 kg	0.420 kg	0.007 kg	5740.000 kg	13.000 kg
Total region	88734.810 kg	89234.540 kg	58756.440 kg	61480.980 kg	185902.400 kg	65462.840 kg

Source: Annual Report Questionnaire if not otherwise indicated

SEIZURES 1996 - 2001
Cannabis resin

Region/country or territory	1996	1997	1998	1999	2000	2001
AMERICAS						
Caribbean						
Antigua and Barbuda	33.000 kg [INCB]	1944.900 kg [ICPO]	No Report	1000.000 kg [CICAD]	No Report	No Report
Aruba	No Report	0.004 kg [INCB]	No Report	No Report	No Report	No Report
Bahamas	No Report	5.030 kg [ICPO]	16.082 kg	2.095 kg [ICPO]	27.900 kg	14.220 kg 31 u.
Barbados	No Report	No Report	No Report	1.270 kg [HONLC]	No Report	No Report
Bermuda	0.975 kg	0.609 kg	0.609 kg	171.002 kg	1.136 kg	No Report
Cayman Islands	0.104 kg	No Report	No Report	No Report	No Report	No Report
Cuba	35.503 kg	No Report	No Report	66.200 kg [F.O]	No Report	No Report
Dominica	No Report	No Report	No Report	0.015 kg [ICPO]	No Report	51.580 kg [ICPO]
Dominican Republic	0.003 kg	No Report	No Report	184.000 kg [ICPO]	No Report	0.008 kg
Jamaica	172.680 kg [ICPO]	67.590 kg [ICPO]	No Report	61.450 kg [ICPO]	20.000 kg [CICAD]	8.100 kg
Netherlands Antilles	No Report	0.354 kg [INCB]	No Report	No Report	0.061 kg [ICPO]	0.104 kg [ICPO]
Saint Lucia	No Report	(2	No Report	No Report	0.071 kg	No Report
Trinidad Tobago	No Report	No Report	2725.305 kg	No Report	No Report	No Report
Turks and Caicos Islands	No Report	No Report	No Report	No Report	0.202 kg [ICPO]	No Report
Sub-Total	242.265 kg	2018.487 kg	2741.996 kg	1486.032 kg	49.370 kg	74.012 kg 31 u.
Central America						
Honduras	No Report	No Report	No Report	1027 u. [CICAD]	No Report	No Report
Panama	No Report	No Report	No Report	No Report	0.002 kg [ICPO]	No Report
Sub-Total				1027 u.	0.002 kg	
North America						
Canada	24655.000 kg	6178.000 kg	15925.320 kg 0.002 lt. 97 u.	6477.000 kg 1.000 lt. 5 u.	16317.600 kg 31 u.	1755.997 kg
Mexico	8.795 kg	115.155 kg	1.743 kg	0.329 kg	0.005 kg	29.507 kg
United States	38205.000 kg	1072.600 kg	No Report	761.000 kg	945.137 kg	56.500 kg
Sub-Total	62868.800 kg	7365.755 kg	15927.060 kg 0.002 lt. 97 u.	7238.330 kg 1.000 lt. 5 u.	17262.740 kg 31 u.	1842.004 kg
South America						
Argentina	6.720 kg [Govt.]	0.060 kg	1.880 kg	5006 u.	9.114 kg	1.219 kg
Brazil	8.509 kg	12.160 kg	No Report	37.550 kg	41.009 kg	43.519 kg [Govt]
Chile	No Report	No Report	No Report	No Report	0.001 kg	No Report
Colombia	13.000 kg [Govt.]	7.000 kg	No Report	338.000 kg	38.000 lt. [CICAD]	0.200 kg
Falkland Islands	No Report	0.122 kg	No Report	0.063 kg	0.120 kg	No Report
Paraguay	0.880 kg	1.780 kg	3.702 kg	2.337 kg	No Report	No Report

Source: Annual Report Questionnaire if not otherwise indicated

SEIZURES 1996 - 2001
Cannabis resin

Region/country or territory	1996	1997	1998	1999	2000	2001
AMERICAS						
South America						
Suriname	No Report	No Report	0.529 kg	No Report	No Report	No Report
Uruguay	0.100 kg ^{Govt.}	No Report	No Report	1.136 kg	0.045 kg	No Report
Sub-Total	29.209 kg	21.122 kg	6.111 kg	379.085 kg 5006 u.	50.289 kg 38.000 lt.	44.938 kg
Total region	63140.270 kg	9405.364 kg	18675.170 kg 0.002 lt. 97 u.	9103.447 kg 1.000 lt. 6038 u.	17362.400 kg 38.000 lt. 31 u.	1960.954 kg 31 u.
ASIA						
Central Asia and Transcaucasian countries						
Armenia	0.516 kg	No Report	No Report	0.178 kg ^{ICPO}	0.169 kg	0.112 kg
Azerbaijan	No Report	No Report	23.256 kg	0.832 kg	No Report	15.500 kg
Georgia	8.568 kg ^{ICPO}	No Report	No Report	0.003 kg ^{ICPO}	0.009 kg ^{ICPO}	No Report
Kazakhstan	1500.000 kg ^{Govt.}	4100.000 kg ^{Govt.}	298.635 kg	145.462 kg	No Report	276.160 kg ^{F.O}
Tajikistan	64.000 kg ^{F.O}	630.311 kg ^{F.O}	726.449 kg ^{F.O}	560.000 kg ^{F.O}	429.981 kg ^{F.O}	No Report
Turkmenistan	No Report	No Report	22249.000 kg ^{Govt.}	l0413.000 kg ^{F.O}	No Report	No Report
Uzbekistan	144.502 kg ^{ICPO}	316.055 kg	No Report	694.000 kg ^{F.O}	65.100 kg	86.000 kg ^{F.O}
Sub-Total	1717.586 kg	5046.366 kg	23297.340 kg	11813.480 kg	495.259 kg	377.772 kg
East and South-East Asia						
Hong Kong SAR, China	27.900 kg	38.900 kg	No Report	14.376 kg	6.004 kg	0.700 kg
Indonesia	2.050 kg	No Report	0.690 kg 230 u.	300.005 kg ^{HNLP}	3.885 kg	5.632 kg
Japan	145.143 kg	107.421 kg	214.560 kg	200.297 kg	185.416 kg	73.499 kg
Korea (Republic of)	No Report	0.635 kg	0.884 kg	1.963 kg	No Report	4.254 kg
Macau SAR, China	4.237 kg ^{ICPO}	No Report	0.995 kg ^{ICPO}	No Report	0.043 kg	0.499 kg
Mongolia	No Report	No Report	No Report	No Report	No Report	2 u.
Philippines	0.031 kg	0.283 kg ^{ICPO}	No Report	No Report	1.770 kg 2 u.	8.015 kg
Thailand	No Report	45.169 kg	20.592 kg	121.220 kg	91.903 kg ^{ICPO}	No Report
Sub-Total	179.361 kg	192.408 kg	237.721 kg 230 u.	637.860 kg	289.021 kg 2 u.	92.599 kg 2 u.
Near and Middle East /South-West Asia						
Bahrain	No Report	0.012 kg	1.036 kg ^{ICPO}	1263.049 kg ^{ICPO}	No Report	No Report
Iran (Islamic Republic of)	13063.000 kg	11095.789 kg	14376.364 kg	18907.000 kg	31581.000 kg ^{NAPOL}	46084.000 kg
Iraq	No Report	No Report	No Report	No Report	569.970 kg	2343.796 kg
Israel	83.578 kg	133.000 kg	60.900 kg	70.000 kg ^{ICPO}	30.218 kg	143.000 kg

Source: Annual Report Questionnaire if not otherwise indicated

SEIZURES 1996 - 2001

Cannabis resin

Region/country or territory	1996	1997	1998	1999	2000	2001
ASIA						
Near and Middle East /South-West Asia						
Jordan	No Report	No Report	166.737 kg	112.410 kg	298.456 kg	785.542 kg
Kuwait	3.668 kg [ICPO]	0.530 kg [ICPO]	214.103 kg	972.878 kg [ICPO]	3488.000 kg [F.O]	No Report
Lebanon	4908.757 kg	1876.281 kg	2492.609 kg	76.698 kg	358.000 kg [ICPO]	307.820 kg
Oman	1500.000 kg [INCB]	1979.000 kg [INCB]	No Report	14335.695 kg	No Report	2382.645 kg
Pakistan	192837.469 kg [ICPO]	107000.000 kg [ICPO]	65909.234 kg	81458.142 kg	129181.626 kg	75161.024 kg
Qatar	No Report	361.692 kg [ICPO]	374.526 kg [ICPO]	680.869 kg [ICPO]	134.586 kg [ICPO]	144.820 kg [ICPO]
Saudi Arabia	3531.225 kg [ICPO]	1321.285 kg [ICPO]	2357.874 kg	2003.000 kg [ICPO]	2719.091 kg 18 u.	1767.430 kg
United Arab Emirates	1377.591 kg	3505.585 kg	7087.219 kg	2530.511 kg	943.405 kg	6113.923 kg
Sub-Total	217305.300 kg	127273.200 kg	93040.600 kg	122410.300 kg	169304.400 kg 18 u.	135234.000 kg
South Asia						
Bangladesh	7.206 kg	No Report	No Report	0.700 kg [F.O]	0.001 kg	133.020 kg [ICPO]
India	6520.000 kg [Govt.]	3281.000 kg	10106.000 kg	3290.000 kg	5041.000 kg	5664.000 kg
Maldives	No Report	No Report	No Report	0.004 kg	No Report	No Report
Nepal	1917.372 kg	981.892 kg [Govt]	2585.886 kg [Govt]	1671.413 kg [Govt]	2539.936 kg [Govt]	No Report
Sri Lanka	11027.420 kg	17.756 kg	No Report	(1	0.011 kg	0.015 kg
Sub-Total	19472.000 kg	4280.648 kg	12691.890 kg	4962.117 kg	7580.948 kg	5797.035 kg
Total region	238674.200 kg	136792.600 kg	129267.500 kg 230 u.	139823.700 kg	177669.600 kg 20 u.	141501.400 kg 2 u.
EUROPE						
Eastern Europe						
Belarus	14.519 kg	5.380 kg [INCB]	0.509 kg	1.949 kg	0.639 kg	669.000 kg [ICPO]
Bosnia Herzegovina	No Report	0.500 kg [NAPOL]	No Report	0.002 kg [NAPOL]	No Report	0.060 kg [ICPO]
Bulgaria	8995.840 kg	533.570 kg	0.680 kg	0.010 kg	514.017 kg	422.584 kg
Croatia	3.104 kg	3.257 kg	2.878 kg	6.555 kg	1.041 kg	4.559 kg
Czech Republic	2.806 kg	0.324 kg	No Report	1.200 kg	23.099 kg	6.850 kg
Estonia	4.462 kg [ICPO]	0.316 kg	0.133 kg 52 u.	1.191 kg 191 u.	9.913 kg 58 u.	0.199 kg
FYR of Macedonia	2.534 kg [ICPO]	No Report	1.164 kg [NAPOL]	0.089 kg [NAPOL]	427.519 kg [NAPOL]	309.846 kg [Govt]
Hungary	816.215 kg	21.739 kg [Govt.]	6.803 kg	5.242 kg	22.538 kg	0.880 kg
Latvia	1.497 kg	0.646 kg	3.150 kg	0.685 kg	0.495 kg	0.191 kg
Lithuania	0.249 kg	0.078 kg	3.780 kg	1.054 kg	0.169 kg	0.260 kg
Poland	5.253 kg	628.000 kg	8.176 kg	49.203 kg	No Report	9.426 kg

Source: Annual Report Questionnaire if not otherwise indicated

SEIZURES 1996 - 2001
Cannabis resin

Region/country or territory	1996	1997	1998	1999	2000	2001
EUROPE						
Eastern Europe						
Republic of Moldova	0.209 kg	No Report	228.000 kg	No Report	523.000 kg ICPO	358.130 kg
Romania	4851.528 kg	1309.792 kg ICPO	1.673 kg	43.530 kg	340.810 kg (3	13871.000 kg
Russian Federation	650.500 kg	887.500 kg Govt.	1588.700 kg	710.895 kg	845.000 kg F.O	1335.671 kg
Serbia and Montenegro	No Report	No Report	No Report	No Report	No Report	4.534 kg
Slovakia	No Report	0.038 kg	0.015 kg	No Report	2.085 kg	0.635 kg
Slovenia	5.438 kg	0.938 kg	1.958 kg	64.622 kg	1.022 kg	2.360 kg
Ukraine	20.816 kg	9.500 kg	6150.100 kg	14.000 kg ICPO. (4	49.316 kg ICPO	11.130 kg
Sub-Total	15374.970 kg	3401.578 kg	7997.719 kg 52 u.	900.227 kg 191 u.	2760.663 kg 58 u.	17007.310 kg
Western Europe						
Andorra	No Report	No Report	1.372 kg ICPO	1.422 kg	3.061 kg ICPO	3.790 kg
Austria	247.039 kg	243.909 kg	124.718 kg	109.996 kg	243.673 kg	137.987 kg
Belgium	49899.000 kg	8980.000 kg	817.622 kg	3130.812 kg ICPO	532.163 kg	532.163 kg UNODC (5
Cyprus	29.905 kg	3.413 kg	1.201 kg	7.291 kg	9.525 kg	1.443 kg
Denmark	1772.400 kg	467.100 kg	1572.455 kg	14021.300 kg	2914.419 kg	1762.742 kg
Finland	99.444 kg	197.659 kg	160.972 kg	492.316 kg	196.540 kg	590.000 kg
France	35575.816 kg	51664.367 kg	52176.426 kg	64096.665 kg	48710.697 kg	58195.515 kg
Germany	3246.536 kg	7327.560 kg	6109.549 kg	4885.200 kg	8525.200 kg	6863.057 kg
Gibraltar	481.431 kg	655.882 kg	163.862 kg	30.171 kg	1.443 kg	1.016 kg
Greece	830.319 kg	6825.727 kg	30.817 kg	55.819 kg	56.120 kg	270.780 kg
Iceland	No Report	No Report	No Report	41.622 kg	26.626 kg	44.140 kg
Ireland	1933.000 kg	1247.244 kg	3179.178 kg	2514.975 kg	379.800 kg	567.026 kg
Italy	5939.923 kg	14740.517 kg 1954 u.	15412.128 kg 711 u.	46780.319 kg ICPO	20725.364 kg 818 u.	16455.477 kg 811 u.
Liechtenstein	0.082 kg	0.008 kg	2.770 kg	No Report	No Report	0.012 kg
Luxembourg	14.419 kg	0.868 kg	1.974 kg	1.270 kg	1.174 kg ICPO	No Report
Malta	1.067 kg	1.788 kg	25.116 kg	1.606 kg	3.913 kg	3.562 kg
Monaco	0.651 kg	0.170 kg	0.396 kg	0.111 kg ICPO	0.512 kg ICPO	No Report
Netherlands	38047.000 kg Govt	30272.000 kg Govt	70696.000 kg Govt	61226.000 kg Govt	29590.000 kg Govt	10972.000 kg
Norway	641.000 kg	904.059 kg	1874.136 kg	1254.762 kg	632.647 kg	808.541 kg
Portugal	5324.091 kg	9621.183 kg	5747.793 kg	10636.075 kg	30467.121 kg	6472.688 kg
Spain	247745.094 kg	315328.000 kg ICPO	428236.375 kg	431165.280 kg	474504.785 kg	514181.600 kg
Sweden	304.112 kg	627.994 kg	390.930 kg	1065.387 kg 26 u.	1206.709 kg	772.462 kg
Switzerland	676.736 kg	653.467 kg	1837.480 kg	651.548 kg	1258.307 kg ICPO	317.550 kg

Source: Annual Report Questionnaire if not otherwise indicated

SEIZURES 1996 - 2001
Cannabis resin

Region/country or territory	1996	1997	1998	1999	2000	2001
EUROPE						
Western Europe						
Turkey	12294.000 kg	10439.201 kg	9434.290 kg	11085.546 kg	28637.130 kg	268.477 kg
United Kingdom	66936.703 kg	118849.203 kg	82837.533 kg	33727.243 kg [ICPO]	48346.903 kg	48346.903 kg [UNODC] (5
				194 u.		
Sub-Total	472039.800 kg	579051.300 kg 1954 u.	680835.200 kg 711 u.	686982.800 kg 220 u.	696973.800 kg 818 u.	667568.900 kg 811 u.
Total region	487414.800 kg	582452.900 kg 1954 u.	688832.900 kg 763 u.	687883.000 kg 411 u.	699734.500 kg 876 u.	684576.300 kg 811 u.
OCEANIA						
Oceania						
Australia	9.195 kg 246 u.	537.289 kg	No Report	4.129 kg	17.972 kg	3266.944 kg
New Caledonia	No Report	0.003 kg [INCB]	No Report	No Report	No Report	No Report
New Zealand	No Report	2.198 kg [INCB]	3.632 kg	0.676 kg	No Report	0.435 kg
Sub-Total	9.195 kg 246 u.	539.490 kg	3.632 kg	4.805 kg	17.972 kg	3267.379 kg
Total region	9.195 kg 246 u.	539.490 kg	3.632 kg	4.805 kg	17.972 kg	3267.379 kg
TOTAL	877973.300 kg 246 u.	818424.900 kg 1954 u.	895535.800 kg 0.002 lt. 1090 u.	898295.900 kg 1.000 lt. 6449 u.	1080687.000 kg 38.000 lt. 927 u.	896768.800 kg 844 u.

1) Small quantity. 2) Including depressants. 3) Including cannabis herb. 4) Provisional figures. 5) Due to unavailability of 2001 data, year 2000 data were used for analysis purposes.

Source: Annual Report Questionnaire if not otherwise indicated

SEIZURES 1996 - 2001
Cannabis oil

Region/country or territory	1996	1997	1998	1999	2000	2001
AFRICA						
East Africa						
Kenya	No Report	No Report	No Report	4.057 kg	No Report	No Report
Sub-Total				4.057 kg		
North Africa						
Morocco	4.295 kg	1.060 kg ^{Govt.}	14.473 kg	19.000 lt.	0.693 kg	0.008 kg
Sub-Total	4.295 kg	1.060 kg	14.473 kg	19.000 lt.	0.693 kg	0.008 kg
Southern Africa						
Zambia	2.000 kg ^{Govt}	0.000 kg ^{Govt}	0.000 kg ^{Govt}	0.000 kg ^{Govt}	0.000 kg ^{Govt}	8.500 kg ^{Govt}
Zimbabwe	2.000 kg ^{ICPO}	No Report	No Report	No Report	No Report	No Report
Sub-Total	4.000 kg					8.500 kg
West and Central Africa						
Benin	No Report	No Report	26.863 kg	No Report	No Report	No Report
Sub-Total			26.863 kg			
Total region	8.295 kg	1.060 kg	41.336 kg	4.057 kg 19.000 lt.	0.693 kg	8.508 kg
AMERICAS						
Caribbean						
Aruba	No Report	No Report	No Report	0.002 kg ^{ICPO}	No Report	No Report
Bahamas	No Report	0.020 kg ^{ICPO}	No Report	104.089 kg ^{ICPO}	0.450 kg	No Report
Cayman Islands	No Report	46.036 kg 2 u.	No Report	No Report	No Report	No Report
Cuba	38.722 kg	No Report	No Report	No Report	No Report	No Report
Haiti	No Report		11.000 kg ^{CICAD}	No Report	No Report	No Report
Jamaica	263.420 kg ^{ICPO}	383.820 kg ^{ICPO}	No Report	371.490 kg ^{ICPO}	579.091 kg ^{ICPO}	210.980 kg
Saint Vincent and the Grenadines	No Report	No Report	No Report	No Report	28375 u. ^{INCSR}	No Report
Trinidad Tobago	No Report	1430.000 kg ^{CICAD}	No Report	No Report	No Report	No Report
Sub-Total	302.142 kg	1859.876 kg 2 u.	11.000 kg	475.581 kg	579.541 kg 28375 u.	210.980 kg
Central America						
Panama	No Report	No Report	No Report	11.360 lt.	No Report	No Report
Sub-Total				11.360 lt.		
North America						
Canada	802.115 kg 114.667 lt.	824.000 kg	524.937 kg 20.166 lt. 2 u.	434.000 kg 55.302 lt. 6 u.	28.000 kg 187.392 lt. 13 u.	120.191 kg 16 u.
United States	248.289 kg	No Report	No Report	490.685 kg	66.152 kg	59.700 kg

Source: Annual Report Questionnaire if not otherwise indicated

SEIZURES 1996 - 2001
Cannabis oil

Region/country or territory	1996	1997	1998	1999	2000	2001
AMERICAS						
North America						
Sub-Total	1050.404 kg	824.000 kg	524.937 kg	924.685 kg	94.152 kg	179.891 kg
	114.667 lt.		20.166 lt.	55.302 lt.	187.392 lt.	16 u.
			2 u.	6 u.	13 u.	
South America						
Chile	No Report	No Report	No Report	0.025 kg [ICPO]	No Report	No Report
Colombia	199.250 lt.	8.000 lt.	No Report	No Report	No Report	No Report
Suriname	No Report	No Report	No Report	No Report	No Report	0.217 kg
Venezuela	No Report	8003.000 kg [CICAD]	No Report	No Report	No Report	No Report
Sub-Total	199.250 lt.	8003.000 kg		0.025 kg		0.217 kg
		8.000 lt.				
Total region	1352.546 kg	10686.880 kg	535.937 kg	1400.291 kg	673.693 kg	391.088 kg
	313.917 lt.	8.000 lt.	20.166 lt.	66.662 lt.	187.392 lt.	16 u.
		2 u.	2 u.	6 u.	28388 u.	
ASIA						
Central Asia and Transcaucasian countries						
Armenia	No Report	No Report	22.353 kg	0.002 kg [ICPO]	0.000 kg [(1]	0.007 kg
Azerbaijan	3.378 kg [ICPO]	1.793 kg [ICPO]	No Report	No Report	No Report	No Report
Georgia	0.002 kg [ICPO]	No Report	No Report	No Report	No Report	No Report
Kyrgyzstan	No Report	603.554 kg	1569.238 kg	No Report	No Report	No Report
Sub-Total	3.380 kg	605.347 kg	1591.591 kg	0.002 kg	0.000 kg	0.007 kg
East and South-East Asia						
Brunei Darussalam	No Report	No Report	No Report	No Report	No Report	0.260 lt.
Indonesia	0.546 kg	4.017 kg	No Report	300.005 kg	3.886 kg [ICPO]	No Report
Japan	0.081 lt.	0.143 lt.	3.750 kg	0.002 kg		0.000 lt.
				0.002 lt.		
Korea (Republic of)	No Report	0.027 kg	No Report	No Report	No Report	No Report
Thailand	32.766 kg [ICPO]	No Report	No Report	No Report	0.516 kg [ICPO]	No Report
Sub-Total	33.312 kg	4.044 kg	3.750 kg	300.007 kg	4.402 kg	0.260 lt.
	0.081 lt.	0.143 lt.		0.002 lt.		
Near and Middle East /South-West Asia						
Iran (Islamic Republic of)	No Report	No Report	No Report	68.000 kg [ICPO]	No Report	No Report
Jordan	No Report	0.145 kg	No Report	No Report	No Report	No Report
Lebanon	6.000 kg	58.000 kg	No Report	No Report	10.000 kg	No Report
Sub-Total	6.000 kg	58.145 kg		68.000 kg	10.000 kg	
South Asia						
Maldives	No Report	No Report	No Report	0.001 kg	No Report	0.003 kg

Source: Annual Report Questionnaire if not otherwise indicated

SEIZURES 1996 - 2001
Cannabis oil

Region/country or territory	1996	1997	1998	1999	2000	2001
ASIA						
South Asia						
Nepal	No Report	1342.492 kg [ICPO]	No Report	2.100 kg	No Report	No Report
Sub-Total		1342.492 kg		2.101 kg		0.003 kg
Total region	42.692 kg 0.081 lt.	2010.028 kg 0.143 lt.	1595.341 kg	370.110 kg 0.002 lt.	14.402 kg	0.010 kg 0.260 lt.
EUROPE						
Eastern Europe						
Albania	No Report	No Report	No Report	13.000 lt. [ICPO]	2.100 lt. [ICPO]	No Report
Belarus	No Report	No Report	No Report	0.002 kg	No Report	No Report
Bulgaria	No Report	No Report	No Report	0.100 kg	0.080 kg	6 u.
Croatia	No Report	No Report	0.008 kg	No Report	No Report	No Report
Estonia	No Report	No Report	No Report	No Report	0.300 kg 2 u.	No Report
Russian Federation	42.200 kg	No Report	102.900 kg [F.O]	141.344 kg	291.000 kg [F.O]	366.590 kg
Slovakia	No Report	No Report	No Report	No Report	64.000 kg	No Report
Sub-Total	42.200 kg		102.908 kg	141.446 kg 13.000 lt.	355.380 kg 2.100 lt. 2 u.	366.590 kg 6 u.
Western Europe						
Austria	0.228 kg	3.164 kg	No Report	No Report	0.750 kg [ICPO]	0.188 kg
Belgium	No Report	No Report	No Report	5.000 kg	No Report	No Report
Cyprus	No Report	No Report	No Report	30.294 kg	No Report	No Report
Denmark	2.420 kg	0.123 kg	0.008 kg	3.910 kg	0.962 kg	0.019 kg
France	5.238 kg	5.442 kg	0.592 kg	1.690 kg	2.830 kg	3.513 kg
Germany	1.786 kg	3.510 kg	0.538 kg	2.300 kg	4.500 kg	0.044 kg
Greece	No Report	No Report	No Report	0.200 kg [ICPO]	1.205 kg	1.910 kg
Italy	0.217 kg	6.259 kg 6 u.	0.635 kg 3 u.	6.772 kg [ICPO]	13.349 kg 5 u.	25.263 kg 171 u.
Monaco	No Report	0.029 lt.	No Report	No Report	No Report	No Report
Netherlands	508.000 lt. [Govt]	No Report	150.000 lt. [Govt]	1.000 lt. [Govt]	No Report	No Report
Norway	0.052 kg	0.308 kg	0.034 kg	0.026 kg	0.028 kg	0.009 kg
Portugal	No Report	No Report	No Report	0.001 kg	0.004 kg	0.134 kg
Spain	962 u.	0.705 lt.	74.970 lt.	2346 u.	0.310 lt.	1915.500 kg
Sweden	0.091 kg	0.019 kg	No Report	0.006 kg	No Report	0.203 kg
Switzerland	1.710 kg	8.607 kg	1.541 kg	0.609 kg	95.082 kg	17.577 kg
Turkey	No Report	No Report	63.411 kg	No Report	2.480 kg	0.001 kg
United Kingdom	17.500 kg	26.600 kg	7.366 kg	No Report	4.491 kg	4.491 kg [UNODC (2]

Source: Annual Report Questionnaire if not otherwise indicated

SEIZURES 1996 - 2001
Cannabis oil

Region/country or territory	1996	1997	1998	1999	2000	2001
EUROPE						
Western Europe						
Sub-Total	29.242 kg	54.032 kg	74.125 kg	50.808 kg	125.681 kg	1968.852 kg
	508.000 lt.	0.734 lt.	224.970 lt.	1.000 lt.	0.310 lt.	171 u.
	962 u.	6 u.	3 u.	2346 u.	5 u.	
Total region	71.442 kg	54.032 kg	177.033 kg	192.254 kg	481.061 kg	2335.442 kg
	508.000 lt.	0.734 lt.	224.970 lt.	14.000 lt.	2.410 lt.	177 u.
	962 u.	6 u.	3 u.	2346 u.	7 u.	
OCEANIA						
Oceania						
Australia	1.095 kg	4.945 kg	No Report	2.650 kg	0.755 lt.	No Report
	40 u.					
New Zealand	No Report	No Report	4.159 kg	0.026 kg	8.305 kg	3.147 kg
Sub-Total	1.095 kg	4.945 kg	4.159 kg	2.676 kg	8.305 kg	3.147 kg
	40 u.				0.755 lt.	
Total region	1.095 kg	4.945 kg	4.159 kg	2.676 kg	8.305 kg	3.147 kg
	40 u.				0.755 lt.	
TOTAL	1476.070 kg	12756.940 kg	2353.806 kg	1969.388 kg	1178.154 kg	2738.195 kg
	821.998 lt.	8.877 lt.	245.136 lt.	99.664 lt.	190.557 lt.	0.260 lt.
	1002 u.	8 u.	5 u.	2352 u.	28395 u.	193 u.

1) Small quantity. 2) Due to unavailability of 2001 data, year 2000 data were used for analysis purposes.

Source: Annual Report Questionnaire if not otherwise indicated

SEIZURES 1996 - 2001

Cannabis plant

Region/country or territory	1996	1997	1998	1999	2000	2001
AFRICA						
East Africa						
Eritrea	No Report	No Report	No Report	No Report	No Report	20.000 kg
Kenya	No Report	5.565 kg 2226 u.	No Report	No Report	No Report	No Report
Mauritius	22066 u.	41316 u.	43294 u.	45444 u.	55038 u.	30788 u.
Seychelles	No Report	No Report	No Report	30.700 kg	7.233 kg	No Report
Uganda	4000 u.	No Report	9411 u.	35000 u.	54700 u.	780000 u.
Sub-Total	26066 u.	5.565 kg 43542 u.	52705 u.	30.700 kg 80444 u.	7.233 kg 109738 u.	20.000 kg 810788 u.
North Africa						
Egypt	231482720 u.	63542820 u.	35150384 u.	No Report	No Report	470 u.
Morocco	No Report	No Report	No Report	No Report	No Report	73810.724 kg
Sub-Total	231482700 u.	63542820 u.	35150380 u.			73810.730 kg 470 u.
Southern Africa						
Angola	No Report	No Report	No Report	5733 u.	No Report	No Report
Lesotho	2625 u. [Govt.]	No Report	No Report	No Report	No Report	No Report
Malawi	22959 u.	1116.725 kg 8313 u.	6371.045 kg	9428.350 kg	61182.146 kg	51611.136 kg
Namibia	No Report	No Report	No Report	25 u.	No Report	67 u.
South Africa	69450.977 kg	243565.688 kg	784201.063 kg	No Report	864234.300 kg	608330.095 kg
Swaziland	No Report	No Report	7517.000 kg	2528136 u.	36665 u.	No Report
Zimbabwe	No Report	No Report	300.000 kg 2936 u.	165 u.	3555 u.	878 u.
Sub-Total	69450.980 kg 25584 u.	244682.400 kg 8313 u.	798389.100 kg 2936 u.	9428.350 kg 2534059 u.	925416.400 kg 40220 u.	659941.300 kg 945 u.
West and Central Africa						
Cameroon	No Report	No Report	No Report	No Report	No Report	2649.008 kg
Congo	No Report	3435.000 kg	No Report	10.000 kg [1	No Report	No Report
Côte d'Ivoire	502 u.	No Report	200 u.	No Report	No Report	No Report
Gambia	No Report	No Report	No Report	834.982 kg	No Report	700.000 kg
Ghana	[2	No Report	No Report	No Report	No Report	No Report
Guinea-Bissau	No Report	No Report	No Report	No Report	No Report	8.000 kg
Nigeria	No Report	No Report	1712580.000 [Govt.] kg	No Report	No Report	270250.000 kg
Saint Helena	No Report	18 u.	17 u.	17 u.	6 u.	5 u.
Togo	No Report	No Report	No Report	No Report	50.000 kg	No Report

Source: Annual Report Questionnaire if not otherwise indicated

SEIZURES 1996 - 2001
Cannabis plant

Region/country or territory	1996	1997	1998	1999	2000	2001
AFRICA						
West and Central Africa						
Sub-Total	502 u.	3435.000 kg 18 u.	1712580.000 kg 217 u.	844.982 kg 17 u.	50.000 kg 6 u.	273607.000 kg 5 u.
Total region	69450.980 kg 231534900 u.	248123.000 kg 63594690 u.	2510969.000 kg 35206240 u.	10304.030 kg 2614520 u.	925473.700 kg 149964 u.	1007379.000 kg 812208 u.
AMERICAS						
Caribbean						
Anguilla	No Report	48 u.	40 u.	No Report	No Report	No Report
Antigua and Barbuda	No Report	No Report	No Report	23384 u. CICAD	9317 u. CICAD	No Report
Bahamas	No Report	No Report	99 u.	No Report	1466 u.	10207 u.
Barbados	No Report	No Report	400 u. CICAD	81 u. HONLC	1078 u. CICAD	No Report
Bermuda	53 u.	871 u.	No Report	268 u.	230 u.	No Report
British Virgin Islands	No Report	No Report	No Report	No Report	No Report	4556 u.
Cuba	3517 u.	No Report	No Report	No Report	No Report	No Report
Dominica	176713 u.	No Report	No Report	55120 u. CICAD	123032 u. CICAD	No Report
Dominican Republic	110 u.	116 u.	346 u.	1991 u.	1114 u. CICAD	6578 u.
Grenada	No Report	No Report	6212.000 kg	12086 u. CICAD	2091 u. INCSR	6611 u.
Haiti	No Report	No Report	No Report	No Report	No Report	1705.000 kg
Jamaica	No Report	6858.300 kg ICPO	No Report	No Report	No Report	34 u.
Montserrat	No Report	No Report	No Report	No Report	1008 u.	No Report
Saint Kitts and Nevis	32926 u. CICAD	126293 u. CICAD	36000 u. CICAD	63911 u. CICAD	34057 u. INCSR	No Report
Saint Lucia	163893 u.	26037 u.	69200 u.	18047 u. CICAD	83090 u.	No Report
Saint Vincent and the Grenadines	No Report	No Report	1500 u. CICAD	4760 u. CICAD	28375 u. CICAD	No Report
Trinidad Tobago	No Report	No Report	2869850 u.	4415958 u. CICAD	7200000 u. INCSR	3122894 u.
Sub-Total	377212 u.	6858.300 kg 153365 u.	6212.000 kg 2977435 u.	4595606 u.	7484858 u.	1705.000 kg 3150880 u.
Central America						
Belize	87546 u. CICAD	294712.000 CICAD kg	202803 u. CICAD	270136 u. CICAD	143000 u. CICAD	70607 u.
Costa Rica	110002 u.	No Report	733089 u.	2153645 u.	2048421 u.	1906454 u.
El Salvador	No Report	No Report	No Report	4688 u.	No Report	1126 u.
Guatemala	1052845 u.	587096 u. Govt.	576060 u.	594378 u.	293897 u.	418097 u.
Honduras	2309.000 kg CICAD	337322 u.	286414 u. CICAD	133680 u. CICAD	83859 u. CICAD	No Report
Nicaragua	53528.000 kg	24239.000 kg	833943 u.	13569 u. CICAD	83070 u. CICAD	No Report
Panama	No Report	No Report	No Report	25102 u.	No Report	36950 u.

Source: Annual Report Questionnaire if not otherwise indicated

SEIZURES 1996 - 2001
Cannabis plant

Region/country or territory	1996	1997	1998	1999	2000	2001
AMERICAS						
Central America						
Sub-Total	55837.000 kg 1250393 u.	318951.000 kg 924418 u.	2632309 u.	3195198 u.	2652247 u.	2433234 u.
North America						
Canada	No Report	776288 u.	1025808 u.	1304477 u.	1199423 u.	86456.827 kg 508039 u.
United States	676866.375 Govt. kg	No Report	No Report	497.366 kg	163.344 kg	4561.900 kg
Sub-Total	676866.400 kg	776288 u.	1025808 u.	497.366 kg 1304477 u.	163.344 kg 1199423 u.	91018.730 kg 508039 u.
South America						
Argentina	2152 u. Govt.	458 u.	1296 u.	1222 u.	676 u.	1687 u.
Bolivia	No Report	3450.000 kg	No Report	No Report	No Report	705.536 kg
Brazil	1523.200 kg	2884811 u.	3371112 u.	3462158 u.	3699601 u.	3823846 u. Govt
Chile	94481 u.	34263 u.	956.942 kg 759 u.	No Report	63621 u.	98892 u.
Colombia	37.000 kg	No Report	No Report	No Report	No Report	No Report
Ecuador	336 u.	1 u.	126 u.	0.339 kg	No Report	No Report
Falkland Islands	No Report	No Report	1 u.	No Report	No Report	No Report
Guyana	52181.000 kg	18993.000 kg ICPO	No Report	No Report	31698 u. CICAD	No Report
Paraguay	749412.500 kg	2009500 u.	1415875.000 kg	3769000 u.	1366500 u. CICAD	No Report
Peru	150481.219 kg	140700.000 kg	No Report	5418.300 kg	29566.400 kg	38106.465 kg 2 u.
Suriname	35.000 kg	65.838 kg	500 u.	No Report	No Report	No Report
Uruguay	16 u. Govt.	No Report	No Report	No Report	5 u.	No Report
Venezuela	No Report	No Report	No Report	No Report	26 u.	No Report
Sub-Total	953669.900 kg 96985 u.	163208.800 kg 4929033 u.	1416832.000 kg 3373794 u.	5418.639 kg 7232380 u.	29566.400 kg 5162127 u.	38812.000 kg 3924427 u.
Total region	1686373.000 kg 1724590 u.	489018.200 kg 6783104 u.	1423044.000 kg 10009350 u.	5916.005 kg 16327660 u.	29729.740 kg 16498660 u.	131535.700 kg 10016580 u.
ASIA						
Central Asia and Transcaucasian countries						
Armenia	No Report	No Report	24.218 kg	No Report	No Report	No Report
Azerbaijan	No Report	507380.000 kg ICPO	489000.000 kg	405669.000 kg	No Report	317000.000 kg
Kazakhstan	No Report	No Report	200.077 kg	1869.000 kg	No Report	No Report
Uzbekistan	No Report	18.930 kg	663.316 kg	238.772 kg	No Report	No Report

Source: Annual Report Questionnaire if not otherwise indicated

SEIZURES 1996 - 2001
Cannabis plant

Region/country or territory	1996	1997	1998	1999	2000	2001
ASIA						
Central Asia and Transcaucasian countries						
Sub-Total		507398.900 kg	489887.600 kg	407776.800 kg		317000.000 kg
East and South-East Asia						
Brunei Darussalam	No Report	1 u.	No Report	No Report	6 u.	No Report
Hong Kong SAR, China	No Report	No Report	No Report	No Report	No Report	2103.900 kg
Indonesia	80823 u.	200000.000 kg 132748 u.	47515 u.	78072 u.	No Report	2061 u.
Japan	7.247 kg 3301 u.	36.922 kg 2232 u.	23.954 kg 1668 u.	26.422 kg	95.617 kg 50 u.	77.020 kg 2022 u.
Korea (Republic of)	47465 u.	31501 u.	3815 u.	10705 u.	No Report	4255 u.
Lao People's Dem. Rep.	104595.000 [Govt.] kg	No Report	No Report	No Report	No Report	No Report
Mongolia	No Report	No Report	No Report	No Report	No Report	5 u.
Philippines	12161117 u.	No Report	518939.000 [ICPO] kg	5005860 u. [(3]	2599724 u.	754223.844 kg
Thailand	No Report	19951.301 kg	13401.892 kg	42996.497 kg	No Report	No Report
Sub-Total	104602.300 kg 12292710 u.	219988.200 kg 166482 u.	532364.900 kg 52998 u.	43022.920 kg 5094637 u.	95.617 kg 2599780 u.	756404.800 kg 8343 u.
Near and Middle East /South-West Asia						
Bahrain	0.164 kg	No Report	No Report	No Report	No Report	No Report
Iraq	5.305 kg	34.812 kg	55.905 kg	No Report	No Report	No Report
Jordan	No Report	No Report	1.120 kg	62.525 kg	18.032 kg	No Report
Lebanon	No Report	No Report	No Report	4445.880 kg	No Report	80.000 kg
Qatar	220.899 kg	No Report	No Report	No Report	No Report	No Report
United Arab Emirates	No Report	No Report	No Report	No Report	No Report	0.214 kg
Sub-Total	226.368 kg	34.812 kg	57.025 kg	4508.405 kg	18.032 kg	80.214 kg
South Asia						
Bangladesh	25307 u.	No Report	No Report	11826 u. [F.O]	1840 u.	No Report
India	No Report	No Report	No Report	No Report	No Report	174818.000 kg
Sri Lanka	65010.000 kg	49900.000 kg	21375.000 kg	372000.000 kg	32524.344 kg	No Report
Sub-Total	65010.000 kg 25307 u.	49900.000 kg	21375.000 kg	372000.000 kg 11826 u.	32524.340 kg 1840 u.	174818.000 kg
Total region	169838.600 kg 12318010 u.	777321.900 kg 166482 u.	1043685.000 kg 52998 u.	827308.100 kg 5106463 u.	32637.990 kg 2601620 u.	1248303.000 kg 8343 u.

Source: Annual Report Questionnaire if not otherwise indicated

SEIZURES 1996 - 2001
Cannabis plant

Region/country or territory	1996	1997	1998	1999	2000	2001
EUROPE						
Eastern Europe						
Belarus	No Report	No Report	117.000 kg	No Report	No Report	No Report
Bosnia Herzegovina	487 u. NAPOL	443 u. NAPOL	1445 u. NAPOL	16222 u. NAPOL	451 u. NAPOL	No Report
Bulgaria	50000.000 kg	127000.000 kg	16000.000 kg	2742 u.	12713.026 kg	21390.000 kg
			10943 u.		3448 u.	
Croatia	4602 u.	31710 u.	5131 u.	3050 u.	1739 u.	2843 u.
Czech Republic	11866.134 kg	No Report	No Report	No Report	No Report	343 u.
Estonia	No Report	72 u.	23.184 kg	41.973 kg	67.647 kg	192.062 kg
			92 u.	175 u.	585 u.	
FYR of Macedonia	No Report	No Report	1457 u.	151262 u. NAPOL	No Report	606 u. Govt
Hungary	140 u.	No Report	1033 u.	620.000 kg	2217 u.	No Report
Poland	200.000 kg	12105.075 kg	1904.362 kg	900.000 kg	1.008 kg	15.000 kg
Romania	No Report	No Report	215.923 kg	No Report	No Report	No Report
Slovakia	No Report	No Report	2830.680 kg	848.797 kg	No Report	817.226 kg
Slovenia	5019 u.	44944 u.	14453 u.	8196 u.	6.011 kg	1925 u.
					3354 u.	
Ukraine	2159.000 kg	6091.000 kg	5103.364 kg	No Report	No Report	No Report
Sub-Total	64225.130 kg	145196.100 kg	26194.510 kg	2410.770 kg	12787.690 kg	22414.290 kg
	10248 u.	77169 u.	34554 u.	181647 u.	11794 u.	5717 u.
Western Europe						
Austria	No Report	No Report	No Report	No Report	7991 u.	35.721 kg
Belgium	No Report	653.000 kg	6280.000 kg	2911.166 kg		UNODC (4
Cyprus	260 u.	787 u.	276 u.	190 u.	493 u.	274 u.
Denmark	2177.600 kg	2692.300 kg	949.969 kg	337.290 kg	No Report	No Report
Finland	2065 u.	82.519 kg	2.334 kg	5.251 kg	14.041 kg	16.000 kg
		2328 u.	2900 u.	2789 u.	5325 u.	4900 u.
France	38341 u.	38115 u.	34266 u.	23287 u.	24295 u.	No Report
Germany	53179 u.	5000.000 kg	81097 u.	168833 u.	25277 u.	68696 u.
		67065 u.				
Gibraltar	1 u.	No Report	13 u.	14 u.	3 u.	10 u.
Greece	15192 u.	11010 u.	9967 u.	46198 u.	49985 u.	18821 u.
Ireland	542 u.	753 u.	400 u.	No Report	98 u.	365 u.
Italy	491390 u.	379851 u.	190240 u.	ICPO	1306469 u.	3219414 u.
Liechtenstein	No Report	No Report	1300.000 kg	3.686 kg	42.600 kg	No Report
Luxembourg	No Report	No Report	222 u.	No Report	No Report	No Report
Malta	100 u.	153 u.	5 u.	35 u.	22 u.	11 u.
Netherlands	1272526 u. Govt	553135 u. Govt	353178 u. Govt	582588 u. Govt	661851 u. Govt	844.000 kg
						884609 u.

Source: Annual Report Questionnaire if not otherwise indicated

SEIZURES 1996 - 2001
Cannabis plant

Region/country or territory	1996	1997	1998	1999	2000	2001
EUROPE						
Western Europe						
Norway	7.300 kg	23.329 kg	23.041 kg	28.546 kg	18.854 kg	17.628 kg 123 u.
Portugal	1646 u.	7982 u.	17316 u.	1184 u.	1.936 kg 2279 u.	3807 u.
Spain	14001.399 kg	1734.002 kg	3072.938 kg	2319.031 kg	18156.043 kg	3907.120 kg
Sweden	4.165 kg	2.426 kg 269 u.	6.890 kg	39.820 kg 249 u.	3.213 kg 251 u.	2.789 kg
Switzerland	32488 u.	313258 u.	26813 u.	79746 u.	227476 u.	189008 u.
Turkey	No Report	52100620 u.	55655864 u.	19736000 u.	327.750 kg 29168530 u.	20243988 u.
United Kingdom	116218 u.	114988 u.	72040 u.	382 u. [ICPO]	47816 u.	47816 u. [UNODC (4]
Sub-Total	16190.470 kg 2023948 u.	10187.580 kg 53590320 u.	11635.170 kg 56444600 u.	5644.790 kg 20641490 u.	18564.440 kg 31528160 u.	4823.258 kg 24681840 u.
Total region	80415.590 kg 2034196 u.	155383.700 kg 53667480 u.	37829.680 kg 56479150 u.	8055.560 kg 20823140 u.	31352.130 kg 31539950 u.	27237.550 kg 24687560 u.
OCEANIA						
Oceania						
Australia	2745.057 kg 187837 u.	4445.335 kg	No Report	176.150 kg	90060 u.	22973 u.
Cook Islands	2 u.	No Report	No Report	No Report	No Report	No Report
Fiji	5388 u.	No Report	No Report	No Report	No Report	No Report
New Zealand	No Report	266867 u.	164531 u.	173277 u.	10157 u.	90857 u.
Sub-Total	2745.057 kg 193227 u.	4445.335 kg 266867 u.	164531 u.	176.150 kg 173277 u.	100217 u.	113830 u.
Total region	2745.057 kg 193227 u.	4445.335 kg 266867 u.	164531 u.	176.150 kg 173277 u.	100217 u.	113830 u.
TOTAL	2008824.000 kg 247804900 u.	1674292.000 kg 124478600 u.	5015527.000 kg 101912300 u.	851759.900 kg 45045060 u.	1019194.000 kg 50890410 u.	2414455.000 kg 35638520 u.

1) Including cannabis seeds. 2) Included in cannabis herb. 3) Includes seedlings 4) Due to unavailability of 2001 data, year 2000 data were used for analysis purposes.

Source: Annual Report Questionnaire if not otherwise indicated

SEIZURES 1996 - 2001

Cannabis seed

Region/country or territory	1996	1997	1998	1999	2000	2001
AFRICA						
East Africa						
Mauritius	167 u.	No Report	No Report	No Report	0.076 kg	No Report
Uganda	10.350 kg	No Report	5.000 kg	No Report	102.800 kg	No Report
Sub-Total	10.350 kg 167 u.		5.000 kg		102.876 kg	
North Africa						
Algeria	No Report	No Report	0.930 kg [ICPO]	No Report	No Report	No Report
Egypt	No Report	33.421 kg	11.504 kg	115.819 kg	24.323 kg	No Report
Sub-Total		33.421 kg	12.434 kg	115.819 kg	24.323 kg	
Southern Africa						
Lesotho	No Report	No Report	No Report	35.280 kg [ICPO]	No Report	No Report
Namibia	278.295 kg	No Report	No Report	No Report	No Report	No Report
Swaziland	No Report	No Report	8.096 kg	No Report	263.840 kg	No Report
Zambia	0.044 kg [Govt]	7.130 kg [Govt]	38.597 kg [Govt]	126.280 kg	52.261 kg	13.500 kg [Govt]
Zimbabwe	No Report	No Report	0.200 kg	No Report	No Report	No Report
Sub-Total	278.339 kg	7.130 kg	46.893 kg	161.560 kg	316.101 kg	13.500 kg
West and Central Africa						
Saint Helena	No Report	No Report	100 u.	80 u.	No Report	No Report
Sub-Total			100 u.	80 u.		
Total region	288.689 kg 167 u.	40.551 kg	64.327 kg 100 u.	277.379 kg 80 u.	443.300 kg	13.500 kg
AMERICAS						
Caribbean						
Anguilla	No Report	No Report	8 u.	No Report	No Report	No Report
Bermuda	0.010 kg	No Report	No Report	No Report	No Report	No Report
Cuba	2836 u.	No Report	No Report	No Report	No Report	No Report
Dominica	4.248 kg	No Report	No Report	No Report	No Report	No Report
Dominican Republic	200 u.	72 u.	1327 u.	3642 u.	679.000 kg [CICAD]	No Report
Grenada	No Report	No Report	0.004 kg	No Report	No Report	No Report
Jamaica	No Report	No Report	No Report	452.630 kg [ICPO]	No Report	No Report
Montserrat	No Report	No Report	No Report	No Report	2500 u.	No Report
Saint Lucia	No Report	No Report	No Report	No Report	0.311 kg	No Report
Sub-Total	4.258 kg 3036 u.	72 u.	0.004 kg 1335 u.	452.630 kg 3642 u.	679.311 kg 2500 u.	
Central America						
Guatemala	427.607 kg	1.840 kg [Govt.]	5.100 kg	78.473 kg	24.200 kg	No Report
Honduras	No Report	3.400 kg	No Report	No Report	2.000 kg [CICAD]	No Report

Source: Annual Report Questionnaire if not otherwise indicated

SEIZURES 1996 - 2001
Cannabis seed

Region/country or territory	1996	1997	1998	1999	2000	2001
AMERICAS						
Central America						
Nicaragua	5.181 kg	2.063 kg	No Report	No Report	1.000 kg CICAD	No Report
Sub-Total	432.788 kg	7.303 kg	5.100 kg	78.473 kg	27.200 kg	
North America						
Mexico	5098.837 kg	3968.381 kg	4948.744 kg	5847.545 kg	10353.807 kg	No Report
United States	229291.750 kg	No Report	No Report	412271.587 kg 451 u.	417120.258 kg 102 u.	No Report
Sub-Total	234390.600 kg	3968.381 kg	4948.744 kg	418119.100 kg 451 u.	427474.100 kg 102 u.	
South America						
Argentina	10.970 kg Govt.	39.440 kg	42.790 kg 1950 u.	0.091 kg	0.276 kg	1.255 kg
Brazil	84.622 kg	68.314 kg	5.179 kg	55.804 kg	99.047 kg	No Report
Chile	0.601 kg	No Report	0.377 kg	No Report	No Report	No Report
Colombia	49.000 kg	120.000 kg Govt.	127.789 kg	25.214 kg	121.000 kg	No Report
Guyana	6.772 kg	No Report	No Report	No Report	No Report	No Report
Paraguay	207.550 kg	167.550 kg	503.110 kg	2130.025 kg	668.000 kg CICAD	No Report
Peru	1.924 kg	9.377 kg	0.241 kg	19.041 kg	2.841 kg	No Report
Suriname	6.000 kg	No Report	No Report	No Report	No Report	No Report
Sub-Total	367.439 kg	404.681 kg	679.486 kg 1950 u.	2230.175 kg	891.164 kg	1.255 kg
Total region	235195.100 kg 3036 u.	4380.365 kg 72 u.	5633.333 kg 3285 u.	420880.400 kg 4093 u.	429071.700 kg 2602 u.	1.255 kg
ASIA						
Central Asia and Transcaucasian countries						
Uzbekistan	No Report	No Report	No Report	No Report	222.900 kg	No Report
Sub-Total					222.900 kg	
East and South-East Asia						
Brunei Darussalam	0.011 kg	No Report	No Report	No Report	No Report	No Report
Hong Kong SAR, China	No Report	8.200 kg	No Report	No Report	No Report	No Report
Indonesia	0.386 kg	1.218 kg	0.329 kg	1.875 kg	No Report	No Report
Korea (Republic of)	13.866 kg	58.789 kg	No Report	46.067 kg	No Report	No Report
Philippines	267.800 kg	No Report	85007.000 kg ICPO 223459 u.	163.000 kg	28.550 kg	No Report
Thailand	3.011 kg ICPO	12.127 kg	1.225 kg	No Report	No Report	No Report

Source: Annual Report Questionnaire if not otherwise indicated

SEIZURES 1996 - 2001
Cannabis seed

Region/country or territory	1996	1997	1998	1999	2000	2001
ASIA						
East and South-East Asia						
Sub-Total	285.074 kg	80.334 kg	85008.560 kg 223459 u.	210.942 kg	28.550 kg	
Near and Middle East /South-West Asia						
Bahrain	No Report	No Report	No Report	0.361 kg ICPO	No Report	No Report
Jordan	26.315 kg	0.770 kg	1.412 kg	61.461 kg	3.589 kg	No Report
Lebanon	No Report	20.000 kg	No Report	270.000 kg	424.000 kg	No Report
United Arab Emirates	4.876 kg	No Report	No Report	No Report	0.135 kg	No Report
Sub-Total	31.191 kg	20.770 kg	1.412 kg	331.822 kg	427.724 kg	
South Asia						
Maldives	No Report	No Report	(1	No Report	No Report	No Report
Sub-Total						
Total region	316.265 kg	101.104 kg	85009.970 kg 223459 u.	542.764 kg	679.174 kg	
EUROPE						
Eastern Europe						
Bulgaria	5.986 kg	1.250 kg	6.556 kg	6.768 kg ICPO	1.872 kg	No Report
Croatia	13.064 kg	38037 u.	0.053 kg 24133 u.	0.868 kg 17054 u.	10437 u.	No Report
FYR of Macedonia	No Report	No Report	0.135 kg 508 u.	0.103 kg NAPOL 696 u.	No Report	0.120 kg Govt 186 u.
Hungary	No Report	No Report	No Report	No Report	10.000 kg	No Report
Poland	150.000 kg	300.000 kg	No Report	4.016 kg	1200 u.	No Report
Russian Federation	No Report	0.021 kg	No Report	No Report	No Report	No Report
Sub-Total	169.050 kg	301.271 kg 38037 u.	6.744 kg 24641 u.	11.755 kg 17750 u.	11.872 kg 11637 u.	0.120 kg 186 u.
Western Europe						
Andorra	No Report	No Report	0.576 kg ICPO	4.900 kg	No Report	No Report
Belgium	No Report	75 u.	48.190 kg	16.250 kg	No Report	No Report
Finland	0.924 kg 1108 u.	0.364 kg 369 u.	0.345 kg 1304 u.	0.100 kg 1150 u.	0.054 kg 1242 u.	No Report
Italy	45227 u.	220.116 kg 47646 u.	No Report	No Report	No Report	No Report
Malta	4.005 kg	0.049 kg	72 u.	5 u.	4 u.	No Report
Portugal	0.464 kg	53 u.	1.563 kg	38.377 kg 45 u.	1.739 kg 201 u.	No Report
Spain	No Report	1.376 kg	No Report	No Report	No Report	No Report

Source: Annual Report Questionnaire if not otherwise indicated

SEIZURES 1996 - 2001
Cannabis seed

Region/country or territory	1996	1997	1998	1999	2000	2001
EUROPE						
Western Europe						
Sub-Total	5.393 kg	221.905 kg	50.674 kg	59.627 kg	1.793 kg	
	46335 u.	48143 u.	1376 u.	1200 u.	1447 u.	
Total region	174.443 kg	523.176 kg	57.418 kg	71.382 kg	13.665 kg	0.120 kg
	46335 u.	86180 u.	26017 u.	18950 u.	13084 u.	186 u.
OCEANIA						
Oceania						
Australia	304.094 kg [2]	No Report	No Report	4.129 kg	5.559 kg	No Report
	39567 u.					
New Zealand	No Report	No Report	244031 u.	253609 u.	No Report	No Report
Sub-Total	304.094 kg		244031 u.	4.129 kg	5.559 kg	
	39567 u.			253609 u.		
Total region	304.094 kg		244031 u.	4.129 kg	5.559 kg	
	39567 u.			253609 u.		
TOTAL	236278.600 kg	5045.195 kg	90765.060 kg	421776.000 kg	430213.400 kg	14.875 kg
	89105 u.	86252 u.	496892 u.	276732 u.	15686 u.	186 u.

1) Small quantity. 2) Including cannabis resin.

Source: Annual Report Questionnaire if not otherwise indicated

2.2.6. Cannabis: Wholesale and street prices

WHOLESALE AND STREET PRICES OF
HERBAL CANNABIS

Retail and wholesale prices and purity levels:
breakdown by drug, region and country or territory
(prices expressed in US$ or converted equivalent, and purity levels in percentage)

Region / country or territory	RETAIL PRICE (per gram)				WHOLESALE PRICE (per kilogram)			
	Range	Average	Purity	Year	Range	Average	Purity	Year
Africa								
East Africa								
Ghana					39.2 - 62.7	51.0		1999
Kenya		0.1	-	1996		119.8	-	1996
Mauritius	9.0 - 12.6	10.8	-	2001	3,600.0 - 5,000.0	4,300.0		2001
Seychelles		6.0	-	1998	3,600.0 - 4,510.0	4,055.0	-	2000
Uganda	30.0 - 50.0	40.0	-	2001	50.0 - 100.0	75.0		2001
North Africa								
Egypt		0.3	-	2001		120.0	50.0	2001
Morocco						426.0	-	1997
Southern Africa								
Malawi		0.1	-	2001		400.0		1999
Namibia	0.4 - 0.8	0.6	-	2001	400.0 - 500.0	450.0	-	2001
South Africa		3.8	-	2001		900.0	-	2001
Swaziland		0.1	-	2001		50.0	-	1998
Zambia		0.6	-	1998				
Zimbabwe		0.2	-	2001	18.2 - 270.0	150.0	-	2001
West and Central Africa								
Benin						8.4	-	1998
Burkina Faso						20.0	-	2001
Congo					20.0 - 30.0	25.0	-	2001
Côte d'Ivoire	0.1 - 136.0	68.1	100.0	2001	140.0 - 1,360.0	750.0	100.0	2001
Ghana					39.2 - 62.7	51.0	-	1999
Nigeria		0.1	-	2001	3.0 - 4.0	3.5	-	2001
Americas								
Central America								
Costa Rica	1.8 - 4.4	1.3	1.0 - 4.0	2001	190.0 - 310.0	101.0	1.0 - 4.0	2001
El Salvador	0.8 - 1.4	1.1	60.0 - 100.0	2001	800.0 - 1,500	1,100.0	80.0 - 100.0	2001
Guatemala	1.3 - 2.6	1.9	100.0	2001	60.0 - 90.0	75.0	100.0	2001
Honduras						39.0	-	1997
Panama	0.5 - 1.0	0.8	60.0 - 80.0	2001	150.0 - 300.0	225.0	-	2001
North America								
Canada	6.5 - 19.6	13.1	3.0 - 18.0	2001	3,900.0 - 5,200.0	4,600.0	3.0 - 18.0	2001
Mexico						80.0	-	2001
United States	2.0 - 130.0	66.0	-	2001	600.0 - 4,000.0	2,300.0	6.0 - 13.0	2001
South America								
Argentina	1.3 - 1.7	1.5	0.5 - 6.0	2001	500.0 - 700.0	600.0	1.0 - 6.0	2001
Bolivia		0.7	100.0	2001		145.0	-	2001
Brazil		0.9	-	1997				
Colombia		0.02	-	2001				
Chile		1.0	-	1996		800.0	-	1998
Ecuador						600.0	-	1999
Guyana		0.2	-	1996	50.0 - 80.0	65.0	-	1996
Paraguay		1.6	-	1999	32.6 - 48.9	40.7	-	1999
Peru	1.0 - 2.0	1.5	95.0	2001	50.0 - 70.0	60.0	95.0	2001
Suriname	0.4 - 0.6	0.5	-	2001	5.0 - 10.0	7.5	-	2001
Uruguay		0.4	-	1999	150.0 - 180.0	165.0	-	1999
Venezuela		1.27	-	2001	222.0 - 296.0	260.0		2000

WHOLESALE AND STREET PRICES OF
HERBAL CANNABIS

Retail and wholesale prices and purity levels:
breakdown by drug, region and country or territory
(prices expressed in US$ or converted equivalent, and purity levels in percentage)

Region / country or territory	RETAIL PRICE (per gram)				WHOLESALE PRICE (per kilogram)			
	Range	Average	Purity	Year	Range	Average	Purity	Year
Caribbean								
Bahamas	5.0 - 10.0	7.5	-	2001	800.0 - 1600.0	1,200.0	-	2001
Bermuda		17.6	-	1999	11,023.1 - 15,432.4	13,227.7	-	1999
Cayman Islands	8.0 - 12.0	10.0	100.0	2001	1500.0 - 2500.0	2,000.0	100.0	2001
Dominican Republic		0.6	-	2001	400.0 - 500.0	450.0	-	1998
Grenada	1.1 - 1.4	1.3	-	2001	400.0 - 600.0	500.0	-	2001
Jamaica					57.0 - 65.0	61.0	-	2001
Saint Lucia		0.8	-	2000	600.0 - 660.0	630.0	-	2000
Trinidad Tobago		5.0	-	2001		3,000.0	-	2001
Turks and Caicos Islands						1,102.0	-	1998
Asia								
Central Asia and Transcaucasia								
Armenia						1,000.0	-	1996
Azerbaijan	2.0 - 4.0	3.0	-	2001	1,500.0 - 2,500.0	2,000.0	-	2001
Kyrgyzstan	0.1 - 0.4	0.3	-	2000	5.0 - 10.0	7.5	8.0 - 10.0	2001
Tajikistan	0.1 - 0.4	0.3	-	2001	50.0 - 200.0	125.0	-	2001
Turkmenistan	0.2 - 1.4	0.8	-	2001	38.0 - 675.0	356.5	-	2001
Uzbekistan					100.0 - 300.0	200.0	-	1998
East and South-East Asia								
Brunei Darussalam		0.1	-	2001		5,297.2	-	1998
Hong Kong SAR, China	7.7 - 9.0	8.3	-	2001	1,440.0 - 2,440.0	1,940.0	-	2001
Indonesia		0.4	-	1999		2,000.0	-	2001
Japan	12.5 - 83.3	47.9	-	2001	5,000.0 - 33,800.0	19,400.0	-	2001
Malaysia	0.5 - 0.6	0.5	-	1997	265.2 - 397.8	331.5	-	1999
Myanmar		0.1	-	2001		30.2	-	1999
Macau SAR, China	10.0 - 15.0	12.5	-	2001	2,240.0	2,240.0	-	2001
Philippines	0.1 - 0.2	0.1	-	2001	41.0 - 81.0	61.0	-	2001
Republic of Korea		0.8	-	2001		100.0	-	2001
Singapore	3.7 - 4.5	4.1	-	2001		1,010.0	-	2001
Thailand	1.2 - 2.4	1.8	-	1999	30.0 -150.0	90.0	-	2001
Near and Middle East /South-West Asia								
Israel		12.1	-	2001	150.0 - 730.0	440.0	-	2001
Jordan	0.3 - 0.7	0.5	-	2001	500.0 - 600.0	550.0	-	2001
Lebanon						1,200.0	-	2000
Syrian Arab Republic		1.1	-	1999		652.2	-	1999
South Asia								
India						40.0	-	2001
Maldives	81.7 - 163.5	122.6	-	2001				
Nepal					7.4 - 14.7	11.0	-	1999
Sri Lanka	21.0 - 23.3	22.1	24.3 - 79.2	2001				
Europe								
Eastern Europe								
Bulgaria		0.7	-	2001	40.0 - 50.0	45.0	-	2001
Croatia	3.0 - 4.1	3.6	-	2001	500.0 - 700.0	600.0	-	2001
Czech Republic	3.9 - 6.5	5.2	-	2001	2,100.0 - 2,600.0	2,300.0	-	2001
Estonia	5.1 - 6.3	5.7	-	2001		1,140.0	-	2001
Hungary	6.1 - 8.5	7.3	-	2001	1,000.0 - 1,400.0	1,200.0	-	2001
Latvia	2.4 - 12.9	7.6	-	2001	300.0 - 1,400.0	900.0	-	2001

WHOLESALE AND STREET PRICES OF
HERBAL CANNABIS

Retail and wholesale prices and purity levels:
breakdown by drug, region and country or territory
(prices expressed in US$ or converted equivalent, and purity levels in percentage)

Region / country or territory	RETAIL PRICE (per gram)				WHOLESALE PRICE (per kilogram)			
	Range	Average	Purity	Year	Range	Average	Purity	Year
Lithuania		1.8	-	2001	1,000.0 - 1,500.0	1,250.0	-	2001
Poland	5.0 - 10.1	7.6	-	2001	2,020.0 - 2,770.0	2,390.0	-	2001
Republic of Moldova		0.05	-	1997		100.0	-	1997
Serbia and Montenegro	5.4 - 10.8	8.1	40.0 - 50.0	2001	100.0 - 200.0	150.0	40.0 - 50.0	2001
Slovakia	0.2 - 4.2	2.2	1.0 - 15.0	2001	200.0 - 4,200.0	2,200.0	1.0 - 15.0	2001
Slovenia		2.0	-	2001	600.0 - 800.0	700.0	-	2001
Romania		2.0	-	2001		1,500.0	-	2001
Russian Federation		1.0	-	1999	100.0 - 500.0	300.0	-	2001
The former Yug.Rep of Macedonia					100.0 - 200.0	150.0	-	2001
Ukraine	0.5 - 1.0	0.8	-	2001	500.0 - 750.0	625.0	-	2001
Western Europe								
Andorra		2.7	-	2001				
Austria	3.6 - 6.3	4.9	9.0	2001	1,300.0 - 3,300.0	2,300.0	1.0 - 20.0	2001
Belgium	3.6 - 6.0	4.8	-	2001	1,200.0 - 1,800.0	1,500.0	-	2001
Cyprus	12.4 - 18.6	15.5	-	2001	4,600.0 - 7,700.0	6,200.0	-	2001
Denmark	8.8 - 9.2	9.0	-	1999				
Finland	6.4 - 9.6	8.0	-	1999				
France	1.8 - 6.3	4.0	-	2001	652.1 - 1,956.3	1,304.2	-	1999
Germany	3.2 - 8.7	5.9	-	2001	1,700.0 - 2,900.0	2,300.0	-	2001
Gibraltar						5,000.0	-	1997
Greece	1.3 - 2.7	2.0	-	2001	263.0 - 789.0	526.0	-	2001
Iceland	16.0 - 22.0	19.0	-	2001	-	-	-	-
Ireland	1.8 - 3.6	2.7	-	2001	2,549.6 - 2,832.9	2,691.2	-	1998
Italy	4.5 - 5.8	5.2	-	2001	900.0 - 1,300.0	1,100.0	4.7	2001
Liechtenstein		8.2	-	1996		3,679.5	-	1996
Luxembourg		2.5	-	1998	1,642.9 - 2,190.5	1,916.7	-	1998
Malta		2.8	17.0	2001		1,700.0	17.0	2001
Netherlands	3.6 - 6.1	4.9	-	1999	1,005.0 - 1,538.5	.	-	1997
Norway	5.7 - 11.4	8.6	-	2000	3,600.0 - 5,400.0	4,500.0	0.2 - 38.5	2001
Portugal		3.26	3.2 - 7.7	2001		890.0	-	2001
Spain		2.6	-	2001		1,020.0	-	2001
Sweden		5.0	-	2001				
Switzerland	2.3 - 8.8	5.6	-	2001	500.0 - 4,100.0	2,300.0	-	2001
Turkey	8.0 - 12.0	10.0	-	2001	400.0 - 600.0	500.0	-	2001
United Kingdom	4.3 - 5.8	5.0	-	2001	2,600.0 - 3,500.0	3,000.0	-	2001
Oceania								
Australia		19.2	-	1999		3,050.0	-	1999
New Zealand					2,100.0 - 5,100.0	3,600.0	100.0	2001

WHOLESALE AND STREET PRICES OF
CANNABIS RESIN

Retail and wholesale prices and purity levels:
breakdown by drug, region and country or territory
(prices expressed in US$ or converted equivalent, and purity levels in percentage)

Region / country or territory	RETAIL PRICE (per gram)				WHOLESALE PRICE (per kilogram)			
	Range	Average	Purity	Year	Range	Average	Purity	Year
Africa								
East Africa								
Seychelles					8,110.0 - 9,010.0	8,560.0	-	2000
Uganda					2,250.0	2,250.0	-	1998
North Africa								
Algeria					2,207.3	2,207.3	-	1999
Egypt	0.1 - 2.3	1.2	-	2001	3,100.0 - 4,200.0	3,700.0	-	2001
Tunisia					1,035.4 - 1,207.9	1,121.7	-	1999
Southern Africa								
South Africa		8.38	-	2001		5,710.0	-	2001
Swaziland		0.2	-	2001				
Zambia	0.7	0.7	-	1998				
Americas								
North America								
Canada	6.5 -39.2	22.9	7.0 - 10.0	2001	3,900.0 - 7,800.0	5,900.0	7.0 - 10.0	2001
United States					2,205.0 - 7,720.0	4,962.5	-	1996
South America								
Argentina	1.8 - 2.2	2.0	-	2001	500.0 - 700.0	600.0	-	2001
Caribbean								
Jamaica					250.0 - 270.0	260.0	-	2001
Asia								
Central Asia and Transcaucasia								
Armenia	5.0	5.0	-	2000	5,000.0	5,000.0	-	1999
Azerbaijan	4.0 - 5.0	4.5	-	2001	2,000.0 - 3,000.0	2,500.0	-	2001
Kyrgyzstan	0.4 - 0.6	0.5	2.0 - 3.0	2001	300.0 - 400.0	350.0	2.0 - 3.0	2001
Tajikistan					70.0 - 90.0	80.0	-	2001
Uzbekistan	0.7 - 1.5	1.1	-	1999	400.0 - 1,000.0	700.0	-	1999
East and South-East Asia								
Hong Kong SAR, China	9.0	9.0	-	1999	21,882.3	21,882.3	-	1999
Japan	16.3 - 56.7	36.5	-	2001	5,830.0 - 16,677.0	11,250.0	-	2001
Republic of Korea	9.5 - 11.1	10.3	-	2001		7,900.0	-	2001
Macau SAR, China	10.0 - 15.0	12.5	-	2001	2,240.0 - 2,490.0	2,365.0	-	2001
Philippines	3.2 - 3.7	3.4	-	2001	3,100.0 - 3,700.0	3,400.0	-	2001
Near and Middle East /South-West Asia								
Afghanistan					28.3 - 69.0	51.7	-	1999
Iran (Islamic Republic of)						390.0	-	2001
Israel	12.1 - 72.8	42.5	-	2001	700.0 - 2,400.0	1,600.0	-	2001
Jordan	0.4 - 0.8	0.6	-	2001	600.0 - 800.0	700.0	-	2001
Kuwait					4,934.2	4,934.2	-	1998
Lebanon	8.0 - 10.0	9.0	70.0 - 90.0	2001	200.0 - 400.0	300.0	-	2001
Oman	26.0 - 52.1	39.1	-	2001	2,600.0 - 3,100.0	2,900.0	-	2001
Pakistan	0.5 - 0.6	0.5	-	2001	50.0 - 60.0	55.5	-	2001
Qatar	6.9 - 8.2	7.5	-	1996	5,995.0 - 6,870.0	6,432.5	-	1996
Saudia Arabia	6.7 - 9.3	8.0	-	2001	1,200.0 - 1,300.0	1,250.0	60.0 - 80.0	2001
Syrian Arab Republic	1.1	1.1	-	1998	663.0	663.0	-	1998

WHOLESALE AND STREET PRICES OF
CANNABIS RESIN

Retail and wholesale prices and purity levels:
breakdown by drug, region and country or territory
(prices expressed in US$ or converted equivalent, and purity levels in percentage)

Region / country or territory	RETAIL PRICE (per gram)				WHOLESALE PRICE (per kilogram)			
	Range	Average	Purity	Year	Range	Average	Purity	Year
South Asia								
India	0.2 - 0.4	0.3	-	1999	**220.0 - 650.0**	**430.0**	-	2001
Nepal	0.1 - 0.2	0.1	-	1999	36.8 - 44.2	40.5	-	1998
Sri Lanka	0.3	0.3	-	1997	244.0	244.0	-	1997
Europe								
Eastern Europe								
Bulgaria		1.8	-	2001		1,380.0	-	2001
Croatia	3.0 - 4.7	3.9	-	2001	1,200.0 - 1,400.0	1,300.0	-	2001
Czech Republic		5.2	1.0 - 20.0	2001	2,800.0 - 3,100.0	3,000.0	3.0 - 20.0	2001
Estonia	11.4 - 14.3	12.8	-	2001		2,000.0		2001
Hungary	5.1 - 10.2	7.7	0.2 - 6.5	2001	1,400.0 - 1,500.0	1,450.0	-	2001
Latvia	9.6 - 17.7	13.7	-	2001	800.0 - 1,600.0	1,200.0	-	2001
Lithuania	1.8 - 2.3	2.0	-	2001	1,000.0 - 1,500.0	1,250.0	-	2001
Poland	5.0 - 11.3	8.2	-	2001	2,000.0 - 3,000.0	2,500.0	-	2001
Republic of Moldova		0.4	60.0	2001		400.0	70.0	2001
Romania		2.0	-	2001		2,000.0	-	2001
Russian Federation	3.0 - 6.0	4.5	-	2001	2,700.0 - 6,500.0	4,600.0	-	2001
Serbia and Montenegro	13.5 - 19.7	16.6	40.0 - 50.0	2001	3,400.0 - 4,800.0	4,100.0	40.0 - 50.0	2001
Slovakia	1.0 - 4.2	2.6	2.0 - 20.0	2001	1,000.0 - 4,200.0	2,600.0	2.0 - 20.0	2001
Slovenia		4.0	-	2001	800.0 - 1,000.0	900.0		2001
Ukraine	3.0 - 5.0	4.0	-	2001	1,000.0 - 1,500.0	1,250.0		2001
Western Europe								
Andorra		2.2	-	2001				
Austria	5.4 - 6.3	5.8	3.0 - 16.0	2001	2,610.0 - 2,930.0	2,770.0	-	2001
Belgium	4.0 - 6.7	5.4	-	2001	1,600.0 - 2,400.0	2,000.0	-	2001
Cyprus	12.4 - 18.6	15.5	-	2001	6,200.0 - 9,300.0	7,700.0	-	2001
Denmark	3.0 - 12.0	7.5	-	2001	1,800.0 - 3,600.0	2,700.0	-	2001
Finland	7.2 - 11.7	9.4	-	2001		2,960.0	-	2001
France	6.3 - 13.5	9.9	-	2001	900.0 - 2,300.0	1,600.0	-	2001
Germany	3.2 - 6.8	5.0	-	2001	1,300.0 - 2,700.0	2,000.0	-	2001
Gibraltar		3.6	-	2001	1,000.0 - 1,500.0	1,250.0	-	1998
Greece	4.0 - 6.5	5.3	-	2001	800.0 - 2,100.0	1,500.0	-	2001
Iceland	16.0 - 22.0	19.0	-	2001				
Ireland	9.0 - 13.6	11.2	-	2001		2,910.0	-	2001
Italy	6.2 - 7.6	6.9	-	2001	1,800.0 - 2,300.0	2,100.0	-	2001
Luxembourg	5.3	5.3	-	1999	2,651.0 - 3,976.5	3,313.7	-	1999
Monaco					5,807.0	5,807.0	-	1997
Netherlands	4.9 - 12.1	8.5	-	1999	1,237.6 - 2,475.2	1,671.7	-	1998
Norway	9.0 - 22.4	15.7	-	2001	4,000.0 - 5,713.0	4,856.0	-	2000
Portugal		3.6	1.0 - 11.0	2001		1,340.0	-	2001
Spain		3.5	-	2001		1,280.0	-	2001
Sweden	7.9 - 9.9	8.9	-	2001	3,000.0 - 4,000.0	3,500.0	-	2001
Switzerland	2.9 - 11.7	7.3	-	2001	1,200.0 - 5,800.0	3,500.0	-	2001
Turkey					500.0 - 1,500.0	1,000.0	-	2001
United Kingdom	4.3 - 5.8	5.0	-	2001	1,440.0 - 3,600.0	2,520.0	-	2001
Oceania								
Australia	32.0	32.0	-	1999	6,550.0	6,550.0	-	1999

WHOLESALE AND STREET PRICES OF
CANNABIS OIL

Retail and wholesale prices and purity levels:
breakdown by drug, region and country or territory
(prices expressed in US$ or converted equivalent, and purity levels in percentage)

Region / country or territory	RETAIL PRICE (per gram)				WHOLESALE PRICE (per kilogram)			
	Range	Average	Purity	Year	Range	Average	Purity	Year
Africa								
Southern Africa								
Zambia		1.3	-	1998	-	-	-	-
Americas								
North America								
Canada	13.1 - 32.6	22.9	3.0 - 28.0	2001	3,300.0 - 9,800.0	6,500.0	3.0 - 15.0	2001
United States	35.0 - 55.0	45.0	-	1996	3,510.0 - 8,820.0	6,165.0	-	1996
South America								
Chile		24.7	-	1996	-	-	-	-
Caribbean								
Jamaica					500.0 - 520.0	510.0	-	2001
Asia								
Near and Middle East /South-West Asia								
Israel		10.0	-	1998	-	-	-	-
Europe								
Eastern Europe								
Bulgaria						2,300.0	-	2001
Western Europe								
Cyprus					8,000.0 - 10,000.0	9,000.0	-	1999
France	13.5 - 40.4	26.9	-	2001				
Iceland		89.3	-	1998	-	-	-	-
Spain		11.4	-	2001		2,300.0	-	2001
Switzerland	8.8 - 29.2	19.0	-	2001	-	-	-	-
United Kingdom	22.9 - 24.4	23.7	-	2000	1,145.0 - 3,817.0	2,481.00	-	2000
Oceania								
Australia		33.3	-	1998	6,666.7 - 9,333.3	8,000.0	-	1998
New Zealand	8.5 - 21.1	14.8	-	2001	250.0 - 510.0	380.0	100.0	2001

2.2.7. Amphetamine-type stimulants: Seizures 1996-2001

SEIZURES 1996 - 2001						
Amphetamine-type Stimulants (excluding 'Ecstasy')						
Region/country or territory	1996	1997	1998	1999	2000	2001
AFRICA						
East Africa						
Eritrea	No Report	No Report	No Report	No Report	6.000 kg [ICPO]	No Report
Sub-Total					6.000 kg	
North Africa						
Algeria	43211 u. [ICPO]	No Report	No Report	No Report	No Report	No Report
Egypt	19.453 lt. 415237 u.	46.565 lt. 94881 u.	15.348 lt.	5.222 kg 19.023 lt.	11.650 lt. 57076 u.	No Report
Morocco	No Report	No Report	49561 u.	73917 u.	No Report	No Report
Sudan	No Report	No Report	No Report	No Report	0.250 kg 38 u.	No Report
Tunisia	3 u. [ICPO]	No Report	No Report	No Report	No Report	No Report
Sub-Total	19.453 lt. 458451 u.	46.565 lt. 94881 u.	15.348 lt. 49561 u.	5.222 kg 19.023 lt. 73917 u.	0.250 kg 11.650 lt. 57114 u.	
Southern Africa						
South Africa	3266 u.	0.280 kg	527 u.	369 u. [ICPO]	0.013 kg [ICPO] 924 u.	59078 u.
Zambia	0.091 kg [Govt]	0.050 kg [Govt]	0.000 kg [Govt]	0.018 kg	0.000 kg [Govt]	270 u. [Govt]
Zimbabwe	No Report	No Report	15.729 kg	No Report	No Report	No Report
Sub-Total	0.091 kg 3266 u.	0.330 kg	15.729 kg 527 u.	0.018 kg 369 u.	0.013 kg 924 u.	59348 u.
West and Central Africa						
Burkina Faso	No Report	40750 u. [ICPO]	No Report	No Report	No Report	2.851 kg
Cameroon	No Report	No Report	No Report	No Report	No Report	1000 u.
Chad	No Report	No Report	No Report	1620 u. [ICPO]	180000 u.	No Report
Côte d'Ivoire	1809 u.	No Report	6385 u.	56.131 kg	0.200 kg [ICPO]	0.124 kg
Gambia	No Report	No Report	No Report	328 u.	No Report	3.000 kg
Niger	220368 u. [ICPO]	186574 u. [ICPO]	No Report	556537 u. [ICPO]	No Report	No Report
Nigeria	10.652 kg [ICPO]	309.525 kg	No Report	322.071 kg	0.580 kg	No Report
Senegal	17 u. [ICPO]	No Report	No Report	No Report	No Report	No Report
Sub-Total	10.652 kg 222194 u.	309.525 kg 227324 u.	6385 u.	378.202 kg 558485 u.	0.780 kg 180000 u.	5.975 kg 1000 u.
Total region	10.743 kg 19.453 lt. 683911 u.	309.855 kg 46.565 lt. 322205 u.	15.729 kg 15.348 lt. 56473 u.	383.442 kg 19.023 lt. 632771 u.	7.043 kg 11.650 lt. 238038 u.	5.975 kg 60348 u.
AMERICAS						
Caribbean						
Bahamas	No Report	0.200 kg [ICPO]	No Report	No Report	60.000 kg [CICAD]	No Report

Source: Annual Report Questionnaire if not otherwise indicated

SEIZURES 1996 - 2001

Amphetamine-type Stimulants (excluding 'Ecstasy')

Region/country or territory	1996	1997	1998	1999	2000	2001
AMERICAS						
Caribbean						
Cayman Islands	0.258 kg	No Report	0.040 kg 120 u.	0.001 kg [ICPO]	No Report	No Report
Netherlands Antilles	No Report	No Report	541.000 kg [F.O]	No Report	No Report	No Report
Sub-Total	0.258 kg	0.200 kg	541.040 kg 120 u.	0.001 kg	60.000 kg	
Central America						
Costa Rica	No Report	No Report	No Report	No Report	195 u.	468 u.
Sub-Total					195 u.	468 u.
North America						
Canada	0.561 kg 1572 u.	2.260 kg 0.225 lt.	0.590 kg 54.500 lt. 11207 u.	20.218 kg 2.306 lt. 4970 u.	29.482 kg 2.798 lt. 8815 u.	53.231 kg 57798 u.
Mexico	180.723 kg	38.891 kg	98.391 kg	926.011 kg 880 u.	714.920 kg	417.944 kg
United States	1469.164 kg 25890 u.	1428.798 kg 84.942 lt. 3747486 u.	1824.363 kg 215.776 lt. 411768 u.	2641.000 kg 20217 u.	2451.383 kg 226.682 lt. 43096 u.	2857.600 kg 5494617 u.
Sub-Total	1650.448 kg 27462 u.	1469.949 kg 85.167 lt. 3747486 u.	1923.344 kg 270.276 lt. 422975 u.	3587.229 kg 2.306 lt. 26067 u.	3195.785 kg 229.480 lt. 51911 u.	3328.775 kg 5552415 u.
South America						
Argentina	480 u. [Govt.]	504 u.	600 u.	4103 u.	10134 u.	3991 u.
Brazil	0.028 kg	No Report	No Report	No Report	No Report	No Report
Chile	17463 u.	55686 u.	0.011 kg 6973 u.	104523 u. [CICAD]	11287 u.	22225 u.
Peru	No Report	No Report	No Report	No Report	No Report	0.063 kg 709 u.
Uruguay	37 u.	No Report	No Report	No Report	No Report	No Report
Sub-Total	0.028 kg 17980 u.	56190 u.	0.011 kg 7573 u.	108626 u.	21421 u.	0.063 kg 26925 u.
Total region	1650.734 kg 45442 u.	1470.149 kg 85.167 lt. 3803676 u.	2464.395 kg 270.276 lt. 430668 u.	3587.230 kg 2.306 lt. 134693 u.	3255.785 kg 229.480 lt. 73527 u.	3328.838 kg 5579808 u.
ASIA						
Central Asia and Transcaucasian countries						
Armenia	No Report	0.040 lt. [ICPO]	No Report	No Report	No Report	No Report

Source: Annual Report Questionnaire if not otherwise indicated

SEIZURES 1996 - 2001

Amphetamine-type Stimulants (excluding 'Ecstasy')

Region/country or territory	1996	1997	1998	1999	2000	2001
ASIA						
Central Asia and Transcaucasian countries						
Georgia	0.051 kg [ICPO]	No Report	No Report	No Report	0.013 kg [ICPO]	No Report
	4.373 lt.					
	224461 u.					
Kyrgyzstan	No Report	0.020 kg	No Report	No Report	No Report	No Report
Uzbekistan	0.358 kg [ICPO]	0.430 kg [ICPO]	No Report	0.031 kg	No Report	No Report
Sub-Total	0.409 kg	0.450 kg		0.031 kg	0.013 kg	
	4.373 lt.	0.040 lt.				
	224461 u.					
East and South-East Asia						
Brunei Darussalam	0.095 kg	0.123 kg	0.237 kg	1.197 kg	1.648 kg	0.661 kg
	6479 u.					375 u.
Cambodia	No Report	13928 u. [ICPO]	No Report	No Report	No Report	No Report
China	1599.000 kg	1334.000 kg	1608.000 kg	16059.000 kg [ICPO]	20900.000 kg [ICPO]	4800.000 kg
Hong Kong SAR, China	46.800 kg	73.600 kg	232.700 kg [Govt.]	No Report	87.600 kg	63.100 kg
	14295 u.	3461 u.			7879 u.	214776 u.
Indonesia	0.334 kg	5.621 kg	7.761 kg [HNLP]	218.625 kg	88.163 kg	48.793 kg
	303 u.			29511 u.		5355 u.
Japan	652.192 kg	173.526 kg	549.702 kg	1994.459 kg	1030.580 kg [ICPO]	419.175 kg
		2.203 lt.	0.788 lt.	0.589 lt.	0.471 lt.	142 u.
		1415 u.	1 u.	4589 u.	954 u.	
Korea (Republic of)	33.250 kg	24.872 kg	28.311 kg	29.233 kg	4.500 kg [ICPO]	169.562 kg
					9240 u.	2095 u.
Lao People's Dem. Rep.	9.698 kg [Govt.]	774714 u. [Govt.]	No Report	1793202 u. [HNLP]	1957929 u. [Govt]	851619 u. [Govt]
Macau SAR, China	0.252 kg [ICPO]	No Report	0.073 kg [ICPO]	No Report	0.272 kg [ICPO]	0.035 kg
			187 u.		785 u.	1732 u.
Malaysia	No Report	2.000 kg	No Report	5.411 kg	208.100 kg	No Report
				329265 u.	195387 u.	
Mongolia	No Report	No Report	No Report	0.100 kg [ICPO]	No Report	4 u.
Myanmar	5906555 u.	5028600 u.	16026688 u.	22.058 kg	6.398 kg	33103548 u.
				28887514 u.	26759772 u.	
Philippines	797.530 kg	694.480 kg [ICPO]	312.929 kg [Govt]	943.700 kg	989.760 kg	1777.642 kg
	2 u.	2.000 lt.	85.730 lt.		30.000 lt.	
Singapore	252 u.	0.090 kg	1.711 kg	1.300 kg	0.759 kg	2.175 kg
		8141 u.	4470 u.	1380 u.	24723 u.	19935 u.
Taiwan province, China	No Report	2256.000 kg [PRESS]	No Report	No Report	836.000 kg [PRESS]	1156.000 kg [PRESS]
Thailand	442.000 kg [Govt.]	2135.889 kg	2827.890 kg	5046.368 kg	7431.147 kg [ICPO]	8338.000 kg [F.O]
Viet Nam	No Report	No Report	No Report	6025 u. [ICPO]	13876 u. [ICPO]	72391 u.

Source: Annual Report Questionnaire if not otherwise indicated

SEIZURES 1996 - 2001
Amphetamine-type Stimulants (excluding 'Ecstasy')

Region/country or territory	1996	1997	1998	1999	2000	2001
ASIA						
East and South-East Asia						
Sub-Total	3581.151 kg 5927886 u.	6700.201 kg 4.203 lt. 5830259 u.	5569.314 kg 86.518 lt. 16031350 u.	24321.450 kg 0.589 lt. 31051480 u.	31584.930 kg 30.471 lt. 28970540 u.	16775.140 kg 34271980 u.
Near and Middle East /South-West Asia						
Bahrain	No Report	No Report	28 u. [ICPO]	No Report	0.005 kg [ICPO]	No Report
Israel	50784 u.	30807 u.	No Report	190 u. [ICPO]	131 u. [ICPO]	0.014 kg
Jordan	2586467 u.	0.290 kg [ICPO] 2794059 u.	262071 u.	518813 u.	5817798 u.	1405872 u.
Kuwait	3.414 kg [ICPO]	No Report	No Report	No Report	110000 u. [ICPO]	No Report
Lebanon	No Report	No Report	No Report	359 u. [ICPO]	41616 u. [ICPO]	No Report
Pakistan	No Report	No Report	No Report	No Report	20.000 kg	No Report
Qatar	27 u.	1026 u. [ICPO]	220 u. [ICPO]	14 u. [ICPO]	448 u. [ICPO]	No Report
Saudi Arabia	4016752 u. [ICPO]	10852279 u. [ICPO]	3553231 u.	7549665 u. [ICPO]	9698370 u. [1]	1.000 kg 6715652 u.
Syrian Arab Republic	1484690 u.	2463977 u.	No Report	1470831 u.	1159065 u. [1]	1911796 u. [Govt 1]
United Arab Emirates	8563 u.	No Report	No Report	No Report	0.107 kg [ICPO]	0.176 kg
Yemen	No Report	3704 u. [ICPO]	972 u. [ICPO]	3020 u. [ICPO]	0.005 kg [ICPO] 3754 u.	No Report
Sub-Total	3.414 kg 8147283 u.	0.290 kg 16145850 u.	3816522 u.	9542892 u.	20.117 kg 16831180 u.	1.190 kg 10033320 u.
South Asia						
India	No Report	No Report	No Report	No Report	3.000 kg [ICPO]	0.965 kg
Maldives	No Report	No Report	No Report	0.001 kg	No Report	6 u.
Sub-Total				0.001 kg	3.000 kg	0.965 kg 6 u.
Total region	3584.974 kg 4.373 lt. 14299630 u.	6700.941 kg 4.243 lt. 21976110 u.	5569.314 kg 86.518 lt. 19847870 u.	24321.480 kg 0.589 lt. 40594380 u.	31608.060 kg 30.471 lt. 45801730 u.	16777.300 kg 44305300 u.
EUROPE						
Eastern Europe						
Albania	No Report	No Report	No Report	0.009 kg [ICPO]	No Report	No Report
Belarus	No Report	No Report	0.282 kg	1.644 kg	1.267 kg [ICPO]	No Report
Bulgaria	No Report	134.293 kg	150 u.	87.192 kg 22928 u.	209.930 kg 18491 u.	64.676 kg [1] 760 u.
Croatia	2075 u.	1.255 kg 1596 u.	0.765 kg 9106 u.	1.110 kg 15429 u.	2.124 kg	0.931 kg

Source: Annual Report Questionnaire if not otherwise indicated

SEIZURES 1996 - 2001

Amphetamine-type Stimulants (excluding 'Ecstasy')

Region/country or territory	1996	1997	1998	1999	2000	2001
EUROPE						
Eastern Europe						
Czech Republic	21.763 kg	0.617 kg 56 u.	76.500 kg [ICPO.]	21.400 kg 673 u.	13.234 kg [ICPO]	23.130 kg
Estonia	0.024 kg [ICPO]	0.725 kg 0.078 lt.	1.955 kg 971 u.	11.507 kg 2707 u.	26.692 kg 955 u.	25.300 kg
FYR of Macedonia	42 u. [ICPO]	No Report	No Report	No Report	No Report	No Report
Hungary	2.465 kg 5818 u.	12.326 kg [Govt.]	7.605 kg	9.257 kg	10.000 kg	1.740 kg 19 u.
Latvia	1.338 kg	0.370 kg	1.395 kg 1.700 lt. 2671 u.	0.493 kg [ICPO]	0.853 kg 1114 u.	3.551 kg
Lithuania	0.054 kg 1.035 lt.	0.205 kg 1.348 lt.	0.013 kg 0.994 lt. 5641 u.	0.077 kg 0.486 lt. 142 u.	19.492 kg 0.482 lt. 2297 u.	6.886 kg 42 u.
Poland	15.253 kg	27.150 kg	51.503 kg	51.453 kg	141.600 kg	194.960 kg
Republic of Moldova	No Report	20.607 kg 1034 u.	No Report	0.105 lt. [ICPO]	No Report	No Report
Romania	11420 u.	3289 u. [ICPO]	No Report	10546 u.	15874 u.	11663 u.
Russian Federation	21.800 kg	No Report	34.000 kg [F.O]	40.500 kg [F.O]	9.000 kg [F.O (2]	13.513 kg
Serbia and Montenegro	No Report	No Report	No Report	No Report	No Report	0.087 kg
Slovakia	No Report	0.094 kg	9.717 kg 35 u.	0.131 kg 22 u.	0.281 kg	0.571 kg
Slovenia	18748 u.	1.410 kg	0.339 kg 267 u.	0.625 kg [ICPO] 818 u.	0.218 kg 28546 u.	0.064 kg 98 u.
Ukraine	7.100 kg	39.500 kg	2.482 kg	No Report	No Report	0.716 kg
Sub-Total	69.797 kg 1.035 lt. 38103 u.	238.552 kg 1.426 lt. 11616 u.	186.556 kg 2.694 lt. 13342 u.	225.398 kg 0.591 lt. 55420 u.	434.691 kg 0.482 lt. 65022 u.	336.125 kg 12540 u.
Western Europe						
Andorra	No Report	No Report	143 u. [ICPO]	43 u.	0.004 kg [ICPO]	No Report
Austria	3767 u.	7895 u.	9763 u.	5165 u.	0.450 kg 1452 u.	2.918 kg
Belgium	24.000 kg 184413 u.	77.000 kg 511 u.	445.000 kg 271080 u.	325.070 kg 489566 u.	75.140 kg [ICPO] 18397 u.	75.140 kg [UNODC (3] 18397 u.
Cyprus	0.004 kg 18 u.	0.050 kg [ICPO]	No Report	0.012 kg	0.005 kg [ICPO]	0.004 kg
Denmark	26.700 kg	119.400 kg	25.236 kg	31.600 kg	57.136 kg	160.640 kg
Finland	22.408 kg 1011 u.	22.189 kg 1101 u.	24.784 kg 1003 u.	140.464 kg 17665 u.	79.565 kg	137.730 kg 14967 u.

Source: Annual Report Questionnaire if not otherwise indicated

SEIZURES 1996 - 2001

Amphetamine-type Stimulants (excluding 'Ecstasy')

Region/country or territory	1996	1997	1998	1999	2000	2001
EUROPE						
Western Europe						
France	127.965 kg 349210 u.	194.047 kg 198941 u.	165.122 kg 1142226 u.	232.941 kg	676.834 kg 2283620 u.	57.420 kg
Germany	159.767 kg	233.633 kg	309.602 kg	360.000 kg	271.200 kg ICPO	262.539 kg
Gibraltar	No Report	0.030 kg	No Report	0.546 kg ICPO	0.209 kg	0.184 kg
Greece	0.013 kg 2104 u.	0.034 kg 958 u.	0.003 kg 5 u.	1.380 kg 257 u.	2.008 kg 30109 u.	0.078 kg 8 u.
Iceland	No Report	No Report	No Report	5.078 kg	10.267 kg	0.132 kg
Ireland	19244 u.	102.585 kg 22191 u.	43.162 kg 46538 u.	13.300 kg ICPO 12015 u.	5.040 kg 568952 u.	17.955 kg
Italy	154503 u.	0.384 kg 10950 u.	2.454 kg 2309 u.	5.131 kg ICPO 16115 u.	0.197 kg 77299 u.	0.924 kg 327 u.
Liechtenstein	122 u.	No Report	No Report	No Report	No Report	12 u.
Luxembourg	No Report	0.010 kg ICPO	No Report	0.016 kg ICPO	0.157 kg ICPO	No Report
Malta	686 u.	0.060 kg 100 u.	No Report	No Report	45 u. (4	No Report
Monaco	1 u.	No Report	No Report	No Report	No Report	No Report
Netherlands	324.000 kg Govt 1025 u.	815.000 kg Govt 102240 u.	1450.000 kg Govt 242409 u.	853.000 kg Govt 45847 u.	293.000 kg Govt	579.000 kg
Norway	30.286 kg	93.241 kg	207.999 kg	52.110 kg 6056 u.	95.506 kg 1147 u.	106.936 kg 2565 u.
Portugal	4093 u.	0.019 kg 549 u.	1131 u. (5	0.087 kg 31393 u.	0.029 kg 22 u.	0.001 kg 35 u.
Spain	53.412 kg	119.584 kg	176.985 kg	49.538 kg 182.000 lt.	23.412 kg	18.700 kg 29711 u.
Sweden	163.780 kg	187.374 kg 16057 u.	134.714 kg	120.310 kg 1099 u.	107.039 kg ICPO	253.161 kg
Switzerland	4.521 kg	7.981 kg	No Report	10.700 kg	39.105 kg	4.608 kg
Turkey	No Report	1020130 u.	No Report	4244493 u.	295037 u.	1090486 u. (1
United Kingdom	2624.700 kg	3295.700 kg	1807.847 kg	1194.938 kg ICPO 25021 u.	1772.344 kg 6541808 u.	1772.344 kg UNODC (3 6541808 u.
Sub-Total	3561.556 kg 720197 u.	5268.321 kg 1381623 u.	4792.908 kg 1716607 u.	3396.221 kg 182.000 lt. 4894735 u.	3508.647 kg 9817888 u.	3450.414 kg 7698316 u.
Total region	3631.353 kg 1.035 lt. 758300 u.	5506.873 kg 1.426 lt. 1393239 u.	4979.464 kg 2.694 lt. 1729949 u.	3621.619 kg 182.591 lt. 4950155 u.	3943.338 kg 0.482 lt. 9882910 u.	3786.538 kg 7710856 u.

Source: Annual Report Questionnaire if not otherwise indicated

SEIZURES 1996 - 2001

Amphetamine-type Stimulants (excluding 'Ecstasy')

Region/country or territory	1996	1997	1998	1999	2000	2001
OCEANIA						
Oceania						
Australia	339.958 kg 0.101 lt. 13742 u.	202.814 kg	182.220 kg Govt. (6	276.288 kg (6	427.312 kg	876.006 kg
Fiji	No Report	No Report	No Report	No Report	0.333 kg ICPO	No Report
New Zealand	No Report	No Report	1.340 kg	1.104 kg 1400 u.	10.175 kg 103 u.	4.170 kg
Sub-Total	339.958 kg 0.101 lt. 13742 u.	202.814 kg	183.560 kg	277.392 kg 1400 u.	437.820 kg 103 u.	880.176 kg
Total region	339.958 kg 0.101 lt. 13742 u.	202.814 kg	183.560 kg	277.392 kg 1400 u.	437.820 kg 103 u.	880.176 kg
TOTAL	9217.763 kg 24.962 lt. 15801030 u.	14190.630 kg 137.401 lt. 27495230 u.	13212.460 kg 374.836 lt. 22064960 u.	32191.170 kg 204.509 lt. 46313400 u.	39252.040 kg 272.083 lt. 55996300 u.	24778.830 kg 57656320 u.

1) Captagon 2) Including other hallucinogens. 3) Due to unavailability of 2001 data, year 2000 data were used for analysis purposes. 4) Duromine 5) Small quantity. 6) Provisional figures.

Source: Annual Report Questionnaire if not otherwise indicated

SEIZURES 1996 - 2001
Depressants (excluding Methaqualone)

Region/country or territory	1996	1997	1998	1999	2000	2001
AFRICA						
East Africa						
Kenya	No Report	No Report	9060 u.	No Report	272 u.	No Report
Mauritius	1886 u.	1886 u.	11694 u.	952 u.	1758 u.	No Report
Sub-Total	1886 u.	1886 u.	20754 u.	952 u.	2030 u.	
North Africa						
Algeria	No Report	No Report	No Report	110786 u.	100555 u. [ICPO]	No Report
Morocco	28988 u. [Govt.]	36236 u. [Govt.]	No Report	No Report	71672 u.	No Report
Sudan	14345 u. [ICPO]	No Report	No Report	No Report	No Report	No Report
Tunisia	4330 u. [ICPO]	No Report	4439 u.	No Report	No Report	No Report
Sub-Total	47663 u.	36236 u.	4439 u.	110786 u.	172227 u.	
Southern Africa						
Botswana	No Report	No Report	No Report	0.073 kg [ICPO] 500 u.	No Report	No Report
Mozambique	No Report	No Report	5080 u. [ICPO]	No Report	No Report	No Report
South Africa	No Report	No Report	No Report	No Report	0.025 kg [ICPO] 3026 u.	No Report
Zambia	0.825 kg [Govt]	0.800 kg [Govt]	0.908 kg [Govt]	4140 u.	0.000 kg [Govt]	0.064 kg [Govt] 3522 u.
Zimbabwe	No Report	No Report	43.640 kg	No Report	No Report	No Report
Sub-Total	0.825 kg	0.800 kg	44.548 kg 5080 u.	0.073 kg 4640 u.	0.025 kg 3026 u.	0.064 kg 3522 u.
West and Central Africa						
Benin	No Report	24 u. [Govt.]	No Report	No Report	No Report	No Report
Cameroon	222 u. [ICPO]	No Report	No Report	No Report	No Report	No Report
Chad	No Report	No Report	No Report	5360 u. [ICPO]	961230 u.	No Report
Congo	No Report	No Report	No Report	No Report	0.003 kg	No Report
Côte d'Ivoire	8290 u.	71.500 kg 44699 u.	23.600 kg 9367 u.	66.690 kg	48.646 kg [ICPO]	298.041 kg
Gabon	100 u. [ICPO]	No Report	No Report	No Report	No Report	No Report
Gambia	18650 u. [ICPO]	No Report	4500 u. [ICPO]	No Report	No Report	3.000 kg
Niger	591703 u. [ICPO]	No Report	679484 u. [ICPO]	367823 u. [ICPO]	No Report	No Report
Nigeria	1183.252 kg [ICPO]	1426.487 kg	No Report	No Report	134.690 kg	282.454 kg
Senegal	No Report	No Report	4063 u. [ICPO]	4737 u. [ICPO]	310 u. [ICPO]	No Report
Togo	9.275 kg	No Report	No Report	No Report	No Report	No Report
Sub-Total	1192.527 kg 618965 u.	1497.987 kg 44723 u.	23.600 kg 697414 u.	66.690 kg 377920 u.	183.339 kg 961540 u.	583.495 kg
Total region	1193.352 kg 668514 u.	1498.787 kg 82845 u.	68.148 kg 727687 u.	66.763 kg 494298 u.	183.364 kg 1138823 u.	583.559 kg 3522 u.

Source: Annual Report Questionnaire if not otherwise indicated

SEIZURES 1996 - 2001
Depressants (excluding Methaqualone)

Region/country or territory	1996	1997	1998	1999	2000	2001
AMERICAS						
Caribbean						
Cayman Islands	No Report	No Report	No Report	0.001 kg	1 u.	No Report
Dominican Republic	No Report	No Report	No Report	8 u. ICPO	No Report	50 u.
Sub-Total				0.001 kg 8 u.	1 u.	50 u.
Central America						
El Salvador	No Report	No Report	40000 u. ICPO	No Report	0.010 kg ICPO 22964 u.	No Report
Guatemala	No Report	No Report	52.000 kg	No Report	No Report	No Report
Honduras	No Report	1 u.	No Report	No Report	No Report	No Report
Sub-Total		1 u.	52.000 kg 40000 u.		0.010 kg 22964 u.	
North America						
Canada	0.265 kg 25183 u.	0.880 kg 0.120 lt. 122359 u.	0.934 kg 0.686 lt. 12033 u.	0.726 kg 2.439 lt. 8355 u.	173.865 kg 4.511 lt. 10921 u.	5.321 kg 18684 u.
Mexico	1108863 u.	117104 u.	1484000 u.	182604 u.	734281 u. ICPO	823726 u.
United States	0.329 kg 442712 u.	0.026 kg 0.867 lt. 709685 u.	No Report	2.646 kg 403724 u.	0.508 kg 0.021 lt. 3338 u.	53385 u.
Sub-Total	0.594 kg 1576758 u.	0.906 kg 0.987 lt. 949148 u.	0.934 kg 0.686 lt. 1496033 u.	3.372 kg 2.439 lt. 594683 u.	174.373 kg 4.532 lt. 748540 u.	5.321 kg 895795 u.
South America						
Argentina	No Report	5759 u.	13125 u.	8055 u.	11779 u.	4795 u.
Chile	48392 u.	No Report	0.002 kg 2545 u.	19813 u. CICAD	6993 u.	9341 u.
Uruguay	2 u.	No Report	No Report	No Report	No Report	No Report
Sub-Total	48394 u.	5759 u.	0.002 kg 15670 u.	27868 u.	18772 u.	14136 u.
Total region	0.594 kg 1625152 u.	0.906 kg 0.987 lt. 954908 u.	52.936 kg 0.686 lt. 1551703 u.	3.373 kg 2.439 lt. 622559 u.	174.383 kg 4.532 lt. 790277 u.	5.321 kg 909981 u.
ASIA						
Central Asia and Transcaucasian countries						
Armenia	No Report	No Report	No Report	1209 u. ICPO	No Report	No Report
Georgia	0.215 lt. ICPO 4956 u.	No Report	180 u. ICPO	0.018 kg ICPO 1060 u.	0.444 kg ICPO	No Report
Kazakhstan	No Report	No Report	No Report	56.000 kg	No Report	No Report

Source: Annual Report Questionnaire if not otherwise indicated

305

SEIZURES 1996 - 2001
Depressants (excluding Methaqualone)

Region/country or territory	1996	1997	1998	1999	2000	2001
ASIA						
Central Asia and Transcaucasian countries						
Uzbekistan	40 u.	970 u.	No Report	No Report	No Report	No Report
Sub-Total	0.215 lt. 4996 u.	970 u.	180 u.	56.018 kg 2269 u.	0.444 kg	
East and South-East Asia						
Brunei Darussalam	No Report	3227 u.	No Report	53 u.	1 u.	1 u.
Hong Kong SAR, China	No Report	512832 u.	162850 u. Govt.	12.208 kg (1 1134461 u.	0.090 kg ICPO 77862 u.	2.000 kg 390550 u.
Indonesia	0.103 kg 48294 u.	No Report	17793 u.	372494 u. ICPO	No Report	37545 u.
Japan	109778 u.	56895 u.	0.024 kg 0.010 lt. 141455 u.	0.003 lt. 97310 u.	0.003 kg 32358 u.	0.002 kg 20545 u.
Korea (Republic of)	130000 u.	681233 u.	1452896 u.	1030567 u.	2176 u. ICPO	No Report
Macau SAR, China	5942 u. ICPO	No Report	4937 u. ICPO	No Report	19421 u.	2583 u.
Philippines	No Report	No Report	No Report	No Report	100000 u. (2	No Report
Singapore	273 u.	582 u.	34911 u.	13069 u.	48061 u.	0.074 kg 1807 u.
Thailand	No Report	No Report	No Report	4.630 kg ICPO	10.524 kg ICPO	No Report
Viet Nam	No Report	No Report	No Report	74274 u. ICPO	115000 u. ICPO	158007 u.
Sub-Total	0.103 kg 294287 u.	1254769 u.	0.024 kg 0.010 lt. 1814842 u.	16.838 kg 0.003 lt. 2722228 u.	10.617 kg 394879 u.	2.076 kg 611038 u.
Near and Middle East /South-West Asia						
Israel	No Report	No Report	No Report	936 u. ICPO	No Report	No Report
Jordan	No Report	2794 u.	No Report	No Report	1014 u.	No Report
Kuwait	No Report	No Report	8943 u.	No Report	No Report	No Report
Lebanon	14510 u.	490 u.	No Report	359 u.	41616 u.	859 u.
Oman	No Report	No Report	No Report	No Report	No Report	1815.000 kg
Pakistan	No Report	No Report	No Report	No Report	20000 u. ICPO	No Report
Qatar	12 u.	No Report	753 u. ICPO	2164 u. ICPO	15 u. ICPO	No Report
Saudi Arabia	23594 u. ICPO	No Report	No Report	No Report	854 u. ICPO	No Report
Syrian Arab Republic	17921 u.	No Report	No Report	15117 u. ICPO	No Report	No Report
United Arab Emirates	No Report	No Report	No Report	No Report	No Report	0.498 kg
Yemen	No Report	No Report	169 u. ICPO	No Report	1486 u. ICPO	No Report
Sub-Total	56037 u.	3284 u.	9865 u.	18576 u.	64985 u.	1815.498 kg 859 u.

Source: Annual Report Questionnaire if not otherwise indicated

SEIZURES 1996 - 2001
Depressants (excluding Methaqualone)

Region/country or territory	1996	1997	1998	1999	2000	2001
ASIA						
South Asia						
Nepal	No Report	No Report	6811 u.	No Report	1654 u. [ICPO]	No Report
Sub-Total			6811 u.		1654 u.	
Total region	0.103 kg	1259023 u.	0.024 kg	72.856 kg	11.061 kg	1817.574 kg
	0.215 lt.		0.010 lt.	0.003 lt.	461518 u.	611897 u.
	355320 u.		1831698 u.	2743073 u.		
EUROPE						
Eastern Europe						
Belarus	No Report	No Report	No Report	0.002 kg	0.100 kg	No Report
Bulgaria	No Report	0.627 kg	93460 u.	1.500 kg	4.682 kg	No Report
					4142 u.	
Croatia	No Report	4915 u.	4358 u.	8335 u.	4778 u.	No Report
Czech Republic	No Report	No Report	No Report	50.000 kg	9450 u.	1119 u.
Estonia	0.016 lt. [ICPO]	9.139 kg	No Report	0.103 kg	1.525 kg [3]	0.184 kg
	120 u.	908 u.		138 u.	846 u.	14571 u.
Hungary	No Report	No Report	No Report	No Report	No Report	0.001 kg
Latvia	0.975 kg	20830 u.	11244 u.	0.171 kg	No Report	9011 u.
	1731 u.			13562 u.		
Lithuania	No Report	No Report	1237 u.	580 u.	106 u.	No Report
Poland	No Report	No Report	No Report	No Report	No Report	8.000 lt.
Republic of Moldova	No Report	No Report	1800 u.	No Report	No Report	No Report
Romania	No Report	No Report	No Report	No Report	No Report	5961 u.
Russian Federation	91.000 kg	975 u.	No Report	39.500 kg [ICPO]	2.420 kg [ICPO]	61.574 kg
Slovakia	No Report	10642 u.	1356 u.	1104 u.		No Report
Slovenia	1138 u.	No Report	5745 u.	621 u.	735 u.	460 u.
Ukraine	36.868 kg	No Report	No Report	0.001 kg [ICPO]	289318 u. [ICPO]	No Report
				8427 u.		
Sub-Total	128.843 kg	9.766 kg	119200 u.	91.277 kg	8.727 kg	61.759 kg
	0.016 lt.	38270 u.		32767 u.	309375 u.	8.000 lt.
	2989 u.					31122 u.
Western Europe						
Andorra	No Report	No Report	No Report	No Report	11 u. [ICPO]	No Report
Austria	No Report	No Report	No Report	No Report	32207 u. [ICPO]	36132 u.
Finland	74997 u.	48395 u.	35664 u.	45448 u.	32148 u.	11700 u.
France	No Report	No Report	No Report	No Report	0.039 kg	No Report
Germany	4195 u.	6035 u.	7071 u.	No Report	No Report	No Report
Gibraltar	569 u.	1058 u.	No Report	64 u. [ICPO]	372 u. [2]	227 u.

Source: Annual Report Questionnaire if not otherwise indicated

SEIZURES 1996 - 2001
Depressants (excluding Methaqualone)

Region/country or territory	1996	1997	1998	1999	2000	2001
EUROPE						
Western Europe						
Greece	6.098 kg 41520 u.	10.400 kg 26403 u.	2.306 kg 18470 u.	80.210 kg 217004 u.	3.700 kg 35354 u.	22.204 kg 43958 u.
Ireland	No Report	0.248 kg 4935 u.	No Report	13793 u. ICPO	1.121 kg	No Report
Italy	2599 u.	14437 u.	0.037 kg 1506 u.	0.232 kg ICPO 3316 u.	0.662 kg 1883 u.	No Report
Liechtenstein	No Report	No Report	No Report	No Report	10280 u. (4	430 u.
Luxembourg	No Report	No Report	145 u.	No Report	No Report	No Report
Malta	14 u.	212 u.	353 u.	8 u.	207 u.	No Report
Norway	53908 u.	130000 u.	0.071 kg 101295 u.	0.012 kg 180500 u.	0.043 kg 413548 u.	11.361 kg 848206 u.
Portugal	1544 u.	1945 u.	2577 u.	2122 u.	0.001 kg 4794 u.	3689 u.
Spain	63543 u.	59352 u.	99126 u.	343974 u.	6.825 lt. (3 132951 u.	595619 u.
Sweden	No Report	No Report	0.302 kg 293508 u.	255000 u.	2.320 kg (3 16.558 lt. 237312 u.	46.570 lt. 271478 u.
Switzerland	No Report	No Report	1204104 u.	554641 u.	1907207 u.	No Report
Turkey	No Report	No Report	3559 u.	No Report	No Report	No Report
United Kingdom	7.700 kg	6.200 kg	No Report	12000 u. ICPO	3.360 kg 37 u.	3.360 kg UNODC (5 37 u.
Sub-Total	13.798 kg 242889 u.	16.848 kg 292772 u.	2.716 kg 1767378 u.	80.454 kg 1627870 u.	11.246 kg 23.383 lt. 2808311 u.	36.925 kg 46.570 lt. 1811476 u.
Total region	142.641 kg 0.016 lt. 245878 u.	26.614 kg 331042 u.	2.716 kg 1886578 u.	171.731 kg 1660637 u.	19.973 kg 23.383 lt. 3117686 u.	98.684 kg 54.570 lt. 1842598 u.
OCEANIA						
Oceania						
Australia	1.823 kg 336 u.	0.380 kg	No Report	No Report	0.117 kg	0.038 kg
New Zealand	No Report	No Report	445 u.	126 u.	317 u.	No Report
Sub-Total	1.823 kg 336 u.	0.380 kg	445 u.	126 u.	0.117 kg 317 u.	0.038 kg
Total region	1.823 kg 336 u.	0.380 kg	445 u.	126 u.	0.117 kg 317 u.	0.038 kg

Source: Annual Report Questionnaire if not otherwise indicated

SEIZURES 1996 - 2001

Depressants (excluding Methaqualone)

Region/country or territory	1996	1997	1998	1999	2000	2001
TOTAL	1338.513 kg	1526.687 kg	123.824 kg	314.723 kg	388.898 kg	2505.176 kg
	0.231 lt.	0.987 lt.	0.696 lt.	2.442 lt.	27.915 lt.	54.570 lt.
	2895200 u.	2627818 u.	5998111 u.	5520693 u.	5508621 u.	3367999 u.

1) Includes mainly benzodiazapines 2) Diazepam 3) Including GHB 4) Rohypnol 5) Due to unavailability of 2001 data, year 2000 data were used for analysis purposes.

Source: Annual Report Questionnaire if not otherwise indicated

SEIZURES 1996 - 2001

Hallucinogens (excluding LSD but incl. "Ecstasy")

Region/country or territory	1996	1997	1998	1999	2000	2001
AFRICA						
North Africa						
Egypt	No Report	No Report	No Report	No Report	3372 u.	70080 u.
Sub-Total					3372 u.	70080 u.
Southern Africa						
Namibia	No Report	No Report	No Report	74 u.	157 u.	546 u.
South Africa	No Report	118784 u.	111733 u.	30132 u. [ICPO]	1.177 kg 297021 u.	95792 u.
Zimbabwe	No Report	No Report	No Report	3 u.	No Report	0.000 kg 6 u.
Sub-Total		118784 u.	111733 u.	30209 u.	1.177 kg 297178 u.	0.000 kg 96344 u.
Total region		118784 u.	111733 u.	30209 u.	1.177 kg 300550 u.	0.000 kg 166424 u.
AMERICAS						
Caribbean						
Aruba	No Report	No Report	No Report	873 u. [F.O]	85279 u. [F.O]	59874 u. [F.O]
Bahamas	No Report	No Report	No Report	No Report	63.000 kg	0.023 kg 0 u.
Bermuda	No Report	No Report	No Report	No Report	No Report	153 u. [F.O]
Cayman Islands	No Report	No Report	No Report	0.030 kg	162 u.	No Report
Dominican Republic	No Report	No Report	No Report	29 u.	125073 u. [F.O]	30903 u.
Guadeloupe	No Report	No Report	No Report	No Report	25540 u. [F.O]	500 u. [F.O]
Jamaica	No Report	No Report	No Report	No Report	No Report	5070 u.
Netherlands Antilles	No Report	No Report	No Report	No Report	15.464 kg [ICPO]	20465 u. [F.O]
Puerto Rico	No Report	No Report	No Report	No Report	No Report	1977 u. [F.O]
Sub-Total				0.030 kg 902 u.	78.464 kg 236054 u.	0.023 kg 118942 u.
Central America						
Costa Rica	No Report	No Report	No Report	No Report	46 u.	87 u.
Panama	No Report	No Report	No Report	No Report	2256 u.	22166 u.
Sub-Total					2302 u.	22253 u.
North America						
Canada	50.261 kg 719 u.	47.703 kg 9288 u.	64.019 kg 0.022 lt. 25451 u.	561.837 kg 0.503 lt. 3427 u.	764.514 kg 0.155 lt. 2136444 u.	459.025 kg 846973 u.
Mexico	No Report	611.380 kg	93.000 kg	No Report	32.302 kg [ICPO]	102.000 kg

Source: Annual Report Questionnaire if not otherwise indicated

SEIZURES 1996 - 2001

Hallucinogens (excluding LSD but incl. "Ecstasy")

Region/country or territory	1996	1997	1998	1999	2000	2001
AMERICAS						
North America						
United States	83.409 kg 53598 u.	44.588 kg 59.968 lt. 151934 u.	No Report	160.515 kg 4745097 u.	9600000 u. [ICPO]	9795741 u.
Sub-Total	133.670 kg 54317 u.	703.671 kg 59.968 lt. 161222 u.	157.019 kg 0.022 lt. 25451 u.	722.352 kg 0.503 lt. 4748524 u.	796.816 kg 0.155 lt. 11736440 u.	561.026 kg 10642710 u.
South America						
Argentina	No Report		No Report	No Report	No Report	No Report
Brazil	No Report	No Report	No Report	59612 u. [ICPO]	36796 u. [(1]	1909 u. [Govt]
Chile	No Report	No Report	2.977 kg	No Report	140 u. [ICPO]	2626 u.
Colombia	No Report	No Report	No Report	1022 u.	83.000 kg	No Report
Ecuador	No Report	No Report	No Report	No Report	No Report	7 u.
Guyana	No Report	No Report	No Report	626 u. [F.O]	124 u. [F.O]	No Report
Peru	No Report	No Report	No Report	No Report	No Report	35 u.
Suriname	No Report	No Report	6000 u.	No Report	61232 u. [INCSR]	No Report
Uruguay	20 u.	No Report	No Report	84 u.	738 u.	No Report
Venezuela	No Report	No Report	No Report	No Report	7985 u. [CICAD]	2 u.
Sub-Total	20 u.		2.977 kg 6000 u.	61344 u.	83.000 kg 107015 u.	4579 u.
Total region	133.670 kg 54337 u.	703.671 kg 59.968 lt. 161222 u.	159.996 kg 0.022 lt. 31451 u.	722.382 kg 0.503 lt. 4810770 u.	958.280 kg 0.155 lt. 12081820 u.	561.049 kg 10788490 u.
ASIA						
Central Asia and Transcaucasian countries						
Kazakhstan	No Report	No Report	No Report	1099.000 kg	No Report	No Report
Sub-Total				1099.000 kg		
East and South-East Asia						
Brunei Darussalam	No Report	No Report	No Report	32 u.	No Report	No Report
China	No Report	No Report	No Report	No Report	200.000 kg [HNLP] 240000 u.	2700000 u.
Hong Kong SAR, China	No Report	49613 u.	265 u. [Govt.]	21202 u. [ICPO]	58.800 kg 378621 u.	0.032 kg 170243 u.
Indonesia	0.444 kg 300052 u.	5.197 kg 89413 u.	119655 u.	32361 u.	383174 u.	No Report
Japan	298 u.	56 u.	16 u. [(2]	5273 u.	0.016 kg 78471 u.	0.121 kg 112542 u.
Korea (Republic of)	No Report	No Report	No Report	No Report	No Report	1672 u.

Source: Annual Report Questionnaire if not otherwise indicated

SEIZURES 1996 - 2001
Hallucinogens (excluding LSD but incl. "Ecstasy")

Region/country or territory	1996	1997	1998	1999	2000	2001
ASIA						
East and South-East Asia						
Macau SAR, China	1452 u. [ICPO]	No Report	64 u. [ICPO]	No Report	2453 u. [ICPO]	1687 u.
Malaysia	No Report	1397979 u.	1733335 u.	55975 u.	49901 u. [ICPO]	No Report
Philippines	No Report	No Report	No Report	No Report	1026 u.	No Report
Singapore	No Report	No Report	2175 u.	5.170 kg 17232 u.	2.566 kg 10339 u.	0.257 kg 23846 u.
Thailand	9687 u. [HNLP]	13.005 kg 80047 u.	10395 u. [Govt.]	269.620 kg [ICPO (3]	70.553 kg [ICPO]	61922 u. [F.O]
Sub-Total	0.444 kg 311489 u.	18.202 kg 1617108 u.	1865905 u.	274.790 kg 132075 u.	331.935 kg 1143985 u.	0.410 kg 3071912 u.
Near and Middle East /South-West Asia						
Israel	No Report	No Report	5.000 kg 118501 u.	130.687 kg [ICPO] 30335 u.	270000 u.	1.504 kg 121695 u.
Jordan	No Report	10178 u.	No Report	5000 u. [ICPO]	No Report	No Report
Sub-Total		10178 u.	5.000 kg 118501 u.	130.687 kg 35335 u.	270000 u.	1.504 kg 121695 u.
Total region	0.444 kg 311489 u.	18.202 kg 1627286 u.	5.000 kg 1984406 u.	1504.477 kg 167410 u.	331.935 kg 1413985 u.	1.914 kg 3193607 u.
EUROPE						
Eastern Europe						
Belarus	0.305 kg	No Report	No Report	No Report	No Report	No Report
Bosnia Herzegovina	No Report	No Report	1041 u. [ICPO]	No Report	No Report	No Report
Bulgaria	No Report	No Report	No Report	No Report	4524 u. [Govt]	7.900 kg 2361 u.
Croatia	No Report	0.004 kg	No Report	0.018 kg [ICPO] 15421 u.	9979 u.	12906 u.
Czech Republic	No Report	0.001 kg 4 u.	No Report	No Report	17502 u.	29.890 kg
Estonia	2058 u. [ICPO]	No Report	No Report	0.000 lt. 1773 u.	0.431 kg 1351 u.	1.714 kg
FYR of Macedonia	65 u. [NAPOL]	184 u. [NAPOL]	1574 u.	5532 u. [NAPOL]	280 u. [NAPOL]	45 u. [Govt]
Hungary	No Report	No Report	11857 u.	510 u.	13616 u.	0.260 kg 18301 u.
Latvia	No Report	0.007 kg 23 u.	No Report	0.749 kg [ICPO] 9625 u.	No Report	1620 u.
Lithuania	56 u.	0.002 kg 1641 u.	831 u.	1122 u. [ICPO]	50724 u. [ICPO]	0.045 kg 514 u.
Poland	No Report	No Report	1736 u.	6319 u.	129513 u.	232735 u.
Romania	No Report	No Report	1093 u.	No Report	10945 u. [ICPO]	67210 u.

Source: Annual Report Questionnaire if not otherwise indicated

SEIZURES 1996 - 2001

Hallucinogens (excluding LSD but incl. "Ecstasy")

Region/country or territory	1996	1997	1998	1999	2000	2001
EUROPE						
Eastern Europe						
Russian Federation	0.800 kg	No Report	No Report	0.153 kg	No Report	0.850 kg
Serbia and Montenegro	No Report	No Report	No Report	No Report	No Report	0.079 kg
						10811 u.
Slovakia	No Report	No Report	No Report	9 u.	493 u. [ICPO]	0.568 kg
Slovenia	No Report	7440 u.	No Report	1749 u. [ICPO]	0.053 kg	1852 u.
					27974 u.	
Ukraine	No Report	No Report	No Report	1.349 kg [ICPO]	0.305 kg [ICPO]	47 u.
				18888 u.	4784 u.	
Sub-Total	1.105 kg	0.014 kg	18132 u.	2.269 kg	0.789 kg	41.306 kg
	2179 u.	9292 u.		0.000 lt.	271685 u.	348402 u.
				60948 u.		
Western Europe						
Andorra	No Report	No Report	88 u. [ICPO]	0.002 kg	0.002 kg [ICPO]	105 u.
				43 u.	283 u.	
Austria	25118 u.	23522 u.	114677 u.	31129 u.	162.093 kg	256299 u.
Belgium	No Report	132.000 kg	33.044 kg	279.620 kg	68.000 kg [ICPO]	68.000 kg [UNODC (4]
		125718 u.		467506 u.	818515 u.	818515 u.
Cyprus	No Report	3 u.	20 u.	0.001 kg	0.005 kg	0.004 kg
				62 u.	3317 u.	2910 u.
Denmark	15262 u.	0.102 kg	27038 u. [(2]	26117 u.	0.279 kg	150080 u.
		5802 u.			21638 u.	
Finland	No Report	0.195 kg	0.130 kg	16578 u. [ICPO]	87393 u.	81228 u.
		3147 u.	2396 u.			
France	1.522 kg	1.607 kg	4.795 kg	14.000 kg	13.314 kg	7.584 kg
				1860402 u.	2283620 u.	1503773 u.
Germany	692397 u.	694281 u.	419329 u.	1470507 u. [Govt]	35.500 kg	21.897 kg
					1634683 u.	4576504 u.
Gibraltar	300 u.	No Report	No Report	1.000 kg	205 u. [(5]	23 u.
				2 u.		
Greece	No Report	0.010 kg	85 u.	3095 u.	53557 u.	58845 u.
		136 u.				
Iceland	No Report	No Report	No Report	7478 u.	22057 u.	93151 u.
Ireland	No Report	9 u.	1.087 kg	74.609 kg	695133 u. [ICPO]	469862 u.
			616439 u.	266462 u.		
Italy	22958 u.	0.034 kg	1.580 kg	0.673 kg [ICPO]	0.492 kg	0.285 kg
		161044 u.	15 u.	272397 u.	502070 u.	308845 u.
Liechtenstein	No Report	565 u.	0.500 kg	No Report	10 u.	No Report
Luxembourg	545 u.	367 u.	No Report	0.167 kg	0.122 kg [ICPO]	No Report
				357 u.	318 u.	
Malta	No Report	247 u.	153 u.	459 u.	5191 u.	2242 u.

Source: Annual Report Questionnaire if not otherwise indicated

SEIZURES 1996 - 2001

Hallucinogens (excluding LSD but incl. "Ecstasy")

Region/country or territory	1996	1997	1998	1999	2000	2001
EUROPE						
Western Europe						
Monaco	No Report	No Report	No Report	3 u. [ICPO]	5 u. [ICPO]	No Report
Netherlands	350.000 kg [Govt] 2302179 u.	703.289 kg [Govt] 870980 u.	1163514 u. [Govt]	3663608 u. [Govt]	632.000 kg [Govt] 5500000 u.	113.000 kg 8684505 u.
Norway	12852 u.	13182 u.	1.081 kg 15647 u.	0.025 kg 24644 u.	0.114 kg 49390 u.	0.492 kg 61205 u.
Portugal	No Report	No Report	10 u.	0.089 kg 31319 u.	1.089 kg 25499 u.	0.091 kg 126451 u.
Spain	340444 u.	184950 u.	194527 u.	357649 u.	914974 u. [ICPO]	860164 u.
Sweden	0.122 kg	0.135 kg 1540 u.	0.579 kg	0.504 kg	0.591 kg [ICPO] 184161 u.	0.887 kg 57750 u.
Switzerland	81917 u.	86676 u.	73914 u.	67353 u.	189569 u. [6]	86959 u.
Turkey	No Report	No Report	477250 u.	No Report	33894 u. [Govt.]	121508 u.
United Kingdom	5798000 u.	1925500 u.	2095879 u. [7]	6323500 u. [NCIS]	6534813 u.	6534813 u. [UNODC] [4]
Sub-Total	351.644 kg 9291972 u.	837.372 kg 4097669 u.	42.796 kg 5200981 u.	370.690 kg 14890670 u.	913.601 kg 19560290 u.	212.240 kg 24855740 u.
Total region	352.749 kg 9294151 u.	837.386 kg 4106961 u.	42.796 kg 5219113 u.	372.959 kg 0.000 lt. 14951620 u.	914.390 kg 19831980 u.	253.546 kg 25204140 u.
OCEANIA						
Oceania						
Australia	2.110 kg 56128 u.	1.394 kg	7.380 kg [Govt. (8)]	57.645 kg [9]	0.773 kg	4.630 kg
New Zealand	No Report	No Report	2665 u.	No Report	0.530 kg [10] 8858 u.	0.483 kg 3.000 lt. 84744 u.
Sub-Total	2.110 kg 56128 u.	1.394 kg	7.380 kg 2665 u.	57.645 kg	1.303 kg 8858 u.	5.113 kg 3.000 lt. 84744 u.
Total region	2.110 kg 56128 u.	1.394 kg	7.380 kg 2665 u.	57.645 kg	1.303 kg 8858 u.	5.113 kg 3.000 lt. 84744 u.
TOTAL	488.973 kg 9716105 u.	1560.653 kg 59.968 lt. 6014253 u.	215.172 kg 0.022 lt. 7349368 u.	2657.463 kg 0.503 lt. 19960000 u.	2207.085 kg 0.155 lt. 33637180 u.	821.621 kg 3.000 lt. 39437400 u.

1) éxtasis 2) Small quantity. 3) Ketamine 4) Due to unavailability of 2001 data, year 2000 data were used for analysis purposes.
5) Psilocibin 6) Includes ecstasy 7) Including other opiates. 8) Provisional figures. 9) Mushrooms 10) Psilocybine

Source: Annual Report Questionnaire if not otherwise indicated

SEIZURES 1996 - 2001
LSD

Region/country or territory	1996	1997	1998	1999	2000	2001
AFRICA						
North Africa						
Egypt	669 u.	15 u.	514 u.	No Report	300 u.	No Report
Sub-Total	669 u.	15 u.	514 u.		300 u.	
Southern Africa						
Namibia	No Report	No Report	No Report	No Report	127 u. [ICPO]	No Report
South Africa	11804 u.	2730 u.	6426 u.	1549 u. [ICPO]	5506 u.	7841 u.
Zambia	0.000 kg [Govt]	0.080 kg [Govt]	0.000 kg [Govt]	0.000 kg [Govt]	0.000 kg [Govt]	0.000 kg [Govt]
Zimbabwe	No Report	No Report	No Report	30 u.	No Report	No Report
Sub-Total	11804 u.	0.080 kg 2730 u.	6426 u.	1579 u.	5633 u.	7841 u.
Total region	12473 u.	0.080 kg 2745 u.	6940 u.	1579 u.	5933 u.	7841 u.
AMERICAS						
Caribbean						
Bermuda	No Report	18 u.	No Report	No Report	No Report	No Report
Sub-Total		18 u.				
Central America						
Costa Rica	No Report	No Report	No Report	No Report	1045 u.	277 u.
Sub-Total					1045 u.	277 u.
North America						
Canada	0.259 kg 17613 u.	22519 u.	0.295 kg 8955 u.	0.098 kg 9852 u.	0.149 kg 5.000 lt. 1592 u.	0.401 kg 2747 u.
Mexico	No Report	No Report	No Report	No Report	No Report	8 u.
United States	0.099 kg 74396 u.	1.488 kg 0.452 lt. 79073 u.	No Report	0.330 kg 165504 u.	0.004 kg 1.296 lt. 28459 u.	97057 u.
Sub-Total	0.358 kg 92009 u.	1.488 kg 0.452 lt. 101592 u.	0.295 kg 8955 u.	0.428 kg 175356 u.	0.153 kg 6.296 lt. 30051 u.	0.401 kg 99812 u.
South America						
Argentina	1291 u. [Govt.]	563 u.	1435 u.	1085 u.	1093 u.	1239 u.
Brazil	No Report	3 u.	No Report	16 u. [Govt.]	2368 u.	No Report
Chile	1205 u.	1764 u.	153 u.	11 u. [CICAD]	33 u.	2 u.
Uruguay	13 u. [Govt.]	72 u.	1 u.	4 u.	143 u.	No Report
Venezuela	No Report	No Report	No Report	No Report	1675 u.	No Report
Sub-Total	2509 u.	2402 u.	1589 u.	1116 u.	5312 u.	1241 u.

Source: Annual Report Questionnaire if not otherwise indicated

SEIZURES 1996 - 2001
LSD

Region/country or territory	1996	1997	1998	1999	2000	2001
AMERICAS						
Total region	0.358 kg 94518 u.	1.488 kg 0.452 lt. 104012 u.	0.295 kg 10544 u.	0.428 kg 176472 u.	0.153 kg 6.296 lt. 36408 u.	0.401 kg 101330 u.
ASIA						
Central Asia and Transcaucasian countries						
Uzbekistan	No Report	No Report	40 u.	No Report	No Report	No Report
Sub-Total			40 u.			
East and South-East Asia						
Hong Kong SAR, China	46 u.	52 u.	No Report	21 u.	27877 u.	6858 u.
Indonesia	3328 u.	No Report	103368 u.	53160 u.	No Report	No Report
Japan	3668201 u.	3471 u.	4802 u.	62618 u.	65043 u.	644 u.
Macau SAR, China	No Report	No Report	No Report	No Report	No Report	8 u.
Singapore	No Report	No Report	No Report	No Report	No Report	807 u.
Thailand	No Report	0.031 kg	No Report	No Report	ICPO	No Report
Sub-Total	3671575 u.	0.031 kg 3523 u.	108170 u.	115799 u.	92920 u.	8317 u.
Near and Middle East /South-West Asia						
Israel	16660 u.	0.040 lt. 7342 u.	10337 u.	7346 u. ICPO	7769 u.	0.003 kg 6266 u.
Kuwait	No Report	13245 u.	No Report	No Report	No Report	No Report
Saudi Arabia	3882730 u. ICPO	No Report	No Report	No Report	No Report	No Report
Sub-Total	3899390 u.	0.040 lt. 20587 u.	10337 u.	7346 u.	7769 u.	0.003 kg 6266 u.
South Asia						
India	1285 u. Govt.	No Report	45 u.	20 u.	No Report	No Report
Nepal	No Report	No Report	9 u.	No Report	No Report	No Report
Sub-Total	1285 u.		54 u.	20 u.		
Total region	7572250 u.	0.031 kg 0.040 lt. 24110 u.	118601 u.	123165 u.	100689 u.	0.003 kg 14583 u.
EUROPE						
Eastern Europe						
Croatia	172 u.	114 u.	86 u.	247 u.	231 u.	154 u.
Czech Republic	No Report	No Report	No Report	19 u.	1001 u.	5 u.
Estonia	4 u. ICPO	No Report	No Report	6 u.	0.022 kg 3 u.	0.002 kg

Source: Annual Report Questionnaire if not otherwise indicated

SEIZURES 1996 - 2001
LSD

Region/country or territory	1996	1997	1998	1999	2000	2001
EUROPE						
Eastern Europe						
Hungary	1079 u.	1450 u. Govt.	3351 u.	1928 u.	1242 u.	973 u.
Latvia	16 u.	205 u.	38 u.	27 u.	14 u.	16 u.
Lithuania	No Report	2 u.	342 u.	164 u.	26 u.	275 u.
Poland	No Report	542 u.	14902 u.	14099 u.	3659 u.	672 u.
Romania	No Report	No Report	No Report	1 u.	1 u. ICPO	No Report
Russian Federation	No Report	No Report	No Report	No Report	0.380 kg ICPO	1.676 kg
Serbia and Montenegro	No Report	No Report	No Report	No Report	No Report	5 u.
Slovakia	No Report	2 u.	63 u.	72 u.	110 u.	60 u.
Slovenia	947 u.	156 u.	53 u.	512 u.	59 u.	No Report
Ukraine	No Report	14 u.	500 u.	36 u. ICPO	No Report	No Report
Sub-Total	2218 u.	2485 u.	19335 u.	17111 u.	0.402 kg 6346 u.	1.678 kg 2160 u.
Western Europe						
Andorra	No Report	No Report	28 u. ICPO	No Report	47 u. ICPO	9 u.
Austria	4166 u.	5243 u.	2494 u.	2811 u.	0.865 kg	572 u.
Belgium	13704 u.	621 u.	2050 u.	1047 u.	1090 u. ICPO	No Report
Cyprus	1 u.	No Report	No Report	2 u.	11 u.	No Report
Denmark	262 u.	381 u.	108 u.	83 u.	1109 u.	156 u.
Finland	41 u.	323 u.	301 u.	50 u.	2355 u.	1026 u.
France	74780 u.	5983 u.	18680 u.	9991 u.	20691 u.	6718 u.
Germany	67082 u.	78430 u.	32250 u.	22965 u.	43924 u.	11441 u.
Gibraltar	3 u.	(1	0.001 kg	No Report	No Report	No Report
Greece	1106 u.	166 u.	44 u.	212 u. ICPO	112 u.	577 u.
Iceland	No Report	No Report	No Report	339 u.	15 u.	No Report
Ireland	5901 u.	1851 u.	792 u.	648 u.	No Report	325 u.
Italy	14191 u.	8140 u.	0.003 kg 9752 u.	5509 u. ICPO	1980 u.	1139 u.
Liechtenstein	No Report	No Report	No Report	No Report	No Report	1 u.
Luxembourg	122 u.	4 u.	0.303 kg	1 u.	21 u. ICPO	No Report
Malta	45 u.	19 u.	123 u.	54 u.	462 u.	No Report
Monaco	No Report	No Report	10 u.	No Report	No Report	No Report
Netherlands	32320 u. Govt	27634 u. Govt	37790 u. Govt	2667 u. Govt	9972 u. Govt	28731 u.
Norway	551 u.	6888 u.	2833 u.	483 u.	893 u.	417 u.
Portugal	705 u.	84 u.	261 u.	1845 u.	6106 u.	3588 u.
Spain	13373 u.	25368 u.	9068 u.	3353 u.	7542 u.	26535 u.
Sweden	2459 u.	1541 u.	0.002 kg 2704 u.	1508 u.	0.000 kg (2 278 u.	635 u.

Source: Annual Report Questionnaire if not otherwise indicated

SEIZURES 1996 - 2001
LSD

Region/country or territory	1996	1997	1998	1999	2000	2001
EUROPE						
Western Europe						
Switzerland	9010 u.	9424 u.	2995 u.	3130 u.	15525 u.	8707 u.
Turkey	No Report	No Report	No Report	61 u.	No Report	105 u.
United Kingdom	216400 u.	164100 u.	40070 u.	67400 u. NCIS	25392 u.	25392 u. (3 UNODC
Sub-Total	456222 u.	336200 u.	0.309 kg 162353 u.	124159 u.	0.865 kg 137525 u.	116074 u.
Total region	458440 u.	338685 u.	0.309 kg 181688 u.	141270 u.	1.267 kg 143871 u.	1.678 kg 118234 u.
OCEANIA						
Oceania						
Australia	0.647 kg 6180 u.		No Report	0.108 kg	0.007 kg	No Report
New Zealand	No Report	No Report	37554 u.	17437 u.	17522 u.	1057 u.
Sub-Total	0.647 kg 6180 u.		37554 u.	0.108 kg 17437 u.	0.007 kg 17522 u.	1057 u.
Total region	0.647 kg 6180 u.		37554 u.	0.108 kg 17437 u.	0.007 kg 17522 u.	1057 u.
TOTAL	1.005 kg 8143861 u.	1.599 kg 0.492 lt. 469552 u.	0.604 kg 355327 u.	0.536 kg 459923 u.	1.427 kg 6.296 lt. 304423 u.	2.082 kg 243045 u.

1) Including depressants. 2) 2 micrograms 3) Due to unavailability of 2001 data, year 2000 data were used for analysis purposes.

Source: Annual Report Questionnaire if not otherwise indicated

SEIZURES 1996 - 2001
Methaqualone

Region/country or territory	1996	1997	1998	1999	2000	2001
AFRICA						
East Africa						
Kenya	(1	5000 u.	No Report	No Report	No Report	52693 u.[Govt]
Uganda	78.354 kg	No Report	No Report	No Report	No Report	No Report
United Republic of Tanzania	No Report	57 u.	4 u.	7 u.	295.000 kg [ICPO]	2.107 kg[Govt]
Sub-Total	78.354 kg	5057 u.	4 u.	7 u.	295.000 kg	2.107 kg 52693 u.
Southern Africa						
Angola	No Report	No Report	1.050 kg [ICPO]	No Report	No Report	No Report
Malawi	1000 u.	185.652 kg 200307 u.	1007 u. [Govt.]	1800 u.	No Report	No Report
Mozambique	No Report	No Report	No Report	No Report	2200 u. [ICPO]	No Report
Namibia	4846 u.	No Report	6318 u.	2611 u.	10430 u. [ICPO]	16675 u.
South Africa	34.200 kg 432807 u.	50.561 kg 1629531 u.	160.000 kg 1307109 u.	2498806 u. [ICPO]	114.507 kg 2669813 u.	7297.837 kg 4202835 u.
Swaziland	7408 u. [ICPO]	15245 u. [ICPO]	12015 u.	1621 u.	6 u. [ICPO]	258 u.
Zambia	2.784 kg [Govt]	0.004 kg [Govt]	0.125 kg [Govt]	2368 u.	0.125 kg 724 u.	0.020 kg[Govt]
Zimbabwe	No Report	No Report	4.300 kg 4431 u.	1701 u.	1500 u.	No Report
Sub-Total	36.984 kg 446061 u.	236.217 kg 1845083 u.	165.475 kg 1330880 u.	2508907 u.	114.632 kg 2684673 u.	7297.857 kg 4219768 u.
Total region	115.338 kg 446061 u.	236.217 kg 1850140 u.	165.475 kg 1330884 u.	2508914 u.	409.632 kg 2684673 u.	7299.964 kg 4272461 u.
AMERICAS						
North America						
Canada	0.002 kg 78 u.		0.007 kg	56.000 kg 123 u.	0.139 kg 46 u.	0.002 kg
United States	80585 u.	1330 u.	No Report	32030 u.	0.002 kg 76 u.	107 u.
Sub-Total	0.002 kg 80663 u.	1330 u.	0.007 kg	56.000 kg 32153 u.	0.141 kg 122 u.	0.002 kg 107 u.
South America						
Chile	No Report	No Report	1390 u.	No Report	No Report	No Report
Sub-Total			1390 u.			
Total region	0.002 kg 80663 u.	1330 u.	0.007 kg 1390 u.	56.000 kg 32153 u.	0.141 kg 122 u.	0.002 kg 107 u.

Source: Annual Report Questionnaire if not otherwise indicated

SEIZURES 1996 - 2001
Methaqualone

Region/country or territory	1996	1997	1998	1999	2000	2001
ASIA						
East and South-East Asia						
Hong Kong SAR, China	25 u.	4 u.	No Report	187 u. [ICPO]	25.000 kg	0.001 kg
						1 u.
Indonesia	53290 u.	No Report	No Report	2018 u.	No Report	No Report
Singapore		No Report	No Report	No Report	No Report	No Report
Sub-Total	53315 u.	4 u.		2205 u.	25.000 kg	0.001 kg
						1 u.
Near and Middle East /South-West Asia						
United Arab Emirates	No Report	6000.815 kg	No Report	No Report	No Report	No Report
Sub-Total		6000.815 kg				
South Asia						
India	2212.000 kg [Govt.]	1740.000 kg	2257.000 kg	474.000 kg	1095.000 kg	2024.000 kg
Sub-Total	2212.000 kg	1740.000 kg	2257.000 kg	474.000 kg	1095.000 kg	2024.000 kg
Total region	2212.000 kg	7740.815 kg	2257.000 kg	474.000 kg	1120.000 kg	2024.001 kg
	53315 u.	4 u.		2205 u.		1 u.
EUROPE						
Eastern Europe						
Romania	No Report	No Report	1924 u.	8487 u. [ICPO]	3981 u. [ICPO]	3 u.
Sub-Total			1924 u.	8487 u.	3981 u.	3 u.
Western Europe						
Belgium	No Report	No Report	11.000 kg	No Report	No Report	No Report
			52 u.			
Greece	No Report	41 u.	No Report	No Report	No Report	No Report
Switzerland	No Report	No Report	4620 u.	No Report	No Report	No Report
United Kingdom				No Report	No Report	No Report
Sub-Total		41 u.	11.000 kg			
			4672 u.			
Total region		41 u.	11.000 kg	8487 u.	3981 u.	3 u.
			6596 u.			
TOTAL	2327.340 kg	7977.032 kg	2433.482 kg	530.000 kg	1529.773 kg	9323.966 kg
	580039 u.	1851515 u.	1338870 u.	2551759 u.	2688776 u.	4272572 u.

1) Small quantity.

Source: Annual Report Questionnaire if not otherwise indicated

SEIZURES 1996 - 2001
Synthetic narcotics

Region/country or territory	1996	1997	1998	1999	2000	2001
AFRICA						
Southern Africa						
Zambia	0.000 kg Govt	0.881 kg Govt	2.300 kg Govt	0.000 kg Govt	0.000 kg Govt	0.000 kg Govt
Sub-Total		0.881 kg	2.300 kg			
West and Central Africa						
Gambia	No Report	1750 u. ICPO	No Report	No Report	No Report	No Report
Mali	No Report	1.100 kg ICPO 3336 u.	No Report	No Report	No Report	No Report
Niger	No Report	752718 u. ICPO	No Report	No Report	No Report	No Report
Nigeria	No Report	760.753 kg ICPO	No Report	No Report	No Report	No Report
Sub-Total		761.853 kg 757804 u.				
Total region		762.734 kg 757804 u.	2.300 kg			
AMERICAS						
North America						
Canada	0.400 kg 1.963 lt. 827 u.	154.121 kg 0.286 lt. 2645 u.	0.281 kg 1764.550 lt. 4231 u.	1.025 kg 2.654 lt. 2461 u.	0.644 kg 2.077 lt. 2719 u.	No Report
United States	767.100 kg 6646 u.	No Report	No Report	2.883 kg 39037 u.	0.314 kg 4.021 lt. 51860 u.	No Report
Sub-Total	767.500 kg 1.963 lt. 7473 u.	154.121 kg 0.286 lt. 2645 u.	0.281 kg 1764.550 lt. 4231 u.	3.908 kg 2.654 lt. 41498 u.	0.958 kg 6.098 lt. 54579 u.	
South America						
Colombia	No Report	No Report	No Report	No Report	No Report	22750 u.
Venezuela	No Report	No Report	No Report	No Report	7985 u.	No Report
Sub-Total					7985 u.	22750 u.
Total region	767.500 kg 1.963 lt. 7473 u.	154.121 kg 0.286 lt. 2645 u.	0.281 kg 1764.550 lt. 4231 u.	3.908 kg 2.654 lt. 41498 u.	0.958 kg 6.098 lt. 62564 u.	22750 u.
ASIA						
Central Asia and Transcaucasian countries						
Armenia	1.023 kg 1550 u.	No Report	No Report	No Report	0.003 kg	0.003 kg
Georgia	0.001 kg ICPO	No Report	No Report	No Report	No Report	No Report
Kazakhstan	No Report	No Report	11.576 kg	3.408 kg	No Report	No Report

Source: Annual Report Questionnaire if not otherwise indicated

321

SEIZURES 1996 - 2001
Synthetic narcotics

Region/country or territory	1996	1997	1998	1999	2000	2001
ASIA						
Central Asia and Transcaucasian countries						
Kyrgyzstan	13.988 kg	0.020 kg	0.000 kg [F.O]	0.692 kg	0.000 kg [F.O]	0.000 kg [F.O]
Uzbekistan	No Report	287 u.	No Report	No Report	No Report	No Report
Sub-Total	15.012 kg 1550 u.	0.020 kg 287 u.	11.576 kg	4.100 kg	0.003 kg	0.003 kg
East and South-East Asia						
China	79373 u.	No Report	No Report	No Report	No Report	No Report
Hong Kong SAR, China	No Report	No Report	No Report	1000 u.	No Report	No Report
Indonesia	138 u.	863 u.	No Report	550 u.	No Report	No Report
Japan	0.031 kg 15098 u.	0.013 kg 8240 u.	0.097 kg 11483 u.	0.048 kg 17968 u.	0.495 kg 77078 u.	No Report
Korea (Republic of)	200 u.	No Report	No Report	0.046 kg	No Report	No Report
Macau SAR, China	No Report	8968 u. [ICPO]	No Report	No Report	No Report	No Report
Philippines	No Report	93 u. [ICPO]	No Report	No Report	No Report	No Report
Singapore	69631 u.	7670 u.	No Report	No Report	No Report	No Report
Thailand	No Report	No Report	593.652 kg	No Report	No Report	No Report
Sub-Total	0.031 kg 164440 u.	0.013 kg 25834 u.	593.749 kg 11483 u.	0.094 kg 19518 u.	0.495 kg 77078 u.	
Near and Middle East /South-West Asia						
Qatar	No Report	2503 u. [ICPO]	No Report	No Report	No Report	No Report
Yemen	No Report	60 u. [ICPO]	No Report	No Report	No Report	No Report
Sub-Total		2563 u.				
South Asia						
Bangladesh	16075 u.	No Report	No Report	No Report	No Report	No Report
Maldives	No Report	No Report	No Report	140 u.	No Report	No Report
Nepal	No Report	6439 u. [ICPO]	No Report	No Report	No Report	No Report
Sub-Total	16075 u.	6439 u.		140 u.		
Total region	15.043 kg 182065 u.	0.033 kg 35123 u.	605.325 kg 11483 u.	4.194 kg 19658 u.	0.498 kg 77078 u.	0.003 kg
EUROPE						
Eastern Europe						
Belarus	No Report	No Report	0.080 kg	0.025 kg	0.101 kg	No Report
Bulgaria	No Report	No Report	No Report	No Report	22.126 kg [Govt]	No Report
Croatia	4438 u.	3554 u.	6252 u.	635 u.	5458 u.	No Report
Estonia	No Report	No Report	0.012 kg 44 u.	0.011 kg 43 u.	0.039 kg 100 u.	No Report
Latvia	0.015 kg	No Report	No Report	No Report	No Report	No Report

Source: Annual Report Questionnaire if not otherwise indicated

SEIZURES 1996 - 2001

Synthetic narcotics

Region/country or territory	1996	1997	1998	1999	2000	2001
EUROPE						
Eastern Europe						
Lithuania	0.022 kg 0.015 lt. 92 u.	0.001 lt. [1] 252 u.	No Report	No Report	25.992 kg	No Report
Romania	No Report	No Report	1003 u.	No Report	No Report	No Report
Russian Federation	No Report	287 u.	10230 u.	No Report	No Report	No Report
Slovakia	No Report	No Report	No Report	1309 u.	No Report	No Report
Slovenia	186 u.	81 u.	No Report	No Report	0.002 lt. 245 u.	No Report
Ukraine	9.782 kg	No Report	No Report	No Report	No Report	No Report
Sub-Total	9.819 kg 0.015 lt. 4716 u.	0.001 lt. 4174 u.	0.092 kg 17529 u.	0.036 kg 1987 u.	48.258 kg 0.002 lt. 5803 u.	
Western Europe						
Belgium	No Report	1100 u.	No Report	9.300 kg	No Report	No Report
France	630 u.	854 u.	5085 u.	521 u.	No Report	No Report
Germany	4443 u.	0.180 kg 0.994 lt. 3482 u.	No Report	No Report	No Report	No Report
Greece	No Report	No Report	20 u.	No Report	No Report	No Report
Ireland	No Report	34.000 lt. 408 u.	0.009 kg 1960 u.	No Report	No Report	No Report
Italy	1.902 kg	0.077 kg 5080 u.	3.045 kg 134359 u.	No Report	No Report	No Report
Malta	94 u.	0.005 kg	0.030 lt. 23 u.	No Report	No Report	No Report
Norway	14431 u.	16076 u.	0.104 kg 17949 u.	0.004 kg 9170 u.	0.008 kg 4942 u.	No Report
Portugal	No Report	0.001 kg 7 u.	2 u.	0.021 kg 27 u.	No Report	No Report
Switzerland	No Report	5.231 kg	33.190 kg	No Report	No Report	No Report
Turkey	259097 u.	No Report	257493 u.	55067 u.	15558 u.	911407 u.
United Kingdom	87.500 kg	117.200 kg	70.584 kg	No Report	No Report	No Report
Sub-Total	89.402 kg 278695 u.	122.694 kg 34.994 lt. 27007 u.	106.932 kg 0.030 lt. 416891 u.	9.325 kg 64785 u.	0.008 kg 20500 u.	911407 u.
Total region	99.221 kg 0.015 lt. 283411 u.	122.694 kg 34.995 lt. 31181 u.	107.024 kg 0.030 lt. 434420 u.	9.361 kg 66772 u.	48.266 kg 0.002 lt. 26303 u.	911407 u.

Source: Annual Report Questionnaire if not otherwise indicated

SEIZURES 1996 - 2001
Synthetic narcotics

Region/country or territory	1996	1997	1998	1999	2000	2001
OCEANIA						
Oceania						
Australia	2.563 kg 0.250 lt. 3 u.	2.259 kg	No Report	0.369 kg	No Report	No Report
Sub-Total	2.563 kg 0.250 lt. 3 u.	2.259 kg		0.369 kg		
Total region	2.563 kg 0.250 lt. 3 u.	2.259 kg		0.369 kg		
TOTAL	884.327 kg 2.228 lt. 472952 u.	1041.841 kg 35.281 lt. 826753 u.	714.930 kg 1764.580 lt. 450134 u.	17.832 kg 2.654 lt. 127928 u.	49.722 kg 6.100 lt. 165945 u.	0.003 kg 934157 u.

1) Including depressants.

Source: Annual Report Questionnaire if not otherwise indicated

SEIZURES 1996 - 2001
Psychotropic substances

Region/country or territory	1996	1997	1998	1999	2000	2001
AFRICA						
East Africa						
Kenya	9 u. [Govt]	No Report	9060 u. [Govt]	No Report	272 u. [Govt]	No Report
Mauritius	No Report	No Report	No Report	No Report	No Report	897 u.
Sub-Total	9 u.		9060 u.		272 u.	897 u.
North Africa						
Morocco	No Report	No Report	No Report	No Report	No Report	135769 u.
Sub-Total						135769 u.
West and Central Africa						
Mauritania	No Report	147 u. [Govt]	135 u. [Govt]	No Report	No Report	No Report
Sub-Total		147 u.	135 u.			
Total region	9 u.	147 u.	9195 u.		272 u.	136666 u.
AMERICAS						
North America						
Mexico	No Report	No Report	1484078 u.	1490152 u.	3418369 u.	No Report
Sub-Total			1484078 u.	1490152 u.	3418369 u.	
South America						
Brazil	No Report	No Report	No Report	No Report	4862 u. [Govt]	No Report
Sub-Total					4862 u.	
Total region			1484078 u.	1490152 u.	3423231 u.	
ASIA						
Central Asia and Transcaucasian countries						
Uzbekistan	No Report	No Report	No Report	0.639 kg	No Report	No Report
Sub-Total				0.639 kg		
Near and Middle East /South-West Asia						
United Arab Emirates	No Report	No Report	No Report	14460 u.	23246 u.	No Report
Sub-Total				14460 u.	23246 u.	
Total region				0.639 kg 14460 u.	23246 u.	
EUROPE						
Eastern Europe						
Russian Federation	No Report	No Report	673.400 kg [F.O]	905.500 kg [F.O]	835.000 kg [F.O]	No Report
Sub-Total			673.400 kg	905.500 kg	835.000 kg	

Source: Annual Report Questionnaire if not otherwise indicated

SEIZURES 1996 - 2001
Psychotropic substances

Region/country or territory	1996	1997	1998	1999	2000	2001
EUROPE						
Total region			673.400 kg	905.500 kg	835.000 kg	
TOTAL	9 u.	147 u.	673.400 kg	906.139 kg	835.000 kg	136666 u.
			1493273 u.	1504612 u.	3446749 u.	

Source: Annual Report Questionnaire if not otherwise indicated

2.2.8. Amphetamine-type stimulants: Wholesale and street prices

WHOLESALE AND STREET PRICES OF
AMPHETAMINE
Retail and wholesale prices and purity levels:
breakdown by drug, region and country or territory
(prices expressed in US$ or converted equivalent, and purity levels in percentage)

Region / country or territory	RETAIL PRICE (*)					WHOLESALE PRICE (**)				
	Range	Average	Purity	Year	Unit	Range	Average	Purity	Year	Unit
Africa										
East Africa										
Seychelles						3,600.0 - 4,510.0	4,055.0		2000	
Uganda						100.0 - 150.0	125.0		2000	
Southern Africa										
South Africa	4.9 - 6.5	5.7	-	1999	T					
West and Central Africa										
Burkina Faso	0.1 - 0.1	0.1	-	2001		20.4 - 24.5	22.4	-	2001	
Côte d'Ivoire	0.1 - 2.7	1.4	100.0	2001		2.7 - 5.4	4.1	100.0	2001	
Nigeria	0.4 - 0.8	0.6	-	2001		392.9 - 480.2	436.5	-	2001	
Americas										
Caribbean										
Saint Lucia	0.7 - 0.8	0.7		2000		600.0 - 660.0	630.0		2000	
North America										
United States	80.0 - 600.0	240.0		2000		24,000.0 - 175,000.0	70,500.0		2000	
South America										
Argentina	3.0 - 5.0	4.0	-	2001		250.0 - 350.0	300.0		2000	
Venezuela	2.2 - 3.0	2.6		2000		222.0 - 295.7	260.0		2000	
Asia										
Central Asia and Transcaucasian countries										
Kyrgyzstan	0.1 - 0.4	0.3		2000		80.0 - 300.0	190.0		2000	
East and South-East Asia										
Brunei Darussalam	9.2 - 15.3	12.2		2000						
Indonesia							500.0	-	2001	
Macau SAR, China	7.0 - 9.0	8.0		2000						
Myanmar	0.2 - 0.5	0.3	-	2001	T	100.0 - 213.1	156.6	-	2001	TT
Vietnam	40.0 - 67.0	53.5	-	2001						
Near and Middle East/South										
Israel						200.0 - 375.0	288.0		2000	
Saudi Arabia	6.7 - 6.9	6.8	-	2001	T	6,666.7 - 6,933.3	6,800.0	40.0 - 90.0	2001	TT
Europe										
Eastern Europe										
Bulgaria	1.8 - 5.5	3.7	-	2001			3,220.0	30.0 - 60.0	2001	
Croatia	11.8 - 17.8	14.8	-	2001			6,520.0	-	2001	
Czech Republic	15.5 - 18.1	16.8	-	2001		11,633.1 - 15,510.8	13,571.9	-	2001	
Estonia	5.7 - 11.4	8.6	6.0 - 100.0	2001		1,996.1 - 2,851.5	2,423.8	2.0 - 100.0	2001	
Hungary	8.5 - 11.9	10.2	1.0 - 76.0	2001		1,704.0 - 3,408.0	2,556.0	1.0 - 29.0	2001	
Latvia	16.1 - 28.9	22.5	-	2001		1,446.3 - 2,731.9	2,089.1	-	2001	
Lithuania	12.5 - 20.0	16.3	35.0 - 60.0	2001		3,750.0 - 7,500.0	5,625.0	35.0 - 90.0	2001	
Poland	5.0 - 20.2	12.6	-	2001		2,520.7 - 5,041.4	3,781.1	-	2001	
Romania	3.0 - 5.0	4.0	-	2001	T	3,000.0 - 5,000.0	4,000.0	-	2001	TT
Slovakia		0.3	90.0	1998	T					
Slovenia	6.5 - 11.1	8.8	20.0 - 25.0	2000		2,780.0 - 4,630.0	3,705.0	20.0 - 25.0	2000	

WHOLESALE AND STREET PRICES OF
AMPHETAMINE

Retail and wholesale prices and purity levels:
breakdown by drug, region and country or territory
(prices expressed in US$ or converted equivalent, and purity levels in percentage)

Region / country or territory	RETAIL PRICE (*)					WHOLESALE PRICE (**)				
	Range	Average	Purity	Year	Unit	Range	Average	Purity	Year	Unit
Western Europe										
Andorra	8.0 - 16.1	12.1	-	2001	T					
Austria	13.5 - 33.6	23.5	-	2000		1,955.2 - 19,552.5	10,753.8	2.0 - 92.0	2001	
Belgium	8.5 - 13.0	10.8	-	2001		1,964.1 - 3,228.7	2,596.4	-	2001	
Denmark	23.9 - 59.8	41.9	-	2001		4,783.9 - 35,879.0	20,331.5	-	2001	
Finland		13.5	40.0	2001			5,381.2	50.0 - 60.0	2001	
France	6.3 - 17.9	12.1	-	2001						
Germany	8.2 - 21.9	15.1	-	2001	T	2,815.0 - 6,777.4	4,796.2	-	2001	TT
Gibraltar	21.6 - 43.2	32.4	2.0 - 60.0	2001						
Greece	2.7 - 4.5	3.6	-	2001		6.2 - 7.9	7.0	-	2001	
Iceland	38.0 - 54.0	46.0	-	2001						
Ireland		5.4	-	2001	D		1,790.0	-	2001	TD
Italy	16.9 - 19.2	18.1	-	2001		6,021.5 - 6,368.8	6,195.1	-	2001	
Luxembourg	13.3 - 26.5	19.9	-	1999						
Netherlands	2.5 - 7.8	5.1	-	1998		2,604.2 - 3,465.3	3,013.3	-	1998	
Norway	22.4 - 89.7	56.1	10.0 - 90.0	2001		8,968.6 - 13,452.9	11,210.8	10.0 - 90.0	2001	
Portugal	5.7 - 14.3	10.0	-	1998						
Spain		23.0	-	2001			15,810.0	-	2001	
Sweden	9.9 - 49.6	29.7	-	2001		4,956.1 - 9,912.2	7,434.2	-	2001	
Switzerland	7.0 - 17.5	12.3	-	2001	T					
United Kingdom	7.2 - 14.4	10.8	7.4 - 13.9	2001		2,160.5 - 3,600.8	2,880.7	15.3	2001	
Oceania										
Australia	44.8 - 191.9	118.4	7.0	1999		12,790.0 - 19,180.0	15,985.0	7.0	1999	
New Zealand	15.3 - 51.6	41.1		2000	T	18,270.0 - 27,410.0	22,840.0		2000	TT

(*) in Gram or otherwise as indicated
(**) in Kilogram or otherwise as indicated
D : Doses unit
T : Tablets unit
TD: Thousand of doses
TT: Thousand of tablets

WHOLESALE AND STREET PRICES OF
METHAMPHETAMINE
Retail and wholesale prices and purity levels:
breakdown by drug, region and country or territory
(prices expressed in US$ or converted equivalent, and purity levels in percentage)

Region / country or territory	RETAIL PRICE (per gram)					WHOLESALE PRICE (per kilogram)			
	Range	Average	Purity	Year		Range	Average	Purity	Year
Africa									
Southern Africa									
Malawi		5.0	-	1997			2,000.0	-	1997
Namibia		10.0	-	1996			2,000.0	-	1996
South Africa	3.4 - 8.9	6.2	-	1997		1,800.0 - 2,700.0	2,250.0	-	1997
West and Central Africa									
Burkina Faso	0.1 - 0.1	0.1	-	2001		20.4 - 24.5	22.4	-	2001
Americas									
North America									
Canada	52.2 - 130.6	91.4	-	2001	T	20,154.2 - 25,912.6	23,033.3	-	2001
United States	20.0 - 400.0	210.0	38.0	2001		6,000.0 - 45,000.0	25,500.0	-	2001
Asia									
East and South-East Asia									
Brunei Darussalam						58,858.2 - 70,629.8	64,744.0	-	1999
Hong Kong SAR, China	12.8 - 57.8	35.3	-	2001		4,365.4 - 6,419.7	5,392.5	-	2001
Japan	41.7 - 833.3	437.5	95.0	2001		15,000.0 - 50,000.0	32,500.0	-	2001
Macau SAR, China	12.5 - 24.9	18.7	-	2001					
Myanmar		1.0	-	2001					
Philippines	32.4 - 40.6	36.5	-	2001		36,500.6 - 44,611.8	40,556.2	-	2001
Republic of Korea	213.2 - 442.3	327.8	98.0	2001		31,592.0 - 47,388.0	39,490.0	-	2001
Singapore	56.2 - 67.4	61.8	73.0 - 80.1	2001		67,415.7 - 84,269.7	75,842.7	-	2001
Thailand	2.4 - 3.6	3.0	-	1998					
Europe									
Eastern Europe									
Czech Republic		25.9	40.0 - 80.0	2001		11,633.1 - 15,510.7	13,571.9	60.0 - 97.0	2001
Lithuania	12.5 - 20.0	16.3	35.0 - 55.0	2001		3,750.0 - 7,500.0	5,625.0	35.0 - 60.0	2001
Russian Federation	15.0 - 20.0	17.5	-	2001					
Slovakia						20,800.2 - 41,600.3	31,200.2	10.0 - 50.0	2001
Ukraine	10.0 - 30.0	20.0	-	2001		1,000.0 - 3,000.0	2,000.0	-	2001
Western Europe									
Finland	18.0 - 36.0	27.0	-	1999		9,892.1 - 12,589.9	11,241.0	31.0	1999
Germany	7.1 - 26.5	16.8	-	2000		3,200.0 - 7,990.0	5,595.0	-	2000
Netherlands	7.3 - 12.1	9.7	-	1999		-	-	-	-
Spain	24.3 - 25.8	25.1	-	1997		21,812.1 - 24,305.6	23,058.8	-	1997
Sweden	14.9 - 24.8	19.8	-	2001		5,947.3 - 9,912.2	7,929.8	-	2001
Switzerland	8.8 - 38.0	23.4	-	2001					
Oceania									
New Zealand	296.0 - 380.5	338.3	-	2001					

WHOLESALE AND STREET PRICES OF
L.S.D

Retail and wholesale prices and purity levels:
breakdown by drug, region and country or territory
(prices expressed in US$ or converted equivalent, and purity levels in percentage)

Region / country or territory	RETAIL PRICE (per dose)				WHOLESALE PRICE (per thousand dose)			
	Range	Average	Purity	Year	Range	Average	Purity	Year
Africa								
Southern Africa								
Namibia	15.2 - 17.8	16.5	-	2001				
South Africa		9.5	-	2001		5,710.0	-	2001
Zambia		42.8	-	1998				
Americas								
Central America								
Costa Rica		15.5	-	2001		15,500.0	-	2001
North America								
Canada	2.0 - 9.8	5.9	-	2001	653.0 - 2,611.9	1,632.5	-	2001
United States	1.0 - 10.0	5.5	-	1996	250.0 - 500.0	375.0	20.0 - 80.0	1996
South America								
Argentina	20.0 - 30.1	25.1	-	2001	450.9 - 551.1	501.0	-	2001
Asia								
East and South-East Asia								
Japan	33.3 - 83.3	58.3	-	2001				
Republic of Korea		15.8	-	2001				
Singapore	19.7 - 30.9	25.3	-	2001	8,427.0 - 11,236.0	9,831.5	-	2001
Near and Middle East /South-West Asia								
Israel	9.7 - 24.3	17.0	-	2001				
Europe								
Eastern Europe								
Bulgaria		13.8	-	2001				
Croatia	11.8 - 14.2	13.0	-	2001	8,292.4 - 10,661.7	9,477.1	-	2001
Czech Republic	3.2 - 6.4	4.8	-	1999				
Estonia		8.6	-	2001				
Hungary	8.5 - 11.9	10.2	-	2001	6,134.4 - 6,816.0	6,475.2	60.0 - 70.0	2001
Latvia		9.6	-	2001		800.0		2001
Lithuania	15.0 - 20.0	17.5	-	2001	10,000.0 - 12,500.0	11,250.0	-	2001
Poland	7.6 - 11.3	9.5	-	2001	5,264.5 - 10,529.1	7,896.8	-	1999
Slovakia	2.1 - 12.5	7.3	-	2001				
Slovenia		10.7	-	2001				
Western Europe								
Austria		9.0	-	2001		1,790.0	-	2001
Belgium	6.7 - 8.9	7.8	-	2001	1,793.7 - 2,242.2	2,017.9	-	2001
Denmark	7.7 - 11.7	9.7	-	1998		4,622.5	-	1999
Finland	9.2 - 19.3	14.1	-	1998	9,174.3 - 9,633.9	9,404.1	-	1998
France	4.5 - 13.5	9.0	-	2001				
Germany	3.6 - 10.0	6.8	-	2001	456.2 - 4,562.4	2,509.3	-	2001
Greece	2.7 - 8.1	5.4	-	2001	2,690.6 - 4,484.3	3,587.4	-	2001
Iceland		17.9	-	1998	-	-	-	-
Ireland	14.1 - 14.6	14.3	-	1998		1,790.0	-	2001
Italy	24.3 - 25.5	24.9	-	2001	2,870.8 - 4,593.3	3,732.1	-	1998

WHOLESALE AND STREET PRICES OF
L.S.D

Retail and wholesale prices and purity levels:
breakdown by drug, region and country or territory
(prices expressed in US$ or converted equivalent, and purity levels in percentage)

Region / country or territory	RETAIL PRICE (per dose)				WHOLESALE PRICE (per thousand dose)			
	Range	Average	Purity	Year	Range	Average	Purity	Year
Luxembourg		12.3	-	1998		9,943.2	-	1998
Netherlands		5.2	-	1998				
Norway	**0.7 - 1.3**	**1.0**	-	**2001**				
Portugal	5.7 - 14.3	10.0	-	1998				
Spain		8.5	-	1998		8,965.5	-	1998
Sweden	6.1 - 12.1	9.1	-	1999				
Switzerland	**8.8 - 11.7**	**10.2**	-	**2001**				
United Kingdom	**2.9 - 7.2**	**5.0**	-	**2001**	**1,440.3 - 4,321.0**	**2,880.7**	**-**	**2001**
Oceania								
Australia	12.4 - 26.7	16.5	-	1998				
New Zealand	**12.7 - 16.9**	**14.8**	-	**2001**	11,421.0 - 20,557.0	15,990.0	-	2000

WHOLESALE AND STREET PRICES OF
ECSTASY

Retail and wholesale prices and purity levels:
breakdown by drug, region and country or territory
(prices expressed in US$ or converted equivalent, and purity levels in percentage)

Region / country or territory	RETAIL PRICE (per tablet)				WHOLESALE PRICE (per thousand tablets)			
	Range	Average	Purity	Year	Range	Average	Purity	Year
Africa								
North Africa								
Egypt	20.9 - 31.3	26.1	-	2001	13,059.7 - 20,895.5	16,977.6	-	2001
Southern Africa								
Namibia	15.2 - 17.8	16.5	-	2001	11,421.3 - 12,690.4	12,055.8	-	2001
South Africa		9.4	-	2001		6,350.0	-	2001
Zimbabwe	45.5 - 54.5	50.0	-	2001	45,454.5 - 54,545.4	50,000.0	-	2001
Americas								
Caribbean								
Bahamas	25.0 - 40.0	32.5	-	2001	25,000.0 - 40,000.0	32,500.0	-	2001
Cayman Islands		30.0	-	2001				
Jamaica	20.0 - 25.0	22.5	-	2001				
Central America								
Costa Rica	10.9 - 15.5	13.2	-	2001	10,856.3 - 15,509.0	13,182.7	-	2001
Panama	5.0 - 12.0	8.5	35.0 - 60.0	2001	6,000.0 - 10,000.0	8,000.0	-	2001
North America								
Canada	13.1 - 32.6	22.9	-	2001	6,529.9 - 9,794.8	8,162.3	-	2001
United States	10,0 - 45.0	27.5	-	2000	2,000.0 - 20,000.0	11,000.0	-	2000
South America								
Argentina	25.1 - 35.1	30.1	-	2001	14,028.1 - 16,032.1	15,030.1	-	2001
Peru	40.0 - 50.0	45.0	95.0	2001	15,000.0 - 25,000.0	20,000.0	95.0	2001
Suriname	9.0 - 11.0	10.0	-	2001				
Venezuela		21.2	-	2001				
Asia								
East and South-East Asia								
China		34.3	-	1999	4,839.1 - 9,678.2	7,258.7	-	2001
Hong Kong SAR, China	7.7 - 38.5	23.1	-	2001	3,851.8 - 15,407.2	9,629.5	-	2001
Indonesia		30.0	-	1996		10,730.0	-	1996
Japan	16.7 - 50.0	33.3	-	2001				
Republic of Korea	39.5 - 79.0	59.2	-	2001	31,592.0 - 39,490.0	35,541.0	-	2001
Macau	18.7 - 31.0	24.9	-	2001				
Philippines	32.4 - 36.5	34.5	-	2001				
Singapore	11.2 - 14.0	12.6	23.6 - 49.6	2001		6,740.0	-	2001
Thailand	10.6	10.6	-	1999				
Near and Middle East /South-West Asia								
Israel	8.5 - 19.4	14.0	-	2001				
Europe								
Eastern Europe								
Bulgaria	6.9 - 9.2	8.1	-	2001	4,141.2 - 13,804.0	8,972.6	-	2001
Croatia	4.7 - 8.3	6.5	-	2001	2,369.3 - 3,553.9	2,961.6	-	2001
Czech Republic	3.9 - 7.8	5.8	20.0 - 40.0	2001	1,292.6 - 2,585.1	1,938.8	-	2001
Estonia	5.1 - 6.8	6.0	15.0 - 68.0	2001	1,425.8 - 3,992.1	2,708.9	11.0 - 68.0	2001
Hungary	8.5 - 10.2	9.4	1.0 - 49.0	2001	1,022.4 - 5,112.0	3,067.2	1.0	2001
Latvia					401.7 - 1,205.2	803.5	-	2001

WHOLESALE AND STREET PRICES OF
ECSTASY

Retail and wholesale prices and purity levels:
breakdown by drug, region and country or territory
(prices expressed in US$ or converted equivalent, and purity levels in percentage)

Region / country or territory	RETAIL PRICE (per tablet)				WHOLESALE PRICE (per thousand tablets)			
	Range	Average	Purity	Year	Range	Average	Purity	Year
Lithuania	6.3 - 8.8	7.5	10.0 - 30.0	2001	2,500.0 - 3,800.0	3,100.0	10.0 - 30.0	2001
Poland	2.5 - 7.6	5.0	-	2001	1,512.4 - 2,016.6	1,764.5	-	2001
Romania	3.0 - 5.0	4.0	-	2001	3,000.0 - 5,000.0	4,000.0	25.0 - 35.0	2001
Russian Federation	15.0 - 20.0	17.5	-	2001				
Serbia and Montenegro	13.5 - 20.2	16.8	-	2001	1,793.7 - 8,968.6	5,381.2	-	2001
Slovakia	4.2 - 10.4	7.3	-	2001				
Slovenia		6.0	-	2001		1,970.0	-	2001
Western Europe								
Andorra	8.0 - 10.7	9.4	-	2001				
Austria	5.4 - 13.5	9.4	90.0	2001	2,690.6 - 3,587.4	3,139.0	-	2001
Belgium	4.5 - 7.8	6.1	-	2001	1,004.5 - 1,452.9	1,228.7	-	2001
Cyprus	12.4 - 18.6	15.5	-	2001				
Denmark	9.6 - 12.0	10.8	-	2001	2,391.9 - 5,979.8	4,185.9	-	2001
Finland	7.2 - 15.2	11.2	-	2001	4,671.4 - 6,229.0	5,450.0	-	2000
France	6.3 - 22.4	14.3	-	2001				
Germany	3.6 - 11.4	7.5	-	2001	1,616.9 - 4,359.8	2,988.4	-	2001
Gibraltar	7.2 - 17.3	12.2	-	2001				
Greece	9.0 - 17.9	13.5	-	2001	8,071.7 - 10,762.3	9,417.0	-	2001
Iceland	22.0 - 38.0	30.0	-	2001				
Ireland		9.0	-	2001		1,790.0	-	2001
Italy	19.5 - 22.7	21.1	-	2001	463.2 - 694.8	579.0	26.0	2001
Luxembourg		13.3	-	1999	6,747.6 - 7,102.3	6,925.0	-	1998
Malta	22.6 - 27.1	24.9	-	2001	13,561.5 - 18,082.0	15,821.8	-	2001
Netherlands	7.8 - 12.4	10.0	-	1998	2,475.5 - 3,465.3	2,848.3	-	1998
Norway	10.8 - 22.4	16.6	20.0 - 50.0	2001				
Portugal		6.2	8.5 - 59.5	2001	1.358.7 - 2,857.1	2,104.7	-	1998
Spain		14.6	-	1999		15,689.7	-	1998
Sweden	9.9 - 19.8	14.9	-	2001		8,489.0	-	1999
Switzerland	8.8 - 23.4	16.1	-	2001				
Turkey	15.0 - 20.0	17.5	-	2001	10,000.0 - 20,000.0	15,000.0	-	2001
United Kingdom	7.2 - 14.4	10.8	-	2001	1,440.3 - 4,321.0	2,880.7	-	2001
Oceania								
Australia	15.6 - 41.7	28.6	-	2001	9,590.0 - 15,980.0	12,785.0	-	1999
New Zealand	33.8 - 42.3	38.1	-	2001	16,913.3 - 29,598.3	23,255.8	80.0	2001

2.3. CONSUMPTION

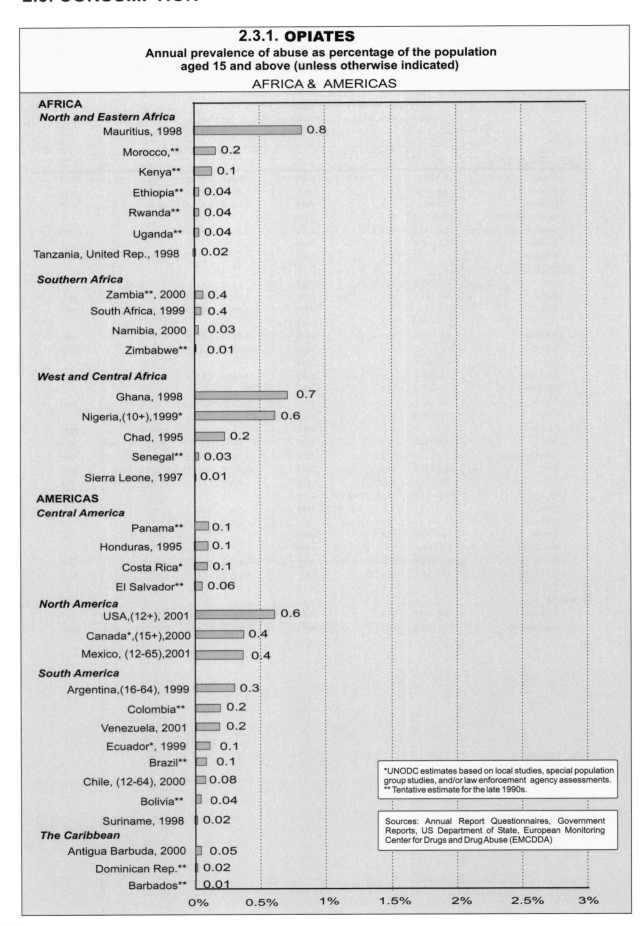

2.3.1. OPIATES
**Annual prevalence of abuse as percentage of the population
aged 15 and above (unless otherwise indicated)**

AFRICA & AMERICAS

AFRICA
North and Eastern Africa
Mauritius, 1998 — 0.8
Morocco,** — 0.2
Kenya** — 0.1
Ethiopia** — 0.04
Rwanda** — 0.04
Uganda** — 0.04
Tanzania, United Rep., 1998 — 0.02

Southern Africa
Zambia**, 2000 — 0.4
South Africa, 1999 — 0.4
Namibia, 2000 — 0.03
Zimbabwe** — 0.01

West and Central Africa
Ghana, 1998 — 0.7
Nigeria,(10+),1999* — 0.6
Chad, 1995 — 0.2
Senegal** — 0.03
Sierra Leone, 1997 — 0.01

AMERICAS
Central America
Panama** — 0.1
Honduras, 1995 — 0.1
Costa Rica* — 0.1
El Salvador** — 0.06

North America
USA,(12+), 2001 — 0.6
Canada*,(15+),2000 — 0.4
Mexico, (12-65),2001 — 0.4

South America
Argentina,(16-64), 1999 — 0.3
Colombia** — 0.2
Venezuela, 2001 — 0.2
Ecuador*, 1999 — 0.1
Brazil** — 0.1
Chile, (12-64), 2000 — 0.08
Bolivia** — 0.04
Suriname, 1998 — 0.02
The Caribbean
Antigua Barbuda, 2000 — 0.05
Dominican Rep.** — 0.02
Barbados** — 0.01

*UNODC estimates based on local studies, special population group studies, and/or law enforcement agency assessments.
** Tentative estimate for the late 1990s.

Sources: Annual Report Questionnaires, Government Reports, US Department of State, European Monitoring Center for Drugs and Drug Abuse (EMCDDA)

0%   0.5%   1%   1.5%   2%   2.5%   3%

OPIATES
Annual prevalence of abuse as percentage of the population aged 15 and above (unless otherwise indicated)
EUROPE & OCEANIA

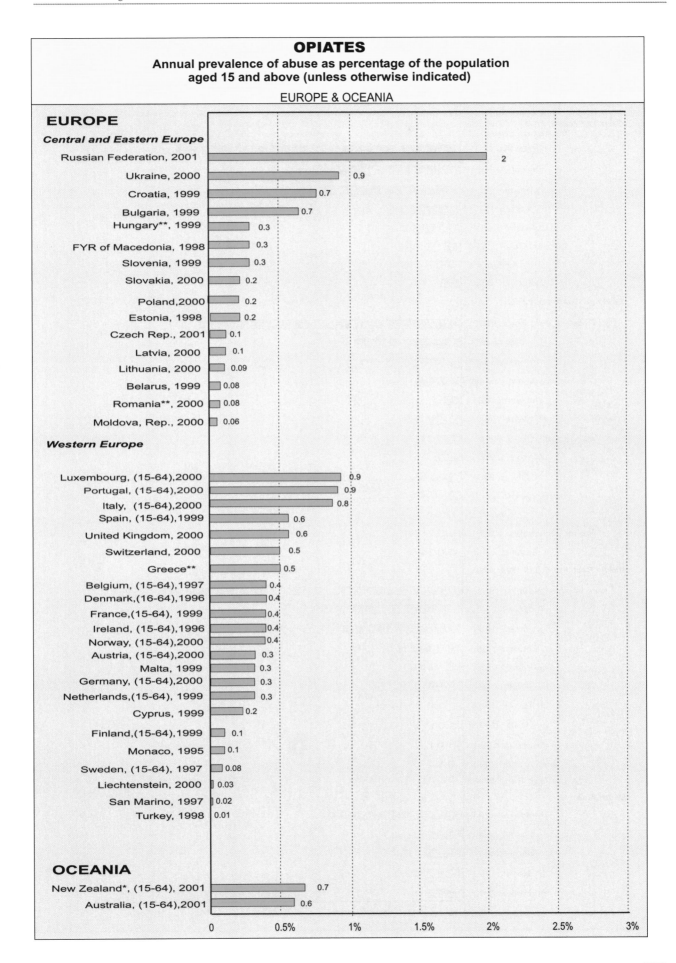

EUROPE

Central and Eastern Europe

Russian Federation, 2001	2
Ukraine, 2000	0.9
Croatia, 1999	0.7
Bulgaria, 1999	0.7
Hungary**, 1999	0.3
FYR of Macedonia, 1998	0.3
Slovenia, 1999	0.3
Slovakia, 2000	0.2
Poland, 2000	0.2
Estonia, 1998	0.2
Czech Rep., 2001	0.1
Latvia, 2000	0.1
Lithuania, 2000	0.09
Belarus, 1999	0.08
Romania**, 2000	0.08
Moldova, Rep., 2000	0.06

Western Europe

Luxembourg, (15-64), 2000	0.9
Portugal, (15-64), 2000	0.9
Italy, (15-64), 2000	0.8
Spain, (15-64), 1999	0.6
United Kingdom, 2000	0.6
Switzerland, 2000	0.5
Greece**	0.5
Belgium, (15-64), 1997	0.4
Denmark, (16-64), 1996	0.4
France, (15-64), 1999	0.4
Ireland, (15-64), 1996	0.4
Norway, (15-64), 2000	0.4
Austria, (15-64), 2000	0.3
Malta, 1999	0.3
Germany, (15-64), 2000	0.3
Netherlands, (15-64), 1999	0.3
Cyprus, 1999	0.2
Finland, (15-64), 1999	0.1
Monaco, 1995	0.1
Sweden, (15-64), 1997	0.08
Liechtenstein, 2000	0.03
San Marino, 1997	0.02
Turkey, 1998	0.01

OCEANIA

New Zealand*, (15-64), 2001	0.7
Australia, (15-64), 2001	0.6

0   0.5%   1%   1.5%   2%   2.5%   3%

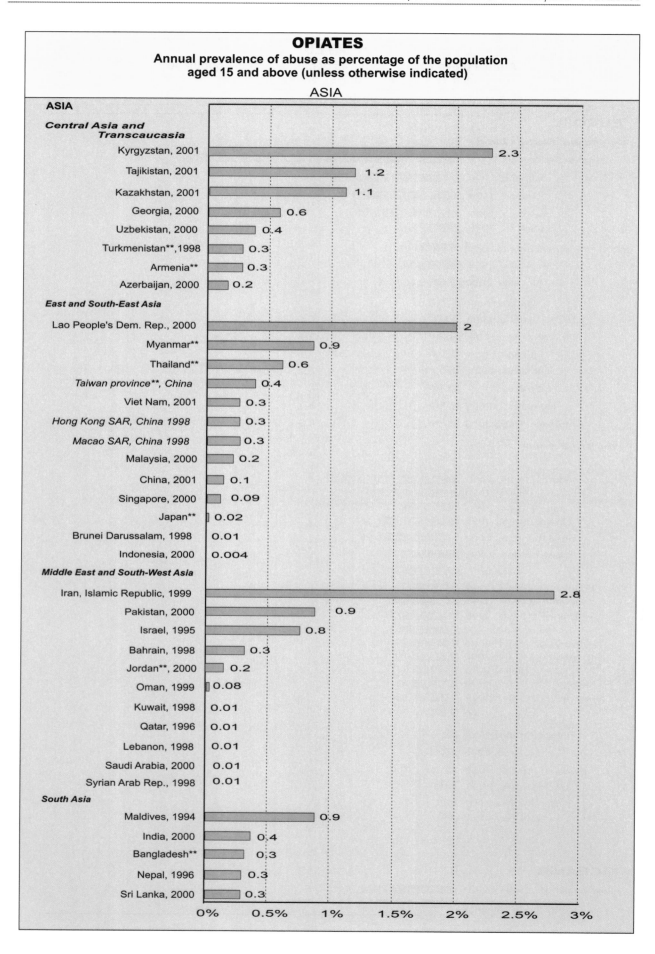

OPIATES
Annual prevalence of abuse as percentage of the population
aged 15 and above (unless otherwise indicated)

ASIA

ASIA

Central Asia and Transcaucasia

Kyrgyzstan, 2001	2.3
Tajikistan, 2001	1.2
Kazakhstan, 2001	1.1
Georgia, 2000	0.6
Uzbekistan, 2000	0.4
Turkmenistan**, 1998	0.3
Armenia**	0.3
Azerbaijan, 2000	0.2

East and South-East Asia

Lao People's Dem. Rep., 2000	2
Myanmar**	0.9
Thailand**	0.6
Taiwan province**, China	0.4
Viet Nam, 2001	0.3
Hong Kong SAR, China 1998	0.3
Macao SAR, China 1998	0.3
Malaysia, 2000	0.2
China, 2001	0.1
Singapore, 2000	0.09
Japan**	0.02
Brunei Darussalam, 1998	0.01
Indonesia, 2000	0.004

Middle East and South-West Asia

Iran, Islamic Republic, 1999	2.8
Pakistan, 2000	0.9
Israel, 1995	0.8
Bahrain, 1998	0.3
Jordan**, 2000	0.2
Oman, 1999	0.08
Kuwait, 1998	0.01
Qatar, 1996	0.01
Lebanon, 1998	0.01
Saudi Arabia, 2000	0.01
Syrian Arab Rep., 1998	0.01

South Asia

Maldives, 1994	0.9
India, 2000	0.4
Bangladesh**	0.3
Nepal, 1996	0.3
Sri Lanka, 2000	0.3

0%   0.5%   1%   1.5%   2%   2.5%   3%

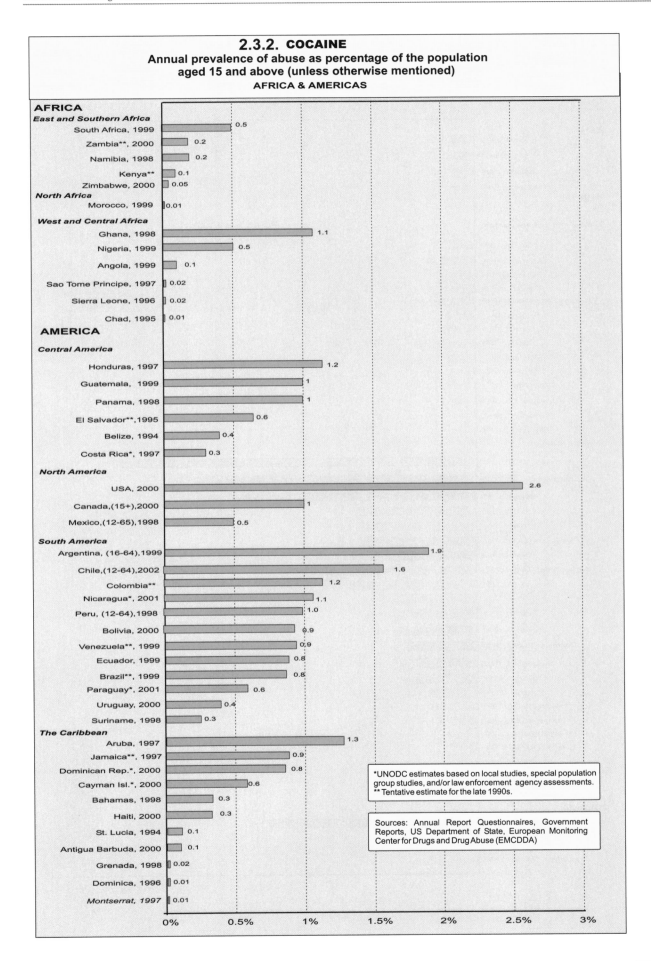

2.3.2. COCAINE
Annual prevalence of abuse as percentage of the population aged 15 and above (unless otherwise mentioned)
AFRICA & AMERICAS

AFRICA

East and Southern Africa
- South Africa, 1999 — 0.5
- Zambia**, 2000 — 0.2
- Namibia, 1998 — 0.2
- Kenya** — 0.1
- Zimbabwe, 2000 — 0.05

North Africa
- Morocco, 1999 — 0.01

West and Central Africa
- Ghana, 1998 — 1.1
- Nigeria, 1999 — 0.5
- Angola, 1999 — 0.1
- Sao Tome Principe, 1997 — 0.02
- Sierra Leone, 1996 — 0.02
- Chad, 1995 — 0.01

AMERICA

Central America
- Honduras, 1997 — 1.2
- Guatemala, 1999 — 1
- Panama, 1998 — 1
- El Salvador**, 1995 — 0.6
- Belize, 1994 — 0.4
- Costa Rica*, 1997 — 0.3

North America
- USA, 2000 — 2.6
- Canada, (15+), 2000 — 1
- Mexico, (12-65), 1998 — 0.5

South America
- Argentina, (16-64), 1999 — 1.9
- Chile, (12-64), 2002 — 1.6
- Colombia** — 1.2
- Nicaragua*, 2001 — 1.1
- Peru, (12-64), 1998 — 1.0
- Bolivia, 2000 — 0.9
- Venezuela**, 1999 — 0.9
- Ecuador, 1999 — 0.8
- Brazil**, 1999 — 0.8
- Paraguay*, 2001 — 0.6
- Uruguay, 2000 — 0.4
- Suriname, 1998 — 0.3

The Caribbean
- Aruba, 1997 — 1.3
- Jamaica**, 1997 — 0.9
- Dominican Rep.*, 2000 — 0.8
- Cayman Isl.*, 2000 — 0.6
- Bahamas, 1998 — 0.3
- Haiti, 2000 — 0.3
- St. Lucia, 1994 — 0.1
- Antigua Barbuda, 2000 — 0.1
- Grenada, 1998 — 0.02
- Dominica, 1996 — 0.01
- Montserrat, 1997 — 0.01

*UNODC estimates based on local studies, special population group studies, and/or law enforcement agency assessments.
** Tentative estimate for the late 1990s.

Sources: Annual Report Questionnaires, Government Reports, US Department of State, European Monitoring Center for Drugs and Drug Abuse (EMCDDA)

0% 0.5% 1% 1.5% 2% 2.5% 3%

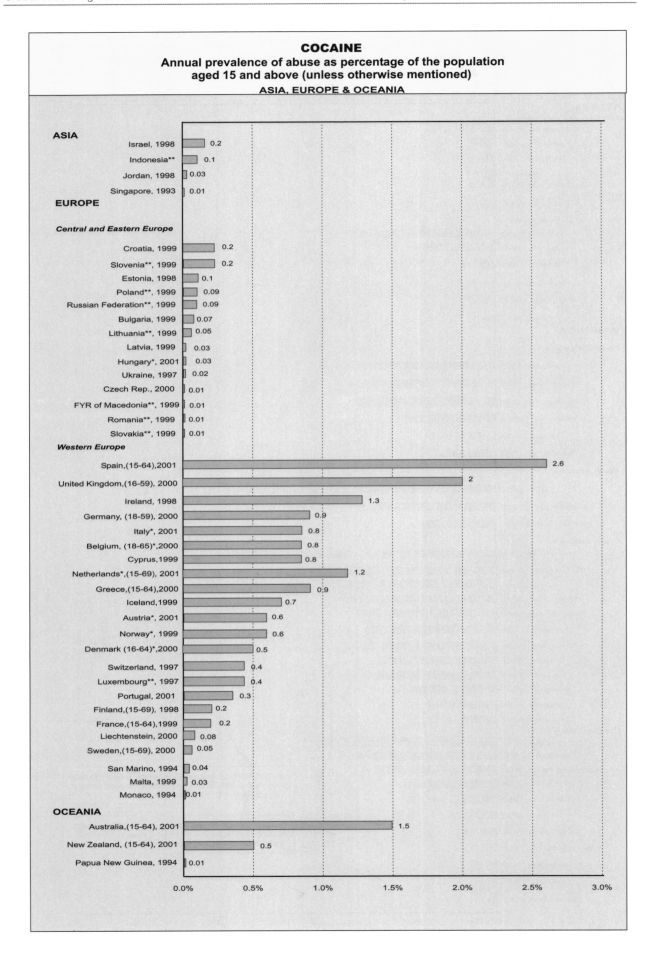

COCAINE
Annual prevalence of abuse as percentage of the population
aged 15 and above (unless otherwise mentioned)
ASIA, EUROPE & OCEANIA

ASIA
- Israel, 1998 — 0.2
- Indonesia** — 0.1
- Jordan, 1998 — 0.03
- Singapore, 1993 — 0.01

EUROPE

Central and Eastern Europe
- Croatia, 1999 — 0.2
- Slovenia**, 1999 — 0.2
- Estonia, 1998 — 0.1
- Poland**, 1999 — 0.09
- Russian Federation**, 1999 — 0.09
- Bulgaria, 1999 — 0.07
- Lithuania**, 1999 — 0.05
- Latvia, 1999 — 0.03
- Hungary*, 2001 — 0.03
- Ukraine, 1997 — 0.02
- Czech Rep., 2000 — 0.01
- FYR of Macedonia**, 1999 — 0.01
- Romania**, 1999 — 0.01
- Slovakia**, 1999 — 0.01

Western Europe
- Spain,(15-64),2001 — 2.6
- United Kingdom,(16-59), 2000 — 2
- Ireland, 1998 — 1.3
- Germany, (18-59), 2000 — 0.9
- Italy*, 2001 — 0.8
- Belgium, (18-65)*,2000 — 0.8
- Cyprus,1999 — 0.8
- Netherlands*,(15-69), 2001 — 1.2
- Greece,(15-64),2000 — 0.9
- Iceland,1999 — 0.7
- Austria*, 2001 — 0.6
- Norway*, 1999 — 0.6
- Denmark (16-64)*,2000 — 0.5
- Switzerland, 1997 — 0.4
- Luxembourg**, 1997 — 0.4
- Portugal, 2001 — 0.3
- Finland,(15-69), 1998 — 0.2
- France,(15-64),1999 — 0.2
- Liechtenstein, 2000 — 0.08
- Sweden,(15-69), 2000 — 0.05
- San Marino, 1994 — 0.04
- Malta, 1999 — 0.03
- Monaco, 1994 — 0.01

OCEANIA
- Australia,(15-64), 2001 — 1.5
- New Zealand, (15-64), 2001 — 0.5
- Papua New Guinea, 1994 — 0.01

0.0%   0.5%   1.0%   1.5%   2.0%   2.5%   3.0%

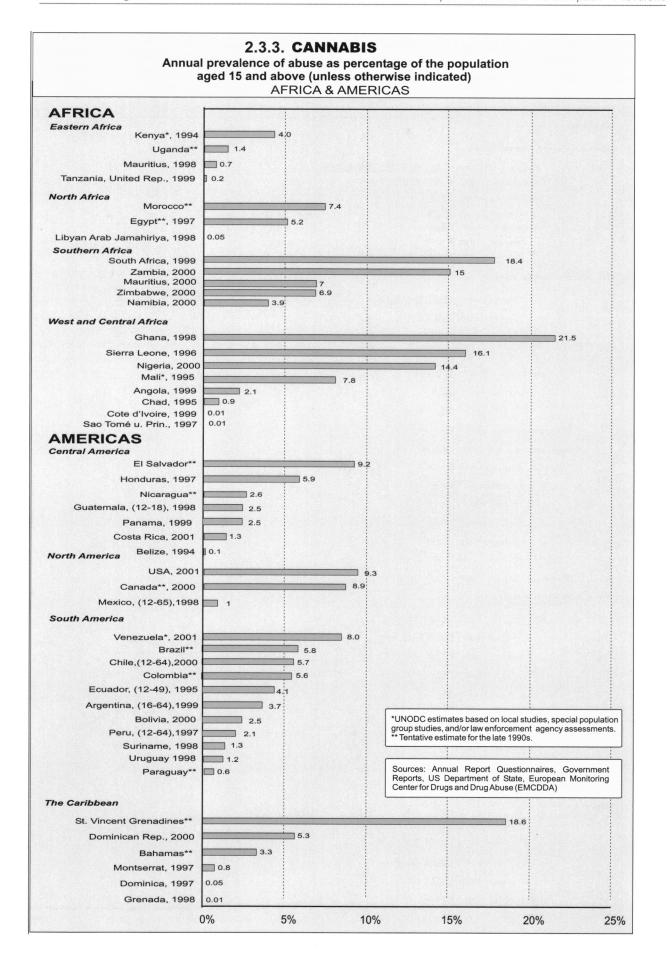

2.3.3. CANNABIS
**Annual prevalence of abuse as percentage of the population
aged 15 and above (unless otherwise indicated)**
AFRICA & AMERICAS

AFRICA

Eastern Africa
- Kenya*, 1994 — 4.0
- Uganda** — 1.4
- Mauritius, 1998 — 0.7
- Tanzania, United Rep., 1999 — 0.2

North Africa
- Morocco** — 7.4
- Egypt**, 1997 — 5.2
- Libyan Arab Jamahiriya, 1998 — 0.05

Southern Africa
- South Africa, 1999 — 18.4
- Zambia, 2000 — 15
- Mauritius, 2000 — 7
- Zimbabwe, 2000 — 6.9
- Namibia, 2000 — 3.9

West and Central Africa
- Ghana, 1998 — 21.5
- Sierra Leone, 1996 — 16.1
- Nigeria, 2000 — 14.4
- Mali*, 1995 — 7.8
- Angola, 1999 — 2.1
- Chad, 1995 — 0.9
- Cote d'Ivoire, 1999 — 0.01
- Sao Tomé u. Prin., 1997 — 0.01

AMERICAS

Central America
- El Salvador** — 9.2
- Honduras, 1997 — 5.9
- Nicaragua** — 2.6
- Guatemala, (12-18), 1998 — 2.5
- Panama, 1999 — 2.5
- Costa Rica, 2001 — 1.3
- Belize, 1994 — 0.1

North America
- USA, 2001 — 9.3
- Canada**, 2000 — 8.9
- Mexico, (12-65),1998 — 1

South America
- Venezuela*, 2001 — 8.0
- Brazil** — 5.8
- Chile,(12-64),2000 — 5.7
- Colombia** — 5.6
- Ecuador, (12-49), 1995 — 4.1
- Argentina, (16-64),1999 — 3.7
- Bolivia, 2000 — 2.5
- Peru, (12-64),1997 — 2.1
- Suriname, 1998 — 1.3
- Uruguay 1998 — 1.2
- Paraguay** — 0.6

*UNODC estimates based on local studies, special population group studies, and/or law enforcement agency assessments.
** Tentative estimate for the late 1990s.

Sources: Annual Report Questionnaires, Government Reports, US Department of State, European Monitoring Center for Drugs and Drug Abuse (EMCDDA)

The Caribbean
- St. Vincent Grenadines** — 18.6
- Dominican Rep., 2000 — 5.3
- Bahamas** — 3.3
- Montserrat, 1997 — 0.8
- Dominica, 1997 — 0.05
- Grenada, 1998 — 0.01

0%   5%   10%   15%   20%   25%

339

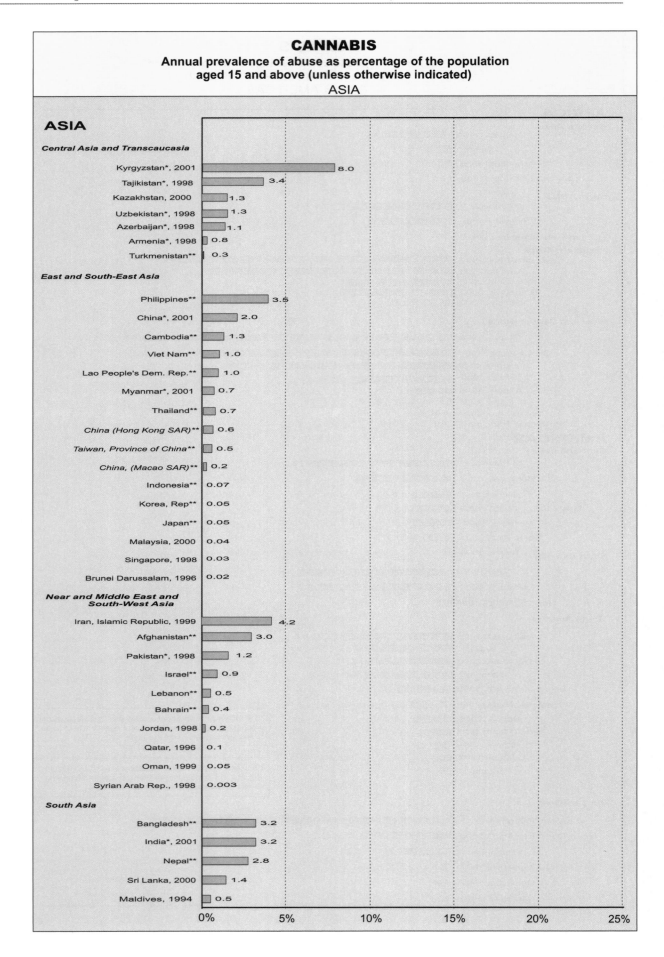

CANNABIS
Annual prevalence of abuse as percentage of the population aged 15 and above (unless otherwise indicated)
ASIA

ASIA

Central Asia and Transcaucasia

Kyrgyzstan*, 2001	8.0
Tajikistan*, 1998	3.4
Kazakhstan, 2000	1.3
Uzbekistan*, 1998	1.3
Azerbaijan*, 1998	1.1
Armenia*, 1998	0.8
Turkmenistan**	0.3

East and South-East Asia

Philippines**	3.5
China*, 2001	2.0
Cambodia**	1.3
Viet Nam**	1.0
Lao People's Dem. Rep.**	1.0
Myanmar*, 2001	0.7
Thailand**	0.7
China (Hong Kong SAR)**	0.6
Taiwan, Province of China**	0.5
China, (Macao SAR)**	0.2
Indonesia**	0.07
Korea, Rep**	0.05
Japan**	0.05
Malaysia, 2000	0.04
Singapore, 1998	0.03
Brunei Darussalam, 1996	0.02

Near and Middle East and South-West Asia

Iran, Islamic Republic, 1999	4.2
Afghanistan**	3.0
Pakistan*, 1998	1.2
Israel**	0.9
Lebanon**	0.5
Bahrain**	0.4
Jordan, 1998	0.2
Qatar, 1996	0.1
Oman, 1999	0.05
Syrian Arab Rep., 1998	0.003

South Asia

Bangladesh**	3.2
India*, 2001	3.2
Nepal**	2.8
Sri Lanka, 2000	1.4
Maldives, 1994	0.5

0%   5%   10%   15%   20%   25%

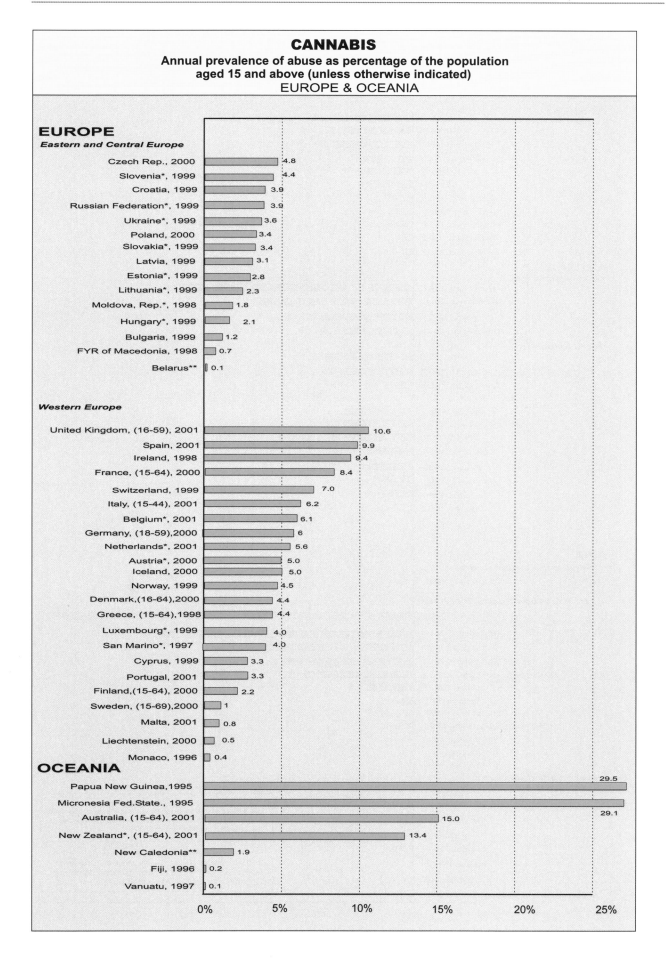

CANNABIS
Annual prevalence of abuse as percentage of the population
aged 15 and above (unless otherwise indicated)
EUROPE & OCEANIA

EUROPE
Eastern and Central Europe

Czech Rep., 2000	4.8
Slovenia*, 1999	4.4
Croatia, 1999	3.9
Russian Federation*, 1999	3.9
Ukraine*, 1999	3.6
Poland, 2000	3.4
Slovakia*, 1999	3.4
Latvia, 1999	3.1
Estonia*, 1999	2.8
Lithuania*, 1999	2.3
Moldova, Rep.*, 1998	1.8
Hungary*, 1999	2.1
Bulgaria, 1999	1.2
FYR of Macedonia, 1998	0.7
Belarus**	0.1

Western Europe

United Kingdom, (16-59), 2001	10.6
Spain, 2001	9.9
Ireland, 1998	9.4
France, (15-64), 2000	8.4
Switzerland, 1999	7.0
Italy, (15-44), 2001	6.2
Belgium*, 2001	6.1
Germany, (18-59), 2000	6
Netherlands*, 2001	5.6
Austria*, 2000	5.0
Iceland, 2000	5.0
Norway, 1999	4.5
Denmark, (16-64), 2000	4.4
Greece, (15-64), 1998	4.4
Luxembourg*, 1999	4.0
San Marino*, 1997	4.0
Cyprus, 1999	3.3
Portugal, 2001	3.3
Finland, (15-64), 2000	2.2
Sweden, (15-69), 2000	1
Malta, 2001	0.8
Liechtenstein, 2000	0.5
Monaco, 1996	0.4

OCEANIA

Papua New Guinea, 1995	29.5
Micronesia Fed.State., 1995	29.1
Australia, (15-64), 2001	15.0
New Zealand*, (15-64), 2001	13.4
New Caledonia**	1.9
Fiji, 1996	0.2
Vanuatu, 1997	0.1

0%   5%   10%   15%   20%   25%

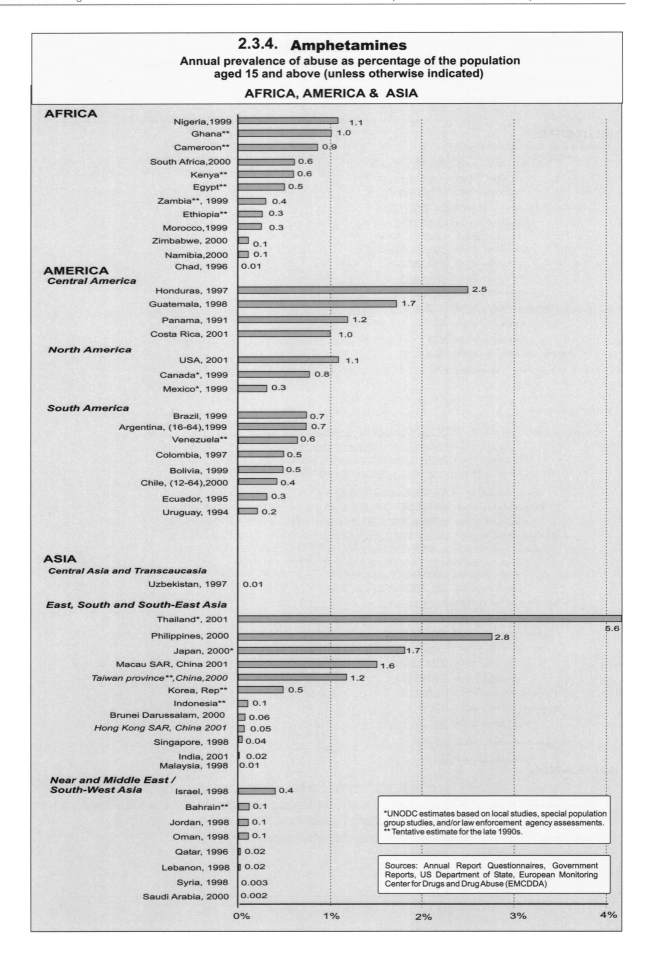

2.3.4. Amphetamines

Annual prevalence of abuse as percentage of the population
aged 15 and above (unless otherwise indicated)

AFRICA, AMERICA & ASIA

AFRICA

Nigeria,1999	1.1
Ghana**	1.0
Cameroon**	0.9
South Africa,2000	0.6
Kenya**	0.6
Egypt**	0.5
Zambia**, 1999	0.4
Ethiopia**	0.3
Morocco,1999	0.3
Zimbabwe, 2000	0.1
Namibia,2000	0.1
Chad, 1996	0.01

AMERICA
Central America

Honduras, 1997	2.5
Guatemala, 1998	1.7
Panama, 1991	1.2
Costa Rica, 2001	1.0

North America

USA, 2001	1.1
Canada*, 1999	0.8
Mexico*, 1999	0.3

South America

Brazil, 1999	0.7
Argentina, (16-64),1999	0.7
Venezuela**	0.6
Colombia, 1997	0.5
Bolivia, 1999	0.5
Chile, (12-64),2000	0.4
Ecuador, 1995	0.3
Uruguay, 1994	0.2

ASIA
Central Asia and Transcaucasia

Uzbekistan, 1997	0.01

East, South and South-East Asia

Thailand*, 2001	5.6
Philippines, 2000	2.8
Japan, 2000*	1.7
Macau SAR, China 2001	1.6
Taiwan province**,China,2000	1.2
Korea, Rep**	0.5
Indonesia**	0.1
Brunei Darussalam, 2000	0.06
Hong Kong SAR, China 2001	0.05
Singapore, 1998	0.04
India, 2001	0.02
Malaysia, 1998	0.01

*Near and Middle East /
South-West Asia*

Israel, 1998	0.4
Bahrain**	0.1
Jordan, 1998	0.1
Oman, 1998	0.1
Qatar, 1996	0.02
Lebanon, 1998	0.02
Syria, 1998	0.003
Saudi Arabia, 2000	0.002

*UNODC estimates based on local studies, special population group studies, and/or law enforcement agency assessments.
** Tentative estimate for the late 1990s.

Sources: Annual Report Questionnaires, Government Reports, US Department of State, European Monitoring Center for Drugs and Drug Abuse (EMCDDA)

0%   1%   2%   3%   4%

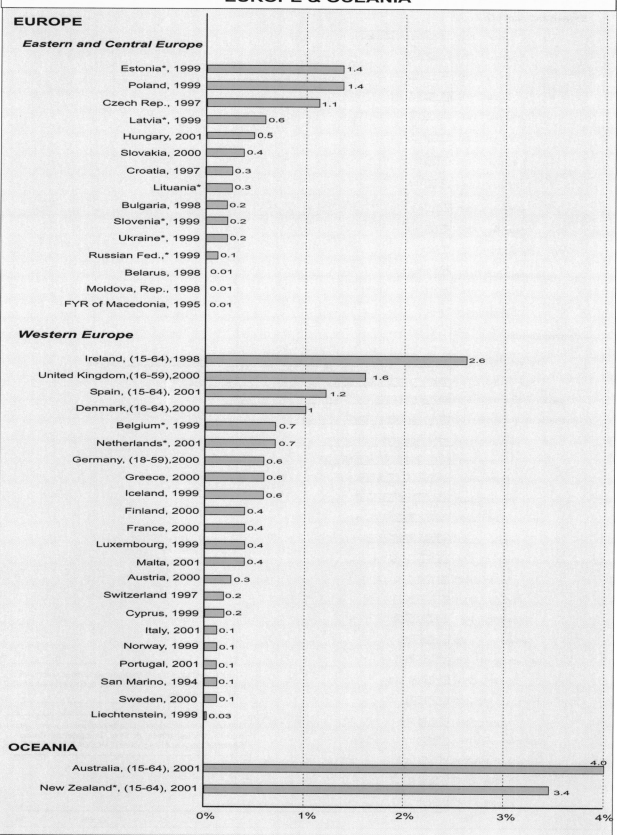

Amphetamines
Annual prevalence of abuse as percentage of the population aged 15 and above (unless otherwise indicated)
EUROPE & OCEANIA

EUROPE

Eastern and Central Europe

Estonia*, 1999	1.4
Poland, 1999	1.4
Czech Rep., 1997	1.1
Latvia*, 1999	0.6
Hungary, 2001	0.5
Slovakia, 2000	0.4
Croatia, 1997	0.3
Lituania*	0.3
Bulgaria, 1998	0.2
Slovenia*, 1999	0.2
Ukraine*, 1999	0.2
Russian Fed.,* 1999	0.1
Belarus, 1998	0.01
Moldova, Rep., 1998	0.01
FYR of Macedonia, 1995	0.01

Western Europe

Ireland, (15-64),1998	2.6
United Kingdom,(16-59),2000	1.6
Spain, (15-64), 2001	1.2
Denmark,(16-64),2000	1
Belgium*, 1999	0.7
Netherlands*, 2001	0.7
Germany, (18-59),2000	0.6
Greece, 2000	0.6
Iceland, 1999	0.6
Finland, 2000	0.4
France, 2000	0.4
Luxembourg, 1999	0.4
Malta, 2001	0.4
Austria, 2000	0.3
Switzerland 1997	0.2
Cyprus, 1999	0.2
Italy, 2001	0.1
Norway, 1999	0.1
Portugal, 2001	0.1
San Marino, 1994	0.1
Sweden, 2000	0.1
Liechtenstein, 1999	0.03

OCEANIA

Australia, (15-64), 2001	4.0
New Zealand*, (15-64), 2001	3.4

0%   1%   2%   3%   4%

343

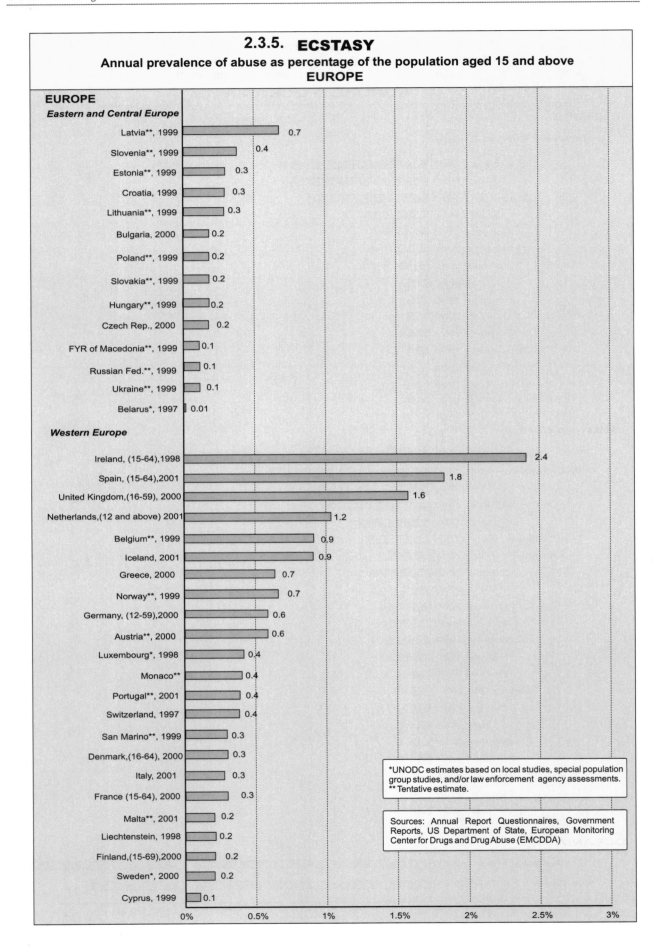

2.3.5. ECSTASY
Annual prevalence of abuse as percentage of the population aged 15 and above
EUROPE

EUROPE

Eastern and Central Europe

Latvia**, 1999	0.7
Slovenia**, 1999	0.4
Estonia**, 1999	0.3
Croatia, 1999	0.3
Lithuania**, 1999	0.3
Bulgaria, 2000	0.2
Poland**, 1999	0.2
Slovakia**, 1999	0.2
Hungary**, 1999	0.2
Czech Rep., 2000	0.2
FYR of Macedonia**, 1999	0.1
Russian Fed.**, 1999	0.1
Ukraine**, 1999	0.1
Belarus*, 1997	0.01

Western Europe

Ireland, (15-64),1998	2.4
Spain, (15-64),2001	1.8
United Kingdom,(16-59), 2000	1.6
Netherlands,(12 and above) 2001	1.2
Belgium**, 1999	0.9
Iceland, 2001	0.9
Greece, 2000	0.7
Norway**, 1999	0.7
Germany, (12-59),2000	0.6
Austria**, 2000	0.6
Luxembourg*, 1998	0.4
Monaco**	0.4
Portugal**, 2001	0.4
Switzerland, 1997	0.4
San Marino**, 1999	0.3
Denmark,(16-64), 2000	0.3
Italy, 2001	0.3
France (15-64), 2000	0.3
Malta**, 2001	0.2
Liechtenstein, 1998	0.2
Finland,(15-69),2000	0.2
Sweden*, 2000	0.2
Cyprus, 1999	0.1

*UNODC estimates based on local studies, special population group studies, and/or law enforcement agency assessments.
** Tentative estimate.

Sources: Annual Report Questionnaires, Government Reports, US Department of State, European Monitoring Center for Drugs and Drug Abuse (EMCDDA)

0%   0.5%   1%   1.5%   2%   2.5%   3%

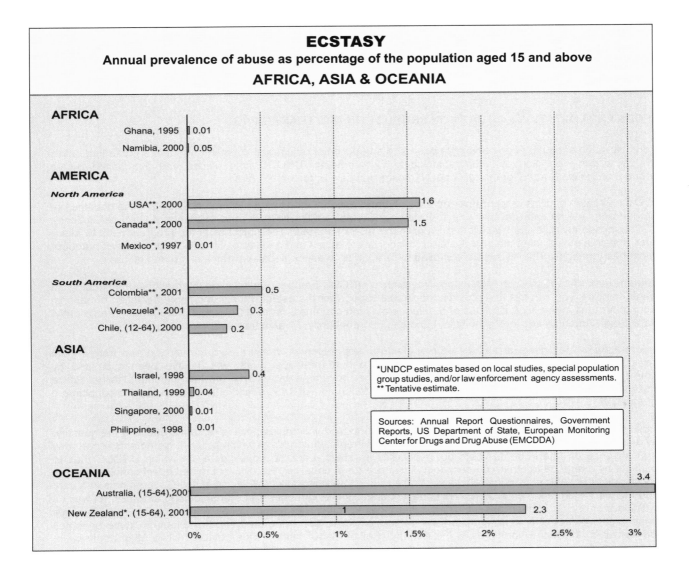

SOURCES AND LIMITATIONS OF DATA

Data presented in this report must be interpreted with caution. All figures provided, particularly those of more recent years, are subject to updating.

SOURCES AND LIMITATIONS OF DATA ON PRODUCTION AND TRAFFICKING

Data on cultivation of opium poppy and coca bush and production of opium and coca leaf, which are presented in this report, are drawn from various sources including Governments, UNODC field offices and the United States Department of State's Bureau for International Narcotics and Law Enforcement Affairs.

UNODC's estimates on illicit crops derive increasingly from national monitoring systems operating in the countries of illicit production. In line with decisions of the Member States (1998 UNGASS and subsequent CND resolutions), UNODC launched an Illicit Crop Monitoring Programme (ICMP) in 1999. The objective of the programme is to assist Member States in establishing national systems to monitor the extent and evolution of the illicit cultivation of narcotics crops on their territories. The results are compiled by UNODC to present global estimates on an annual basis.

In the framework of its Illicit Crop Monitoring Programme, UNODC has been developing international methodological standards for illicit crop surveys and providing technical support for the establishment and implementation of national monitoring systems in the six main coca and opium producing countries, namely Colombia, Peru, and more recently, Bolivia in South America, and in Afghanistan, Laos and, more recently, Myanmar in Asia.

The information on trafficking (and partly on manufacture), as presented in this report, is mainly drawn from annual reports questionnaires (ARQ), relating mostly to 2001 and to previous years, which have been submitted by Governments to UNODC. Additional sources, such as other governmental reports, the International Criminal Police Organization (Interpol), the World Customs Organization (WCO) and UNODC's field offices, were used to supplement the information.

The main problems with regard to data relate to the irregularity and incompleteness in reporting affecting the quantity, quality and comparability of information received. First, the irregular intervals at which some Governments report may result in absence of data in some years but availability in others. Lack of regular data, for which UNODC tries to compensate by reference to other sources, could influence trend patterns. Second, submitted questionnaires are not always complete or sufficiently comprehensive. While data on seizures are provided by many Governments in a very detailed manner, information on production of drugs, clandestine laboratories and manufacturing activities, as well as on particulars of prices, is often absent. Third, differences in criteria of reporting between countries, or from single countries over a period of time, may distort the trafficking picture and trend analysis. For example, some countries include so-called "kitchen" laboratories in the total number of manufacturing sites detected while others only count fully equipped clandestine laboratories. By the same token, a country which in the past has included "kitchen" laboratories may then change its reporting practice and omit such detections. Also, the extent to which seizure statistics from some countries constitute all reported national cases, regardless of the final destination of the illicit drug, can vary and make it difficult to assess international trafficking.

The utilization of data which are available through the various sources is limited due to two main shortcomings. First, some available information is not fully reliable due to the complexity of the drug phenomenon and problems in assessing the specific nature of an illicit activity. analysis of illicit drug cultivation/production, for example, rely on estimates and cannot be treated as hard data. Second, data (for example on seizures) reflect different factors, such as changes in reporting modalities or variations in law enforcement practices. However, where such factors do hold constant, changes in seizure statistics can indicate trends in trafficking, and some inferences in the present report are drawn on this very basis.

Despite these limitations, comparisons, on a time-series basis, of different indicators with statistical dependence show high correlations, thus supporting their statistical worth.

SOURCES AND LIMITATIONS OF DATA ON CONSUMPTION

Drug abuse in the general population

Assessing the extent of drug abuse (the number of drug abusers) is a particularly difficult undertaking because it involves measuring the size of a hidden population. Margins of error are considerable, and tend to multiply as the scale of estimation is raised, from local to national, regional and global levels. Despite some improvements in recent years, estimates provided by member states to UNODC are still very heterogeneous in terms of quality and reliability. These estimates cannot simply be aggregated globally to arrive at the exact number of drug users in the world. Yet it is both desirable and possible to establish basic orders of magnitude - which are obviously subject to revision as new and better information is generated. Estimates of illicit consumption for a significantly large number of countries have been received by UNODC over the years (in the form of annual reports questionnaires (ARQ) submitted by Governments, as well as from additional sources, such as other governmental reports and research results from scientific literature, often received via UNODC's field offices. Detailed information is available from countries in North America, a number of countries in Europe (mostly West Europe), some countries in South America, a few countries in the Oceania region and a limited number of countries in Asia and in Africa. For several other countries, available qualitative information on the drug abuse situation only allows for making a 'guess estimate'. In the case of complete data gaps for individual countries, it was assumed that drug abuse was likely to be close to the respective subregional average, unless other available indicators suggested that they were likely to be above or below such an average.

The most widely used indicator at the global level is the "annual prevalence" rate: the number of people who have consumed an illicit drug at least once in the last twelve months prior to the survey. As "annual prevalence" is the most commonly used indicator to measure prevalence, it has also been adopted by UNODC as the key indicator for the extent of drug abuse and is part of the Lisbon Consensus (20-21 January 2000) on core epidemiological demand indicators (CN.7/2000/CRP.3). The use of "annual prevalence" is a compromise between "life-time prevalence" data (drug use at least once in a life-time) and data on current use. Life-time prevalence data are, in general, easier to generate but are not very illustrative. (The fact that a 50-year-old person smoked marijuana at the age of 20 does not provide much insight into the current drug abuse problem). Data on current use (e.g. monthly prevalence) are of more value. However, they often require larger samples in order to obtain meaningful results, and are thus more costly to generate.

The "annual prevalence" rate is frequently shown as a percentage of the population aged 15 years and above, or 12 years and above, though a number of other age groupings are used as well. In this report prevalence data, in general, have been presented as reported; the age group was cited. In cases where studies were based on significantly different age groups, the data were adjusted to the age group of 15 years and above (see below), taking into account that drug abuse is usually greater among younger age groups.

The methods used for collecting data on illicit activities vary from country to country. In some cases, strongly differing results have been obtained for the same country. In order to arrive at basically comparable results, it is necessary in a number of cases to extrapolate from reported current use or life-time prevalence to annual prevalence rates and/or to adjust results for differences in age groups. These operations can potentially lead to over-estimation or under-estimation. One key problem in currently available prevalence estimates is still the level of accuracy which varies strongly from country to country. While a number of prevalence estimates are based on sound epidemiological surveys, some are obviously the result of guesses. In other cases, the estimates provided simply reflect the aggregate number of drug addicts found in some drug registries which probably cover only a small fraction of the total drug abusing population in a country.

Even in cases where detailed information is available, there is often considerable divergence in definitions used - registry data (people in contact with the treatment system or the judicial system) versus survey data (usually extrapolation of results obtained through interviews of a selected sample); general population versus specific surveys of groups in terms of age (e.g. school surveys), special settings (such as hospitals or prisons), life-time, annual, or monthly prevalence, etc.

In order to reduce the error from simply aggregating such diverse estimates, an attempt was made to standardize - as a far as possible - the very heterogeneous data set. Thus, all available estimates were transformed into one single indicator – annual prevalence among the general population age 15 and above - using transformation ratios derived from analysis of the situation in neighbouring countries, and if such data were not available, on estimates from the USA, the most studied country worldwide with regard to drug abuse.

In order to minimize the potential error from the use of different methodological approaches, all available estimates for the same country - after transformation - were taken into consideration and - unless methodological considerations suggested a clear superiority of one method over another - the mean of the various estimates was calculated and used as UNODC's country estimate.

All of this - pooling of national results, standardization and extrapolation from subregional results in the case of data gaps - does not guarantee an accurate picture. But it should be sufficient to arrive at reasonable orders of magnitude about the likely extent of drug abuse in the general population.